THE

WYCLIFFE

HISTORICAL GEOGRAPHY

OF BIBLE LANDS

CHARLES F. PFEIFFER

HOWARD F. VOS

THE
WYCLIFFE
HISTORICAL GEOGRAPHY
OF BIBLE LANDS

MOODY
PRESS
Chicago

WYCLIFFE HISTORICAL GEOGRAPHY OF BIBLE LANDS, *First Printing*

Pfeiffer and Vos

Library of Congress Catalog Card Number 67-14382

Manufactured in the United States of America

Color maps by arrangement with Oxford University Press
Drawings by Ben Wood

PICTURES ON TITLE PAGE

A war chariot of Ashurbanipal (the Asnapper of Ezra 4:10), king of Assyria. Courtesy of the Louvre

Samaria from the Shechem Road. Courtesy Matson Photo Service

Preface

A survey of the history and geography of all the Bible lands in one volume is long overdue. Numerous books have been written on Palestine, but few have recognized that such widely separated places as Iran, Egypt, Greece and even Italy also provided a geographical stage on which the biblical drama was enacted. In recent years Bible dictionaries, encyclopedias and atlases have been published in increasing numbers. While they have often provided information on all the Bible lands, their approach has been either topical or very largely geographical. In the present volume the writers have sought to bring together historical, geographical, biblical and archaeological material on all ten areas of the Near Eastern and Mediterranean world that might properly be called "Bible Lands."

Separate chapters have been written on each of these lands, and the areas have been discussed in the order in which they figure most significantly in the biblical narrative. The earliest events occurred in Mesopotamia. Although the Patriarchs lived in Palestine for a while, the Children of Israel were rather firmly anchored in Egypt for a more extended period of time. The spotlight then focused on Palestine for several hundred years. Developments in Phoenicia and Syria were both closely entwined with Palestinian history; but intimate relations between Phoenicia and Palestine came during the United Monarchy, a little earlier than those between Palestine and Syria. Syrian and Palestinian affairs were most closely linked during the days of the separate history of Judah and Israel. Not long after the fall of Samaria and Jerusalem, Persia won control of the whole Near East for some two hundred years, and ruled the area at the close of the Old Testament narrative. When the curtain rose on the New Testament, Palestine again figured prominently during the life of Christ, but the country was not free to initiate action. Rome was in control. Soon a new message of salvation through Christ was being proclaimed, the church was founded and missionary crusades were being launched. The Apostle Paul led in these church-expansion movements. Cyprus, Asia Minor, Greece and Italy, in that order, assumed prominence in his missionary endeavors.

As to arrangement of material within the chapters of this book, there is some difference of outlook between areas. Commonly, a brief geographical survey appears first, followed by a historical outline. Thereafter, divergence frequently occurs because some areas lend themselves to a different sort of treatment than others. In some instances historical developments received greater prominence, in others geographical concerns predominated. As to authorship, Dr. Pfeiffer has written the chapters on Mesopotamia, Egypt, Palestine and Iran; and Dr. Vos has written those on Asia Minor, Greece, Italy, Cyprus, Syria and Phoenicia.

As any author finishes a manuscript, he recognizes how indebted he is to the many

v

who have helped to make his work possible. Several have read this entire work and have made numerous and valuable suggestions. A larger number have helped the writers in significant ways in their travel and research in the Near East. To all of these the authors express their gratitude again. But a special word of appreciation is due the Moody Press for helping to make possible some of the research for this book and for their efforts in bringing together an outstanding collection of illustrative material.

Contents

Illustrations

ABBREVIATIONS: *BM*, The British Museum; *IIS*, Israel Information Services; *MPS*, The Matson Photo Service; *ORINST*, The Oriental Institute of the University of Chicago. Photographs for which credits are not given below were taken by Howard F. Vos.

ix

Maps

1. Great human-headed winged bull from the palace of Sargon II, probable Assyrian conqueror of Samaria

Mesopotamia

The Fertile Crescent

Stretching northwestward from the Persian Gulf is a narrow strip of land which skirts the Arabian and Syrian deserts and descends to the border of Egypt. James H. Breasted named this region "The Fertile Crescent." Along its northern boundary lie the 3,000-foot-high tablelands of Anatolia and Iran, separated from each other by the mountains of Armenia, the Urartu of ancient cuneiform inscriptions and the Ararat of the Bible (Gen. 8:4).

South and east of the Fertile Crescent are the desert areas which forbid access to the merchant and the soldier alike. The famous trek of Abraham from Ur of the Chaldees through Haran to Canaan approximates the way by which people have journeyed from southern Mesopotamia to Palestine since the beginning of history. As man moved from either the mountains or the desert into the river valleys of the Fertile Crescent, he became a part of the culture which early produced separate city-states and later on the Assyrian and Babylonian empires. In these valleys of the Tigris and the Euphrates rivers—two of the four rivers of Eden (Gen. 2:14)—were found the earliest evidences of complex civilization. In this region also the early narratives of Genesis occurred.

If the Euphrates River were followed as it swings northwestward, one would reach a point in northern Syria not far from the Mediterranean coast. Here rainfall is more plentiful, and the summer drought is shorter than in the regions farther south. Here too there is only one mountain barrier, and the rain is carried farther inland, so that a broad area of fertile steppeland connects the Mediterranean with the Euphrates.

As the Fertile Crescent turns southwestward along the coasts of Syria and Palestine, rainfall diminishes and cultivated land gradually passes into desert. Along the Mediterranean Sea the desert begins at Gaza (cf. Acts 8:26), and this, technically speaking, also marks the end of the Fertile Crescent. Actually, however, the fertile delta and valley of the Nile are but a short distance southwest. The Fertile Crescent has historically been the connecting road between the nations of the Nile and of the Tigris-Euphrates valleys. It connects Asia to Africa, which dangles from Asia by a mere thread of less than one hundred miles of land north of the Gulf of Suez. The Suez Canal has eliminated even that tenuous connection.

Palestine, at the southwestern end of the Fertile Crescent, could not avoid contact with the great powers of biblical times, for their armies were constantly on her doorsteps. The proper home of ancient Israel was in the central mountain range rather than in the coastal region; yet she was never far removed from the major imperial strug-

1

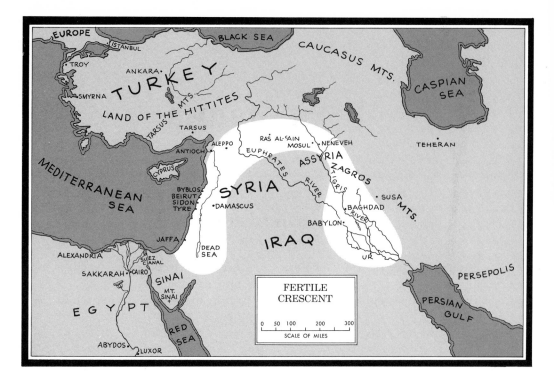

EUROPE · ISTANBUL · TROY · BLACK SEA · CAUCASUS MTS. · CASPIAN SEA · ANKARA · TURKEY · SMYRNA · MTS. · LAND OF THE HITTITES · TARSUS MTS. · TARSUS · RAS AL-SAIN · MOSUL · NENEVEH · TEHERAN · ALEPPO · ANTIOCH · EUPHRATES · ASSYRIA · ZAGROS · MEDITERRANEAN SEA · CYPRUS · BYBLOS · BEIRUT · SIDON · TYRE · SYRIA · RIVER · TIGRIS RIVER · SUSA · BAGHDAD · MTS. · DAMASCUS · BABYLON · JAFFA · DEAD SEA · IRAQ · UR · PERSEPOLIS · ALEXANDRIA · SUEZ CANAL · SAKKARAH · CAIRO · SINAI · MT. SINAI · EGYPT · RED SEA · PERSIAN GULF · ABYDOS · LUXOR

FERTILE CRESCENT

0 50 100   200   300
SCALE OF MILES

gles of the day. Egypt, Assyria, Babylonia, Greece, and Rome in their turn were able to subdue Palestine. Africa, Asia, and Europe meet at the place where the events of Old and New Testament history occurred. From this center of the ancient world, God in His providence revealed Himself through inspired prophets and, in the fullness of time, through his incarnate Son.

Geographical Features

Scripture places the cradle of the human race in a land watered by four rivers, two of which are the well-known Tigris (Hiddekel) and the Euphrates (Gen. 2:8-14). The "mighty hunter" Nimrod ruled a kingdom which included "Babel, and Erech, and Accad [or Akkad] and Calneh, in the land of Shinar" (Gen. 10:10). These brief references to events at the dawn of history take us to the land north of the Persian Gulf which the Greeks called "Mesopotamia," meaning "land between the rivers."

Mesopotamia, in the language of the Greek historian Polybius and of the geographer Strabo, was the land extending southward from the Armenian highlands to modern Baghdad. The name Mesopotamia was used in the Septuagint Version of the Old Testament to translate the Hebrew *Aram Naharaim*, "Aram of the two rivers" (Gen. 24:10). This is the section of northern Mesopotamia around the junction of the rivers Habor and Euphrates, a district also known as Paddan-Aram ("the fields of Aram," Gen. 25:20; 28:2, etc.) which included the biblical city of Haran, where Abraham and the

THE WYCLIFFE HISTORICAL GEOGRAPHY OF BIBLE LANDS

patriarchal family stopped while on the way to Canaan.

In modern use, the name Mesopotamia applies to the entire Tigris-Euphrates region from the mountains of the north to the marshlands at the head of the Persian Gulf. By the Third Dynasty of Ur (c. 2060-1950 B.C.), at the beginning of the biblical age of the Patriarchs, Lower Mesopotamia was known as "Sumer and Akkad," Sumer being the territory north of the Persian Gulf, and Akkad being the region around modern Baghdad. Later, when the city-state of Babylon rose to prominence, Lower Mesopotamia became known as "Babylonia." Modern Iraq occupies most of the territory of ancient Mesopotamia, which stretched some 600 miles north and south and 300 miles east and west.

The rivers. Both the Tigris and the Euphrates rivers have their sources in the mountains of Armenia, which reach heights of 10,000 feet. The ancient name for Armenia was Urartu, of which the biblical Ararat is a variant. "Upon the mountains of Ararat" (Gen. 8:4) the ark of Noah rested following the flood. From these mountains the Tigris descends in a fairly straight course of about 1,000 miles to the Persian Gulf. Along its upper reaches lay the most important cities of ancient Assyria such as Nineveh, Ashur, and Calah. The Euphrates took a more leisurely course to the sea, meandering for almost 1,800 miles. Along the lower Euphrates rose the city of Babylon and other great centers of Babylonia.

Before entering the Persian Gulf, the Tigris and the Euphrates unite to form the

2. Sunset on the Euphrates

CASPIAN SEA

PERSIAN GULF

SUSA

KURDISTAN

ELAM

ZAGROS MTS.

MTS. OF NISIR

ESHNUNNA
BAGHDAD
JEMDET NASR

UMMA
LAGASH

BASRA

TEPE GAWRA
CALAH
KIRKUK
JARMO
NUZU
TIGRIS

KISH
NIPPUR
ISIN
URUK
LARSA
UR
ERIDU
TELL EL-OBEID

BABYLON

A S S Y R I A

KHORSABAD
NINEVEH
TELL HASSUNA
ASHUR
SAMARRA
R.
SIPPAR
AGADE

EUPHRATES R.

BABYLONIA

M E S O P O T A M I A

MARI

TELL HALAF
HARAN

CARCHEMISH

MESOPOTAMIA

0   50   100   200
SCALE OF MILES

Shatt-al-Arab at Kurna, southwest of Basra. It flows through a region of marshes, where the so-called "marsh Arabs" eke out a precarious existence. Modern marsh dwellers follow many of the customs of their ancestors who populated the area during Sumerian times. The boats in use there today are identical in design to those illustrated in tombs from ancient Ur.

As the snows of the north melt, the waters of the Tigris and Euphrates rise, reaching flood stage in April and May. Starting with the month of June, the waters again subside. Floods may do much damage because the water hardly penetrates the sunbaked soil.

The flood situation is aggravated when unusually heavy rain coincides with the melting of snow in the Taurus and Zagros Mountains. As recently as 1954, such a flood destroyed part of Baghdad. A system of canals, dikes, and dams was early devised to regulate the available water during the dry period, bringing fertility to the soil and protection from flood damage. Efficient governments took pride in such projects. Rim-Sin of Larsa boasted that he had "dug the canal of abundance, the canal of the plain as far as the sea." The lawgiver Hammurabi named the canal which he built "Hammurabi is the prosperity of the people." A later ruler, Siniddina, boasted, "Indeed I have provided waters of everlastingness, unceasing prosperity for my land of Larsa."

Rainfall. The importance of the Tigris and Euphrates to the existence of civilization in the Mesopotamian Valley is underscored by a look at rainfall statistics for the region. In Babylonia, rainfall averages six inches a year and comes mainly during the winter and spring. In some years there is none at all during the summer. In the hill country of Assyria the annual average is 15 to 16 inches. In the mountains the amount may be 30 inches a year.

The dryness of Lower Mesopotamia is responsible for the dust storm (known as

3. The "treasury" at Ur made from clay brick, illustrating the fact that Mesopotamians were "people of the soil"

idyah) which occurs each spring and summer. Blowing in from the west, the wind removes sand from the desert, depositing it in the river valley and forming immense mounds and dunes.

Through the centuries, both the Tigris and the Euphrates have changed their courses. Aerial photography helps the modern archaeologist to trace abandoned riverbeds and to note how great cities were first bypassed by the river and then abandoned by a people that needed water for subsistence.

People of the soil. From Samarra, on the Tigris River north of Baghdad, to the head of the Persian Gulf is the 400-mile-long Mesopotamian plain, built largely by alluvial silt. Here the inhabitants were literally "people of the soil." They made their building materials from clay bricks and raised their food and clothing on the soil, the latter largely on the backs of animals. Likewise, they made their pottery from clay, and their writing material consisted of clay tablets.

In Assyria the situation was somewhat different. There abundant supplies of limestone and alabaster and some marble changed methods of construction. But the population was still a people of the soil and still very dependent on the rivers.

Periodic invasion. As already intimated, mountains rose to the north of the Mesopotamian Valley. They also lay all along the eastern edge of the prosperous lowlands. These mountainous regions bred a hardy type of people who found their meager lands insufficient for an expanding population and who found themselves being pushed from behind by other tribes. This double incentive plus the attraction of the wealth of the valley brought periodic inva-

sions of Mesopotamia. Once in the valley, these invaders tended to intermingle with the older population over a fairly large area because there were no natural barriers in Mesopotamia. Thus the population and culture of the region were constantly infused with new blood and new ideas, in contrast with the homogeneous development of Egypt.

Historical Developments

A Historical Overview

Professor Robert Braidwood of the University of Chicago believes that the beginnings of village life will be found in northern Mesopotamia and adjacent regions, and that these early villages will date somewhere between 10,000 and 7,000 B.C.; and he has expended considerable effort to prove it. A Bible student would expect village life to begin at an early time in this region because here Noah's ark rested and the repopulation of the earth started. Of this early Neolithic development little is as yet known.

4. Royal sled from tomb at Ur, c. 2500 B.C.

Sumerians. The first people of the Mesopotamian Valley important for the development of civilization were the Sumerians, who came from the Caucasus region during the fourth millennium B.C. or possibly a little earlier. Who they were is still a puzzle, but their achievements are more familiar. They developed cuneiform writing, introduced the wheel, the arch, and the vault, produced a calendar and a system of mathematics based on the number 60, and contributed much more to the rise of civilization in this area of the world. Learning how to irrigate the lower reaches of the valley, they built city-states for the growing population of the area. 'Obeid, Ur, Erech, Eridu, Lagash, Nippur, and other city-states became important in the fourth and third millennia B.C.

Sargon of Akkad. During the third millennium B.C., Semites became more numerous in the Mesopotamian Valley and controlled the area during the Old Akkadian Period, 2360-2180. Sargon of Akkad, operating from his capital south of modern Baghdad, was the guiding light to empire at the beginning of the period. He was the first empire builder in the region.

Ur's revival. Thereafter, the city-state of Ur sparked a Neo-Sumerian revival during the city's golden age, 2060-1950 B.C. How much actual political power Ur exercised over Mesopotamia during this time is problematical. Perhaps her hegemony was largely a result of economic and commercial success.

Hammurabi. The next great historical development came during the Old Babylonian Period, 1830-1550 B.C. Babylon was raised from the position of an insignificant town along the Euphrates to that of the capital of an empire. Hammurabi (1728-1686 B.C.) was the great empire builder and lawgiver. About 1650 the Kassites descended from the mountain rim surrounding Mesopotamia and eventually established a kingdom that ruled at least Babylonia for about a half millennium. Details of this era are meager.

Assyrian Empire. Meanwhile Assyria gradually rose in power, contesting with the Hittites, Hurrians, Egyptians, and others for a place in the sun. Finally Tiglath-pileser I launched the Assyrian Empire about 1100 B.C. But after his death the nation slumped into a rather moribund condition for about 200 years. Then in 883 Ashurnasirpal came to the throne and established Assyrian military power and put Assyria on the road to imperial development. Babylonia, Syria, Phoenicia, Palestine, and Egypt all fell under her sway.

Neo-Babylonian Empire. Revolts against Assyrian power were numerous, but finally a coalition of Babylonians, Scythians, and Medes took Nineveh in 612 B.C. and brought the empire to an end. The Neo-Babylonian, or Chaldean, power then controlled Mesopotamia, as well as Syria, Phoenicia, and Palestine, until Babylon fell to the Medo-Persians in 539 B.C. The Babylonian Empire was, of course, essentially the empire of Nebuchadnezzar, and it disintegrated shortly after his death.

Persian Empire. Under the Persians, whose great capitals were located in the Iranian highlands, the great cities of Mesopotamia lost much of their former glory. Nineveh had been destroyed in 612 B.C., and Babylon was destroyed by Xerxes early in the fifth century B.C. The interest of Alexander the Great in rebuilding Babylon never came to fruition.

5. Alexander coin from Persepolis

Alexander and the Seleucids. Persian hosts fell before Alexander the Great on several occasions, but for all practical purposes the empire was Alexander's after the Battle of Arbela in 331 B.C. The conqueror did not live long enough to establish his power effectively over the Near East, however. On his death in 323 B.C., his generals began to squabble over the immense territory conquered. Seleucus managed to take Mesopotamia with most of the rest of the old Persian Empire. But his successors were ineffective in maintaining the empire, and the Parthians gained control of Mesopotamia about the middle of the third century B.C. and held it until Rome won Mesopotamia by force of arms early in the second century A.D.

Beginnings

Both in southern Mesopotamia and in Egypt by about 3000 B.C., man had learned to keep meaningful records which became

6. Stone house foundations, Jarmo, Iraq, *c.* 6500 B.C.

the raw material from which later history was written. Much is known about the people who lived before 3000 B.C., but such knowledge comes from the study of their buildings, tools, jewelry, and other artifacts, and even from the animal and human bones discovered in ancient communities.

Before man settled in the Tigris-Euphrates and Nile river valleys, he already had developed a fairly high degree of culture. He acquired food by hunting and fishing, and ate the grains and berries which he could gather in season. Civilization, as now known, could develop only as man abandoned the nomadic life and settled in one place. As long as he was constantly on the move, food-gathering occupied most of his time, and the arts had no place to take root.

Jarmo. In 1948 Robert J. Braidwood began a series of expeditions for the Oriental Institute of the University of Chicago at Jarmo, in the highlands of eastern Iraq, thirty miles from modern Kirkuk, looking for the beginnings of village life in the Near East. During successive years, Braidwood excavated Jarmo, where he found fifteen different levels of occupation, the top five of which contained pottery. But the lower levels dated from a period before pottery had been invented. Even in the earliest levels, the people of Jarmo had tools made from flint and obsidian.

Although most of the earliest houses were crudely built of packed mud, some had stone foundations, making it possible for modern archaeologists to trace their plans.

THE WYCLIFFE HISTORICAL GEOGRAPHY OF BIBLE LANDS

The people of Jarmo ground their cereals between grindstones; but they do not appear to have used hoes, a fact which suggests that grains were gathered wild. One of the flint sickles bears evidence that it had been fastened into a wooden handle with bitumen.

The presence of clay figurines of animals (goats, sheep, dogs, and pigs) and of pregnant women suggests that the people of Jarmo practiced a fertility cult. They used stone in making decorative beads, rings, and armbands which probably served both a magical and an ornamental purpose. Bones of sheep, goats, pigs, and oxen discovered on the mound provide evidence that some progress had been made in the domestication of animals.

Tools made of obsidian indicate that the people of Jarmo were engaged in trade with other peoples, for obsidian is not native to the Jarmo area and had to be imported from the region around Lake Van, 250 miles away, or from some more remote source. The carbon 14 method of dating organic materials, applied to snail shells from ancient Jarmo, gives evidence that the settlement dates from the period just before 6500 B.C.[1] Dr. Braidwood and his staff continue to excavate at other sites in northeastern Iraq and across the border in Iran.

Hassuna. About two thousand years passed between the prepottery Neolithic settlement at Jarmo and the beginnings of history among the Sumerians of southern Mesopotamia. The study of pottery forms a convenient basis for following this period of great cultural development. The Jarmo culture appears to have been succeeded by one which was first identified at the mound of Tell Hassuna, northwest of ancient Ashur on the Tigris River. The Iraq Museum excavated Hassuna in 1943/44 and found at its lowest level flint tools and coarse earthenware jugs. Stone axes may have been used for breaking the ground in a crude type of agriculture. No metal was yet in use, but Hassuna illustrates the existence of a village culture based on small farming during the Neolithic Period or Late Stone Age. Pottery similar to that from Hassuna has also been discovered in Syria and Palestine, suggesting that the Hassuna culture was widespread.

Remains from seven layers were found above the earliest Hassuna settlement, showing a succession of cultures in which people lived in permanent houses, some of which had several rooms and an open courtyard. Pottery also was improved in design and texture, some having incised or painted decorations. Flint-toothed sickles were used for reaping, and grain was stored in spherical clay bins. The women of Hassuna ground their flour between flat rubbing stones and baked their bread in clay ovens. Infants were buried in pottery jars, and other jars—perhaps for food and water—were placed nearby. Beads, amulets, and figurines used in a fertility cult were also part of the culture which left its remains at Hassuna.

The upper levels at Hassuna yielded pottery of a type that was first identified by Ernst Herzfeld in his excavations at Samarra, on the Tigris north of Baghdad. Herzfeld was investigating Islamic ruins in the area, but he was attracted to the five-foot layer of debris between the pavements of the houses and virgin soil. In the debris he found badly preserved graves containing painted pottery in a variety of forms: plates, dishes on high bases, hemispheric bowls, widemouthed pots, and squat jars. The pottery was of medium thickness, and much of it was overfired. It was distinctive in that it was covered with drawings of plants, animals, and people in bright red and purple-brown. Geometric motifs also appear. This Samarra type pottery has been found at various sites between the Tigris River and northern Syria.

[1]Robert J. Braidwood, *Prehistoric Men* (3rd ed.; Chicago: Chicago Natural History Museum Press, 1957), pp. 127, 130.

Halaf. The pottery next in chronological sequence to that of Samarra comes from Tell Halaf (Gozan), near the headwaters of the Khabur River in northern Mesopotamia, which was excavated over a period of years (1911-13, 1927, 1929) by Baron Max von Oppenheim. In one of the oldest strata, Oppenheim discovered fine painted pottery decorated with black and orange-red paint. Some of it was geometrical in design, but more often the painting was of birds, animals (frequently horses), or human beings. The pottery appeared in a variety of forms: beakers, basins, plates, bowls, and jugs. The pottery had a porcelain-like finish and had been fired in intense heat in closed kilns. Similar ceramic ware was found at Hajji Muhammed and at Eridu in southern Mesopotamia.

The excavations at Tell Halaf yielded knives and tools made of flint and obsidian. A Halafian vase depicts a man riding a chariot, the first such representation in the history of art. The chariot had two wheels with eight spokes each. Amulets, clay figurines, and stamp seals were also found. Houses at Tell Halaf were small and made of mud brick, but larger buildings were erected on stone foundations and were circular in shape. The Halafians appear to have been a peaceful agricultural people.

Arpachiya. In 1932 the British School of Archaeology began excavations at Arpachiya, about four miles north of Nineveh, after learning of the discovery of Tell Halaf type pottery there. The archaeologists found evidence of sixteen levels of occupation, the sixth to the tenth of which were from the period of the Halafian culture. Particularly interesting was a craftsman's shop which had been burned, its charred remains scattered in the ashes. In a debris was a piece of red ocher clay, flat palettes for mixing paint, and bone tools for shaping the clay. Pieces of earthenware pottery bore white, black, and red decorations. Geometric designs, flowers, trees, and dancing girls were used for ornamentation. Arpachiya appears to have suffered at the hands of a people whose culture bears the type name of Tell 'Obeid. The sixth occupation level of Arpachiya gives evidence of the introduction of this new cultural element.

7. Head of bronze bull, 'Obeid, third millennium B.C.

'Obeid. The ruins of Tell 'Obeid, located on the Lower Euphrates River above ancient Ur, were discovered by H. R. Hall in 1919, and systematic excavations were conducted in 1923/24 and 1937 by Sir Charles Leonard Woolley for the Joint Expedition of the British Museum and the University of Pennsylvania. 'Obeid pottery was pale green in color, painted with free geometric designs in black or dark brown. Some of it was made by hand and the remainder fashioned on a slow, hand-turned wheel. Human and animal figurines were also molded in clay.

'Obeid type pottery has also been discovered at Ur, Erech, Eridu, Lagash, Susa, Persepolis, and numerous other places. The discovery of a peculiar variety in the fourteenth to eighteenth levels at Eridu has caused some scholars to suggest that there is a proto- or pre-'Obeid period which was

8. Copper panel from Sumerian temple lintel at 'Obeid (2600 B.C.), showing the god Im-du-gud and stags

contemporary with Tell Halaf. 'Obeid pottery, although for the most part later than Halaf, is aesthetically less attractive. The use of the wheel and the ability to maintain uniform heat in a closed oven were, however, important technical advances in the ceramic art.

Houses at 'Obeid were made of reeds plastered with mud, and larger buildings were made of sun-dried bricks. Mud-plastered walls were decorated with mosaics of small, slender, pencil-like cones of baked clay. The ends, some of which were painted, provided valuable waterproofing for the houses and served as decoration for otherwise drab walls.

Tepe Gawra. Man's discovery of the usefulness of metal marked one of the greatest cultural advances of prehistoric times. The oldest known brass ax came to light during excavations at Tepe Gawra, fifteen miles northeast of Nineveh. Metal was introduced from some unknown mountain area and was first used for weapons, while stone continued to be used for household tools. Ephraim Speiser of the University of Pennsylvania discovered Tepe Gawra in 1927, and he con-

ducted a series of campaigns there from 1931 to 1938 under the sponsorship of the American Schools of Oriental Research and the University Museum. The oldest pottery from Tepe Gawra was of the Halaf type, and the ax came from the 'Obeid level.

Eridu. A few miles south of Ur is the mound of Tell Abu Shahrain, ancient Eridu, the site of the first ruling dynasty according to the Sumerian King List. Eridu was excavated from 1946 to 1949 by Faud Safar for the Iraq Department of Antiquities. Its lower levels, dating from 4500 B.C., contained pottery with ornamental designs which are earlier than 'Obeid ware. There are also remains of a shrine, ten feet square, built of sun-dried bricks. Successive levels at Eridu reveal a series of fourteen shrines from the prehistoric period.

Uruk. Thirty-five miles up the Euphrates from Tell 'Obeid is ancient Uruk or Erech (Gen. 10:10; modern Warka), one of the oldest of Mesopotamian cities and one which flourished well into Hellenistic times. The period of Uruk and the following Jemdet Nasr period comprise the Late Prehistoric period in Mesopotamia.

Excavations at Uruk began in a small way in 1850, but serious work was commenced in 1912 by Julius Jordan for the Deutsche Orient-Gesellschaft. The work was interrupted by World War I, but it was resumed in 1928, continuing until 1939 when World War II halted the work again. Excavation was resumed in 1954. Two ziggurats[2] have been cleared, along with several temples from the late fourth and early third millennia. At one point, a shaft was dug to virgin soil, 70 feet below the surface, revealing eighteen levels of occupation. The original village, Kullab, was founded by 'Obeid people around 4000 B.C. Erech itself was founded by Meskiaggasher early in the third millennium. His successors included such heroes as Enmerkar, Lugalbanda, and Gilgamesh.

The pottery of prehistoric Uruk was made on a spinning potter's wheel and baked in a kiln smothered down to make the smoke penetrate and color the clay. It was highly polished but unpainted. Rough limestone blocks forming a small pavement constitute the oldest stone structure in Mesopotamia, and the Erech ziggurat is the oldest staged temple tower.

The introduction of the cylinder seal and of cuneiform script form the most notable of Uruk's contributions to culture and to history. Stone stamp seals were impressed in clay to indicate ownership as early as the Halaf period. The flat seals of the Halaf period were replaced by a domelike shape in the 'Obeid era. At Uruk, however, we find the first seals made by cutting a design into a small stone cylinder so that it would leave an impression when rolled across a soft surface. The seals introduced a new art form, for each seal had to have a distinctive design to identify its owner and his property. The religion and mythology of the day provided motifs which artists carved into their cylinder seals.

In one of the temples excavated at Uruk, there were a number of flat clay tablets inscribed in a crude pictographic script, representing the earliest stage of the cuneiform syllabary which was used throughout the Fertile Crescent until the Persian Period. The language of these earliest tablets was Sumerian, but the cuneiform syllabary was later adopted by Babylonians, Assyrians, and other Fertile Crescent peoples.

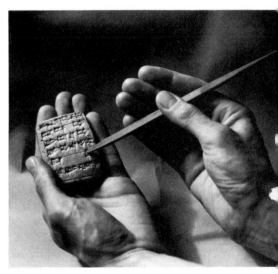

9. Babylonian clay tablet with stylus in correct position for writing cuneiform

Jemdet Nasr. The last period of Mesopotamian prehistory bears the type name of Jemdet Nasr, a mound near ancient Babylon. Jemdet Nasr pottery was painted with black and yellow designs, and a rapidly developing culture produced utensils of bronze as well as stone. The pictographic cuneiform script, first seen at Uruk, appeared in a more advanced form during the Jemdet Nasr period, and sculpture in stone developed into a fine art. Trade was highly developed among the Jemdet Nasr people, and the art of writing spread to the point where one enters the full light of history for the first time.

---

[2]Towers with each successive story smaller than the one beneath it and capped with a temple.

The Sumerian City-States

The people who lived in Lower Mesopotamia at the dawn of history are known as Sumerians. Their system of wedge-shaped characters inscribed on clay tablets constitutes man's earliest written records, and their culture became as normative to the ancient Fertile Crescent as that of Greece and Rome in the life of modern Europe. The Sumerians seem to have migrated into the lower Tigris-Euphrates Valley from the Caucasus Mountain region.[3] In the Sumerian language, the words for "country" and "mountain" are identical, suggesting that they originally represented one concept. Sumerians were the first people to build immense artificial mountains called ziggurats as foundations for the temples of their gods, who were thought to be most at home in mountain sanctuaries. Sumerians termed themselves "the black-headed" people, a fact which suggests that at one time they distinguished themselves from fair-haired neighbors.

The Sumerians were not alone in the lower Tigris-Euphrates Valley, however, because Iranians from the east and Semites from the Arabian Peninsula to the west contested their control of this area. Properly speaking, Sumer was the region from Baghdad to the Persian Gulf, the territory north of Sumer being known as Akkad (or Agade). The proximity of peoples of diverse ethnic backgrounds brought inevitable friction; but in time, the culture of the lower Tigris-Euphrates Valley tended to become unified. The sharing of a common system of writing and, to a large extent, common religious and mythological ideas, hastened the process.

Sumer comprised a group of city-states which, in theory, belonged to the gods. Nippur was the city of Enlil and Ninlil; Erech of Anu and Inanna; Ur of Nanna, the moon god, and his wife, Ningal. The

10. Impression of a Sumerian cylinder seal. Liberation of the sun-god, *c.* 2250 B.C.

head of state was known as the *lugal* ("great man") or king. The Sumerian King List asserts that kingship came directly from heaven, but there is evidence that prehistoric Sumerian cities were governed by city assemblies. The legend of Gilgamesh and Agga describes a threat to the state of Uruk which first came to the attention of the city elders and then was discussed by the men of the city, presumably those who bore arms.[4]

In historic times, the ruler was either the *lugal* ("king") or the *ensi*, a term used of the priest of the local temple who acted as viceroy of the city god. The city and its adjacent lands were regarded as the estate of its god, and it was the responsibility of the *ensi* to look after the god's interests. The most important building was the temple, which served as a commercial as well as a religious center. Farmers either brought a fixed proportion of their produce to the temple or served as direct temple employees. The temples maintained workshops where craftsmen were busy weaving, brewing, or laboring at carpentry, metalwork, stonecutting, or jewel setting. Wages were paid from the produce brought to the temple, which had storehouses filled with the excess barley, wool, sesame oil, and dates. Trading caravans carried surplus products northward where they were exchanged for metal, stone, and wood, none of which was native to southern Mesopotamia.

[3]Samuel N. Kramer, *American Journal of Archaeology,* LII (1948), 156-64.

[4]T. Jacobsen, "Primitive Democracy in Ancient Mesopotamia," *Journal of Near Eastern Studies,* II (1943), 159-72.

Periodically, ambitious rulers of Sumerian city-states made war on one another. The gods were expected to fight on behalf of their cities, and defeat in battle was regarded as punishment for some serious offense. Although a number of Sumerian states governed large territories, none established an empire comparable to those of the later Assyrians and Babylonians.

Settlement in the Tigris-Euphrates Valley encouraged a rapid development in culture among the Sumerian city-states. The erratic nature of the Tigris and Euphrates rivers forced the settlers on its banks to devise a system of dams and canals if they were to make efficient use of the available water supply. Early in Sumerian history, canals were dug and laws were enforced to control the use of the water. Cooperation was also necessary in procuring materials for hoes, sickle blades, spades, and hammers which were used on the farms. Since the metals and stone used in farm implements were not native to southern Mesopotamia, the Sumerian farmers were dependent on the imports which resulted from trade and commerce for their livelihood. Standard weights and measures were adopted and controlled by the temple officials. Taxes were heavy, and the tax collector was no more popular in Sumer than in modern Western countries.

The period from about 3000 to 2300 B.C. is known as the Classical Sumerian, or Early Dynastic, Age. Excavations at Tell Asmar, ancient Eshnunna, fifty miles northeast of Baghdad in the Diyala River area, show a transition from the Jemdet Nasr period, attested by the typical polychrome pottery of the time, to the first stage of Sumerian Early Dynastic history. Henri Frankfort, the excavator of Tell Asmar, discovered a number of well-preserved statues under the floor of an early dynastic temple. Among them are a fertility god with a full black beard and his consort, the mother goddess, wearing a one-piece cloak which passes under her right arm and is fastened on the left shoulder. The cult statues from Tell Asmar are the earliest of which there is knowledge.

The city-state of Ur. In 1854 the British Consul at Basra (or Busra), J. E. Taylor, dug into the mound known as el-Muqayyar ("mound of pitch"), 200 miles north of the Persian Gulf, and identified it as the site of the ancient Sumerian city of Ur. Interest developed because of biblical references to Ur of the Chaldees as the place from which Abraham began the trek that took him ultimately to Canaan. The University of Pennsylvania and the British Museum conducted preliminary work there during the 1918/19 season, and a prolonged series of campaigns was conducted by the two institutions under the leadership of Sir Charles Leonard Woolley from 1922 to 1934.

Woolley found evidence of a settlement at Ur during the 'Obeid Period (before 3500 B.C.). Flint objects, clay figurines, and pottery of the 'Obeid type were made by the pre-Sumerian settlers at Ur, who engaged in trade and already showed signs of a high culture. Above this 'Obeid level, Woolley found a layer of silt from three to eleven feet thick which he thought to be the remains of the biblical flood.[5] Captain E. Mackay and Stephen Langdon, excavating at Kish, also came upon flood deposits, but pottery evidence indicates that the two floods did not take place at the same time or even in the same century. The Tigris and Euphrates rivers changed their beds several times, and the so-called flood silt may have been formed when the rivers inundated parts of the land that had earlier been inhabited. Martin Beek suggests that the so-called flood silt was not caused by water at all. In his opinion it was produced by the dust storms which occur in southern Mesopotamia each spring and summer.[6]

[5]C. L. Woolley, *Ur of the Chaldees* (London: Ernest Benn, 1930), p. 29.
[6]*Atlas of Mesopotamia* (New York: Thomas Nelson and Sons, 1962), p. 12.

Above Woolley's flood silt there were further levels showing that Ur was occupied successively by people who used the Uruk and Jemdet Nasr type of pottery, building techniques, and funerary practices. From the Jemdet Nasr level (c. 3000 B.C.), Woolley found traces of a ziggurat, inscribed cuneiform tablets, and cylinder seals.

During his 1927-30 campaign, Woolley cleared the remarkable "Royal Cemetery" of Ur, which ranks as one of the great discoveries in Near Eastern archaeology. Under a layer of graves containing seals and inscriptions of the Akkad dynasty were

Above the vault of Abargi was the tomb of a lady who was identified by a blue stone cylinder as Shubad. Her body had been placed on a wooden bier with a gold cup in her hand. She wore an elaborate headdress made from nine yards of gold band. The "Spanish comb" in her hair had five points which ended in gold flowers with centers of lapis lazuli. Lady Shubad was further adorned with crescent-shaped earrings.

Near the tombs were death pits containing the remains of chariots which had been driven into them, treasures which seem to have been placed there in honor of the de-

11. Gaming board from Ur, c. 2500 B.C.

tombs from about 2500 B.C. Many of them were burial places of commoners whose bodies had been wrapped in matting or placed in coffins of wood, wickerwork, or clay. The graves contained the personal belongings of the deceased—bracelets, necklaces, vanity cases, tools, weapons, food, and drink. Each body was placed on its side, in a sleeping position, with the hands holding a cup to the mouth.

Near the graves of the commoners, Woolley came upon the so-called "Royal Tombs" made of native sun-dried brick or stone imported from the western desert. One tomb, identified by a cylinder seal as belonging to a man named Abargi, had been partially plundered. Against the tomb wall, however, there stood the silver model of a boat like those which can be seen today plying the marshes of southern Mesopotamia.

12. Queen Shubad of Ur, c. 2500 B.C.

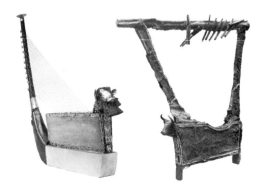

been priests and priestesses who were sacrificed in fertility rites.[7]

Some knowledge of music in ancient Sumer is gained from the harps, or lyres,

15. Royal lyres from Ur, *c.* 2500 B.C.

13. Queen Shubad, detail of the headdress

ceased, and large numbers of people who were evidently killed at the time of the funeral. It appears that the servants of a king (or priest) went into the grave voluntarily in the hope of continuing to serve their master in the next life. On the other hand, the bodies in the death pit may have

found in the "Royal Tombs." They are normally decorated with heads of animals including a bearded bull, a cow, and a stag. Two statues depict a goat standing in front of a bush from which it seems to be eating leaves. Woolley likened these to the biblical "ram in the thicket," although the Sumerian statues are at least five hundred years before Abraham.

16. Dagger of Mes-kalam-dug, hilt of lapis lazuli, sheath of gold filigree 14½ inches long

14. A death pit at Ur

A beautiful golden dagger, one of the finest art objects of the ancient East, came from the tomb of "Mes-kalam-dug, hero of the Good Land." The hero's body was in the usual position, and between his hands there was a beautiful cup of heavy gold.

[7]Cf. E. A. Speiser, *Antiquity*, VIII (1934), 45.

17. Helmet of Mes-kalam-dug

The dagger hung from a broad silver belt at his side. Over the skull was a helmet in the shape of a wig, with locks of hair hammered in relief and individual hairs engraved in delicate lines.

In one of the large stone tombs, Woolley discovered the Standard of Ur, a wooden panel twenty-two inches long by nine inches high, which was probably carried by the ancient Sumerians on a pole during their processions. It was inlaid with mosaic work on both sides, one of which depicted scenes of war, and the other of peace. The wooden background had rotted away, but the pieces of inlay kept their relative positions, and skillful work on the part of the archaeologists made it possible to restore the mosaics with perfect fidelity. Each side comprised three rows made of shell figures set in a lapis lazuli background.

The "war" panel begins with a representation of the king, distinguished by his height, dismounting from his chariot. Soldiers lead to him a group of naked captives with arms tied behind their backs. In the second row appears the phalanx of the royal army advancing. Warriors wear long cloaks and copper helmets and are armed with axes. Ahead of them the men of the light-armed infantry fight without cloaks, armed with axes or short spears. The third row depicts chariots of javelin throwers who break into an excited gallop as they encounter corpses strewn on the ground.

The reverse side of the panel, dedicated to peace, shows the king and his family at a banquet. Musicians play their instruments, and servants bring in food. Spoils captured from the enemy are also in evidence. The people are dressed in the characteristic Sumerian sheepskin kilts with the upper part of their bodies bare.

The Sumerians of Ur were conquered by

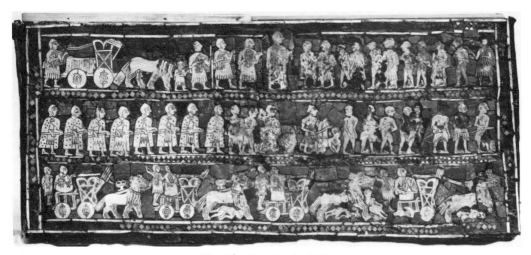

18. The Standard of Ur

19. The ziggurat at Ur

the Semitic ruler Sargon of Akkad (or Accad) and, like their neighboring states, were ruled by the Akkadians from about 2360 to 2180 B.C. While Ur was not the center of government, Woolley found remains there dating from the Sargonid period.

The last great period of Sumerian power and cultural growth is known as the Third Dynasty of Ur (2060-1950 B.C.), founded by Ur-Nammu. He was able to wrest power from the Gutians, a little-known mountain people who had overrun lower Mesopotamia following the breakup of the Akkadian dynasty. Ur-Nammu rebuilt the walls of Ur, its ziggurat, palace, and numerous public buildings.

A contemporary record of the building of the ziggurat is given on the Stele of Ur-Nammu, a slab of white limestone nearly five feet across and ten feet high. The top panel depicts the king in an attitude of prayer. Above him are flying angels carrying vases from which water is flowing.

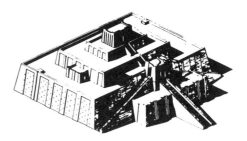

20. Ziggurat at Ur, reconstruction

THE WYCLIFFE HISTORICAL GEOGRAPHY OF BIBLE LANDS

These are the first known artistic representations of angels. The king appears to be thanking his god for the gift of water, so needful in southern Mesopotamia. A series of panels is then devoted to the building of the ziggurat. In the first of these, Ur-Nammu stands before the goddess Ningal and the god Nanna receiving orders for the building of the ziggurat. The next panel shows the king with compasses, mortar basket, pick, and trowel on his way to begin work. And the final panel, although poorly preserved, shows one of the baskets of the workmen leaning against the side of the rising structure.

An extensive sacred area developed as other buildings were erected around the ziggurat. One of these, the Gig-par-ku temple, dedicated to Ningal, the moon goddess, had a well-equipped kitchen with a well for water, fireplaces for boiling water, a bitumen-covered brick table for cutting up the carcass of an animal, a flat-topped cooking range, and a domed bread oven. The kitchen was an important part of ancient temples since animals were offered in sacrifice, and the cooked flesh was meant to be shared among the god, the priests, and the worshipers.

Present knowledge of business life in the Ur III Period comes largely from two thousand cuneiform tablets which record the offerings and taxes given to Nanna, the moon god. Records were carefully kept by the temple scribes, who compiled weekly, monthly, and annual reports. There are also records of a weaving factory which produced twelve varieties of woolen cloth. Cuneiform tablets give the names of the women who did the weaving, the rations allotted to them, the quantity of wool issued to each, and the amount of cloth manufactured.

Ur was a center for commerce and trade. Ships from the Persian Gulf brought to Ur diorite and alabaster stone, gold, copper ore, ivory, and hardwoods. Products of Egypt, Ethiopia, and India reached the

21. Street of Ur in Abraham's day. Note windowless house fronts. Houses faced inward on courtyards.

trading houses of Ur during the time that Abraham lived there.

Fragments of the law code of Ur-Nammu have been identified among the Sumerian texts at the Museum of the Ancient Orient in Istanbul. The texts state that Ur-Nammu was chosen by the god Nanna to rule over Ur and Sumer. Ur-Nammu boasted that he removed dishonesty and corruption from government and established honest weights and measures. The few laws which have been preserved mention fines to be imposed upon men who had caused certain injuries to others. In the temple area was the Sumerian law court, with its Dublal-mah, or "Great House of Tablets," in which the clay tablets recording legal decisions were kept. From the door of the Dublal-mah, judges announced their decisions to the waiting crowds.

Following the death of Ur-Nammu, the city of Ur began to lose its prestige. His son, Shulgi, proclaimed himself "the divine Shulgi, god of his land," but his greatest monument was his mortuary temple and sepulcher which Woolley excavated. Shulgi was followed successively by Bur-Sin, Gimil-Sin, and Ibi-Sin.

Changes were taking place in southern Mesopotamia in the days of Ibi-Sin. Ishbi-Irra, an Amorite from the city-state of Mari on the middle Euphrates, overran Akkad and occupied the city of Isin. Elamites crossed the Tigris, took Sumer, and placed their vassal on the throne at the city of Larsa. Ur was sacked and Ibi-Sin taken captive. Subsequently the city of Ur, the Nannar temple, and the great ziggurat were rebuilt, but catastrophe struck Ur again in 1737 B.C. when its rulers rebelled against Samsu-iluna, the son of Hammurabi who had brought Sumer into the Babylonian Empire. Samsu-iluna destroyed Ur, and little is heard of it for some centuries.

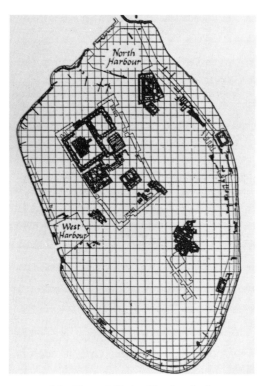

22. Plan of Ur in Abraham's day

About 1400 B.C., a Kassite ruler named Kurigalzu restored the Ningal Temple in Ur and rebuilt the great gateway into the sacred area and the House of Tablets. The next mention of the city is made when Nebuchadnezzar rebuilt its main temples and Nabonidus (or Nabu-naid, or Naboni-dus) (556-539 B.C.) increased the height of the ziggurat to seven stages and installed his daughter Belshalti-Nannar as high priestess to the moon god. Belshalti-Nannar collected antiquities and maintained a private museum. A clay tablet which lists the

objects in her collection is the earliest known museum catalog. Included were a Kassite boundary stone, a statue of Shulgi, copies of Ur III documents, some of which are extant in their earlier originals, and many other objects. Neo-Babylonian interest in Ur continued under the early Persians, but the latest document from the city is dated 316 B.C. About that time the Euphrates seems to have changed its course, for the ruins of Ur are now ten miles from the river on which it was once situated. This may be the reason Ur was abandoned and became but a "mound of pitch" until nineteenth century archaeologists determined to unlock its mysteries.[8]

Lagash. Fifty miles north of Ur is the mound of Telloh, ancient Lagash, which was first settled during the 'Obeid period. A dynasty was founded at Lagash about 2500 B.C. by Ur-Nanshe, who has left inscriptions describing the temples and canals which he built. His grandson, Eannatum, commemorated his conquest of neighboring Umma by erecting the Stele of the Vultures, one of the great art treasures from ancient Sumer.

The eighth ruler of Lagash, Urukagina (24th century B.C.), sought to free the land from corrupt tax collectors and other graft in political life. His reforms are the earliest mentioned in historical times. A few years after Urukagina's death, Lagash fell to its northern rival, Umma, whose ruler, Lugal-zaggisi, became king of Uruk and Ur and conquered territory as far as the Mediterranean.

Best known of the rulers of Lagash was Gudea, who established Sumerian power after a period of decline caused by the

[8]Biblical "Ur of the Chaldees" (Gen. 11:28) has been generally equated with Sumerian Ur since the extensive excavations at that site. An older view located biblical Ur at Urfa (Edessa), twenty miles northwest of Haran. While contemporary scholars do not locate Ur at Urfa, Cyrus H. Gordon maintains that the biblical Ur was located in northern Mesopotamia. Cf. Cyrus H. Gordon, *The World of the Old Testament* (New York: Doubleday & Co., 1948), p. 132.

THE WYCLIFFE HISTORICAL GEOGRAPHY OF BIBLE LANDS

Gutian invaders. Gudea's inscriptions indicate that he imported gold from Anatolia and Egypt, silver from the Taurus Mountains, cedars from the Amanus Range, copper from the Zagros Mountains, black diorite stone from Ethiopia, and timber from Dilmun.

Soon after Gudea's reign, Ur-Nammu of Ur gained control of the entire land of Sumer, including Lagash. Lagash continued, however, as an important Mesopotamian city until the second century B.C. It has been excavated by the French during a series of campaigns since 1877. A score of inscribed statues of Gudea make him the best-known figure in Sumerian history.

24. Gudea

23. A governor of Lagash, c. 2200 B.C.

Babylon and Its Environs

Babylon was located on the Euphrates River, fifty-one miles south of modern Baghdad, which is on the Tigris River. Its shorter form, Babel, appears in Genesis 10:10 as one of three cities ruled by Nimrod at a remote period of prehistory. The Akkadian form of the name is Bab-ili, a translation from the Sumerian *Ka-dingir-ra*, "gate of god." Babylon is a later Greek form of Bab-ili, Hebrew Bab-el. The biblical writer drew an analogy between Babel and the Hebrew verb *balal*, "to confuse," for *Babel* was the place of the confusion of tongues (Gen. 11:9).

According to Babylonian tradition, the city was founded by Marduk, who became the god of Babylon. Sargon of Akkad is said to have destroyed the city (c. 2350 B.C.) and to have carried soil from Baby-

25. The god Marduk

and Larsa in lower Mesopotamia. About 1830 B.C. an Amorite ruler, Sumu-abum, established a dynasty at Babylon which reached its zenith under Hammurabi (1728-1686 B.C.). Hammurabi controlled the territory from Mari on the Euphrates and Nineveh on the Tigris southward to the Persian Gulf.

lon to his new city of Akkad which he built nearby. The exact location of Akkad is unknown, but it was probably a part of greater Babylon. A text from Sargon's successor, Sharkallishari (c. 2250 B.C.), mentions the restoration of the temple tower (ziggurat) of Babylon, which evidently existed much earlier. Most biblical scholars think of the ziggurat of Babylon as the biblical Tower of Babel, although a number of ruins in the vicinity of Babylon have at various times been identified with the tower.

Troops from Ur attacked Babylon during the Ur III dynasty, and Shulgi of Ur appointed governors to rule the city on his behalf. The Sumerians at Ur were unable to maintain their power against Semitic invaders from the northwest known as Amorites, whose rulers controlled the city-state of Mari on the middle Euphrates, and Isin

26. Code of Hammurabi

27. Upper part of the Code of Hammurabi. Hammurabi receiving his laws from the sun-god

The rule of Hammurabi. Under Hammurabi, Babylon was a flourishing city with great palaces and temples. The E-temen-an-ki, "House of the Foundation of Heaven and Earth," with its ziggurat was one of the wonders of the age; and Marduk, the god of Babylon, was honored throughout Mesopotamia. The Babylonian account of creation, known from this time, names Marduk as the god who created the universe. The Babylon of Hammurabi also produced dictionaries, mathematical treatises, astronomical texts, and cuneiform documents dealing with a wide variety of scientific and pseudoscientific knowledge.

Best known of the texts from Hammurabi's Babylon is the famed law code discovered by Jacques de Morgan in 1901. The Code of Hammurabi was not an original production but a reformulation and application of a legal tradition which reached far back into the third millennium B.C. The same or similar traditions appear in the Ur-nammu, Lipit-Ishtar, and Eshnunna law codes. Hammurabi sought to provide stand-

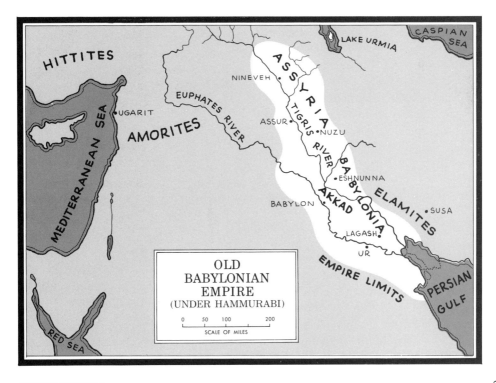

OLD
BABYLONIAN
EMPIRE
(UNDER HAMMURABI)

0   50   100   200

SCALE OF MILES

28. Kassite boundary stone. Melishi-pak presenting his daughter to goddess Nanar

sites, fell before the powerful Hittites from distant Anatolia. The Hittites retreated into Asia Minor, but Kassites controlled southern Mesopotamia until the twelfth century B.C.

Assyrian domination. By about 1150 B.C. Babylon had been able to shake off the Kassite yoke and establish a native dynasty. She was conquered again by Tiglath-pileser I (1116-1078 B.C.), the Assyrian empire builder whose campaigns took him

ard legal procedures throughout his realm and, by erecting a stele containing the recognized laws, to inform the people of the rights and obligations which they had as citizens of Babylon.

Kassite control. The period of Hammurabi was Babylon's first great period of cultural flowering. The second such period was not to take place for another millennium. Hammurabi's immediate successors enlarged the city of Babylon, but they soon faced a challenge from the non-Semitic Kassites, who emerged from the mountains of Luristan and began to make themselves masters of southern Mesopotamia. About 1530 B.C. Babylon, weakened by the Kas-

29. Boundary stone of Nebuchadnezzar I of Babylon, king during the twelfth century B.C.

northward into Armenia and Asia Minor, and westward to the Mediterranean. Under pressure from the rising Aramaean states, however, Assyria was forced to retreat to her own borders. Although she was later to emerge as a powerful empire, the Assyria of 1000 B.C. was quiescent. It was at this time that the Kingdom was established in Israel, and Babylon, too, had a period of respite.

The respite was brief, however. Shalmaneser III (859-824 B.C.) and Adad-nirari III (811-782 B.C.) campaigned vigorously and sought to restore Assyria to a place of world power. The Assyrians incorporated Babylon into their empire, but Babylon was continually restive. Sargon II, the conqueror of Samaria, had to put down a rebellion in Babylon led by Marduk-apal-iddina (biblical Merodach-baladan; II Kings 20:12; Isa. 39:1). For about twelve years Babylon successfully maintained its independence against the Assyrian overlords. She fell to Sargon, however, when he sacked the city and deported some of her population to Samaria.

When Sargon was succeeded by his son Sennacherib, Marduk-apal-iddina again rebelled and, with help from the Elamites, established himself as king. It was during this period that Marduk-apal-iddina sent envoys to Hezekiah (II Kings 20:12-19), seeking his aid. The Babylonians, hoping to stimulate simultaneous revolts against Assyria in Judah and other states in western Asia, felt that they could humble their Assyrian overlords. Egypt, under Shabaka (c. 710-695 B.C.), could be expected to lend support. The revolt failed, however. Although Sennacherib did not occupy Jerusalem, all of the remaining provinces in the West fell to him, and within a few months the rebellion in Babylon was put down. Marduk-apal-iddina was replaced by a puppet ruler, Bel-ibni. When Bel-ibni rebelled (c. 700 B.C.), Sennacherib replaced him with his own son Asshur-nadin-shum. Uprisings continued, however. About 694 B.C.

the king of Elam encouraged Babylon to rebel. A usurper, Nergal-ushezib, was placed on the throne, and Sennacherib's son was taken prisoner, later to be killed. Nergal-ushezib was quickly punished, but another usurper, Mushe-zib-Marduk, arose and all Babylonia was in rebellion. Sennacherib attempted to quell the revolt, but he was defeated by a coalition of Babylonians, Elamites, and their allies. Sennacherib did not give up, however, and in 689 B.C. he succeeded in conquering Babylon. He destroyed its temples and carried the statue of Marduk into Assyria. The people were treated with cruelty by the Assyrians, who were determined to put down revolt in Babylon once and for all.

Esarhaddon, a son of Sennacherib who succeeded to the throne of Assyria, undertook to stabilize the situation in Babylon by restoring the city and rebuilding the Marduk temple. Babylon became a vassal city under Shamash-shum-ukin, Esarhaddon's son. Shamash-shum-ukin quarreled with his brother Ashurbanipal, who succeeded his father Esarhaddon as king of Assyria. Rebellion broke out in Babylon and throughout the Assyrian Empire. After a bitter struggle, Ashurbanipal took Babylon in 648 B.C. Shamash-shum-ukin, who had defied his brother during the two years when the city was besieged, committed suicide. The Assyrians appointed Kandalanu as their governor in a chastened Babylon.

The Assyrian Empire fell within two decades after the death of Ashurbanipal. The Babylonians again sought independence, this time under a Chaldean prince, Nabopolassar, who defeated the Assyrians at Babylon in October, 626 B.C., and took the throne. The Chaldeans appear first in history as a seminomadic tribe occupying the desert regions between northern Arabia and the Persian Gulf (cf. Job 1:17). After the tenth century B.C. the Chaldeans (*Kaldu* in Assyrian texts) are found in the area south of Babylon. With the growth of

30. Reconstruction of Babylon from the Euphrates with the ziggurat in the foreground. Procession Street runs up the center of the picture.

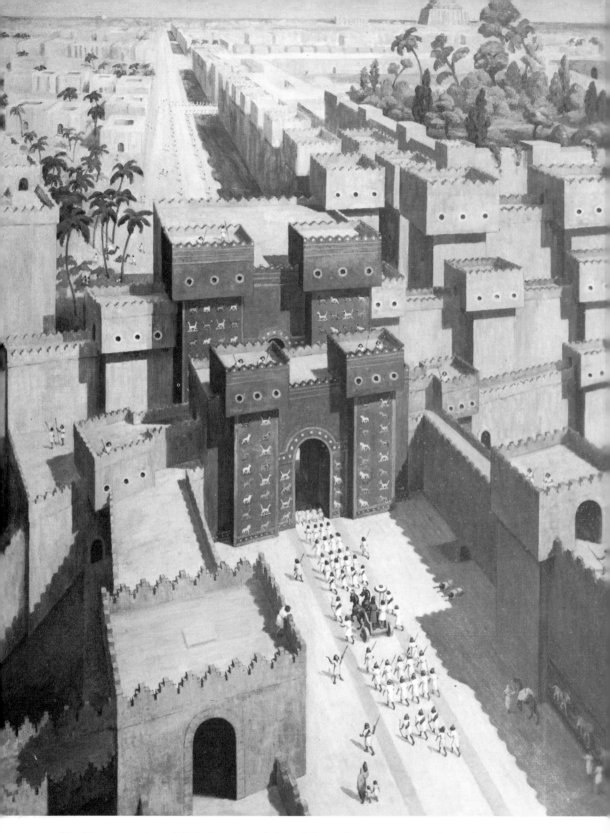

31. Reconstruction of Babylon viewed from Ishtar Gate. Procession Street leads out
to the Euphrates and the ziggurat.

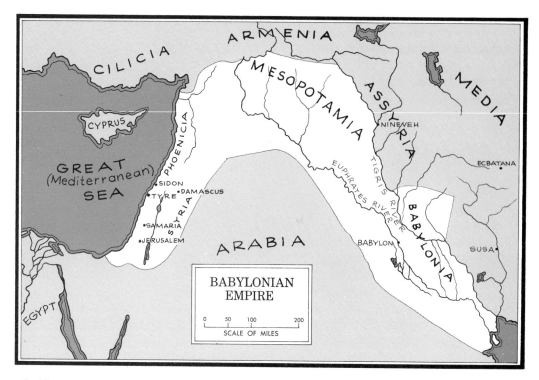

BABYLONIAN
EMPIRE

0   50   100   200
SCALE OF MILES

Chaldean power, Chaldean princes extended their power to Babylon itself, and in later usage the terms *Chaldean* and *Babylonian* are synonymous. Nabopolassar, through his conquest of Babylon, became the founder of the Neo-Babylonian or Chaldean Empire. Not only were Assyrian efforts to dislodge him unsuccessful, but he joined forces with the Medes in attacking Assyria. In 614 B.C. Cyaxeres, the Mede, took Asshur, the ancient capital of Assyria, by storm. Two years later, Nabopolassar joined Cyaxeres in the siege of Nineveh, which fell after a three-month siege (612 B.C.). Nineveh was completely destroyed; and although an attempt was made at Haran to make a last stand, the Assyrian Empire came to an end within three years.

The greatness of Nebuchadnezzar. Under Nabopolassar's son, Nebuchadnezzar (605-561 B.C.), the city of Babylon reached its zenith. This was the city whose glory has been discovered by the archaeologist's spade. Here were the famed walls and the "hanging gardens" of which Herodotus spoke. The Ishtar Gate, leading into the elevated Procession Way, must have filled the visitor with wonder. He could walk down this stone-paved street to the ziggurat and the principal temples of the city. Jerusalem, which successfully defied Sennacherib, fell to Nebuchadnezzar, and her exiles wept by the waters of Babylon. While most of the Jews were settled in other cities of Babylonia, King Jehoiachin and the Prophet Daniel were among those who lived in Babylon itself. Daniel tells us of Nebuchadnezzar's boast: "Is not this great Babylon which I have built by my power as a royal residence and for the glory of my majesty?" (Dan. 4:30).

Nebuchadnezzar was followed by a succession of weak rulers. His unworthy son Amel-Marduk (Evil-merodach, II Kings 25:27) ruled 561-559 B.C. Amel-Marduk's brother-in-law, Neriglisar (Nergal-sharezer of Jer. 39:3), proved to be much more successful during his short reign (559-555 B.C.). His young son was soon disposed of. Nabonidus, Babylon's last king, turned the government over to his son Belshazzar, whose drunken revelry is described in Daniel 5.

Foreign domination again. As Daniel had prophesied, Babylon fell to the Persians (Dan. 5:30), and she was never again to be the seat of a mighty empire. The Persians sought to maintain Babylon as an administrative center and subsidiary capital. Jews and other captive peoples were permitted to return to their homes.

The Babylonian love of independence continued to assert itself, however. Rebellion was as common against Persia as it had been against Assyria. Persian arms had to put down revolts by Nidintu-Bel (522 B.C.), Araka (521 B.C.), Bel-shimanni, and Shamash-eriba (482 B.C.). The latter rebellion, during the reign of Xerxes, resulted in the destruction of the city in an effort to

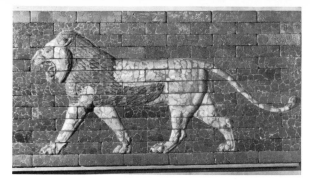

32. A lion in enameled brick from the Ishtar Gate

eradicate the Babylonian menace permanently.

Babylon never really recovered from the devastation wrought by Xerxes' armies. Alexander the Great was impressed with Babylon's glorious history and planned to reconstruct the buildings of Babylon, but he died there before the work had pro-

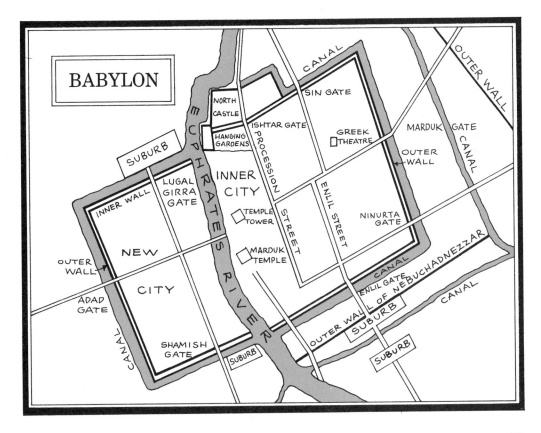

33. Tablet relating accession of Nebuchadnezzar II to the throne of Babylon
and his capture of Jerusalem in 597 B.C.

gressed very far. Alexander's successor,
Seleucus I, founded Seleucus on the Tigris
a short distance away. Slowly Babylon declined in importance. In the years that followed, a few people lived among the ruins
of the once great city. The Bel temple was
in use as late as A.D. 75. Babylon, however,
became but a symbol of past greatness.

Recovery of Babylonian antiquities. The
site of Babylon was never forgotten, and it
has been visited through the centuries by a
succession of distinguished visitors. Herodotus visited Babylon about 460 B.C. and
described it in his *History* (I, 178-88). The
twelfth century Jewish traveler, Benjamin
of Tudela, mentions Babylon in his book of
travels, which was first published in 1543.
The German physician Leonhart Rauwolff
visited Babylon during a three-year trip
through the Orient (1573-76). This visit
was described in his book *Itenerarium* (or
Rayssbuchlein), which was published in
1583. Carsten Niebuhr, a German traveler,
describes Babylon in his *Reisbescreibung
nach Arabien und andern umliegenden
Landern,* published in Copenhagen in 1778.
He had visited the ruins of Babylon in
1765 and sought to identify the hanging
gardens and the "Temple of Belus" of which
Herodotus wrote.

The Pope's vicar-general of Babylonia,
Abbe De Beauchamp, who lived in Baghdad between 1780 and 1790, made two
visits to the ruins of Babylon and published
the results of his observations in *Journal
des Savants,* May, 1785 and December,
1790. Although these reports contained
much that was inaccurate, they did give the
people of western Europe some idea of the
size and significance of the ruins of Babylon, and they created an interest that resulted in the series of studies and excavations undertaken during the nineteenth century.

Claudius James Rich, a precocious youth
who mastered Italian, Arabic, and Turkish
before accepting the position of Resident of
the East Indian Company at Baghdad, was
the first to make a thorough examination of
the ruins of Babylon. Such free time as
Rich could spare from his official duties he
gave to historical, geographical, and archaeological studies. In December, 1811, he
spent ten days among the ruins of Babylon, after which he wrote accurate descrip-
tions of the ruins as he saw them, augmented by maps, drawings, and plans. He
gathered together the sculptures and cuneiform tablets he discovered for future study.
Rich died of cholera at the age of thirty-
four. His *Memoir on the Ruins of Babylon*
was published in Vienna in 1813, and re-
published with corrections in London in
1816. A second *Memoir* appeared in London in 1818. A definitive edition, including
Rich's diaries and other materials, was published by his widow in 1839. Mrs. Rich also
published her husband's *Narrative of a
Residence in Koordistan and on the Site of
Ancient Nineveh,* in London in 1836.

Sir Robert Ker Porter, a man of great artistic ability who had married a Russian princess, did much to popularize Near Eastern studies among the classes of European society best able to finance them. After extensive travels in Georgia and Persia, Porter arrived at Baghdad in 1818. He spent six weeks with Rich during which time he made extensive visits to the ruins of Babylon and made drawings of the more interesting mounds and objects discovered.

34. Austen H. Layard in Bakhtiyari costume, from a portrait in his *Early Adventures*

In 1850, Sir Austen Henry Layard, who had enjoyed great success in the excavation of the ruins of Nineveh, conducted an unprofitable campaign at Babylon. Aside from some bricks inscribed with Nebuchadnezzar's name, bits of pottery and seal cylinders, Layard had nothing to show for his work at Babylon. He was not well at the time, and seems to have been relieved when he was able to leave.

In August, 1851, the French government decided to send an archaeological expedition to the lands of "Mesopotamia and Media," and appointed Fulgence Fresnel, former consul at Jidda, as director and Jules Oppert as Assyriologist and assistant to Fresnel. A third member, Felix Thomas, served as architect. The expedition worked at Babylon from 1852 to 1854 with minimal results. While the archaeologists had merely scratched the surface of the vast mounds at Babylon, they did motivate later and more thorough work. Oppert published the report of the expedition in a two-volume work entitled *Expedition Scientifique en Mesopotamie* (Paris, 1859, 1863).

The definitive campaign at Babylon was begun in 1899 by Robert Koldewey for the Deutsche Orient-Gesellschaft. Koldewey's work continued until 1917, and during those years he recovered much of Nebuchadnezzar's Babylon. The remains of the great walls of the city, buttressed by towers at intervals of about 165 feet, were found to be much like those described by Herodotus. The inner wall was of crude mud brick, and the outer walls of burned brick. The width of the wall, with rubble filling, was about eighty feet. In the northern wall was the Ishtar Gate, a double gateway forty feet high covered with enameled brick reliefs of bulls and dragons in vivid colors. The Ishtar Gate led to the Procession Way, a road paved with limestone slabs three feet square, bearing an inscription crediting the building of the road to Nebuchadnezzar. The walls along the Procession Way were decorated with enameled bricks portraying 120 lions, representing Ishtar; 575 dragons, representing Marduk; and bulls representing Bel. The road led to the temple of Marduk and its adjacent ziggurat with another temple at the summit.

Koldewey's excavations located the citadel, known as Qasr, and the market area known as Merkez. The vast palace of Nebuchadnezzar with its "hanging gardens" has also been located. Koldewey's work is summarized in his book, *Das Wieder Erste-*

hende Babylon published in Leipzig in 1913, with a second edition in 1925. German archaeologists returned to Babylon in 1956 and excavated there for two more seasons.

Seven miles southwest of Babylon is the mound of Birs Nimrud, ancient Borsippa. As early as 1850, A. H. Layard and Hormuzd Rassam began work among the ruins of Birs Nimrud, where a mass of jagged masonry rises 150 feet above the plain. This "tower" was long thought to be the biblical Tower of Babel, but biblical scholars now discredit that idea and look for the tower in Babylon itself. The excavators of Borsippa have unearthed the Ezida ("the enduring house"), the temple of Nebo built by Nebuchadnezzar, the palace of Nebuchadnezzar, and the city wall.

Nippur, southeast of Babylon, was inhabited by people using the 'Obeid type of pottery, around 4000 B.C. From the early third millennium to the time of Hammurabi, Nippur was the cultural center of Sumer. Its gods Enlil and Ninlil were honored throughout the land, and the famed E-kir, or mountain house, of Enlil became Sumer's leading shrine.

Parts of the E-kur and its ziggurat have been excavated in a series of campaigns at Nippur beginning in 1889 by the Babylonian Exploration Fund, and continued since 1948 by the Oriental Institute of Chicago and the University Museum of Pennsylvania. From thirty to forty thousand clay tablets have been discovered, including about four thousand containing Sumerian literary works.

The Land of Ashur

Ashur. The city-state of Ashur (cf. Gen. 10:11) was located on the western bank of the Tigris, above the Little Zab River, about sixty miles south of Nineveh. The city seems to have been colonized by Sumerians as early as the third millennium

B.C. The remains of temples to the gods Ishtar and Ashur date from about 3000 B.C. Ashur is first mentioned by name on a cuneiform tablet from Nuzi written during the Old Akkadian period (*c.* 2350 B.C.).

35. The god Ashur

The site of Ashur was identified in 1853 when Hormuzd Rassam dug under the base of the ziggurat at Qalat Sharqat and found two cylinders of Tiglath-pileser I (1115-1077 B.C.) which mentioned Ashur by name. Robert Koldewey and Walter Andrae conducted systematic excavations for the Deutsche Orient-Gesellschaft from 1903 until the outbreak of World War I in 1914. During those years the excavators were able to plot the successive layers of the city and study the plans of its palaces and temples.

One of the finest examples of Assyrian architecture is the Anu-Adad temple built on a double ziggurat at Ashur during the twelfth century B.C. Among the literary discoveries is an Assyrian version of the Babylonian Creation Epic written about 1000 B.C. While the Babylonian version exalts Marduk, god of Babylon, as the supreme deity, the god Ashur is the hero of the Assyrian account.

Our knowledge of Assyrian law comes from Andrae's excavations at Ashur. Two large tablets and a number of fragments dating from the time of Tiglath-pileser I (12th century B.C.) give us a corpus of law which is about one-quarter the length of the better-known Code of Hammurabi. It is thought that the laws themselves may go back to the fifteenth century B.C.; but the tablets are badly broken, and the lacunae have not yet been filled. The penalties of the Assyrian code were more severe than those of their Babylonian counterparts.

The kings of Ashur ruled over a limited area until the end of the Ur III period, when they began a policy of conquest. Assyrian merchants established settlements at Kanish, Kultepe, and other centers in Cappadocia (eastern Turkey) which brought prestige and wealth to Ashur. Although we do not know the reasons, within three generations the Assyrian merchants were prevented from communicating with their capital, and Ashur entered a period of decline.

Shamshi-Adad I (c. 1812-1780 B.C.) extended Assyrian power by subduing Mari and placing his son Yashmakh-Adad on its throne. Caravan routes stretched from Ashur to the Mediterranean and Asia Minor during his reign. Shamshi-Adad built the great Enlil temple in Ashur. After his death, however, the empire disintegrated. Hammurabi of Babylon became master of Mesopotamia, and after him the Hittites sought to control the entire Fertile Crescent.

During the Amarna Age, Ashur-uballit I (1365-1330 B.C.) of Ashur corresponded with Pharaoh Amenhotep IV of Egypt, and Assyria emerged from a period of quiescence. From the fourteenth to the seventh centuries B.C., the armies of Assyria periodically spread panic through much of western Asia. Assyrian kings imposed heavy tribute on subject people and sent punitive expeditions to collect tribute when it did not arrive on time. The Assyrian monarchs boasted of their cruelty in the annals which recorded their expeditions.

Rise of Assyrian Empire. Tiglath-pileser I (1115-1077 B.C.) campaigned vigorously

36.   Tiglath-pileser III in a war chariot

throughout western Asia, but he met fierce resistance from the Aramaean states, which temporarily checked Assyrian imperialism. During this period Israel was able to emerge as an independent monarchy and, under David and Solomon, actually struck into Syria. With the rise of Tukulti-Ninurta II (890-885 B.C.), Assyria began to take more vigorous action against her foes. Rulers such as Ashurnasirpal II (885-860 B.C.), Shalmaneser III (859-824 B.C.), Shalmaneser IV (781-772 B.C.), Tiglath-pileser III (745-727 B.C.), Shalmaneser V (727-722 B.C.), and Sargon II (722-705 B.C.) administered the empire during the period when Assyria demanded tribute of the states of western Asia and succeeded in conquering Damascus (732 B.C.) and Samaria (722 B.C.).

Shalmaneser III had met and defeated a Syrian coalition at Qarqar in 853. Ahab

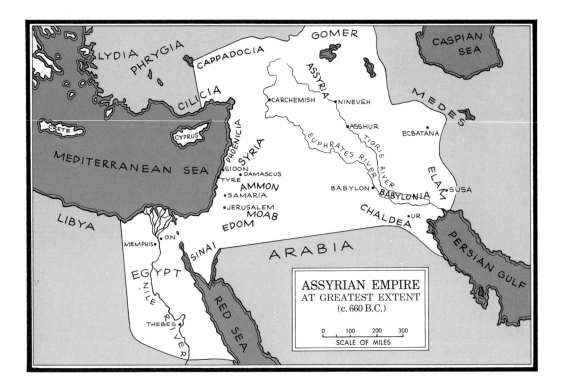

37. A clay prism from Sennacherib's palace, telling of his attack on Judah in 701 B.C.

was one of his most powerful foes on that occasion. Subsequently Shalmaneser brought Jehu to heel and exacted tribute from him. Tiglath-pileser III (referred to as Pul in II Kings 15:19; I Chron. 5:26) wrung tribute out of Menahem of Israel (II Kings 15:19) and conquered the northern part of Israel in the days of Pekah (II Kings 15:29). Ahaz of Judah became tributary to Tiglath-pileser in order to enlist his help against an invasion of Syria and Israel (II Kings 16:7-10). Shalmaneser V and Sargon II were presumably both involved in the conquest of Samaria, the former investing the city and the latter completing the conquest after his predecessor's death. While most accept at face value Sargon's claim to taking Samaria, some believe evidence is strong that Shalmaneser really took the city before he died.

Assyria was at the zenith of its power in the years following the fall of Samaria. Sennacherib (705-681 B.C.) conquered most

38. A fragment of the Babylonian creation epic from Ashurbanipal's palace

39. Part of the Babylonian flood account from Ashurbanipal's palace

of Judah but was unable to take Jerusalem (II Kings 18:17—19:9). The Assyrians had to lift their siege, and Sennacherib returned home where he was murdered by his own sons (II Kings 19:36-37).

Esarhaddon (680-669 B.C.) continued his father's policies, but met increasing opposition. His son Ashurbanipal (669-627 B.C.; Asnapper, Ezra 4:10) fought hard to maintain the power of Assyria which was slipping rapidly. He enjoyed a great victory over the Egyptians and sacked Thebes. Ashurbanipal gave attention to his library, thereby making his name respected among modern students of ancient Assyria because in it he preserved thousands of documents important for the study of Mesopotamia and of the Bible. Especially interesting among the accessions are early creation and flood accounts.

The kingdom, however, was fast approaching its end. Cyaxeres the Mede and Nabopolassar of Babylon took the city of Ashur in 614 B.C., and Nineveh itself fell in 612 B.C. By 609 B.C. the Assyrians had been defeated at Haran, and their empire had come to an end.

Calah. On the east bank of the Tigris, twenty-four miles south of Nineveh, at the point where the Great Zab River joins the Tigris, was the city of Calah (Kalakh; modern Nimrud) which, along with Nineveh, was built by Nimrod (Gen. 10:11). Excavations at Calah were begun by Austin Henry Layard in 1845 and were resumed in 1949 by the British School of Archaeology in Iraq under the direction of M. E. L. Mallowan.

The main citadel of the city was built by Shalmaneser I about 1250 B.C. and subsequently restored by Ashurnasirpal II (c. 879 B.C.). The great palace of Ashurnasirpal II covered four thousand square feet. Its completion was commemorated by the Banquet Stele, discovered by the British excavators in 1951, which depicts the king surrounded by symbols of the gods and describes a feast to which 69,574 guests were invited. They came from all parts of the empire and spent ten days consuming 2,200 oxen, 16,000 sheep, 10,000 skins of wine, and 10,000 barrels of beer. The walls of the palace courts and rooms were adorned with alabaster panels and reliefs, some of which contained inscriptions. The colossal winged lions and bulls reflected Hittite influence on the art of the land.

The Black Obelisk of Shalmaneser III originally stood in the main square of Calah. It depicts subject princes, including Jehu of Israel or his representative, bowing before Shalmaneser while bringing tribute. Under the representation of Jehu, or his emissary, are the words "Tribute of Jehu, the son of Omri."

Nineveh. On the east bank of the Tigris River opposite Mosul are two mounds which contain the remains of ancient Nineveh, surrounded by walls eight miles in circumference. One of the mounds, Nebi Yunus ("the Prophet Jonah"), is occupied by a modern village and has not been excavated. The second, Quyunjiq, yielded some of the most impressive remains of antiquity (including the palaces of Senna-

41. Black Obelisk of Shalmaneser, detailed view showing Jehu or his representative prostrated before Shalmaneser

cherib and Ashurbanipal) when P. E. Botta began work at the site in 1842. Many of the great names in Assyriology have been active in the excavation of Nineveh: A. H. Layard and H. Rassam (1845-54); George Smith (1873-76); Wallis Budge (1882-91); L. W. King (1903-5) and R. Campbell Thompson (1927-32).

According to Genesis 10:11, Asshur founded the city of Nineveh along with

40. Black Obelisk of Shalmaneser

42. Ashurbanipal in his war chariot

43. Prisoners of war represented on a relief in the palace of Ashurbanipal, Nineveh

other cities in its environs. Asshur cannot positively be identified with any character of history, but historians note that his career parallels that of the first Semitic empire builder, Sargon of Akkad.

In 1931/32 M. E. L. Mallowan conducted archaeological soundings at Nineveh on behalf of the British Museum. He dug a pit ninety feet from the highest point to virgin soil only slightly above the level of the surrounding plain. The earliest levels of Nineveh yielded 'Obeid and Samarra type pottery, causing archaeologists to date its earliest occupation somewhere around 4500 B.C. The first and second levels at Nineveh parallel levels one to five at Hassuna. An inscription from the time of Naram-sin (c. 2200 B.C.) has been discovered at Nineveh, and Gudea of Lagash is known to have campaigned in the area (c. 2100 B.C.). Nineveh had commercial contacts with the Assyrian colony at Kanish in Cappadocia early in the second millennium B.C. The Code of the Babylonian king Hammurabi mentions an Ishtar temple at Nineveh.

Sennacherib made Nineveh the capital of the Assyrian Empire (cf. Isa. 37:37; II Kings 19:36), and the spoils of conquest continued to flow into the city during the reigns of Esarhaddon and Ashurbanipal. By tracing the ruins of Nineveh's ancient walls, archaeologists have been able to determine that the city extended about two and one-half miles along the river. The eastern wall was three miles long. The Israelite prophets Jonah and Nahum pronounced judgment upon Nineveh for her atrocities when her armies seemed invincible.

By 612 B.C., however, Assyria was on the defensive. Her cruelties were known throughout western Asia, and she had no allies when she had to face the combined might of Babylon and Media. The destruction of Nineveh was final. When Xenophon

44. Reconstruction drawing of the palace of Sargon II of Assyria at Khorsabad

and his Ten Thousand Greeks fought their way through the wilderness and mountains to the Black Sea (401/400 B.C.), they passed the ruins of Nineveh but were not aware that some two centuries earlier the greatest city of the world had stood on the site. Xenophon does not even mention Nineveh. An Englishman, Sir Anthony Shirley, journeyed in the East at the close of the sixteenth century and observed, "Nineveh, that which God Himself calleth That great Citie, hath not one stone standing which may give meaning to the being of a town."

Khorsabad. Sargon II (mentioned in Isa. 20:1) moved his capital from Nineveh to a site twelve miles north of the city and named it Dur-Sharrukin ("Sargon's burg"). The ruin was later mistakenly associated

46. Sargon and his commander in chief, Khorsabad

45. Assyrian warrior, Sargon's palace

with the Persian king Khosroes and named "Khorsabad." Its discovery dates from 1843 when Paul Emile Botta, the French consul at Mosul, decided to excavate the site. Almost immediately he came upon walls with reliefs and cuneiform inscriptions which identified the structure as Sargon's palace. Reliefs from Khorsabad depict Assyrian warriors, including Sargon himself, with bow and arrow, sword, and club. Khorsabad inscriptions record the annals of Sargon in which he claimed credit for the fall of Samaria and the deportation of its inhabitants.

47. Assyrian naval expedition, Sargon's palace

Mari and Mitanni

Mari. The ancient caravan route from the Tigris-Euphrates Valley westward to the Mediterranean intersected at the city of Mari, on the Middle Euphrates, with the main route which extended southward from the Khabur and the Upper Euphrates to Babylon and the Persian Gulf. The first known conqueror of Mari, modern Tell Hariri, was Eannatum of Lagash (*c.* 2500 B.C.) who boasted of his victory on a cuneiform inscription. In subsequent years, Mari was controlled by Sargon of Akkad and governors appointed by Sumerian kings of the Ur III dynasty.

About 1955 B.C., however, Ishbi-Irra of Mari conquered the city of Isin and brought about the downfall of the Third Dynasty of Ur. But Mari's period of independence was short because she soon fell to Iahdun-Lim of Khana. In turn, Iahdun-Lim was defeated by Shamshi-Adad of Assyria, who placed Ismah-Adad, his son, on the throne of Mari. At the death of Shamshi-Adad I (*c.* 1786 B.C.), Iahdun-Lim's son, Zimri-Lim, regained control of Mari. His dynasty lasted until 1728 B.C. when Hammurabi of Babylon conquered the city. In 1546 B.C. it was conquered and destroyed by the Kassites.

Archaeological interest in Tell Hariri began in 1933 when Bedouins of the area discovered a headless stone statue while quarrying for building material. Excavations began the same year by the French archaeologist André Parrot, who represented the Louvre. Work continued until the outbreak of World War II in 1939 and was resumed, following the war, from 1951 to 1956.

THE WYCLIFFE HISTORICAL GEOGRAPHY OF BIBLE LANDS

During the years prior to World War II, Parrot excavated the ziggurat at Mari with its adjoining shrines. Remains of four temples to the goddess Ishtar were found at one site, indicating a succession of superimposed sanctuaries. More important, however, was the palace complex, which covered fifteen acres. Among the three hundred rooms of the palace was a throne room with wall paintings. The royal archives yielded about twenty thousand cuneiform tablets from the time of Ismah-Adad and Zimri-Lim, including correspondence between Zimri-Lim and Hammurabi. The texts dealt largely with administrative matters, but personal and geographic names provide interesting parallels with the patriarchal records of Genesis. Most of the Mari texts were in the Akkadian language, but a few were written in Hurrian, and there are several Sumero-Akkadian bilinguals. The palace included a school for scribes.

Mari had commercial relations with Susa, Babylon, Byblos, Ugarit, and Crete. As an Amorite city-state it used a Semitic language and had religious institutions similar to those of Israel's neighbors in Old Testament times. Dagan was one of the favorite

gods of Mari. Liver divination seems to have been common, as evidenced by thirty-two liver models which have been excavated. The Mari tablets mention a people known as Benjaminites, and some scholars feel that these Benjaminites are related to the Israelite tribe of that name.

49. Lamgi-Mari, early king of Mari in the time of Hammurabi

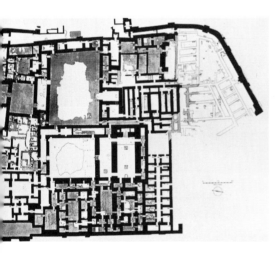

48. Mari Palace plan

Mitanni. About 1500 B.C. when the Kassites were taking over power in southern Mesopotamia, a people known as Hurrians, or the long-lost biblical Horites, became the dominant cultural element in the northern Mesopotamian state of Mitanni. The rulers of Mitanni were Indo-Aryans who worshiped the Vedic gods. They were surrounded by a feudal nobility known as *maryannu,* or chariot warriors, who constituted the power behind the throne. The Indo-Aryan ruling class intermarried with the dominant Hurrian element in the population.[9]

The Mitannian capital of Wassukkanni has not yet been identified, but it is thought to have been located on the upper Khabur River. Hurrian influence extended over a wide area and reached Nuzi and Arrapkha in Assyria and Alalakh in Syria. Abdi-Hepa, the fourteenth century king of Jerusalem who wrote several of the Amarna Letters, was evidently named for Hepa, the Hurrian mother goddess. The name "Araunah" (II Sam. 24:16), the Jebusite from whom David bought the threshing floor on which the Solomonic temple was later built, is the Hurrian word for "lord." The Jebusites, who occupied Jerusalem prior to the time of David, appear to have been a division of the people known as Horites or Hurrians.

[9]Roger T. O'Callaghan, *Aram Naharaim* (Rome: Pontifical Biblical Institute, 1948), p. 64.

During Egypt's Empire Period her troops reached the Euphrates and occupied Mitannian territory west of the river. In time the relations between the two nations became normalized, for the Amarna Letters show that the kings of Mitanni gave daughters as brides to the Egyptian Pharaohs. The position of Mitanni, however, was vulnerable. Exposed to the rising power of both Assyria to the east and the Hittites who were expanding from their Anatolian strongholds, Mitanni lost her political independence about 1350 B.C., when the Hittite king Suppiluliumas conquered Tushratta of Mitanni. The Amarna Letters contain correspondence of both Tushratta of Mitanni and the Hittite ruler Suppiluliumas, with Amenhotep IV of Egypt.

Nuzi. Twelve miles southwest of modern Kirkuk, near the foothills of southern Kurdistan, is the mound of Yorgan Tepe, which had been occupied since prehistoric times and became an important Hurrian center

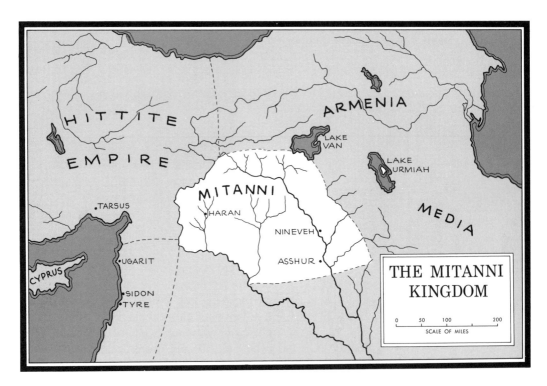

THE MITANNI KINGDOM

during the middle of the second millennium B.C. The site was excavated from 1925 to 1931 by the late Edward Chiera for the American Schools of Oriental Research in Baghdad in cooperation with the Oriental Institute (Chicago), the Iraq Museum, Harvard University, and the University Museum (Pennsylvania).

The earliest cuneiform documents from the site, including a clay map, date from the time of Sargon of Akkad when Yorgan Tepe was known as Gasur. Of even greater interest, however, were several thousand unearthed cuneiform texts from public and private archives of the fifteenth and fourteenth centuries B.C., when the site, known as Nuzi, an eastern province of Mitanni, had a predominantly Hurrian population. Although at the extreme eastern end of the Mitanni territory, the Nuzi tablets show a social structure remarkably similar to that of the biblical patriarchs who made their home for a time in the Haran area of western Mitanni. Marriage customs and matters of adoption and birthright mentioned in the patriarchal records find parallels in the customs reflected in the Nuzi Tablets. Following conquest by the Assyrians in the late fourteenth or early thirteenth century, however, Nuzi entered a period of decline and never recovered. Her major importance rests in the fact that the Nuzi Tablets preserve an authentic picture of life in an ancient Hurrian community.

Haran. In western Mitanni, about sixty miles north of the point where the Balikh River empties into the Euphrates, was the important trading center of Haran (or Harran), where Abraham and Terah settled after leaving Ur (Gen. 11:31-32). The Haran region was known in Old Testament times as Paddan-Aram, "the fields of Aram," and it was occupied by people known as Aramaeans who were closely related to the Israelites. Laban, Jacob's father-in-law, was an Aramaean (Syrian, Gen. 31:20). Haran, like Ur, was devoted to the worship of the moon god. The Mari Texts indicate that

Amorite tribes were in the area early in the second millennium B.C. Among the townspeople of the Haran area were Serug, Nahor, and Terah, all immediate ancestors or relatives of Abraham.

Excavations at Haran have brought to light remains of the Roman city near which the Parthians slew Crassus in 53 B.C. The site was known as Carrhae in later Islamic times. Its strategic location on the main road connecting Nineveh, Ashur, and Babylon with Aleppo, Damascus, Tyre, Egypt, and Asia Minor made Haran an important trading center throughout its history. It served as a provincial capital in Assyrian times and was fortified by Adad-nirari I (c. 1310 B.C.). Tiglath-pileser I (c. 1115 B.C.) boasted that he embellished the temple of Sin, the moon god. The people of Haran rebelled against Sennacherib, but the Assyrians regained control. The Rab-shakeh mentioned Haran as one of the cities whose gods were powerless to stop the Assyrian advance (II Kings 19:12). Revolts continued, however. The Assyrians sacked Haran in 763 B.C., but Sargon II, sensing its value to the empire, began to rebuild the city, and repaired and refurnished its temple. Following the fall of Nineveh (612 B.C.), Haran served as the Assyrian capital, but it fell to the Babylonians in 609 B.C., and Assyrian power was forever broken.

Citizens of Haran, like the Babylonians, respected the cult of the moon god. The mother of King Nabonidus served as a priestess in the temple to Sin at Haran, and his daughter became a priestess at the corresponding temple in Ur. Haran continued as a center for the worship of the moon god well into Christian times.

* * *

Although western man is indebted to Greece and Rome for much of his culture, it was in the lands at the head of the Persian Gulf that man first used symbols inscribed on clay tablets as a system of written communication. Here among the Sumerians and the cultures influenced by them are found the earliest recorded law codes, the earliest mathematical systems, and the literary texts that were to influence the ancient Near East in much the same manner that the classics of Greece and Rome influenced the West. With the passing of the centuries, Western man all but forgot the culture of the lands of the Fertile Crescent. Only the Bible provided a link with that part of his cultural heritage until archaeologists of the nineteenth and twentieth centuries discovered the documents and artifacts which throw new light on the all-but-forgotten peoples.

Bibliography

BRAIDWOOD, LINDA. *Digging Beyond the Tigris*. New York: Henry Schuman, Inc., 1953.

BRAIDWOOD, ROBERT J. *Prehistoric Men* (3rd ed.). Chicago: Chicago Natural History Museum Press, 1957.

CHAMPDOR, ALBERT. *Babylon*. Translated and adapted by ELSA COULT. New York: G. P. Putnam's Sons, 1958.

CONTENAU, GEORGES. *Everyday Life in Babylon and Assyria*. London: Edward Arnold, Ltd., 1954.

DROWER, E. S. *The Mandaeans of Iraq and Iran*. Oxford: Clarendon Press, 1937.

Iraq and the Persian Gulf. London: Naval Intelligence Division, 1944.

KIRK, GEORGE E. *A Short History of the Middle East*. New York: Frederick A. Praeger, Publishers, 1960.

KRAMER, SAMUEL NOAH. *From the Tablets of Sumer*. Indian Hills, Col.: Falcon's Wing Press, 1956.

———. *The Sumerians*. Chicago: University of Chicago Press, 1964.

LASSOE, JORGEN. *People of Ancient Assyria*. Translated by F. S. LEIGH-BROWNE. New York: Barnes and Noble, Inc., 1963.

MOSCATI, SABATINO. *The Face of the Ancient Orient*. London: Routledge & Kegan Paul, 1960.

O'CALLAGHAN, ROGER T. *Aram Naharaim*. Rome: Pontificium Institutum Biblicum, 1948.

OLMSTEAD, A. T. *History of Assyria*. New York: Charles Scribner's Sons, 1923.

OPPENHEIM, A. LEO. *Ancient Mesopotamia*. Chicago: University of Chicago Press, 1964.

ROUX, GEORGES. *Ancient Iraq*. London: George Allen and Unwin, Ltd., 1964.

RUTTEN, MARGUERITE. *Babylone*. France: University of France Press, 1948.

SAGGS, H. W. F. *The Greatness That Was Babylon*. New York: Hawthorn Books, Inc., 1962.

SCHMOKEL, HARTMUT. *Ur, Assur und Babylon*. Stuttgart: Gustav Kilpper Verlag, 1955.

50. The papyrus (left) and lotus, symbols of Upper and Lower Egypt

Egypt

The Land and Its People

STRETCHING A DISTANCE of six hundred miles, from Aswan (ancient Syene, Ezek. 29:10; 30:6) at the First Cataract of the Nile northward to the Mediterranean, is the narrow strip of cultivable land that was ancient Egypt.[1] The Greek historian Herodotus stated that Egypt is the gift of the Nile, for the fertile land produced by the flooding of the Nile is the only break in the Sahara and Libyan deserts which extend across North Africa to the Red Sea. The deserts which stretch interminably to the east and west of the Nile Valley made access to ancient Egypt quite difficult, and they explain in part the isolation of the country in early times.

Name of Egypt. The English name "Egypt" is derived from the Greek and Latin forms of the ancient Ha-ku-ptah, an early name for the city of Memphis, across the Nile from modern Cairo. When Memphis served as capital of Egypt, its name came to be applied to the whole country, just as the city of Babylon gave its name to the Babylonian Empire. Egypt was also known to its own people as Ta-meri, "the beloved land," and as Kemet, "the black country," a name descriptive of the black soil of the Nile Valley which contrasted with the nearby Deshret, or "red country," producing the English word *desert*. The Hebrews and other Semites use the name Misrayim which, in the form Mizraim, appears in the English Bible as the name of the second son of Ham and the progenitor of the Ludim, Anamim, Lehabim, Naphtuhim, Casluhim, and Caphtorim (Gen. 10:6, 13-14).

The Nile. From Mount Ruwenzori ("Mountain of the Moon"), near the equator, the Nile Valley extends 2,450 air miles northward to the Mediterranean. The actual mileage, however, including the numerous twists and turns in its tortuous route, amounts to about four thousand miles, making the Nile the longest river on earth. The valley, formed as water cut its way through sandstone and limestone, is traversed in six places by granite and other hard stones which create cataracts, interfering with navigation and serving as natural boundaries for Nile Valley peoples. The region of the Fourth Cataract was settled by the people known in the Bible as Cushites, whose kingdom became known as Cush or Ethiopia. Between the Fourth and Third Cataracts is Gebal Barkal, the southernmost point of Egyptian rule during the New Kingdom, when Cush was under an Egyptian viceroy. The land of Nubia, rich in gold, lay between the Third and First Cata-

[1] *Herodotus,* I, Book II, Sections 5-10.

47

51. Part of the first cataract is still visible but much of it has been submerged by the first Aswan dam.

from four sources at the Twelfth Gate of the netherworld.[2] Legend also suggested that it emerged from the netherworld at the First Cataract, near modern Aswan. Even Herodotus was puzzled at conflicting views concerning the sources of the Nile. One, which he affirms is "most in error," holds

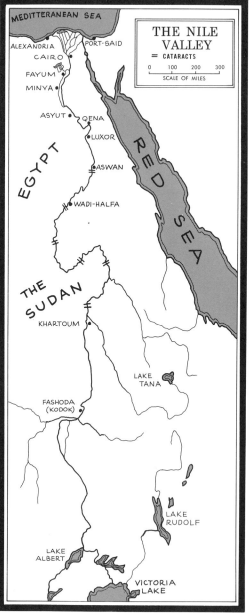

racts. The remains of Abu Simbel, two huge shrines hewn out of living rock by Ramses II, are north of the Second Cataract. Their chapels, stelae, and inscriptions portray the history that took place up and down the Nile.

The Nile Valley from Aswan at the First Cataract to the Mediterranean Sea provided Egypt with about 13,300 square miles of cultivable land, roughly equivalent in area to Belgium or the American states of Massachusetts and Connecticut. Only the northern part of the Nile Delta lies within reach of the winter rains of the Mediterranean. Alexandria in the western Delta has about eight inches of rain annually, falling during the late autumn and early winter. Cairo, at the head of the Delta, has only one and one-half to two inches, mostly in January; and rain is so rare in Upper Egypt that it is looked upon as a miracle. Often years pass with no rain at all. The only fertility that comes to the land is brought by the floodwaters of the Nile which deposit on its banks both moisture and rich alluvial soil washed down from central Africa.

The Egyptians were puzzled concerning the source of the Nile, flowing as it does northward from the central part of Africa. Mythology suggested that the river had its origin in heaven and that it fell to the earth far to the south of their land. *The Book of the Dead* states that the Nile River sprang

[2] E. W. Budge, *The Book of the Dead*, Chap. 146 (2nd ed.; New York: Barnes & Noble, Inc., 1951).

52. The Nile at Luxor

that "the Nile flows from where snows melt." This is impossible, according to Herodotus, for the river flows "from the hottest places to lands that are for the most part cooler." Herodotus, of course, did not know of the snowcapped mountains which actually do provide one of the sources of the Nile.[3]

The main stream, known as the White Nile, flowing from the mountainous region of central Africa, provides a steady flow of water throughout the year. This is augmented by the Blue Nile, flowing from Lake Tana in the Ethiopian Plateau, which becomes a mountain torrent from June to September as a result of heavy spring rains. Near Khartoum, in the Sudan, the Blue Nile joins the White Nile in its northward course. Two hundred miles farther down-

[3]Herodotus, *History*, Book II, Sections 20-24, contains a full discussion of Greek and Egyptian ideas concerning the source of the Nile. The subject seems to have fascinated Herodotus.

stream, from the Atbara, the Nile's only significant tributary, additional flood waters pour into the Nile from the highlands of Ethiopia. It is these waters from the Blue Nile and the Atbara, added to the more steady stream of the White Nile, that bring about the annual inundation on which the economy of Egypt depends.

The Nile flood and famine. Although an annual flood was predictable, its extent varied from year to year. Too much water would sweep away dikes and canal banks and destroy the mud-brick homes in Egyptian villages. Too little water would result in famine and starvation.

Such a famine is known to have taken place during the reign of Pharaoh Djoser, the builder of the famed Step Pyramid, who reigned about 2600 B.C. An inscription discovered near the First Cataract of the Nile, dating from about 100 B.C., says:

53. The nilometer on the island of Elephantine at Aswan, used for measuring the Nile flood

of June, and the Nile continues to rise until early in September, falling slowly during October and November. At Cairo the flood stage is reached almost a month later. By building dams, dikes, and canals, the Egyptians were able to control the flooding and to reduce the rate at which the waters would normally subside. The digging of Lake Moeris in the Faiyum, the predecessor of the modern Birket Qarun, was praised by classical writers as the earliest attempt to use the floodwaters to provide for irrigation on a prolonged basis. Pharaohs of the Twelfth Dynasty had seen the possibilities of diverting the waters of the Nile into the Faiyum area during the inundation period.

The necessity for control of the Nile was a factor in uniting Egypt and encouraging a tendency toward centralized authority. A strong government could sponsor a program of public construction to make the best use of the Nile. During the inundation season, when agricultural work was at a standstill, the peasants' time could be utilized in building drainage canals and other public works. Herodotus says that the laborers who built the Great Pyramid worked during three-month shifts. Pyramid construction probably took place during the inundation season when labor in the fields was impossible. Pyramid building hurt the economy, not because the fields were neglected but because the labor could have been expended in more productive ways. Had energy been spent on developing irrigation projects rather than building tombs for the Pharaohs, the standard of living for the entire people could have been raised significantly. This judgment is a modern one, to be sure. Those who believed that Pharaoh was a god worked on his pyramid with the same devotion that medieval Christians expended on the building of great cathedrals.

I was in distress on the Great Throne, and those who are in the palace were in affliction of heart because of a very great evil, for in my time the Nile has not overflowed for a period of seven years. There was scarcely any grain; fruits were dried up; and everything which they eat was short. Every man robbed his neighbor. . . .[4]

Djoser lived nearly a thousand years before Joseph, the Hebrew slave who became prime minister of Egypt. Joseph gained the confidence of the Pharaoh by interpreting his dreams and suggesting a plan whereby food might be stored during the years of prosperity so that there would be ample supplies during the famine years which would follow (Gen. 41:28-57).

The annual inundation usually begins at Aswan at the end of May or the beginning

The Nile Valley. The valley floor of Upper Egypt is from one to twenty-four miles in width, hugging the shores of the Nile.

[4]A translation of the text, first published by H. K. Brugsch in 1891, appears in James B. Pritchard (ed.), *Ancient Near Eastern Texts Relating to the Old Testament* (Princeton, N. J.: University Press, 1955), p. 31.

From his fertile valley the Egyptian could look to the east or the west and see barren desert cliffs as high as 1,800 feet. Quite naturally he regarded Egypt as the one land particularly blessed of the gods. Even the border at the First Cataract was protected by a series of cascades and rapids which served as a natural barrier to the movement of hostile peoples from the south.

The Delta. The Egyptian Delta area had been a large gulf in remote prehistoric times when the area around Cairo bordered the Mediterranean. As the Nile waters made their way to the sea, however, they deposited alluvium in the gulf at their mouth; and the Delta slowly emerged as the Lower Egypt of historical times. As the Nile waters entered the Delta, they were diverted into a number of branches, only two of which have persisted into modern times. Most of the others have largely dried up. This pie-shaped region is about 125 miles north and south and 115 at its greatest width.

Because of its proximity to the Mediterranean, the Delta had contacts with the outside world; and its inhabitants did not enjoy the isolation which characterized the people of Upper Egypt. The Delta was the great reservoir of land in ancient Egypt. It had a dozen or so important towns, each of which was surrounded by fertile soil suitable for agriculture or for the grazing of cattle. Pharaohs and their nobles enjoyed hunting in the thickets of the Delta where the jackal, fox, hyena, lion, lynx, and leopard were common. The reeds of the Delta marshes were used in making papyrus, the writing material of ancient Egypt which was the forerunner of modern paper. Papyrus was also used in making baskets, sandals, small ships, and rope.

Sinai Peninsula. Bordering Egypt to the northeast was the Sinai Peninsula, an arid region which served as a buffer zone between Egypt and the nations of Asia. The civilized Egyptians built a wall on their border and sought to keep the nomadic people of the desert from their land. But in times of Egyptian weakness, the Bedouin were able to enter and settle permanently. Through the centuries Egypt was invaded by a succession of Hyksos, Assyrians, Persians, and Arabs who crossed the Sinai Peninsula and occupied Egypt. Conversely, during Egypt's Empire Period, she penetrated western Asia as far as the upper reaches of the Euphrates. Nevertheless, the Sinai Peninsula discouraged such contacts, and military ventures often had to be supplemented by naval activities in the eastern Mediterranean.

Peoples and their livelihood. Paleolithic man lived on the desert plateau which today stretches along both sides of the Nile Valley. Although the Libyan and the Sahara deserts are now barren except for a few oases, in Paleolithic times they received enough rain to make life possible on a relatively large scale. While Europe was going through a succession of ice ages, North Africa had a corresponding rainy, or pluvial, period. In regions now completely barren, Paleolithic strata reveal the presence of hippopotami, buffalo, wild asses, gazelles, and ostriches. At the end of the Ice Age, African climate changed markedly, because the rain belt shifted, the wells began to dry up, and man and beast had to retreat to regions which afforded a means of livelihood. As bordering lands became desert, the Nile Valley continued to provide fertile ground.

People of differing races moved into the Nile Valley long before recorded history. The earliest inhabitants appear to have been a hunting people of the "brown Mediterranean" type. Their tombs have yielded hunting knives and the remains of dogs which were domesticated and trained as companions on the chase. After settling in the Nile Valley, the earliest Egyptians domesticated cattle and subsequently became cultivators of the soil.

54. The Stele of the Cartouches of Amenemhet III. The hieroglyphic script was
devised by Egyptians early in their history and was used at least on official inscriptions
until the third century A.D.

Early in man's history the basic Mediterranean population of Egypt was modified by groups of Asiatics of Anatolian and Semitic descent who settled periodically on the eastern frontier of the Delta. They are known to have been in Egypt at the end of the Sixth Dynasty (c. 2250 B.C.), and the Asiatic Hyksos actually ruled Egypt from about 1720 to 1570 B.C. During the time of Joseph, a Semitic Israelite who became prime minister of Egypt, the Israelite tribes settled in the district of the eastern Delta known as Goshen (Gen. 46:28-34).

The ancient Egyptian was usually characterized by his reddish-brown skin and long, curly black hair, full lips, a long skull, and almond-shaped eyes. His hands were quite small. The ancient Egyptians spoke a Hamito-Semitic language which has been preserved in writing since about 3000 B.C. Its latest form, Coptic, is still used as a liturgical language in the Coptic church. The Egyptian language seems to have been built on a Hamitic African base to which numerous Semitic elements were added. These include a considerable amount of vocabulary, as well as prefixes, suffixes, and verb forms. The Egyptian verb, like that of the Semitic languages, is based on a tri-consonantal root.

The alluvium which provided Egypt with excellent soil determined her agriculture-based economy. Egyptians lived in small villages which they left each morning to tend their farms. Although theoretically all land belonged to the king, in practice the Egyptians treated their soil, cattle, and homes as private property, paying the required taxes to the government. Barley was the principal agricultural crop, with wheat and emmer occupying subordinate positions. Egyptian flax made possible the manufacture of a high grade of linen for which Egypt became famous. Fruits and melons were also grown in considerable quantity. Although the Egyptian became a food-producer before recorded history, the abundance of life in the Nile made it inevitable

55. The Rosetta Stone, used by Champollion to decipher Egyptian

that he would not abandon hunting entirely. Fish, geese, and ducks supplemented the food grown by Egyptian peasants on their small farms.

The Bible mentions the antipathy felt by the Egyptians of the Nile Valley toward the Bedouin who tended flocks of sheep and goats (Gen. 46:34). Not only did Israel settle in the land of Goshen, in the eastern part of the Delta, but Bedouin have kept their flocks in that general area throughout history. Even today, Arab Bedouin regularly appear in the Wadi Tumilat area between Lake Timsah and the Delta. The pastureland is covered with clumps of bulrushes, papyrus, and shrubs.

While the Egyptian frowned upon the nomadic Bedouin with his sheep and goats, large cattle were raised in Egypt itself; and they were so abundant that their hides became an export commodity. The Hyksos invaders introduced the horse into Egypt (c. 1700 B.C.), and in subsequent years Egypt was noted for its fine horses (cf. I Kings 10:28-29). The donkey was the

56. Plowing in the land of Goshen

caravan animal of ancient nomads who entered Egypt, as is known from the Beni Hassan tomb painting (about 1890 B.C.) which depicts Semitic traders with their retinue. The camel was rare in Egypt until Persian times.

Natural resources. Egypt had a decided advantage over Mesopotamia in her natural

supply of stone from nearby cliffs. Whereas Sumer and Babylon built their temples and palaces of mud brick, Egypt could use limestone, alabaster, granite, and basalt in her major buildings. Copper was available from the mines of Sinai, and Nubia was a ready source of gold, which was also mined in the hills between the Nile and the Red Sea. Egypt, however, did not have a native supply of iron. With the beginnings of the Iron Age, she was at a disadvantage because all her iron had to be imported. Egypt was also poor in wood. Her papyrus shrubs could serve some minor needs, but good wood had to be imported from Phoenicia. Early in her history, Egypt maintained trade relations with Byblos (ancient Gebal) on the Syrian coast where she secured the famed cedar trees of Lebanon, along with fir and cypress trees.

Historical Outline

Before the beginnings of recorded history, the small states or nomes of ancient Egypt were united into two kingdoms: Lower Egypt, comprising the Delta; and Upper Egypt, the Nile Valley from Memphis at the apex of the Delta to Aswan, at the First Cataract. Even in historical times when the states were united under one Pharaoh, Egyptians spoke of their country as "The Two Lands," and the ruler bore the title "King of Upper and Lower Egypt," and wore a double crown.

The history of Egypt is traditionally divided into thirty dynasties, extending from the time when Upper and Lower Egypt were unified under Menes (c. 2980 B.C.) to Alexander's conquest (332 B.C.). The first two dynasties, which ruled from This, or Thinis, are known as the Early Dynastic or Thinite Period. Dynasties three to six (c. 2676-2194 B.C.) comprise the Old Kingdom, or Pyramid Age, when Pharaohs reigned from Memphis with unchallenged power.

The absolutism of the Old Kingdom ended in a time of social upheaval known as the First Intermediate Period (c. 2160-1991 B.C.) during which local princes gained power at the expense of the central government. One of them boasted, "I rescued my city in the day of violence from the terrors of the royal house." The rule of the princes covers Dynasties seven through eleven. The establishment of the powerful Twelfth Dynasty (c. 1991 B.C.) ushered in the brilliant Middle Kingdom (c. 1991-1730 B.C.) during which literature and the arts flourished.

Egypt experienced her most trying hour during the Second Intermediate Period (c. 1730-1568 B.C.), comprising Dynasties thirteen to seventeen, when Asiatic Hyksos seized control and reigned from Avaris in the eastern Delta. Most biblical scholars suggest that Joseph rose in power and became prime minister of Egypt during Hyksos times. Kings of the Seventeenth

Dynasty began the liberation of Egypt, and Ahmose, founder of the Eighteenth Dynasty, expelled the Hyksos and ushered in Egypt's New Kingdom, or Empire Period (1568-1085 B.C., Dynasties 18-20). Egyptian armies marched into western Asia and controlled Palestine and Syria as far north as the Euphrates River. Dynasties nineteen and twenty mark the Ramesside Age. The exodus from Egypt probably took place at this time. At the end of the Ramesside Age a period of decline began from which Egypt never fully recovered. Dynasties twenty-one to twenty-three (1085-718 B.C.) were a period of transition, in the early years of which Israel became a monarchy under Saul and David. Solomon married an Egyptian princess, but relations with Egypt subsequently deteriorated. Jeroboam was able to find a place of asylum there, from which he returned to challenge Rehoboam's right to the throne. Egypt sought to control Palestine through invasions and alliances designed to restrain the rival Assyrian Empire in the East.

Dynasties twenty-five and twenty-six comprise the Late Period (750-525 B.C.) during which Ethiopian kings from Napata struggled with Assyrians for lordship over Egypt, and Saite kings, including Necho and Apries (Hophra), fought on Palestinian battlefields and promised aid to the states of western Asia that would resist Assyria and Babylonia. Dynasties twenty-seven to thirty comprise the Persian Period (525-341 B.C.) following the conquest of Egypt by Cambyses. Egypt tried to discard the Persian yoke and was periodically successful until 332 B.C. when Alexander the Great conquered Egypt. Alexander's people looked upon him as a deliverer; at this time the Hellenistic Age began.

Regional Surveys

The Nile Delta

The fertile Delta area which comprised Lower Egypt has fewer remains of the past than does the Nile Valley south of Cairo. Being more exposed to its enemies than Upper Egypt, the Delta communities were more frequently ravaged by war. Also, in the natural course of events, the Nile floods bring an annual layer of alluvium which slowly submerges the remains of earlier cultures. As a result, the Delta possesses almost no free standing monuments above ground, such as those which can be seen farther south at Karnak and Luxor.

The principal roads of Lower Egypt have always run in a north-south direction toward the apex of the Delta, near modern Cairo. The great conquerors who entered Egypt from western Asia traveled through the eastern Delta, past Bubastis, and on to Memphis or Thebes.

Periodic times of famine in Canaan and the Sinai Peninsula brought Bedouin to Egypt in quest of food (cf. Gen. 12:10-20). Egyptian documents tell us that frontier officials frequently allowed such Bedouin to settle in the area known in Scripture as the land of Goshen (Gen. 46:28-34). The alternate names, "the land of Rameses" (Gen. 47:11) and "the field of Zoan" (Ps. 78:12), indicate that Goshen was located in the eastern Delta not far from the border of Sinai. The region is now known as the Wadi Tumilat. It extends westward from Lake Timsah to the neighborhood of Bubastis.

Bubastis. Bubastis is the Pi-beseth mentioned by Ezekiel as an idolatrous city ripe

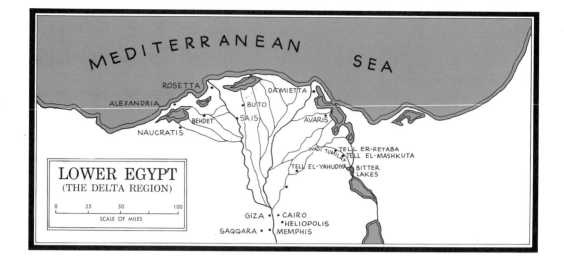

LOWER EGYPT
(THE DELTA REGION)

for divine judgment (Ezek. 30:17). It was dedicated to the worship of Bast, the cat-headed goddess. So popular was the worship of Bast that, according to Herodotus' figures (doubtless greatly exaggerated), as many as seven hundred thousand pilgrims would come to the annual festival at Bubastis. Herodotus described the pilgrimage:

> Now when they are being conveyed to the city of Bubastis, they act as follows: for men and women embark together, and great numbers of both sexes in every barge: some of the women have castanets on which they play, and the men play on the flute during the whole voyage; the rest of the women and men sing and clap their hands together at the same time. When, in the course of their journey, they come to any town, they lay their barge near to land, and do as follows: some of the women do as I have described; others shout and scoff at the women of the place; some dance, and others behave in an unseemly manner; this they do at every town by the river-side. When they arrive at Bubastis, they celebrate the feast, offering up great sacrifices; and more wine is consumed at this festival than in all the rest of the year. What with men and women, they congregate, as the inhabitants say, to the number of seven hundred thousand.[5]

The foundation stones of the famous temple at Bubastis date from the time of the Old Kingdom Pharaoh Khafra. The Libyan

[5]Herodotus, *History*, Book II, Section 60.

kings of the Twenty-second Dynasty, including Shishak, made Bubastis their capital city and enhanced its prestige by enlarging the Bast temple. Bubastis was the key to the Delta from the east, and it was called upon to withstand many sieges during its long history.

Napoleon's savants visited and described the ruins of Bubastis during their expedition in Egypt (1798), although the discovery of the Rosetta Stone at the Rosetta mouth of the Nile had such far-reaching consequences that their other discoveries are often overlooked. Bubastis was also visited by Sir Gardner Wilkinson in 1840 and was the subject of systematic excavation by Edouard Naville for the Egypt Exploration Fund from 1887 to 1889. Unfortunately the ruins had been used by the local population as a source of building material, and Naville had to be content with tracing the general outlines of the temple during its various stages. The site of ancient Bubastis, now known as Tell Basta, is located about a mile from modern Zagazig (or Zakazik), a town of about 80,000 people.

Ismailia Canal. Near Zagazig is the Ismailia Canal, which connects the Nile with the Red Sea. A canal was built in this area as early as the time of Ramses II, and it was cleared and deepened in turn by Pharaoh Necho, Darius the Great, and Ptolemy II. This canal, an ancient forerunner of the Suez Canal, ran from the Nile, past Bubastis, through the Wadi Tumilat into the Bitter Lakes, and then southward to the Red Sea. Remains of the masonry work indicate that the canal was 150 feet broad and sixteen to seventeen and one-half feet deep. Herodotus states that 120,000 Egyptians perished while working on the canal during the reign of Necho, who abandoned the project when an oracle told him that he was working for a barbarian. The barbarian was none other than the Persian Darius, who completed the work.[6]

Zoan. Near the northeastern frontier of Egypt on the east bank of the Tanaitic branch of the Nile, about thirty miles due west of ancient Pelusium, was the city of Zoan (Num. 13:22, Ps. 78:12, 43; Isa. 19:11-13; 30:4), or Tanis, which had been settled at least as early as the Sixth Dynasty of Pharaoh Pepi I (c. 2300 B.C.). It was rebuilt and enlarged by the Twelfth Dynasty Pharaohs (c. 1990-1785 B.C.), Amenemhet and his successors, who left large statues of themselves in Tanis. Ramses II (c. 1250 B.C.) practically reconstructed the place, erecting obelisks and statues with pompous inscriptions boasting about his accomplishments, real and fancied.

The temple at Tanis was one of the largest structures of ancient Egypt, measuring about 1,000 feet from end to end. In the temple was a colossal statue of Ramses II which originally stood 92 feet high and weighed about 900 tons. Its large toe was the size of a man's body. The stone was all quarried at Aswan and floated six hundred miles down the Nile to Tanis.

The Hyksos invaders of Egypt established their capital in the eastern Delta at Tanis, which they renamed Avaris. Its position on the northeast border of Egypt gave them ready access both to their Asiatic holdings

[6]*Ibid.,* Book II, Section 158.

57. The Syene quarry at Aswan furnished much of the best granite for Egyptian construction. A large cracked obelisk was left in the quarry thousands of years ago.

and to Egypt. The store city of Ramses (Exodus 1:11), on which the Israelites were forced to perform slave labor, is identified by most scholars as Tanis, although others locate it at Quantir, a few miles farther south.

Tanis continued to be an important town as late as Roman times. Among the bishops who attended the Council of Chalcedon (A.D. 451) was Apollonius, Bishop of Tanis. Arab writers spoke favorably of the climate of Tanis, but its significance declined until it became a heap of ruins in the midst of a small village bearing the name San— reminiscent of ancient Zoan.

San was visited by the Frenchman Auguste Mariette who became Director of the Service of Antiquities in Egypt in 1858 and sought to develop among the Egyptians an interest in their own antiquities. Extensive excavations began at San in 1884 when Sir W. M. Flinders Petrie reached the mound. In those days, such an expedition was virtually isolated from society. Once a week a man was sent on the forty-mile journey to Faqus, the nearest town, in order to maintain communications with the outside world and to bring needed provisions. The excavation of Tanis was Petrie's first mission for

the Egypt Exploration Society; and although he labored under great hardships, he was able to reconstruct much of its history. Many of his Tanis finds are now in the Cairo Museum. More recently the French archaeologist Pierre Montet explored the ruins of ancient Tanis. Before World War II Montet discovered in the temple precincts the remains of six kings from the Twenty-first Dynasty. Although the burials had been violated, Montet found much gold and silverwork showing something of the art, beliefs, and resources of the age contemporary with Solomon.

Pithom. Although the exact location of Pithom is not known, there can be no doubt that it was located in the Wadi Tumilat. In 1883 Dr. Edouard Naville began the excavation of Tell el-Mashkuta for the Egypt Exploration Fund, finding inscriptions which suggested that in ancient times the place was called Per-Atum, "the house of Atum," a close approximation to Pithom. Years before, Karl R. Lepsius, leader of a German expedition in Egypt, had identified the site of Tell el-Mashkuta with Ramses, second of the two store cities mentioned in Exodus 1:11. Naville found at the site a number of rectangular chambers, without doors, separated from one another by thick walls of crude brick. These he assumed to be the storerooms which the Hebrews were forced to build during the days of their slavery.

Grain, according to the usual Egyptian custom, had been poured into the storerooms through openings in the roof.

The bricks used at Tell el-Mashkuta are of three varieties. Those at the lowest level were made of clay mixed with chopped straw; higher up when the straw seems to have been used up, the clay was found mixed with reeds, and at the top level, Nile mud was used for the bricks with no binding substance added. It will be remembered that the Egyptian taskmasters withheld straw from their Israelite slaves (Exodus 5:10-21). Nile mud coheres in such a way that bricks can be made without straw, but the biblical record implies that straw was normally used. Although the bricks of Tell el-Mashkuta cannot be identified as Israelite in origin, they illustrate the different kinds of bricks which were used by the ancient Egyptians and may possibly be connected with the Israelite construction at the site.

Alan Gardiner is not satisfied that the Tell el-Mashkuta site is the biblical Pithom, preferring a mound eight and one-half miles west, known as Tell er-Retaba. Earlier, Sir W. M. Flinders Petrie had identified Tell er-Retaba with biblical Ramses. Some identify Tell el-Mashkuta with Succoth, the first stop of the Israelites after they escaped from Pharaoh (Exodus 12:37).

Naville's "store chambers" have been questioned by recent archaeologists who suggest that the walls of the cells which he discovered were really foundations of a strong fortress. T. Eric Peet states, "These late Egyptian fortresses were built up on massive brick platforms containing hollow compartments." No one who examines Naville's plan can remain in doubt as to the real nature of what he found.[7]

Flinders Petrie excavated Tell er-Retaba in 1905-6, finding evidence that the site had been occupied since Old Kingdom times. A temple was discovered, dating to the time of Ramses II and adorned with red granite and sandstone. A double statue represented Ramses and the god Atum. Baikie mentions a curious tradition dating from the fourth century A.D. when a woman pilgrim was told that the statue depicted Moses and Aaron.[8]

Petrie noted that human sacrifices had been offered at the dedication of the first wall of the town, a custom otherwise unknown among the Egyptians but common among the Canaanites. Macalister had discovered evidences of such human sacrifice at Canaanite Gezer, and it appears that Canaanite influence had been exerted at Tell er-Retaba at an early date.

Among the more colorful discoveries of Petrie at Tell er-Retaba was a bowl of blue glaze with nineteen frogs sitting around the bowl and others scrambling up the sides of the interior. In the middle of the inside a large frog sits enthroned upon a pedestal. The bowl probably dates from the Twenty-second Dynasty (c. 945-745 B.C.).

Tell el-Yahudiya and the Jewish temple in Egypt. In 162 B.C., Antiochus V (Eupator) of Syria appointed a man named Alkimus as high priest in Jerusalem, although he was not of the priestly family. Alkimus was regarded as a usurper by many pious Jews, and Onias IV, the son of the High Priest Onias III who had earlier been deposed by

Antiochus IV (Epiphanes), fled to Egypt with the hope of establishing a center of true worship there. According to Josephus, Onias addressed a letter to the Egyptian ruler, Ptolemy VI (Philometor) and his wife, Cleopatra, requesting permission to build in Egypt a temple similar to that in Jerusalem, with Levites and priests serving as ministrants.[9] The reply was brief and favorable:

> King Ptolemy and Queen Cleopatra to Onias, greeting. We have read your petition asking that it be permitted you to cleanse the ruined temple at Leontopolis in the nome of Heliopolis, called Bubastis-of-the-Fields. We wonder, therefore, whether it will be pleasing to God that a temple be built in a place so wild and full of sacred animals. But since you say that the prophet Isaiah foretold this long ago [cf. Isa. 19:19], we grant your request if this is to be in accordance with the law, so that we may not seem to have sinned against God in any way.[10]

Josephus tells us that Onias built a temple at Leontopolis "similar to that at Jerusalem, but smaller and poorer."[11] Although the letters which Josephus records are not accepted as authentic, a Jewish temple is known to have been built in Egypt, and Tell el-Yahudiya is its traditional site.

The tell, just north of Heliopolis, was excavated in 1887 by E. Naville and Llewellyn Griffin with no significant results, although the excavators were satisfied that they had identified the site of ancient Leontopolis. Flinders Petrie was more successful in his work there in 1906. He discovered the remains of a large building and later observed, "The plan of the whole hill is strikingly modelled on that of Jerusalem; the temple had inner and outer courts, like that of Zion, but it was smaller and poorer in size. . . . The whole site was formed in imitation of the shape of the Temple hill of the Holy

---

[7]*Egypt and the Old Testament* (Liverpool: University Press, 1922), p. 86, note 2.
[8]James Baikie, *Egyptian Antiquities on the Nile Valley* (London: Methuen and Co., 1932), p. 16.

[9]Josephus, *Antiquities,* Book XIII, Chap. III, Sections 1-3.
[10]*Ibid.,* Book XIII, Chap. III, Section 2.
[11]*Ibid.,* Section 3.

City. It was, in short, a New Jerusalem in Egypt."[12]

Petrie also discovered remains of a large Hyksos fortified encampment, a mile in circumference, at Tell el-Yahudiya, with a Hyksos cemetery nearby. He considered this as evidence that he had discovered the Hyksos capital city, Avaris; but more recent scholars tend to identify Avaris with Tanis. It is reasonably certain, however, that the Hyksos maintained a stronghold at Tell el-Yahudiya, whatever its name in ancient times.

Tahpanhes. In the eastern Delta, twelve miles north of Tell-el-Mashkuta, the mound known as Tell Defenneh is located on the Pelusiac branch of the Nile. Tell Defenneh is thought to mark the site of ancient Tahpanhes, the Egyptian city to which the Jews of Jeremiah's day fled in order to escape Nebuchadnezzar's wrath following the murder of Gedaliah (Jer. 40–41). Jeremiah accompanied the Jewish community which fled to Tahpanhes and prophesied to them:

> Take in your hands large stones, and hide them in the mortar in the pavement which is at the entrance to Pharaoh's palace at Tahpanhes, in the sight of the men of Judah, and say to them, 'Thus says the Lord of hosts, the God of Israel: Behold I will send and take Nebuchadnezzar the king of Babylon, my servant, and he will set this throne above these stones which I have hid, and he will spread his royal canopy over them. He shall come and smite the land of Egypt, giving to the pestilence those who are doomed to the pestilence, to captivity those who are doomed to captivity, and to the sword those who are doomed to the sword . . .' (Jer. 43:8-11, RSV).

Flinders Petrie arrived at Tell Defenneh in the spring of 1886 and learned that the largest mound in the area bore the name Qasr Bint el-Yahudi, "The Palace of the Jew's Daughter." Remembering the biblical reference to the Jewish settlement at Tahpanhes (Daphnae), Petrie's interest in the site quickened. In excavating the mound, he came upon the entrance to an ancient fort with a door and a stairway. Parallel to the stairway, and projecting from the main tower, was a large brick platform suitable for the loading and unloading of baggage trains and other work connected with the garrison. Its shape was such that Jeremiah could have built into it such witness stones as the Scripture mentions (Jer. 43:9). At a later time Nebuchadnezzar may well have pitched his royal tent on this very spot in front of the frontier stronghold which he had captured.

The *Histories of Herodotus* contain two references to Daphnae, the Greek form of the biblical Tahpanhes. The first reads:

> In the reign of King Psammetichus, garrisons were stationed at Elephantine against the Ethiopians, and another at the Pelusiac Daphnae against the Arabians and Syrians.[13]

It is known that Psammetichus made use of Ionians and Carians in his garrison "near the sea, a little below the city of Bubastis, on that which is called the Pelusiac mouth of the Nile . . . these were the first people of a different language who settled in Egypt."[14]

A second reference in Herodotus states that a Pharaoh named Sesostris was nearly burned alive at Daphnae through his brother's treachery. Two of the Pharaoh's six sons made a living bridge over the flames and the rest of the family escaped, although the two were burned to death.[15]

Excavations proved that Herodotus was correct in his statement concerning a garrison at Daphnae in the days of Psammetichus. Ruins of the fortress indicate that it contained a superstructure with living quarters for the garrison. It rose to a height of forty feet and provided an unobstructed view of the plain for miles around. The

---

[12]W. M. Flinders Petrie, *Hyksos and Israelite Cities* (London: Office of School of Archaeology, University College, 1906), publication no. 12.

[13]Herodotus, *History*, Book II, Section 30.
[14]*Ibid.*, Section 154.
[15]*Ibid.*, Section 107.

fortification was surrounded by a wall forty feet thick, and its foundation deposit mentions the name of Psammetichus.

The heroic tale allegedly from the time of Sesostris is probably to be dismissed as fiction. The identity of Sesostris is not at all certain. There are, however, traces of a building earlier than that of Psammetichus at Daphnae. Bricks discovered there are traceable to the Ramesside period, and earlier attempts to identify Sesostris with Ramses II are not historically improbable although most recent scholars identify him with Senwosret III of the Twelfth Dynasty.

The fact that Greeks settled at Daphnae found abundant attestation in Petrie's excavations, for pottery shows a curious combination of Greek and Egyptian motifs. The Greek influences at Daphnae ended, however, in 564 B.C. when Ahmose II decreed that Naucratis (Naukratis), in the western Delta should be the sole Greek treaty port.

Alexandria. When Alexander of Macedon reached Egypt in 322 B.C., he was warmly received as a deliverer from the rule of the hated Persians. Making a pilgrimage to the Oasis of Ammon, west of the Delta, he was formally recognized there as a divine king and successor to the Pharaohs. While on that journey, he passed the small Egyptian port of Rakotis at the Canopic mouth of the Nile, near the western extremity of the Delta. Phoenicians had earlier made use of its harbor, and Alexander determined to enlarge it and make it a model Hellenistic city. It is blessed by a more temperate climate than most of Egypt, and rain often falls during November, December, and January.

The city which soon arose on the site of Rakotis was named for Alexander himself and became the most successful of the many Alexandrias established throughout the Near East. Egyptian Alexandria was about four miles long, built with streets intersecting at right angles. These streets were

adorned with colonnades. In order to preserve the best in Hellenistic culture, Alexander encouraged Greeks to settle in Alexandria, although the city continued to have an Egyptian substratum, and a few years later a large and influential Jewish element moved into its northeastern sector. This intermingling of Greek, Jew, and Egyptian made Alexandria the most cosmopolitan city of the ancient world.

Located on a narrow isthmus between the Mediterranean Sea and Mareotis Lake, Alexandria soon became a major port; and within thirty years after it was founded, Ptolemy I (Soter) made it his capital, a position it held throughout the Ptolemaic Era (304-30 B.C.).

During those years Alexandria was the literary and scientific center of the Greek world. A great library and museum were founded by Ptolemy I; they were enlarged by his successor, Ptolemy II (Philadelphus). Alexandria became an academic center in which mathematics, art, physics, philosophy, poetry, astronomy, and grammar were studied. Legend states that it was Ptolemy Philadelphus who arranged for the translation of the Hebrew law into Greek, known as the Septuagint. Although the initiative was probably taken by the Jewish community in Alexandria, it is likely that the Jewish Scriptures found their way into the great Alexandrian library.

59. Alexandrian waterfront and skyline

Many of the great names of antiquity were associated with the Alexandrian library. Its first librarian, Zenodotus of Ephesus, made a specialty of the classification of poetry. Callimachus, a poet, classified, arranged, and labeled a library which numbered 100,000 manuscripts. Eratosthenes, Strabo, Hipparchus, Archimedes, and Euclid were among the scholars who used its facilities. The library, which is said to have numbered 750,000 volumes, was destroyed at the time of Julius Caesar's siege of Alexandria (48 B.C.).

Ptolemy II employed a noted architect, Sostratus of Cnidus, to construct a famed lighthouse on an island off the coast of Alexandria. The Pharos, as it was called, made use of a variety of architectural designs, and is regarded as one of the wonders of the ancient world. The lowest level was in the form of a rectangle, the second level an octagon, and the upper level a circle with a fire beacon, amplified by a mirror, which flashed out into the sea. Its 600-foot height makes it comparable in size with a thirty-six-story building of modern times.

Another engineering feat was the hepastadium (i.e., seven stades), a causeway which joined the island of Pharos to the Alexandrian mainland. The causeway, built either by Ptolemy Soter or Ptolemy Philadelphus, made two harbors, one facing east which was largely used for small Egyptian boats, and a larger western harbor, bearing the name Eunostos, which was protected by a breakwater. Into this harbor vessels from the entire Mediterranean world brought their wares to Alexandria.

One of the most beautiful buildings of the ancient world was the Serapeum, built near Rakotis, east of Alexandria, by Ptolemy Soter. The Serapeum was built to house the statue of a god from Sinope whom the Egyptians called Osiris-Apis, or Serapis. Eventually the shrine was filled with statuary and other works of art, and it had a library of 300,000 manuscripts in its own right. The Serapeum was destroyed by Theophilus, Patriarch of Alexandria during the reign of Theodosius II. Theophilus was intolerant of the pagan nature of the Serapeum and thought of himself as a partisan for true Christianity. The library was burned by another religious reformer, 'Amr ibn el'Asi, the Arab commander under Calif Omar (A.D. 641). Legend says that a request was made to Omar asking that the library be spared, whereupon he replied, "If these writings of the Greeks agree with the book of God, they are useless and need not be preserved; if they disagree, they are pernicious and ought to be destroyed." The volumes of paper and parchment were then distributed to the 4,000 baths of the city, and they provided fuel to heat the public baths for six months!

After the Ptolemaic period, Alexandria had a checkered history. In 48 B.C. Caesar landed his troops, 4,000 in all, on the famed island and stated:

> I immediately embarked some troops, and landed them on Pharos. The island of Pharos gives its name to a lighthouse, a miracle of size and engineering. Lying opposite Alexandria, it forms one side of the harbor, and earlier monarchs had connected it with the city by means of a narrow causeway. The channel (of the harbor) is so narrow that anyone controlling the Pharos may close the harbor to shipping from whatever quarter. This alarming prospect decided me . . . to land troops on the island; a move that ensured the safe arrival of our food and reinforcements, which had been ordered by the neighboring provinces.[16]

Although Caesar destroyed the great Alexandrian library, Mark Antony rebuilt it and gave to Cleopatra 200,000 volumes which he brought from Pergamum. The library there had been built by Eumenes II in 197 B.C.

Following the defeat of Cleopatra at the Battle of Actium (31 B.C.), Alexandria fell to Octavian, who was later to be known as the Roman Emperor Augustus. Egypt was under Roman control, made subject to a Roman prefect.

[16]Caesar, *The Civil Wars,* iii, 10.

Christian tradition states that Mark preached in Alexandria. The city became a Christian center, and the church suffered there under Decius (A.D. 250), Valerian (A.D. 257), and Diocletian (A.D. 304). It was a center of controversy between Arius and Athanasius.

With the disintegration of Roman power in the East, Alexandria fell to Chosroes of Persia, A.D. 619. Persian power was short-lived, however. Islam was on the march, and 'Amr ibn el'Asi took the city in the name of Omar in A.D. 641. The Muslim conquerors moved their capital to Cairo at the head of the Delta, and Alexandria declined in importance. At the time of the conquest, Alexandria had a population of 300,000, and that progressively decreased until the early nineteenth century saw but 12,000 people there. During the fourteenth century the canal to the Nile River was silted up, and this hastened Alexandria's decline. The canal was reopened under Mohammed Ali in the nineteenth century, and today the city has grown to a population of 1,000,000 and serves as Egypt's major seaport once more.

Behdet. In the vicinity of modern Damanhur, an important cotton-growing center thirty-eight miles southwest of Alexandria, is the ancient Teme-en-Hor ("City of Horus"), earlier known as Behdet. In predynastic times, Behdet was the capital of Lower Egypt. It was devoted to the falcon god Horus who became the royal god of Pharaonic Egypt. Horus, in the form of a winged disk, remained a patron deity of the Pharaohs throughout the history of ancient Egypt. In later times Edfu in Upper Egypt became the chief center of the Horus cult, and Behdet lost its earlier importance. There are not even any ruins to remind one of Behdet's illustrious past.

Naucratis. According to Herodotus, Naucratis, west of the Rosetta branch of the Nile, was established by Ahmose II of the Twenty-sixth Dynasty as the exclusive Greek trading port in Egypt.[17] Ahmose had been assisted by Ionian and Carian mercenaries in his bid for the crown, and the assignment of a Greek port may have been in the interests of repaying them for their loyalty. During the years 1884-86 Sir Flinders Petrie and E. A. Gardner excavated Naucratis, finding traces of a Greek colony there at the time of Psammetichus I. Hogarth continued the excavations (1899, 1903) discovering potsherds with dedications to Greek gods including Hera, Apollo, and Aphrodite. Some of these were dated as early as the seventh century B.C. and indicate that Greeks were at Naucratis before the reign of Ahmose. Either Herodotus was in error regarding this city's founding, or Ahmose rebuilt Naucratis and gave it its privileged position.

The city of Naucratis flourished during classical times, but its trade passed to Alexandria, which became the most important city of Hellenistic Egypt. Naucratis boasted an important structure known as the Panhellion which contained the central altar of the Greek community in Egypt.

60. The cobra of Buto on the head of Thutmose III, great Egyptian Empire builder, thought by many to be the Pharaoh of the Oppression

[17]Herodotus, *History*, Book II, Section 179.

Buto. The prehistoric capital of Lower Egypt under the Bu or Hornet kings was Buto, a city whose mound is near modern Tell el-Fara'in. Although Buto did not remain an important city, the Cobra of Buto gleams on the forehead of every pictorial or statuary representation of an Egyptian Pharaoh. In Herodotus' day, Buto was a flourishing city with a noted oracle in the temple of Edjo, the cobra goddess of the city and presiding genius of Lower Egypt. From the top of the temple pylon, it was possible to see the distant Mediterranean.

Sais. On the Rosetta branch of the Nile south of Buto is the ancient city of Sais, capital of Egypt during the Twenty-sixth (or Saite) Dynasty. Sais was devoted to Neith, the creator goddess who is said to have woven the world as a piece of cloth. According to another tradition, Neith is "the mother who brought forth the sun." Neith was also associated with warfare and is symbolically represented by a shield with crossed arrows.

Sais was once the greatest of Egyptian cities. Because of the danger of flooding, it was built on an artificial mound and is said to have had walls one hundred feet high and seventy feet thick. It was a priest of Sais who conversed with Herodotus concerning the wonders of the Nile River. Another priest from that city told Solon the story of the Lost Atlantis. Herodotus describes the famed temple of Neith at Sais but maintains a discreet silence concerning the mystery plays which were performed there in honor of Neith. He speaks rather of the shrines and obelisks of the Sais temple and of the sacred lakes associated with it. Herodotus claims to have seen tombs of ancient kings during his visit at Sais, but nothing remains of the city or temple today.

Busiris. Busiris, west of the Damietta branch of the Nile, was the site of an ancient passion play entitled "The Setting-up of the Backbone of Osiris," reflecting a tra-

dition that the backbone of Osiris was buried there. The city was dedicated to Osiris and his devoted wife, Isis. Herodotus observed the great feast at Busiris and noted that "all the men and women, to the number of many ten thousands, beat themselves after the sacrifice."

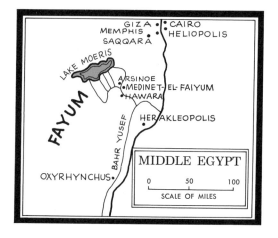

From Heliopolis to the Faiyum

The strategic area at the apex of the Nile Delta, marking the border between Upper and Lower Egypt, has been the scene of some of Egypt's most colorful history. Here the priests of the sun god Re officiated at ancient Heliopolis, and here at Memphis, Old Kingdom Pharaohs wielded absolute power.

From Abu Roash, opposite modern Cairo, southward to Hawara and El-Lahun, on the borders of the Faiyum, stretch a series of funerary mastabas and pyramids which stand as monuments to the skill and determination of their builders after 4500 years. The Faiyum itself serves as a different type of monument—one of a more practical nature—which speaks of the knowledge and ability of ancient Egyptians to dredge canals and engage in engineering projects which could make productive soil out of swampland.

Heliopolis. When Midianite traders brought the youthful slave Joseph to Egypt, they sold him to an Egyptian officer named Potiphar (Gen. 37:36). Potiphar's name means "the gift of Re," the Egyptian god of the sun whose worship centered in On, the city known to the Greeks as Heliopolis, "The City of the Sun." A variant of Potiphar is Potipherah, the name of the priest of On, who gave his daughter Asenath in marriage to Joseph (Gen. 41:45). On was sometimes given the fuller name On-mehit, "the northern On" to distinguish it from a southern On which the Greeks called Hermonthis. Jeremiah uses the Semitic name Beth-shemesh, "House of the Sun," in referring to Heliopolis (Jer. 43:13).

Modern Heliopolis is located about seven miles northeast of the center of Cairo, not far from what is now the main airport. There are few ancient remains, and the "city of the sun" is now a fashionable modern suburb. Tradition says that the holy family sojourned at Heliopolis following the flight into Egypt (Matt. 2:13-14). The visitor may still see the so-called "Virgin's Tree" and the well where Mary and the Infant Jesus are said to have refreshed themselves during their journey. Actually the sycamore tree which supposedly shaded Mary was planted during the seventeenth century, and the "Virgin's Well" was associated in pre-Christian times with the worship of the sun god to whom Heliopolis was dedicated. Christian legend says that the Child Jesus miraculously created the well, after which His mother washed His garments in it. A much older Egyptian legend states that the sun god bathed his face in the well when he rose upon the earth for the first time.

About 730 B.C. a Sudanese (Cushite) warrior named Pi'ankhy marched northward from Napata in ancient Ethiopia and gained control of Egypt. The Libyan dynasties which preceded him had left the nation in disorder and disunion so that Pi'ankhy met no united resistance. After bringing local rulers into subjection, he made a pilgrimage to Heliopolis where, in the words of his commemorative stele, "his purification was performed, and he was cleansed in the pool of Kebeh, and he bathed his face in the river of Nun, in which Re bathes his face." The legend of the river of Nun reflects the Egyptian concept of a primeval chaos from which the sun is said to have emerged. This legend was embellished in Christian times and applied to Christ. According to the legend all the idols of Heliopolis fell upon their faces before the virgin and her Child.

Of the ancient splendor of Heliopolis, nothing remains above ground today except a red granite obelisk which had been imported from Aswan and erected to celebrate the sed-festival, or jubilee of Pharaoh Sesostris I (c. 1950 B.C.). Originally this obelisk marked the entrance to the great temple at Heliopolis which was second in size to that of Amun at Thebes. It was in this temple that Potipherah, Joseph's father-in-law, functioned as a priest of Re.

Thutmose III erected additional obelisks at Heliopolis, two of which were taken to Alexandria by the Roman prefect Barbarus in 23 B.C. One of them was knocked down during the earthquake of A.D. 1301. Mohammed Ali, Egyptian governor from 1805 to 1849, presented this fallen obelisk to the British, who did nothing with it until 1877 when Sir Erasmus Wilson paid John Wayman Dixon, an engineer, to move it to the Thames embankment in London. The second obelisk was taken to New York in 1880 by Lieutenant Commander H. H. Gorringe of the United States Navy, and it now is located in Central Park of that city. These obelisks are popularly known as "Cleopatra's needles." A third obelisk built by Thutmose III at Heliopolis was discovered in 1912 during excavations conducted by Flinders Petrie and R. Engelbach for the British School of Archaeology. The fragments have been removed to the Cairo Museum.

Throughout the history of ancient Egypt,

Heliopolis was noted for its temple and the wisdom of its priests. Herodotus made their acquaintance and incorporated many of their tales into his histories. He says, "I went to Heliopolis . . . for the Heliopolitans are esteemed the most learned of all the Egyptians."[18] A tradition, which has no basis in fact, states that Plato studied there for thirteen years.

61. A column base in the cornfields where Memphis once stood

Memphis. Shortly before 3000 B.C. a ruler named Menes or Narmer unified Egypt and became the first in the series of rulers known to history as Pharaohs. Herodotus states that he founded Memphis ("white walls") as his royal city on ground reclaimed by diverting the course of the Nile at the head of the Delta where Upper Egypt and Lower Egypt meet. The city was built on the west bank of the Nile and came to be known as Men-nefru-Mire, of which Memphis (Hosea 9:6) is a corruption. The common Old Testament form of the name is Noph (cf. Isa. 19:13; Jer. 2:16; 44:1; 46:14, 19; Ezek. 30:13, 16). Herodotus wrote:

> Menes, who was the first king of Egypt, separated Memphis from the Nile by a dam; for the whole river formerly ran close to the sandy mountain on the side of Libya [i.e.,

[18]Herodotus, *History*, Book II, Section 3.

to the west]; but Menes, beginning about a hundred furlongs above Memphis, by damming the stream, dried up the old channel, and conducted the river into a canal, so as to make it flow between the mountains. . . . When the part cut off had become dry land, this Menes, who was first king, founded upon it the city that is now called Memphis. . . .[19]

Memphis early became a center for the worship of Ptah and his living emblem, the Apis bull. Even after the seat of government was removed from Memphis, the Ptah sanctuary maintained its importance. In later times it ranked third in Egypt, after the great temples at Thebes and Heliopolis.

With the period of instability at the close of the Sixth Dynasty (c. 2180 B.C.) the glory of Memphis faded. The seat of government was transferred to Lisht, twenty miles south of Memphis, during the Middle Kingdom, and the great Pharaohs of the New Kingdom ruled from Thebes. Yet Memphis, because of its strategic location and religious associations, remained one of the most important and populous cities of Egypt until the founding of Alexandria.

Memphis, located at the head of the Delta on the main route to Upper Egypt, was frequently exposed to invaders. The city was sacked by the Assyrian rulers Esarhaddon and Ashurbanipal. Although neither Assyria nor Babylonia succeeded in destroying Egyptian independence, Cambyses, the son of Cyrus, invaded Egypt and incorporated it into the Persian Empire. After gaining a decisive victory at the frontier city of Pelusium, he marched on Memphis, killed its priests and magistrates, and is said to have wounded the Apis bull, bringing about its death. This was regarded as inexcusable sacrilege, and the authenticity of the tradition has been challenged. During Persian times Memphis was a political center as the seat of a satrap. Although its great palaces were deserted during Hellenistic and Roman times, Memphis prospered until Emperor Theodosius (A.D. 379-

[19]*Ibid.*, Section 99.

THE WYCLIFFE HISTORICAL GEOGRAPHY OF BIBLE LANDS

395), in his effort to destroy paganism and establish Christianity, ordered the destruction of its temples and the desecration of their statues. The ruin of Memphis was completed when Calif Omar's general, 'Amr ibn el 'Asi, captured the city in the name of Islam (A.D. 640). The Arabs established their capital at nearby Fostat, replaced in 969 B.C. by Cairo on the east bank of the Nile. Stones from old Memphis provided a ready source of building material, with the result that the ancient capital is almost totally demolished.

The destruction of Memphis is without parallel in the ancient world. Nineveh was destroyed, but its ruins remained for the modern archaeologist to excavate. This was not so with the destruction of Memphis. Jeremiah's prophecy has been literally fulfilled: "Memphis (Noph, AV) shall become a waste, a ruin, without inhabitant" (Jer.

63. An Apis bull

46:19). Ezekiel also spoke of the desolation of Memphis: "I will destroy the idols, and put an end to the images, in Memphis" (Ezek. 30:13a, RSV).

A. F. F. Mariette discovered the Sepulcher of Apis at Memphis in 1861, and subsequent excavations were conducted there by Sir Flinders Petrie and by the University Museum of Philadelphia. Petrie gave particular attention to the site of the Ptah temple and did much to corroborate the accuracy of Herodotus. A red granite sphinx dating from Ramses II, discovered at the north gate of the temple, is now in the University Museum in Philadelphia.

Two colossal statues of Ramses II have been excavated at Memphis. The first, discovered by Giovanni Caviglia in 1820, was left in a mudhole for sixty-six years. Caviglia was an Italian sailor in the employ of Henry Salt, the British Consul General in Cairo in 1820. During the rainy season the statue was covered with water, but at other times of the year visitors could descend into the hole to examine it. Finally, in 1887, Sir Frederick Stephenson collected a sum of money in Great Britain and had the statue raised and placed on a brick pedestal. A second granite colossus was discovered in

62. Entrance to the sepulcher of Apis

1888, and an alabaster sphinx was excavated nearby in 1912. One of the colossi has been set up in the Cairo railroad station. A colossus and the sphinx are the only contemporary remains of Memphis, once the greatest city on earth.

Pyramids. A line of pyramids once stretched all the way from the head of the Delta, near modern Cairo, southward to Meroe, between the Fifth and Sixth Cataracts of the Nile, in the vicinity of Khartoum. Each of these pyramids was the center of a necropolis, and each had a funerary temple in which offerings were made on behalf of the dead person entombed in the pyramid. Although the Giza pyramids near Cairo are the best known, they are but the largest of many built by the Pharaohs of ancient Egypt.

64. The Giza Pyramid group

The great epoch of pyramid building came during the Egyptian Old Kingdom, Dynasties Three and Four according to Manetho's reckoning, covering the period from about 2660 to about 2500 B.C. Although the Pharaohs used forced-labor batallions in building their pyramids, Israelites did not work on them, for the Pyramid Age ended at least five centuries before the time of Abraham. The biblical record speaks of Israelite slaves working on "treasure [store] cities" (Exodus 1:11), but there is no hint that they had anything to do with the pyramids.

The Great Pyramid of Khufu (Cheops) was probably built about the middle of the twenty-fifth century before Christ. It covers an area of about thirteen acres and contains more than 2,300,000 blocks of stone, each weighing an average of two and one-half tons. It has been computed that the blocks, if cut into sections one foot square, would reach two-thirds of the way around the earth at the equator.

The physical labor required to construct the Great Pyramid staggers the imagination, for the lever, roller, and inclined plane were the only mechanical devices known to the ancient Egyptians. Petrie found evidence that copper saws, at least nine feet in length, were used to cut great blocks of stone. The Egyptians also used tubular drills in hollowing out stones such as those used for a royal sarcophagus.

Herodotus reports the tradition that 100,000 men worked for twenty years in building the Great Pyramid. They labored, however, only three months a year. This was evidently the season when the Nile floods made work in the fields impossible. Although laborers were certainly forced to work on the royal pyramid of Khufu, the Pharaoh evidently felt he was using manpower that would not otherwise have been usefully employed. The pyramids had religious significance, and the workers doubtless felt they were contributing to the well-

65. The Great Pyramid from the Nile

being of Egypt as they labored for the Pharaoh.

The second pyramid, built for Pharaoh Khafre (Khephren), successor to Khufu (c. 2525 B.C.), had a base measurement nearly fifty feet less than that of the Great Pyramid, but its perpendicular height was only ten feet less. It was first opened in modern times by the Italian archaeologist Giovanni Belzoni on March 2, 1818.

Nearby is the famous sphinx, also associated with Khafre, in the form of a recumbent lion with a human head adorned with the royal headdress and its uraeus (serpent). The sphinx rises sixty-six feet from the pavement to the crown of its head and is 240 feet long. There are many smaller sphinxes throughout Egypt, but the sculptors of Khafre were able to make use of a natural outcrop of gray and yellowish limestone for their most impressive tribute to the Pharaoh. They shaped the limestone into a portrait of Khafre, whose head towers above a lion's body with outstretched paws. Through the years it has been weathered and abused, but it still stands in majestic calm among the pyramids. Under the Mamluk rulers of Egypt the head of the sphinx was actually used as the target for musketry practice!

The desert sands habitually encroach upon the sphinx with the result that its base is periodically covered. An Egyptian record tells us that the sphinx was cleared of desert stand by Pharaoh Thutmose IV (*c.* 1440 B.C.). Excavations were again made during Ptolemaic and Roman times. Early in the nineteenth century (1818) an English group paid £ 450 sterling to have the sphinx cleared, and the work had to be done again by Gaston Maspero in 1886. The Egyptian Department of Antiquities undertook the most recent clearing in 1925/26. Since Egyptians as well as Europeans now appreciate the value of the monuments of antiquity, the government of Egypt will certainly do its best to keep them in a proper state of repair.

67. The Step Pyramid of Djoser

66. The Sphinx

The third pyramid of the Giza group is that of Menkure, the Mycerinus of Herodotus, who succeeded Pharaoh Khafre. His pyramid, built about 2500 B.C., is much smaller than its companions, ranking ninth in size among existing pyramids.

Of equal interest with the Giza pyramids is the older step pyramid at Saqqara, in the

desert west of Memphis. The step pyramid, built by Djoser (*c.* 2640 B.C.), is the earliest large stone building known to man. It is actually a succession of bench-shaped tombs known as mastabas, built one above another. Architecturally the step pyramid served as the transition between the mastabas in which earlier Pharaohs were buried and the pyramids which were built by Djoser's successors.

The ground plan of the step pyramid measures 413 by 344 feet. It is surmounted by six steps, each set back 6½ feet from the next lower level. The lowest step is 37½ feet high, but successive steps decrease in size, the topmost being only 29 feet high. All six steps have a combined height of 200 feet. True pyramids developed when steps were filled in and leveled off, as was done by the engineers of Khufu who designed the Great Pyramid.

The Faiyum. A few miles west of the Nile is an oasis known as the Faiyum, with a ninety-square-mile lake, the Birket Qarun, 147 feet below sea level. In prehistoric times the Nile flowed into this depression, which is the most easterly of the oases of the Libyan tableland; but silting produced an undesirable marsh country until the Twelfth Dynasty when energetic Pharaohs deepened the channel connecting the lake with the Nile River. The Lake of Moeris which was formed in this way became a valuable reservoir and a means of siphoning off Nile waters to prevent Lower Egypt from experiencing excessive floods. Supplies of water conserved after the passing of the flood season could be used for irrigation. The Greek historian Diodorus Siculus, who visited Egypt in 57 B.C., described the operation of the canal:

> Through this canal he [Moeris] directed the water of the river at times into the lake, at other times he shut it off again. He furnished the farmers with an opportune supply of water by opening the inlet and closing it by a skilful device and yet at considerable expense; for it cost no less than fifty talents if a man wanted to open or close this work.[20]

Earlier, Herodotus felt constrained to comment on the remarkable lake:

> The water of the lake is not natural (for the country here is exceeding waterless) but brought by a channel from the Nile; six months it flows into the lake, and six back into the river. For the six months that it flows from the lake, the daily take of fish brings a silver talent into the royal treasury, and twenty minae for each day of the flow into the lake.[21]

The kings of the Twelfth Dynasty, although native to Thebes, ruled chiefly from Memphis and Faiyum. Amenemhet I, founder of the Twelfth Dynasty, may have been responsible for the reclamation of Shedet (Medinet el-Faiyum), the chief town of the Faiyum whose Egyptian name actually means "reclaimed." The work was continued by Sesostris II, who moved his capital from Memphis to El-Lahun in the Faiyum. Sesostris set up an obelisk at Begig and colossi at Biahmu, which seems to have marked the limit of Twelfth Dynasty reclamation work. Such projects were virtually abandoned until Ptolemaic times when Macedonian veterans were settled on reclaimed land in the Faiyum.

68. The mortuary temple of Djoser adjacent to his pyramid

The Romans were impressed by the pleasant climate and fertility of the Faiyum. Strabo mentions olive groves, grain, and legumes, which had probably been planted by Greek settlers.[22] As early as Neolithic times, fishing was a favorite occupation in the Faiyum. Certain fish, however, notably the oxyrhynchus and lepidotus, were regarded as sacred, and it was illegal to catch them. The marshes around the lakes and pools of the Faiyum boasted some of the finest hunting ground in Upper Egypt.

The prosperity of the Faiyum during Ptolemaic and Egyptian times has had an important bearing on modern knowledge of the Greek language and, indirectly, on New Testament scholarship. Papyri written in the common, or Koiné form of Greek have been discovered in large quantities in ancient cemeteries and rubbish heaps of the Faiyum. Unlike the Greek classics, they represented the everyday language of the Hellenistic world, and had a grammar and vocabulary comparable to those of the New Testament itself.

The provincial capital of the Faiyum district is known as Medinet el-Faiyum, ancient Shedet. The Greeks named the town "Crocodilopolis" because Sobkh, the crocodile god was worshiped there. It was rebuilt by Ptolemy Philadelphus in honor of

[20]Diodorus Siculus, Book I, Section 52, p. 83.
[21]Herodotus, *History*, Book II, Section 149.
[22]Strabo, Book XVII, Part I, Section 35, p. 97.

69. A papyrus fragment of Hebrews

his sister-wife, and named "Arsinoe" after her. Even in Roman times, the visitors to Arsinoe made it a point to see the sacred crocodiles. A letter from Hermias, a high official at Alexandria, to Asclepiades of Arsinoe reads:

> To Asclepiades: Lucius Memmius, a Roman senator, who occupies a position of great dignity and honor, is making the voyage from Alexandria to the Arsinoite nome to see the sights. Let him be received with the utmost magnificence, and take care that at the proper spots the guest-chambers be prepared, and the landing stages to them be completed, and that the appointed gifts of hospitality be brought to him at the landing place, and that the things for the furnishing of the guest chamber, and the customary tid-bits for Petesuchos [Sobkh, the crocodile god] and the crocodiles, and the necessities for the view of the Labyrinth, and the offerings and sacrifices be provided. In short,

take the greatest pains in everything that the visitor may thereby be well satisfied, and display the utmost zeal.[23]

The mounds of Arsinoe were the first to yield papyri manuscripts which illustrated the use of the Koiné Greek. Letters, contracts, title deeds, and other writings from the rubbish heaps of the Faiyum give the fullest picture of life in Hellenistic Egypt and a wealth of information concerning the Greek language.

Herodotus, in describing Lake Moeris, makes the observation:

> About the middle of the Lake stand two pyramids, each rising fifty fathoms above the surface of the water, and the part built under water extends to an equal depth: on each of these is built a stone statue, seated on a throne.[24]

Although no such pyramids are to be found in the middle of the lake, tradition links them with two piles of stone half a mile north of Biahmu in the northern Faiyum. In 1888, Flinders Petrie, while excavating in the area, found two sandstone colossi with thrones and parts of an inscription of Amenemhet III. The two piles of stone were evidently pedestals in the form of truncated pyramids which served as bases for the colossi. From a distance they appeared to Herodotus as though they were in the water, although actually they were on the edge of the lake. The colossi themselves show Amenemhet's interest in the reclamation projects which changed the swampy Faiyum district into a fertile and prosperous province.

During excavations at Hawara, Flinders Petrie discovered the pyramid of Amenemhet III which, like most of the other Egyptian tombs, had been rifled in antiquity. South of the pyramid, Petrie came upon the ruins of a building which had traditionally been identified as the Labyrinth, the build-

[23]Quoted in James Baikie, *Egyptian Antiquities in the Nile Valley* (London: Methuen and Co., 1932), p. 204.
[24]Herodotus, *History*, Book II, Section 149.

ing which fascinated ancients and moderns alike. Herodotus described it in glowing terms:

> Yet the labyrinth surpasses even the pyramids, for it has twelve courts enclosed with walls, with doors opposite each other, six facing the north and six the south, contiguous to one another; and the same exterior wall encloses them. . . . The passage through the corridors, and the windings through the courts, from their great variety, presented a thousand occasions of wonder, as I passed from a court to the rooms, and from the rooms to the hall, and to the other corridors from the halls, and to other courts from the rooms.[25]

The description of the Labyrinth given by Herodotus does not give information concerning its purpose or its floor plan, and Strabo and Pliny, the other classical writers who describe it, do not provide much more information. Petrie's own description, based on his studies of the Hawara ruins, supplements and corrects those of his predecessors:

> From the scanty indications of the levels of the ground, and the fragmentary accounts of ancient authors, it appears as if the Labyrinth were a peristyle temple, with a central passage and two great crossways: the first crossway with courts or small temples opening on each side of it; the second crossway being a hall with a long row of columns, and with courts opening on the farther side of it, much like the temple of Abydos.[26]

Petrie considered his greatest success at Hawara to be the discovery of about sixty mummies from the Roman period, each with a painted portrait on a wooden panel over the face of the deceased. The style was strictly classical, and there is no evidence of Egyptian influence. Similar mummy portraits have been discovered at the necropolis of El-Rubiyat in the far north of the Faiyum.

Mummification was a long and costly process taking seventy days, according to Herodotus. The brain was removed through the nose and the viscera through an incision in the side. The stomach was filled with pure ground myrrh, cassia, and other spices, and then sewn up. The viscera were placed in four so-called canopic jars with lids in the form of images of the four sons of the god Horus. What was left of the corpse was then impregnated with salt and steeped for seventy days in natron, according to Herodotus. After this time the body was washed and wrapped in gauze bandages. Sometimes several hundred yards of finely woven cloth were used in wrapping the body. Between the layers of bandages, amulets of semiprecious stones were placed to assure the preservation and protection of the deceased.

70. A Canopic jar

[25]*Ibid.*, Section 148, pp. 23-25.
[26]W. M. Flinders Petrie, *Kahun, Gurob, and Hawara*, p. 16.

Mummies were evidently kept for many years above ground in an anteroom to the house. Great care was taken in mummification and in the funerary art which accompanied it. It was probably under the influence of Christianity that immediate burial began, about the time of Constantine. The deceased were buried in richly woven garments with articles which they loved while alive. Children had their toys buried with them. Dolls and toy furniture were placed in the grave of little girls who had used them. A copy of the second book of *The Iliad* was found under the head of a lady.

Semites—including the Israelites—did not normally embalm their dead. Burial usually took place a few hours after death, the body being simply wrapped in a cloth. When Jacob died in Egypt, however, he was embalmed (Gen. 50:2) before being taken to Canaan for burial. Before his death, Joseph insisted that his brothers promise not to leave his mummified body in Egypt. At his death he too was embalmed and placed in a coffin (Gen. 50:26) until his descendants could take the body with them at the exodus.

Upper Egypt

From Memphis to Aswan, at the First Cataract, the Nile flows for 500 miles through a narrow strip of arable land dotted by villages, some of which have been occupied since prehistoric times. All traffic moved on the river, for the land was too precious to be used for roads. Towns were built in the fertile valley, but the dead were buried in the adjacent deserts, and it is from the tombs that present knowledge of ancient Egyptian life is gained.

Heracleopolis. The Pharaohs of Egypt's Ninth and Tenth Dynasties were natives of Heracleopolis, the metropolis of the twentieth nome of Upper Egypt. The Egyptian name of the town was Neni-nesu, and it claimed the distinction of having the right leg of Osiris in its necropolis. The left leg was thought to have been buried at Philae, the beautiful island beyond the First Cataract.

Edouard Naville excavated the remains of Heracleopolis during the 1892/93 season for the Egypt Exploration Fund, and his work was continued in 1904 by Flinders Petrie. The most significant discovery was a Twelfth Dynasty temple which had been rebuilt and enlarged in the Eighteenth Dynasty, and again by Ramses II of the Nineteenth Dynasty. The forecourt was adorned with a colonnade of red granite columns with palm leaf capitals. The temple's hypostyle court had twenty-four columns. It included a small pronaos and a sanctuary with three chambers.

Petrie discovered important statuary remains including a granite statue of Ramses II between the gods Ptah and Herishef, the ram god of Heracleopolis. A gold statuette of Herishef is thought to date from the Twenty-third Dynasty. Petrie returned to Heracleopolis in 1920/21 to excavate the necropolis, situated on the left bank of the Bahr Yusuf, a Nile tributary on which Heracleopolis is located. Tombs from the Old Kingdom were identified in the necropolis.

Oxyrhynchus. Ancient Oxyrhynchus, known to the Egyptians as Per-medjet, the capital of the nineteenth nome, occupied the site of modern El Bahnasa on the west bank of the Bahr Yusuf. Its Greek name is derived from the oxyrhynchus fish, which was regarded as sacred. In early Christian times, Oxyrhynchus was a center of Egyptian monasticism, with as many as 10,000 monks and 12,000 nuns in the district.

Beginning in 1897, B. P. Grenfell and A. S. Hunt conducted excavations at Oxyrhynchus which produced valuable papyri, including two series of logia, or sayings attributed to Jesus, and fragments of several apocryphal gospels. Thus far 2,506 individual papyri manuscripts and fragments have been published in twenty-nine volumes bearing the collective title *Oxyrhynchus Papyri*. Some of the papyri contain biblical texts which date as early as the third century. Important classical manuscripts from Oxyrhynchus include Plato's *Symposium* and the *Hellenica*, a copy of the work of an unknown Greek historian. Manuscripts of poems by Bacchylides, the Paeans of Pindar, and fragments from the writings of Sappho and Callimachus are among the *Oxyrhynchus Papyri*. The papyri illustrate the use of the Greek language as it developed during the New Testament period and the centuries immediately following. Vocabulary in the papyri has been of considerable value to New Testament scholars in the study of the vocabulary of the Greek Testament.

Beni Hasan. The rock tombs of Beni Hasan extend several miles along the face of cliffs on the eastern bank of the Nile in central Egypt, 168 miles south of Cairo. The northernmost tombs date from the Second and Third Dynasties, and the most southerly are from the Fifth Dynasty. Other tombs in the area date as late as the Thirtieth Dynasty. Of particular interest, however, is a series of Twelfth Dynasty tombs excavated from 1902 to 1904 by Professor John Garstang, comprising the necropolis of courtiers and officials of the Oryx nome.

In all, there are thirty-nine Middle Kingdom tombs at Beni Hasan, twelve of which mention the names of those for whom they were made. Eight of these were chieftains or nomarchs, two were princes, one the son of a prince, and one a royal scribe. The tombs are cut from limestone and decorated with some of the finest examples of Egyptian art. Wrestlers, dancers, and girls playing ball are depicted with a naturalism only paralleled by that of the Greeks in their finest period of vase painting.

Beni Hasan tomb three, belonging to Khnumhotep, contains the famous painting of a Semite named Ibsha coming to Egypt with his retinue to trade stibium, a black eye cosmetic which the Egyptians enjoyed using. Under the painting is an inscription which reads, "The arrival, bringing stibium, which thirty-seven Asiatics brought to him."[27] The Semites are pictured in their colorful dress. The men are bearded, and a donkey is their beast of burden. The tomb dates from about 1892 B.C., giving a contemporary picture of Semites in Egypt during patriarchal times.

Tell el 'Amarna. On the east bank of the Nile, 190 miles south of Cairo, is the mound of Tell el 'Amarna, anciently known as Akhetaton, "the horizon of Aton," where the flanking cliffs on the eastern bank of the

[27]Cf. James B. Pritchard (ed.), *Ancient Near Eastern Texts Relating to the Old Testament* (Princeton: University Press, 1955), p. 229.

Nile recede to leave a semicircle eight miles long. Here the reforming Pharaoh, Amenhotep IV (Akhnaton) built his new capital after renouncing the Amun priesthood at Thebes and devoting himself exclusively to the worship of Aton.

71. The model of a house and estate at Amarna, c. 1375-1330 B.C.

The ruins of Akhetaton are not imposing today. Excavations begun in 1891 by Flinders Petrie were continued until 1937, except for the World War I years, by the Egypt Exploration Society. The city may be traced for about five miles along the east bank of the Nile, but its width was only about 1,100 yards. The lines of the streets and the ground plan of the houses of Akhetaton may still be traced. Little remains of the great temple to the Aton, but the lines of the royal palace are clear. Flinders Petrie discovered four pavements of painted stucco during his first expedition at Tell el 'Amarna in 1891. They were maliciously destroyed by a disgruntled guard in 1912, and the portions that were salvaged were sent to the Cairo Museum. The excavations revealed a number of palaces and temples, along with mansions of the functionaries and a workmen's village. The Temple to Aton was 200 yards long.

To the east of the palace was the so-called House of Rolls, which contained records of the Egyptian foreign office of Akhnaton's time. While digging in this area in 1887, a woman accidentally came upon the first of the now famous *Amarna Letters*. They comprise about three hundred clay tablets inscribed in cuneiform characters and addressed to Akhnaton and his father Amenhotep III by kings of city-states in Palestine and more remote lands. These texts show that during the days of reform the empire was allowed to disintegrate; and they mention the movement of Habiru, which some have identified with the Hebrews, into Palestine.

Akhnaton is usually thought to have been a conscientious reformer. While his break with the priesthood at Thebes certainly had political overtones, the sincerity of Akhnaton's religious convictions has never been doubted. His solar monotheism, however, was far removed from the faith of Israel's prophetic spokesman who insisted that the true God could not be represented by things in heaven, on earth, or under the earth (Exodus 20:4).

In the sixth year of his reign, Akhnaton moved his capital from Thebes to Akhetaton, about midway between Memphis and Thebes. Excavations at Tell el 'Amarna suggest that the city was built in haste. The workmanship is shoddy, although this fact is often disguised by the beauty of the naturalistic pictures of birds and vegetation painted on plaster walls and floors. The story of the founding of the city is related on boundary stelae, fourteen of which have been discovered.

Cut into the side of the hills to the east of Akhetaton were tombs in which Akhnaton's family and officials were buried. The tombs were numbered from one to twenty-five by N. de G. Davies who made an extensive study of their contents. The summation of this study was published in his book, *Rock Tombs of El Amarna*. Akhnaton's second daughter, who died prematurely, is buried in the family tomb.

Davies comments on the method of decorating the tombs:

![An Amarna letter](...)

72. An Amarna letter

The rock in which they are hewn is far from having the uniform good quality which would invite bas-reliefs of the usual kind. Nor was Akhnaton willing, it appears, to employ the flat painting on plastered walls, which was much in vogue, and which the artists of Akhetaton also employed at times with good effect. The idea of modelling in plaster was conceived or adopted; and, since figures in plaster-relief would have been liable to easy injury, the outline was sunk so far below the general surface as to bring the parts in highest relief just to its level. Nor was this the only measure taken to ensure durability. The whole design was first cut roughly in sunk-relief in the stone itself. Then a fine plaster was spread over it, covering all the inequalities and yet having the support at all points of a solid stone core.

While the plaster was still soft, it was moulded with a blunt tool into the form and features which the artist desired. Finally the whole was painted, all the outlines being additionally marked out in red, frequently with such deviations as to leave the copyist in dilemma between the painted and the moulded lines.[28]

[28]Norman de Garis Davies, *Rock Tombs of El Amarna* (London and Boston: Sold at the offices of the Egypt Exploration Fund, 1903-8), I, 18.

During the German experition of 1911/12, the ruins of a sculptor's studio were discovered with a number of plaster casts and portrait heads including the famous bust of Queen Nefertiti.

The Amarna tombs lack the variety of those at Thebes. They afford little knowledge concerning life in Akhetaton, for mention of the royal family and the worship of the Aton appear with monotonous regularity. These Amarna tombs do give some concept, however, of life in the royal court—of Akhnaton and his beautiful wife, Nefertiti.

Hermopolis. Opposite Amarna, on the west bank of the Nile, was Hermopolis (Eshmunein), where the ibis-headed Thoth was worshiped. The Greeks equated Thoth with their god Hermes. The region around Hermopolis was dotted with provincial towns during the First Immediate Period and the early years of the Middle Kingdom. During the Middle Kingdom, Hermopolis was capital of the Hare district, and its princes were buried in rock tombs nearby. Ramses II erected a temple at Hermopolis, built largely of stone taken from Amarna.

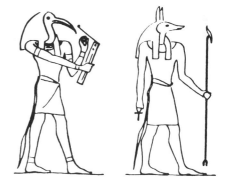

73. Thoth and Anubis in their stylized form

Asyut. Asyut, about 250 miles from Cairo and the largest town in Upper Egypt today, was the capital of the thirteenth nome of ancient Egypt, and the city of the jackal-headed god Anubis. The Greeks termed it Lycopolis, "wolf city." Near Asyut are rock tombs which date from the First Intermediate Period and the famous Twelfth Dynasty.

One of Egypt's oldest cultures, dating back to Chalcolithic times, centered in Badari, twenty miles south of Asyut. Badarians were known for their fine pottery and for the green malachite which they ground on slate palettes for eye paint.

On the east bank of the Nile about thirty miles north of Luxor is the village of Nag Hammadi, near the site of ancient Chenoboskion, "geese pasture." In the days of Thutmose III a yearly tax of 500 geese was paid to the Pharaoh from the town of Hatweret-Amenemhet, "the great stronghold of Amenemhet."

Monastery of Pachomius. The monastery of Pachomius was located at Chenoboskion during the fourth century of the Christian Era, and the manuscripts which are now associated with the town probably date from that time. In 1946, peasant laborers accidentally dug into an early Christian tomb and found a jarful of ancient books in the Coptic language, the latest form of the language of ancient Egypt. There were eleven volumes in all, comprising about one thousand pages of text written on papyrus and bound in leather. Nine of the volumes were complete, and two lacked their binding. They were in the book form known as the codex and not on scrolls such as those used among the Jews in pre-Christian times. The volumes comprised about forty-nine works, all of which probably had been translated from Greek originals. Although most of them are still unpublished, scholars have access to the books known as "The Gospel of Truth" and "The Gospel of Thomas." Both of these are Gnostic works which purport to contain traditions concerning the teachings of Christ not preserved in the canonical Gospels. Although they have no value in helping in the understanding of Christ and the earliest church, they do pro-

vide background material for the study of Gnosticism which was regarded by the church fathers as a dangerous heresy.

Thinis. Manetho's first two dynasties comprised rulers from the city of This, or Thinis, near Abydos. This was the political center, and Abydos the religious center and the place where early dynastic Pharaohs were buried. As usually happens in Egypt, the ruins of the city of the living have long since disappeared; but Abydos, the city of the dead, continues to have important remains. Burial at Abydos continued during the First and Second Dynasties, but it was discontinued when the Third Dynasty Pharaohs began the practice of building pyramids for themselves in the desert west of Memphis.

Abydos. In 1897, E. Amelineau began the excavations which uncovered the royal tombs at Abydos. To the west of the temple of Seti I, he discovered a huge deposit of potsherds and a number of subterranean tombs with burial chambers constructed with beams and planks. The chambers had been destroyed by fire, but one of them was found to contain a granite bier with a figure of Osiris. This was thought to be the grave of Osiris, and to the ancient Egyptians, it was the most sacred spot in Abydos. It is now known to be one of the royal tombs.

In 1897, Kurt Sethe, a noted German Egyptologist, read the tomb inscriptions and proved that the Abydos tombs comprised the royal necropolis of the Thinite Pharaohs. Among the more significant names are Narmer (Menes), Aha, Zer, Khasti, and Khasekhemui. Around the royal tombs were the graves of members of the court, servants, attendants, and even dogs. Following Amelineau, Flinders Petrie, Edouard Naville, and T. E. Peet did significant archaeological work at Abydos.

The earliest known deity at Abydos was a black, doglike god named Wepwawet, "the opener of the ways." He served as a guide for the dead, a function which seems to be derived from the jackal's habit of prowling at night around the cemeteries on the edge of the desert. With the rise of the Third Dynasty, when Abydos ceased to be the royal burial place, Wepwawet was replaced by the god Khenti-Amentiu, "Chief of the Westerners," whose temple at Abydos seems to have been built by Khufu (Cheops), the builder of the Great Pyramid. Khenti-Amentiu did not last long in the popular affection, however, for he was replaced by Osiris, the god originally associated with the Delta city of Busiris. Around the name of Osiris the tradition developed that he was the first king of Egypt and the instructor of the people in all useful arts. Since the earliest historical kings had been buried at Abydos, it was natural that the cult of Osiris should flourish there. Osiris was identified with Khenti-Amentiu, and he is designated "First of the Westerners" as early as the pyramid texts.

According to the Osiris myth, the king had been murdered and dismembered. Various cities claimed the honor of being places where some part of the dead god's body was buried. Abydos claimed the honor of having the head of Osiris. By the Fifth Dynasty, the tomb of King Zer was mistakenly identified as the burial place of Osiris' head, and succeeding generations brought their votive offerings in honor of the deity.

By the Sixth Dynasty, devout Egyptians wished to be buried near the tomb of Osiris at Abydos. If this was impractical, the body of the deceased might be taken on a pilgrimage to Abydos. Another alternative was to erect a memorial stele in the necropolis at Abydos. Poorer people might leave a votive pot in the necropolis area, and Pharaohs gained merit by adding buildings to the temple complex.

During the chaotic First Intermediate Period, Abydos was the subject of dispute between the rulers of Heracleopolis and

74. Horus (left), Osiris (center), Isis (right)

Thebes. Soldiers of Heracleopolis violated the Abydos tombs, although the ruler of their city was innocent in the matter. In a work known as *The Instruction for King Merikere*, the king took responsibility for the misdeeds of his soldiers and interpreted the misfortunes which befell him as punishment for this sin.

Abydos became the chief of Egypt's holy places during Middle Kingdom times. The middle classes as well as the rich aspired to be buried there so that they might hear the blessed dead of earlier generations utter the greeting "Welcome in peace." Every dead person buried in accord with the Osiris ritual symbolically took a pilgrimage to Abydos. The models of barques found in tombs all over Egypt were provided for this symbolic journey, as were pictures of journeys of the soul of the deceased painted on the walls of tombs.

The zenith of Abydos' influence was reached during the Ramesside Age when Seti I rebuilt the Osiris temple and provided it with a heavy endowment. Seti depicted seventy-six of his predecessors in reliefs in the Abydos temple, and he even built a palace there so that he could supervise the work. The limestone reliefs are the best preserved of any from pre-Ptolemaic times.

Seti I died before his temple could be completed, but the work was continued by Ramses II who left an inscription of 116 lines describing his labors. A short distance to the north of the Seti temple, Ramses built a second temple for himself. It was beautifully landscaped and richly endowed according to an inscription which Ramses left on the exterior of the south wall.

After Ramses II, apparently there was little further work at Abydos. With the decline of Egyptian power, the magnificence of gifts to Osiris inevitably diminished. Other centers gradually replaced Abydos. Beautiful Philae Island became the center for Osiris worship in the days of the Ptolemies and the Romans. In the development of Egyptian religious thought, Osiris came to be regarded as the husband of Isis, and ultimately her popularity became such that he took second place.

Thebes. During the four centuries between the expulsion of the Hyksos (*c.* 1575 B.C.) and the death of Ramses III (*c.* 1511 B.C.), Thebes was Egypt's capital and, during much of that time, the political center of an empire which extended to the Euphrates. Unlike the cities of Babylon and Nineveh, whose remains were hidden until modern times in mounds of rubbish, the glory of Thebes was always visible in the ruins of its great temples standing on the east bank of the Nile, 450 miles south of Cairo.

The modern city of Luxor covers only a small portion of the area occupied by ancient Thebes. The name Luxor is derived from the Arabic El-Uqsur, "the castles," a reference to the ruins of the great temples which still dominate the site. In ancient times the city and district of Thebes bore the name Weset, or Newt ("the city"). From the latter name the Bible designates the city as No (Ezek. 30:14-16) and No-Amon, the city of the god Amon (Nahum 3:8, marg. ref.).

Another ancient name for Thebes was "the two apts," a reference to the two dis-

75. A contingent of Egyptian troops

THE WYCLIFFE HISTORICAL GEOGRAPHY OF BIBLE LANDS

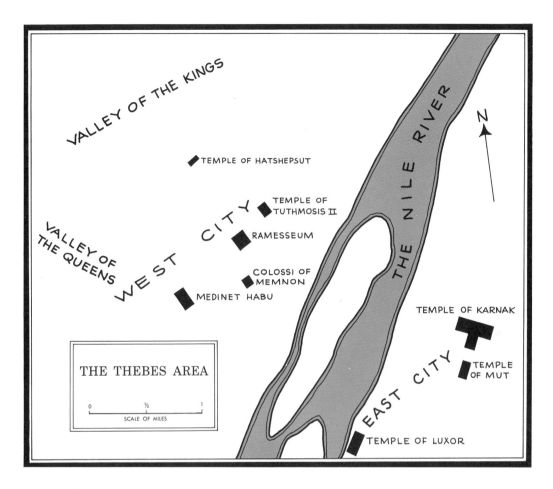

THE THEBES AREA

0   ½   1
SCALE OF MILES

tricts of the city corresponding to the ruins of Karnak and Luxor. Some Egyptologists suggest that the Greeks called the city Thebes (after Grecian Thebes) because of the native *ta ape*, Tape ("the apts"). Egyptian Thebes was familiar to the Greeks as early as Homer, who speaks of its heaps of precious golden ingots. *The Iliad* further describes "hundred-gated Thebes from which valiant men with steeds, . . . march through each massive gate."[29]

The Greeks identified the great Egyptian god Amon with their Zeus and referred to Thebes as Diospolis Magna, "the great city of the god." Across the river from Thebes was Weset Amentet ("Western Thebes") or Per Hathor ("House of Hathor"), the

[29]Homer, *The Iliad,* Book IX, ll. 381-84, and *The Odyssey,* Book IV, l. 127.

city of the dead in which the tombs of the Pharaohs were located.

Although the origin of Thebes goes back to predynastic times and traces of a Second Dynasty temple can still be seen at Karnak, it was not until the Eleventh Dynasty that a Theban prince took to himself the title "King of Upper and Lower Egypt." Thebes maintained its importance during the period of Hyksos rule in Egypt although its local ruler was forced for a few decades to admit the suzerainty of the hated foreigners. It was a Theban prince, Kamose, who ultimately freed Middle Egypt of Hyksos power. Ahmose I, founder of the Eighteenth Dynasty, succeeded in driving the Hyksos from their Delta stronghold at Avaris, and Egypt once again was ruled by a native dynasty. Ahmose restored Luxor,

76. Gold statuette of the god Amon

The conquests of Thutmose III brought added glory to the Amon temple at Karnak. Under Amenhotep II, Thutmose IV, and Amenhotep III, the city of Thebes continued to expand and the glory of Amon was enhanced.

Amenhotep III connected the temples of Luxor and Karnak by a wide avenue beautified by flower gardens and bordered with sphinxes. Across the river he built a mortuary temple of which the so-called Colossi of Memnon are the remaining monuments. A palace for himself, another for his favorite wife, Tiy, and a pleasure lake on which he and she could sail, were among the other construction projects of Amenhotep III.

Under Amenhotep IV (Akhnaton), Thebes was abandoned as a royal city. The son of Amenhotep III renounced the Amon priests, left Thebes, and built his new capital Akhetaton at Tell el 'Amarna. For about a dozen years, Thebes was purposely neglected, and Aton of Akhetaton replaced Amon of Thebes as the royal deity.

At the death of Akhnaton the Amarna revolt was ended. His successor Harmhab (Horemhab) moved the capital back to Thebes and made additions to the temples at Luxor and Karnak. Ramses I, Seti I, and Ramses II added to the huge hypostyle hall

and the Pharaohs Amenhotep I and Thutmose I built monuments at Karnak which still stand. Queen Hatshepsut is also honored by an obelisk at Karnak. Her successor, Thutmose III, extended Egyptian power into Asia and returned with trophies of victory that made Thebes the grandest capital in the ancient world.

At this time, Amon, the god of Thebes, attained the position of chief deity of Egypt. Prior to the Twelfth Dynasty, Amon was a lesser god of Thebes. It may have been Amenemhet I, founder of the Twelfth Dynasty, who first raised the Amon cult to a place of importance, because temples to Amon were first built at Karnak during his reign.

77. Columns with lotus capitals and headless statues of Ramses II, Luxor Temple

THE WYCLIFFE HISTORICAL GEOGRAPHY OF BIBLE LANDS

which became the most noteworthy feature of the Karnak temple. West of the Nile, successive Pharaohs continued to build funerary temples. The Rameseum of Ramses II was adorned with the largest granite colossus of ancient Egypt.

After Ramses II, however, the power of Egypt quickly declined, and with it faded the glory of Thebes. Ramses III built the gigantic Medinet Habu temple, but he could not arrest the decay in Egyptian prestige. The priests of Amon gained power, and the high priest Herihor was able to dethrone the last of the Ramesside rulers. The Amon priesthood controlled most of the wealth of Egypt. As a result, both Thebes and Egypt suffered.

79. The Colossi of Memnon

78. Amenhotep II, who some think was the Pharaoh of the Exodus, stands in his chariot and shoots arrows at a copper target.

With the rise in power of the Amon priests of Thebes, a rival dynasty was established at Tanis in the Delta. The god Amon continued to be reverenced, and Thebes was recognized as a religious center, but the political center shifted to the north. Under the Ethiopian Pharaohs of the Twenty-fifth Dynasty, the seat of government was returned to Thebes; but the results were disastrous. Shabaka, Taharka, and Tanutamun attempted to interfere in the affairs of Syria and Palestine, but in doing so they angered Assyria, whose King Ashurbanipal sacked Thebes in 663 B.C.

The Prophet Nahum taunted proud Nineveh by reminding the Assyrian capital of the fate of Thebes:

> Are you better than Thebes
>   that sat by the Nile
>   with water around her,
>   her rampart a sea,
>   and water her wall?
> Ethiopia was her strength,
> Egypt too, and that without limit;
> Put and the Libyans were her helpers.
>   —Nahum 3:8-9, RSV

After the sack of Thebes, efforts were made to restore the city, but it never regained its former strategic importance. Cambyses, the son of Cyrus the Persian,

80. Pylon entrance to the Luxor Temple. The twin flanking obelisk was taken to Paris in 1831.

Vestiges of its magnitude still exist, which extend 80 stadia [about 9 miles] in length. There are a great number of temples, many of which Cambyses mutilated. The spot is at present occupied by villages.[31]

From Roman times to the present, Thebes has served as a tourist attraction. Its temples have been desecrated by Muslim and Christian alike, and nature has also taken its toll of the monuments of Egypt's past. The city remains a witness to the fact that human glory is short-lived, that earthly fame lasts at most but a few generations, although its site is inundated much of the year, since the construction of the High Aswan Dam.

sacked Thebes 136 years after Ashurbanipal's expedition, and Egypt was incorporated into the Persian Empire.

The Ptolemies sought to enhance Thebes, but the city lived in the afterglow of former glories. When Diodorus visited the town in 57 B.C., he was shown its splendid ruins. He observed:

> The Thebans boast that they were the most ancient philosophers and astrologers of any people in the world, and the first that found out exact rules for the improvement both of philosophy and astrology.[30]

In 24 B.C., Strabo visited the city and commented:

82. Medinet Habu in western Thebes, pylon entrance

81. Court of Amenhotep III in the Luxor Temple, showing papyrus bundle columns

During the period of Thebes' glory, her Pharaohs were buried across the Nile from Thebes in the famed Valley of the Kings. Although elaborate precautions were taken to guarantee that their mummies would remain undisturbed, only one of them—that of the famed Tutankhamen—was preserved substantially intact until modern times. The painted walls of the tombs preserve the names of the Pharaohs and give some idea of their lives, but most of the costly furnishings were looted long ago.

In addition to the carefully concealed tombs, the Pharaohs built for themselves

[30]Diodorus Siculus, Book I, Section 45, p. 46.

[31]Strabo, Book XVII, Part I, Section 46, pp. 121-123.

83. Gold mask of Tutankhamen

84. Ramses II, whom some identify as Pharaoh of the Exodus

ornate funerary temples to which their departed spirits might go to receive the offerings that future generations would provide for their welfare. Ramses II built the Rameseum in which he commemorated his prowess on the field of battle. The temple complex at Medinet Habu includes temples of Thutmose III and Ramses III. One of the finest of funerary temples is that of Hatshepsut at Deir el-Bahri which was built in stages at the foot of a cliff with courts connected by flights of steps. It was designed by an architect named Senmut and was built of fine limestone. In front of the temple is an avenue of sandstone sphinxes and two obelisks. Wall sculptures in the temple commemorate the return of Egyptian soldiers from a successful military expedition to Punt, modern Somaliland.

Idfu. Idfu (Edfu), on the west bank of the Nile halfway between Luxor and Aswan, was capital of the second nome of Upper Egypt. The Greeks called it Appolinopolis Magna, equating the god Horus of Idfu with Apollo. Auguste Mariette discovered Idfu in 1860 and cleared the temple of Horus which is the most perfectly preserved monument of the ancient world. It was begun by Ptolemy III (Euergetes)

in 237 B.C. and not completed until 57 B.C. Its towers rise to a height of one hundred twelve feet, and the walls enclose a space four hundred fifty by one hundred twenty feet. Earlier temples had been built at Idfu by Pharaohs Seti I, Ramses III, and Ramses IV, but there are no remains today.

Horus, the god of Idfu, is represented on the monuments of Egypt by a winged solar disk. Legend says that he waged war with the god Seth and his followers, and was assisted by men who understood the use of metal. The legend seems to reflect a time when primitive users of stone weapons and implements were defeated by people who had learned to use metal.

85. The Valley of the Kings at Thebes. In foreground is tomb of Tutankhamen, behind which is tomb of Ramses VI.

86. The first Aswan dam

Aswan. Ancient Aswan marked the frontier between Egypt and Nubia. It was located at the First Cataract of the Nile, where red granite, syenite, and other hard stone formed a natural boundary between the two peoples. It early became a center for trade and warfare. Princes of Elephantine bore the titles "Caravan Conductor" and "Keeper of the Gate of the South" and conducted expeditions from Egypt into the unknown southern regions to enhance the glory and comfort of Egypt. Located on the east bank of the Nile at the First Cataract, Aswan was largely a commercial city. Elephantine Island was the religious and military center of its district and is presumed to have been the older settlement.

Elephantine. The origin of the name "Elephantine" is itself problematic. Some scholars relate it to the fact that Egyptians first saw the elephant there. Others follow the suggestion of Arthur Weigall that the name comes from the totem of the tribe which settled at Elephantine. There are numerous drawings of elephants on the rocks near Elephantine, many dating to prehistoric times. The Egyptian word for "elephant" is *yeb* or *yebu*, and it was that name which the town bore in ancient times.

Because the island was probably crowded, Nubian traders brought their wares to the mainland market town which came to be called Swn ("market"). The Egyptians pronounced the name as though it were spelled Swani, and the Greeks gave as their approximation Syene (cf. Ezek. 30:6, RSV). In Coptic it was called Swan.

The area around Aswan is rich in hard stone; red and gray granite, and diorite are plentiful. The Egyptians were the great builders of antiquity, and they were not slow in learning to quarry stone from Aswan and float it northward on Nile barges. As early as the First Dynasty, the tomb of Den Semti at Abydos was provided with a red granite floor. This red granite became the most familiar of hard stones to the craftsmen of the Egyptian Middle Kingdom and Empire Period.

The pyramid builders made use of limestone and sandstone which were quarried locally. Nevertheless, they appreciated the value of the harder granite and used it for linings and other furnishings. Mycerinus attempted to encase his entire pyramid in granite, although this project was never completed.

During the Pyramid Age, Aswan was evidently an important quarrying community. As the need arose, local workmen would be augmented by special gangs sent in by the reigning Pharaoh who had a special project to be accomplished.

87. Roman tombs on the Island of Elephantine

THE WYCLIFFE HISTORICAL GEOGRAPHY OF BIBLE LANDS

During the latter days of the Old Kingdom, Aswan and Elephantine became important centers of military expeditions. From Aswan, the frontier lords led Egyptian soldiers deep into Nubia, and there is some evidence that expeditions reached as far as central Africa.

Pharaoh Pepi I used Nubian mercenaries as the spearhead of the forces which he put into the field from time to time. Uni, an officer of Pepi, traveled south to Elephantine to organize a force to repel "the Asiatic Sand-dwellers." Ultimately his army included the Arthet, Mazoi, Yam, Wawat, and Kau Negroes and the Temeh of Libya.[32] Aside from the Libyans, all these warriors were recruited from the Negro tribes south of Aswan.

Throughout subsequent history, the Nubian mercenaries played an important role in Egyptian military campaigns.

Philae. The island of Philae ("the frontier"), located at the head of the First Cataract, six miles south of Aswan, was once the beauty spot of Upper Egypt. It did not achieve importance before the fourth century B.C., but the Ptolemies and the Romans made it a holy place second to none. The beautiful temple to Isis was begun by Ptolemy II Philadelphus and his wife Arsinoe.

[32]James A. Breasted, *Ancient Records of Egypt* (Chicago: University of Chicago Press, 1906), Vol. I, Section 311, p. 142.

88. Hatshepsut, who some think was the daughter of Pharaoh who adopted Moses

Osiris worship flourished at Philae until A.D. 453, seventy years after Theodosius issued his edict against the religion of Egypt. Both Egyptians and Ethiopians esteemed Philae as one of the burial places of Osiris. His left leg was thought to have been buried there, the right leg being at

89. Terraced Temple of Hatshepsut at Deir el-Bahri

Heracleopolis. The temples of Philae have become a casualty to the need for irrigation in modern Egypt. The lake created by the construction of the Aswan Dam now covers the island, and during much of the year Philae's ancient monuments are under water.

90. Temple to Isis on the Island of Philae

The Sinai Peninsula

The Sinai Peninsula comprises a barren wilderness south of the land bridge which connects Egypt with the lands of the Fertile Crescent. The Brook of Egypt, or Wadi El 'Arish, flowing northward from the Wilderness of Paran, marks the geographical boundary between Canaan and Egypt. However, contact between the two lands was continuous, for the distance between major cities was relatively short. El Kantara, in the eastern Delta is only 117 miles from Raphia in southern Canaan. The Roman general Titus took just five days to march from Sile in Egypt to Gaza.

Three ancient roads traverse the land bridge between Egypt and her Asiatic neighbors. Skirting the Mediterranean is the Via Maris, "the way of the sea," which was used by the armies of Egypt when they campaigned in Asia. Scripture calls it "the way of the land of the Philistines" (Exodus 13:17-18), asserting that the Israelites avoided this road at the direction of God. The former slaves to Pharaoh were in no condition to wage full-scale warfare, which would have been unavoidable had the route of the exodus followed the coastal road.

South of the Via Maris was the "way to Shur" (Gen. 16:7), the road which Hagar took as she fled from her mistress Sarah. Hagar, an Egyptian, was evidently on the way to her homeland when an angel stopped her, and told her to return to the home of Abraham. The Egyptians maintained a wall at the frontier to control traffic from the East. As the word *Shur* means "wall," the road seems to have terminated at the checkpoint garrisoned by Egyptian troops. The Egyptian terminus was in the region of modern Ismailia on the Suez Canal. In southern Canaan the "way to Shur" connected with roads leading northward to Beersheba, Hebron, and Jerusalem.

A third route, the biblical "way of the wilderness" known in modern times as the Darb el-Haj, "the pilgrim's way," runs across the Sinai Peninsula from the head of the Gulf of Suez to Ezion-geber (Elath) at the head of the Gulf of Aqaba. These two gulfs, extending like rabbit ears in a northwesterly and a northeasterly direction from the Red Sea, bound the Sinai Peninsula.

91. Model of a ship sent by Hatshepsut to land of Punt

92. Reconstruction of Hatshepsut's temple

The exodus did not take Israel along any of the well-traveled roads, and it is difficult for modern geographers to trace the route of the exodus with any certainty. The starting point was Ramses in the eastern Delta (Num. 33:5), perhaps to be identified with Egyptian Per-Ramses, the capital city which Ramses II built at or near the site of ancient Tanis. It was in this region that the patriarch Jacob had settled some centuries before (Gen. 47:11) when it was described as the "choicest part of the land."

Stops were made at Succoth (Exodus 12:37), Egyptian Tkw, in the eastern part of the Wadi Tumilat, and at Etham "in the edge of the wilderness" (Exodus 13:20), a site which has not been identified. From Etham they turned back to Pi-hahiroth, which may have been the name of a canal linking the Bitter Lakes to the Nile. The Israelite encampment was "by the sea, beside Pi-hahiroth, before Baal-zephon" (Exodus 14:9). The exact location of Baal-zephon is uncertain. In recent times it has been identified with Ras Qasrun, on the Mediterranean forty-three miles east of Port Said. Baal-zephon is a Semitic name meaning "Baal of the North." In Hellenistic times a temple to Zeus Casius was located there. Nearby was another place bearing a Semitic name: Migdol, meaning "tower." Migdol was a common place-name, for the ancient world had many watchtowers. There are records of a tower of Seti and a tower of Merneptah, identified with modern Tell el-Heir, five miles north of Sile between El Kantara and Pelusium. Migdol was doubtless the site of a tower in the northern sector in the ancient wall of Egypt, maintained primarily to control the movements of Bedouin tribes.

Israel left Egypt "by the way of the Reed Sea" (Exodus 13:18), but the exact location of the crossing is not known. Although traditionally known as the Red Sea, the Hebrew text of Exodus may best be translated the "Sea of Reeds." The term aptly describes the lake region north of the Gulf of Suez comprising the Bitter Lakes

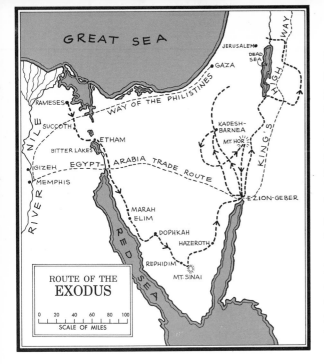

ROUTE OF THE
EXODUS

SCALE OF MILES

ly dynastic times. In the center of the mining region was the famed temple to the goddess Hathor at Serabit el Khadim. Hundreds of inscriptions have been identified at the temple and at the entrances to the mines. Although most of them are in hieroglyphic Egyptian characters, about forty are in the so-called Proto-Sinaitic alphabetic script from the fifteenth century B.C. They represent one of the earliest attempts at developing a purely alphabetic means of writing.

The last stop before Mount Sinai was at Rephidim (Exodus 17:1), possibly modern Wadi Refayid in the southwestern part of the peninsula. Here Moses smote the rock (Exodus 17:1-7) in order to obtain water to supply the demands of his people. Shortly afterward the Israelites met their first enemies, the Amalekites, and gained a victory after a difficult battle (Exodus 17:8-16).

Since the fourth century A.D., tradition has located Mount Sinai in the southern part of the Sinai Peninsula. A legend states

and Lake Timsah. The crossing must have occurred to the north of the Sinai Peninsula, for the Israelites found themselves in the Wilderness of Shur after crossing the sea (Exodus 15:22). The Wilderness of Shur covers the area south of the Mediterranean coast, extending from the Wadi El 'Arish ("brook of Egypt") to the line of the modern Suez Canal. All of the direct routes from Egypt to Canaan passed through the Wilderness of Shur.

Instead of taking one of the direct routes eastward, however, the Israelites turned southward into the Sinai Peninsula, taking a route parallel to the Gulf of Suez. Brief stops were made at Marah, where the bitter waters were made sweet (Exodus 15:23-26), and at the oasis of Elim (Exodus 15:27) with its twelve springs and seventy palm trees.

In the heart of the Sinai Peninsula, south of the Wilderness of Shur, is the region known as the Wilderness of Sin in which Dophkah was located (Num. 33:12). Dophkah is thought to have been located near the famed copper and turquoise mines which were operated by Pharaohs from ear-

93. The Oasis of Elim

94. Mount Sinai

that Catherine of Alexandria, after her martyrdom, was carried by angels to the top of the mountain which now bears her name. A monastery has been located there continuously since the fourth century, although the Christians have undergone periods of severe persecution. Massacres are recorded in the time of the monk Ammonius (A.D. 373) and some years later in the days of St. Nilus (390). Following the Muslim conquest, Christians in the area suffered considerable persecution. The present Monastery of St. Catherine, on the northwest slope of Jebel Musa, a 7,500-foot mountain, was founded about A.D. 527 under Emperor Justinian who established it on the site where Helena, the mother of Constantine, had erected a small church two centuries earlier.

Approaching Jebel Musa from Serabit el Khadim, the traveler enters a fairly wide valley called er-Raha, two miles long and one-third to two-thirds of a mile wide. This would be the natural place for Israel to have encamped (Exodus 19:1-2; Num. 33:15). Towering above the plain are three summits, Ras es-Safsaf to the northwest, Jebel Musa to the southeast and, still higher, Jebel Katarin rising 8,500 feet to the southwest. While Jebel Musa, "the mount of Moses," is the favored location, one cannot be positive concerning the original Sinai. The church historian Eusebius preferred still another site, Jebel Serbal west of the Wadi Feiran; and some scholars abandon the Sinai Peninsula entirely, preferring a site in northwestern Arabia or in the vicinity of Kadesh-barnea. The southern part of the Sinai Peninsula is still favored, however; and Jebel Musa may well be the real Mount Sinai, or Horeb, where the law was received by Moses.

After the encampment at Sinai, the Israelites moved northeastward and entered the Wilderness of Paran, which is bordered on the east by the extension of the Jordan–Dead Sea valley known as the Arabah, and its southern extension, the Gulf of 'Aqaba. To this Wilderness of Paran, Hagar and Ishmael fled after they were expelled from the household of Abraham (Gen. 21:21); and from the same region, Moses sent men to spy out the land of Canaan (Num. 10:12; 12:16). On the northern border of the Wilderness of Paran, where it touches the Wilderness of Zin, was Kadesh-barnea (Num. 20:1, 22). Kadesh-barnea was evidently an ancient holy place, known by the alternate name En Mishpat ("spring of judgment") at the time of Abraham (Gen.

14:7). In 1842 Rowlands discovered a spring with the name Ain Qudeis about fifty miles southwest of Beersheba, and scholars have tended to equate this with biblical Kadesh-barnea. The paucity of water at the site argues against the identification, however. A more suitable location would be Ain Qudeirat, five miles northwest of Ain Qudeis, which has an abundance of water and vegetation. It must have been somewhere in this general area that Israel encamped several times during the period of wilderness wandering (Num. 13:26; 20:1; Deut. 1:19, 46). Here Miriam died and was buried (Num. 20:1), and Aaron was buried in nearby Mount Hor (Num. 20:22-29).

Kadesh-barnea might well have served as a base for the invasion of Canaan, had not the Israelites accepted the report of the majority of the spies who expressed fear that they could not overcome the enemy (Num. 13:25—14:3). An attempt was made to penetrate southern Canaan (Num. 14:45) but Israel suffered defeat at the hand of the Amalekites and the Canaanites. The generation which had left Egypt did not enter the land of promise. Most of the years of wandering seem to have been spent in the vicinity of Kadesh. When the time came for making a fresh attempt to enter Canaan, the direct route from the south was rejected and the tribes crossed the Arabah and circled around Edom (Num. 21:4) as they prepared to enter Canaan from the east.

The proximity of Egypt to Palestine could be a blessing or a curse to the Israelites. When the Holy Land suffered famine, food might be available in the fertile Nile Valley.

Both Abraham and the sons of Jacob found it wise to look for food in Egypt when Canaan produced no crops. On the other hand a powerful Egypt could force its will on the less cohesive peoples of Syria and Palestine. During much of the second millennium before Christ, Egypt was at least nominally in control of Canaan.

While Egypt's great age of empire ended before the establishment of the Israelite monarchy, Egypt sought to regain her lost prestige and regain control of Syria and Palestine during the first half of the first millennium B.C. Pharaoh Shishak (Sheshonk) took advantage of the disrupted state of affairs after Solomon's death to launch a disastrous attack. With the rise of power in Assyria and, subsequently, in Babylon, Israel was torn between factions favorable to Egypt and those who preferred alliances with the Mesopotamian powers. The pro-Egyptian parties won out, but Egypt proved a broken reed. She was unable to provide effective aid to Israel or Judah, and those nations fell successively to Assyria and to Babylon. A Pharaoh Necho or a Pharaoh Hophra (Apries) might try to reassert Egyptian influence in Asia, with resulting failure. Babylon went down in defeat, but it was to Cyrus of Anshan, founder of the Persian Empire. Cambyses, the son of Cyrus, invaded Egypt and brought it into his empire. Until the Arab conquest, Egypt was a state subject to the Persians, the forces of Alexander and their successors, the Ptolemies, and the Romans. Egypt's period of glory was not forgotten, but neither could it be revived.

Bibliography

ALDRED, CYRIL. *The Egyptians*. London: Thames and Hudson, 1961.

BAIKIE, JAMES. *Egyptian Antiquities in the Nile Valley*. London: Methuen and Co., Ltd., 1932.

———. *The Amarna Age*. London: A. and C. Black, Ltd., 1926.

BREASTED, JAMES HENRY. *A History of Egypt*. New York: Charles Scribner's Sons, 1954.

DRIOTON, ETIENNE, and VANDIER, JACQUES. *Les Peuples de L'Orient Mediterraneen:L'Egypte*. Paris: Les Presses Universitaires de France, 1938.

EDWARDS, AMELIA B. *A Thousand Miles up the Nile*. Vol. 1. Leipzig: Bernhard Tauchnitz, 1878.

EDWARDS, I. E. S. *The Pyramids of Egypt*. London: Penguin Books, 1955.

EMERY, WALTER B. *Archaic Egypt*. Baltimore: Penguin Books, 1961.

FAIRSERVIS, WALTER A., JR. *The Ancient Kingdoms of the Nile*. New York: New American Library, 1962.

FAKHRY, AHMED. *The Pyramids*. Chicago: University of Chicago Press, 1961.

GARDINER, ALAN. *Egypt of the Pharaohs*. Oxford: Clarendon Press, 1961.

HURST, H. E. *The Nile*. London: Constable Publishers, 1957.

KEES, HERMAN. *Ancient Egypt*. Chicago: University of Chicago Press, 1961.

MONTET, PIERRE. *Eternal Egypt*. Translated by DOREEN WEIGHTMAN. London: Weidenfeld and Nicolson, 1964.

MOOREHEAD, ALAN. *The Blue Nile*. New York: Harper & Row, Publishers, 1962.

———. *The White Nile*. New York: Harper and Brothers, 1960.

RIEFSTAHL, ELIZABETH. *Thebes in the Time of Amunhotep III*. Norman, Okla.: University of Oklahoma Press, 1964.

STEINDORFF, GEORGE, and SEELE, KEITH C. *When Egypt Ruled the East*. Chicago: University of Chicago Press, 1958.

WILSON, JOHN A. *The Burden of Egypt*. Chicago: University of Chicago Press, 1954.

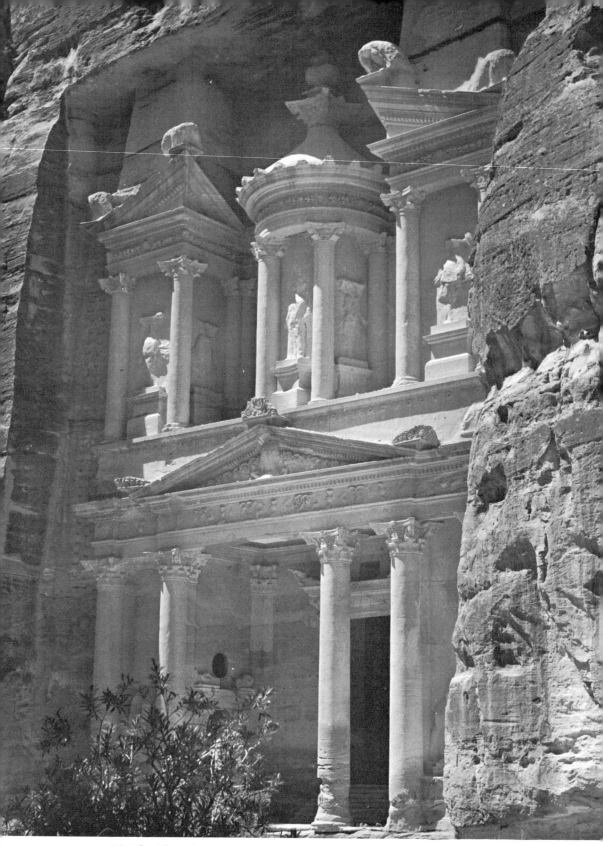

95. The Khazneh, or treasury, at Petra, probably the tomb of a Nabataean king

Palestine

Geographical and Historical Summary

PALESTINE, known in the Old Testament as Canaan, extended from Dan at one of the Jordan's sources to Beersheba in the northern Negeb, a distance of only 150 miles. From Dan to Ezion-geber on the Gulf of 'Aqaba (Akaba), where Solomon maintained a merchant fleet, is about 300 miles. From the Mediterranean to the edge of the Transjordan desert at the latitude of Jerusalem is only 75 miles.

Within this small area, however, occurs a great variety of topography and climate. The narrow coastal plain yields to the western highlands, extending southward from the Lebanon Range through the hill country of Upper and Lower Galilee and then, after a break at the Esdraelon Valley, continuing into Samaria and Judaea as far as Hebron. The eastern slopes of the highlands descend rapidly toward the Jordan Valley which is 230 feet above sea level at Lake Hule (Waters of Merom), 695 feet below sea level at the Sea of Galilee, and 1285 feet below sea level at the surface of the Dead Sea, with the bottom 1300 feet lower than the surface.

Rising from the Jordan Valley eastward is the plateau of Transjordan. The fertile lands of Bashan and Gilead were east of the Jordan River, with Moab and Edom occupying territory east and south of the Dead Sea. The famed Nabataean city of Petra marks the southern extremity of cultivated ground in the Transjordan Plateau.

Numerous streams flow westward into the Jordan River and the Dead Sea. The most important of these rivers are the Yarmuk, the Jabbok (Wadi Zerqa), the Arnon (Wadi Mojib), and the Zered (Wadi Hesa). East of the plateau is desert, which cannot maintain a settled population. Even the camel cannot traverse the sharp rocks and slippery ground which characterize much of this part of Transjordan.

The name "Palestine" is derived from the Philistines, a people who came in large numbers to southwestern Canaan from Caphtor (Amos 9:7), usually identified with the island of Crete, during the twelfth and eleventh centuries B.C. At this time Israel was attempting to strengthen and enlarge her holdings in the hill country west of the Jordan. The low hills known as the Shephelah, between the hill country, occupied by Israel, and the coastal plain, occupied by the Philistines, formed a transition zone whose ownership alternated between the warring peoples. It was not until the time of David that Israel subdued the Philistines and gained effective control of the whole of Canaan-Palestine.

Palestine, the territory west of the Jordan, was occupied in very ancient times. Excavations by Dorothy Garrod in the vicinity of Mount Carmel have yielded some of the earliest human remains, and Kathleen Ken-

96. The Neolithic level at Jericho

yon has shown that Jericho was a town in the seventh millennium before Christ.

During the fourth and third millenniums before Christ, town life developed in Palestine. The people who settled the land at this time are thought to have been Semites, although proof is lacking. The third millennium was the time of Egypt's Old Kingdom, or Pyramid Age, and Egypt probably attempted to control Palestine during that time. Beginning around 2300 B.C., a people known as Amorites occupied much of Palestine. They were a pastoral people who formed loose federations of tribes. The Semitic place-names which the Israelites found as they entered Canaan under Joshua may go back, in part at least, to these early settlers.

From about 1900 to 1200 B.C., a people known as Canaanites, related to the Phoenicians of the Syrian Coast, entered Palestine and established a series of communities. They left, in addition to numerous place-names, the religion in which the fertility god Baal (Hadad) held a conspicuous place.

Egyptian rise and decline. During this same period, the Hyksos—partly Semitic and partly Hurrian—founded a warrior aristocracy in Palestine. After centuries of gradual infiltration, they seized control of Egypt and ruled for about a century and a half

(c. 1730 to 1580 B.C.). When a native dynasty expelled the Hyksos, Egypt entered Palestine and sought to bring it under effective Egyptian control. During the fifteenth century, in the days of Thutmose III, Egyptian armies fought their way to the upper reaches of the Euphrates River, and Egyptian power reached its zenith. Egypt was not to maintain her control, however, for the fourteenth century revolutionary Akhenaton (Ikhnaton) was not particularly interested in the affairs of empire. Marauding Habiru threatened the city-states of Canaan, as we know from the Amarna Tablets. The Habiru included many more tribes and covered a wider area than the biblical Israelites, or "Hebrews," but they probably included some of the ancestors of the Israelites who entered Canaan under Joshua.[1]

Hebrew rise and decline. About 1200 B.C. the so-called "Sea Peoples" from Crete and the Aegean region settled along the southern coasts of Canaan, ultimately giving the country their name—Palestine, the land of the Philistines. About the same time the Israelite tribes under Joshua were gaining victories and slowly emerging into a state. By 1000 B.C. the Israelites established their monarchy. David, their second king, made Jerusalem his capital and succeeded in making surrounding nations tributary. The glory of David and his son Solomon was short-lived, however. By the time of Solomon's death, the nation was virtually bankrupt. Dissension was so great that the northern tribes withdrew support from the Davidic dynasty and established their independent rule. Thereafter, the Northern Kingdom was known as Israel, and the Southern Kingdom as Judah. The South, loyal to the Davidic line, remained independent somewhat longer than the North. Israel fell to the Assyrians in 722 B.C., while Judah maintained her independence (al-

---

[1]Biblical Eber is listed as a son of Shem (Gen. 10:21). His descendants are therefore more inclusive than those of Abraham.

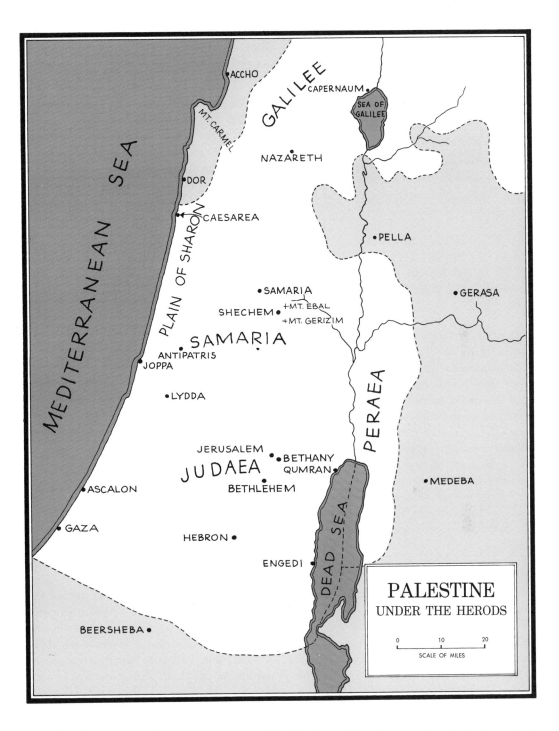

PALESTINE
UNDER THE HERODS

SCALE OF MILES

0   10   20

though often in a tributary status) until
Nebuchadnezzar's armies destroyed Jerusalem in 587/586 B.C.

The Assyrians deported the people of the

Northern Kingdom and settled their land
with other captive peoples. The resulting
fusion of remnants of the northern tribe and
other peoples settled in the land became

97. Samaritan priests celebrating the Passover

known as Samaritans, because they were settled in the region of Samaria. Several hundred Samaritans continue to live in this area.

Hebrew restoration. All but the poorest people of Judah were taken to Babylon by Nebuchadnezzar's armies. Babylon did not repopulate Judah, however, with the result that the exiles in Babylon could one day return to their country. When the Persian king Cyrus conquered Babylon, he issued a decree permitting the Jews to return (538 B.C.), and many chose to do so. Over a number of years the Temple and the walls of the city were rebuilt and Jerusalem again became the center of Jewish religious life. Politically the Jews were subject to Persia, but their high priests were given authority to handle many matters of civil as well as religious concern.

The Hellenistic period. With the conquest of Palestine by Alexander the Great (333 B.C.), Persian power was ended and Palestine fell first to Alexander's successors in Egypt, known as the Ptolemies, and then to the Seleucid rulers of Syria. When the Seleucid prince Antiochus Epiphanes attempted to proscribe Judaism and force Hellenistic practices upon the Jews, he met swift resistance (167 B.C.). A priest named Mattathias, followed by his son Judas, surnamed "the Maccabee," conducted guerilla warfare against the Syrians, and the sons of Mattathias lived to see the establishment of an independent Jewish state.

The Roman period. The successors of Mattathias and Judas did not always live up to the high ideals of the early days of the revolt. Internal dissension gave the Romans an opportunity to intervene in Palestine, and in the year 63 B.C. Pompey took Jerusalem. In 40 B.C. the Romans appointed Herod the Great as sole ruler of Judaea, subject to Rome. It was during the last days of Herod's rule that Jesus was born. Following Herod's death (4 B.C.), the kingdom was divided into tetrarchies, each under a separate ruler. The power of the Roman governor became progressively greater, and Jewish unrest continued to grow until open revolt resulted in the destruction of Jerusalem by the Roman general Titus in A.D. 70. Meanwhile Christianity had made its advent and was rapidly expanding around the eastern Mediterranean. A second Jewish revolt (A.D. 132-135) under a man named Bar Cocheba (Bar Kokhba), who thought of himself as Israel's Messiah, was also suppressed and the Jews were scattered. With Jerusalem out of bounds, Rabbinical schools were established in Tiberias in Galilee.

Islam and the Crusades. Christianity continued to flourish in Palestine as in other parts of the Roman Empire. When the Empire was divided, Palestine was part of the Byzantine East, but Christendom was in a precarious position there. Early in the seventh century Chosroes of Persia ravaged the country, and within a few decades Omar, the second caliph of Islam, conquered Palestine for Allah and Muhammad. Western Christendom attempted to take the holy places from the Muslims in a series of Crusades after 1095, and by the twelfth century Christian princes from the West had established a Christian enclave in the East. Their victories were temporary, however, and Pal-

THE WYCLIFFE HISTORICAL GEOGRAPHY OF BIBLE LANDS

estine has continued to be basically a Muslim land with significant Christian minorities.

The contemporary scene. In 1516 Palestine was taken by the Seljuk Turks, who ruled it until World War I. After the war Britain accepted Palestine from the Jordan River to the Mediterranean as a mandated territory. The land east of the Jordan was ruled by an Arab prince of the Hashemite house as the Emirate of Transjordan. Through the centuries of Arab rule, some Jews had lived in Palestine, but it was not until the nineteenth and twentieth centuries that large-scale migration took place. The Balfour Declaration, establishing Palestine as a national homeland for the Jews, encouraged many to flee from persecution in Europe to Palestine, where they settled largely along the coastal plain. Increased immigration caused the Arabs to grow apprehensive concerning Jewish aims, and violence resulted. In 1948 Britain resigned her mandate, after which the Jews and Arabs engaged in a bitter war (1948/49). The land was divided along truce lines in 1949, the western sector becoming the state of Israel, and the eastern sector being united with Transjordan to become the Hashemite kingdom of Jordan.

Regional Surveys

The Coastal Plain

The coast of Palestine, unlike that of Phoenicia to the north, is destitute of natural harbors. Except for the point where Mount Carmel protrudes into the Mediterranean, the Palestinian coast is perfectly straight. A harbor existed at Joppa in Old Testament times, and at Caesarea under the Romans; but neither of these could rank with Tyre and Sidon farther north on the Phoenician coast. None of the ancient Israelite harbors is of any significance today. Modern Israel has developed her Mediterranean harbor facilities at Haifa at the foot of Mount Carmel. Tel Aviv, the metropolis of modern Israel, has some harbor facilities; but the superior port of Haifa is used for all major shipping. The Palestinian shore, in the words of J. Howard Kitchen, "is strewn with the wrecks of harbors where other shores might show instead the wrecks of ships."[2]

The waters of the Mediterranean extended as far as the Judaean foothills in relatively recent geological times. With the passing of the centuries, however, the silt of

[2]*Holy Fields* (Grand Rapids: Wm. B. Eerdmans Publishing Co., 1955), p. 70.

the Nile River not only filled its mouth to become the Egyptian Delta but also deposited in the Mediterranean the sediment which was carried by ocean currents to the coasts of Syria and Palestine.

The proper home of the ancient Israelites was in the mountainous interior of the country. The Phoenicians on the Mediterranean coast north of Palestine were never subdued; and the Philistines, rivals of Israel through much of Old Testament history, always bothered Israel. The Plain of Sharon, the one sector of the coastal plain under Israelite control, was an exception. It is significant that when Solomon wished to engage in maritime traffic, he did not consider building a Mediterranean port but rather used the port of Ezion-geber on the Gulf of 'Aqaba.

Mount Carmel

Mount Carmel, jutting out into the Mediterranean, splits the Palestinian coastal plain into two sectors and forms a barrier to communication between the two. Commer-

98. Mount Carmel with Haifa at its foot

Elijah gave Mount Carmel its grandest moment when he challenged the prophets of Baal to a showdown encounter. Ahab and Jezebel had encouraged the cult of the Canaanite fertility god Baal, with the result that Israel's God was largely forgotten. Elijah, however, proved the futility of Baal worship (I Kings 18:19-40) and demonstrated the fact that Yahweh, the God of Israel, was the living God who answered by fire.

cial and military traffic usually crossed the Carmel Range through passes leading to such points as Taanach, Megiddo, and Ibleam. The range extends southeast from the Mediterranean (at modern Haifa) for approximately thirteen miles. The maximum height is 1,742 feet. In ancient times, as at present, Carmel was covered with luxuriant foliage.

Somewhat isolated from the normal flow of traffic, Mount Carmel, the western sector of the Carmel Range, was sparsely occupied in ancient times. The lower western slope, however, contains caves in which remains of a Stone Age culture were discovered by Dorothy Garrod of the British School of Archaeology in Jerusalem and Theodore McCown, representing the American School of Prehistoric Research.

The Plain of Asher

The sector of the coastal plain north of Mount Carmel is known as the Plain of Asher. It extends twenty-five miles north from the Gulf of Accho to Ras en Naqura, the ancient "Ladder of Tyre," and has a maximum width of eight miles. Its principal city and only port was known in Old Testament times as Accho, during New Testament times as Ptolemais, and during the Middle Ages as Acre.

Accho. A prince of Accho is mentioned in Egyptian execration texts of the eighteenth century B.C. During the Amarna Age (c. 1450-1400 B.C.), Zatatna, prince of Accho, pledged his loyalty to Akhenaton, assuring the Egyptian ruler that "Accho is [as Egyptian] as Magdol."[3] In another letter, however, a prince of Accho named Zurata is accused of disloyalty.[4]

With the division of Canaan among the tribes, Accho was assigned to Asher, whose men were unable to occupy the city (Judges 1:31) with the result that Accho remained in Phoenician hands throughout Old Testament times. When the Assyrian king Sennacherib recorded his campaigns in western Asia, he mentioned that Accho was part of the territory ruled by Luli, King of Sidon.

99. The Carmel Caves

[3]I.e., Migdol in Egypt, possibly the town of Exodus 14:2. The text is translated in James Pritchard, *Ancient Near Eastern Texts*, pp. 484 f.
[4]*Ibid.*

In Hellenistic times the name of Accho was changed to Ptolemais, probably in honor of Ptolemy Philadelphus (who reigned 285-246 B.C.), and it bore that name during the Maccabean period (cf. I Macc. 5:15; 12:45-48) and in the New Testament period (Acts 21:7). Toward the end of his third missionary journey, Paul stopped briefly en route from Tyre to Caesarea and spent a day in fellowship with a group of Christians at Ptolemais. At that time Ptolemais was a Roman colony with a population which included war veterans who had received grants of land from Emperor Claudius.

The name was changed back to Accho in early Arabic times. The Crusaders conquered the city and made it one of their strongholds under the name of "Acre." The Israeli city is known as "Accho," but it is no longer a port city, since major harbor facilities have been installed at nearby Haifa at the southern end of the Bay of Accho.

100. Crusaders' Wall, Accho

Achzib. About ten miles north of Accho at the mouth of the Wadi Qarn, stood the town of Achzib, assigned to Asher (Joshua 19:29) but never occupied (Judges 1:31). Sennacherib mentions Achzib as one of the cities taken during his campaign in Syria and Palestine (701 B.C.). The Wadi Qarn offers access to the hill country of Upper Galilee. Near the beginning of the Galilean hills, four miles inland from Achzib, is the mound known as Khirbet Abdeh, identified as Abdon, a Levitical city in Asher's territory (Joshua 21:30).

The Plain of Dor

The narrow coastal plain extending about twenty miles south of Mount Carmel was known in ancient times as "the coasts of Dor." Mount Carmel, at the north, formed a natural boundary as did the marshes of the Crocodile River (Nahr ez-Zerka) at the south. These extensive marshes actually blocked a two-mile area which extended from the mountains to the sea. Dor, the only town in this region mentioned in the Bible, was inhabited by the Tjeker, sea people who, like the Philistines, settled in various places in Asia Minor, Syria, and Palestine between the fifteenth and twelfth centuries B.C. The king of Dor joined Jabin of Hazor as part of a confederacy of kings from northern Canaan who determined to block Joshua in his plans for the conquest of the land (Joshua 11:1-2; 12:23). The confederacy was defeated, but Israel did not gain possession of Dor for several generations. In the division of the land, (Judges 1:27) Dor, although on the border of Asher, was assigned to Manasseh.

The Egyptian tale of Wen-Amon tells how an official by the name of Wen-Amon of the Amun temple at Karnak journeyed to Phoenicia to procure lumber for the ceremonial barge of his god. He stopped at Dor, "a town of the Tjeker," and was given a fitting reception by its prince, who evidently felt it necessary to show honor to a visiting Egyptian dignitary. While at Dor, one of Wen-Amon's men stole the gold and silver which was to have been used in paying for the lumber and ran away. The prince of Dor was courteous, but he disclaimed any responsibility in the matter.

A king of Sidon wrote in praise of his gods in the fifth century B.C.: "And further, the lord of kings gave to us Dor and Jaffa, the glorious cornlands which are in the field of Sharon, in accordance with the great things which I did; and we added them to the borders of the land that they might belong to the Sidonians."[5] Dor had access to the Plain of Esdraelon through the Fureidis Gap in the Carmel Range, but it could not compete with the port of Accho, which was superior to Dor and which provided a more natural outlet from Esdraelon.

The Plain of Sharon

The fertile Plain of Sharon extends southward along the Mediterranean from the Crocodile River to the valley of Aijalon (Ajalon) and Joppa, a distance of about fifty miles. Sharon varies in width from nine to ten miles and includes an area of red sand which was once covered with oak forests which made it comparable to Carmel and Lebanon (Isa. 33:9; 35:2).

101. Modern Jaffa and ancient ruins

[5]Inscription from Eshmunezer's coffin, now in the Louvre. Cited in G. A. Cooke, *A Text-Book of North-Semitic Inscriptions* (Oxford: Oxford University Press, 1903), p. 32.

Joppa. Joppa, in the Plain of Sharon, served as the seaport for Jerusalem, thirty-five miles distant. It was a walled town as early as the reign of Pharaoh Thutmose III (1490-1435 B.C.), who mentions Joppa in his town lists. The conquest of Joppa by Thoth, a general of Thutmose III, became the subject of a popular folktale. Thoth had two hundred of his soldiers placed in baskets and ordered five hundred men to carry them. Then he feigned a surrender, pretending that the baskets were filled with booty which the Egyptians were bringing to their conquerors. The gates of Joppa were opened to receive the men carrying the baskets, but once inside the city, the Egyptians released their men from the baskets and took the city of Joppa in the name of Thutmose.

At the division of the land, Joppa was assigned to Dan (Joshua 19:46), but it did not come under Israelite control until David gained effective control of the coast. Hiram of Tyre had timber floated from Lebanon to the seaport of Joppa for Solomon's Temple (II Chron. 2:16). In the time of Cyrus, cedars were again transported by water to Joppa for the building of the second temple (Ezra 3:7). When Jonah embarked for Tarshish in order to avoid going to Nineveh, he boarded a ship at Joppa (Jonah 1:3). Here Peter spent some time in the house of a tanner named Simon (Acts 9:43) and received the vision which told him he should not term unclean that which God had cleansed (Acts 10:5-16). Joppa was twice destroyed by the Romans and changed hands several times during the Crusades. Jaffa, or Yafa, now forms the southern part of the combined Israeli metropolis Tel Aviv-Jaffa.

Lydda. Eleven miles southeast of Jaffa is the town of Lydda, Old Testament Lod, mentioned by Pharaoh Thutmose III in the list of Palestinian towns conquered by his generals. Lydda was in territory assigned to Benjamin and was one of the most westerly of the Jewish towns of the postexilic period. It was strategically located at the junction between the road from Egypt to Babylon and the Joppa to Jerusalem highway. Peter cured a palsied man at Lydda and saw many of its people converted to Christ (Acts 9:32-35).

After the destruction of Jerusalem (A.D. 70), Lydda served as a center for Rabbinical studies, but Judaism was evidently short-lived there, for by the third century, Lydda, renamed "Diospolis," became a Christian center. It is the traditional site of the martyrdom of St. George (A.D. 303), who was honored by the Crusaders and, through Richard Coeur de Lion, was adopted as the patron saint of England. The Church of St. George was built by the Crusaders at Lydda during the twelfth century.

During the fourth century, Diospolis became the seat of a bishopric. At the synod held there in A.D. 415, Pelagius was tried for heresy. During the Middle Ages it was an Arab town, and in modern times it has survived as the Israeli town of Lod, situated two and one-half miles from Israel's principal airport, known as the Lod (or Lydda) Airport.

Caesarea. About halfway between Joppa and Dor, Herod the Great built the city of Caesarea at a site which was earlier known as Strato's Tower. Herod named it for Caesar Augustus and intended it to serve as the center of the Roman provincial government in Judaea. The Herodian kings and the Roman procurators had their official residences there. Stone breakwaters were built to the north and south of the harbor so that Caesarea could serve as a major Mediterranean port. Its position on the main caravan route between Tyre and Egypt made it a center for inland traffic as well.

Caesarea served as a showpiece for Roman culture. It contained an enormous amphitheater and a huge temple, dedicated

102. Temple of Augustus, Caesarea

to Caesar and Rome, with huge statues of the emperor. In New Testament times Caesarea was a mixed city, with Jews and non-Jews in its population. Pilate, the procurator of Judaea, resided in Caesarea; and Philip the deacon made his home there (Acts 21:8) as did Cornelius the centurion, whom Peter brought to Christ (Acts 10:1, 24; 11:11). Having escaped his Jewish enemies at Damascus, Paul departed for Caesarea on his way to Tarsus (Acts 9:30) and made the city his port of landing on returning from his second and third missionary journeys (Acts 18:22; 21:8). Paul stood trial before Felix at Caesarea (Acts 23:23-35), where he was imprisoned for two years. His defense before Porcius Festus and Agrippa took place at Caesarea (Acts 25:11), and from its harbor he sailed on his voyage to Rome.

Difficulties between Jews and Romans at Caesarea sparked the Jewish revolt (A.D. 66) which ended in the destruction of Jerusalem by the armies of Titus (A.D. 70). Caesarea was the headquarters of the Roman legions which were sent to crush the uprising, and many captured Jewish zealots were tortured in its prisons. After the Romans crushed the revolt, both Jews and Gentiles continued to live in Caesarea. It became an important Christian center and was the home of Eusebius, the church father who wrote his *Ecclesiastical History* and

Onomasticon, which give much information about Palestinian geography. The city became a Crusader stronghold in the twelfth century, but it was destroyed by the Muslims in 1291. The Antiquities Department of the state of Israel has been excavating ancient Caesarea, and Israeli farmers work the fertile land nearby.

Antipatris. Antipatris (Antipatria), about twenty-six miles south of Caesarea on the road to Lydda, was the site of a Canaanite stronghold as early as 2000 B.C. Known in the Old Testament as Aphek, Antipatris was the site where the Israelites suffered the tragic loss of the ark to the Philistines (I Samuel 4). Herod the Great rebuilt the city about 35 B.C. and named it "Antipatris" for his father Antipater. Here the Apostle Paul stopped on his way from Jerusalem to Caesarea (Acts 23:31). Ancient Antipatris is now known as Ras el-'Ain, and its water is piped thirty miles upland to Israeli Jerusalem.

The principal stream of the southern Sharon is the Yarkon River, which has its source near Antipatris and enters the Mediterranean north of Tel Aviv. In biblical times it marked the boundary between the tribes of Dan and Ephraim. About one and one-quarter miles from the mouth of the Yarkon, excavators have come upon a site which was occupied from Philistine to Roman times. The ancient name is not yet known, but it bears the modern name "Tel Qasile." The Israel Exploration Society, assisted financially by the municipality of Tel Aviv, began work there in 1949 under the direction of Benjamin Mazar. The stratification of the mound reveals remains from Philistine, Israelite, Persian, Hellenistic, and Roman periods.

South of Joppa there is a rise in the land as one enters the Philistine Plain where the rainfall decreases and the influence of the desert becomes more and more apparent. Trees are rare as one moves southward, but the open country is good for the raising of grains and makes possible the development of large and prosperous communities.

The Plain of Philistia

The Philistine Plain is named for its ancient inhabitants of the same name. Their appellation survives in the name "Palestine." The Prophet Amos asserted that the Philistines had come from Caphtor, the Hebrew name for the island of Crete (Amos

9:7). Minoan Crete was one of the great cultural centers of the second millennium B.C., and the Philistines brought their arts, crafts, and literary traditions with them to southern Canaan. Deuteronomy states that the Caphtorim (another name for the Philistines) dispossessed the aboriginal Avvim (biblical Avim) "who lived in villages as far as Gaza" (Deut. 2:23).

Gerar. During the Patriarchal Age the Philistine center in Palestine was at Gerar, in the foothills of the Judaean mountains south of Gaza. Both Abraham and Isaac enjoyed cordial relations with Abimelech of Gerar, although Isaac's relations were strained because he had lied concerning the identity of his wife (Gen. 21:32, 34; 26:1, 8). Although there are no extrabiblical references to Philistines in Canaan before the twelfth century B.C., it is known that trade was common between western Asia and Crete early in the second millennium. One of the Mari Tablets (18th century B.C.) records the sending of gifts by the king of Hazor to Kaptara (Caphtor). Philistines did not have a dominant position in southern Palestine during the Patriarchal Age, but early trading centers appear to have been established at that time.

The site of Gerar has been identified with Tell Jemmeh, about eight miles south of Gaza. This mound was excavated in 1922 by W. J. Phythian-Adams and in 1927 by W. M. Flinders Petrie. Petrie's excavation produced remains from the time of Egypt's Eighteenth Dynasty (16th to 14th centuries B.C.). More recently, however, Y. Aharoni has argued that Gerar should be located at Tell Abu Hureira, a mound about eleven miles southeast of Gaza.[6] An Israeli archaeologist, D. Alon, made a survey of Tell Abu Hureira and found evidence from potsherds that the city had enjoyed a period of prosperity during the Middle Bronze Age, the period of the biblical Patriarchs.

The twelfth century B.C. was a time of much mobility in the lands of the eastern Mediterranean. Greece was invaded from the north; Achaeans launched their Trojan War by attacking Troy (traditionally, 1194 B.C.); the Hittite Empire was overcome by Sea Peoples from the west; and the Egypt of Ramses III was attacked by the same Sea Peoples among whom were the *PRST* (Semitic *PLST*), the Egyptian form of the word *Philistine* (1165 B.C.). These Philistines were repulsed by the Egyptians but succeeded in occupying the coastal areas of southern Palestine and dispossessing the Canaanites who had been settled there.

The main road from Egypt to the north passed through the land of the Philistines which was open country, protected by no natural barriers at either end. Once an Egyptian army had taken Gaza, there was nothing to stop it until it reached Megiddo which guards the pass to the valley of Esdraelon. Conversely, having passed Megiddo, an army from the north could readily move on toward Gaza. At the time of the exodus, the Israelites did not travel "through the way of the land of the Philistines, although that was near" (Exodus 13:17) because of the danger of warfare which would result from a frontal movement into Canaan.

At the conquest of Canaan, Joshua did not encounter the Philistines; but when he was an old man, he noted that the Philistines were settled in the five cities with which they were subsequently identified: Gaza, Ashdod (ancient Greek Azotos), Ascalon (Ashkelon), Gath, and Ekron (Joshua 13:1-3, RSV). Throughout the period of the Judges, the Philistines occupied the coastal plain, the Israelites occupied the hill country, and the low hills known as the Shephelah constituted a no-man's-land whose possession passed back and forth between the two peoples and served as an indicator of their relative strength.

[6]Y. Aharoni, "The Land of Gerar," *Israel Explorations Journal*, VI, 1956, 26-32.

Gaza. Gaza was the southernmost of the cities of the Philistine pentapolis (the five cities of Joshua 13:1-3) and marked the southern limit of Canaan on the Mediterranean coast (Gen. 10:19). It was the center of busy caravan routes which led southwest into Egypt, south to Arabia by way of Beersheba, southeast into Edom, and north along the Mediterranean and then overland to Damascus and beyond. In the days of the Egyptian Empire (1550-1225 B.C.), Gaza served as an administrative center for protecting Egyptian interests in Canaan. When the Philistines were repulsed in their attempt to enter Egypt during the reign of Ramses III, they moved northward and occupied Gaza and its environs.

During the period of the Judges, Gaza

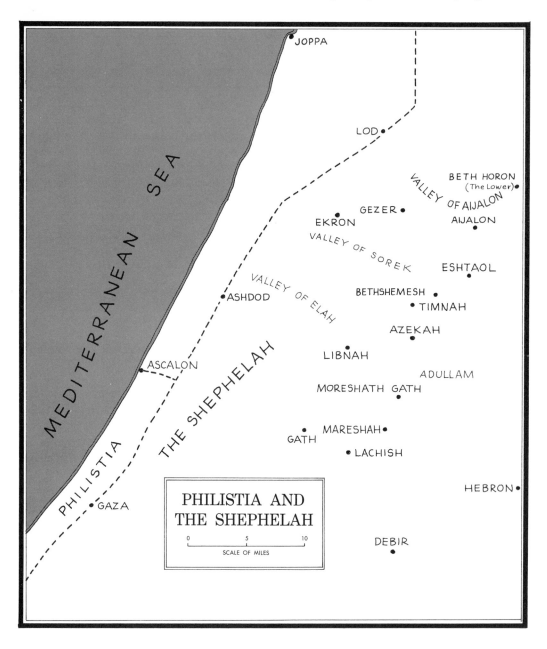

PHILISTIA AND THE SHEPHELAH

THE WYCLIFFE HISTORICAL GEOGRAPHY OF BIBLE LANDS

was a Philistine stronghold. There blinded Samson worked in the prison mill (Judges 16:21); and when his strength was revived, he caused the death of the assembled multitude (Judges 16:28-30).

Although Gaza was nominally a part of the kingdoms of David and Solomon (cf. I Kings 4:24), Israelite control of the city was tenuous. The Assyrian annals record a series of battles for Gaza. Tiglath-pileser III captured it in 734 B.C., but Hanno, the ruler of Gaza, succeeded in fleeing to Egypt. When Assyrian pressure was relieved, Hanno returned to support a rebellion against Assyria. Sargon marched against the city in 722 B.C. and took Hanno as a prisoner to Assyria. At the time of Sennacherib's campaign against Judah (701 B.C.), Gaza was evidently loyal to Assyria, for Sennacherib gave to Sillibel, king of Gaza, territory which was taken from Judah. By the time of Jeremiah, Gaza had fallen into Egyptian control (Jer. 47:1). It was nominally a part of the Persian Empire until it fell to Alexander the Great after a five-month siege (332 B.C.). Alexander colonized Gaza as a Hellenistic city, but sovereignty was disputed by the Egyptian Ptolemies and the Syrian Seleucids after his death. In 198 B.C. it was annexed by Antiochus III of Syria. Under the Maccabean ruler Alexander Jannaeus, Gaza was destroyed along with other coastal cities (93 B.C.). Pompey, however, declared Gaza a free city in 61 B.C.

Gaza became an important trading city in the days of the Nabataean Arabs. In 57 B.C. Pompey's general, Aulus Gabinius, rebuilt the city at a new site south of the old location and nearer the ocean. It was on the road to the old, or "desert," Gaza that Philip met an Ethiopian (i.e., Nubian) eunuch and led him to Christ (Acts 8:26-40). Gaza is now the principal city of the Gaza Strip, administered by Egypt and populated largely by Arab refugees.

The mound Tell el-'Ajjul, long assumed to be the site of ancient Gaza, was excavated by Flinders Petrie from 1930 to 1934.

Pottery indicated settlements from the Middle Bronze and Late Bronze Ages, and there was evidence that the site had once been a Hyksos stronghold, but nothing was found to identify the mound with Gaza. The numerous artifacts which Petrie found there included gold jewelry and bronze daggers, toggle pins, and horse bits. Tel el-'Ajjul is now tentatively identified with Beth-eglaim.

Ashdod. Eighteen miles northeast of Gaza was Ashdod, the Philistine city with the famed temple of Dagon (Dagan) to which the ark was taken following the Israelite debacle at Aphek (I Sam. 5:1-5). The history of Ashdod was largely parallel to that of other Philistine city-states. Its governor rebelled against Sargon II (711 B.C.), after which the Assyrians sacked the city (Isa. 20:1). Jeremiah spoke of "the remnant of Ashdod" (Jer. 25:20), implying that the city was weak in his day. Following the exile, Nehemiah was shocked to learn that Jews had married women of Ashdod and that their children spoke the language of Ashdod rather than that of Judah (Neh. 13:23-24).

According to Herodotus, Ashdod was besieged for twenty-nine years by Psamtik (Psammetichos) of Egypt.[7] The city was conquered and partially destroyed by the Maccabees (I Macc. 5:68; 10:84). It flourished, however, following reconstruction by Herod. The Roman governor Gabinius beautified the inner city which was presented by Augustus to Salome, Herod's sister. In New Testament times, the city was known as Azotus. Following the conversion of the Ethiopian eunuch, Philip preached in the communities between Azotus and Caesarea (Acts 8:40).

Today a village known as Esdud, inhabited by Arabs before the establishment of the state of Israel, occupies the ancient site of Ashdod. A Jewish settlement nearby is Sede-Uzziah ("fields of Uzziah"), named

---

[7]Herodotus, *History*, Book II, Section 157.

104. Ashkelon Antiquities
Park

after the Judaean king who "went forth and warred against the Philistines and broke down the wall of Ashdod" (II Chron. 26:6). Under the direction of David Noel Freedman, excavations have been conducted at Ashdod since 1962.

Ashkelon. Excavations at Ashkelon, about twelve miles north of Gaza, show that the site was occupied as early as 2000 B.C. Its king is mentioned in Egyptian execration texts and the Amarna Letters. In 1280 B.C. Ashkelon was sacked by Ramses II. During the time of the Judges it was temporarily occupied by Judah (Judges 1:18) but had reverted to Philistine rule by the time of Samson (Judges 14:19).

Under Tiglath-pileser III, Ashkelon became a vassal to Assyria (734 B.C.), but it later rebelled and, after a brief period of freedom, was sacked by Sennacherib. By 630 B.C. Ashkelon regained its independence from the disintegrating Assyrian Empire. Babylonia, however, attempted to regain in her own name the lands that had once paid tribute to Assyria, and Ashkelon was again sacked in 604 B.C. This time it was the army of Nebuchadnezzar that destroyed Ashke-

lon, slew its king, and took prisoners to Babylon (cf. Jer. 47:5-7).

Ashkelon was the birthplace of Herod the Great and the residence of his sister Salome. Herod embellished the city with ornate buildings and colonnaded courts. It is Herodian Ashkelon that has yielded the most impressive ruins.

The excavation of Ashkelon began at the beginning of the nineteenth century when Lady Hester Stanhope, an English noblewoman, began excavating the site in the hope of finding silver and gold which tradition said were buried there. Although this romantic adventure proved fruitless, scholarly work began in 1920 under John Garstang representing the Palestine Exploration Fund. Garstang discovered remains of Roman Ashkelon on the summit of the mound. A sampling of the other levels was gained by cutting sections in the face of the mound which revealed a succession of settlements. A complete break marked the period between the end of the Late Bronze Age and the beginning of the Early Iron Age. This probably marks the disruption caused by the invading Philistines and their subsequent settlement at Ashkelon.

Gath. The Philistine city of Gath ("wine press") is best known as the home of Goliath, the giant who was felled by a stone from David's sling (I Sam. 17). Later, in fleeing from Saul, David came to Gath and feigned madness before Achish, the king of the city (I Sam. 21:10-15). David, with a company of six hundred men, spent over a year in Gath, where they were safe from Saul's murderous intent (I Sam. 27). After the death of Saul, David was able to add Gath to his own territory (I Chron. 18:1). Throughout life David seems to have maintained friendly relations with the people of Gath, who are known in Scripture as Gittites. At the time of Absalom's rebellion, David had six hundred Gittites among his mercenaries (II Sam. 15:18).

Rehoboam fortified Gath (II Chron. 11:8), but the city fell to Hazael of Damascus in the ninth century (II Kings 12:17). It was evidently in Philistine hands again when Uzziah broke down its walls (II Chron. 26:6). It was besieged and conquered by Sargon II of Assyria in the eighth century, and subsequently dropped out of history (cf. Amos 6:2). The exact location of Gath is still not known. Excavations have been conducted by the Israeli Department of Archaeology under S. Yeivin at Tell el-'Areini, twenty miles northeast of Gaza, which the excavators assumed to be Gath. The work, begun in 1956, included diggings both at the top and the foot of the mound. The archaeologists uncovered foundations of buildings made of clay bricks, potsherds, and Hebrew seals on jar handles from the time of the kingdom of Judah. The fact that no Philistine remains have been found leads many scholars to doubt the identification of the site with Gath. The nearby mound 'Araq el-Menshiyeh is another possible location of Gath, but this is still uncertain.

Ekron. During the period of the Judges, Ekron, the northernmost city of the Philistine pentapolis, was occupied by the men of

105. The Mound of Gath

Judah (Judges 1:18), but it did not remain in Israelite control. It was close to Israelite territory but remained essentially Philistine. When the ark was removed from Gath, it was taken to Ekron, the last of the Philistine cities, and then sent on to Beth-shemesh in Israel (I Sam. 5:10—6:12).

The fortunes of Ekorn, like the other Philistine cities, varied through its long history. Padi, its king in the days of Sennacherib, remained loyal to the Assyrians, but a group of rebels seized the throne and turned Padi over to Hezekiah, who was evidently a leader in the opposition to Sennacherib. The *Annals of Sennacherib* tell how the Assyrians took Ekron and restored Padi to his throne as a loyal vassal. Esarhaddon also mentioned Ekron as a Philistine city, loyal to its Assyrian overlord.

The god of Ekron was Baal-zebub (Beelzebub). Ahaziah of Israel was on his way to consult the shrine of Baal-zebub when he was intercepted by Elijah who demanded to know if Israel was without a god and why the god of Ekron must be consulted (II Kings 1:1-6, 16). *Baal-zebub* ("lord of flies") may be an intentional Hebrew alteration of the Canaanite *Baal-zebul* ("Lord of the High Place," or "Exalted Baal"). Baal-zebub (or Baal-zebul) is used in the New Testament as a synonym for Satan, and is rendered "the prince of the devils" (Matt. 12:24-29).

In 147 B.C., Alexander Balas, king of Syria, transferred Ekron to the Maccabean ruler Jonathan (I Macc. 10:89). According to Eusebius, it had a large Jewish population in the third century A.D. Ekron has long been in ruins, however, and positive identification has not been possible. Edward Robinson, in the nineteenth century, plausibly suggested that it be identified with 'Akir, ten miles northeast of Ashdod. Some scholars identify Ekron with Khirbet el-Muqenna', six miles southeast of Akir, although el-Muqenna' is usually thought to contain the ruins of Eltekeh.

The Shephelah

East of the coastal plain, extending southward from the valley of Aijalon (Ajalon) toward Gaza, is the Shephelah, comprising a rocky plateau which reaches heights of fifteen hundred feet in the south, cut across by several parallel valleys. The Shephelah served as a buffer zone between the Israelites, who controlled the hill country of the central range, and the Philistines, who occupied the coastal plain. In ancient times, it was covered with sycamore forests (I Kings 10:27).

North of Joppa the coastal plain adjoins the slopes of the central range, but south of the valley of Aijalon, the Shephelah is a region distinct from the mountains of Judah. The Philistines frequently overran the Shephelah, but seldom did they penetrate beyond its eastern border where many of their battles with Israel were fought.

Fortified Towns

The line between Judah and the Shephelah was marked by a series of fortified towns. The northernmost was Aijalon, a town commanding the valley of the same name. Aijalon was fortified by Rehoboam to guard the northwestern approaches to Jerusalem (II Chron. 11:10), but it had fallen into Philistine hands by the time of Ahaz (II Chron. 28:18). The history of Aijalon goes back to the time of the biblical Patriarchs, and it is mentioned in the Amarna Tablets as the town of Aialuna.

Farther south were Zorah and nearby Eshtaol in the region where Samson spent his early life. Then came Zanoah (Khirbet Zanu'), two miles south of Beth-shemesh, and Tappuah (Beit Nettif), east of Azekah. Adullam, the site of the cave in which David hid from Saul (I Sam. 22:1), had also been fortified by Rehoboam (II Chron. 11:7). It has been identified with Tell esh-Sheikh Madhkur, midway between Jerusalem and Lachish. Next was Keilah (Khirbet Qila) which was attacked by the Philistines during the reign of Saul and temporarily relieved by David (I Sam. 23). East of Lachish was Nezib (Khirbet Beit Nasib), two and one-quarter miles south of Keilah (Joshua 15:44). Then, nearby, was Iphtah (biblical Jiphtah) (Joshua 15:43), possibly modern Tarqumiya. Beyond Iphtah there is a break in the valley which interrupts the line of towns.

The southernmost fortified town between Judah and the Shephelah was Debir, also known as Kirjath-sepher. Debir was probably located at Tell Beit Mirsim, twelve miles southwest of Hebron, a mound excavated by W. F. Albright and Melvin Grove Kyle beginning in 1924. The site was occupied as early as 2200 B.C., and during the Hyksos period it covered nine acres. Late Bronze Age and Israelite settlements are identified by remains of pottery, Astarte figurines, and evidences of a wool industry. A jar handle bears the inscription "[Belonging] to Eliakim, steward of Yaukin," probably Jehoiachin, the king of Judah who was taken to Babylon in 597 B.C. From Debir it was possible to approach the highlands of Judah from the south, by way of Hebron.

Valleys of the Shephelah

The Shephelah was crossed by a series of narrow valleys which provided access to the Judaean hill country. The most important of these, the valley of Aijalon, is named for the fortress city on the border of the Judaean hill country. About eleven miles northwest of Jerusalem was Upper Beth-horon (Joshua 16:5), and one and three-quarter miles farther was Lower Beth-horon. These were ancient towns named for the Canaanite god of the underworld, Horon. Joshua pursued the coalition of Amorite kings from southern Canaan past the two Beth-horons (Joshua 10:10-11) in the battle during which he called upon the sun to stand still until the day's work was finished (Joshua 10:10-14). The towns were assigned to the tribe of Ephraim (I Chron. 7:24) and were fortified in the days of Solomon (II Chron. 8:5). Pharaoh Shishak (Sheshonk) mentions the Beth-horons in the inscription at Karnak which records his successful campaign in Palestine. After the exile, Sanballat "the Horonite," a native of Beth-horon, (Neh. 2:10) attempted to prevent the Israelites from rebuilding the walls of Jerusalem. During Maccabean times, the Maccabees fought the Syrians at Beth-horon (I Macc. 3:16, 24; 7:39). East of the Beth-horons, the valley of Aijalon divides, providing access northward to Bethel and southward to Jerusalem.

South of the valley of Aijalon is the Sorek Valley, in which many of the exploits of Samson took place (Judges 16:4). Eshtaol and Zorah were on the north of the valley, and Timnah (biblical Timnath), where Samson sought a wife (Judges 14:1), is located farther southwest, near the mouth of the valley.

106. Valley of Aijalon, where the sun stood still

Beth-shemesh. Up the valley from Timnah was Beth-shemesh, an Israelite border town. When the Philistines returned the ark to Israel, it was taken first to Beth-shemesh (I Sam. 6:12). It is identified with Tell er-Rumeileh, just west of the settlement known as 'Ain Shems. Excavations were conducted there by the Palestine Exploration Fund in 1911/12 and by Haverford College 1928-32. Beth-shemesh was a flourishing Canaanite city during most of the second millennium B.C. A clay tablet discovered there was written in the alphabetic cuneiform script which was in use in Ugarit during the fourteenth and fifteenth centuries B.C. The presence of Philistine pottery indicates that Beth-shemesh was at one time occupied by Philistines, but by the time of the Judges it appears to have been firmly in Israelite hands. Although set apart as a Levitical city (Joshua 21:16), proximity to the Philistines made heavy fortifications necessary. Casemate (fortified) walls discovered during excavations at Beth-shemesh apparently date from the time of David.

Beth-shemesh seems to have been destroyed by Pharaoh Shishak during his invasion of Judah in Rehoboam's fifth year (I Kings 14:25-28), but it was rebuilt; and a century later it was the scene of a battle in which Joash of Israel defeated Amaziah of Judah (II Kings 14:11-13). The Philistines took Beth-shemesh and other Judaean cities early in the reign of Ahaz (II Chron. 28:18), but they were driven out by Tiglath-pileser III who restored the city to Ahaz, his vassal. The city was finally destroyed by Nebuchadnezzar.

Among the archaeological remains at Beth-shemesh are installations for making copper which date back to the Bronze Age and a refinery for olive oil. A number of Hebrew seals from the eighth century B.C. bear inscriptions which identify their owners.

107. Abu Ghosh

Kirjath-jearim. Farther up the Sorek Valley was the town of Kirjath-jearim ("city of forests") where the ark was kept for twenty years (I Sam. 7:1-2). The exact site of Kirjath-jearim is not certain, but it has been traditionally identified with a village nine miles west of Jerusalem now known as Abu Ghosh (Tell el-Azhar). Abu Ghosh is named for an Arab family which exacted a toll from pilgrims to Jerusalem in the early nineteenth century. Since the road from Jaffa to Jerusalem passed through their village, the Abu Ghosh family amassed a considerable fortune. The Arabs of Abu Ghosh did not leave the land at the time of the war between the Arabs and Israel, and they still occupy their village.

In 1889 a railway to Jerusalem from the coast was built in the Sorek Valley, and it still runs from Tel Aviv to Israeli Jerusalem. The Sorek is now known as the Wadi al-Sarar.

Libnah. The third valley connecting the coastal plain with the Judaean highlands is the Vale of Elah ("Terebinth Valley"), known in modern times as Wadi es-Sant. The point where the valley leads into the Philistine Plain is the site of Libnah, modern Tell es-Safi, the town known to the Crusaders as Blanchegarde. The Hebrew, Arabic, and French names all mention the white limestone cliffs which characterize the region. Joshua captured Libnah (Joshua 10:29) and evidently destroyed the city. Bliss and Macalister, the excavators of Tell es-Safi, found evidence of a well-built fortress that was badly burned about 1230 B.C.

At the division of the land, Libnah was assigned to Judah, but it later became a City of Refuge inhabited by priests of the Levitical line (Joshua 21:13; I Chron. 6:57). Libnah joined the Edomites in revolt against Jehoram (or Joram) of Israel (II Kings 8:22). At the time of the Assyrian campaign in Judah, Sennacherib attacked Libnah on his way to Jerusalem (II Kings 19:8).

108. Mound of Azekah

Azekah. A short distance up the valley from Libnah was Azekah, modern Tell ez-Zakariyeh, the city toward which Joshua pursued the Amorites after their attack on Gibeon (Joshua 10:10-11). Rehoboam fortified Azekah to make it a Judaean stronghold (II Chron. 11:9), and it was able to hold out, along with Lachish and Jerusalem, after all the other cities of Judah had fallen to Nebuchadnezzar (Jer. 34:7). One of the Lachish Letters notes the failure of the smoke signals from Azekah, suggesting that Azekah had finally succumbed to the might of Babylon. Lachish was the next to fall,

110. Vale of Elah. Philistines camped on right, Israelites on left.

109. Brook in Vale of Elah where David may have gathered stones to kill Goliath

and Jerusalem, the capital, was finally taken in 587/586 B.C.

It was between Socoh and Azekah in the Vale of Elah that the Philistines encamped with their champion Goliath. Socoh (Khirbet 'Abbad) commands the Vale of Elah from the south, at the place where it is joined by wadis coming down from the hills west of Bethlehem. Here young David met the challenge of Goliath and brought victory to Israel (I Sam. 17).

Mareshah. The fourth valley from the Philistine Plain to the mountainous interior bore the name of Zephathah (modern Wadi Zeita) and was the shortest route inland to Hebron and southern Palestine. Its principal town was Mareshah, on the edge of the Shephelah. Its Arabic name, *Tell Sandahannah*, is a corruption of Saint Anna, the name of an ancient church. Mareshah was excavated in 1900 by the Palestine Exploration Fund.

Mareshah, the home of the Prophet Micah (Micah 1:1), had been fortified in the days of Rehoboam (II Chron. 11:8). Early in the reign of Asa the armies of Judah gained a victory over "Zerah the Ethiopian" in the neighborhood of Mareshah (II Chron. 14:9). Zerah was probably an Ethiopian commander in the army of the Egyptian Pharaoh Osorkon I who was attempting to follow up the victories of his father Shishak in Palestine. Although Zerah's army outnumbered that of Asa two to one, the invaders were defeated and pursued down the coastal road toward Gerar. One and one-half miles north of Mareshah, the Romans later rebuilt an older town and gave it the name Eleutheropolis (modern Beit Jibrin, "City of Liberty"). Now its old Semitic name, Beit Guvrin, has been restored, and it is an important communal settlement in modern Israel.

Lachish. The important fortress of Lachish was located in the Wadi Qubeiba south of the valley of Zephathah. The eighteen-acre mound of Tell ed-Duweir, ancient

Lachish, covers a city which was larger than either Davidic Jerusalem or Megiddo. It had been occupied before the Patriarchs entered Canaan, and was a military stronghold during the Hyksos period (*c.* 1720-1550 B.C.). During the Amarna Age, Lachish was sympathetic with the seminomadic Habiru who were disturbing the peace of Canaan, with the result that other states asked for Egyptian help against both Lachish and the Habiru.

111. Mound of Lachish

Japhia, king of Lachish, joined the kings of Jerusalem, Hebron, Jarmuth, and Eglon in attacking Joshua following Israelite victories at Jericho and Ai and the capitulation of Gibeon (Joshua 10:1-5). After Joshua's victory over this confederation in the valley of Aijalon, he pursued the kings to Makkedah (possibly Khirbet el-Kheishum, northeast of Azekah). Lachish, along with other rebel cities, was taken and totally destroyed by Joshua (Joshua 10:31-32; cf. 11:10-13). There are traces of burning from the period of 1220 to 1200 B.C. at the mound of Lachish which may date from the period of Joshua or from the troubled period of the Judges.

Lachish was fortified by Rehoboam (II Chron. 11:9) as a protection against attacks from the Philistines and from Egypt. When Sennacherib attacked Judah in 701 B.C., he laid siege to Lachish to prevent Egyptian aid from reaching Jerusalem

(II Kings 18:13-17). The walls of Sennacherib's palace at Nineveh (ancient Ninus) were decorated with scenes from the siege of Lachish which are now in the British Museum. An inscription reads, "Sennacherib, King of Assyria, sitting on his throne while the spoil from the city of Lachish passed before him." After the fall of Lachish, Sennacherib appointed Assyrian governors and used the city as an administrative center for the collection of tribute from the Philistine country.

With the lapse of Assyrian power, Lachish again became a Judaean stronghold. Nebuchadnezzar attacked it in 597 B.C. during the campaign against Judah which resulted in the deportation of Jehoiachin and the appointment of Zedekiah as king in his place (II Kings 24). A decade later (589-587 B.C.) the Babylonian armies again besieged Lachish which, along with Azekah and Jerusalem, held out against Nebuchadnezzar as long as possible (Jer. 34:7). Shortly before the fall of Jerusalem, Lachish fell to Nebuchadnezzar, its walls were demolished, and the city was reduced to rubble.

Lachish was subsequently rebuilt, but it never regained its position of importance. A seal found above the debris of the destruction in 587/586 B.C. bears the inscription "Gedaliah, who is over the house." This is the name of the governor appointed by

112. Sennacherib's siege of Lachish

113. Ruins of Sun Temple at Lachish, Persian period

Nebuchadnezzar after the destruction of Jerusalem (II Kings 25:22-25), and this evidence suggests that the town was quickly occupied after the war. Ruins of a Persian villa built on the summit of the mound date from about 400 B.C. and may have been the residence of Geshem (Gashmu), the Arabian governor of Idumaea (Neh. 6:1).

The mound known as Tell ed-Duweir, now identified with Lachish, was excavated by the Wellcome-Marston Archaeological Expedition from 1933 to 1938 under the direction of James L. Starkey whose murder by bandits halted the work. Caves in the area of Lachish were occupied during the Early Bronze Age, and a succession of cities occupied the mound down to late biblical times. The Lachish of the Late Bronze Age, the period of Joshua's conquest, had a temple with stone walls plastered with lime. Its floor was of hard clay, and it had a roof supported by wooden columns. A small vestibule led into the sanctuary where there was a raised shrine which is presumed to have contained a cult statue. Around the shrine and in rubbish pits connected with the building were large quantities of bones of sheep, oxen, and other animals. Most of the bones were of the right foreleg which, according to biblical law, was assigned to the priest (Lev. 7:32). The presence of these bones helps to confirm the antiquity of the Levitical law and suggests that the

Israelites and Canaanites had similar forms of sacrifice.

A scarab discovered at Lachish recounts the feat of Amenhotep III of Egypt who personally killed one hundred and two lions during the first ten years of his reign. A scarab of Ramses II suggests Egyptian dominance of Lachish as late as the thirteenth century, and a broken bowl contains the words "year four" in a form of Egyptian writing which dates from Pharaoh Merneptah. Year four of Merneptah's reign would be about 1221 B.C. The fragments of the bowl were found together in the debris of the burned city, and this evidence has caused some archaeologists to date the fall of Lachish to Joshua about 1221 B.C.[8]

114. A Lachish Letter

A bowl and a jar discovered in the temple at Lachish bore inscriptions in the early type of Canaanite script identical with that discovered at Serabit el-Khadim in the Sinai Peninsula. The most sensational discovery, however, was a group of eighteen ostraca (potsherds used as ballots) inscribed in a cursive Hebrew script, found in a small guardroom under the gate tower of the city, later augmented by three other fragments. These proved to be letters addressed to Yaosh, the military governor of the city, by

[8]Cf. W. F. Albright, *Bulletin of the American Schools of Oriental Research,* 68 (Dec., 1937), pp. 23-24; 74 (April, 1939), pp. 20-22; 132 (Dec., 1953), p. 46; Raymond S. Haupert, *Biblical Archaeoogist,* 1 (1938), p. 26.

115. Lachish Gate near where the Lachish Letters were found

Hoshaiah, an officer stationed at a military outpost during the period immediately before the fall of Lachish to Nebuchadnezzar. Letter four mentions that no smoke signals had been sighted from Azekah, suggesting that the city had already fallen. The Lachish Letters help one visualize life outside the capital at the time Jeremiah was ministering in Jerusalem. They are the only extant letters in classical Hebrew and are valued for the light they throw on Hebrew vocabulary and epigraphy.

The Valley of Esdraelon

The road through the Plain of Esdraelon and the valley of Jezreel was the only readily accessible route from the coastal plain of Palestine to the Jordan Valley and beyond; it was used throughout history by travelers, merchants, and conquerors. Although *Esdraelon* is the Greek form of the Hebrew *Jezreel* ("God sows"), the two terms acquired specialized meanings. Esdraelon is the alluvial plain which is shaped like a triangle with its point directed to the Mediterranean north of Mount Carmel. Along its southwestern flank were the strategically situated cities of Jokneam, Megiddo, Taanach, and Ibleam at the base of the Carmel Range. The plain was bounded on the northwest by the mountains of Galilee. At the base of the triangle was Jezreel (modern Zerin), the city which guarded the narrow valley of Jezreel to Bethshean and the Jordan Valley. In biblical times, Esdraelon was a region of marshes through which the Kishon River flowed, the terrain in which the chariots of Sisera were mired (Judges 1:31; 4:14-16; 5). The valley of Jezreel was then, as now, a fruitful area rich in agricultural crops.

The Kishon River rises in the hills of Samaria and flows northwestward through the Plain of Esdraelon past Taanach and Megiddo before emptying into the Bay of Accho (Acre) north of Mount Carmel. The flooding of the Qishon (biblical Kishon) River made possible the victory of Barak and the Israelites taken from Naphtali and Zebulon (biblical Zebulun) in their battle with Sisera, commander of the forces of Jabin of Hazor and his Canaanite allies (Judges 4; 5). Deborah, a Judge in Israel, summoned Barak and ordered him to assemble the Israelites at Mount Tabor, a mountain rising 1,843 feet in the northeastern sector of Esdraelon. The army of Sisera, with nine hundred chariots, moved from Harosheth in the Plain of Asher near the entrance to the Esdraelon Plain to attack Israel. Barak, with ten thousand Israelites,

116. Mount Tabor

left his encampment on Mount Tabor and headed toward Esdraelon to confront the invading enemy. In the meantime, a storm caused the Qishon to overflow its banks, turning nearby fields into quagmires. The chariots, normally of great value to the Canaanites in their wars with Israel, became a liability as they became stuck in the mud. The drivers had to abandon the chariots and flee, leaving the Israelites in undisputed possession of the valley. Sisera escaped, only to meet death at the hand of Jael, the wife of Heber the Kenite (Judges 5:24-27).

Jokneam, on the northern slopes of the Carmel Range, was located at the junction of two important roads. One is the chief route through the Esdraelon Valley from Accho (modern Acre) to Megiddo, Taanach, and Jenin. The second is the pass through the Carmel Range east of Dor which connects the Plain of Sharon with the valley of Esdraelon. Jokneam, modern Tell Qeimun, was conquered by the Egyptian empire builder Thutmose III. In Israelite times, this community marked the western limit of the territory of Zebulun (Joshua 19:10-11) and became a Levitical city (Joshua 21:23).

Megiddo. Seven miles southeast of Jokneam, at the head of a mountain pass which led to the coastal plain and on a hill overlooking the main road through the Plain of Esdraelon, was the fortress city of Megiddo.

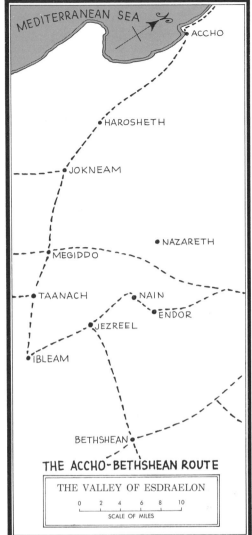

THE ACCHO-BETHSHEAN ROUTE

THE VALLEY OF ESDRAELON

0 2 4 6 8 10
SCALE OF MILES

117. Plain of Esdraelon

PALESTINE

Through the centuries, it witnessed a succession of conquerors: Egyptians, Canaanites, Israelites, Philistines, Assyrians, Persians, Greeks, and Romans. In 1918 the Allied forces under Allenby entered northern Palestine through the Megiddo Pass to wrest it from the Turkish forces. The British commander subsequently was named Viscount Allenby of Megiddo.

118. Limestone altar of incense, Megiddo

When Edwin Robinson stood on the imposing hill known as Tell el-Mutesellim in 1838, he jotted these words in his diary: "I wonder where Megiddo could have been!" Without knowing it, he was standing on the mound of Megiddo, which rose nearly seventy feet above the surrounding plain and covered an area of ten acres at its summit, with lower levels even larger.

Serious archaeological work began at Tell el-Mutesellim in 1903 when Gottlieb Schu-

macher began excavating for the Deutsche Orientgesellschaft. During almost three years of work at Megiddo, Schumacher dug a trench across the top of the mound and identified seven occupation levels, the fifth of which was from the Israelite period. Schumacher discovered pottery remains, a bronze knife, and some scarabs set in gold in a stratum which he dated prior to 2000 B.C. Among the Israelite remains he found a seal depicting a lion with the inscription "Belonging to Shema, the servant of Jeroboam." The seal was discovered among the remains of an Israelite palace.

Schumacher's work at Megiddo showed the importance of the mound, but the limited knowledge of pottery at the time seriously handicapped scholars in properly appraising the results. In 1925, however, the Oriental Institute of Chicago, directed by J. H. Breasted, began a series of major excavations under the leadership, successively, of C. S. Fisher (1925-27), P. L. O. Guy (1927-35), and G. Loud (1935-39). It was the purpose of the Chicago excavators to clear the entire mound, level by level, to its base. They succeeded in identifying twenty occupational levels, the earliest of which dated back to the early part of the fourth millennium. The top four were completely removed, but work was stopped by the outbreak of World War II, and the excavation of pre-Iron Age sites was not completed. In 1958, the Commission for Landscaping and Preservation of Antiquities of the Israel Government resumed work, and Yigael Yadin conducted a brief excavation in 1960.

The first historical reference to Megiddo occurs during the reign of the Egyptian Pharaoh Thutmose III, who defeated a coalition of Canaanite rulers led by the prince of Kadesh in 1468 B.C. The record of this victory was later inscribed on the walls of a corridor of the temple of Amun at Karnak. Thutmose's son, Amenhotep II, campaigned in the same region thirty years later and boasted that he sat in judgment on "rebellious princes" in the vicinity of Megiddo.

A letter discovered at Taanach, southeast of Megiddo, dating from about 1450 B.C., mentions an Egyptian general who urged the king of Taanach to pay his tribute: "Send me your charioteers and horses, presents for me, and send all your prisoners. Send them tomorrow to Megiddo."[9] Megiddo appears to have served as an Egyptian administrative center during the fifteenth century B.C.

Conditions in Megiddo during the fourteenth century B.C. are revealed in the Amarna Letters, discovered in Egypt in 1887. Six of the letters were sent to Phar-

aoh Amenhotep IV (Akhenaton) by Biridiya, king of Megiddo. Biridiya affirmed his unswerving loyalty to Egypt and paid his tribute faithfully. He warned Akhenaton, however, that he needed a contingent of one hundred men to save Megiddo from hostile insurgents in the area. The Amarna Age was one in which Egyptian power was waning in Palestine, and Biridiya had difficulty continuing as a vassal to Akhenaton.

During the conquest of Canaan, Joshua effected a temporary victory over the king of Megiddo (Joshua 12:21). Later, Megiddo was assigned to Manasseh (Joshua 17:11), but Manasseh was unable to occupy the city (Judges 1:27). Canaanite forces held control of the area during the time of the conquest. In the days of Deborah, the Canaanites fought "in Taanach, by the wa-

[9]W. F. Albright, "A Prince of Taanach in the Fifteenth Century B.C.," *Bulletin of the American Schools of Oriental Research*, 94 (April, 1944), 12-29.

119.   Reconstruction of Solomonic gate, Megiddo

ters of Megiddo" (Judges 5:19), but no mention is made of Megiddo itself, which may not have been occupied at the time.

During the tenth century B.C., Solomon rebuilt and fortified Megiddo, making it one of his chariot cities (I Kings 9:15). A century later, Ahaziah of Judah was struck by an arrow from the bow of Jehu, who brought the Omri dynasty in Israel to a violent end. Ahaziah reached the fortress of Megiddo and died there (II Kings 9:27). Megiddo was also the site of the tragic death of Josiah in 609 B.C. Josiah had hurried to Megiddo to prevent Pharaoh Necho II (609-593 B.C.) of Egypt from helping Assyria resist Babylonian power. The godly Josiah was wounded, "and his servants carried him in a chariot dead from Megiddo, and brought him to Jerusalem, and buried him in his own sepulchre" (II Kings 23:30).

The Hebrew *Har Megiddon*, "the hill of Megiddo," is the basis for the New Testament Armageddon, the assembly point for the great apocalyptic battle in which God's power will be manifested in the destruction of His foes. The scene, described in Revelation 16:16, is comparable to that of Ezekiel 39:1-6, where the foe from the north comes "upon the mountains of Israel" (Ezek. 39:4).

Along the path toward the northern slope of the mound a few yards beyond the present Megiddo Museum, there is a roadway which served as the main approach to the ancient city. To the left are remains of the Solomonic double gateway. An enemy who forced his way past the first gate would find himself in a small paved and walled enclosure, with the great walls and bastions of the real gate into the city still towering above him. This latter gate was more massive than the first, with guardrooms on either side. In plan and style the gate to Megiddo is similar to the gates at Hazor and Gezer, two other chariot cities of King Solomon.

The Prophet Ezekiel described similar gates as he depicted the eastern wall of the

120. Reconstruction drawing of an ivory plaque, Megiddo

Temple in his prophetic vision: "Then came he unto the gate which looked toward the east, and went up the stairs thereof, and measured the threshold of the gate. . . . And the little chambers of the gate eastward were three on this side, and three on that side" (Ezek. 40:6-10). Ezekiel was probably familiar with the ruins of the Solomonic Temple in Jerusalem, and his vision reflected a similar pattern. The eastern gate of Solomon's Temple evidently made use of the same architectural pattern that was used in Megiddo and other Solomonic cities.

East of the gate are remains of the stone wall of Solomon's city with its wide ramparts. Northwest of Solomon's gate stood an earlier Canaanite wall, near which were

THE WYCLIFFE HISTORICAL GEOGRAPHY OF BIBLE LANDS

the palaces of the Canaanite kings. In one of these palaces, later removed to expose lower strata, the excavators came upon a collection of two hundred and eighty-two carved ivories dating to the thirteenth and twelfth centuries B.C. Included were a pen case, cosmetic dishes or spoons, ivory carved with Egyptian hieroglyphs, and a plaque depicting a victory celebration of a king or prince. The latter object gives a picture of social life in a Canaanite court. The ruler, seated on a throne with a sphinx-shaped side, is drinking from a bowl. Behind him are two servers, a large jar, and a bird. In front of the king stands an attendant, followed by a woman playing a lyre. Behind her is a procession headed by a soldier armed with shield and spear. Next come two prisoners with hands bound behind them, joined by a rope to a chariot drawn by two horses. Seated in the chariot is a man whose dress and general appearance are similar to the king on his throne. Probably this represents the king returning in victory. Behind the chariot stands a soldier with drawn sword. The plaque is both an example of ancient Canaanite art and a document depicting military practices and concepts of luxury in an ancient Canaanite palace.

At the western edge of the Megiddo mound are the well-preserved remains of a water system which dates back to the twelfth century B.C. The ancient engineers sank a large shaft to a depth of one hundred twenty feet. From the bottom of the shaft they cut a tunnel through the rock for a distance of three hundred feet to a spring outside the city so that water could be brought into Megiddo even during times of siege. The opening to the spring was hidden by a wall and a covering of earth so that besieging forces would not notice it.

At the southern edge of the mound are ruins of stables which once housed Solomon's horses. These are identical in plan to other stables unearthed near the gate and removed after excavation. In front of the stable compound was an enclosed courtyard, one hundred eighty feet square, with a lime plaster floor, in the center of which was a huge cistern for watering the horses. The stables themselves are recognizable from the rows of stone pillars alternating with mangers. The pillars served as supports for the roof and also as tethering posts for the horses. There were five parallel sheds in all, each containing twenty-two stalls in parallel rows of eleven. East of the stable area, in the southern sector of

121. Solomon's stables
Megiddo

PALESTINE

the mound, are remains of a large building surrounded by a square wall. This building, also dated to the Solomonic period, is believed to have been the residence of the governor at Megiddo.

In the center of the mound are remains of a large eighth century silo shaped like an inverted cone with steps leading down from two sides. The most ancient buildings, at the east side of the mound, include the ruins of three Canaanite temples from the third millennium B.C. Each consisted of a large chamber with an altar at the southern side, flanked by two large pillar bases. The southeast temple, dated about 2700 B.C., had steps leading up to a circular "high place." A second temple, built of mud brick, faces due east, and was probably dedicated to the sun god. The altar of this temple commands a view of the sunrise over Mount Tabor and the Jordan Valley.

Seldom do all scholars agree on the significance and dating of archaeological discoveries, and Megiddo is no exception. J. W. Crowfoot argued that the so-called Solomonic buildings, including the stables, are actually from the time of Omri and Ahab. P. L. O. Guy, however, maintained that they were Solomonic, and his interpretation has been followed by most contemporary archaeologists. Yigael Yadin, following his work at Megiddo, dated the stables during the reign of Ahab, who is known to have had a chariot force of two thousand in his battle with Shalmaneser III at the battle of Karkar. Megiddo is perhaps the most thoroughly studied site of the ancient Bible world, but all of its mysteries have not yet been resolved.

Taanach. Four miles southeast of Megiddo was Taanach, modern Tell Ta'annak, guarding the pass across Mount Carmel which follows the route of the Wadi Abdullah. This narrow and steep route is the least attractive means of access to the Plain of Esdraelon. Throughout history, the proximity of Taanach to Megiddo made them

122. Shishak leads Palestine towns captive, Thebes

rivals; and it appears that when one of the towns flourished, the other was in eclipse. In his account of campaigns in western Palestine, Thutmose III mentions a campaign at Taanach (c. 1465 B.C.). In one of the Amarna Letters, the prince of Megiddo, avowing loyalty to Egypt, complained of a raid by the men of Taanach upon his city. After the Israelite conquest, Taanach was assigned to Manasseh, but it remained in Canaanite hands during the period of the Judges (Joshua 12:21; 17:11; Judges 1:27) Sisera, the Canaanite general who oppressed Israel during the judgeship of Deborah, suffered a crushing defeat at Taanach (Judges 5:19). Shishak (Sheshonk I), who invaded Palestine during the fifth year of

Rehoboam (I Kings 14:25-26), mentioned the conquest of Taanach, along with other towns of Judah and Israel, on the relief which he had carved at the Amun temple in Thebes.

Professor Ernst Sellin was attracted to the mound of Taanach during a visit to Palestine in 1899, and during 1902 and 1903 he began there the first excavations in northern Palestine. Sellin's work was primitive by modern standards, for scientific stratigraphy was not yet known. His work, however, uncovered impressive remains of early life in the Plain of Esdraelon.

Sellin discovered the walls of Taanach which had been built in the so-called Cyclopean style—huge, irregularly shaped blocks of stone fashioned into a wall, with the spaces between the stones filled with small stones. A palace of a fourteenth century king was discovered, along with a collection of cuneiform texts written in a script similar to that of the Amarna Letters.[10] W. F. Albright made a detailed study of four of the twelve Taanach Letters.[11] Letter 1, addressed to Rewashsha,

123. Detail of Shishak's relief

the ruler of Taanach, contains this request: ". . . if there is a wizard of Asherah, let him tell our fortunes, and let me hear quickly, and the [oracular] sign and interpretation send to me" (lines 19-24). Oracles were given in the name of the goddess Asherah who, along with Baal, was represented by prophets at Mount Carmel in the time of Ahab (I Kings 18:19, RSV). Asherah was a mother goddess whose worship was a stumbling block in Israel. The "groves" mentioned in II Kings 17:10 (AV) are, literally, the *Asherim,* plural of *Asherah,* and were probably trees or poles which served as cult objects for the goddess.

The Israelite settlement of Taanach may be represented by the brick houses which Sellin found during his excavations. In what appears to have been a private house, he came upon a terra-cotta incense altar, three feet high and eighteen inches in diameter at the base, adorned with protruding animal heads. One side has the picture of a palm tree with two ibexes descending a mountain. Concordia Seminary and the American Schools of Oriental Research excavated at Taanach during the summer of 1963.

About five miles southeast of Megiddo were the twin cities of Engannim (modern Jenin) and Ibleam guarding the narrow defile which leads to Dothan and, ultimately, the coastal plain. Engannim is about seven miles southwest of Mount Gilboa on the road from Esdraelon, through Samaria to Jerusalem. Ibleam, now known as Khirbet Bil'ameh, was assigned to Manasseh (Joshua 17:11), but the Canaanites were not expelled during the time of the Judges (Judges 1:27).

[10]Cf. F. Hrozny, *Tell Ta'annek* (*Denkschriften der Kaiserlichen Akademie der Wissenschaften,* phil.-hist. Klasse, L, Vienna, 1904, Part IV), pp. 113 ff., and in *Eine Nachlese auf dem Tell Ta'annek in Palastina* (Denkschriften, LII, 1906, Part III).

[11]"A Prince of Taanach in the Fifteenth Century B.C.," *Bulletin of the American Schools of Oriental Research,* 94 (April, 1944), 12-27.

Battles of Gideon and Saul

The road from the Plain of Esdraelon into the valley of Jezreel passes between the hill of Moreh and Mount Gilboa. In their encounter with the Midianites, Gideon and his men camped beside the spring, or well, of Harod, the modern Ain Jalud, at the foot of Mount Gilboa. Two miles to the north, the Midianites were encamped in the valley by the hill of Moreh (Judges 7:1). After reducing the size of his forces, Gideon made a surprise attack on the sleeping Midianites who, in their confusion, fled down the valley of Jezreel (Judges 7:22).

In this same area Saul faced his final encounter with the Philistines (I Sam. 28:4). The enemy marched through the Plain of Esdraelon and camped at Shunem on the southwestern foot of the hill of Moreh, three miles north of Jezreel. Saul assembled his Israelite forces on Mount Gilboa, a thousand feet above the plain, where he could watch every movement of the enemy. On the north shoulder of the hill of Moreh, barely four miles from the Philistine camp, was the town of Endor, to which Saul went by night to inquire of a witch the outcome of the ensuing battle. The witch of Endor gave Saul a message of doom, and the next day the Israelites fled before the Philistines (I Sam. 31:1). Saul and his three sons were killed. The Philistines stripped Saul's body, hung it on the walls of Bethshean, and placed his armor in the temple of the goddess Ashtaroth, or Astarte (I Sam. 31:8-10).

The city of Jezreel guards the western entrance to the valley of Jezreel which leads from Esdraelon into the Jordan Valley. Before Saul's battle at Mount Gilboa, the Israelites encamped at Jezreel, and in later years, kings of Israel built luxurious winter palaces there because of its mild winters. Ahab desired to add Naboth's vineyard to his estates at Jezreel, but Naboth determined to maintain his holdings in defiance of the king's wishes. When Jezebel effected the judicial murder of Naboth to secure his vineyard for her husband, she brought judgment upon herself and also upon the dynasty of Omri and Ahab (I Kings 21:1-24).

Bethshean

At the junction between the valley of Jezreel and the Jordan stood the fortified city of Bethshean, identified with Tell el-Husn, adjacent to modern Beisan. The city, known as Scythopolis ("City of the Scythians") in Hellenistic and Roman times, has both a strategic location and also the benefit of several springs in addition to the waters of the river Jalud. The intense heat of the Jordan Valley combines with the fertile soil of Jezreel to produce rich, subtropical vegetation. One of the sages of Israel said, "If the Garden of Eden is in the Land of Israel—then its gate is at Bethshan."

In 1921, Clarence Fisher, representing the University Museum of Philadelphia, began at Bethshean the first American archaeological mission in Palestine after World War I. He worked for three summer seasons, each one lasting from two to five months. After 1923, Fisher was succeeded by Alan Rowe, who was in charge of the work from 1924 to 1929. G. M. Fitzgerald continued the work in 1929 and was leader of the excavations until 1931, and again in 1933 when the work stopped.

Eighteen levels of occupation were identified, ranging from the Chalcolithic period (c. 3500 B.C.) to the time of the Byzantines and the Arabs who conquered Palestine in A.D. 637. Levels 17 and 18 were identified as Chalcolithic; level 12 represents the great Twelfth Dynasty of Egypt (c. 2000 B.C.); and level 11 contains Hyksos remains. Bethshean was an Egyptian stronghold during the second half of the second millennium B.C. when the city attained a high degree of prosperity. This affluence is observed in the remains of its temples and houses, in the cult objects, jewelry, household equipment, and inscriptions which have been excavated. An impressive stele of Pharaoh Seti I (1309-1290 B.C.) depicts the king presenting an offering to his god, Re-Harakhti,

124. Mound of Bethshean, Roman theater in foreground

after the suppression of a revolt among the city-states of northern Palestine. A second stele was erected by Ramses II (1290-1224 B.C.), and a statue of Ramses III (1175-1144 B.C.), gives further evidence of Egyptian control.

At the division of the land following the victories of Joshua, Beth-shean was assigned to Manasseh; but the Canaanites were not immediately dispossessed (Judges 1:27), because they had an advantage over Israel in their horse-driven chariots (Joshua 17:16). Stables belonging to the period of the Israelite conquest were discovered by Clarence Fisher at Bethshean in 1923. They had a row of stone pillars for tethering the horses, and the floors were paved with cobblestones.

Toward the end of the eleventh century, Bethshean was in the hands of the Philistines. By the time of David, however, Beth-shean was in Israelite control; it is mentioned at the time of Solomon's division of the country into administrative districts (I Kings 4:12). The remains of a city gate and walls from the Israelite period were discovered on the western edge of the mound.

Two mud brick temples, built in the fourteenth century B.C., have been excavated, one dedicated to Mekal, "the lord of Bethshan," and the other to Astarte. It was in the latter temple, termed "the house of Ashtaroth" in I Samuel 31:10, that Saul's armor was placed after his death on Mount Gilboa.

Nomadic Scythians invaded the Bethshean area during the seventh century B.C., and their name was applied to the city as late as Hellenistic and Roman times when it was called Scythopolis. During the third and second centuries B.C., Scythopolis was

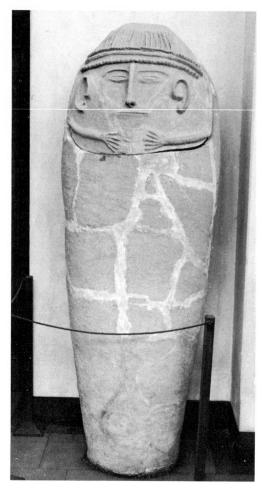

a thriving city with a marble-columned temple dedicated to Dionysus. In 107 B.C., John Hyrcanus added Scythopolis to the Maccabean state, and it was part of the Hasmonaean Kingdom until 64 B.C. when the Romans occupied Palestine. In New Testament times, it was the leading member of the league of Hellenistic cities known as the Decapolis. A theater, hippodrome, aqueduct, and other public buildings date from the Roman period. At the end of the fourth century, A.D., Scythopolis became the capital of a new province, Palaestina Secunda, which comprised the Plain of Esdraelon, Galilee, and parts of northern Transjordan.

During the Byzantine period, Scythopolis became a Christian center with its own bishop. A round church, excavated at the summit of the mound, is similar in plan to the original Church of the Holy Sepulchre in Jerusalem. Across the valley, north of the mound, was a sixth century monastery with mosaic floors. During the early Arab period, the name "Scythopolis" was replaced by "Beisan," a contraction of "Bethshean." The city was destroyed, however, by the Crusaders, and has never regained its past importance. In 1949, the state of Israel established a town named "Beit-Shean" at Beisan.

125. Pottery coffin, Bethshean

Galilee

North of the Plain of Esdraelon and the valley of Jezreel was the fertile hill country known as the *galil*, literally "the circle" or "the district." It is a land of rivers and wells, and the olives of Galilee were so numerous that the ancient rabbis maintained that it was easier to support an entire legion there than to raise one child in the more barren country to the south.

In preexilic times, the tribes of Asher, Zebulun, Issachar, and Naphtali occupied the area north of Esdraelon. These were the tribes most exposed to the nearby Phoeni-

cians and Syrians, as well as to the more distant Assyrians who periodically invaded western Asia. Following the exile, comparatively few Jews settled in Galilee, and even they were resettled in Judaea in 164 B.C. by Simon the Maccabee (I Macc. 5:21-23). Under John Hyrcanus and his successors, Galilee was incorporated into the Hasmonaean State, and many Jews settled there. The inhabitants of Judaea, however, continued to look upon the Jews of Galilee as slightly unorthodox. Jesus and his disciples were despised as Galileans, who were iden-

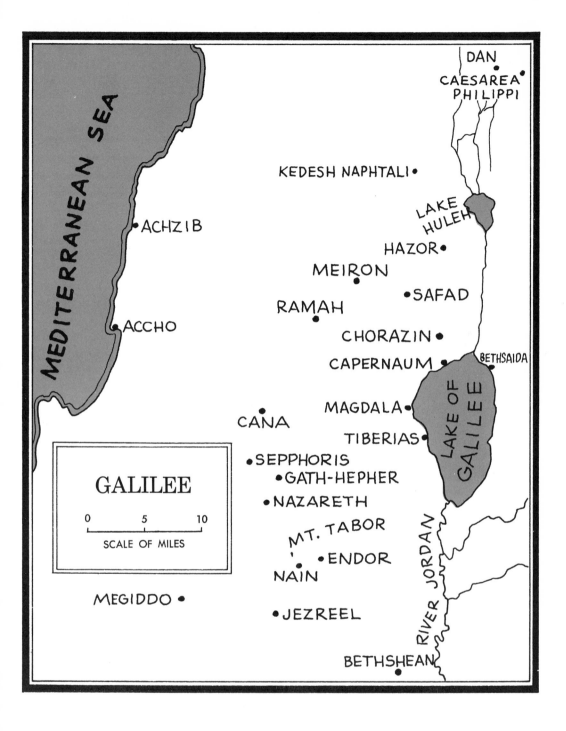

MEDITERRANEAN SEA

DAN
CAESAREA
PHILIPPI

KEDESH NAPHTALI •

LAKE
HULEH

• ACHZIB

HAZOR •

MEIRON

RAMAH

• SAFAD

• ACCHO

CHORAZIN •

CAPERNAUM •

BETHSAIDA

MAGDALA •

LAKE OF GALILEE

CANA

TIBERIAS

• SEPPHORIS
• GATH-HEPHER

GALILEE

• NAZARETH

0   5   10

MT. TABOR

SCALE OF MILES

• ENDOR

NAIN

RIVER JORDAN

MEGIDDO •

• JEZREEL

BETHSHEAN

tified by a peculiar accent (cf. Mark 14:70).
Nothing good could be expected from
Nazareth (John 1:46), and the claims of a
Messiah who was from Nazareth in Galilee

could not be taken seriously (cf. Matt.
21:11).

The people of Galilee, however, were as
intensely loyal to the Jewish faith, and as

intensely anti-Roman, as any in Judaea. Judas of Galilee[12] was the founder of the Zealots, an intensely anti-Roman sect whose fanaticism and violence under Florus, the last of the procurators, brought on the war with Rome. Although Josephus was writing with a view to winning the favor of the Romans, he made it clear that these Galilean insurrectionists were motivated by the same spirit as their Maccabean predecessors. It was loyalty to the Jewish law, the Torah, that proved the rallying point for the Zealots.[13]

Galilee awakes within the Christian the reminiscence of Jesus' boyhood in Nazareth, His ministry at Capernaum, and His miracles and teaching along the shores of the Sea of Galilee. To the Jew, also, Galilee

[12]Josephus, *Jewish Wars*, Book II, Chap. viii, Section 1; cf. Acts 5:37.
[13]Josephus, *Life*, Section 12 (65); Section 13 (74); Section 27 (134).

ultimately became a place of sanctified associations, because the Rabbinic sages migrated northward following the destruction of Jerusalem. Tiberias, on the western shore of the Sea of Galilee (Sea of Tiberias), became a center of Talmudic scholarship and the capital of Jewish Palestine. The families of Ben Asher and Ben Naphtali at Tiberias made important contributions to the preservation of the traditional (or Masoretic) text of the Old Testament. During the fifteenth century, Safad in Upper Galilee was the home of Jewish mystics whose religious ideas found expression in the Cabala.

During the time of Christ, the province of Galilee was a rectangle, forty miles from north to south and twenty-five miles from east to west. It was bounded on the east by the Jordan River and the Sea of Galilee, and on the west by the Coastal Plain which

126. Nazareth with Church of St. Joseph in foreground

had been assigned to the tribe of Asher. South of Galilee was the fertile Plain of Esdraelon with the main road from the coast to the Jordan Valley. Galilee itself is divided into two parallel strips, comprising Upper Galilee and Lower Galilee. Between them is the fault of Esh-shaghur, now known as the Plain of er-Rameh, cutting across the country from Accho (Acre) to the region south of Safad. North of this plain the plateau of Upper Galilee reaches 3,000 feet, with its highest point, Jebel Jarmuk, 3,900 feet above the Mediterranean. The hills of Lower Galilee, however, have no elevations in excess of two thousand feet. The border between modern Israel and Lebanon passes through Upper Galilee. In New Testament times, however, Upper Galilee extended northward to the gorge of the Leontes River which enters the Mediterranean north of Tyre.

127. Mary's Well, Nazareth

Nazareth. About midway between the Sea of Galilee and the Mediterranean, in the hill country north of the Esdraelon Plain, was Nazareth, the boyhood home of Jesus. Nazareth is situated in a basin enclosed by hills except on the south where a narrow rocky gorge leads to the plain. The village itself is on a hillside facing east and southeast. It was separated from, but near, the important trade centers of that day. From the hills surrounding Nazareth, Jesus could look northward over rich plains to the snowcapped Mount Hermon. Westward, His eye could take in majestic Mount Carmel and, looking eastward, He might have observed Tabor's wooded heights. Looking southward, Jesus would have seen the Plain of Esdraelon.

Although in no sense isolated from the world, the Nazareth in which Jesus grew up was a small village with only one spring of water from which Mary certainly drew water for her household. Today it is appropriately named "Mary's Well." The French Bishop Arculf, who visited the Holy Land in the seventh century, described

Nazareth as a city of large stone houses and two fine churches. One of these was built over the traditional site of the house of Mary.

Nazareth suffered during the years of Muslim control. Its religious shrines were desecrated during the tenth century, but the Crusaders took it a century later and made it the political and religious center of Galilee. The Crusaders ruled Nazareth until it was recaptured by Muslims in the thirteenth century. With the expulsion of the Crusaders (or "Franks" as they were called), Nazareth again deteriorated; and only since the eighteenth century has it shown signs of revival. In the days of the British Mandate, Nazareth was the center for the administration of Galilee. In July, 1948, the Israeli army took the city. It now has a population of about thirty-two thousand.

About two miles southeast of Nazareth is Jebel Kafsy, the traditional "Mount of Precipitation" from which the people of

Nazareth tried to cast Jesus at the time of their rejection of Him (Luke 4:29). Like many so-called holy places, the tradition which identifies the place cannot be either confirmed or denied.

Sepphoris. When Jesus lived at Nazareth, the chief town of the region was situated about four miles northwest at Sepphoris (modern Saffurye), south of the main Roman road from Ptolemais (Accho) to Tiberias. In 1931, the University of Michigan conducted excavations around the citadel at Sepphoris and discovered Roman remains which were in a poor state of preservation. Among these were an amphitheater and a basilica dating from the second century A.D. The small fort standing on top of the mound was built by the Turks in 1745 from ancient stones collected on the spot.

Tradition states that the virgin Mary was a native of Sepphoris, and a church now marks the site of the house of her parents, Anna and Joachim. The city also became a spiritual center for Palestinian Judaism. Rabbi Judah the Prince compiled and edited the Mishnah in Sepphoris during the second century.

Nain. Southeast of Nazareth, at the edge of the Hill of Moreh, is the village of Na'im, probably to be identified with biblical Nain (Luke 7:11) in which Jesus raised the son of a widow. The Hebrew form *Na'im,* means "pleasant," and the village was known to the Arabs as Nein. A Franciscan church marks the traditional site of the miracle.

Cana. The exact location of Cana in Galilee, the site of the first miracle of our Lord, is still in dispute. Khirbet Kana is a mound nine miles north of Nazareth which local Arabs call "Cana of Galilee." Tradition favors Kefr Kenna, four miles northeast of Nazareth where the Greek church has preserved ancient stone vats which are reputed to have been used by Jesus when he

changed water into wine at the wedding feast (John 2). A Franciscan church in the heart of the village makes the same claim for an old jar which it possesses. The Franciscans believe their church to be built on the actual remains of the house in which the miracle took place. Cana was the home of the disciple Nathanael (Bartholomew, John 21:2), and it was the place where Jesus healed with a word a nobleman's son who lay sick in Capernaum (John 4:46-50).

During an archaeological survey of Galilee, the Israelite archaeologist Yohanan Aharoni examined fifty sites and made two trial digs. He found evidence that Lower Galilee was first settled by Israelites during the twelfth and thirteenth centuries B.C. Upper Galilee, however, had a string of Canaanite strongholds in pre-Israelite times.

Hazor. The most powerful Canaanite center in Upper Galilee at the time of Joshua was Hazor, a short distance southwest of Lake Hule. The Amarna Letters indicate a rivalry during the fourteenth century B.C. between the king of Hazor and the king of Tyre. At the time of Joshua, Jabin of Hazor organized a coalition of Canaanite rulers to prevent Israel from expanding into northern Palestine (Joshua 11:1-5). Joshua surprised his foes at the Waters of Merom (Joshua 11:7), once identified with Lake Hule, north of the Sea of Galilee, but now more plausibly associated with the springs which flow southward by the village of Meiron. The battle turned into a rout as the Canaanites fled northwestward toward the Phoenician coastal cities. Thereupon, "Joshua . . . turned back, and took Hazor, and smote the king thereof with the sword" (Joshua 11:10). The city was destroyed by Joshua, but it was evidently rebuilt soon afterward, because another Jabin of Hazor oppressed Israel during the period of the Judges (Judges 4:2). This time Hazor appears to have been permanently crushed (Judges 4; 5), because it was incorporated into the tribe of Naphtali and was fortified by Solomon (I Kings 9:15).

Located in the far northern part of Israel, Hazor was exposed to dangers of invasion, and during the eighth century B.C. Tiglath-pileser III of Assyria conquered the city (II Kings 15:29). Its inhabitants were taken into exile, and the city never regained its earlier importance.

128. Cultic objects from the temple at Hazor

The site of Hazor was identified by John Garstang with the mound known as Tell el-Qedah, five miles southwest of Lake Hule, during a trial dig in 1926. Garstang returned to Tell el-Qedah in 1928, but the major archaeological undertaking there began in 1955 when Professor Yigael Yadin conducted the first of a series of excavations for the James A. de Rothschild—Hebrew University Archaeological Expedition. The mound of the acropolis was one of the most impressive in Palestine covering twenty-five acres and reaching a height of one hundred thirty feet.

Yadin set out to locate the boundaries of ancient Hazor, to investigate the levels of occupation, to fix the date of the final destruction of the city, and to learn all that could be discovered about the social, economic, political, and military history of Hazor. Before the excavation began, there was ample evidence that Hazor was one of the important cities of the past. It is mentioned in Egyptian execration texts written about 1900 B.C. which list some of the provinces as potential enemies of the Egyptian Empire. Several letters from Mari (Tell Hariri) on the Middle Euphrates (c. 1700 B.C.) mention Hazor. Somewhat later, we read of ambassadors who journeyed from Babylon to Hazor to see the king of Hazor.

During the fifteenth and fourteenth centuries, Hazor was incorporated into the Egyptian Empire, and it is mentioned among the cities conquered by Pharaohs Thutmose III, Amenhotep II, and Seti I. Four of the Amarna Letters mention Hazor, and it also is mentioned in the famous papyrus from thirteenth century Egypt known as Papyrus Anastasi I.

The excavators worked in two distinct places at Hazor. The first was the bottle-shaped tell itself, and the second was a rectangular plateau immediately to the north of the mound. Excavations began on the mound proper near a row of columns discovered by John Garstang in 1928. During 1955, Yadin uncovered four strata, the topmost of which proved to be the remains of a humble settlement of the late eighth and early seventh centuries B.C. The second level appears to have been that of the Israelite city destroyed by Tiglath-pileser III in 732 B.C. It contained beautiful basalt and pottery vessels, along with loom weights and other handicraft tools. Many were intact and in their original positions, suggesting that the population fled in haste and did not return. One interesting object from the third level (8th and 9th centuries B.C.) was a handle of a mirror or a scepter made of bone depicting a winged deity grasping a "Tree of Life" of a type known from Phoenicia. The fourth level is from the period of Ahab (874-852 B.C.). Its most imposing structure was a public building, about forty-nine by sixty-six feet, containing two rows of stone columns, nine pillars to the row, each six and one-half feet high. Most were still intact.

The rectangular enclosure to the north of the mound yielded remains of a well-built city which was destroyed during the thirteenth century and never again occupied. Floors of the houses were littered with Mycenaean pottery from the Late Bronze Age. Two small Canaanite temples were also discovered on successive levels from the fourteenth and thirteenth centuries B.C. One of them contained a sculptured male figure in basalt, seated on a throne in a central niche high above the floor. He holds a cup, and to the left are basalt stelae, one of which depicts two hands outstretched in prayer, surmounted by a sun disk within a crescent. At the end of the row of stelae is a basalt orthostat bearing a sculpture of the head and forelegs of a lion on the narrow side, and a relief of a crouching lion with its tail between its legs on the wide side. These are representative of the religion and art of Hazor before its conquest.

Excavations at the central and eastern parts of the enclosure revealed thirteenth century buildings constructed on the ruins of earlier cities, the oldest dating back to the Hyksos period (eighteenth century B.C.). A Middle Bronze Age cemetery had rock-hewn tombs with pottery and scarabs near the skeletons. Two furnaces were discovered, one was used for smelting metals, and the other probably as a pottery kiln. Three Late Bronze Age arrowheads were found in an excellent state of preservation.

Kedesh. Northwest of Lake Hule, now greatly reduced in size as the result of the drainage of malaria-infested swamps, is the mound of Tell Qades, probably to be identified with Kedesh-Naphtali. Soundings and surface finds by the Israeli archaeologist Y. Aharoni show that the city was occupied in the Early and Late Bronze Ages. At the time of the conquest it was ruled by a Canaanite king (Joshua 12:22), and archaeological soundings indicate that it was surrounded by a thick wall. Under Joshua it became a Levitical city and a City of Refuge (Joshua 20:7; 21:32). Kedesh is said to have been the home of Barak (Judges 4:9-11), but Aharoni suggests that this was probably another Kedesh in Lower Galilee. Kedesh, meaning "holy," was a common place-name for ancient shrine cities. There is no doubt, however, that it was Kedesh-Naphtali in Upper Galilee that fell to Tiglath-pileser III in 734-732 B.C. (II Kings 15:29).

Safad. Safad (Safed), traditionally identified as the "city that is set on an hill" (Matt. 5:14), is perched high among the mountains of northern Israel. Although not mentioned in Scripture, the Talmud says it was one of a chain of high places on which beacons were lit to signal the arrival of the New Year. During the sixteenth and seventeenth centuries A.D., Safad gained renown as one of four holy cities in Palestine and the center of Cabalist mysticism. Jews, suffering from persecution in Europe, looked for the imminent appearance of their Messiah, and spiritual leaders found in Safad a center from which to write and teach. In the late sixteenth and early seventeenth centuries there were eighteen Talmudic colleges there. The historian Cecil Roth terms this "the most vital movement in Judaism which had come forth from Palestine since the

129. Safad

THE WYCLIFFE HISTORICAL GEOGRAPHY OF BIBLE LANDS

days of the Second Temple." The first printing press in all Asia was installed in sixteenth century Safad. The first Hebrew book to be printed in Palestine was published in 1578. Safad is the northernmost city in modern Israel. Its old synagogues still show a concern for the traditions of the past, but its modern artists' colony blends the contemporary with the old.

Meiron. Five miles northwest of Safad is the holy city of Meiron, a town known from Egyptian inscriptions of the second millennium B.C. and conquered by Tiglath-pileser III in 732 B.C. It is not mentioned in Scripture, although the Waters of Merom where Joshua defeated the Hazor Confederacy are nearby. A spring pours water into the Wadi Meiron ten and one-half miles northwest of Capernaum. This may be the area in which Joshua fought. Jewish tradition states that Rabbi Simeon ben Yochai compiled the Zohar ("Book of Splendor"), from which Jewish mysticism draws its inspiration, in a cave at nearby Peki'in to which he was forced to flee from Meiron because of outspoken opposition to the Romans. Each year on Lag ba-Omer, twenty-six days after Passover, thousands of Orthodox Jews make a pilgrimage from Safad to Meiron where they honor Simeon ben Yochai at his tomb.

Other sages, including Rabbi Hillel and Rabbi Shammai, heads of contending schools of Pharisees during the first century B.C., are allegedly buried on the Meiron hillside. Eliezer, the son of Simeon ben Yochai, buried with his father, shares the honors of the great annual pilgrimage. Meiron contains the ruins of a synagogue from the second century B.C. Its central doorway is made of huge single stones upon which rests the lintel, also a huge monolith, now dangerously cracked. Tradition says that if it falls of its own accord, it will presage the coming of the Messiah. There is a story that an earthquake once moved the lintel slightly and the people began to

130. Tiberias and the Sea of Galilee

celebrate, for they were sure that Messiah would soon come.

Tiberias. Although the ministry of Jesus covered much of Galilee, He does not appear to have visited one of its chief cities, Tiberias. This town, along the western shore, was built by Herod Antipas around A.D. 25 to serve as capital of the tetrarchy of Galilee and Peraea, and was named for Tiberius Caesar. The city had not been built when Jesus was a boy, and in His manhood He seems never to have visited it.

South of Tiberias are sulphur springs which were used by the Romans and evidently had been known as early as Joshua, who mentions a town of Hammath (Joshua 19:35) in the region. The Romans called the place "Therma." During the building of Tiberias, the workmen discovered an ancient cemetery, presumably connected with Therma, and the Jews considered the city unclean for that reason. Before the destruction of Jerusalem in A.D. 70, Tiberias was a strictly Gentile city; but subsequently it became a center of Talmudic Judaism. The Palestinian Talmud was compiled there and, significantly, the great medieval Jewish scholar Maimonides was buried at Tiberias in the twelfth century.

Tiberias gave its name to the Sea of Galilee which became known as the Lake of

131. Hot Springs, Tiberias

it is almost seven hundred feet below sea level and the summer heat is almost unbearable.

Magdala. Two miles north of Tiberias was Magdala, known to the Greeks as Tarichea, a center of the fishing industry and the home of Mary of Magdala, who is known in the New Testament as Mary Magdalene. Magdala is at the junction of the lake road from Tiberias and a road coming down from the western hills. Since *Magdala* is the Aramaic word for "tower," it is likely that the town was named for an important watchtower.

Tiberias. The city is mentioned only once in the New Testament when the followers of Jesus took Tiberian boats to journey from the east side of the sea to Capernaum (John 6:23).

Its geographical position, surrounded by mountains and the waters of the sea, made Tiberias easy to defend, a fact which probably caused Herod Antipas to choose the site for his capital. The region around Tiberias has few other advantages because

Capernaum. About three miles farther north, along the shores of the Sea of Galilee, was Capernaum, modern Tell Hum, the place where Jesus made His home after leaving Nazareth (Matt. 4:12-13). Capernaum was an important town in New Testament times. It stood on an important highway and was provided with a custom-house and a military guard.

Jesus performed some of his greatest miracles at Capernaum (Mark 2:1-12; Luke 4:23; John 4:46-54), and He ministered in its synagogue (John 6:16-59). In 1865, Charles Wilson discovered ruins of a synagogue at Tell Hum and identified it with the syna-

132. Capernaum synagogue

gogue in which Jesus ministered. Later excavations by Heinrich Kohl and Carl Watzinger in 1905 showed that the synagogue dates from the third century A.D., although it may have been built on the site of the earlier synagogue in which Jesus ministered.

Chorazin. Chorazin (probably to be identified with Kerazeh), in the basalt hills two miles north of Capernaum, was a scene of Jesus' preaching (Matt. 11:21). Like Capernaum, it still has the remains of a fourth century synagogue, evidence of its earlier prosperity. Second century rabbis were enthusiastic in their praise of the wheat from Chorazin, but today the town is only a ruin.

Bethsaida. The home of Simon Peter was at Bethsaida, "house of fishing," most likely situated on the north shore of the Sea of Galilee a few miles east of the point where the Jordan River flows into the sea. Philip the Tetrarch rebuilt the town and named it "Julius" in honor of Julia, the daughter of Augustus. Ain Tabgha, west of the Jordan, is sometimes identified as "Bethsaida of Galilee" (John 12:21), but the proximity of Bethsaida Julias to Capernaum may account for the reference to Galilee.

Samaria

The highlands south of Esdraelon, assigned by Joshua to Manasseh and Ephraim, comprise the territory which was known after the division of Solomon's kingdom and in New Testament times as Samaria. The name "Samaria" applied in the first instance to the city which Omri chose as his capital. The name of the capital city then was applied to the entire territory of the ten tribes—the Northern Kingdom of Israel. Sometimes the name of the principal tribe, Ephraim, was also applied to the entire country (Isa. 9:9-12).

Shechem. Shechem (modern Nablus), in a fertile valley dominated by the twin mountains, Gerizim (Jebel et Tur) and Ebal, is the first Palestinian site mentioned in the Bible. Here at the "plain of Moreh" Abraham stayed for a time (Gen. 12:6). The sacred historian reminds us that at that time "the Canaanites were in the land," and Abraham received it only by promise. On his return from Paddan-Aram, Jacob purchased a plot of ground from the Canaanites of Shechem (Gen. 33:18-19). The aftermath was tragic, however, for Dinah, a daughter of Jacob by Leah, was seduced by

one of the Shechemites; and her two brothers, Simeon and Levi, retaliated by killing the men of the city and plundering it. Jacob realized that this act would turn the other Canaanites of central Palestine against him, and he prepared to move farther south to Bethel (Gen. 34:1—35:1). In response to a theophany which directed him to move on, Jacob urged his household to put away their idols and ceremonially purify themselves before setting out for Bethel. The idols which had been brought from Paddan-Aram were gathered together and hidden

133. Mount Gerizim

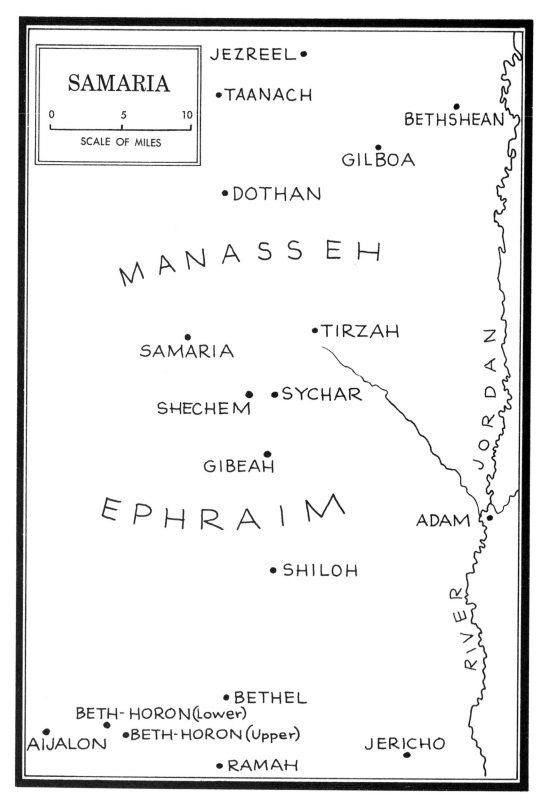

SAMARIA

0   5   10
SCALE OF MILES

JEZREEL •

• TAANACH

BETHSHEAN •

GILBOA

• DOTHAN

M A N A S S E H

• TIRZAH

• SAMARIA

• SYCHAR
SHECHEM •

GIBEAH •

E P H R A I M

ADAM •

• SHILOH

JORDAN

RIVER

• BETHEL
BETH-HORON(Lower)
• BETH-HORON(Upper)
AIJALON •
JERICHO •
• RAMAH

THE WYCLIFFE HISTORICAL GEOGRAPHY OF BIBLE LANDS

"under the oak which was by Shechem" (Gen. 35:1-4).

A stele found at Abydos in Egypt records a campaign in Asia by Pharaoh Senusret III (Senusert, c. 1887-1849 B.C.) during which the Egyptians took a country called "Sekmem," which may be a variant of Shechem. Egyptian execration texts from the nineteenth or eighteenth centuries B.C. clearly identify Shechem as an enemy or a potential enemy of Pharaoh. In the Amarna Letters, Abdu-Heba of Jerusalem charged that Lab'ayu of Shechem had turned his city over to the 'Apiru; and Biridiya of Megiddo complained that he was unable to pass through his city gate because of the hostility of Lab 'ayu. Shechem had developed into a powerful city-state, and Lab-'ayu successfully raided the lands of his neighbors on all sides.

135. Tomb of Joseph

134. Shechem flanked by Gerizim (l.) and Ebal (r.)

At the time of the conquest of Canaan, Shechem seems to have been friendly to Joshua, for there is no record of a battle there. After Joshua had secured a foothold in central Palestine with the conquest of Jericho and Ai, he moved into the pass of Shechem and assembled the people in the natural amphitheater formed by the mountains Gerizim and Ebal. There, in a covenant renewal ceremony, sacrifices were offered and a copy of the law was inscribed on stone and read in the hearing of "all the assembly of Israel, and the women, and the little ones, and the sojourners who lived among them" (Joshua 8:30-35). At some time after the entrance of Israel to Canaan, the body of Joseph, which was mummified and buried temporarily in Egypt (cf. Gen. 50:26), was taken to the plot of ground which Jacob had purchased near Shechem and buried there. At the division of the land among the tribes, Shechem lay in Ephraim near the Manasseh border. It served as a Levitical city and a City of Refuge (Joshua 20:7; 21:21).

The mother of Gideon's son Abimelech was a Shechemite woman, and Abimelech persuaded the Shechemites to support him in his bid for the throne (Judges 9). As tangible evidence of their loyalty, the Shechemites gave Abimelech money from their temple of Baal-berith (Judges 8:33; 9:4; cf. 9:46 where the name is rendered El-berith in RV and RSV). When Jotham, the only surviving son of Gideon, heard what had happened, he stood on Mount Gerizim and addressed the people of Shechem. His parable of the trees was designed to show that a man who tried to rule others was himself good for nothing. The address did not produce immediate results, but after three years the men of Shechem renounced Abimelech (Judges 9:22-23),

136. Excavating the Temple of Baal-
berith

temple at nearby Mount Gerizim.[14] The
temple was never rebuilt, but the Samaritan
community continues to this day to revere
its holy mountain. The Roman general (later emperor) Vespasian encamped near ancient Shechem during his war with the
Jews. After his victory he built the town of
Flavia Neapolis near older Shechem, and
the name "Nablus," a contraction of Neapolis, "new city," is used to this day.

who in turn destroyed the city and its temple (Judges 9:46-49).

Shechem comes into the biblical history
again after the death of Solomon when
Rehoboam journeyed there to be confirmed
as king by the northern tribes (I Kings
12:1). Its sacred associations and its central
location made it a natural choice for such
a gathering. When Rehoboam refused to
pledge a reform in the tax structure, Israel
rebelled, rejected the Davidic dynasty, and
anointed Jeroboam as king. Shechem then
became the first capital of the Northern
Kingdom (I Kings 12).

When the capital was moved to Tirzah,
and then to Samaria, Shechem declined in
importance. Yet after the fall of Samaria
(722 B.C.), people from Shechem continued
to send offerings to Jerusalem (cf. Jer. 41:
5). In postexilic times, Shechem became
the major religious center of the Samaritans
who built their temple on Mount Gerizim
which they regarded as the sacred mount
on which God was to be worshiped (cf.
John 4). The Jerusalem Jews not only
spurned help from the Samaritans in building their temple but they looked upon "the
foolish people that dwell in Shechem"
(Sirach 50:26) as contemptible foes. In
128 B.C., the Hasmonaean ruler John Hyrcanus captured Shechem and destroyed the

137. Samaritan high priest and
Samaritan Pentateuch

The ruins of ancient Shechem have been
buried in the mound known as Tell Balata,
one mile east of modern Nablus. Excavations were begun in 1907 by Carl Watzinger
for the Deutsche Orientgesellschaft, but
major discoveries awaited the labors of
Ernst Sellin who worked from 1913 until
the outbreak of World War I (1914). He

[14]Josephus, *Antiquities,* Book XIII, Chap. ix,
Section 1.

THE WYCLIFFE HISTORICAL GEOGRAPHY OF BIBLE LANDS

excavated there again from 1926 to 1928. Dr. Welter-Mauve worked at Balata for a season in 1928; but neither he nor Sellin had taken advantage of methods of dating strata on the basis of pottery, therefore the chronology of the mound was confused. The work of the Germans at Balata ended in 1934. During their years of labor they had excavated walls and gateways of the city dating to the 1700-1500 B.C. period. In 1926 Sellin discovered a massive wall and a palace with masonry that was partly cyclopean in form. He also discovered a building which was identified as the El-berith Temple constructed about 1300 B.C., renovated a century later, and burned about 1150 B.C. Two cuneiform tablets discovered at the same time were written in the same style as the Amarna Tablets. Names appear to be Hittite in origin.

In August of 1956, the joint expedition of the American Schools of Oriental Research, Drew University, and McCormick Theological Seminary reopened the mound of Balata under the direction of G. Ernest Wright. The Drew-McCormick Expedition has traced the history of Shechem from the middle of the fourth millennium B.C., when the earliest inhabitants seem to have settled there, through its period of prosperity in the Middle Bronze Age to its zenith in the Hyksos period (1700-1550 B.C.). About 1550 B.C., Shechem was completely destroyed, perhaps by the Egyptians. It was rebuilt on a smaller scale during the Late Bronze Age (1500-1225 B.C.). Interestingly the Bible makes no reference to any battle between Joshua and Shechem, and this fact has caused many Bible students to surmise that the Shechemites came to a friendly agreement with the Israelites.

After the eighth century B.C., archaeological remains indicate that a period of deterioration set in, corresponding with the moving of the Israelite capital from Shechem and the ultimate rise of Samaria as the capital of the Northern Kingdom. During the fourth century B.C., Shechem experi-

138. Fortress temple, Shechem

enced a revival, doubtless because of its proximity to the Samaritan sanctuary on Mount Gerizim. The capture of the city by John Hyrcanus (128 B.C.) marked the end of the settlement of Tell Balata, although Nablus nearby was to perpetuate the history of ancient Shechem.

Samaria. About 880 B.C., Omri of Israel moved his capital from Tirzah to Samaria, a three-hundred-foot-high hill seven miles northwest of Shechem. The hill is located in a wide basin formed by a valley which runs from Shechem to the coast, and this elevation commands the main trade route to Esdraelon. The hill was easily defensible, being surrounded by valleys on all sides. From the summit there is a clear view to the Mediterranean.

The work of Omri (I Kings 16:21) was continued by his son Ahab who is known for the ivory palace which he built at Samaria (I Kings 22:39). The "ivory palace" reference may be to the rich ivory inlay which was used in the palace furnishings, many of which have been discovered in recent years. Under Ahab, Baalism became a prominent element in the life of Samaria, and idolatrous cult objects were erected in the capital (cf. II Kings 3:2).

The city was unsuccessfully besieged by

139. Samaria

Ben-hadad of Damascus (I Kings 20;
II Kings 6:24). With the growth in Assyrian power, Menahem thought it would be
wise to pay tribute to Pul (Tiglath-pileser
III), king of Assyria (II Kings 15:17-20);
but Pekah adopted an anti-Assyrian policy,
trusting Egypt to offer aid in the event of
an emergency. Shalmaneser V besieged
Samaria with his Assyrian armies (725-722
B.C.), and the city finally was taken by
Sargon II (II Kings 17:6). Its people were
transported to other areas subject to Assyria, and new colonists were settled in
Samaria and its environs. These settlers
(II Kings 17:24), who were augmented
periodically by others (cf. Ezra 4:2, 9-10),
formed the people later known as Samari-

140. Palace area, Samaria

tans. The area was also colonized by
Greeks following Alexander's conquest (331
B.C.). John Hyrcanus besieged Samaria
(111-107 B.C.) and incorporated it into his
Hasmonaean Empire. The city was rebuilt
by Pompey (Pompeius) and Gabinius and
later embellished by Herod who named it
"Sebaste Augusta" for his emperor. The village today still bears the name "Sebastiyeh."

Excavations began at Sebastiyeh in 1908
under the auspices of Harvard University.
The first director was D. G. Lyon, followed
in 1909 and 1910 by G. A. Reisner. Work
was resumed in 1931 by J. W. Crowfoot
representing Harvard University, the Palestine Exploration Fund, the Hebrew University, and the British School of Archaeology,
Jerusalem. Excavations were conducted
during the summers of 1931, 1932, and
1933, and part of the 1935 season.

The history of Israelite Samaria began
with Omri's purchase of the site, although
there is evidence of some occupation during the Early Bronze Age (3000-2000 B.C.).
Seven Israelite levels of occupation have
been traced, followed by Hellenistic and
Roman levels. The two lowest levels (designated I and II) are from the time of
Omri and Ahab. They include the city
walls—inner walls five feet thick and outer
walls nineteen and one-half feet thick. The
main gateway had a columned entrance
court. The palace also had a wide court
and a pool, or reservoir, thirty-three and
one-half by seventeen feet (cf. I Kings
22:38). The palace has additions from the
time of Jeroboam II.

In a storeroom near the palace, about
two hundred plaques and ivory pieces were
discovered. Some of these objects have
Hebrew letters scratched on their backs.
Many of these plaques were apparently attached to furniture, but most seem to have
been affixed to the paneling of the room.
They are of Phoenician workmanship with
many Egyptian motifs. They may have
given rise to the name of the "ivory house"

which Ahab is said to have built (I Kings 22:39).

Near the west end of the Israelite citadel, the excavators found about seventy broken pieces of pottery inscribed with official records in the Old Hebrew script. Twenty-two villages in the territory of Manasseh are mentioned, along with several of the revenue officers. These villages probably date from the reign of Jeroboam II.

141. "Pool" of Samaria

The third level marks the period of Jehu, and some of the earlier buildings were adapted for the new dynasty. Levels four through six cover the period of Jeroboam II and the eighth century B.C. The destruction level seven marks the fall of the city to the Assyrians.

The Hellenistic remains include a round tower, earlier thought to date from Jeroboam II. Ben Dor of the Hebrew University discovered Hellenistic pottery in the masonry, which would date it no earlier than 325 B.C. The same level has yielded remains of a fortress, a city wall, stamped jar handles, and Hellenistic pottery. During Hellenistic times the city of Samaria was Greek in culture, while the Semitic Samaritans found their cultural and religious center at Shechem. The jar fragments, when pieced together, indicate a type of wine jar that was used on the island of Rhodes. Much of the pottery was of an Athenian type. It is obvious that Samaria had commerce with the Hellenistic world and that she had little cultural contact with either the Jew or the Samaritan of the period.

John Hyrcanus destroyed the Hellenistic city and sold its inhabitants into slavery. For nearly half a century the city was unoccupied. Then in 63 B.C., Pompey and his Roman army invaded Judaea and annexed Samaria to the province of Syria. In 57 B.C., Gabinius, the provincial governor of Syria, rebuilt Samaria on a small scale. In 30 B.C., Octavian, later to become Augustus Caesar, presented Samaria to Herod who settled the city with discharged mercenaries and renamed it "Sebaste," the Greek equivalent of Augustus, in honor of his friend and patron. Herod's mercenaries included Gauls, Thracians, and Germans; and the city assumed a thoroughly cosmopolitan atmosphere. Over the remains of earlier Israelite palaces there arose a Roman temple to Augustus. The city boasted a basilica, a forum, a stadium, and an aqueduct—all representative of Roman influence. Roman Samaria boasted a nine-hundred-yard-long colonnaded street with adjacent shops.

142. Inside facing of the round tower, Samaria

Sychar. John 4 records the encounter of Jesus with a Samaritan woman from the town of Sychar who came to draw water from the well named for the Patriarch Jacob. The name "Sychar" does not appear elsewhere in Scripture, and it has been traditionally identified with Shechem. Excavations at Shechem indicate that the town was not occupied in New Testament times, and current scholarship tends to identify Sychar with the village El-Askar on the eastern slope of Mount Ebal about half a mile north of Jacob's Well and just east of Shechem.

144. Jacob's Well

143. Sychar

Tirzah. The site of Tirzah, which became the capital of Israel during the reign of Baasha (I Kings 15:21, 33; 16:6), is not certain although it is usually identified with Tell el-Far'a, seven miles northeast of Shechem. The king of Canaanite Tirzah, a city noted for its beauty (Song of Solomon 6:4), was captured by Joshua at the time of the conquest (Joshua 12:24). Jeroboam maintained a home there after the division of the Israelite kingdom (I Kings 14:17), and it was the capital of the Northern Kingdom from the days of Baasha until Zimri burned its palace over his own head during a dy-

nastic struggle with Omri (I Kings 16:17-18). Although victorious, Omri moved his capital a few years later to Samaria. Tirzah appears in biblical history again when one of its native sons, Menahem, went to Samaria, slew King Shallum, and usurped the throne (II Kings 15:14, 16).

The excavation of Tell el-Far'a was begun in 1946 by Father Roland de Vaux of the Dominican Ecole Biblique in Jerusalem. Pottery remains indicate that a city flourished there during the ninth century B.C., the period when it served as Israel's capital, after which it deteriorated rapidly. The site was occupied as early as the fourth millennium B.C., and an important city was located there throughout the Bronze Age.

145. Dothan

THE WYCLIFFE HISTORICAL GEOGRAPHY OF BIBLE LANDS

Dothan. About eleven miles north of Samaria is a magnificent mound rising nearly two hundred feet above the surrounding plain. The mound, known as "Tell Dotha," has been identified with biblical Dothan, the place to which Joseph went in search for his brothers (Gen. 37:17) and where he was sold into slavery. The mound covers about ten acres, and the slopes almost fifteen more.

Professor and Mrs. Joseph Free have directed a series of excavations at Dothan since 1953. The site was evidently occupied as early as 3000 B.C. The discovery of bowls and juglets from the Middle Bronze Age (2000-1500 B.C.) along with later discoveries confirms the fact that Dothan was occupied during the time of the biblical Patriarchs. From about 3000 B.C., Dothan had a continuous history, with periodic destruction and rebuilding, down to the period of the divided kingdom (900-700 B.C.). Dothan is mentioned in connection with Elisha's disclosure of the secret movement of the Syrian army (II Kings 6:12-13). The Wheaton Archaeological Expedition is continuing excavation at Dothan.

Shiloh. On a hilltop three miles east of the main road, about twelve miles south of Shechem, is the Arab village of Seilun, occupying the site of ancient Shiloh (cf. Judges 21:19). In this isolated spot the Israelites assembled after the division of Canaan among the tribes and erected the tabernacle which was to serve as their national shrine (Joshua 18:1). The tabernacle, or "tent of meeting," had been a portable sanctuary during the years of wandering, but at Shiloh it became the more permanent structure (Judges 18:31) to which pilgrims came for their annual feasts (I Sam. 1:3). Although the nature of this "house of God" at Shiloh is not known, the Scripture speaks of "the doorpost of the temple of the Lord" (I Sam. 1:9, RSV) beside which Eli the priest sat. During the

146. Level of Elisha's day, Dothan

wilderness period the tabernacle was a portable shrine. Alterations were apparently made after Israel settled in the land of Canaan.

Scripture does not mention the destruction of Shiloh, but it is clearly implied. Israel took the sacred ark into battle at Aphek, and it fell into the hands of the Philistines (I Sam. 4). When they determined to return the ark to Israel, it was not returned to Shiloh but was placed instead in the house of a man named Abinadab at Kirjath-jearim, west of Jerusalem. It is probable that Shiloh was destroyed during the Philistine wars, a fact which seems to have been well known in the time of Jeremiah, for the prophet addressed the Jerusalemites of his generation with the warning concerning the Temple: "I will make this house like Shiloh" (Jer. 26:6; cf. 7:12; 26:9).

In September, 1922, H. Kjaer and Aage Schmidt sank a number of trial pits through the debris at Seilun and found pottery from the Arabic, Greco-Roman, and Early Israelite (1200-1050 B.C.) periods. Schmidt periodically renewed the excavation of Shiloh until his death in 1952. Although no major discoveries were reported, the evidence from pottery tallies perfectly with what might be expected from the biblical record. There is no evidence that there was ever a Canaanite settlement at Shiloh. It seems to have been purposely selected as a centrally located place for the ark, and the town then grew around the sanctuary which was built to house the ark. After the ark was taken by the Philistines, the priesthood seems to have settled at Nob (I Sam. 22:11) in the environs of Jerusalem. The pottery indicates no settlement at Shiloh from about 1050 B.C. to about 300 B.C., although the possibility of an unimportant town at the site cannot be ruled out. The prophet who told Jeroboam that he would become king of the ten tribes is named "Ahijah the Shilonite" (I Kings 11:29), a name which suggests that there was some community at Shiloh as late as the time of Solomon. Subsequently, however, the town existed only in the memory of Israel's prophets and psalmists (cf. Ps. 78:60).

Bethel. On the point of a low, rocky ridge twelve miles north of Jerusalem was the city of Bethel, near which Abraham pitched his tent after leaving Shechem (Gen. 12:8) and to which he returned after his stay in Egypt (Gen. 13:3). Bethel is particularly associated with Jacob, who spent the night in the vicinity of the city during his journey from Beersheba to Paddan-Aram and dreamed of a ladder which reached from earth to heaven (Gen. 28:11-12). Years later, after Jacob's unfortunate experience with the men of Shechem, God brought him back to Bethel where the covenant made with Abraham was renewed and the descendants of Jacob were given the land of Canaan as an inheritance (Gen. 35:1-15).

At the time of the conquest, Bethel was assigned to the tribe of Benjamin (Joshua 18:11-13), but the town was on the Ephraim border and was absorbed into that tribe

147. Shick's model of the tabernacle

THE WYCLIFFE HISTORICAL GEOGRAPHY OF BIBLE LANDS

(Judges 1:22-26). During the time of the Judges, the sacred ark was located at Bethel (cf. Judges 20:18-28). It was regarded as a holy place (I Sam. 10:3) and was one of three cities in which Samuel sat to judge Israel (I Sam. 7:16).

With the establishment of David's political and religious center at Jerusalem, Bethel lost its importance. Jeroboam, however, in revolting against the house of David re-established Bethel as a cult center for the Northern Kingdom (I Kings 12:28-33), and it became a rival shrine to Jerusalem. The golden calves at Bethel evoked the wrath of the prophets Hosea and Amos. Hosea gave Bethel ("House of God") the nickname "Beth-aven" ("House of Iniquity," Hosea 10:5). And Amos sarcastically urged Israel, "Come to Bethel, and transgress" (Amos 4:4). Abijah of Judah captured and temporarily held Bethel (II Chron. 13:19), and the city probably changed hands more than once during the border disputes between Israel and Judah. After the fall of Israel to the Assyrians, when new settlers were brought into the land, the Assyrian king allowed one of the priests of Bethel who had been taken into exile to return to "teach them the law of the god of the land" (II Kings 17:27-28). The result was a mixture of pagan worship and biblical monotheism. During the revival under King Josiah of Judah, the idolatrous altar and the high place at Bethel were destroyed (II Kings 23:15-20). But shortly afterward the armies of Nebuchadnezzar invaded western Asia and destroyed Bethel along with Jerusalem and other cities that resisted his conquests. Following the exile, Bethel was resettled (Neh. 11:31), but the Jews of that period looked to Jerusalem as their spiritual center.

The ruins of ancient Bethel have been identified on the north side of the Arab village of Beitin where W. F. Albright made soundings during 1927 while he was director of the American Schools of Oriental Research in Jerusalem. Full-scale excavations were conducted from July to September, 1934, by Albright and J. L. Kelso of Pittsburgh-Xenia Theological Seminary (now Pittsburgh Theological Seminary).

The earliest level contained a Middle Bronze Age wall and houses with some of the best-laid masonry of that period yet discovered in Palestine. This was the Bethel of the age of the biblical Patriarchs. Its occupation is thought to have begun about 2200 B.C. During the thirteenth century the Canaanite city was destroyed in a tremendous conflagration which left debris five feet high in places. Albright attributes this to the Israelites at the time of their conquest of Palestine. The Israelite levels that follow are inferior in workmanship to the Canaanite city. Twice Bethel seems to have been burned by the Philistines or other early enemies of Israel. The city of the ninth century—the time of Jeroboam I—was built with evidences of finer workmanship than that in the comparatively primitive levels of the earliest Israelite period. Early in the sixth century the city was again burned, this time by the armies of Nebuchadnezzar. For a time the site was unoccupied, but a humble village was built there during the Persian period. Vespasian captured it in A.D. 69, and it was reoccupied as a Roman town and continued to flourish until the Arab conquest.

During the 1960 excavation at Bethel sponsored by the Pittsburgh Theological Seminary and the American Schools of Oriental Research, a gateway dating late in the eighteenth century B.C. was excavated. The gateway was destroyed in the mid-sixteenth century. Beneath the gateway the archaeologists came upon bedrock stained with blood. This seems to indicate that Canaanite Bethel had an open-air sacrificial holy place sacred to the God El. At a later time Baal replaced El as the major Canaanite deity, and it was Baal worship that the Israelites had to combat from the entrance into Canaan under Joshua to the destruction of Jerusalem in the days of Nebuchadnezzar. The sanctuary at Bethel dates at least to Patriarchal times. Jacob worshiped God (El) there (Gen. 28:18-22).

148. James Kelso excavating a worship center at Bethel

Ai. Two miles east of Beitin (ancient Bethel) rises the mound et-Tell, usually identified with Ai, the site of Joshua's second encounter with the Canaanites (Joshua 7; 8). In 1928 Professor John Garstang, while director of the Department of Antiquities in Palestine, did some superficial digging on the et-Tell mound. On the basis of ceramic evidence, he and Professor Albright of the American Schools concluded that the city fell to Joshua in the sixteenth or fifteenth century B.C.[15]

[15]Cf. *Bulletin of the American Schools of Oriental Research*, 56, 1934 ff.

From 1933 to 1935 the Rothschild Expedition excavated et-Tell under the direction of Madame Judith Marquet-Krause and Mr. S. Yeivin. Excavations proved conclusively that Ai was a thriving city during the third millennium B.C. It had strong walls, well-constructed stone houses, and a porticoed palace on top of the hill. Ivories and stone bowls discovered there give evidence of contacts with Egypt at this early period. Some time before 2200 B.C., however, Ai was destroyed. Except for a small settlement which made use of the earlier ruins (*c.* 1100 B.C.), there is no archaeological evidence that the site was ever occupied again.

Many biblical scholars suggest that the story of Joshua's conquest of Ai should actually be applied to nearby Bethel. Father Hugues Vincent has suggested that the Canaanites of Bethel used the site of the Bronze Age city at et-Tell as a military outpost at the time of the Israelite conquest and that the battle was actually fought there.[16] On the other hand, the identification of Ai with et-Tell has itself been challenged. J. Simons insists that the expression "beside Bethel" in Joshua 12:9 requires a location for Ai closer than the two miles which separate et-Tell from Bethel.[17] Yehezkel Kaufmann[18] denies the identity of Ai with et-Tell and insists that the term "Ai" does not mean "ruin" but "a heap" in the sense of a pile of stones, rejecting the idea that Ai stood on the mound of an ancient city. In the light of present archaeological knowledge it seems apparent that Ai has not yet been identified. Joseph A. Callaway, director of the 1964 excavations at et-Tell, found nothing at the site to warrant identification of the village with the biblical Ai.

[16]*Revue Biblique*, 1937, pp. 231-66.
[17]J. Simons, *The Geographical and Topographical Texts of the Old Testament* (Leiden: E. J. Brill, 1959), p. 270.
[18]Y. Kaufmann, *The Biblical Account of the Conquest of Palestine* (Jerusalem: Magnes Press, 1953), p. 77, n. 64.

The Hill Country of Judah

The tribe of Judah occupied the mountainous tract of land west of the Dead Sea which was half desert and half cultivable land. At best, however, Judah provided a precarious existence, and its material prosperity never was comparable to that of northern Palestine. It had one supreme advantage, however. Judah with its mountain strongholds was easily defended. It did not, like the Esdraelon Valley, attract potential empire builders, and all who attempted to invade its mountainous terrain found the going difficult indeed.

The Dead Sea stretches almost the full length of Judah's eastern border. The Judaean wilderness, which extends along the western bank of the Dead Sea, had no cities, but it had a fascination for the ascetically minded. The Qumran community lived its monastic life near the northwest corner of the Dead Sea during the first and second centuries B.C. and the first century A.D. Later, Christian monks—four thousand strong—lived in the nearby Mar Saba monastery.

The wilderness also provided a place of escape for political exiles and lawless men. Saul pursued David to Ziph, in the wilderness three miles southeast of Hebron (I Sam. 23:24). David then fled into the wilderness of Maon, the pasturelands adjacent to Khirbet Ma'in, eight and one-half miles south of Hebron. When Saul was attacked by the Philistines, David made his escape to the Oasis of En-gedi (modern 'Ain Jidi) midway down the west bank of the Dead Sea. The Judaean wilderness began a short distance east of Jerusalem. The traditional site of the temptation of Jesus may be seen from the road between Jerusalem and Jericho.

The southern border of Judah was in the steppeland south of Beersheba which had been occupied by Israel's perennial enemy, the Amalekites. Israel's first military en-counter after the exodus was with the Amalekites (Exodus 17:8-16), and the presence of Amalekites, Edomites, and other hostile peoples in southern Palestine forced Israel to enter the land of promise by a circuitous route through Transjordan. The region south of Beersheba is now known as the Negeb, and the modern state of Israel is expending much effort to irrigate and render productive this area which has been a wasteland for centuries.

The western defense line of Judah comprised the hills of the Shephelah, the lowlands which were separated from the Ju-

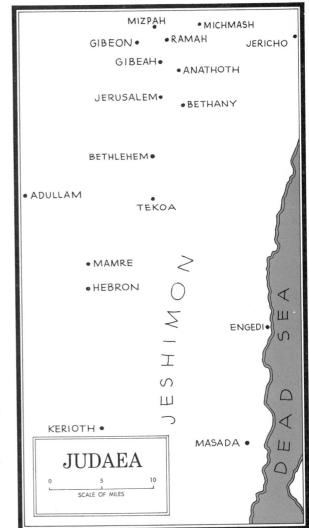

149. Traditional Mount of Temptation with its Greek Orthodox monastery

daean highlands by several cross valleys running north and south. A potential invader from the coastal plain would first have to conquer the Shephelah before he could begin an assault on the principal Judaean cities in the central range. This was accomplished by such conquerors as Sennacherib and Nebuchadnezzar, but Jerusalem was not nearly so vulnerable as were the cities of Esdraelon and Galilee.

The northern border of Judah was not well defined, however, and it was the weakest link in the defenses of the Southern Kingdom. Geba, at the northern frontier of Judah, was only five miles south of Bethel on the southern edge of Israel. Jerusalem was just seven miles south of the frontier. Geba was fortified in the days of Asa, and the Southern Kingdom was designated as the land "from Geba to Beer-sheba" (II Kings 23:8).

Gibeon. Six miles northwest of Jerusalem lies the mound El Jib, identified with biblical Gibeon. Following the fall of Jericho and Ai, the Hivites of Gibeon induced Joshua to make a treaty with them on the pretense that they had come from a great distance and were not inhabitants of nearby Canaanite cities (Joshua 9). The treaty was honored even after the deceit of the Gibeonites was apparent, but they were reduced to the status of servants.

At the division of the land, Gibeon was assigned to Benjamin and set apart as a Levitical city (Joshua 18:25; 21:17). During the conflict between the partisans of Ishbosheth, Saul's son, and the partisans of David, the two sides met at Gibeon. Twelve warriors from each met at the pool of Gibeon, and in the contest that ensued, each killed his opposite number (II Sam. 2:12-17). Amasa, who had commanded Absalom's rebel army, was later murdered by Joab at "the great stone which is in Gibeon" (II Sam. 20:8).

Saul, who was evidently intolerant of non-Israelites in his kingdom, had put to death a number of Gibeonites (II Sam. 21:1). During a period of famine, David became aware of the complaint of the Gibeonites at this breach of treaty with Israel. Interpreting the famine in Israel at that time as a punishment for this treaty violation, David asked the Gibeonites what reparation might be made to them (II Sam. 21:3). They suggested that seven "sons" (i.e., descendants) of Saul be given to them so that they might be put to death as a suitable punishment for Saul's misdeed (II Sam. 21:6-9). The seven men were delivered, and the Gibeonites hanged them on the hill (II Sam. 21:9).

Gibeon appears in the list of cities which Pharaoh Shishak (Sheshonk I) captured during his campaign in Palestine. The city is again mentioned following the destruction of Jerusalem when the assassins of Gedaliah were overtaken by the "great pool which is in Gibeon" and their prisoners were set· free (Jer. 41:11-14). Gibeonites helped Nehemiah in the work of rebuilding the walls of Jerusalem (Neh. 3:7).

James B. Pritchard has conducted excavations since 1956 at El Jib on behalf of the University Museum of Philadelphia and the Church Divinity School of the Pacific. Pritchard has shown that El Jib was occupied during the Early Bronze Age. A large part of the mound was occupied during the third millennium B.C. (c. 3000-2500 B.C.), and there is evidence of violent destruction at the end of the period. In one room more than a dozen jars were crushed by the collapse of the roof. The site was then abandoned until the eighteenth century B.C. when it was rebuilt and occupied for two or three centuries. Except for a Cypriot milk bowl found in a dumping area outside the Iron Age city wall, there are no further remains until about 1200 B.C.

150. Gibeon

During the Iron Age, beginning about 1200 B.C., Gibeon was resettled and encircled by a wall built on the edge of the rock scarp of the natural hill. Just inside the wall on the north side of the mound, a pool was hewn from the native rock thirty-seven feet in diameter and more than thirty-five and one-half feet deep. A spiral stairway was cut along the east side of the pool, and a balustrade provided protection for those who used the stairs. At the bottom of the pool, a tunnel was cut downward almost forty-four feet farther, and the steps of the pool continue to form a stairwell to the water chamber.

Pritchard is puzzled about the purpose of this pool, but he feels that it may have been the place where the twelve warriors lost their lives in the battle to determine whether Ishbosheth or David would rule Israel. The north wall of Gibeon was later moved outward to enclose a larger area, and a second tunnel was cut from inside the city wall to a spring which flows from the base of the mound. The city appears to have been continuously occupied from early in the twelfth century until the end of the seventh century.

During the eighth and seventh centuries B.C., Gibeon was a commercial center particularly noted for its wine industry. Grapes were crushed by foot in wine presses, and

151. Pool of Gibeon

the juice was dipped out and placed in large jars which were stored in underground cellars. The excavations have produced not only jars but also funnels used in pouring the wine, wine vats cut into bedrock, and ninety-five stamped jar handles bearing either a royal seal or the owners' names and the word *Gibeon*.

Gibeah. Three miles north of the Damascus Gate in Jerusalem, rises a limestone hill with a mound on the summit which is known to the Arabs as "Tell el-Ful" ("hill of beans"). This is almost certainly the site of the Benjamite city of Gibeah, also known as "Gibeah of Saul." Situated away from running water, Gibeah does not appear to have been occupied until the Iron Age when cisterns were first dug in Palestine to conserve rainwater.

Gibeah first appears in Scripture as the place where an unnamed Levite passed the night while journeying with his concubine from Bethlehem to the hill country of Ephraim. The men of Gibeah seized the concubine and repeatedly attacked her until she was dead (Judges 19). Thereupon the Levite cut her body into pieces, sent them to the Israelite tribes, and thereby urged a war upon Benjamin to punish Gibeah for its sin. The city was destroyed, and the tribe of Benjamin was almost annihilated in the civil war which followed.

As the birthplace and residence of Israel's first king, Saul, Gibeah became a city of importance during his reign (I Sam. 10:26; 15:34). After Saul's death, however, nearby Jerusalem became the capital, and Gibeah became a city of comparative insignificance, although it continued to be occupied until Maccabean times.

W. F. Albright excavated Tell el-Ful for the American Schools of Oriental Research during 1922 and 1923, and returned for a short campaign in 1933. The results indicate that Tell el-Ful (Gibeah) experienced seven periods of occupancy. The earliest, during the twelfth century B.C., was a small Benjamite village which was destroyed by fire, probably during the warfare that broke out following the abuse of the Levite's concubine. The next village (c. 1050 B.C.) contained a fortress built of massive polygonal masonry. This was doubtless the castle which Saul occupied as king of Israel. It originally had two stories which were connected by a stone staircase. In the audience chamber of this castle, young David played his harp to ease the spirit of troubled Saul (I Sam. 16:23). Storage bins found in the castle bore evidence that they had been used for oil, wine, and grain. Other objects discovered included spinning whorls, grinding stones, cooking pots, burnished ware, and a gaming board.

Saul's castle was destroyed and imme-

152. An ancient wine-press in Jerusalem

153. Gibeah

diately rebuilt of massive but better-laid masonry. This may have occurred after the death of Saul, during the contest between David and Ishbosheth. The rebuilt fortress, however, was abandoned during the period when Jerusalem was the capital. During the late ninth or eighth century, a watchtower was built at one of the corners of Saul's castle. This watchtower (or *migdal* as it is termed in Hebrew) was a part of the northern defenses of Jerusalem. It was destroyed and rebuilt, probably during the seventh century. The tower seems to have become the center of a village in late preexilic times, but Nebuchadnezzar's armies destroyed the tower and the village.

The last remains of Tell el-Ful date from the Persian and Hellenistic periods, when it was evidently the site of a prosperous village. The fort was rebuilt, but the defenses of Gibeah were no match for the Romans; the final destruction probably dates from A.D. 70 when the armies of Titus moved against Jerusalem. Since then it has been simply a place on which to grow beans!

Mizpah. "Mizpah," meaning "watchtower," was a common biblical name. Palestine was constantly being invaded and was struggling internally through dynastic and intertribal wars. For this reason it was necessary to build and man watchtowers at strategic positions throughout the land. One town named Mizpah was located in the territory of Benjamin near Gibeon and Ramah (Joshua 18:25-26; I Kings 15:22). Mizpah seems to have been a place of assembly for Israel. In the days of the Judges when some lewd Benjamites (mentioned earlier) outraged the Levite's concubine, the men of Israel assembled at Mizpah to plan their punishment (Judges 20:1, 3; 21:1, 5, 8). In the days of Samuel, Israel gathered at Mizpah for prayers twenty years after the ark had been returned by the Philistines (I Sam. 7:5-6). The Philistines attacked the assembled Israelites, but they were repulsed and Samuel was able to erect a stone commemorating divine aid at nearby Ebenezer ("Stone of Help"). Saul, a native of Gibeah, was presented to Israel at Mizpah (I Sam. 10:17) and there acclaimed king.

In his controversies with Baasha of Israel, Asa of Judah fortified Mizpah as an important border town (I Kings 15:22). Following the destruction of Jerusalem by Nebuchadnezzar, Mizpah had a brief period of importance when it served as the capital ruled by Gedaliah (II Kings 25:23, 25). Jeremiah and other refugees migrated to Mizpah, but a group of Zealots killed Gedaliah and thereby brought an end to the last vestige of Israelite independence (Jer. 41).

Mizpah's history continued into Maccabean times. When Judas the Maccabee realized the strength of his Syrian opposition, he called his partisans together for prayer: "So they assembled and went to Mizpah opposite Jerusalem, because Israel formerly had a place of prayer in Mizpah" (I Macc. 3:46).

The location of Mizpah in Benjamin is still uncertain, although contemporary biblical scholarship prefers the mound of Tell en-Nasbeh, about eight miles north of Jerusalem. Traditionally Mizpah has been identified with a mound four and one-half miles northwest of Jerusalem known as "Nebi Samwil" ("the Prophet Samuel"). Nebi Samwil, rising about three thousand fifty feet, above sea level, was named "Mount Joy" by the Crusaders because from its summit they caught their first view of the Holy City. It is one of the highest spots in Judaea and is as yet unexcavated. Eusebius identified Nebi Samwil with Mizpah, as did Edward Robinson and George Adam Smith during the nineteenth century.

Since the excavation of Tell en-Nasbeh by W. F. Bade of the Pacific School of Religion, scholars have tended to identify this mound with Mizpah. Bade worked on Tell en-Nasbeh for five seasons: 1926, 1927, 1929, 1932, and 1935. He died before publication of the results of his work could be begun, but his assistant, J. C. Wampler, and C. C. McCown inherited the task of editing the reports.

A number of caves and tombs in the limestone rock of the hill on which Tell en-Nasbeh is located contain pottery, implements, and ornaments of Early Bronze Age settlers. A small town, probably founded by Israelites, existed there during the twelfth century B.C. It was defended by means of a wall about a yard thick built of rubble.

Excavations indicate that much stronger walls, between fifteen and twenty feet thick, were built about 900 B.C., enclosing an area of eight acres. At important salients, towers projected as much as seven feet beyond the wall. They were made of large blocks of stone, fitted together and laid in clay mortar. The outside was covered with lime plaster to a height of fifteen to eighteen feet.

At the northeast side of the city, the ends of the wall overlapped, and a large city gate occupied the thirty-foot space between the walls. Inside the gate were guardrooms; on the outside, benches lined the court. The gate of an oriental city was the place where business and legal transactions were conducted, and the Tell en-Nasbeh gate gives an excellent illustration of that practice (cf. Deut. 22:24; Ruth 4:11; II Sam. 19:8).

Tell en-Nasbeh was occupied to Hellenistic times, although the population was greatly reduced after the fifth century. Over eighty jar handles from the period shortly before the exile bear the words "for the king" (Hebrew *lemelech*), perhaps an indication that their contents were assigned to the king in payment of taxes. This inscription occurs on other jars from cities of Judah and is evidence that Tell en-Nasbeh belonged to the Southern Kingdom. None were found at Bethel, only three miles to the north, indicating that the border between North and South lay between the two cities. Pottery of a later, postexilic type, was stamped with the word *Yehud* (Judah), showing that Tell en-Nasbeh belonged to Judah during the Persian period.

Other pottery from the Persian period bears an inscription which may be read *m s h* or *m s p*. Scholars who suggest the reading *m s p* see in the letters the name Mispah, thus identifying the mound. Specimens of the same inscription have been found at Jericho and at Gibeon, so the identification with Mizpah cannot be proved. N. Avigad, an Israeli archaeologist, suggests that the letters refer to the city Mozah (Joshua 18:26) and that products of that town were exported to the places where the inscriptions were found.

Jerusalem. High in the mountains of Judaea, just east of the watershed, is the city of Jerusalem which, since the time of David, has been sacred to all who trace their spiritual origins to ancient Israel. Jerusalem, with an altitude of twenty-five hundred feet, is located at the junction of ancient roads which ran southward from Shechem to Hebron and westward from the Jordan Valley and Jericho to the Mediterranean coast.

The city is first mentioned in Egyptian execration texts from the nineteenth century B.C. where one of Egypt's enemies in

154. Jerusalem from the Mount of Olives

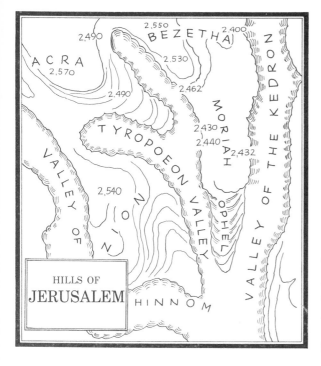

HILLS OF
JERUSALEM

Canaan bears the name "Urushalim." At about the same time, the Patriarch Abraham visited a king of Salem named Melchizedek (Gen. 14). "Salem" is probably a shortened form of Jerusalem, a city devoted to the ancient Semitic god Shalem who was associated with peace and prosperity. The Amarna Letters, written about five centuries later, mention Bethshalem, "the House of Shalem," which may be either a variant of the name "Jerusalem" or another town dedicated to the god Shalem.

Deep ravines provide a system of natural defenses to the east, south, and west of the city, leaving the north as the one vulnerable border. The Kidron Valley separates Jerusalem from the Mount of Olives which dominates the eastern horizon. West and south of the city is the valley of Hinnom (Greek Gehenna) which joins the Kidron near the site of Job's Well, the biblical

THE WYCLIFFE HISTORICAL GEOGRAPHY OF BIBLE LANDS

En-rogel (II Sam. 17:17; I Kings 1:9), to the southeast. In ancient times the Holy City was dissected by the Tyropoeon Valley (i.e., "the Valley of Cheesemakers"), but the debris of the centuries has filled the valley so that its lines can no longer be traced.

During the latter part of the fourth millennium B.C., a Semitic people occupied the hill to the southeast of the present city of Jerusalem. At the foot of the hill on its eastern slope is an intermittent spring, 'Ain Sitti Miryam ("the Virgin's Spring"). This is the biblical Gihon spring which, along with Job's Well farther south, provided water for the city. The earliest settlers used both pottery and metal, and the remains of these assist the modern archaeologist in reconstructing the history of the site.

Melchizedek, king of the Salem-Jerusalem of Abraham's day, had a Semitic name, but the city is known to have been occupied by Hurrians (biblical Horites) after the time of the biblical Patriarchs. The Amarna Letters show that Hurrian Jerusalem was a vassal of Egypt during the fourteenth century B.C. Hurrian fortifications have been excavated on the eastern slope of the Ophel (II Chron. 27:3), between the southeastern hill and the Temple mount.

The ruler of Jerusalem at the time of the conquest of Canaan bore the Semitic name Adoni-zedek. Alarmed at the fall of Jericho and the defection of the Gibeonites, he joined four other Canaanite kings in attacking Gibeon (Joshua 10:1-5). Events following the defeat of Adoni-zedek are not recorded, but it is known that a Canaanite people known as Jebusites continued to occupy the site of Jerusalem until the time of David. Judah and Simeon defeated these Canaanites (Judges 1:1-8), but Israelite victories were short-lived until David and his men took the Jebusite stronghold (II Sam. 5:6-8).

Jerusalem was ideally situated to serve as David's capital. It was centrally located

155. Jebusite Jerusalem (foreground), now barren, and Valley of Hinnom

in the United Kingdom, yet on the border of Judah. Since it had not been previously occupied by either Judah or Benjamin on whose borders it stood, David was able to make it a royal enclave. Because of this unique position, it became known as "the City of David." David built his palace there and tried to make Jerusalem the spiritual center of his kingdom by bringing the sacred ark into the city. David built a magnificent palace and planned to build a temple, but the Prophet Nathan insisted that the Temple should not be built until David was succeeded by his son Solomon (II Samuel 7).

The building and fortification of Jerusalem, begun by David, were continued by Solomon, who built a magnificent temple on the mountain to the north of the older Jebusite and Davidic city. He then extended the city walls northward to protect the Temple precincts. The Solomonic Temple stood until the destruction of Jerusalem by the army of Nebuchadnezzar (587 B.C.), and a second temple, built by the Jews who returned from Babylon following the decree of Cyrus (536 B.C.), stood on the same site until the Romans destroyed Jerusalem (A.D. 70). It was this second temple, later rebuilt by Herod, which was standing during the period of Jesus' ministry. The site is now occupied by the Muslim shrine known as the "Dome of the Rock."

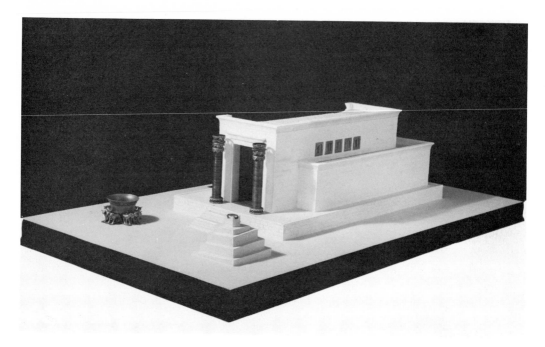

156. Howland-Garber model of Solomon's Temple

157. Howland-Garber model interior

158. Dome of the Rock

With the disruption of the kingdom following the death of Solomon, Jerusalem was no longer a centrally located capital. It was dangerously close to the fluctuating borders of the Northern Kingdom, and it was periodically threatened. Encouraged by Jeroboam of Israel, Pharaoh Sheshonk I marched against Jerusalem and plundered both the Temple and the palace during the reign of Solomon's son Rehoboam. In subsequent years, Jerusalem was attacked by Syrians (II Chron. 24:17-24), Assyrians (II Kings 18), and Babylonians (II Kings 25). Although miraculously delivered from Sennacherib's siege in 701 B.C., Jerusalem fell slightly more than a century later to Nebuchadnezzar of Babylon. Hezekiah built a pool and a tunnel to bring water into the city from the Gihon spring (II Kings 20:20; II Chron. 32:30). The tunnel, which exists today, is nearly 1800 feet long and about 6 feet high. In 597 B.C., Nebuchadnezzar took King Jehoiachin into exile. A decade later, after the Jews revolted against Babylonian rule, the city was destroyed and its people deported.

With the fall of Babylon (539 B.C.), the Persian conquerors adopted a new policy toward deported peoples, and Jews were encouraged to return to Jerusalem and rebuild their temple (Ezra 1:1-4). Those who returned met opposition from Samaritans and other peoples who had profited from the Jews' absence. Although the work of rebuilding the Temple was temporarily stopped, the preaching of Haggai and Zechariah was instrumental in restoring the people's confidence, with the result that the

159. Mount of Olives with the Church
of All Nations and Garden of Gethsemane

second temple was completed during the
sixth year of Darius (515 B.C.; cf. Ezra
6:15).

Not until the visit of Nehemiah, a Persian Jew from the court of Artaxerxes
Longimanus, were the walls of Jerusalem
rebuilt (about 445 B.C.) and the city restored to something of its earlier luster.
The city, however, was not the capital of
a sovereign state but rather the center of
a struggling province of the Persian Empire. Its earlier glory was never fully restored. With the fall of Persia, Jerusalem
was subject first to Ptolemy I of Egypt (320
B.C.) and then to the Seleucids of Syria
(198 B.C.). The tyrannies of the Syrian
despot Antiochus Epiphanes reduced much
of Jerusalem to rubble, but Judas Maccabaeus and his compatriots fought a guerrilla
war and in 164 B.C. dedicated the purified
Temple. Jerusalem was again the capital
of an independent state during the century
of Hasmonaean rule until the Roman general Pompey invaded Palestine and occupied Jerusalem in 63 B.C.

New Testament Jerusalem was subject to
Rome. Herod the Great (37-4 B.C.) had rebuilt and enlarged the Temple to make it
equal in beauty to the Hellenistic temples
which were being built throughout the
Near East. In this temple Jesus conversed
with doctors of the Jewish law when He

was a boy of twelve, and from the same
temple He later drove out money changers.
At the moment of Jesus' death, the thick
veil which divided the Holy Place from the
Most Holy Place in the Temple was torn
in two from top to bottom, a fact which the
New Testament writers interpreted to mean
that the way into God's presence is now
open to all who approach Him through the
Person of Jesus Christ (cf. Heb. 9).

East of the city is a mile-long ridge of
limestone hills known collectively as "the
Mount of Olives." The mountain dominates
the eastern horizon of Jerusalem, and in
ancient times the coming of each new moon
was announced by signals from the mount.
Jesus frequently visited the Mount of
Olives and the Garden of Gethsemane at
its western base. From the mount, Jesus
could look upon the beautiful city of Jerusalem with its ornate Herodian buildings.
Prophetically He looked into the heart of
the city and saw its hypocrisy and the ex-

160. Herodian family tomb, Jerusalem
(illustrates a "rolling stone" that would
seal a tomb)

161. The Garden Tomb

trial. Burial was in a nearby tomb; but on the first day of the week, the tomb was found to be empty and the risen Christ appeared to His disciples. Forty days later, Jesus again led His disciples to the Mount of Olives from which He made His ascent to the Father's right hand.

ternalism of its religious life. In His Olivet Discourse (Matt. 24-25), Jesus pronounced impending judgment upon the city which had rejected Him.

The Garden of Gethsemane was the site of the Saviour's agony and betrayal (Matt. 26:47-65). From there He was taken to be crucified the following day after a mock

163. Via Dolorosa

162. Chapel of the Ascension atop the Mount of Olives

Around the shoulder of the Mount of Olives, about two miles from Jerusalem, was the village of Bethany, where Jesus enjoyed the fellowship of Mary, Martha, and Lazarus. A footpath led from Bethany across the Mount of Olives to Jerusalem. It was on this path that the Palm Sunday procession to the Holy City began.

164. Bethany

166. Bethlehem

Bethlehem. About six miles south of Jerusalem, a third of the way along the road to Hebron, is the "little town of Bethlehem," noted by Micah (5:2) as "little among the thousands of Judah," yet the birthplace of King David (I Sam. 17:12, 15; 20:6, 28) and of David's greater Son (Matt. 2:1-16; Luke 2:4-15). From Bethlehem Elimelech's family (Ruth 1:1-2) went to Moab in a time of famine, and to the same city his bereaved widow, Naomi, returned with her faithful daughter-in-law, Ruth (Ruth 4:11). Nearby is the traditional tomb of the beloved Rachel, whose passing brought such grief to Jacob.

Yet the prime interest in Bethlehem will always center in the nearby fields where shepherds first heard the announcement of the Saviour's birth and in the Church of the Nativity which marks the spot where tradition affirms that Mary "brought forth her firstborn son . . . and laid him in a manger."

165. Tomb of Lazarus

167. Tomb of Rachel

THE WYCLIFFE HISTORICAL GEOGRAPHY OF BIBLE LANDS

168. Shepherds' Fields

170. Hebron

Hebron. Hebron, nineteen miles southwest of Jerusalem, is 3,040 feet above sea level, the highest town in Palestine. It was known to the biblical Patriarchs as "Kirjath-Arba" ("tetrapolis"). Abraham spent much of his time in the vicinity of Hebron and purchased his family burial plot from a Hittite chieftain named Ephron who lived nearby (Gen. 23:8; 25:9).

At the time of Joshua's invasion, Hebron was allied with Adonizedek of Jerusalem in an attempt to halt the Israelite advance (Joshua 10:1-27). After Joshua's death, Caleb succeeded in conquering the Hebron region from the Anakim (Joshua 14:6-15; cf. Num. 13:22, 28, 33).

David ruled as king of Judah from He-

bron for seven and one-half years before moving his capital to Jerusalem farther north. Absalom was born in Hebron; and when he revolted against his father David, he attempted to establish headquarters there (II Sam. 15:7-10).

169. Church of Nativity

171. Entrance to the mosque at Hebron covering the traditional tomb of Abraham and Sarah

Hebron did not occupy an important place in later Old Testament history, and it is not mentioned in the New Testament. The city seems to have had a royal pottery factory during the eighth century B.C.; numerous jar handles have been found throughout Palestine bearing the inscription "Belonging to the King: Hebron."

In July, 1964, the American Expedition to Hebron began the first of a contemplated series of eight archaeological expeditions to the Hebron region. A mud brick wall built on bedrock, discovered at Hebron, gives evidence that the site was occupied by 3000 B.C. Successive expeditions will attempt to fill in the gaps in our knowledge of Hebron's history.

Following the exile, Jews resettled in Hebron (Neh. 11:25) but in subsequent years the Idumaeans pushed northward as far as Hebron when their homeland south of the Dead Sea was taken by the Nabataean Arabs. During the Maccabean wars, Hebron was conquered by the Jews (164 B.C.). And in subsequent years, Herod the Great erected an imposing structure at the traditional site of the Cave of Machpelah (Gen. 23:19) and another at Mamre (Gen. 13:18).

The Wilderness of Judaea

From the eastern terraces of the Judaean mountains on the west to the barren shores of the Dead Sea on the east, stretches the hot and dry Wilderness of Judaea, the Jeshimon (I Sam. 23:24; 26:1) of Old Testament Scripture. Arid soil and naked rocks characterize this desolate region which has been a refuge for fugitives from society throughout history. David was forced to flee to this general region to escape the jealous wrath of Saul. And here, centuries later, the Essenes of Qumran, the followers of Bar Cocheba, and the Christian monastics of Mar Saba found a place of escape from the world.

The Judaean wilderness is never more than twelve and one-half miles wide, and the cities of Jerusalem and Hebron are within easy reach of any spot in the wilderness. Unlike most desert areas, the Judean wilderness is not isolated. On its borders are such well-known oases as Jericho and En-gedi (I Sam. 23:29). Joshua lists a chain of Israelite cities in the wilderness: Beth-arabah, Middin, Secacah, Nibshan, the City of Salt (Ir-Hammelach), and En-gedi (Joshua 15:61-62). "The City of Salt" may be an earlier name for the site now known as Qumran.[19]

En-gedi, the largest oasis on the western shore of the Dead Sea, is watered by a spring which causes narrow green belts of vegetation to spring up in the barren wasteland. The fame of the En-gedi Oasis caused the author of the Song of Solomon to exclaim, "My beloved is unto me as a cluster of henna blossoms in the vineyards of En-gedi" (1:14, RSV). Yet the region around En-gedi was anything but fruitful. David fled to its barren wastes when Saul was seeking his life; the former shepherd boy found a place of refuge in one of its numerous caves (I Sam. 24:1-6).

Although David's flight to En-gedi was a temporary expedient, and even though he left the wilderness as soon as it was safe to do so, others in Israel looked upon the Judaean wilderness as an ideal abode because of its remoteness from the corrupting influences of society. Such were the Rechabites, who determined to live a life of asceticism in an environment removed from

[19]Cf. Frank M. Cross, Jr. and J. T. Milik, *Bulletin of the American Schools of Oriental Research*, 142 (April, 1956), 5 ff.

172. Climbing up from Cave Four

the temptations of civilized life. They lived in tents and abstained from the fruits of the vineyard and crops that were sowed by man (cf. II Kings 10:15-18; Jer. 35:5-10).

The Rechabites were forerunners of the Essenes who established a communal settlement at Qumran, north of En-gedi, within sight of the Dead Sea. To the people of Qumran, the wilderness was the ideal place to live in pious preparation for the advent of the Messiah. In their *Manual of Discipline* they quote Isaiah 40:3: "Clear ye in the wilderness the way of the Lord, make plain in the desert a highway for our God."[20]

Eight miles south of Jericho, in the Ju-

[20]*Manual of Discipline,* VIII, 13-14.

daean wilderness, are the caves and ruins associated with the Dead Sea Scrolls which were discovered in 1947 and subsequent years. After the announcement of the discovery, excavations were conducted at Khirbet Qumran, the mound near the cave where the first scrolls were discovered. Excavations were conducted by G. Lankester Harding of the Jordan Department of Antiquities and Roland deVaux of the Ecole Biblique in Jerusalem.

Vestiges of occupation during Israelite times (8th or 7th century B.C.) were discovered, and it is conjectured that these may mark the site of the City of Salt (Ir-Hammelach) mentioned in Joshua 15:62. The site was abandoned and was not occu-

173. The "school" at Qumran

pied again until the second century B.C. when a sectarian Jewish community, usually identified with the Essenes, built a large community center and evidently occupied the nearby caves. The community center contained facilities for dining and for religious devotion. A scriptorium with tables and inkpots served as the place where copyists produced many of the Dead Sea Scrolls. Around the central building were smaller buildings and cisterns, some of which may have been used in ceremonial bathing, a part of the religious ritual of the members of the community. The excavators explain the cracks in the cisterns as the result of an earthquake which struck the area in 31 B.C. and caused the community center to be temporarily abandoned. About the beginning of the Christian Era, repairs were made and the Qumran community continued to observe its communal life until A.D. 68 when the Tenth Roman Legion occupied the site during the Jewish revolt against Rome. At the approach of the Roman soldiers, the Jewish community apparently fled. The library of sacred scrolls was concealed in nearby caves, doubtless with the thought that the Jews would return after the Romans had gone. The Roman garrison occupied the center, however, and used it as military headquarters. During the second Jewish-Roman war (A.D. 132-135),

Jews again occupied Qumran, but they were not related to the earlier religious settlement. At the end of the war, Qumran was again abandoned. Aside from providing shelter for an occasional Arab, it was not used again and remained an obscure mound until the discovery, by an Arab boy, of the now-famous Dead Sea Scrolls.

South of En-gedi is a rocky cliff where the Zealots who attempted to defy the armies of Rome made their last stand after the destruction (A.D. 70). The Hasmonaean ruler Jonathan had earlier erected a fortress there which he named "Masada." King Herod saw the strategic importance of Masada and strengthened its fortifications, making it a secret storehouse for supplies and a refuge for the royal household in the event of revolt.

Masada's hour of fame came during the Jewish revolt (A.D. 66-70) when it was seized by Jewish rebels against Rome and made a base for surprise attacks on Roman troops. In one daring episode, the Zealot Menahem ben Judah of Galilee took the fortress, distributed its weapons among his men, and led them to the gates of Jerusalem.

Deeds of heroism, however, were no match for the Roman legions. The initial victories of the Zealots had the advantage of surprise. When the Roman legions started pouring out of Caesarea with their

174. Qumran scriptorium where many Dead Sea Scrolls were copied

175. Qumran structures (airview)

first put to the sword, then the men killed one another. When the Romans eventually broke into the fortress, they gazed upon the corpses with amazement. Food supplies had been left as evidence that the people of Masada had died willingly, choosing death rather than slavery. Archaeological work has revealed signs of ash in the rubble at Masada, confirming the account of Josephus who mentions that the last of the Zealots completely razed the palace. The site has now been almost completely excavated under the direction of Yigael Yadin of the Hebrew University in Jerusalem. Extensive light has been thrown on Jewish life of the first century A.D.

En-gedi, which fell to the Romans along with Masada, became an important base during the second Jewish revolt (A.D. 132-135) led by Shimeon ben Cosba (Bar Cocheba). Many in Israel, including the renowned Rabbi Akiba, looked upon Bar Cocheba as the promised Messiah and deliverer of his people. Letters recently discovered in caves near En-gedi, in the Judaean desert, contain orders to the commander and people at En-gedi to provide supplies for the Jewish army. Bar Cocheba exercised control for about two and a half years, but again the might of Rome prevailed, and En-gedi suffered defeat along

heavy war machines, the Zealots had to retreat. On the ninth of Av, A.D. 70, Jerusalem fell to the Romans; and in subsequent weeks the city and its temple were completely destroyed.

After the fall of Jerusalem, a heroic Zealot leader, Eleazer Ben Yair, determined to defend Masada. When every other stronghold had fallen to Rome and it was obvious that the Zealots could not keep Masada, they chose to die by their own hands rather than fall to the enemy. By agreement the women and children were

176. Masada with outline of a Roman army camp in right foreground

with Jerusalem and the rest of Jewish Palestine.

Later Roman writers continued to speak of the date palms of En-gedi, and as late as the fifth century, Jerome spoke of En-gedi as a "large Jewish village," famous for its henna, dates, and vineyards. During Roman times En-gedi served as the agricultural, commercial, and territorial administrative center for the west coast of the Dead Sea.

The Jordan Valley

The Jordan Valley is part of a great rift in the earth produced by two parallel geological faults. North of Palestine the rift separates the Lebanon Mountains from the Anti-Liban Range. The Orontes and the Leontes rivers flow through the northern rift. South of the Jordan the rift continues and forms the Dead Sea and the Arabah (Wadi el'Araba). It can be traced in the Gulf of 'Aqaba, the Red Sea, and southwestward where it becomes the Great African Rift.

From its principal source at the foot of snowcapped Mount Hermon, which rises 9,232 feet above sea level, to its mouth at the northern tip of the Dead Sea, the Jordan flows only eighty air miles. Its tortuous, winding course, however, gives it a total length of about two hundred miles. The Jordan Valley is marked by a rapid descent. By the time it reaches the Sea of Galilee, it is 695 feet below sea level, and it continues to descend until it is 1285 feet

below sea level when it enters the Dead Sea. No spot on the earth, uncovered by water, sinks to such depths. The floor of the Dead Sea itself is 1300 feet deep.

There are four principal sources of the Jordan, the easternmost of which, issuing from a cave at the foot of Mount Hermon, marked a holy place dedicated to the Canaanite Baal and, in Roman times, to Pan, the god of pastures, flocks, and shepherds. The name of Pan continues in the Arab name, "Nahr Banias," which is still used of the six-mile stream. The ancient town along its banks bore the name of "Panias." Herod the Great built a marble temple to Augustus Caesar at Panias, and his son Philip the Tetrarch further adorned the city and named it "Caesarea" in honor of the Roman emperor. To distinguish it from Caesarea on the Mediterranean coast, it was given the fuller name "Caesarea Philippi." Jesus and His disciples journeyed in the district of Caesarea Philippi, and it was there that Peter confessed his faith in Jesus as the Messiah, the Son of the living God (Matt. 16:13-20). Caesarea Philippi marks the northern limit of the Saviour's travels in the Holy Land. The little village of Banias still marks the site of the ancient city.

Two miles west of the Nahr Banias is the Nahr Leddan, a second source of the Jordan, west-southwest of the city of Dan which marked the northern border of Israel (cf. Judges 20:1; I Sam. 3:20). The Leddan has a course of only four miles before it joins the Banias. A third source, the

177. Mount Hermon

178. Gladioli harvest in the Hule Valley

Nahr Hasbany, descending from the western foot of Mount Hermon, flows a distance of twenty-four miles before joining the other streams a short distance below their junction. The westernmost source of the Jordan, the Nahr Bareighit, is a short stream which empties into the Nahr Hasbany near its end. The junction of these four streams forms the Jordan River which flows southward into the Dead Sea.

The Jordan flows seven miles southward before it enters a triangular-shaped body of water known as Lake Hule (Waters of Merom), two hundred thirty feet above sea level. The region is one of lush vegetation with reeds, bulrushes, and papyrus growing in abundance. In ancient times hyenas, jackals, and boars roamed in the marshes of the Hule district. Since the establishment of the state of Israel, the swamps have been drained and the region has been cultivated. Northwest of Hule was the town of Abel-beth-maacah (modern Tell Abil), which was besieged by Joab during Sheba's revolt against David (II Sam. 20:1-26).

Continuing southward from Lake Hule, the Jordan flows about ten miles to the Sea of Galilee where it is 695 feet below sea level. The first two of these miles see a steady flow of water to the site of a bridge known as the "Bridge of the Daughters of Jacob" which is part of the road between

Galilee and Damascus. For the next seven miles the Jordan cuts its way through a gorge in the black basalt rock, tumbling and cascading as it goes. Then it emerges into a plain and flows through a delta into the Sea of Galilee.

Closely shut in by hills around its entire circumference, the heart-shaped Sea of Galilee is thirteen miles long and as much as seven miles broad. Around the sea were the towns in which Jesus ministered—Capernaum, Bethsaida, Chorazin—towns which prospered because of the fishing industry and the possibilities of trade across the lake. Tiberias, a Gentile city in New Testament times, built by Herod Antipas between A.D. 17 and 22, is the one town on the Sea of Galilee which is still an important community in Israel. Since it was built on the site of an old cemetery, the Jews of New Testament times considered Tiberias unclean and avoided living there.

In the course of sixty-five miles from the Sea of Galilee to the Dead Sea, the Jordan drops 590 feet, an average of nine feet to the mile. The valley of the Jordan is from three to fourteen miles wide. As it approaches the Dead Sea several levels appear. The trench in the soft alluvium on both sides of the river bank is known as "the Zor," or the "jungle of the Jordan" (Jer. 12:5, RSV). This wild region has an abundance of vegetation—dense thickets of tamarisks, oleanders, willows, poplars,

179. Sea of Galilee

180. Jordan River

vines, thorns, and thistles. Here wild beasts lurked, and life was difficult for man.

At a higher level, however, was the fertile Ghor (Aulon) with its plantations and pastureland. The Ghor is located on the sides of the hills which bound the Jordan on both the east and the west.

Although the channel of the Jordan is too deep to make irrigation practical, it has a series of tributaries below the Sea of Galilee from which water for irrigation may be more easily obtained.

From the hills of Bashan, the Yarmuk River flows westward to unite with the Jordan about five miles south of the Sea of Galilee. Eight miles farther south, the Jalud River in the valley of Jezreel flows into the Jordan from the northwest, past Bethshean. A series of lesser tributaries— the Jurm, the Yabis, the Kufrinjeh, and the Rajib—join the Jordan from the east; but its major eastern tributary is the Jabbok River (modern Wadi Zerqa), which rises near the town of Amman and has a course of over sixty miles before joining the Jordan some twenty miles north of the Dead Sea. A few miles farther south the Far'a River joins the Jordan from the west.

The Jabbok was crossed by Jacob in his flight from Laban (Gen. 32:22-32). At some spot along its northern banks he had his mysterious encounter with the Lord,

following which he continued with a limp and a blessing to meet his estranged brother Esau (Gen. 33:1-15). As he entered western Palestine, Jacob probably used the Far'a; and Joshua probably used the same route in going to Mount Ebal and Mount Gerizim where Israel heard the blessings and curses of the law after entering the land of promise (Joshua 8:30-39).

The Jordan Valley has been inhabited since very early times. Prehistoric men from the area used flint and basalt axes. In prebiblical times, elephants and rhinoceroses roamed the Jordan Valley. Skeletons of these beasts have been found near the Bridge of the Daughters of Jacob. During biblical times. important communities were located on both sides of the Jordan.

East of the Jordan, on the north side of the Wadi Yabis, is the mound known as "Tell Abu-Kharaz," an isolated hill which

181. Sheep grazing along the Jabbok

THE WYCLIFFE HISTORICAL GEOGRAPHY OF BIBLE LANDS

dominates the surrounding country. It was heavily fortified in Israelite times and has plausibly been identified with biblical Jabesh-gilead where Saul routed the Ammonites (I Sam. 11). The towns of Zaretan (Joshua 3:16) and Adam were important places at the time of Joshua's invasion of Canaan. Adam is usually identified with Tell ed-Damiyeh, east of the Jordan near the mouth of the Jabbok. Joshua also mentions Zaphon in "the valley" (Joshua 13:27), i.e., the Jordan Valley.

Succoth. This city of Gad incurred the anger of Gideon when its inhabitants failed to assist him in the pursuit of Zebah and Zalmunna (Judges 8:15-16) The site has not been positively identified, but it may be the place known as "Tell Akhsas" or the mound Tell Deir Allah, north of the Jabbok River. H. J. Franken of Leiden, in the Netherlands, has discovered the remains of a large sanctuary from the Late Bronze Age at Deir Allah, and he considers this evidence that Deir Allah should not be identified with Succoth.[21]

Bethshean and Jericho. These two most imporant cities of ancient Palestine were located in the valley west of the Jordan. Fourteen miles south of the Sea of Galilee, at the junction of the Jezreel and Jordan valleys was the fortified city of Bethshean. The name is preserved in the modern village of Beisan near the mound of Tell el-Husn, ancient Scythopolis. Excavations conducted by the University of Pennsylvania between 1921 and 1933 at Tell el-Husn have shown that the site was occupied from 3500 B.C. to the Christian Era. Between the fifteenth and the twelfth centuries B.C., Bethshean was a fortified Egyptian outpost. Among the Canaanite temples discovered at Bethshean were shrines of Ashtaroth (I Sam. 31:10) and Dagon (I Chron. 10:10). After the debacle of Mount Gilboa, the Philistines

placed Saul's armor in the temple of Ashtaroth and fastened his body to the wall of Bethshean. The city was destroyed between 1050 and 1000 B.C., at the time David was consolidating his rule over Israel, and it is possible that the destruction should be attributed to David. Bethshean subsequently became an Israelite stronghold (I Kings 4:12). In Hellenistic times it was known as "Scythopolis" and was a member of the league of cities known as the Decapolis.

Seven miles north of the Dead Sea, five miles west of the Jordan, is Jericho, "the city of palm trees" which is an oasis in the parched valley eight hundred feet below sea level. Radiocarbon dating places the earliest settlement of Jericho during the seventh and sixth millennia B.C. when it was occupied by a prepottery Neolithic people. The city of Old Testament times was situated on the mound known as "Tell es-Sultan," a mile north of the modern town of Er Raha. New Testament Jericho is on a higher elevation nearby.

182. Looking through a cut in the mound of Old Testament Jericho toward the Mount of Temptation

[21]H. J. Franken, "Excavations at Deir 'Alla, Season 1964," *Vetus Testamentum* XIV (1964), 417-22.

Jericho's strategic importance may be traced to its location near a ford of the Jordan. The ancient trade routes from the East crossed the Jordan near Jericho and then branched out in three directions. The northern route went in the direction of Bethel and Shechem; the westward road led toward Jerusalem, and the southern route went to Hebron. Jericho controlled all of these access routes to the hill country of Palestine.

The strategic position of Jericho plays an important part in the record of the Israelite conquest. By taking Jericho (Joshua 6), Joshua drove a wedge into the land of Canaan and struck terror into the hearts of its inhabitants. Canaanite Jericho was completely destroyed, and for centuries no attempt was made to rebuild the town (cf. Joshua 6:26), although the spring and the oasis located there were frequented. In the days of the Judges, Eglon of Moab temporarily occupied the oasis (Judges 3:12-13). It was not until Ahab's reign that the city proper was rebuilt (I Kings 16:34), only to be destroyed again by the Babylonians in 587/586 B.C. After the exile, Jericho was inhabited by Israelites again, and by New Testament times it had become a thriving town. Herod the Great and his successors maintained a winter palace at Jericho and augmented its natural water supply by means of an aqueduct which brought water from the Wadi Qelt.

New Testament Jericho lay to the southeast of the Old Testament city. Modern

183. Airview of Old Testament Jericho

184. Excavating New Testament Jericho

185. Herodian palace, New Testament Jericho

Jericho was founded in the time of the Crusaders and lies to the east of New Testament Jericho, and to the southeast of Old Testament Jericho. Herod's winter palace, with a facade 330 feet long, was excavated in 1950/51 by the American Schools of Oriental Research under the direction of J. L. Kelso and J. B. Pritchard.

Gilgal. The site of Israel's first encampment after crossing the Jordan (Joshua 4:19-20), Gilgal was located between Jericho and the Jordan, but its exact location is not known. In subsequent years Gilgal became an important town. Samuel included it in his judicial circuit (I Sam. 7:16), and Saul's kingship was confirmed there (I Sam. 11:14-15). David, who fled across the Jordan at the time of Absalom's revolt, was welcomed back to his own tribe at Gilgal (II Sam. 19:15, 40).

In later years, however, Gilgal gained infamy because of the idolatry practiced there. The memorial stones erected at Gilgal to commemorate the crossing of the Jordan (Joshua 4:19—5:10) became a pagan shrine which was denounced by Hosea (4:15) and Amos (4:4).

All or most of the Dead Sea south of the Lisan, a peninsula that juts out from the eastern shore of the sea opposite the village of Masada, was once a plain. Sodom, Gomorrah, and their sister cities are prob-

ably to be located in this area. Scripture mentions bitumen pits nearby (Gen. 14:10), a fact which correlates with the nature of this region as it is known today.

Extending along the southwestern shore of the Dead Sea for more than five miles is a one-hundred-foot stratum of crystalline salt, surmounted by layers of clay and limestone cap rock. The Arabs call this formation "Jebel Usdum," "Mount Sodom."

At its southern end, the Dead Sea gives way to an area of salt marshes, known as "es-Sebkha," which are filled with water during times of flood. When the water level returns to normal, the terrain again becomes marshy. Es-Sebkha extends south about eight miles before it is terminated by

186. Statuary niches in facade of Herod's palace at Jericho

187. The Dead Sea

188. Sodom

cliffs which mark the beginning of Wadi el 'Araba (biblical Arabah), a continuation of the rift valley which produced the Jordan Valley and the Dead Sea depressions farther north. Veering slightly southwest, the 'Araba continues about one hundred miles to the head of the Gulf of 'Aqaba.

The 'Araba is largely desert, with a few oases to make possible the Bedouin life still observable. In Nabataean times irrigation projects made some agriculture possible. Copper and iron, mined from the hills of the 'Araba (cf. Deut. 8:9), made the region particularly valuable. Edom vied with Ju-

dah for control of the region in Old Testament times. After the third century B.C. it was occupied by Nabataean Arabs.

The Negeb

South of the Judaean Shephelah and hill country is an area of arid terrain that appears on modern maps as an inverted triangle. It is bounded on the east by the extension of the Jordan Valley known as the "Wadi el 'Araba," and on the west by the Sinai Peninsula. The apex of the triangle is at the head of the Gulf of 'Aqaba where the Israeli city of Eilat is located. The northern boundary of the Negeb is not clearly defined. It follows an irregular line extending eastward from the coastal plain north of Beersheba to the western shore of the Dead Sea.

Although geologists state that heavy rains fell in the Negeb when Europe was experiencing the Ice Age, the area is arid today; and it is necessary to pipe water from a distance to make the land productive. One of the great challenges faced by the state of Israel is to irrigate the Negeb and encourage pioneers to farm this difficult terrain.

The word *Negeb* (or *Negev* in Hebrew) means "dry," and it is usually used in the Bible to describe the arid terrain south of Judah where the biblical Patriarchs lived. Abraham settled for a time in the northern Negeb, at Beersheba (Gen. 13:1). As semi-nomads, the Patriarchs moved from place to place with their flocks and herds, seeking adequate supplies of water and pasturage.

By the time of the exodus, the Negeb was inhabited by seminomadic Amalekites who were inveterate foes of the Israelites. Hebrew spies passed through the Negeb as they surveyed the promised land (Num. 13:17). They reported that the people were so formidable that Israel could not hope to enter the land of promise. Although a few, notably Caleb and Joshua, were willing to trust God and move right in to Canaan, the majority prevailed; and, after a generation in the wilderness, Joshua's army crossed the Jordan opposite Jericho and invaded Canaan from the east. The Amalekites who had frightened the spies (Num. 13:29) continued to be bitter foes of Israel. In the days of Saul, the Israelite army defeated the Amalekites and captured Agag their king. Samuel personally slew Agag and rebuked Saul for sparing him (I Sam. 15).

Although assigned to the tribes of Simeon (Joshua 19:1-9) and Judah (Joshua 15:20-31), the Negeb was marginal territory which was not easily controlled. During the time of his flight from Saul, David served as a vassal of the Philistines at Ziklag, northwest of Beersheba (I Sam. 27:6). At that time he "invaded the Geshurites, and the Gezrites, and the Amalekites: for those nations were of old the inhabitants of the land, as thou goest to Shur, even unto the land of Egypt" (I Sam. 27:8).

The road from the Judaean highlands to Egypt, passing through Beersheba, is known as "the Way to Shur." When Hagar, Sarah's Egyptian handmaid, fled from her mistress, she took the road to Shur (Gen. 16:7), doubtless thinking she should head in the direction of her homeland. After leaving the Negeb, the traveler could continue westward to the borders of Egypt or turn southwestward into the Sinai Peninsula. The word *Shur*, meaning "wall," is evidently named for the fortifications built by the Egyptians across the isthmus of Suez to protect Egypt from intrusion of the Asians. Another important road in the Negeb went southeastward toward Eziongeber and then into the Arabian Peninsula.

Communities were settled and roads were built in those places in the Negeb where there was water. Wells were highly prized possessions, and places such as Beersheba, where water was plentiful, invariably became major settlements. Since 1952 Nelson Glueck has identified hundreds of sites in the Negeb that once were occupied. Some of these date back to Paleolithic times, and many are from the seventh to the fifth millennium B.C., the period known as the Neolithic age. There were extensive settlements there during the twenty-first to the nineteenth centuries B.C. When Abraham journeyed through the Negeb to and from Egypt, he found numerous cities and pastures which supplied the needs of his servants and animals.

The book of Joshua mentions twenty-nine cities in the Negeb (Joshua 15:21-32). Most of their sites are not known today. The best known is Beersheba which often marked the southern boundary of Israel (cf. Judges 20:1) and continues today to serve as the metropolis and market town of the northern Negeb. Archaeological work continues at Arad, east of Beersheba. Southeast of Beersheba is Khirbet Ar'areh, one of three biblical towns which bore the name "Aroer."

The Nabataeans, who founded a kingdom in southern Transjordan with its capital at

189. Abraham's Well, Beersheba

190. Beersheba

Petra, settled in the Negeb; and by carefully conserving its meager water supply, they brought it to a high point of productivity. The Nabataeans were extensive traders, and they used the overland route from 'Aqaba to Gaza, through the Negeb, to reach the Mediterranean. Among the towns which date to Nabataean times are Mampsis (Mamshit), Avdat (Abde), Shivta (Subeita), Nessana (Uja-el-Hafir), Rehovot, and Halutza.

The Nabataeans were succeeded by the Romans and the Byzantines in the rule of the Negeb, but the area continued to prosper. Each city had its water reservoirs and wells, some of which were adjacent to private homes. Water from wells, rain, and torrential flooding was collected in carefully planned systems of dams and reservoirs. The church father Jerome, who studied in Palestine during the early part of the fifth century A.D., speaks of the "vines of Halutza" as particularly fruitful. This good productivity probably resulted from one of the water systems of that time.

Excavations at Mampsis have yielded water cisterns and the remains of the city wall and of churches. Avdat, in the central Negeb, was settled by the Nabataeans during the third century B.C. At first it was merely a road station, but by the first century B.C. a Nabataean temple occupied a site on the north end of the hill. A potter's house, discovered nearby, yielded evidence of the high standards of Nabataean artisans. A layer of ash showed that the Romans destroyed the Nabataean city, after which Avdat was unoccupied for a century and a half. When the Romans rebuilt the city, they erected temples to Zeus and Aphrodite, waterworks, and a bathhouse. During the Byzantine period the town reached the peak of its development. Among its buildings were two churches, a monastery, a citadel, and a market. Farms dotted the neighborhood. The hundreds of caves in the area were used for processing and storing agricultural produce.

Shivta has left remains of a complete city, with streets, reservoirs, and three beautiful churches. At Nessana archaeologists have studied the remains of a fort, a town wall, and two churches. The site also yielded legal, administrative, and religious documents written on papyri during Greek, Roman, and Arabic times.

During the Arabic period the towns of the Negeb gradually sank into insignificance. There was no policy of destruction, but the Arabs had no need of the difficult roads through the Negeb, and the centers of their culture focused upon Baghdad, Damascus, and Cairo. Not until recent times when necessity has forced Israel to seek more farmland and a sea route to Africa and the East has a fresh attempt been made to rebuild the Negeb, causing the desert to blossom as the rose.

Transjordan

The country east of the Jordan, extending about one hundred fifty miles from the base of Mount Hermon to the southern edge of the Dead Sea, is an elevated plateau which becomes higher as it moves southward. Its width, from the Jordan Valley to the desert, ranges from thirty to eighty miles, and it has an average elevation of about two thousand feet above sea level. The climate is quite temperate, and it is not surprising that Reuben, Gad, and the half tribe of Manasseh were content to settle there instead of seeking territory west of the Jordan.

There are no natural boundaries between the Transjordan country and the Arabian Desert to the east. Nomadic Ishmaelites and Midianites who lived in the desert invaded periodically the more fertile areas adjacent to their normal habitat. During the time of the Judges, the Midianites came up "like grasshoppers" (Judges 6:5) and seized the produce of the Israelites in Canaan. The population of Transjordan was largely migratory, and as a result its cities were insecure.

The region of Transjordan, or Abarim, "the region beyond," is divided by the deep gorges of the Yarmuk, the Jabbok, and the Arnon rivers and their tributaries. South of the Zered was the land of Edom.

Hauran-Bashan. The territory from Mount Hermon southward to the Yarmuk, which enters the Jordan south of the Sea of Galilee, is the fertile Hauran, the southern part of which was known as Bashan in Old Testament times. The Hauran has rich volcanic soil over a limestone base. This plain was known for its well-fed bulls (cf. Ps. 22:12; Amos 4:1; Ezek. 39:18) and boasted some of the best farmland in western Asia.

The center of the Hauran is a treeless plain, fifty miles long by twenty wide. To the west of this plain was the Jaulan, which was well wooded in ancient times. To the east are extinct volcanoes, and to the southeast were Jebel Hauran and Jebel Druze with thick forests comparable to those of Lebanon (Nahum 1:4; Zech. 11:1-2). Beyond these is the desert, which extends eastward to the Euphrates. Somewhere in this region was the land of Tob to which Jephthah fled when his brothers rejected him. There Jephthah led a band of renegades, robbing caravans until he was called home to deliver Israel from her Ammonite oppressors (Judges 11:3).

Bashan was a constant battleground between Israel and Syria. The Yarmuk River posed no natural obstacle to opposing armies, which fought on its banks and crossed it at will. The name of "Argob" is applied to Og's kingdom (Deut. 3:4, 13-14) which included not only territory in Bashan but extended south to the Jabbok River. Og was a confederate of the Amorite ruler Sihon in a joint attempt to halt Joshua's advance through eastern Palestine. The Israelite victory over Sihon at Heshbon and over Og at Edrei (modern Der'aa), on the upper reaches of the Yarmuk, struck terror in the hearts of the Canaanites of western Palestine who feared the Israelite advance into their country. Ashtaroth (Deut. 1:4) and Golan (Deut. 4:43) were important towns in Bashan, but scholars have not agreed on their sites. Old Testament Bashan was known as "Batanaea" in New Testament times, and the territory in the Jordan Valley between Mount Hermon and the Yarmuk was named "Gaulanitis."

Gilead. Eighteen miles south of the Yarmuk, the plains of Bashan end at the mountains of Gilead, through which the Jabbok River passes. Gilead is an oval-shaped land, thirty-five miles from north to south and twenty-five from east to west. Gad and half the tribe of Manasseh settled in Gilead

(Num. 32:40; Deut. 4:43) which was famed for its forests (Jer. 22:6) that produced a medicinal balm (Jer. 8:22; 46:11). Pomegranates, apricots, and olives were also plentiful, and Gilead boasted excellent pastureland (Num. 32:1).

Both Ammon to the east and Syria to the north attempted to control Gilead. During the time of the Judges, Jephthah, a Gileadite, succeeded in driving out the Ammonite oppressors (Judges 11:29-33). They were back, however, by the time of Saul, who first came to the attention of Israel as a mighty warrior when he repulsed the Ammonites at Jabesh-gilead (I Sam. 11:1-15) in the Jordan Valley.

When conventional defenses failed, the mountains of Gilead provided a sanctuary for refugees from west of the Jordan. After the debacle at Mount Gilboa, Saul's son Ishbosheth fled to Mahanaim in Gilead (II Sam. 2:8-9). David also crossed the Jordan into Gilead when he was forced to flee from his son Absalom (II Sam. 17:21-22). In the "wood of Ephraim," probably near Mahanaim, Absalom's head was caught in the branches of a tree, and he was killed (II Sam. 18:6-13). When the kingdom was divided, Gilead became a part of the Northern Kingdom, Israel.

Ammon. Southeast of Gilead, bordering the desert, was the land of Ammon, home

192. Circular forum, Jerash

of the Ammonites, a people frequently at war with Israel. Their chief town was Rabbah, or Rabbath-Ammon (modern Amman), twenty-two miles east of the Jordan. David's general, Joab, besieged and finally took Rabbath-Ammon for Israel (II Sam. 12:26-31), but the Ammonites were able to regain their independence after Solomon's death. It was during the siege of Rabbath-Ammon that Uriah the Hittite was sent into the center of the battle so that his death would make it possible for David to marry his wife, Bath-sheba. David's adultery and murder evoked stern condemnation from Nathan, and David's latter years were marked by tragedy and heartache. Ptolemy Philadelphus (285-246 B.C.) rebuilt Rabbath-Ammon and renamed it "Philadelphia." It became an important trading center and a member of the Decapolis.

The term "Decapolis" ("ten cities") refers to a league of Greek cities, all of which except Bethshean (Scythopolis) were located east of the Jordan, an area which had been occupied by Greek colonists as early as 200 B.C. In the Maccabean struggle they came under Jewish rule, but Pompey "liberated" three of the cities—Hippos, Scythopolis, and Pella. He then annexed them to the province of Syria with guarantees of municipal freedom. About the beginning of

191. Roman theater, Amman

the Christian Era, these Greek cities formed a league for mutual defense. Pliny states that the original members included Scythopolis, Pella, Dion, Gerasa, Philadelphia, Gadara, Raphana, Kanatha, Hippos, and Damascus. In the second century A.D., Ptolemy listed eighteen towns south of Damascus in the Decapolis. Philadelphia was the old Rabbath-Ammon, chief city of the Ammonites of Old Testament times. Pella was probably founded by Greeks and named for Pella in Macedonia, the birthplace of Alexander the Great. The Jewish Christians fled to Pella before the destruction of Jerusalem (A.D. 70).

The Decapolis city of Gerasa, now known as Jerash, was located about thirty-five miles southeast of the Sea of Galilee, twenty-six miles north of Amman, two thousand feet high on the Transjordan Plateau. It lies in the valley of the Barada River (Greek Chrysorrhoas), a tributary to the

194. Temple of Zeus, Jerash

Jabbok. During the early Iron Age a simple Ammonite village occupied the site of Gerasa. From the third century B.C., it was occupied successively by the Egyptian Ptolemies, the Syrian Seleucids, the Jewish Maccabeans and, after 63 B.C., by the Romans. Gerasa was in reality a city-state with authority over territory around it.

In Roman times Gerasa became an important center of trade. It reached its zenith in the second century A.D. A triumphal arch commemorating the visit of Emperor Hadrian (A.D. 129) still stands. Toward the end of the second century a magnificent temple to Artemis was built in the heart of the city. By the fourth century, Gerasa was a Christian center, and pagan temples were transformed into churches. After the Muslim conquest (635) Gerasa declined in importance. In 726 a disastrous earthquake ended the history of Gerasa.

The very abandonment of the site has made it possible for archaeologists to work freely among its ruins, with the result that Gerasa is now regarded as one of the most magnificent of ancient cities. Many of the columns of its first century forum have remained in place through the ages. Beside

193. Main street, Jerash

195. South theater, looking toward the
stage, Jerash

the Temple of Zeus are the remains of a
theater seating three thousand persons. Remains of eleven churches, dating from the
fourth to the sixth centuries, have been
identified at Gerasa.

In New Testament times the region between the Jabbok and the Arnon, roughly
corresponding to Old Testament Gilead,
was known as Peraea, the land "beyond
Jordan." In the time of Christ, Peraea was
inhabited by Jews and ranked with Galilee
and Judaea as a Jewish province. In order
to avoid contact with the despised Samaritans, the people of Galilee crossed the Jordan and traveled southward through Peraea, then recrossed again into Judaea to
observe the religious festivals at Jerusalem
(cf. Christ's last journey to Jerusalem, Mark
10:1).

Moab. The region south of Gilead and
east of the Dead Sea was the land of Moab.
The terrain is largely bare and treeless,
bleak in winter but quite pleasant in summer. The land was good for grazing, and
the king of Moab was himself a sheep
breeder (II Kings 3:4). Moab proper was
the plateau east of the Dead Sea between
the Arnon, which enters the Dead Sea
about halfway down its east bank, and the
Zered, the southernmost stream entering
the Dead Sea. In periods of political

strength Moab occupied territory well to
the north of the Arnon. Prior to the exodus,
the lands north of the Arnon as far as the
Jabbok were wrested from the Moabites by
Sihon, king of the Amorites (Num. 21:21-
31). After Sihon's defeat, the territory east
of the Dead Sea and north of the Arnon
became the possession of the tribe of Reuben. The Israelites did not claim territory
south of the Arnon, although Moab and
Edom were subject to Israel during periods
of Israel's political strength.

The Moabite city of Dibon was captured
by the Israelites (Num. 21:26, 30) and
occupied for a time by the tribe of Gad
(Num. 32:34). At the time of the division
of the land of Canaan among the tribes,
Dibon was a part of the territory assigned
to the Reubenites (Joshua 13:15-17). The

196. The Moabite Stone

THE WYCLIFFE HISTORICAL GEOGRAPHY OF BIBLE LANDS

Moabite Stone, a black basalt stele containing thirty-four lines of preexilic Hebrew script, tells how the Moabites reconquered Dibon from Israel. The Moabite Stone was discovered in 1868 by a German missionary, F. Klein, at Dhiban, the Arabic form of the biblical name. Excavations at Dhiban have revealed ruins from Nabataean times. The Moabite remains are buried under these ruins.

Edom. South of the Zered (Num. 21:12), also called the "Brook of Willows" (Isa. 15:7), was the land of Edom with dark-red sandstone cliffs rising 5600 feet above sea level. The barren terrain of Edom was not conducive to agriculture or cattle-raising, but its hills yielded copper and its geographical position astride the King's Highway (Num. 20:17; 21:22) made it a center of commercial activity on the road from Damascus to southern Arabia and Africa.

The King's Highway is the most important route from north to south through Transjordan, going from Damascus to the Gulf of 'Aqaba by way of Rabbath-Ammon (modern Amman), Heshbon, and Dibon (modern Dhiban), and past Petra. Its entire length can be traced by the ruins of cities, some of which date back to the fourth millennium B.C. Chedorlaomer and his confederates used the road in their attack on Sodom and her allies during the time of Abraham (Gen. 14). At the time of the exodus the Israelites asked permission to use the King's Highway, but the Edomites and Sihon of Heshbon refused access through their land (Num. 20:17-21; 21:21-23). As a result, Israel had to travel around Edom, taking a more difficult route. The Emperor Trajan made the King's Highway a paved Roman road in the second century A.D. The road is now hard-topped, and it continues to be the principal north-south road in Jordan.

In the heart of the Mount Seir region, about halfway between the southern border of the Dead Sea and the Gulf of 'Aqaba, is

197. The King's Highway and the mountains of Gilead

the rock city of Petra, identified by many scholars with Sela (II Kings 14:7; II Chron. 25:11-12; Isa. 16:1; 42:11; Jer. 49:16; Obadiah 3).

Petra, in the western part of the Old Testament land of Edom, is reached by traveling up the Wadi Musa, a name reminiscent of the tradition that Moses passed through this valley during the exodus. Jebel Harun (Mount Hor), near Petra, may be the Mount Hor where Aaron died and was buried (Num. 20:22-29; 33:37-41). The Wadi Musa passes through a narrow gorge which opens into a plain about one thousand yards wide surrounded by massive cliffs of red and variegated limestone. Hewn from the rock are structures which impress the modern visitor with the artistic ability and ingenuity of the ancient Nabataeans.

The description of the Edomites building their nests like eagles in the clefts of the rocks (Obadiah 3-4) is in perfect accord with the geography of the region. Petra is in an irregular valley of trapezoidal shape, surrounded on all sides by lofty hills, with only a few narrow gorges leading into the area. Edomite remains have been found on top of the Umm el-Bayyarah, a towering mountain inside the Petra area, whose summit is a plateau that is difficult to reach.

Sometime around 300 B.C., Nabataean Arabs drove the Edomites to the west and occupied Petra. By 100 B.C., Petra was the capital of a powerful Nabataean kingdom and the center of a large commercial empire. In 87 B.C. the Nabataeans conquered Damascus. Their territory reached from Gaza on the Mediterranean to central Arabia. Their wealth came from the caravans passing through Petra en route from southern Arabia to Damascus and other markets in the North. Under the Nabataeans, Petra became a beautiful city with temples, houses, tombs, and a theater cut out of the solid rock. More than a thousand ancient structures, mostly those cut from the rocks, survive to this day. The rocks are of varying colors—red, brown, purple,

and yellow—adding to the picturesqueness of the city's remains.

In A.D. 105 the Romans conquered Petra and incorporated it into the province of Arabia Petraea. With the decline in use of the caravan routes, the city lost its significance. It fell into ruins after the Muslim conquests of the seventh century and was forgotten in the West until 1812 when J. L. Burckhardt, an explorer, rediscovered Petra.

The Israelites did not lay claim to Edom when they divided Canaan among the tribes, but both David and Solomon conquered Edom and made it a vassal to Israel (II Sam. 8:13-14; I Kings 9:26-28). The conquest of Edom made it possible for Solomon to maintain a port at Ezion-geber, on the Gulf of 'Aqaba at the southern end

198. Tombs carved from the mountainside at Petra

THE WYCLIFFE HISTORICAL GEOGRAPHY OF BIBLE LANDS

of the 'Araba. The Edomites rejoiced when Jerusalem fell to the Babylonians (Ps. 137:7), and some Edomites moved into southern Judaea, settling in the region of Hebron. Between the fifth and the third centuries B.C., Edom proper, west of the 'Araba, fell into the hands of the Nabataean Arabs, and the Edomites were pressed into the area of southern Palestine which came to be called Idumaea. The Idumaeans were subdued by John Hyrcanus (c. 126 B.C.), and they were forcibly incorporated into the Jewish state. Antipater, a native of Idumaea, is known as the father of Herod the Great, king of the Jews between 40 and 4 B.C.

199. The great high place, or worship center, Petra

Teman, in northern Edom, dominated a well-watered area which was thickly populated in ancient times. It was the meeting place of important trade routes. Temanites were famous for their wisdom (Jer. 49:7). One of Job's friends, Eliphaz the Temanite, may have come from Teman (Job 2:11).

About thirty miles north of Petra is the village of El Buseira, identified with ancient Bozrah, an important Edomite city (Gen. 36:33; I Chron. 1:44; Isa. 34:6). Amos predicted the destruction of Bozrah's palaces because of the sins of the Edomites (Amos 1:11-12).

Palestine, now comprising the Jewish state of Israel and the sector of Arab Jordan west of the Jordan River, continues to be a focal point of international concern. East and West still meet on soil over which Egyptian, Assyrian, Babylonian, Persian, Macedonian, and Roman marched in quest of power. Sacred to Jew, Christian, and Muslim, the faithful of the world's three monotheistic religions still regard Palestine as the Holy Land. They look upon its hills and valleys with sacred affection and consider it their spiritual home.

Bibliography

ABRAMSKY, SAMUEL. *Ancient Towns in Israel.* Jerusalem: Youth & Hechalutz Department of the World Zionist Organization, 1963.

ALBRIGHT, WILLIAM FOXWELL. *The Archaeology of Palestine.* London: Penguin Books, 1960.

BALY, DENIS. *Geographical Companion to the Bible.* New York: McGraw-Hill Book Co., 1963.

———. *The Geography of the Bible.* New York: Harper & Brothers, 1957.

———. *Palestine and the Bible.* London: Lutterworth Press, 1960.

BLISS, FREDERICK JONES. *A Mound of Many Cities.* London: A. P. Watt & Son, 1894.

DALMAN, GUSTAF. *Sacred Sites and Ways.* Translated by Paul P. Levertoff. New York: Macmillan Co., 1935.

GLUECK, NELSON. *The Other Side of the Jordan.* New Haven: American Schools of Oriental Research, 1940.

———. *Rivers in the Desert.* New York: Farrar, Straus & Cudahy, 1959.

———. *The River Jordan.* Philadelphia: Westminster Press, 1946.

HARDING, G. LANKESTER. *The Antiquities of Jordan.* London: Lutterworth Press, 1959.

JACK, J. W. *Samaria in Ahab's Time.* Edinburgh: T. & T. Clark, 1929.

JOIN-LAMBERT, MICHEL. *Jerusalem.* New York: G. P. Putnam's Sons, 1958.

KENYON, KATHLEEN. *Archaeology in the Holy Land*. London: Ernest Benn, Ltd., 1960.

KITCHEN, J. HOWARD. *Holy Fields*. Grand Rapids: Wm. B. Eerdmans Publishing Co., 1955.

KYLE, MELVIN GROVE. *Excavating Kirjath-Sepher's Ten Cities*. Grand Rapids: Wm. B. Eerdmans Publishing Co., 1934.

MACALISTER, R. A. S. *A Century of Excavation in Palestine*. London: Religious Tract Society, n.d.

MACGREGOR, M. A. *The Rob Roy on the Jordan*. New York: Harper & Brothers, 1870.

MONTGOMERY, JAMES A. *Arabia and the Bible*. Philadelphia: University of Pennsylvania Press, 1934.

———. *The Samaritans*. Philadelphia: John C. Winston Co., 1907.

MORRIS, YAAKOV. *Masters of the Desert*. New York: G. P. Putnam's Sons, 1961.

MOSCATI, SABATINO. *Ancient Semitic Civilizations*. London: Elek Books, 1957.

Palestine and Transjordan. London: Naval Intelligence Division, 1943.

PORTER, J. L. *The Giant Cities of Bashan*. New York: T. Nelson & Sons, 1886.

PRITCHARD, JAMES B. *Gibeon: Where the Sun Stood Still*. Princeton: Princeton University Press, 1962.

ROBINSON, GEORGE LIVINGSTON. *The Sarcophagus of an Ancient Civilization*. New York: Macmillan Co., 1930.

SIMONS, J. *The Geographical and Topographical Texts of the Old Testament*. Leiden: E. J. Brill, 1959.

———. *Jerusalem in the Old Testament*. Leiden: E. J. Brill, 1952.

SMITH, GEORGE ADAM. *The Historical Geography of the Holy Land*. London: Hodder & Stoughton, 1910.

STAPFER, EDMOND. *Palestine in the Time of Christ*. New York: A. C. Armstrong & Son, 1885.

VAN ZYL, A. H. *The Moabites*. Leiden: E. J. Brill, 1960.

Western Arabia and the Red Sea. London: Naval Intelligence Division, 1946.

WOOLLEY, C. LEONARD, and LAWRENCE, T. E. *The Wilderness of Zin*. London: Jonathan Cape, 1936.

200. Cedars of Lebanon

Phoenicia

PHOENICIA HAS A SPECIAL APPEAL to some Bible students because of her role in furnishing Solomon with cedars and other materials for his magnificent temple and palace. It is significant to others as a source of Baal worship, which flooded the kingdom of Israel in the days when Jezebel ruled as Ahab's queen. It serves others as a good example of the fulfillment of God's prophetic judgment on a pagan society. Though small, Phoenicia played an important part in the biblical narrative—much greater than any or all of these three functions suggest. It also played a significant role in the affairs of the ancient world in general.

Phoenicia, along with Palestine, is commonly classified by geographers as a part of Syria. However, in many periods of history it has been politically separated from Palestine and Syria. For purposes of organization and simplification of treatment, Phoenicia, Palestine, and Syria are given separate consideration in this volume.

Geographical Features

During most of her history, Phoenicia occupied a strip of the Syrian coastal plain roughly compassed by the present north and south boundaries of Lebanon. But at her height she extended her control south to Mount Carmel and north to Arvad —a distance of some 200 miles. Nowhere is this coastal plain—opposite the Lebanon Mountains—more than four miles wide, and it averages little over a mile. It is known that the Phoenicians controlled part of the Lebanon Range because they possessed substantial timber resources in the cedar forests. How far inland their boundaries extended is not known; certainly they were largely shut up to the coastal plain. Ancient Phoenicia probably never exceeded in area more than half of modern Lebanon and therefore would have approximated the size of the state of Delaware or the country of Luxembourg.

The Coastal Plain. It is somewhat misleading to refer to a Phoenician "coastal plain" because it is far from being one continuous stretch of plain. Rather, it is a series of pockets of plains surrounding the lower basins of rivers or rivulets, their existence being made possible by the mountains' slight withdrawal to the east. These plains came to be known for the principal cities located in them. For instance, on the south lay the Plain of Accho (modern Acre), then the Plain of Tyre, followed by the Plain of Sidon (or Zidon) and the Plain of Beirut, and so on up the coast. None of these plains was very extensive. Sidon's was about ten miles in length, Tyre's about fifteen; neither was more than about two miles in width.

Rivers. Fortunately for the inhabitants, the coastal plain was extremely fertile and well watered. Average annual rainfall at

Beirut is about thirty-eight inches. The rivers that cross the plain on their way to the sea are no more than mountain torrents. Fall rains and melting snows of spring render them unfordable near their mouths, and no boat can survive in them. But the rivers did bring down new deposits of rich soil and plenty of water for irrigation. Most important of the rivers of Lebanon are the Nahr el Litani (ancient Leontes), which enters the sea about five miles south of Sidon; and Nahr el Kelb (Dog River, ancient Lycus), which flows into the Mediterranean about seven miles north of Beirut.

Barriers to communication. Not only did these mountain streams prove to be a hindrance to communication, at least at certain seasons of the year, but rocky spurs posed more effective barriers. In fact, during the centuries before man learned to modify the configuration of the land, it was difficult—in some places impossible—to follow the coast by land. At Nahr el Kelb, for instance, the mountains wash their feet in the ocean, forming a virtually impassable promontory. Although the natives were thus inconvenienced, they had a strategic position for intercepting invaders. And conquerors made it a practice of carving inscriptions on the cliffs at the Dog River Pass after signal victories. A total of twelve inscriptions may be seen there—ranging in date from the time of the Egyptian, Assyrian, and Babylonian empires to the 1946 Lebanese inscription commemorating the evacuation of all foreign troops from the country. The Romans were the first to overcome the dangers of the precarious path of ancient times at Nahr el Kelb by building a road along the coast. The new Lebanese highway completed in 1960, made possible by the blasting away of cliffs there, leaves the visitor entirely unappreciative of the difficulty of moving through this area when Phoenicians ruled the coast.

201. The Dog River, Dog River Pass and Lebanon Mountains

Unpromising shoreline. Since the Phoenicians were the finest sailors of antiquity, it is surprising that they had hardly a natural harbor to use as a maritime base. The coast is one of the straightest on the map, without a single deep estuary or gulf. The man-made harbors which played so important a part in antiquity are nearly all silted up. Only Beirut offers safe anchorage for large modern vessels.

Phoenician cities. Silting and the activities of conquerors, such as Alexander the Great, have also joined to the mainland islands on which Sidon and Tyre were originally built. Phoenicians preferred such sites because they were convenient for shipping and easily defensible against attack. Other important cities of ancient Phoenicia included Accho (modern Acre, Roman Ptolemais), Berytus (Biruta in Egyptian, Biruna in Amarna Tablets, now Beirut), Gebal (Greek Byblos, modern Jubayl), Tripoli, and Arvad.

The Lebanon Mountains. To the east of the coastal plain lay the virtually impassable Lebanon Mountains. If the Phoenicians wanted to penetrate the interior, they usually had to wait until summer, then make their way along the beds of dried-up mountain streams. There were two places, however, which gave easy access to the interior: at Accho in the south along the Nahr al Muqatta (biblical Kishon) and at Tripoli in the north along the Nahr al Kabir. Understandably these became important trade routes of antiquity. Even today, with the aid of modern engineering, there are few roads that cross the Lebanons.

The Lebanon Mountains are part of the western ranges of Syria, which consist of a number of separate groups divided by river valleys. The northernmost are the Amanus Mountains (modern Alma Dag), which begin in the Anti-Taurus and extend south to the Orontes River. The second are the Nusairiyah Mountains, extending from the Orontes to Nahr al Kabir. Next come the

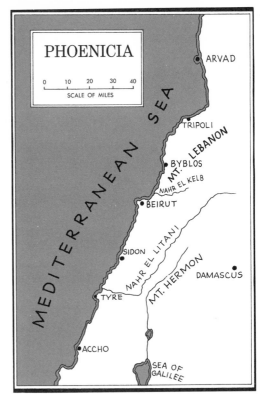

Lebanons proper, bounded by the Nahr al Kabir (near modern Tripoli) and the Nahr el Litani (near Tyre), a distance of 105 miles. South of the Litani rise the mountains of Galilee.

The Lebanons are the highest, steepest, and largest of the western Syrian ranges. As already indicated, they are over 100 miles in length. Their width varies from about 35 miles in the north to 6 on the south. They have many peaks as high as 7,000 to 8,000 feet, and in the north a few peaks 10,000 feet or more. The highest of these is just over 10,000 feet. Geologically, the Lebanons are composed of upper and lower strata of limestone, with an intermediate layer of sandstone.

The name "Lebanon" is derived from a Semitic word meaning "to be white." This whiteness refers to the snow-capped peaks of these mountains, which retain their blanket of snow for several months of the year. Melting snows, augmented by spring rains, send hundreds of rivulets, some of considerable size, tumbling down the Lebanons toward the Mediterranean. Some of these rivers continue to flow throughout the year, and many of them have cut substantial gorges in the mountain chain.

While the western side of the Lebanons is well watered and descends in a series of ledges to the Mediterranean, the eastern side is without substantial water supply and its steep slopes rise almost vertically from El Beqa', or the valley, between the Lebanon and anti-Liban Mountains.

Cedars of Lebanon. The Phoenicians, confined to a narrow plain by such formidable mountains, had to trade or die. They traded, becoming the finest mariners of antiquity. They were aided in their conquest of the sea by having some of the finest timber of the Near East at hand. The timber was not only of value to them for shipbuilding but was much sought after by neighboring monarchs for shipbuilding and construction of important buildings.

Egyptians, Assyrians, Hebrews, and others desired this valuable wood. Darius I, from far away Persia, brought cedars of Lebanon for his winter palace at Susa (biblical Shushan). Bible readers are naturally most familiar with the Hebrews' use of cedar during the days of their greatest kings—a use made possible by David's and Solomon's alliances with Tyrian kings. David built a palace of cedar in Jerusalem after he captured the city from the Jebusites (II Sam. 5:11; 7:2). Solomon built a palace largely of cedar, which must have been very beautiful indeed (for a description see I Kings 7). It is interesting to note in passing that it was called "the house of the forest of Lebanon." Best known of Hebrew structures built largely of cedar was Solomon's Temple, which was at least faced on the interior entirely with cedar (I Kings 6:18). In the days of Solomon or soon after, cedar was extensively used in construction at Megiddo—one of the cities Solo-

mon rebuilt and fortified. In the second temple, Zerubbabel employed cedars of Lebanon (Ezra 3:7).

Best known of the remaining cedars is the stand near Besharreh, about 100 miles northeast of Beirut. This grove of 400 trees is the most beautiful, the most ancient, and the most accessible to the modern tourist. It is located at an altitude of 6,300 feet. Another grove of about 400 trees may be seen near Barook, southeast of Beirut, at an altitude of about 6,000 feet. The wind has twisted and stunted these. A third group of cedars is located near Hadet at 5,000 feet altitude, just a few miles west of the Besharreh stand. The Hadet group is more numerous than those of Besharreh but not so beautiful. Cedars of Lebanon (*Cedrus Libani*) are also found on the Taurus and Amanus Mountains in Turkey.

Cedars of Lebanon may live to be 1500 years old, and about a dozen of those at Besharreh are over 1000 years old. The youngest at Besharreh are said to be 200 years old. These cedars can reach a height of over 100 feet and a girth at the base of 40 to 45 feet. They may have a branch circumference of 200 or 300 feet. Their trunks are unusually straight; their branches are horizontal and shaped like fans. Cedarwood is hard, smooth, and reddish, and finds its chief protection in its bitter taste which repels worms.

The cedar forests of ancient Phoenicia must have been extensive indeed because extremely slow growth would have prevented substantial replacement of depleted stands of timber. In recent years reforestation efforts have resulted in the planting of cedar seeds all over the Lebanon Mountains. A grove of tiny trees may be seen near the Besharreh group. But they are only a few inches high, illustrating the slow growth of these majestic trees.

Cedar was not the only timber grown in ancient Phoenicia. Aleppo pine and cypress are still widely grown on the slopes of the Lebanons.

Historical Developments

Beginnings

The stream of Phoenician history, flowing so close to the stream of Hebrew development, could hardly avoid overflowing its banks on occasion and spilling over on the Hebrews. This contact is intimated in numerous biblical passages. The town name of Sidon appears as early as the Table of Nations in Genesis 10, and Tyre figures in the biblical narrative as late as the end of Paul's third missionary journey (Acts 21: 2-4). Along the way came the Phoenician alliances with David and Solomon, the marriage of the Phoenician Jezebel to Ahab of Israel, and prophecies of Isaiah and Ezekiel against the cities of Tyre and Sidon.

The name "Phoenician," according to some, is traceable to the ancient Egyptians, who called the people of the Syrian coast "Fenkhu," meaning "shipbuilders." This name the Greeks rendered as "Phoinikes" (plural of *Phoinix*), from which comes the English name for the people and area. Others do not find any connection between the Egyptian and Greek names. But they do find the origin of the English name for the inhabitants of the area in the Greek name. The singular form of the word, *phoinix*, may mean "dark red" or "purple" and may refer to the extensive production and export of reddish-purple dye obtained from Tyrian sea snails (murex). A secondary meaning of *phoinix* is "palm"; the name "Phoenicia" might then signify "the land of palms."

While Paleolithic remains have been found in Lebanon, they need not concern us here. It seems that the earliest and basic ethnic element in the eastern Mediterranean area was a Mediterranean stock. They were white men, of the Caucasian race, of short to medium height, of slight or moderate build. Their heads were long with black or dark brown hair. They appeared in Leb-anon by 4000 B.C. or shortly thereafter. Byblos seems to have achieved a fair degree of importance during the fourth millennium; the necropolis there goes back to the first half of that millennium.[1]

But Phoenicia did not begin to assume a position of any importance in international affairs until the third millennium B.C. And its rise occurred under the Canaanites, who occupied the Lebanese littoral about 3000 B.C.—approximately the same time they moved into western Syria and Palestine. According to the Table of Nations, Sidon was the "firstborn" of Canaan (Gen. 10:15). And the city he founded gradually assumed domination of the Phoenician coast and maintained it for several centuries, finally losing it to Tyre. So marked was this ascendancy that "Sidonian" and "Phoenician" largely became interchangeable terms. This was true during the early period when Sidon was predominant in Phoenicia (Deut. 3:9; Joshua 13:4, 6; 19:28) as well as long after Tyre attained the hegemony. Thus Ethbaal, king of Tyre, is called "king of the Sidonians" in I Kings 16:31.

202. Phoenician fortifications, Gebal

[1]Philip K. Hitti, *Lebanon in History* (London: Macmillan and Co., Ltd., 1957), p. 60.

Phoenicia never attained full political unity. Its city-states maintained a considerable degree of independence, with Byblos, Sidon, and Tyre, in that order, achieving partial or total ascendancy over the others. Phoenician society was therefore urban and its economy industrial and commercial. Jealousy and competition between the coastal cities contributed to military weakness and political instability.

The Phoenician Canaanites are often called Semites, even though they were descendants of Ham. The explanation for this switch is that at an early date an admixture of Semites and Canaanites occurred in Phoenicia, with the result that the Semites became predominant. Semitic supremacy occurred as a result of a great Amorite invasion of Phoenicia, Syria, and Palestine a century or two before 2000 B.C.

Early Relations with Egypt

Earliest known contacts between Phoenicia and a foreign power occurred with Egypt. Even before Upper and Lower Egypt combined to form a united nation (c. 3000 B.C.), the people of the Delta area had trading relationships with Phoenicia.[2] The Phoenician trading capital of these early days was Gebal (Greek Byblos), twenty-five miles north of Beirut. It sent wine, oils used in the mummification process, and cedarwood for ships, coffins, and choice furniture. In exchange, the Egyptians sent gold, fine metalwork, and especially papyrus. In fact, so large was the volume of papyrus that flowed into Gebal that its Greek name "Byblos" came to be synonymous with papyrus, or book; our word *Bible* ("the Book") perpetuates the name of the ancient port.

Throughout the Old Kingdom of Egypt (2700-2200 B.C.), extensive trade relations with Byblos continued to such a degree that

Egyptian long-distance sailing vessels came to be named "Byblos travelers." Naturally such extensive commercial relations brought cultural interchange. In religion, in writing, and in decorative motif, the Phoenicians borrowed heavily from the Egyptians, whereas the Egyptians learned certain techniques of metalworking from the Phoenicians. V. Gordon Childe holds that this highly advanced metal industry was an independent development, not influenced by Mesopotamian culture, and that even Aegean metalwork may have been derived from this industry.[3] Steindorff and Seele suggest that possibly Byblos was an Egyptian colony during the Old Kingdom period. Its prince was proud to refer to himself in Egyptian as "the Son of Re [chief solar deity of Egypt], beloved of the gods of his land."[4]

Mention of "Byblos travelers" excites some curiosity as to the nature of early Egyptian freighters. From an inscription and a pictorial representation left in Pharaoh Sahure's pyramid (c. 2500 B.C.), taken in conjunction with other information on Egyptian shipping, the following facts appear. The Egyptians, unlike other ancient shipbuilders, did not use a keel and ribs as a framework for their ships. Quiet waters of the Nile had not necessitated such quality of construction. They built their ships by fastening planks together, without keel and with few ribs, furnishing added stiffening by means of beams which supported the deck.

As a substitute for keel and ribs, Sahure's men had looped an enormous hawser around one end of the ship, carried it along the center of the deck and looped it around the other end of the ship. When tightened by means of a pole thrust through the strands of the hawser, the hawser acted

[3]*New Light on the Most Ancient East* (London: Routledge and Kegan Paul, Ltd., rewritten 1952), p. 224.

[4]George Steindorff and Keith C. Seele, *When Egypt Ruled the East* (Chicago: University of Chicago Press, 1942), p. 21.

[2]S. R. K. Glanville (ed.), *The Legacy of Egypt* (Oxford: The Clarendon Press, 1942), p. 6.

203. Model of Sahure's ship

as an enormous tourniquet. Moreover, a netting ran horizontally around the upper part of the hold, either as chafing protection or as an aid in holding the ship together. Because there was no keel, there was nothing in which to set a single mast. Therefore a double mast was used and held in place by lines fore and aft. On it was hung a square sail with yards at head and foot. The ship was also propelled by rowers when sailing became difficult. How large these ships were we do not know; but "The Story of the Shipwrecked Sailor," dating to the Old Kingdom period, shows that ships could be as much as 180 feet in length and 60 in beam.[5]

Plenty of tangible evidence of contacts between Egypt and Phoenicia in these early days could be given. A few examples will suffice. Pharaohs began to send offerings to the temple of Baalat (Baalath) at Gebal as early as the Second Dynasty

(shortly after 3000 B.C.).[6] Pharaoh Snefru, founder of the Fourth Dynasty, about 2650 B.C., in the second year of his reign brought from Lebanon forty ships filled with cedarwood. In the third year of his reign, he built a ship of cedar; in the fourth year of his reign he mentions making doors of cedar for his palace.[7] The visitor to Egypt can see cedar beam supports still in use in Snefru's burial chamber in his pyramid at Dahshur, a few miles southwest of Cairo. About fifty years later Khufu (Cheops), builder of the great pyramid, also imported cedars from Lebanon. This is known from the discovery in 1954 of his sixty-foot funerary boat of cedar, which had been housed for four and one-half millennia in its limestone vault adjacent to the great pyramid.

Although Sargon of Akkad carved out an empire (c. 2360 B.C.) stretching from

[5]Lionel Casson, *The Ancient Mariners* (New York: The Macmillan Co., 1959), pp. 14-15.

[6]Hitti, p. 72.
[7]James H. Breasted, *Ancient Records of Egypt* (Chicago: University of Chicago Press, 1906), I, 66.

204. Temples of Gebal, third millennium
B.C.

beset with enemies on every side—and within—as the execration texts show. These texts ceremonially and magically cursed all royal enemies, including those apparently involved in palace intrigues. It is interesting to observe that Byblos is among the places cursed.[8]

The Hyksos

Peacefully infiltrating Egypt much earlier, the Hyksos thoroughly overwhelmed the land by military force about 1730 B.C. After an orgy of pillage and destruction, they must have decided that they could never so effectively rebuild as they could tear down; therefore they changed their tactics. Becoming a ruling caste which controlled the Delta, they utilized very largely the bureaucratic machinery of their Egyptian predecessors to rule the kingdom on the Nile. While never successful in thoroughly conquering southern Egypt, the Hyksos ruled Palestine, Phoenicia, and much of Syria, as well as achieving some control on Cyprus.

The last word is still to be written as to exactly who the Hyksos were. Whether or not they were originally a homogeneous people is not at all certain. At any rate, their movement into Greater Syria and Egypt was part of a series of migrations in the eastern Mediterranean world during the eighteenth century B.C. And on the way they became "an unclassified goulash of humanity," as Hitti says,[9] with a preponderant Semitic racial strain. Hitti observes that as far as Lebanon is concerned, the Hyksos seem to have been responsible for the injection of a large Armenoid element into the area.[10]

The Egyptians hated the Hyksos. Naturally no people likes to have its soil occupied by foreigners. But the Hyksos made

the Persian Gulf to the Mediterranean, and although he claimed control of "the forests of cedar," Egyptian influence in Phoenicia reigned supreme during the Old Kingdom and for some time thereafter. The Phoenician city-states were protected from Mesopotamian encroachment by the lofty Lebanons. Moreover, the forests of cedar which Sargon valued may have been located on the slopes of the Amanus Mountains in Asia Minor.

The Egyptian Middle Kingdom

Having declined somewhat during Egypt's First Intermediate period (2200-2050 B.C.), Egyptian commerce with and interest in Phoenicia were thoroughly rehabilitated during the Middle Kingdom years (2050-1800 B.C.). Egyptian Pharaohs now exercised stronger suzerainty in Phoenicia as well as in Syria and Palestine, but it can hardly be said that they brought these areas within the bounds of their empire. Rather, they brought them within the Egyptian sphere of political and cultural influence—to the extent that natives of those areas were willing to send gifts and/or tribute to Egypt and were careful not to offend the Egyptians.

Around 1800 B.C. the Egyptian Middle Kingdom began to disintegrate. Egypt was

[8]John A. Wilson, *The Burden of Egypt* (Chicago: University of Chicago Press, 1951), p. 156
[9]Hitti, p. 77.
[10]*Ibid.*

themselves additionally obnoxious by remaining a caste largely aloof from the native Egyptians in a feudal type of society and by largely ignoring the worship of the Egyptian gods. To be defeated by foreigners, which had not occurred during Egypt's more than 1200 years of national life, to have her culture ignored, and to find her weapons ineffective against the superior arms of the Hyksos, was almost too much for the Egyptians.

The war of revenge began about 1600 B.C., spearheaded by Theban rulers, who had never been more than nominally under the control of the Hyksos. The Egyptians were successful because they effectively turned against their overlords the weapons they had introduced to Egypt. These included the horse and war chariot, the composite bow, and better swords.

The Egyptian Empire Period

Once the Egyptians had ejected the Hyksos, they continued advancing into Palestine and Syria. A good case may be developed for the thesis that the Egyptian Empire was a natural result of the pursuit and defeat of the Hyksos, whose fortresses dotted the landscape of Palestine and Syria. But the Egyptians also may have desired a more extensive buffer area to forestall a future invasion. Also, they may have been interested in controlling more firmly some of the resources they knew existed in such places as Lebanon.

Conquest of Phoenicia. At any rate, the Pharaohs of the Eighteenth Dynasty kept moving farther and farther north. The military expeditions of Ahmose I, Amenhotep I, and Thutmose I and II into Palestine and Syria were in the nature of punitive raids. Thutmose I, shortly after 1525 B.C., penetrated as far as the Euphrates River. But it was Thutmose III (1490-1436 B.C.) who, conducting almost annual campaigns into Syria

for twenty years, broke the last remnants of Hyksos power and established the Egyptian Empire there. His annals mention successful campaigns against several Phoenician towns, including Tyre, Aradus (modern Arwad, biblical Arvad) and Simyra. The last two are the Arvadite and Zemarite of Genesis 10:18.

The booty Thutmose records shows something of the cosmopolitan elegance of Phoenicia at that time. Her princes had chairs of ivory and ebony decorated with gold and accompanied by footstools, tables of ivory and carob wood decorated with gold, and many other objects of great value.

In order to insure the maintenance of his empire, Thutmose, "Napoleon of ancient Egypt," gave much attention to the Phoenician ports. In each, adequate food supplies were stored, harbors were outfitted, and ships were commandeered to maintain communications with Egypt. Gradually, in Lebanon as well as throughout the rest of Greater Syria, Thutmose was able to keep the area in subjection by means of small contingents of soldiers stationed in each town. Behind these stood all the military power of Egypt, which could rapidly be brought into action. And with his sixth campaign, Thutmose inaugurated the practice of carrying sons of the kings of the northern city-states to Egypt as hostages. There he educated them and thoroughly indoctrinated them with the Egyptian viewpoint. When the fathers of these princes died, he sent the sons home to rule as loyal subjects of Egypt. The system worked quite effectively, as future events would demonstrate. Meanwhile, large quantities of agricultural commodities, metal goods, cedar logs, and other Lebanese products found their way annually to Egypt, as booty or tribute or in exchange for Egyptian goods.

Despite Thutmose's prodigious and effective show of might in Phoenicia, his son Amenhotep II (1439-1406 B.C.) also found it necessary to rattle the sword under the noses of the Phoenicians. Probably the area was generally docile during his reign, but his eulogist tried to show him as a fierce conqueror. The eulogies of the Pharaohs are quite misleading because they overplay the power demonstrated by the Egyptian kings, and they do not give a true picture of conditions in lands invaded.

Decline of Egyptian control. But liberty like truth when crushed to earth will rise again. During the Amarna Age (*c.* 1400-1350 B.C.), luxury-loving Amenhotep III and IV were more engrossed in religious reform, building a new capital, or sailing around on a private yacht on an artificial lake, than they were in maintaining their empire. Subject peoples would naturally become restive.

The rise of new forces further complicated the situation in Lebanon during the first half of the fourteenth century B.C. To the north the Hittites attained their height of power. Suppiluliumas strode out of his Asia Minor homeland, toppled the Mitanni Kingdom to the east, and advanced south to face the Egyptians. Nomads (the Habiru) moved in from the desert to the east.

Caught in the power struggle between the Hittites and Egyptians and seized with a desire to obtain their freedom, the Phoenicians were tempted to play off one major power against the other—to their own advantage. Some of the city-states openly revolted. The documents which tell the

most about the developments during the period are the Amarna Letters (about 300 in number), found by an Egyptian peasant woman in the ruins of Amarna in 1887. These letters were written by petty rulers of Palestine and Syria to Amenhotep III and IV pleading for help against insurrectionists and invaders. Written in cuneiform, they demonstrate by that fact the extensiveness of Mesopotamian influence on Greater Syria at this time.

The story told in the Amarna Tablets runs something like this. A certain Abdashirta, an Amorite with headquarters on the upper Orontes River in Syria, attempted to extend his domain by employing Machiavellian tactics. Professing allegiance to Egypt or to the Hittites, whichever best suited his purposes at the moment, he managed to enlarge his territory until it included such important Syrian cities as Qatna and Damascus.[11] His successes along the Phoenician coast were likewise significant. Whether the coastal cities made league with him because he pressured them by overpowering arms, or whether they felt he espoused their cause of independence from Egypt, is not certain.

At any rate, biblical Arvad (Aradus) and Sidon early threw off the Egyptian yoke and became active foes of the Pharaohs. Perhaps their anti-Egyptian feeling was related to their trade rivalry with Gebal (Byblos). Soon they made common cause with Abdashirta, who proceeded to conquer the coastal towns of Lebanon.

The center of pro-Egyptian power was at Byblos. Nor was that hard to understand. Her economy was tied to trade with Egypt. Her culture was strongly influenced by that of Egypt. Ribadda of Byblos was chief spokesman for the Egyptian faction. As pressure against his city and opposition to his cause mounted, he sent appeals to Egypt for help—some fifty in all—almost without response. After a courageous stand, Ribadda was forced to flee when Byblos

205. Phoenician tombs, Gebal

[11]Hitti, p. 83.

was isolated from her hinterland. The southward march of the Abdashirta forces (now headed by his sons who took over after the death of their father) sent Ribadda fleeing from his refuge in Beirut. Ultimately, at Sidon, his enemies sealed his fate. Subsequently the Sidonians and the Amorites besieged Tyre. During the protracted siege, Abimilki, the king of Tyre, sent repeated pleas to Egypt for help, without response. Finally Tyre, the last great Egyptian stronghold on the Lebanese littoral, fell. Soon Egyptian power in all of Greater Syria was dead. Aziru, son of Abdashirta, had established a hegemony over Phoenicia; but he was himself a vassal of the Hittites.

Resurgence of Egyptian Power. About a half century later (*c.* 1300 B.C.), Seti I of Egypt again subdued the coastal cities of Phoenicia and had some success in reestablishing the empire in Asia. His son and successor, Ramses II, ran into trouble. After making his power felt in Phoenicia, where he placed his inscription beside the Dog River (Nahr el Kelb), he determined to halt the Hittite advance into Syria.

Marching east from Lebanon, Ramses II was ambushed by the Hittites at Kadesh on the Orontes in 1286 B.C. By exercising unusual courage, he was able to save himself from annihilation and went home to carve on the temple walls a claim of great victory in classic Egyptian braggadocio. The Hittites also went home claiming a victory. The truth is that the outcome of the battle was a draw. Intermittent fighting between Egyptians and Hittites continued for a few more years, and the two powers signed a nonaggression pact about fifteen years later. By the terms of the pact Egypt retained control of Palestine and Syria. It was obvious that neither power could topple the other. Alas, a new threat on the horizon, the Sea Peoples (Philistines), seemed to require that both empires reserve their strength for a coming showdown with them.

206. Ramses II, Luxor Temple, Egypt

During the remainder of Ramses' reign, the pact with the Hittites was honored. His successor, Merneptah, concerned himself with a brief struggle with enemies in southern Palestine and claimed a devastating defeat of the Hebrews. At the beginning of the twelfth century, Ramses III with great effort turned back an invasion of his northern coasts by the Sea Peoples (Peleset, or Philistines) who subsequently occupied the Philistine plain in southern Palestine.

After the days of Ramses II, the Phoenicians were no longer disturbed by either Egyptians or Hittites. By 1200 B.C., or shortly after, the Hittite Empire was convulsed in dying gasps. The Egyptian Empire was declining. About 1100 B.C., when the Pharaonic envoy Wen-Amon came to Byblos to obtain cedar, he was at first told to go home and then was made to wait for days before having his request granted. Ultimately he paid a handsome price for the Pharaoh's cedar logs. By now the Aramaeans had occupied Syria, the Hebrews the highlands of Palestine, and the Philistines the southwest coast of Palestine. The Egyptian Empire in Asia had come to an end.

The Sea Peoples who splashed ashore in Palestine after defeat at the hands of the Egyptians continued to move northward. They sacked Tyre and Sidon and became masters of the Phoenician coast. Ethnic assimilation gradually produced a new race. But while the ethnic composition of Phoenicia was somewhat changed, the culture remained Canaanite. Establishing control over the Mediterranean, the Phoenicians launched their golden age.

Phoenician Independence

The period of Phoenician independence (*c.* 1200-880 B.C.) is probably the era of Phoenician history most appealing to the Bible student. It was during these centuries that David and Solomon, Israel's greatest monarchs, allied themselves with Tyre and used Phoenician knowledge and cedars to construct buildings on land and ships at sea.

Perhaps it would be well to review the international conditions which permitted both the Phoenician and Hebrew developments at this time. These conditions allowed the expansion of the Hebrew kingdom to the Euphrates on the north and the border of Egypt on the south and permitted the Phoenicians under the leadership of Tyre to achieve a maritime supremacy of the Mediterranean that was not to be broken completely until the days of Alexander the Great.

Imperial weakness. There was a power vacuum in the Mediterranean world during these centuries. About 1200 B.C. the Hittite Empire collapsed. The traditional date for the fall of Troy, on the Hittites' western border, is 1184. Their destroyers, the Mycenaeans, passed off the scene about 1100, and Greece went through a period of readjustment until 800 or after—often called the "Greek Middle Age." Also about 1100 the

Egyptian Empire disintegrated. Babylonian power had disappeared and would remain ineffective until shortly before 600. Assyria, after a brief spurt of activity under Tiglathpileser I about 1100, went into eclipse for more than 200 years. In the West there was nothing of significance. While the traditional date of the founding of Rome is 753 B.C., we now know there were some insignificant villages on the hills of Rome as early as 1000. Elsewhere in the western basin of the Mediterranean there were a few tribes scattered around. Even Phoenician colonies like Carthage were not founded until about 800 or possibly later. So it is quite obvious that there was little in the Mediterranean world to stop Phoenician or Hebrew expansion at the beginning of the first millennium B.C.

Dearth of information. Unfortunately our sources of knowledge for the period of Phoenician independence are quite sketchy, as is true of many other periods of Phoenician history. Little has been done in the way of archaeological investigation. One of the most extensive excavations has been conducted at Byblos intermittently by the French since 1924. Among the directors of this work have been Pierre Montet and Maurice Dunand. Diggings at the site have uncovered layers of occupation dating from the second millennium to the Roman period. Some work has been done at Tyre since 1947. There the Lebanese Department of Antiquities has uncovered ruins of the Byzantine and Greek periods. Excavation has not yet reached the Phoenician levels. Not much excavation has been done elsewhere.

For information on Phoenician history prior to the Assyrian period, the greatest help comes from Josephus (who alludes to some historical works extant in his day) in both his *Antiquities* (VIII,5) and *Against Apion* (I, 14-18); Justin, a Roman historian of the third century A.D., who wrote *Historiarum Philippicarum* (see XLIV); and the Bible. From the available materials it is possible to sketch an outline history of the period of independence.

As has been noted, the indication in Genesis 10:15 of the priority of Sidon (or Zidon) seems supported by the common equation of "Phoenician" and "Sidonian"—in Scripture, in Homer, and in other ancient sources. While the Phoenicians called their land "Canaan," their name for themselves was "Sidonians."[12] Moreover, Isaiah speaks of Tyre as "daughter of Zidon" (23:12).

In connection with this latter assertion, it should be noted that Josephus claimed that Tyre was founded 240 years before the building of the temple at Jerusalem (*Antiquities*, VIII, 3). And Justin asserted that Tyre was founded one year before the destruction of Troy (XVIII, 3). Both of these notations would put the founding of Tyre about 1200 B.C., at the beginning of the period of independence. However, it has been noted that Tyre was besieged by Sidon during the Amarna Age. Herodotus, in his history of Greco-Persian wars, supports a date of about 2750 for the founding of Tyre (II, 44).

The truth of the matter seems to be that both Tyre and Sidon were founded very early, Sidon achieving an ascendancy much earlier than Tyre. During the Amarna Age, Sidon was successful in its siege of Tyre. How much destruction was done at Tyre then is not known. At any rate, Sidon continued in a predominant position. At the end of the thirteenth century the Sea Peoples began to make raids on Egypt and the Syrian coast. One of these peoples, the Philistines, organized a league of five cities in southern Palestine. The king of one of these cities, Ascalon (biblical Ashkelon), sacked Sidon and left it very largely in ruins about 1200 B.C. At about the same time Greek expansion in the Aegean and the fierce rivalry of the mariners of Crete and Cyprus drastically cut the prosperity of the beleaguered city-state. At the time of

her military defeat, many Sidonians migrated to Tyre. In this sense Tyre could be called the "daughter of Sidon." And in this sense the city could be said to have a founding about 1200, as Josephus and Justin indicate. In this way all of the historical indications are cared for, and it is explained how Sidon lost her ascendancy to Tyre early in the period of independence.

Spotlight on Tyre. The story of the period of Phoenician independence is largely the story of the expansion of Tyre. Perhaps this is true to some extent because the available sources do not permit a rounded-out history of the Lebanese littoral. As a result of excavations at Byblos, for instance, it is apparent that she had kings of her own. Probably other city-states in the area did also. But certainly a greater knowledge of the times would not rob Tyre of her place of preeminence. She was clearly ascendant over Sidon. Byblos, tied largely to Egyptian trade, apparently decayed with the decline of the colossus to the south. Moreover, it was Tyre that was largely responsible for the extensive Phoenician colonization and maritime activity that occurred soon after the end of the period. Says Warmington, "It is probable that Tyre exercised some sort of control over almost all the cities of Phoenicia from the time of Hiram to the seventh century; there was a common system of weights and measures, and it is impossible as yet to distinguish

207. Harbor of Tyre

[12]B. H. Warmington, *Carthage* (London: Robert Hale Limited, 1960), p. 16.

between the products of the different cities."[13]

Phoenician sea power rapidly expanded about 1100-1000 B.C. This may have occurred because of land need or the pressure of the Aramaeans in the hinterland. Or possibly, as Arthur Evans and Hogarth suggested, this advance came as a result of immigration of peoples from Aegean lands.[14]

Phoenician ships. What sort of ships the Phoenicians sailed is a matter of some interest, since they dominated the Mediterranean for several centuries. Phoenician ships of about 1350 B.C. are pictured on an Egyptian inscription. These were deep-bellied freighters with curved ends that terminated in straight stem and sternposts. Their substantial holds were covered with flush decks and surrounded with a high railing that permitted a large deck load. They carried broad square sails bent to two yards, along the top and foot.[15] A clay model of a boat uncovered at Byblos shows an undecked merchantman with high sides, giving the appearance of an elongated bowl.[16] The latter was probably used for short coastal hauls as it would easily have swamped on the open sea. Presumably Phoenician ships of the period of independence were similar to those pictured earlier on the Egyptian tomb wall, though Aegean influence may have modified them somewhat.

While the Greeks used galleys powered by rowers for warships (and perhaps the Phoenicians did also before the days of Hiram and Solomon), merchantmen of the pre-Christian era do not seem to have changed much from the slow sail-powered vessels of the late second millennium B.C.

Hiram the Great. The best days of Tyre probably began during the reign of Hiram I.[17] When he took the reins of government, Tyre consisted of a small island about a half mile from the Phoenician coast, with a yet smaller island lying to the southwest. (Whether or not was a Tyre on the mainland at the time is uncertain; at least it is commonly agreed that the island Tyre was founded earlier than the town on the mainland.) Hiram I joined these two islands and then claimed from the sea an area on the east of the larger island. The total circumference of the island was now about two and one-half miles. Then he proceeded to rebuild and beautify the temples, the most famous being to the god Melkart; this latter temple had long stood on the smaller island.

Subsequently attention was given to the harbors and fortifications of the city, the inhabitants constructing by means of piers the Sidonian harbor on the north and the Egyptian harbor on the south. The existence of these harbors was confirmed by Father Poidebard in three aerial and underwater expeditions in 1934-36. He found that in some places the well-built breakwater extended to a depth fifty feet below the surface of the water.[18] A wall eventually rose to a height of 150 feet on the mainland side of the island. This was surmounted by battlements. Just when the breakwaters and fortifications were constructed is not known, though Hiram is given credit for enlarging earlier harbors and is sometimes credited with constructing the wall.

When Hiram I ruled is somewhat problematical. Josephus says that Hiram ruled for thirty-four years and that he was in his twelfth year when Solomon began the Temple. According to I Kings 6:1 the Temple was begun in Solomon's fourth year.

---

[13]*Ibid.*, p. 19.
[14]As cited by Albert A. Trever, *History of Ancient Civilization* (New York: Harcourt, Brace and Co., 1936), I, 80.
[15]Casson, p. 25.
[16]*Ibid.*

[17]For documentation on the ruling dynasty and the development of the city of Tyre, see especially Josephus (who quotes ancient authorities) *Antiquities*, VIII, 2, 5, 7 and *Against Apion*, I, 17-18; see also Wallace B. Fleming, *The History of Tyre* (New York: Columbia University Press, 1915), pp. 4, 16.
[18]Emily D. Wright, "News About Old Tyre," *Biblical Archaeologist*, May, 1939, pp. 20-22.

208. Excavations at Tyre, Byzantine
level

This would mean that Hiram began his reign eight years before Solomon began his and therefore overlapped David's reign by that much. It would seem, however, that David enjoyed the assistance of Hiram for longer than eight years. Indications in II Samuel 5:11-12 (in context) and I Chronicles 14:1-2 (in context) imply that Hiram furnished David with cedar and artisans for the construction of his palace soon after David's conquest of Jerusalem, in about the eighth year of his forty-year reign. One might suggest that Hiram rendered this assistance while he was still crown prince and perhaps coregent with his father Abi-baal. But Hiram was only about twenty when his father died and he assumed full control of the government. Perhaps it is assumed incorrectly that Hiram I had associations with David before the middle of the reign of the latter. Possibly Josephus is in error in stating that the Temple was begun during the twelfth year of Hiram's reign.

At any rate, Josephus supports the Scripture in asserting the overlapping of the reign of Hiram I with that of both David and Solomon. That is really all the situation absolutely demands. When Hiram is dated will depend on what biblical chronology one adopts. If one follows E. R. Thiele, who would begin Solomon's reign in 970, Hiram began his reign about 978. If W. F. Albright is followed, Hiram's reign began about 970.

Hiram's successors. The successors of Hiram were not able to retain the purple as long as he (thirty-four years). Either they were not such hardy souls, or they were not so adept in squelching revolution. After Hiram died, his son Beleazarus (Baalusur) ruled for seven years. His son Abd-Astartus ruled nine years and was assassinated by four of his sons. The eldest of these, Deleastartus ruled twelve years and was succeeded by his son Astartus, who likewise ruled twelve years. Astartus' brother, Aserymus, then ruled nine years and was murdered by his brother Pheles, who lasted only eight months and was in turn assassinated by Ithobalus (Ethbaal), priest of Astarte, who ruled thirty-two years. His son Badezorus ruled six years and Badezorus' son Matgenus nine years. It was Ethbaal's infamous daughter, Jezebel, who married Ahab of Israel (I Kings 16:31).

Relations between Phoenicians and Hebrews. Having noted the dynastic development at Tyre during the period of independence, let us return to a consideration of relations between the Phoenicians and Hebrews during the days of Hiram and the successes of the Phoenicians in industrial and commercial activity during the period.

After David had become king over all Israel and while he was enjoying evident success in warfare against his neighbors, Hiram of Tyre sent a friendly embassy to David to open negotiations with him. The result was that cedar trees and Tyrian carpenters and masons were supplied to David for the construction of his royal palace (II Sam. 5:11-12; I Chron. 14:1-2). Some have suggested that the close relations between the Tyrians and Hebrews during the reigns of David and Solomon involved an alliance against the Philistines, their common enemy. While this is plausible, there is no indication that this pact ever issued in anything but peaceful pursuits. Initially Hiram may have desired to gain favor with a rising potential enemy by sending an em-

209. Byzantine mozaic, Tyre

bassy to David, but soon it must have become evident that both powers would benefit economically from such an alliance. Of course the biblical account is extremely abbreviated. We need not assume that David got his new palace as a gift from Hiram; he may have had to pay dearly for it.

In David's later years he made preparation for construction of the Temple in Jerusalem. His collection of materials included a large amount of cedarwood furnished by Tyre and Sidon (I Chron. 22:4). Prevented by God from building the Temple because he was a warlike man, David under divine orders passed the task on to his son Solomon (I Chron. 22:5-12).

Solomon accepted the charge and shortly after the beginning of his reign sent to Hiram to make specific arrangements for actual construction. The correspondence between the two kings appears in II Chronicles 2 and I Kings 5:1-12. Solomon needed wood, gold, and artisans in various trades.

In exchange for the wood and skilled labor Solomon furnished agricultural products, for the gold a section of land.

The wood desired included cedar, fir (or perhaps cypress), and algum (or almug, probably red sandalwood, II Chron. 2:8). Solomon was to send woodcutters to Phoenicia to help fell the timber, which was then to be floated to Joppa (modern Jaffa). Stonecutters and other workers were to be sent from Phoenicia. Solomon was especially desirous of having a master workman to direct all the artistic work in gold, silver, brass, iron, stone, wood, and cloth. The man chosen for this task was a certain Hiram (not the king; see I Kings 7:13-14), whose specialty seems to have been "brass" (copper) casting. Solomon also needed a considerable amount of gold for decoration of the Temple and his palace. King Hiram also agreed to furnish this.

The total amount of what Solomon agreed to pay annually for the wood and laborers was 20,000 measures (Hebrew *kor*, 10-11 bushels each) of wheat, 20,000 measures of barley, 20,000 measures (Hebrew *bath*, 4½ gallons each) of wine, and 20,000 measures of oil (thought to be a textual corruption; the amount is seemingly too much; II Chron. 2:10).

The fact that this payment differs from that mentioned in I Kings 5:11 seems easily explained. The latter reference speaks of a payment of 20,000 measures of wheat and twenty measures of pure oil and says this was for "his [Hiram's] household." The II Chronicles statistics probably include receipts for public expenditures as well. For gold Solomon gave a tract of land in Galilee to Hiram; this encompassed twenty towns. Upon seeing this district, Hiram was quite unhappy and called it *cabul*. According to Josephus this word is a Phoenician term meaning "that which does not please" (I Kings 9:10-14; Josephus, *Antiquities*, VIII, 5).

Every indication is that the Temple was a remarkable structure indeed and that the craftsmanship of the Phoenicians greatly impressed the Hebrews. Every indication also points to the influence or adoption of Phoenician architectural and artistic design. Since the subject of this chapter is Phoenician rather than Hebrew history, the construction of the Temple will not be discussed. Let it suffice here to mention an article which describes some of this probable Phoenician influence: Paul L. Garber, "Reconstructing Solomon's Temple," *Biblical Archaeologist*, January-March, 1951. For the style of architecture Garber suggests, see Illustrations 156 and 157 in this book.

Having established an agreement for building purposes, Solomon and Hiram also seem to have drawn up a pact for joint commercial endeavor. Solomon's conquest of the Edomites gave him access to the Red Sea. There he constructed the port of Ezion-geber and built a fleet of ships for trade in eastern and southern waters (I Kings 9:26-28). Up to this point, the Hebrews had never possessed good port facilities and had never engaged extensively in travel by sea. When constructing a port and fleet, the most natural place for the Hebrews to turn for skilled technicians was to the Phoenicians, acknowledged leaders in the field. And the Phoenicians were glad to cooperate in construction of a southern fleet because, on the one hand, such a fleet would not contest their mastery of the Mediterranean, since there was no Suez Canal. On the other hand, the Phoenicians would in this way have access to goods of Arabia and Africa for their Mediterranean trade; these products they previously had had to do without. The land of Ophir mentioned in I Kings 9:28 was located in southwest Arabia (modern Yemen) and perhaps included the adjacent coast of Africa. The Phoenicians also seem to have helped Solomon develop his copper smelting industry in the area south of the Dead Sea.

It has been thought, on the basis of II Chronicles 9:21, that Solomon had a fleet in the Mediterranean which accompanied Tyrian fleets to Tarshish. Many identify Tarshish with Tartessus, not far west of Gibraltar in southern Spain. If one compares II Chronicles 9:21 with a parallel passage in I Kings 10:22, he seems to arrive at a different opinion. The latter reference alludes to a navy or ships *of* Tarshish (Tharshish) rather than to ships *to* Tarshish. Ships of Tarshish seem to have been a special kind of ship for long hauls,[19] just as "Byblos travelers," alluded to earlier in this chapter, referred to a kind of ship (see I Kings 22:48). Our conclusion is, then, that the ships of Tarshish actually sailed in the Red Sea and probably even out into the Indian Ocean. Certainly the products brought back were not for the most part of Mediterranean origin (ivory, apes, and peacocks—native to India and Ceylon) but freight which would more likely dock at Ezion-geber.

Not only did Hiram and Solomon have a public commercial alliance; they seem to have had a private tilt of shrewdness over solving riddles. Josephus records that the two monarchs exchanged riddles or enigmatical sayings, with the understanding that the one who could not solve those submitted to him was to forfeit a money payment. At first Hiram seems to have been the substantial loser; but later, with the help of a certain Abdemon of Tyre, he managed to solve the riddles. Later Hiram proposed a number of riddles which even wise Solomon could not unravel, and Solomon paid considerable sums of money to Hiram (Josephus, *Antiquities*, VIII, 5; *Against Apion*, I, 17).

[19]Unger points out that *Tarshish* is a Phoenician word from the Akkadian meaning "smelting plant" or "refinery" and that Tarshish fleets were originally large ships constructed for the purpose of bringing smelted ore to Phoenicia from the mining towns of Sardinia and Spain. "Smeltery fleets" would be a good synonym for "Tarshish ships." Eventually all large ships were referred to as "Tarshish ships," regardless of the nature of their cargo or destination. Merrill F. Unger, *Unger's Bible Dictionary* (2d ed.; Chicago: Moody Press, 1959), pp. 1070-71.

As indicated in Scripture, Solomon reaped substantial wealth from his joint maritime exploits with the Phoenicians (e.g., I Kings 9:28). And we may be sure that the Phoenicians were reaping much more wealth from their commercial endeavors than previously was the case. Not only were they middlemen for a large percentage of the commerce of the Near East but they also dominated the trade of the entire Mediterranean world.

Phoenician commerce. The Phoenicians were intrepid seafarers. After the fall of Cretan and Mycenaean sea power, they became predominant in the Mediterranean world and the Near East. Goods which they secured from Egyptian or Mesopotamian sources or produced in their own shops, they carried into the Aegean Sea and throughout the Mediterranean and even beyond the Pillars of Hercules at Gibraltar. They sailed in ships with Solomon's men down the coasts of Africa and Arabia and perhaps as far as India and Ceylon. How early and how close they got to tin-producing Cornwall in England is a matter of some controversy.

Their crowning achievement (if indeed they accomplished it) was the circumnavigation of Africa during the reign of Pharaoh-Necho of Egypt (609-593 B.C.). Necho, who reopened the ancient canal between the

Nile and the Red Sea, suggested the project to the Phoenicians. They took the canal route and then went south along the east coast of Africa, returning to Egypt in the third year after departure. The trip took so long because they stopped to plant wheat on the way and wait for a harvest. Herodotus, who reported the event, commented, "There [Egypt] they said (what some may believe, though I do not) that in sailing round Libya [Africa] they had the sun on their right hand" (IV, 42). But Hitti observes, "This last detail which made Herodotus suspect the veracity of the story is precisely what confirms its authenticity. As ships sail west around the Cape of Good Hope, the sun of the southern hemisphere would be on their right."[20]

The important discovery which made possible greater maritime success for the Phoenicians was that one could lay a course by the polestar, especially in conjunction with other heavenly bodies. The Greeks named the polestar the "Phoenician Star." Prior to this discovery, it was common to sail by day along the shore or within sight of land, to beach or anchor a boat at night, or to engage in island hopping (in places such as the Aegean).

As Phoenician commercial contacts became more frequent in various areas, they tended to plant trading stations which in many instances grew into full-fledged colonies. Formerly it was commonly claimed that Phoenicians planted colonies in the West as early as 1100 or 1000 B.C. The tendency now is to place the dates considerably later. This question is examined in the next section of this chapter. However, even if the Phoenicians did not plant colonies in the West around 1000, they were making trade contacts there shortly after. Colonies in the East, in such places as Cyprus, Rhodes, and Crete, antedate those in the West.

The Phoenicians were the great middlemen of culture and commerce. Their civil-

[20]Hitti, p. 114.

ization was blended under Egyptian, Babylonian, and Greek influence; and what they learned from the older peoples they put to good use in the development of their culture and in the products they produced for export throughout the Mediterranean. As the middlemen of commerce, they carried the goods of the Nile and Tigris-Euphrates valleys, of Syria, of the Red Sea area (transshipped through Solomon's domain) of the Aegean, and of the lands around the Mediterranean.

While the Phoenicians were more skillful as traders than as manufacturers, they were skillful at making a number of commodities. In metallurgy, especially in connection with copper and bronze, the Canaanites were probably unequalled from about 2100 to 1200 B.C. They were very skilled in the casting and engraving of metals and in the making of jewelry. They learned from Egypt the manufacture of glass and glazed ware, perfected the art, and marketed the product. They also excelled in needlework and the production of linen and woolen cloth.

Perhaps the Phoenicians' most famous product was purple dye. The Minoans and Greeks had utilized the mollusk in making purple dye before them; but the Phoenicians, especially of Tyre and Sidon, had a superior grade of the shellfish with which to work. So much work was involved in dyeing a single piece of cloth, because only a few drops of dye could be obtained from one mollusk, that only the wealthy could afford such material.

It would be tedious indeed and quite unnecessary to enumerate all of the products carried in Phoenician ships. It is sufficient to say that their imports were mainly raw materials, metals (for instance, silver, iron, tin, and lead from Tartessus in Spain), and slaves. They seem to have organized the first widespread trade in slaves.[21] Of course, slaves, like all other imports, were geared to the export market. The most important exports were timber, metal goods, glass products, jewelry, and purple textiles.

Though Ezekiel 27 refers to a time some three centuries later than the period now under discussion, it is a remarkable description of the cosmopolitan character and extent of the trade of Tyre (and, by extension, all of Phoenicia). There was little difference between the nature of Phoenician trade in 900 and in 600; the former date preceded the greatest days of Phoenician prosperity, the latter followed it. There was one difference in shipping, however, as intimated in the Ezekiel passage. In 1000 B.C., Phoenician merchantmen depended almost exclusively on sail; by 600 B.C., galleys run by oars were in common use.

The Assyrian Period

To a large degree, the development of Greater Syria was made possible by the fact that Assyria was quiescent. Although Tiglath-pileser I (*c.* 1114-1076 B.C.) gave promise of building a formidable empire, his successors for some 200 years were not at all of his mettle and posed little threat to surrounding lands. Everything changed, however, with Ashurnasirpal II (883-859). Having developed a powerful army, he proceeded to use it especially against the westland. About 868 he "washed his weapons in the great sea"[22] and received tribute from Arvad, Byblos, Tyre, Sidon, and other nearby towns.

While the Phoenicians could fight if they had to, as history well demonstrates, they were a commercial rather than a warlike people. They apparently felt that parting with a little cash was better than destruction; the Assyrians never dealt lightly with those who dared to oppose them. Then, too,

[21]Ralph Turner, *The Great Cultural Traditions* (New York: McGraw-Hill Book Co., Inc., 1941), I, 238.

[22]For inscriptions of the kings of Assyria see James B. Pritchard (ed.), *Ancient Near Eastern Texts* (2d ed.; Princeton: Princeton University Press, 1955); Daniel D. Luckenbill, *Ancient Records of Assyria and Babylonia* (Chicago: University of Chicago Press, 1926), 2 vols.

by paying tribute, they purchased immunity from undue interference. Moreover, a strong power controlling western Asia meant more stable conditions, which were favorable for commercial relations. Besides, when powerful rulers died, there was always the hope that their successors would be weak and incapable of controlling subject powers.

Shalmaneser III (858-824) continued the expansionist policies of his father, Ashurna-

211. Monolith Inscription of Shalmaneser III

sirpal. Shalmaneser was apparently more of a threat to Syrian independence than his father had been; for when he marched west, a coalition of twelve kings met him at Karkar (Qarqar) in 853. Leading the forces was Benhadad II of Damascus with 20,000 infantry and 1200 chariots. Ahab of Israel provided the next largest force: 10,000 infantry and 2,000 chariots. Several Phoenician city-states sent contingents to the 60,000-man army. The battle seems to have ended in something of a draw. While the Assyrian king claimed a total victory, he found it necessary to make repeated expeditions into Syria. About 842 he recorded having received tribute from Tyrians, Sidonians, and Jehu of Israel. In the twenty-first year of his reign, he records having crossed the Euphrates for the twenty-first time and having received tribute from Tyrians, Sidonians, and Byblians.

It is quite possible that at least during the early part of the Assyrian period Phoenicia had a considerable amount of local autonomy. And it is quite probable that the sway of Assyria was favorable to the land commerce of Tyre by making caravan routes more safe. Phoenicia attained the height of her prosperity during the eighth century—under Assyrian suzerainty. Near the end of the eighth century, Isaiah wrote of Tyre, "The harvest of the river, is her revenue; and she is a mart of nations . . . the crowning city, whose merchants are princes, whose traffickers are the honourable of the earth" (23:3-8).

Perhaps another reason for the general prosperity and peace in Phoenicia during the first half of the eighth century is that Assyria was moribund during the reigns of the three kings who ruled from 782 to 745 B.C. But with Tiglath-pileser III (745-727) the empire came to life once more. About 740 (scholars vary on the date between 743 and 738), he had a successful western campaign during which he received tribute from, among others, Rezin of Damascus, Menahem of Samaria, and Hiram II of

Tyre. In 732 he destroyed the kingdom of Syria; before that year he had annexed northern Israel. It was only a matter of time until Assyria effectively controlled Phoenicia. During his Philistine campaign in 734, Tiglath-pileser received tribute from Arvad, Byblos, and Tyre. The fact that Sidon is missing from the tribute lists of Tiglath-pileser has been taken by some as an indication that Tyre controlled Sidon at the time.

During the reign of Shalmaneser V (727-722 B.C.) Phoenicia again felt the heavy hand of Assyria. According to Josephus (*Antiquities*, IX, 14, 2), whom some scholars doubt at this point, Shalmaneser overran all Phoenicia. Sidon, Palaetyrus (mainland Tyre), and other nearby towns under Tyre's control capitulated to Assyria. Island Tyre refused to surrender. Subsequently Shalmaneser gathered a fleet to attack the island. Repulsed, the Assyrian settled down to an unsuccessful five-year siege of the island. It is not unreasonable to accept Josephus' account of this struggle. Shalmaneser was active in the West during his reign. It was he who initiated the three-year siege of Samaria.

Subsequently Phoenicia seems to have been unmolested for some twenty years, while Eluleus (Luli), king of Tyre (725-690 B.C.), regained control over much of the adjacent mainland. Sargon II (722-705), King of Assyria, devoted his energies to the conquest of Cyprus, or at least the southern part of the island, which was in Phoenician hands, and accomplished his aim in 709.

Sennacherib (705-681 B.C.) had to face one of those ever recurring rebellions in the West. Eluleus of Tyre, supported by other Phoenician city-states, was one of the leaders of the defection. The Philistines, the Egyptians, Hezekiah of Judah, and others cooperated in the venture. "The Assyrian came down like the wolf on the fold" in 701, defeated the Egyptians before Ekron, ravaged Judaea and shut up Hezekiah "like a bird in a cage" in Jerusalem, and completely subdued Phoenicia. Eluleus fled to Cyprus, or possibly just to island Tyre; the situation is not clear. Sennacherib destroyed the powerful combination of Tyre and Sidon and placed a pro-Assyrian king on the throne of Sidon.

But Phoenician efforts to retain liberty would not forever be blocked. With a change of rulers in Assyria, the caldron of liberty boiled over again along the Lebanese littoral. Sidon led the revolt (c. 678 B.C.) against Esarhaddon, king of Assyria (681-668). In his fury the Assyrian absolutely obliterated the city. Most of the inhabitants were killed or sold into slavery; some escaped to nearby cities. Such barbarity had an immediate though temporary effect. The other towns of Phoenicia submitted to Esarhaddon, only to rebel again in 672 under the leadership of King Baal of Tyre and in alliance with Taharka (biblical Tirhakah) of Egypt. Though he claimed to have done so, the Assyrian probably did not defeat either Baal or Taharka at the time. But Ashurbanipal (668-633) finally conquered Egypt and the indomitable Tyrians. The princes of Gebal and Arvad and other Canaanite chiefs, as well as Manasseh of Judah, capitulated. The return of peace brought a return of commercial prosperity and a reduction of military expenditure at Tyre. And after the middle of the seventh century the power of Assyria declined; Tyre certainly obtained her independence by about 625 and held it for most of the following forty years. Her greatness, while tarnished, still remained. Ezekiel, who lived during these decades of independence, penned a remarkable description of her attainments (chapter 27).

Any discussion of the Assyrian period of Phoenician history would be quite incomplete without a brief treatment of three topics: Phoenicia's export of Baal worship, which would affect religious developments in Israel; her export of people to establish colonies, which would affect the subsequent history of the Mediterranean world; and her

212. Hunting scene mosaic, Carthage

export of the alphabet, which would affect cultural developments throughout the world.

Phoenician colonies. The when and why of Phoenician colonial expansion have been the subject of much study in recent years. For some generations it has been the practice to accept the date of 814 B.C. for the founding of Carthage and a date of about 1100 for the founding of Gadir (modern Cadiz) and Utica. These dates were based on the writings of Timaeus, a Sicilian Greek of the third century B.C. Archaeological investigation has raised numerous· questions about the traditional picture. Warmington observes, ". . . the cumulative effect of the archaeological evidence that there were no Phoenician settlements in the west before the middle of the eighth century is impressive."[23] Carpenter asserts that Utica and Carthage were not settled before the latter part of the eighth century; from Carthage western Sicily was settled in the seventh century, Sardinia late in the seventh or early in the sixth century, and the Balearic Islands and southern Spain still later in the sixth century.[24] Carpenter tends toward a very compressed chronology in all of his

writing, and his reckonings are probably too late. W. F. Albright has described new Phoenician materials discovered in Spain which put Phoenician occupation there at least as early as the ninth century B.C.; probably some of these materials go back to the tenth century B.C.[25] So the problem rests. Some scholars are impressed that the evidence points to a late date for Phoenician occupation of the western Mediterranean. Others feel that the evidence tends to confirm approximately the traditional dates.

Many reasons have been given as to why the Phoenicians settled their many colonies. Some have emphasized population surplus and social discord at home. Others have urged that Assyrian pressure was largely the reason. But the key reasons seem to have been economic and commercial: the exploitation of metals of a given region and the provision of supply stations or stopping points on their trade routes.

The alphabet. In their commercial contacts with the Greeks, the Phoenicians passed on to them their consonantal alphabet, to which the Greeks added vowels and which they spread farther afield. There has been some controversy as to just when the Greeks borrowed the alphabet. Some have placed the date as early as 1100 or 1000 B.C. It seems best, however, to hold with Albright to a date in the late ninth or early eighth century.[26] Some put it about 750.

Some have claimed that the Phoenicians invented the alphabet and have considered it their great contribution to culture. But this is open to question. The famous Ahiram sarcophagus inscription (from Byblos) dates about 1000 B.C.; none of the other Byblos alphabetic inscriptions date before the thirteenth century B.C. Alphabetic ma-

---

[23]Warmington, p. 29.
[24]Rhys Carpenter, "Phoenicians in the West," *American Journal of Archaeology*, 62 (January, 1958), 53.

[25]These materials were excavated during the three years just prior to Albright's lecture at the Archaeology Conference at Wheaton College (Ill.), October 16, 1961, and were reported in that lecture.
[26]W. F. Albright, *Archaeology of Palestine* (rev. ed.; Harmondsworth, England: Penguin Books Inc., 1960), p. 196.

terials at Ugarit (Ras Shamra) in Syria were penned during the fifteenth century. The Sinai inscriptions date about 1500 (formerly dated about 1900). Three other alphabetic inscriptions, dating between 1800 and 1500 B.C., have been found at Gezer, Shechem (modern Nablus), and Lachish in Palestine. Clearly, then, the earliest alphabetic inscriptions do not come from Phoenicia proper. When and where the alphabet was invented is not now known—possibly in Egypt during the Hyksos period, possibly in Palestine or Phoenicia during the Hyksos era, or slightly earlier.[27] In passing, it is of some interest to note that alphabetic Hebrew is called in Scripture the "language of Canaan" (Isa. 19:18). Apparently the Patriarchs (with an Akkadian background) found it there and carried it with them to Egypt. While we cannot claim that the Phoenicians invented the alphabet, we do know that at the minimum they fulfilled the very important function of transmitting the Semitic alphabet to the Greeks, who added vowels and in turn introduced it to many other peoples.

Phoenician religion. Because Jezebel, daughter of Ethbaal of Tyre, married Ahab and introduced Baal worship to Israel, and because Ahab and Jezebel's daughter Athaliah married Jehoram of Judah and introduced Baal worship there, Phoenician religion holds considerable interest for most Bible students. Father of the gods and head of the Phoenician pantheon was El. Baal, his son, was one of the chief male deities and served as god of agriculture. As such he was responsible for fertility of the field and was associated with human and animal reproduction. Baalath, who seems to have been the consort of Baal, represented the principle of fertility and generation. Actually, Baal simply means "lord" and Baalath, "lady."

Every community had its own Baal and

[27]*Ibid.*, pp. 188-91, and correspondence addressed to the author by Dr. Albright.

Baalath. Melkart (Melqarth) was the supreme deity or Baal of Tyre and was styled "lord of the sun, supreme ruler, giver of life, embodiment of the male principle, god of productivity." He was identified by the Greeks with Heracles or Hercules. Eshmun, god of vital force and healing, was worshiped at Sidon and identified by the Greeks with Asclepius. Reshef, the lightning god, was especially popular in Cyprus and identified with Apollo by the Greeks. The Baalath of Gebal, Ashtaroth (or Astarte), a fertility goddess, was the most popular Baalath of Phoenicia.

The places for worship of Baal were often merely high places in the hills, consisting of an altar, a sacred tree or pole, and a sacred stone pillar. The pillar represented the Baal, and the tree or pole symbolized the Baalath. But commonly the Phoenicians, an urban people, worshiped in temples consisting of a court or enclosure and a roofed shrine at the entrance of which was a porch or pillared hall. The altar, conical stone pillar, and pole or tree stood in the court. A statue of the deity was housed in the shrine. In one of the temples excavated at Gebal about twenty stone pillars came to light. Cut in the general form of obelisks, the highest was ten feet high.

As to the worship connected with Baalism, it will be recognized immediately that one important feature was sacrifice of ani-

213. Ahiram Sarcophagus, Gebal

mals, food, and drink. Human sacrifices seem to have been offered too, though very rarely and only in time of greatest calamity.

Religious festivals, associated with the rhythm of the seasons, were also connected with Baal worship. That is to say, the god was viewed as dying in the fall and arising in the spring. (Perhaps Elijah was referring to these festivals in I Kings 18:27). The fall festival was accompanied by great mourning, funeral rites, and perhaps self-torture or mutilation. Sacramental sex indulgence was characteristic of the spring festival. Temple prostitutes, both men and women, were attached to all of the temples, where chambers for sexual intercourse were available. Women commonly sacrificed their virginity at the shrines of Astarte in the hope of winning the favor of the goddess. Says Lucian of the festival at Byblos: "But when they have bewailed and lamented, first they perform funeral rites for Adonis as if he were dead, but afterward upon another day they say he lives, . . . and they shave their heads as the Egyptians do when Apis dies. But such women as do not wish to be shaven pay the following penalty; on a certain day they stand for prostitution at the proper time and the market is open for strangers only, and the pay goes as a sacrifice to Aphrodite."[28] The

214. Temple of the Obelisks, Gebal

[28]W. B. Fleming, *History of Tyre* (New York: Columbia University Press, 1915), p. 151.

festival of Adonis was regularly held at Byblos or Gebal, and the festival of Melkart at Tyre. The debased and debasing worship of Phoenicia deserved the total condemnation meted out to it in the Old Testament.

The Neo-Babylonian Period

After the fall of Nineveh (612 B.C.), the Assyrian Empire was replaced by the Neo-Babylonian. But remnants of the Assyrian army held out in the upper Euphrates region until 609/608 B.C. In the confusion of that three-year period, the Egyptians under Necho (609-594) tried to reestablish their power in Palestine and Syria. During the first year or two of his reign, Necho penetrated to the Euphrates River. Seemingly several of the Phoenician cities came under his sway but retained their autonomy and secured conditions favorable to trade.

The Babylonians were not long in meeting the threat. Nebuchadnezzar, son of the ruling monarch Nabopolassar, advanced to wrest from the Egyptians the area once controlled by the Assyrians. He defeated Necho at the famous Battle of Carchemish in 605 and in short order marched to the very borders of Egypt. The city-states of Phoenicia capitulated and paid tribute, retaining a semi-independent status under their own rulers.

Just as Nebuchadnezzar reached the borders of Egypt, he received news of his father's death and had to hurry home to forestall any moves against his kingly rights. In the process of subduing the Westland in 605/604, he apparently besieged Jerusalem and deported many of her best citizens (e.g., Daniel, Dan. 1:1-3). Subsequent disorders in the West resulted in Nebuchadnezzar's again besetting Jerusalem and carrying off a large number of hostages (including Ezekiel) in 597. The Egyptians were not yet over their expansionist dreams, and Hophra (Apries, 588-569) in 588 successfully attacked Tyre and Sidon and managed to intimidate most of the Phoenician coast. But Nebuchadnezzar responded promptly to this threat, as well as to the revolt of the Judaeans, who had allied themselves with Hophra. He destroyed Jerusalem, her walls, and the Temple in 587/586. Phoenicia fell next.

A few years before this Babylonian attack, Ezekiel had prophesied the ultimate ruin of Tyre and Sidon (26:3-12, 14, 19; 28:21-23). Sifted and itemized, these verses present several predictions. The first group is against Tyre: (1) her strongholds to be destroyed; (2) many nations to come up against her; (3) dust to be scraped from her until she would be as bare as the top of a rock; (4) her ruins to provide a place for spreading of nets; (5) Nebuchadnezzar to descend and cast battlements against her; (6) Nebuchadnezzar to break through the walls, tread the streets, and kill the garrisons, taking much spoil; (7) ruins of the city to be dumped in the water; (8) Tyre to be desolated and uninhabited. Others are against Sidon: (1) judgments to be executed in her; (2) pestilence and slaughter to descend upon her.

Sweeping into Phoenicia, Nebuchadnezzar took Sidon and then settled down to a thirteen-year siege of Tyre (585-572). It seems that ultimately Nebuchadnezzar was successful in taking the mainland part of

216. Phoenician harbor, Sidon

Tyre. But without a fleet he could not take the island city, which surrendered on conditions favorable to the citizens of the island. Mainland Tyre remained in ruins until the days of Alexander the Great.[29] In this way the first stage of Ezekiel's prophecy against Tyre was fulfilled.

Tyre's greatest days were gone. Her commerce was ruined by the siege as well as by Greek capture of Phoenician trade in the northeastern Mediterranean and to some extent elsewhere. Tyre's role in international trade was further usurped on land by Aramaean merchants and on sea by the Carthaginians. Temporarily Sidon assumed Phoenician leadership. Although the Assyrians had destroyed Sidon and built a small post on the site populated by foreigners, it had again gradually become a relatively prosperous Phoenician city.

The Persian Period

Transition from Babylonian to Persian rule of Phoenicia seems to have been peaceful. Cyrus' policy of leniency toward all his foreign subjects produced favorable conditions for Phoenicia, whose cities seem to have enjoyed a practical independence and were ruled by their own kings. Treated more like allies than subjects, they furnished the Persians with a fleet on numerous occasions, especially during Persian attacks on Greece. On the other hand they

215. Sculptured lion, Sidon

[29]*Ibid.*, p. 56.

217. Sarcophagus of Eshmunazar of Sidon, third century B.C.

perish with them. It is said that over 40,000 died in the horrible conflagration.[31] Certainly this was sufficient fulfillment of Ezekiel's prophecy against the city. After this terrible catastrophe, the other Phoenician cities had no heart to continue the rebellion against Persia.

The Greek Period

In 334 B.C. Alexander the Great crossed the Hellespont (Dardanelles) to begin his conquest of the Persian Empire. His victory at the Granicus River opened Asia Minor to him. Near the end of the following year, his victory at Issus gained Syria for him. Seeking to neutralize or control the Persian fleet, Alexander chose to continue south around the coast of the Mediterranean. Since he had no fleet, the only way Alexander could conquer the Persian fleet was to conquer its bases. For this reason Alexander moved south into Syria and Egypt before pursuing the Persians eastward.

Sidon, now largely rebuilt, was still bitter over the destruction in the days of Artaxerxes Ochus and welcomed the conquerors. Byblos and other cities of the coast offered no opposition. Tyre alone opposed Alexander. The Tyrians initially offered submission and tribute to him, thinking they would thereby gain substantial freedom, as they had before. But when they saw that Alexander intended personally to occupy the city, they determined to resist.

Hope of Tyrian success in withstanding the siege was not unfounded. Their city was located on an island a half mile from shore; the current in the channel which separated it from land was swift. Their fleet controlled the sea. The city wall on the landside rose to 150 feet. There were assurances of help from Carthage and elsewhere. But Alexander devised unexpected tactics. He resolved to construct a causeway 200

received the protection of a strong empire. During this entire period, Sidon was the predominant city. It even served as a royal residence when Persian kings carried out duties in the West. Of the twenty satrapies or administrative areas into which Darius divided the empire, Phoenicia was in the fifth, which also included Palestine, Syria, and Cyprus.

During the fourth century, the Phoenicians grew increasingly restless under Persian rule. Perhaps this was due in part to increasing relations with the Greeks. Phoenicians began to settle in large numbers in Attica.[30] At least Tyre (how voluntarily we do not know) participated in the unsuccessful revolt of Evagoras in Cyprus in 392, which was also supported by the Greeks and Egyptians. The Phoenicians participated in the War of the Satraps in 362—a rebellion which the Persians also effectively subdued. Then in 352 B.C., after suffering extremely insolent treatment at the hands of the Persians, the Phoenicians determined to revolt. They were aided in the struggle by Egypt. When the Persian army stood before the city of Sidon, the leaders defected to save their own lives. Robbed of all protection, the people determined to set fire to their own homes and

[30]Frederick C. Eiselen, *Sidon A Study in Oriental History* (New York: Columbia University Press, 1907), p. 64.

[31]*Ibid.*, p. 66.

feet wide out to the island, on which he could plant his siege engines. Ruins of mainland Tyre furnished material for the causeway. The Tyrians fought heroically. They destroyed the engines of war by fire-ships and damaged the mole, or causeway. They hurled pots of burning naphtha, sulfur, and red-hot sand from catapults. Seeing that the battle could not be won without the use of a fleet, Alexander obtained contingents from Sidon, Greek allies, and Cyprus. After a siege of seven months, the wall was breached and the city taken after savage fighting. It is reported that 8,000 were killed in the fighting, 2,000 were later executed, 30,000 were sold into slavery, and 15,000 were secretly smuggled away by attacking Sidonian ships whose sailors were sympathetic with the defenders.[32] Previously thousands of women, children, and older people had been evacuated to Carthage.

For all practical purposes it can be said that the prophecies of Ezekiel had been fulfilled. The mainland city had been scraped bare as the top of a rock in building the causeway to the island city. The island city had been destroyed. And though the city was rebuilt once more and was fairly prosperous by 315 B.C., the colonists were large-

218. Modern buildings on the causeway Alexander built to Island Tyre

ly Carian rather than Phoenician. Therefore it can be said that little ethnic connection existed between the old and new cities and that although the city was rebuilt, it was not to be another Phoenician city—mart of nations.[33] In fact, Phoenicians tended to lose their racial characteristics altogether during the Greek period, when the area was merged with Syria. Continued invasions had even before that time considerably diluted the racial stock. With Alexander's conquest, the Greeks were definitely supreme in the Mediterranean; the old Phoenician mercantile and maritime supremacy was forever broken. Rhodes later attained the position proud Tyre had enjoyed.

With the death of Alexander in 323 B.C., Phoenicia once again became an international football, passed from one to another of Alexander's generals. The military activities of those years were hard on the prosperity of the area. Finally in 286 the Ptolemies of Egypt gained firm control. Sidon again achieved supremacy among the Phoenician city-states. With Ptolemaic decline, the Seleucids of Syria became masters of Phoenicia in 198. Under the Seleucids the

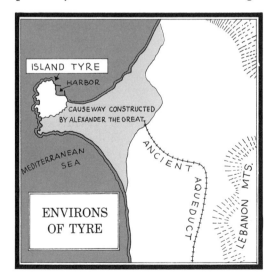

ISLAND TYRE
HARBOR
CAUSEWAY CONSTRUCTED
BY ALEXANDER THE GREAT
MEDITERRANEAN SEA
ANCIENT AQUEDUCT
LEBANON MTS.

ENVIRONS OF TYRE

[33]Tyre suffered several attacks and partial destructions in subsequent centuries, suffering almost complete destruction at the hands of the Muslims in 1291, after which it lay in ruins for centuries. Today Tyre has a population of some 12,000 and occupies the site of the ancient island city and Alexander's mole—now considerably widened by sands which have drifted against it. The site of the mainland city is largely unoccupied; the island site has been partially excavated.

[32]Fleming, p. 64.

219. Graeco-Roman theater, Byblos

Phoenician city-states one by one obtained autonomous status. But while they attained a degree of prosperity, the old glory was gone. With the demise of the Seleucids, Pompey occupied Phoenicia for Rome in 64 B.C.

The Roman Period

Officially Phoenicia ceased to exist, being incorporated with Palestine and Syria proper into the Roman province of Syria. Although Phoenicia suffered during the Roman civil wars, a new era of prosperity dawned with the victory of Augustus, the *Pax Romana*, and imperial reorganization. The peace was kept by the four legions stationed in Syria. Aradus, Sidon, Tyre, and Tripolis were given rights of self-government. Commerce was facilitated by the new road system. Phoenician industrial and commercial activity again became widespread. Mommsen observes that Tyrians had factories (trade depots) in the two great import harbors of Italy, Ostia and Puteoli. Berytus (Beirut) had similar factories in Italian ports.[34] The wine of Byblos and Tyre was especially valued by the Romans. Byblos, Tyre, and Berytus sent their linen all over the world. Tyrian purple was still much in demand and continued to be the city's most significant export. At Tyre

[34]Theodor Mommsen, *The Provinces of the Roman Empire from Caesar to Diocletian*, trans. William P. Dickson (New York: Charles Scribner's Sons, 1906), I, 151, 152.

and Aradus, both of which were located on islands, houses and other buildings rose skyscraperlike in several stories.

The literary activity in Phoenician cities during the early Roman period excelled that of any earlier period. Strabo (d. A.D. 24) eulogized the Sidonian philosophers in the sciences of astronomy and arithmetic. Other classical writers referred to celebrated Phoenician poets whose names are not known. Sidon, Byblos, Berytus, and Tyre seem to have contributed most to the intellectual production of the age.[35] Sidon had a law school which was famed throughout the classical East. Two early Stoic philosophers of Tyre are known: Antipater, an intimate of Cato; and Apollonius, who wrote a work about Zeno and compiled a bibliography of Stoic philosophy.

During the Roman period the whole character of Phoenicia changed. Hellenization went on apace. The native language fell into disuse and was replaced by Aramaic, Greek, and Latin for official documents. Roman rule tended to obliterate the characteristic features of national life. Roman colonies were established at Berytus, Accho (Ptolemais), Tyre, and Sidon.

Phoenicia figures inconspicuously in the New Testament narrative. Jesus went to the region of Tyre and Sidon (Matt. 15:21; Mark 7:24, 31), where He healed a Syro-Phoenician woman's daughter. Whether he actually went into Phoenicia or just to the borders of it is an open question. Numbered among the followers of the Master were inhabitants of Phoenicia (Mark 3:8).

Christianity came to Phoenicia shortly after Pentecost. The persecution accompanying the stoning of Stephen scattered believers to Phoenicia, among other places (Acts 11:19). Barnabas and Saul preached there briefly on their return to Jerusalem from their period of ministry in Antioch (Acts 15:3). At the close of Paul's third missionary journey, he stopped at Tyre for a week while his ship unloaded her cargo.

[35]Hitti, p. 201.

There he seems to have contacted a considerable number of believers (Acts 21:2-7). The apostle stopped briefly at Sidon on his way to Rome and met certain friends there (Acts 27:3).

Tyre was the early center of Christianity in Phoenicia, and she became the seat of a Christian bishop late in the second century. Sidon also became an important center of Christianity, as is demonstrated by the fact that she had a bishop present at the Council of Nicaea (modern Nice) in A.D. 325.

While men tend to judge the importance of a country by its size or its ability to control its neighbors, Phoenicia cannot be so judged. If she did not invent the alphabet, she at least developed it and passed it on to the Greeks. She made significant achievements in production of both molded and blown glass; some would credit her with having invented these processes.[36] Having learned from Babylonian astronomers to use the stars as a guide to navigation, she passed this knowledge on to Greeks and Romans and thereby revolutionized navigation. Phoenician ships controlled the Mediterranean for almost half a millennium and the Aegean for some three centuries.

In her merchant role she bartered ideas as well as goods, bringing ideas of the East to the West and vice versa. In this way she sped the progress of culture in the ancient world. The Bible student is also alert to Phoenician impact on Hebrew cultural and religious development. So notorious is the latter involvement that the name Jezebel has become a byword in western Christian culture—both as the wife of wicked Ahab and as a synonym for a shameless woman.

[36]Dimitri Baramki, *Phoenicia and the Phoenicians* (Beirut: Khayats, 1961), p. 112.

Bibliography

ALBRIGHT, WILLIAM F. *Archaeology of Palestine.* Harmondsworth, England: Penguin Books Inc., rev. ed. 1960.

BARAMKI, DIMITRI. *Phoenicia and the Phoenicians.* Beirut: Khayats, 1961.

BOUCHIER, E. S. *Syria as a Roman Province.* Oxford: B. H. Blackwell, 1916.

BREASTED, JAMES H. *Ancient Records of Egypt.* Vols. 1, 2. Chicago: University of Chicago Press, 1906.

CARPENTER, RHYS. "Phoenicians in the West." *American Journal of Archaeology,* 62 (Jan., 1958).

CASSON, LIONEL. *The Ancient Mariners.* New York: Macmillan Co., 1959.

CHILDE, V. GORDON. *New Light on the Most Ancient East.* London: Routledge and Kegan Paul, Ltd., rewritten 1952.

CONTENAU, GEORGES. *La Civilisation phénicienne.* Paris: Payot, 1926.

DUNAND, MAURICE. *De l'Amanus au Sinai.* Beirut: Catholic Press, 1953.

———. *Fouilles de Byblos.* Paris: P. Geuthner, 1937.

DUSSAUD, RENE. *Topographie historique de la Syrie antique et médiévale.* Paris: P. Geuthner, 1927.

EISELEN, FREDERICK C. *Sidon, a Study in Oriental History.* New York: Columbia University Press, 1907.

FLEMING, WALLACE B. *The History of Tyre.* New York: Columbia University Press, 1915.

HARDEN, DONALD. *The Phoenicians.* New York: Frederick A. Praeger, 1962.

HITTI, PHILIP K. *History of Syria.* London: Macmillan & Co., Ltd., 1951.

———. *Lebanon in History.* London: Macmillan & Co., Ltd., 1957.

———. *The Near East in History.* Princeton: D. Van Nostrand Co., Inc., 1961.

MOMMSEN, THEODOR. *The Provinces of the Roman Empire from Caesar to Diocletian.* Translated by WILLIAM P. DICKSON. Vol. 2. New York: Charles Scribner's Sons, 1906.

MONTET, PIERRE. *Byblos et l'Egypte.* 2 vols. Paris: P. Geuthner, 1928, 1929.

PERROT, GEORGES, and CHIPIEZ, CHARLES. *History of Art in Phoenicia and Its Dependencies.* 2 vols. London: Chapman and Hall, Ltd., 1885.

WARMINGTON, B. H. *Carthage.* London: Robert Hale Limited, 1960.

220. Six columns of the Temple of Jupiter still stand majestically among the ruins of Baalbek.

Syria

Some have called Syria an international football kicked around by the major powers surrounding her. Others have described Syria as a crossroads of civilization. However one looks at her, Greater Syria has commonly been acted upon in history rather than acting upon her neighbors. The existence of a strong power in Asia Minor, Mesopotamia, or Egypt would mean aggressive action against Syria. With a strong power on both the northern and southern borders, Syria became a battleground. Sargon of Akkad (or Accad), Hammurabi of Babylon, the Egyptians, Hittites, Assyrians, Chaldeans, Persians, Greeks, and Romans—all in their turn conducted military campaigns there, sent in their cultural influences, or politically dominated the area. In 1958 Egypt and Syria joined politically to form the United Arab Republic. And today Egypt seems to be Syria's polar magnet. But if the past few years are a proper example, Syria takes her role of being dominated with no better grace now than in ancient times.

Strategic position. Syria has held too good a position for neighboring countries to ignore her. A land bridge between Asia and Africa, she naturally provided a route for conquering armies. Arteries of trade from Mesopotamia, Asia Minor, and Egypt converged on such cities as Damascus. Although the Syrian coast is not hospitable, throughout Syrian history, people have been coming to it and from it; and almost every town on the coast has had its heyday of maritime activity.

Wealth. Moreover, Syria had too many riches to be left to her own fate. There was the wealth of the forests, especially in the Lebanon region and north Syria. The cedars and cypresses of Lebanon, Amanus (Alma Dag), and the regions near Damascus, together with their resin and oil were used in many countries. The wood and resin of the Syrian terebinth and sumac were likewise well known. The laurel wood near Daphne was famous. Syrian figs were renowned, and olive culture was widespread, as was the culture of the vine. Plums, pears, apples, and dates produced in the area were much in demand, especially in the Roman period. Syrian wines were the only ones imported by all countries of the ancient world. Papyrus was also grown in Syrian fens and here as in Egypt was used as a writing material. One must not neglect to mention the products of medicinal and aromatic plants which were a most important source of revenue for the country. Note especially the Syrian styrax (storax), nard, silphion (silphium), and magydaris. The vegetables of the area were apparently superior to those of Egypt. Well-known Syrian centers of cattle breeding were Damascus and Apamea. The exploitation of the mineral wealth of the region in ancient times is not so widely known, but cinnabar, alabaster, amber, and gypsum were extensively produced in Syria.[1]

[1] For documentation and summary on the wealth of Syria, see especially F. M. Heichelheim, "Roman Syria," *An Economic Survey of Ancient Rome*, ed. Tenney Frank (Baltimore: Johns Hopkins Press, 1938), IV, 127-40, 152, 156, and the whole section 123-257.

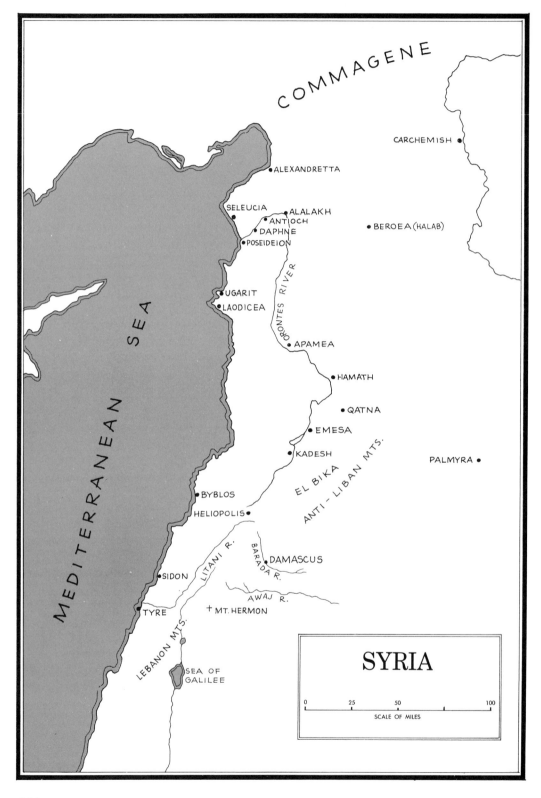

COMMAGENE

CARCHEMISH •

• ALEXANDRETTA

SELEUCIA   • ALALAKH
        • ANTIOCH   • BEROEA (HALAB)
        • DAPHNE
        • POSEIDEION

ORONTES RIVER

• UGARIT
• LAODICEA

        • APAMEA

                • HAMATH

                        • QATNA

                • EMESA

        • KADESH   PALMYRA •

                EL BIKA

                ANTI - LIBAN MTS.

• BYBLOS

HELIOPOLIS •

                LITANI R.   BARADA R.   • DAMASCUS

• SIDON   AWAJ R.

• TYRE   + MT. HERMON

LEBANON MTS.

        SEA OF
        GALILEE

MEDITERRANEAN SEA

SYRIA

0   25   50   100

SCALE OF MILES

Geographical Features

The boundaries of Syria. The boundaries of Syria have fluctuated over the centuries according to political arrangements. When the power of the central government has been strong, it has exerted its control over the nomadic peoples of the desert; so the boundary line has moved east. When the central government has weakened, the nomads have pushed the boundary line westward. During the days of David and Solomon, the Hebrew kingdom virtually engulfed Syria. In days of Assyrian strength, the northern boundary of Syria was pushed southward. In days of Israelite weakness, Syrian kings were able to push their southern boundary southward. When Seleucid kings ruled from Antioch (modern Antakya), they managed, at least temporarily, to control most of the old Persian Empire (including Phoenicia and Palestine). Roman provincial organization also gave Syria a rather large territory.

Originally "Syria" was a term which applied only to a powerful state whose center was in the Lebanon district and whose capital was Damascus. The Assyrians called this country west of the Euphrates "the Land of Amurrû." But geographers, following such ancient authorities as Strabo (who wrote during the lifetime of Jesus Christ) and the Arab geographers, commonly consider the limits of Syria to be the Taurus Mountains and the Euphrates River on the north, the Sinai Desert on the south, and the Mediterranean Sea and the Syrian Desert on the west and east. Strabo divided Syria into four regions: Commagene (a district between the Taurus and the Euphrates), Seleucid Syria (the central section around Antioch and Latakia), Coele-Syria (including the valley between the Lebanon and Anti-Lebanon [Anti-Liban] Mountains and much of southern Syria), and Phoenicia-Palestine.[2]

But biblical students generally—and many others as well—make a distinction between Syria and Palestine. Syria is restricted to the territory at the arch of the Fertile Crescent, bounded on the west by the Mediterranean, on the south by what became known as Galilee and Bashan, on the east by the Syrian Desert, and on the north by the Euphrates River and the Amanus Mountains. Sometimes it is considered to include Phoenicia. In this volume Syria is not generally used to include either Palestine or Phoenicia; separate sections are devoted to those areas. The southwest boundary is set at the Lebanon Mountains, which effectively shut off Syria from the coast.

The Regions of Syria. Syria consists of a series of strongly marked zones—coastal plain, mountain ranges, valleys with luxuriant vegetation, and stony or sandy tracts in the east which are either desert or largely unproductive.

The coast of the eastern Mediterranean, some 440 miles from Alexandretta to the Egyptian border, is one of the straightest in the world, with no deep estuary or gulf and no protecting island of any size. However, at Carmel and northward, where hills approach the coast, short capes jut out and there are a few bays and islets that formed harbors sufficient for the ships of antiquity. In Syria proper there were small harbors at such places as Latakia (ancient Laodicea) and Ras Shamra (ancient Ugarit). Seleucia (the port for Antioch) was hardly more than a roadstead. The coastal plain, never more than a few miles wide, was

[2]René Dussaud, *Topographie Historique de la Syrie Antique et Médiévale* (Paris: Paul Geuthner, 1927), pp. 1-2.

largely inconsequential in Syrian history. Much of it is merely a broad strip of sand dunes covered by short grass and low bushes.

Overlooking the coastal plain is a line of mountains that begins with the Amanus Mountains in the north and extends all the way to the towering massif of Sinai in the south. The Amanus (rising to a height of some 5,000 feet) are a southward offshoot of the Tauric system. Separating Syria from Asia Minor, the Amanus is cut on its southern fringe by the Orontes gorge and is crossed by roads to Antioch and Aleppo. The chief pass over the mountains is at Beilan, the Syrian Gates, at an altitude of 2,400 feet. South of the Orontes the range is continued by Jebel Akra ("the bald," classical Casius), which rises to a height of 5,750 feet and extends to Latakia, south of which it bears the name of Nusayriyah (Bargylus). The Nusayriyah chain is broken on the south by the Nahr el Kebeer (the Kebeer River), which today forms the border between Syria and Lebanon and to the south of which extend for 105 miles the Lebanon Mountains (with peaks over 10,000 feet).

Behind the western mountain range is a deep valley, a great fault extending from Armenia to the Gulf of 'Aqaba on the Red Sea and containing the deepest ditch on the earth's surface. One may start along this third topographical region of Syria in the neighborhood of Antioch, where the Orontes River turns westward to cut through the mountains to the sea. Here the plain is broad and extremely rich, none of it more than 600 feet above sea level. From Antioch the valley of the Orontes ascends slowly between the western range and the high plateau of north Syria. At Hama (Hamath) the altitude is 1,015 feet, and at Homs (ancient Emesa) it rises to 1,660 feet.

After Homs the valley becomes El Bika (El Beqa', "the cleft") between the Lebanon and Anti-Liban Mountains. Varying in breadth from six to ten miles, El Bika rises around Baalbek (ancient Heliopolis) to over 3,770 feet. Here is the watershed; to the north flows the Orontes (246 miles long and largely unnavigable), to the south flows the Litani (90 miles long). Both rivers eventually turn westward and flow into the Mediterranean. El Bika is some seventy-five miles long and has always been a rich agricultural and pastoral region. Its grazing land supports large flocks of sheep and goats. Its vines and other fruits flourish, and there is good wheatland. Here, as well as along the lower course of the Orontes,

221. El Bika and the Lebanon Mountains

there are abundant ruins of ancient towns, testifying to the fact that this whole area was prosperous in ancient times—much more so than at present.

The eastern mountain range (Anti-Liban) constitutes the fourth topographical region of Syria. But it has no counterpart to the northernmost sections of the western mountain range. Rising from the Syrian plateau south of Homs, it opposes the Lebanons in almost equal length and height. This mountain complex is divided into two parts by the broad plateau and gorge of the Barada (biblical Abana) River. To the north is the Jebel esh Sherqi ("Eastern Mountain"), the uppermost ledge of which is a high plateau some twenty miles broad and about 7,500 feet high. It is a stony desert resting on a foundation of chalky limestone. Its western flank falls steeply to El Bika and is virtually uninhabited; the eastern side is more accessible.

The southern part of the eastern range, Jebel esh Sheikh, or Mount Hermon, rises to a height of 9,232 feet and is one of the highest and most majestic peaks of Syria. Here snow settles deep in winter and hardly disappears from the summit in summer. In contrast with the northern part of the Anti-Libans, Mount Hermon has more villages on its western slopes and fewer on its eastern.

On the south and east, the slopes of Hermon fall swiftly to the vast plateau of Hauran, the treeless surface of which is volcanic and its soil a rich, red loam. The lava field covers an area almost sixty miles long by as many wide. On the east the Hauran is bounded by the mountain of Hauran, or the "Mountain of the Druzes." This bulwark is about thirty-five miles north and south and twenty east and west, with a summit that rises to 6,000 feet. In the north the Hauran is two to three thousand feet above sea level, but on the south it shelves off to its limit in the deep valley of the Yarmuk. Known in classical times as "Auranitis" and in biblical times as "Bashan,"

222. Damascus

the Hauran has some of the best wheatland in the Near East. It was one of the granaries of the empire during the Roman period.

The Anti-Libans collect their waters and send them southward into the Jordan system and eastward far into the desert (Damascus is about thirty miles east of Hermon) in the channel of the Barada River. On a lofty and drainable plateau some 2,200 feet in altitude, the Barada has created 150 square miles of fertility, the Ghûtah, from which rises the city of Damascus, civilization's outpost in the desert. Though defenseless and on no natural line of commerce, Damascus has learned to exploit the fertility of her hinterland and to bend to herself much of the traffic between Egypt and Mesopotamia, as well as points west. In this way she has retained her prosperity over the centuries and today has a population well in excess of a half million. The Barada River (c. 45 miles long) divides into five branches in the Damascus oasis and finally loses itself in the desert. Another river which rises in the Anti-Libans is the biblical Pharpar, identified with the Awaj, which flows some distance south of Damascus and disappears in swamps east of the city. Naaman was immensely proud of both of these life-giving rivers of his homeland (II Kings 5:12).

East of the Hauran Plateau and its boundary of Jebel ed Druz (Jebel Druze) lies the Syrian Desert, which is a continuation of the great Arabian Desert. The Syro-Iraqi Desert forms a huge triangle whose base rests on the Gulf of Aqaba on the west and the Gulf of Kuwait on the east and whose apex reaches toward Aleppo on the north. At its widest this desert stretches about 800 miles.

Trade routes. Numerous trade routes crossed the sands of Syria. A Transjordanic route led from the Gulf of Aqaba to Petra and from there to Damascus. A coastal route ran from Gaza to Carmel, across Esdraelon, and in Galilee divided into two branches, one to Damascus and the other north along the Orontes. The northern road to Mesopotamia led from Damascus north and passed through Homs (ancient Emesa), Arabian Haleb (Aleppo, ancient Beroea) and then east down the Euphrates River. Another link between Syria and Mesopotamia by a more southerly track took off from Damascus or Homs and proceeded by way of Palmyra to ancient Dura-Europos. In the days of the Sino-Roman world peace (1st and 2d centuries A.D.), the Aleppo Road formed the last stage of the "silk route" from the Yellow Sea to the Mediterranean.

Climate. It seems that the climate of Syria has changed since New Testament times. Large sections of areas which are now mere desert were formerly cultivated. East of Homs, where there is now not a green leaf nor a drop of water, the heavy basalt slabs of former oil presses are found in quantities.[3] But it is not clear how much of the change is related to rainfall and to what extent the change is due to lack of water regulation brought about by erratic political conditions.[4] The Syrian summer is hot and long (May to September), its winter being short and mild. But there is considerable regional variation. Rainfall on the western mountain slopes and in the north of Syria is adequate. The eastern slopes have less precipitation. While Latakia on the coast enjoys over thirty inches of rainfall per year, the average at Damascus is about nine inches and at Aleppo approximately eighteen inches. Most of the population of the country lives in areas where the average winter temperature is 42 to 43 degrees, the average summer temperature 83 degrees, and the average annual temperature 61 to 63 degrees. These figures apply to both Aleppo and Damascus and would include many of the towns of interior Syria.

[3]Theodor Mommsen, *The Provinces of the Roman Empire from Caesar to Diocletian,* trans. William P. Dickson (New York: Charles Scribner's Sons, 1906), II, 148.

[4]M. Cary, *The Geographic Background of Greek and Roman History* (Oxford: At the Clarendon Press, 1949), p. 165.

223. The Barada River as it flows through downtown Damascus

Historical Developments

The Beginnings

The origins of life in Syria are lost in the mists of prehistory. While there are remains classified as Paleolithic from the Carmel, Galilee, and Lebanon caves and Neolithic materials from excavations at such early sites as Jericho and Gezer, not quite so much is known about early Syria proper. This area has not commanded any archaeological interest like that bestowed on her neighbor to the south. But the highland triangle of north Syria between Tarsus, Damascus, and Nineveh was doubtless occupied in very early times, perhaps in the Neolithic age. Carchemish, on a hill thirty feet above the Euphrates at the present Syro-Turkish border, began its existence in the fifth millennium B.C. with a Chalcolithic culture. The same is true of Ras Shamra on the coast. Sakje Geuzi, to the northwest of Carchemish, likewise went through a Chalcolithic period but it had two earlier levels of occupation.

Around 4000 B.C. copper began to be more or less widely used in Syria and Palestine, and the fourth millennium may be designated the Chalcolithic age.[5] About 3000 B.C. the Copper Age began, at which time copper became the dominant material for tools and weapons. From Syria the knowledge of copper spread in all directions. Probably Egypt and Mesopotamia received their knowledge of this metal from north Syria, from which region also came the domestication of wheat.[6] North Syrian monochrome pottery probably dates as early as 5000 B.C., painted pottery coming about 500 years later. The potter's wheel must have been invented a little before 4000.

During the third millennium an event of major significance occurred in Syria—the coming of the Semites. These people, looked upon from the biblical standpoint as descendants of Noah's son Shem, are commonly viewed by modern scholars as those who speak or spoke a Semitic tongue. The Semitic family of languages includes Assyro-Babylonian (Akkadian), Canaanite, Aramaic, Hebrew, Arabic, and Ethiopic. The Semitic homeland is believed by some to be the Arabian peninsula, by others to be the hill country north or south of the Euphrates Valley.

The Amorites

The first major Semitic group to move into Syria was the Amorites, who began to arrive about the middle of the third millennium. Probably they roamed El Bika and the northern regions for some time as Bedouins following their flocks and herds before settling down to a more sedentary life. There they intermarried with an earlier Armenoid population.

The Amorite language belonged to the west Semitic group and was therefore related to Phoenician, Canaanite, and the later Hebrew and Aramaic. "Amorite" is a non-Semitic word meaning "westerner." This is what the Sumerians of Mesopotamia called them; what the Semitic group called themselves is not known. The name of their country came to be known as "Amurrû" or "Martu" ("westland").

The Semites' chief deity was Amor, or Amurrū, a god of war and hunting. His consort was Ashirat, goddess of the waste places and lusty energy. Her name corresponds to the asherah, the sacred pole or tree trunk, a well-known cult object con-

[5]Philip K. Hitti, *History of Syria* (New York: The Macmillan Co., 1951), p. 23.
[6]*Ibid.*, p. 24.

224. Head of the god Hadad, from Carchemish

demned in the Old Testament. The Amorites introduced into southern Syria the cult of the sacred pillar or monolith, apparently representing the tribal deity, which was erected with altars in caves and other worship centers. Another important deity of their pantheon was the rain god Hadad or Adad, also known as Rimmon. Grain was personified in Dagon.

Meanwhile, probably during the first half of the twenty-fourth century B.C., the Sumerian Lugal-zaggisi in a remarkable twenty-five-year reign which constituted the third dynasty of Uruk, northwest of Ur, claimed control over a vast territory which included Syria. He asserted that his conquests ranged from the "Lower Sea" to the "Upper Sea,"[7] obviously from the Persian Gulf to the Mediterranean.

Meanwhile, Semitic strength in Mesopotamia was increasing. However, the Semites there perpetuated the old Sumerian

civilization, so it is accurate to speak simply of Mesopotamian civilization. With Sargon of Akkad (or Accad) a dynasty of Semitic-speaking kings came to power in Mesopotamia (about the middle of the 24th century B.C.). Sargon toppled Lugal-zaggisi and thereby extended his authority eastward into Elam and westward as far as Syria and the Mediterranean. One of his inscriptions gives credit to the god Dagon of the Semites of north Syria for bestowing on him the Syrian coastlands.[8] When Sargon occupied Amurrû, he destroyed a Sumerian dynasty that ruled at Mari, its capital.

During the twentieth century B.C., Amorites established themselves at Mari and its environs, imposing themselves on a more civilized Mesopotamian society. They overran the rest of Mesopotamia and Syria, as well as moving south into Palestine. Among the dynasties they established in the Fertile Crescent during the period 2100-1800, the Babylonian was the most important. There Hammurabi was the guiding light to empire. About 1700 he took Mari and consigned it to oblivion until André Parrot rescued it with the excavator's pick in the 1930's.

Fortunately Parrot turned up the archives of Mari's kings. These more than 20,000 cuneiform tablets show that during the eighteenth century the entire area from the Mediterranean to the highlands of Elam was under the control of Amorite princes. Shamshi-Adad I, an aggressive Assyrian ruler of the latter eighteenth century, was an Amorite. Aleppo (or Haleb) appears as the capital of an Amorite kingdom; and the biblical Haran (ancient Carrhae), where Abraham stopped, was an Amorite princedom. Byblos (modern Jubayl) under control of an Amorite king, was a center for manufacturing cloth and garments. Qatna (northeast of Homs, its modern successor) was another important Amorite town.[9]

[7]Jack Finegan, *Light from the Ancient Past* (2d ed.; Princeton: Princeton University Press, 1959), p. 44.

[8]*Ibid.*, p. 47.
[9]Hitti, p. 68.

Qatna is one of the best-known sites of Syria in this period. As usual, the most thoroughly explored part of the ruins is the palace complex. The palace and temple formed one great center and sat on a raised clay platform 400 feet east and west and about 230 feet north and south. The main entrance on the south gave access to a court about 66 by 33 feet, on the east side of which two large doors led to the royal apartments. To the west of the court a passageway led to the throne room, from the anteroom of which access was gained to the temple court. At the northeast corner of the temple court was a holy place separated by a curtain from the holy of holies where stood a small golden statue of the goddess Nin-egal, "Lady of Qatna."[10]

Amorite prosperity was based partly on agriculture and partly on commercial advantage. The Amorites occupied good farmlands in Syria and Palestine (where rainfall was sufficient for good crops) and along the Euphrates (where an irrigation culture existed). As to commercial advantage, the Gulf of Issus, or Alexandretta (Turkish Iskenderon), is only about one hundred miles from the western bend of the Euphrates at Carchemish. Here the land forms a natural corridor connecting the Mediterranean Sea and the Mesopotamian Valley. Called the "Syrian Saddle," this corridor lies between the Taurus Mountains on the north and the desert on the south.

The eastern terminus of the east-west corridor is Carchemish on the Euphrates. From there the line of communication passes through Haran and Halaf and turns south to Nineveh (ancient Ninus) and then down the Tigris River. The ease of communication across this area of north Syria was facilitated not only by geographical considerations but also by the climate. The north Syrian plain received ten to twenty inches of rainfall per year, enough to provide pasture for animals and passing caravans. Cities were sustained by waters from the Taurus Mountains and the Euphrates River. This important region was fought over by Akkadians, Babylonians, Egyptians, Hittites, Assyrians, Chaldeans, Persians, Greeks, and Romans. To all it was valuable as a transit land.

225. Lion's head from a statue base at Carchemish

Egyptian Control

Before Hammurabi invaded Syria, the Egyptians had come to dominate the Phoenician coast and were to do so, with interruptions, from about 2400 B.C. to 1200 B.C. Twelfth Dynasty Pharaohs (c. 2000-1775 B.C.) claimed and probably exercised loose control over Palestine and a large part of Syria as well. According to the place-names on Egyptian lists of about 1800 B.C., the Egyptian Empire included Damascus and most of El Bika.

[10]A. T. Olmstead, *History of Palestine and Syria* (New York: Charles Scribner's Sons, 1931), pp. 82-83.

Canaanites

Early in the second millennium B.C., the Canaanites established themselves in Palestine and Syria. Perhaps they arrived at an earlier time. At least in Palestine they seem to have preceded the Amorites. Where they came from is a question not answered with certainty, but some scholars are currently suggesting that they originated in Arabia. The meaning of their name is likewise uncertain. An older view is that their name is related to the Hebrew *kanan* ("to be made low") and that Canaanites therefore were "lowlanders," as opposed to the Amorites, who lived in the higher regions. A newer view is that Canaan should be related to the Hebrew *Kena'an* which came from a Hurrian and Akkadian word for the purple dye for which Phoenician city-states became famous. The term is confusing because sometimes it is used to apply linguistically to northwest Semitic dialects and sometimes culturally to distinguish the people whom the Hebrews found in Palestine.

Historical and archaeological sources portray the Canaanites as Semites. The Old Testament points to Hamitic rather than Semitic extraction for Canaan (Gen. 10:6). There is no necessary contradiction here because whatever their origin may have been, the Canaanites did not long remain in their early "pure" state but soon were racially and culturally mixed with other tribes of Palestine and Syria.

The Canaanites were not greatly different from the Amorites. Linguistically they were both from the northwest Semitic family and differed only dialectically. Ethnically they were not very dissimilar either. But gradually the Amorites assimilated Sumerian and Hurrian elements, and the Canaanites absorbed other local elements. Culturally the difference between them arose from the fact that the Amorites came more under the influence of the Sumerians and Babylonians while the Canaanites were influenced by Egyptian culture.

But the latter generalization is not completely accurate, for the Canaanites of Palestine and Syria did not have a homogeneous culture. Egyptian culture had more influence in Palestine, Mesopotamian in Syria. The regional differences in Canaanite culture may be readily seen by a study of excavations at two typical towns: Bethshean (modern Beisan) in the south and Ugarit (modern Ras Shamra) in the north. The former, located just south of the Sea of Galilee, was under Egyptian political domination c. 1450 to 1200 B.C. While the five temples of the town were patterned after

226. Reshef

Egyptian models, they were built of brick with wood pillars rather than stone. Within the temples Canaanite deities were worshiped, but they were modeled in the Egyptian style. The chief Canaanite deities were Reshef, a war and storm god; Astarte, the fertility goddess; and Mekal, possibly the Semitic Hercules.

Excavations at Ugarit have demonstrated how Canaanite culture in the north differed from that in the south. Farther away from Egyptian influence than the southern Canaanites, and farther from the Mesopotamians than the southern Canaanites were from Egypt, the northern Canaanites had sufficient independence to create a complex and influential civilization. This was true in spite of the fact that Ras Shamra was a vassal of Egypt from 1500 to 1350 B.C.

The city traded extensively with Cyprus and other Mediterranean islands and Egypt. Copper from Cyprus made possible a sizable copper-smelting industry. Other metal goods, cosmetics, and purple dye were also among the town's industries. Her commercial and industrial activities were similar to those of the Canaanite towns of Phoenicia. At the head of the Ugaritic pantheon was El, and his consort was Athirat, or Ashera, equatable with Aphrodite. There was also the grain god Dagon and his son Baal, or Adonis. The latter's consort was Anat, identifiable with Artemis. How much of the religion of Ugarit was Canaanite and how much Hurrian is yet to be determined. Ugarit is later discussed at more length.

The Canaanites never succeeded in establishing a strong unified state. Their political fragmentation in city-states may be explained variously, but more important is the fact that this division left the country at the mercy of neighboring powers, whether conquerors like the Egyptians or Mesopotamians or new settlers like the Hebrews. Sometimes, however, leagues of Canaanite cities were formed under the leadership of a strong center (such as Ugarit, Byblos,

227. A deity in bronze, Ugarit, second millennium

Tyre, or Hazor) which established a political hegemony. Sometimes these leagues were organized under the stress of mutual danger, as was the case when Kadesh (Qadesh) on the Orontes River led a coalition against Thutmose III early in the fifteenth century.

Basically an agricultural people, the Canaanites also developed various crafts to a very high degree of perfection. Their pottery was made by a wheel early in the second millennium, and styles and decoration were influenced by Egyptian, Minoan, Mycenaean, and Cypriot ware. Their metallurgy was probably unexcelled during most of the second millennium B.C. They were excellent goldsmiths and silversmiths. Copper and bronze working was common among them, and they knew how to use tin for hardening iron.[11] The Canaanites excelled in the manufacture of glass too, as well as in the production of woolen cloth and dyestuffs.

One of the most important cultural contributions of the Canaanites to the Hebrews was their language. The Akkadian-speaking Patriarchs apparently borrowed the alphabetic "language of Canaan" (Isa. 19:18) and carried it with them into Egypt, retained it during their long sojourn there, and then brought it back to Palestine at the time of the conquest.[12]

Aleppo and Alalakh

With the demise of the Egyptian Middle Kingdom, the vassals were free to assert themselves once more, and there must have been a great shuffling of thrones and frontiers. One of the more important powers of Syria during the eighteenth century was the kingdom of Aleppo, or Yamkhad. Aleppo was the capital, and the city-state asserted power over the Amq plain

[11]Hitti, p. 87.
[12]For a discussion of the origins of the alphabet, see section on Phoenicia, pp. 206-207.

228. Idrimi, king of Alalakh, sixteenth century B.C.

to the west and controlled territory all the way to the Mediterranean.

To a considerable degree, light on this kingdom has come from Sir C. Leonard Woolley's excavations at Tell Atchana (ancient Alalakh) during seven seasons of excavation between 1936 and 1949. Alalakh was located by the Orontes River northeast of Ugarit and about forty miles west of Aleppo, and was for a while a secondary capital of the kingdom. The town stood in the Amq plain, a wide flat alluvial area, about 30 by 30 miles, in northwest Syria—occupying the greater part of the Turkish province of Hatay. That the Amq plain was prosperous in antiquity is indicated by the fact that some 200 mounds containing ancient cities dot its landscape.

The buildings which Woolley excavated at Alalakh were the royal palace, the city temple, and the city gate. The palace was quite sumptuous, measuring 320 by 50 feet, and was divided into two parts, official and private quarters, separated by a courtyard. Most, if not all, of the better rooms of the palace were adorned with frescoes painted with an architectural design like some of those in the royal palace of Minos in Crete.[13] Moreover, the methods of construction employed are the same as those of Knossos. In fact, the similarities between the palaces at Alalakh and Knossos were so evident that Woolley suggests that trained experts from the former actually may have been involved in construction of the latter.[14]

Adjacent to the palace was a temple courtyard from which one entered the almost square single-room sanctuary about sixty feet on a side. This was equipped with raised benches along its sides and a stepped altar of basalt stones on the side opposite the entrance.

Alalakh's wealth was based largely on international trade, which was considerable because the city stood astride both the north-south and east-west routes. But its prosperity was short-lived. About 1700 a great catastrophe overtook the city. Its temple and palace were thoroughly plundered and burned. Whether the Babylonians, the Hyksos, or an internal revolution was responsible is not known, but Woolley argues cogently for the third possibility. He points out that the ruling caste was from Aleppo and was not native, that pottery styles revert mostly to local styles after the destruction, and that the palace and temple areas were unoccupied for long thereafter as if cursed.[15] Aleppo itself shows no sign of violence at this period.

Jones points out that a large number of the people at Alalakh were Hurrians, but that their rulers bore west Semitic names.[16]

The Hurrians, biblical Horites, presumably entered the Fertile Crescent from the mountains of Armenia and apparently adopted much of the Amorite culture they found there. One of their great centers was Nuzi, southeast of Nineveh. During the sixteenth century the Hurrians established a kingdom known as Mitanni, about which something is said later.

The Hyksos

Jones also suggests that it was the successes of Hammurabi against such towns as Mari and the political decline of Alalakh which created a vacuum that permitted the Hyksos to come in from the desert.[17] Exactly who the Hyksos were and exactly where they came from is still shrouded in mystery. Since they appeared in the Fertile Crescent and Egypt long before 1700, it would seem that Hammurabi's victories and other troubles in the area had little to do with their entrance. They infiltrated for a long time before they became conquering hordes. The fact that an eighteenth century B.C. fortress excavated at Alalakh employed typically Hyksos construction features[18] leads the writer to question whether the Hyksos were not an important element in the Kingdom of Aleppo. They infiltrated Egypt for much more than a century before they took over there about 1730.

The Hyksos brought to Egypt and Syria as war implements the horse and the horse-drawn chariot, the composite bow, and the curving iron sword. They also developed a new type of fortification which used the glacis principle. Usually employing a rectangular area for a fort, they surrounded it with a high wall that was faced with a sloping revetment on the exterior. Therefore an advancing enemy would be brought into the direct line of the defenders' fire and would also find it virtually impossible

[13]C. Leonard Woolley, *A Forgotten Kingdom* (Harmondsworth, England: Penguin Books Ltd., 1953), p. 73.
[14]*Ibid.*, p. 74.
[15]*Ibid.*, pp. 81-82.
[16]Tom B. Jones, *Ancient Civilization* (Chicago: Rand McNally & Co., 1960), p. 111.

[17]*Ibid.*
[18]Woolley, pp. 66-67.

to tunnel under the fortification walls. Moreover, this whole military complex was normally surrounded by a great moat that would naturally be created in the process of scooping up earth for fortification walls. Numerous sites in Palestine and Syria contain remains of Hyksos fortresses. Among those located in Syria proper are Carchemish (on the Euphrates River at the current Syrian-Turkish border), Qadesh (15 miles southwest of modern Homs, or ancient Emesa) and Qatna (about 15 miles northeast of Homs), which was probably their capital.

Although the Hyksos were known as a warlike people, they had a fairly highly advanced culture and made numerous contributions to Syrian culture of the period. They developed metallurgy to new levels, introduced new pottery forms, made progress in production of jewelry, ivory work, and faience. Burrows thinks they may have introduced the art of inlay to Syria and Palestine.[19]

Egyptian Empire

The expansion of the Egyptian Empire up into Palestine and Syria was almost a natural outcome of Egyptian expulsion of the Hyksos from the land of the Nile. Having defeated the Hyksos in Egypt, the Egyptians proceeded to attack them in their northern strongholds. About the middle of the sixteenth century B.C., Ahmose began the subjection of the Asiatic provinces for Egypt. Thutmose I marched as far as the Euphrates in 1520. But the restless inhabitants of the area did not long remain subdued. Thutmose III found himself making seventeen sorties into Palestine and Syria in almost as many years. One of his greatest battles was fought at Megiddo in 1479 when he met a confederation of some 300 princes of Palestine and Syria and vanquished them. In subsequent campaigns he took Aradus (biblical Arvad, modern Arwad) on the Mediterranean and Qadesh on the Orontes, the prince of which had been the leader of the confederation that had met Thutmose at Megiddo. In fact, Thutmose III traversed Syria all the way to the Euphrates River.

Syrians could be momentarily impressed with Egyptian might. But when Egyptian Pharaohs left the country and/or when there was a change of rulers in Egypt, Syrians commonly entertained ideas of revolt. This tendency is well illustrated in the Amarna Letters, which address frantic pleas for help to Amenhotep III and Amenhotep IV. But these luxury-loving kings who ruled during the first half of the fifteenth century B.C. had no interest in helping their loyal vassals in Palestine and Syria and in maintaining the empire. By the middle of the century, Syria had passed completely out of Egyptian control. Later kings, such as Seti I and Ramses II, tried to restore Egyptian power there, but their success was restricted very largely to the Phoenician coast.

The Mitanni

Decline of Egyptian strength in Syria on any occasion provided opportunity for other powers to take over there or for native dynasts to assert themselves. One of the people who came in from the outside were the Hurrians who around 1500 B.C. established the powerful Mitanni Kingdom that stretched from the Mediterranean to the highlands of Media and included Assyria. Its capital was presumably at Washshukanni in the upper reaches of the Khabur River,[20] a tributary of the Euphrates. When Thutmose III campaigned in Syria,

---

[19]Millar Burrows, *What Mean These Stones?* (New Haven: American Schools of Oriental Research, 1941), p. 190.

[20]Biblical Habor. It was to this region that many of the Israelites were deported when Samaria fell in 723/722 (II Kings 17:6).

he produced great havoc in Mitannian domains west of the Euphrates and brought that area within the Egyptian Empire. Apparently a treaty was made between the two powers at that time, accompanied by a royal marriage. At least Mittanian princesses appear in the Egyptian harem in subsequent decades.

The Hittites

When Egyptian power in Syria declined during the Amarna Age, the Hittites moved into northern Syria and warred effectively against the Mitanni. Frantic appeals from the latter to Amenhotep III and Amenhotep IV (in the Amarna Letters) brought no help from the colossus on the Nile. Advancing from their Asia Minor strongholds, the Hittites were successful under Suppiluliumas about 1375 B.C. in carving out a Syrian empire, which by the end of the Hittite king's reign stretched south of Byblos. The Hittites were able to control most of this area unhindered by outside interference for about a century. Then in the thirteenth century Ramses II attempted to restore Egyptian authority in Syria. Meeting the Hittite Muwatallis at Kadesh on the Orontes River in 1286, Ramses claimed an important victory— which was more nearly a draw. From this battle a nonaggression pact eventually ensued, according to the provisions of which the Hittites retained nearly all of Syria north of Palestine.

Ugarit

In the middle of all the Hittite, Hurrian, and Egyptian power struggle, Ugarit (modern Ras Shamra) maintained a precarious but prosperous existence. Located on a sixty-five foot hill a half mile from the Mediterranean, just across from the eastern

229. Mycenean ivory of the great goddess, Ugarit

tip of Cyprus, the city derived its wealth largely from the trade which flowed through its port, Minet el-Beida. Today Minet el-Beida ("the white harbor") is neither a large or safe harbor. The white chalk cliffs from which it received its name have become eroded and have tumbled into the sea. Also the shoreline has advanced some 400 feet since the town ceased to exist.

Almost ever since a Syrian peasant accidentally broke into an ancient tomb with his plow at the site in 1928, excavations have been going on there. In 1929, C. F. A. Schaeffer of the Strasbourg Museum initiated the excavations, which continued until the outbreak of World War II and resumed again in 1950. However, only a small part of the work has yet been completed. Excavation at the royal necropolis, less than a mile north of the harbor town, netted a considerable number of jars, vases, and idols. Adjacent to the cemetery was a large temple-like structure under the floor of which the kings themselves were buried.

230. Reception hall at the palace,
Ugarit

On the mound the most significant finds include large temples of Dagon and Baal. Associated with the latter were a school and library where a great many tablets were found written in Sumerian, Hurrian, Egyptian, Hittite, a Cypro-Minoan script, and a previously unknown "Ugaritic" Semitic language. Most of the tablets, religious in nature, were written in the "Ugaritic" Semitic and dated from the fifteenth and fourteenth centuries.

The Ugarit mound is the grave of five cities lying one on top of the other. The earliest goes back to the fifth or sixth millennium, and the latest dates to the period 1500-1200 B.C. The last city is best known and is chiefly under consideration here. Its history begins with the establishment of Egyptian power in this area during the Empire period and ends with the destructive activities of the sea peoples about 1200 B.C.

During the Middle Kingdom period of Egypt (c. 2000-1775 B.C.) Ugarit attained great prosperity as a crossroads of trade flowing between Mesopotamia and Egypt. Contacts with the Minoan civilization on Crete also proved to be lucrative. Suffering a commercial eclipse during Hyksos domination, Ugarit revived when Egypt gained effective control of the Syrian coast during the Empire period. Allied with Egypt, Ugarit benefited greatly from Egyp-

tian alliance with the Mitanni (c. 1440-1380). And fortunately for the city she remained unmolested by the Hittites for several decades after the Hittite defeat of the Mitanni (1375 ff.). During the fifteenth and fourteenth centuries, then, Ugarit enjoyed a golden age, with Syrians, Cypriots, Cretans, Greeks, Hurrians, and Egyptians living together amicably there.

As Egyptian power in Syria declined during the Amarna age, the Hittites took over at Ugarit (c. 1360 B.C.). As a tribute-paying vassal of the Hittites, Ugarit was unmolested and she prospered. After Ramses II engaged the Hittites at the battle of Kadesh in 1286 B.C., Ugarit found herself in the delicate position of having to maintain good relations with both Egyptians and Hittites. This she seems to have managed fairly successfully. But around 1200 B.C. Aegean peoples destroyed Ugarit, and she never recovered her earlier prosperity.

The discoveries at Ugarit display Canaanite culture at its height and provide an excellent backdrop for the biblical narrative. They spell out much of the detail of Canaanite religion and do so in a language akin to biblical Hebrew. But scholars are especially interested in what light the Ugaritic epics can throw on Hebrew religion and language. The Ugaritic Texts[21] serve along with the Dead Sea Scrolls to provide a means of arriving at an understanding of what Old Testament words meant to the people to whom the Old Testament was addressed. These texts help in understanding Hebrew grammar too, as well as the poetic structure of vast portions of the Old Testament.

Moreover, discoveries at Ugarit have revealed a sacrificial system with interesting affinities to the Mosaic system. They speak of such sacrifices as the burnt offering,

[21]For translations see especially H. L. Ginsberg, "Ugaritic Myths and Legends," *Ancient Near Eastern Texts*, ed. J. B. Pritchard (Princeton: Princeton University Press, 1953); Theodor Gaster, *The Oldest Stories in the World* (New York: Viking Press, 1952).

whole burnt offering, the wave offering, and numerous others. The existence of such practices among the Canaanites even before the days of Moses has necessitated revision of some of the older Wellhausenian higher criticism which said these "Mosaic" practices came late in Hebrew experience and must date to the Persian period.

Some Bible students have been embarrassed by the similarity of the Ugaritic and biblical sacrificial systems and have felt that the distinctiveness of the Mosaic legislation has now been destroyed. It should be noted, however, that marked differences existed between the Ugaritic and biblical rituals. Moreover, one may note with Pfeiffer, "Elements which Israelites and Canaanites held in common may be traced to the common traditions possessed by the two peoples concerning worship. The New Testament insists that there was a genuine revelation of God to the pre-Abrahamic peoples which was never completely forgotten (Rom. 1:21-32)."[22]

The Aramaeans

The Aramaeans (whose ancestry is traced to Shem, Gen. 10:22-23) were Bedouins who probably spread from the fringe areas north of the Syro-Arabian desert into the more settled region of the Fertile Crescent. They were established in upper Mesopotamia from early Patriarchal times, as the accounts of Isaac and Jacob and a Naram-Sin inscription indicate.[23] There Aram Naharaim (Nahor, Gen. 24:10), or Padan-Aram (Gen. 25:20; 28:2), had as its center the biblical Haran (ancient Carrhae). Perhaps the Aramaeans moved into north and central Syria earlier, but events of the twelfth century offered them an unparalleled opportunity to settle in the area. Hit-

tite power had collapsed; the Egyptian Empire in West Asia was gone; the Hebrews were a politically ineffective collection of tribes living under the leadership of the Judges.

Most powerful of the Aramaean kingdoms of Syria in the late eleventh century was that of Zobah (Zoba) which now is known to have been considerably north of Damascus, probably in the region of Emesa (modern Homs).[24] Damascus must at that time have been part of the kingdom of Zobah. The states of Maacah (Deut. 3:14; Joshua 12:5; 13:11, 13), Geshur, and Tob (Judges 11:3 ff.) are located by Unger to the east of the Jordan and south of Damascus (Esh Shâm).[25]

Hebrew Advance into Syria

After a seven-year reign over Judah at Hebron, David became king over all Israel about 1000 B.C. Taking Jerusalem from the Jebusites and making it his capital, he proceeded to subdue the peoples surrounding the Hebrew kingdom. As internal strength of Israel grew and as one after the other of David's adversaries fell before him in battle, other nations became fearful. Con-

231. A gate in the city wall, Ugarit

[22]Charles F. Pfeiffer, *Ras Shamra and the Bible* (Grand Rapids: Baker Book House, 1962), p. 58.
[23]Merrill F. Unger, *Israel and the Aramaeans of Damascus* (Grand Rapids: Zondervan Pub. House, 1957), p. 39.

[24]*Ibid.*, p. 43.
[25]*Ibid.*, p. 45, map opposite p. 47.

sequently, when David sent an embassy with condolences to King Hanun of Ammon upon the death of his father, Hanun treated the Hebrew king's representatives in a manner calculated to instigate war (II Sam. 10:1-7).

Then Hanun quickly made an alliance with the Aramaean kingdoms of Zobah, Rehob, Tob, and Maacah (II Sam. 10:8), which were no doubt also fearful of the increasing Israelite power. David thoroughly defeated the Aramaeans, with heavy

232. Baal of Thunder, Ugarit

casualties suffered both by Zobah and Damascus, and the Hebrew king stationed occupation troops in the latter city (II Sam. 8:3-6). After David worsted Zobah (which lay to the north of Damascus, as noted above), King Toi of the Hittite kingdom of Hamath apparently acknowledged Hebrew suzerainty (II Sam. 8:9-11). It would seem that the districts under Israelite rule in the days of David can be divided into two categories: those in which occupation troops were stationed (e.g., Damascus) and those which were satellites (e.g., Zobah).

Apparently Solomon (970-931 B.C.) expanded the kingdom bequeathed to him and ruled the entire area from the border of Egypt to the Euphrates River, including Transjordan (II Chron. 9:26). He even brought the Phoenicians within his sphere of influence. His geographical position gave him a good opportunity to make his state chief middleman for overland trade among Arabia, Egypt, Phoenicia, and the Hittite and Aramaean states of Syria and Asia Minor. Under the Pax Hebraica the whole area enjoyed a remarkable prosperity.

However, this is not to imply that all peoples of Palestine and Syria were docile followers of the great king in the Holy City. Apparently Zobah rebelled against Solomon and had to be subdued (II Chron. 8:3). As the state disintegrated late in Solomon's reign, Rezon[26] of Zobah headed a rebel movement that captured Damascus (I Kings 11:23-25). There Rezon established a new dynasty. With the death of Solomon the subject-states all seem to have reestablished their independence.

[26]In I Kings 15:8 the descent of the royal line in Damascus is from Hezion to Tabrimon to Benhadad. No mention is made of Rezon as founder of the dynasty. Mazar is of the opinion that Hezion is the founder's proper name and Rezon his royal title (Benjamin Mazar, "The Aramaean Empire and Its Relations with Israel," *Biblical Archaeologist*, Dec., 1962, p. 104). Some assume that after Rezon, Hezion was the founder of a new dynasty. The problem is as yet unsolved. The votive stele of Benhadad I confirms the I Kings 15:18 account (Unger, pp. 56-57).

Hittite City-States

This study now shifts the spotlight for a moment from the Aramaeans to the Hittite states of north Syria. The fall of the Hittite Empire shortly after 1200 B.C. did not spell the end of the Hittites. Indeed, they appear in various places for almost 500 years more. This "Indian summer" of Hittite power has bequeathed more monuments than did the empire. Assyrian records continue to refer to Syria and Asia Minor just east of the Taurus as the "Land of Hatti" and mention rulers with names identical to those of the Imperial period. The list of Hittite city-states is long, but a few examples will suffice. On the fringe of Cappadocia a Hittite state was established at the classical Tyana. At the eastern edge of the Taurus, Hittite cities stood at Adana (or Seyhan) and Zinjirli. In north Syria proper, important Hittite settlements appeared at Carchemish and Tell Ahmar on the Euphrates and at Aleppo to the southwest. Most southerly of all was the important kingdom of Hamath (modern Hama, classical Epiphania).

Some of these city-states were large; others were unpretentious. Never achieving any political unity, they managed in spite of that fact to resist the Assyrians with a determined opposition that kept them independent of Assyria until about 875 B.C. Even after that time, they were in almost continuous revolt for a half century or more and enjoyed a degree of freedom again during the middle of the eighth century when the Urartaeans invaded Assyria. But finally these city-states were effectively annexed one by one by Sargon II of Assyria (722-705), losing their independence. Zinjirli probably fell in 724 B.C., Hamath in 720, Carchemish in 717. All of the rest probably capitulated by 709 B.C.

In passing, it should be noted that the Aramaeans clashed with the newly established Hittite principalities and overthrew the ruling houses of some of them in the eleventh or tenth century B.C. Other Hittite territories maintained themselves until toppled by the Assyrians.

When the Hebrews controlled Syria, they came in contact with the Hittites, conducting business with them (II Chron. 1:17) and using such Hittite mercenaries as Uriah (II Sam. 11:3 ff.) and Ahimelech (I Sam. 26:6) in their military forces. Solomon introduced Hittite women into his harem (I Kings 11:1).

Al Mina[27]

An infrequently told chapter in Syrian history concerns the port of Al Mina on the south bank of the Orontes at its mouth. The site was located about four miles south of the later Seleucia, destined to be the great harbor for Antioch during the Seleucid and Roman periods. Actually the port was a double town: the harbor itself which lay on very low ground at the mouth of the Orontes, where the warehouses were located, and the residential area on an easily defensible and healthful height three miles inland. The double town served as the port for the old town of Alalakh which has been noted above and which was destroyed about 1200 B.C.

Presumably Al Mina was also destroyed about the same time, but it was rebuilt again and had a continuous history until its abandonment about 300 B.C. During its later years the town was known by the Greek name of Poseideion. One of its most prosperous periods came during the first half of the eighth century B.C., when the Assyrian grip on Syria relaxed because of the rise of the kingdom of Urartu (Hebrew Ararat) and its incursions on Assyrian territory. At that time Syria was in a sense split in two. South Syria was controlled by Aramaeans. North Syria was still largely Hittite and seemingly confederate with

[27]For documentation on this section and further description of the town see Woolley, pp. 165-81. Woolley excavated at the site.

Urartu. The trade of north Syria moved through Poseideion.

This prosperity was seriously affected when Tiglath-pileser III about 742 B.C. marched into the westland in the third year of his reign to subdue Syria once for all. Sarduris (Sardur) of Urartu came in person to defend his vassals there, but he was ignominiously defeated. By 740 all Syria was effectively under the heel of Assyria once more.

Poseideion continued to be a fairly busy port under Assyrian rule and became the emporium for the manufactures of eastern Greece. The wares of Rhodes were especially prominent in the ruins of the town. And, unbelievable as it may seem, it was a thriving port under Persian control, even during the period when the Greeks and Persians were at war. Apparently both powers needed or at least wanted the goods that could be obtained through the commerce of Poseideion enough to permit this trade to continue. The town finally withered and died in 301 B.C. when Seleucus Nicator built his new port at Seleucia. Probably he even forcibly deported the population from the old town to his new site to serve as a nucleus of population for Seleucia.

Israel and the Kingdom of Damascus

After the revolt of Rezon (or Hezion) against Solomon, his son Tabrimon and grandson Benhadad I ruled after him (I Kings 15:18). Apparently Rezon set a pattern of Syrian animosity to the Hebrews from the beginning (I Kings 11:23-25). Although the kingdom of Damascus gradually increased in power, its big chance came as a result of the animosity between Israel and Judah. As war progressed between the northern and southern kingdoms, Judah found herself in trying circumstances. Baasha of Israel advanced to within five miles of Jerusalem and proceeded to fortify Ramah as a border fortress. In desperation, Asa of Judah sent a large gift to Benhadad of Syria and asked him to break his alliance with Israel and establish a compact with Judah instead.

Benhadad did this with eagerness. He advanced into Israel and took several cities in the north with their rich farmlands and at the same time secured the important trade route to Acre on the Phoenician coast (I Kings 15:16-20). This occurred in the thirty-sixth year of Asa's reign or about 885 B.C. (II Chron. 16:1).

Within a decade or so Omri established a new dynasty in Israel and launched his kingdom on an imperialist road once more. He made an alliance with Ethbaal of Tyre, thereby seeking to counteract Syrian trade with southern Phoenicia; he gained control of northern Moab and relocated the capital of the realm on the impressive hill of Samaria. The kingdom of Damascus, alarmed by the advance of Assyria, did not try to curb the Israelites during the reign of Omri or in the early days of his son Ahab. But finally, near the end of Ahab's reign (*c.* 855 B.C.), Benhadad advanced on Ahab but met defeat. Seeking revenge in the following year, the Syrians attacked again and suffered even worse defeat.

Ahab was now in a position to humiliate his northern rival, but he chose not to do so because it was quite clear that all possible aid would be needed to meet the imminent Assyrian invasion of the westlands (I Kings 20). So in 853 the inveterate enemies marched side by side in the coalition that met Shalmaneser III at Qarqar north of Hamath (modern Hama). The Assyrian apparently won a victory on that occasion, but it was not sufficiently overwhelming to assure him control of Syria. Benhadad had supplied 1,200 chariots and 20,000 men for the battle, Ahab 2,000 chariots and 10,000 infantry. Irhulenu (Irhuleni) of Hamath contributed 700 chariots and 10,000 men.

Five years later, Shalmaneser met another Syrian confederacy of twelve kings, again headed by Benhadad. Three years after that (845 B.C.) Shalmaneser found it necessary to engage in another major campaign against Syria. Again he met and defeated a coalition of a dozen kings headed by Benhadad of Damascus and Irhulenu of Hamath. Apparently the Assyrian's victories were not sufficiently decisive to give him assured possession of Syria.

Finally, about 843, Benhadad of Damascus met his end at the hands of the usurper Hazael, and a new dynasty came to power in Syria. Within a couple of years Jehu had dispatched the house of Ahab and initiated a new dynasty in Israel. At this juncture, with new dynasties trying to establish themselves in Syria and Palestine and with the populace of both countries shaken by revolution, Shalmaneser elected to come against Damascus. Hazael tried, like his predecessor, to pull together an alliance. But the other kings of the area would not stand with him. Fighting alone, he suffered a costly defeat at the hands of the Assyrians. But the Assyrians, either because they could not or did not have the will to destroy Damascus, circled eastward and received the tribute of the Phoenician towns and Jehu of Israel. In 837, the twenty-first year of his reign, Shalmaneser made one last move against Hazael; again Hazael stood alone, again Shalmaneser defeated but did not destroy him.

Revolts within Assyria and other bothersome problems occupied the attention of Assyria until about the end of the ninth century; so there were no more thrusts into Syria for the moment. Hazael determined to settle a score with Jehu for refusing to aid him against Shalmaneser. He took all of Israel's holdings east of the Jordan in Gilead and Bashan (II Kings 10:32-33). Hazael continued to attack Israel in the days of Jehu's son Jehoahaz (814-798). As indicated in II Kings 13:1-9, 22, Hazael brought Israel very low indeed, apparently

233. A Baal altar, Ugarit

reducing her to a puppet. With Israel on her knees, Hazael was free to move southward. Taking the Philistine stronghold of Gath, he turned upon Judah and exacted tribute from King Jehoash (Joash) (II Kings 12:17-18). Hazael was now master of south Syria and Palestine.

But the fortunes of Syria took a downturn once more. The vigorous Hazael finally died about 800 B.C. after a long reign. Moreover, Adadnirari (or Hadad-nirari) III of Assyria, during the last years of Hazael, campaigned against Syria and sufficiently weakened Israel's northern adversary to enable a Hebrew comeback.

Joash, or Jehoash, of Israel (798-782 B.C.) faced Benhadad II, son of Hazael, in three battles and overcame the Syrian in all three. The result was considerable expansion of the Israelite state, as territory lost previously was retrieved from the Damascenes (II Kings 13:24-25). Joash built a substantial military capability as evidenced by the fact that he hired out 100,000 men to Amaziah of Judah, who wanted them for his campaign against Edom. Warned by a prophet of God not to use these men in the war, the Judean king sent the Israelite mercenaries home again (II Chron. 25:5-10).

The result of this insult was bitter Israelite animosity against Judah. And after the Judean victory over the Edomites, the Israelites turned upon the Judeans, worsted them, and virtually made the Southern Kingdom a vassal of Israel (II Kings 14:8-14). In this manner Joash defeated both Syria and Judah.

However, the kingdom of Damascus was by no means on her knees. The Old Testament itself indicates that Israelite victory over Benhadad was partial (II Kings 13:19). It is known too that Adadnirari III of Assyria had not effectively cowed Syria. The Damascenes soon managed to slip out from under the burden of tribute to Assyria. Benhadad appeared at the head of a Syrian coalition preying on a principality southwest of Aleppo.[28] Apparently the Damascene was worried about the expansion of the kingdom of Hamath, which threatened to upset the balance of power in Syria. Benhadad lost. He may have died in this battle or soon thereafter.

Weakened as it was by Adadnirari III, Joash, and the kingdom of Hamath, the kingdom of Damascus was easy prey for Jeroboam II (793-753 B.C.), successor of Joash of Israel and for some years coregent with him. Jeroboam continued to chip away at the southern boundaries of Damascus. Assyria was in no position to prevent the rise of the Hebrews because of the inroads of the kingdom of Urartu, or Ararat. Established on the shore of Lake Van (ancient Thospitus) about 840 B.C., the Urartian Kingdom invaded Assyria and some

[28]Unger, p. 85.

areas of north Syria in 772 B.C. Under Jeroboam II of Israel and his contemporary Uzziah in Judah, the two prosperous Hebrew kingdoms controlled approximately the same territory ruled over by David and Solomon. Details are wanting, but Damascus and Hamath apparently became tributary to Jeroboam II for a time (II Kings 14:28).

Probably about 750 B.C. Damascus became independent of Israel, with Rezin as king. Soon after, Tiglath-pileser III (745-727) determined to bring the moribund Assyrian Empire back to vigorous life. The westland was hardly ready for him. Hamath and Damascus were just emerging from subject status; Israel was harassed by internal strife. When Tiglath-pileser advanced into north Syria in his third year, Rezin of Damascus and Menahem of Israel (II Kings 15:19; "Pul" is the name by which Tiglath-pileser was known in Babylon) were among those who were forced to pay tribute to him.

Then Tiglath-pileser turned his attention to the destruction of the kingdom of Urartu and crushingly defeated it around 740 B.C. or a little later. During this respite Rezin and Pekah of Israel moved to punish Ahaz of Judah for refusing to support them in the struggle against Assyria. The allies besieged Jerusalem and pushed past the capital to take Judah's Red Sea port, Eziongeber (Elath, II Kings 16:5-6). The slaughter and pillage in Judah were great (II Chron. 28:5-15). Desperate, Ahaz sent an embassy to Tiglath-pileser, professing to be a vassal of Assyria and bearing tribute (II Kings 16:7-8).

The Assyrian gladly intervened. He descended on the foes of Judah, destroying the rich gardens of the Ghûtah (Damascus oasis), slaying Rezin, and bringing the kingdom of Damascus to an end in 732 B.C. (II Kings 16:9). He annexed the whole northern portion of Israel and carried off thousands of captives and resettled them in Assyria (II Kings 15:29).

The Last Days of Assyria

Syrian history now became identified with that of Assyria. The kingdom of Damascus was carved into four Assyrian provinces. Six had already been formed out of the northern part of Syria. However, Syrian freedom died hard. In 727 B.C. there was a revolt in Damascus that was quickly put down. A revolution in Israel terminated with the destruction of Samaria by Assyrian forces no later than 722 B.C. In 720 Hamath led an insurrection against Assyria in which Damascus and Samaria were involved, along with others. In a battle at Qarqar the allies were completely routed and the survivors cruelly treated. Sargon II of Assyria, who was then on the throne, marched to the southwest and defeated Gaza and her confederates.

For about another seventy years Syria was more or less effectively controlled by Assyria. The major excitement in the area involved the humiliation of Judah, which would later be destroyed by the Babylonians.

Then about 650 B.C. the Scythians, proto-Russians or proto-Turks from behind the Caucasus Mountains, rushed down on the seats of luxury in the most fruitful parts of the Assyrian Empire. The invasion itself probably occurred about 635 to 625 in the form of a series of inroads. The whole of Syria was subject to Scythian rule for about twenty-eight years, and this Scythian dominion extended south to the Egyptian border. Babylon asserted her independence under Nabopolassar in 626. And in 612 B.C. the Scythians joined the Babylonians and Medes under Cyaxares in the destruction of the Assyrian capital. The terrifying might of the hordes of Ashur and Nineveh had come to an end.

The Neo-Babylonian Period

When Nineveh fell, the Medes occupied the northern and eastern parts of the Assyrian Empire, leaving the task of wiping out remaining Assyrian resistance to the Babylonians. Ashuruballit II, the last king of Assyria, set up his capital at Haran in western Assyria. There he was defeated by a coalition of Babylonians and Scythians in 609 B.C., who then returned home while the Assyrians retreated westward.

At this juncture Pharaoh-Necho of Egypt rushed to the assistance of Ashuruballit. Marching up the Palestinian coast with a large army whose flank was covered by a well-equipped fleet, he pushed across Mt. Carmel. On the plain of Megiddo, Josiah of Judah met Pharaoh-Necho with an army in an effort to prevent aid from reaching the Assyrian enemy (see II Kings 23:29ff.; II Chron. 35:20-24). Josiah's efforts cost him his life, and Necho brushed past his attackers. The Egyptians then moved up the Beqa' (El Bika) and advanced through Riblah (on the present northern border of Lebanon) and Hamath to the Euphrates River at Carchemish. The combined Egyptian and Assyrian forces were unsuccessful in recapturing Haran.[29]

But the Egyptians did not return home. As a by-product of their northward march, they carved out for themselves a Syrian empire which included Phoenicia, most of Palestine, and the kingdom of Damascus. Riblah was probably the administrative capital of this territory and Carchemish the military headquarters. This empire was destined to be short-lived, however, enjoying an existence of only some three years, 608-605 B. C. Its story is one of the most obscure chapters in the history of the Mediterranean world. Nebuchadnezzar II, crown prince of Babylon, crushed Necho's forces in a strategic battle at Carchemish (605) and chased him back to Egypt (cf. II Kings 24:7; Jer. 46:2).

While Nebuchadnezzar was campaigning in the westland, he received news of his father's death and hurried home to establish his claim to the throne. Hope

[29]Finegan, pp. 129-30.

of a war of liberation rose in the breasts of Syrians. Tyre and Judah were among the rebels, and Egypt was counted on as a source of aid. Ultimately Jerusalem was destroyed by Babylon in 587/586 B.C. Mainland Tyre suffered the same fate in 572 B.C. Syria seems to have been generally quiet during the next two decades of Babylonian rule. But Nabonidus, last king of Babylon, was called upon to quell a revolt there in 553.

The Persian Empire

About 700 B.C. Achaemenes came to the throne of Anshan in Persia and established the Achaemenid line. Long a tributary to the Medes, the Persians broke with their servile past under Cyrus the Great. Cyrus became king in Anshan about 559 B.C. When the Median king Astyages realized that Cyrus intended revolt, he decided to attack first. Unfortunately, however, his army mutinied, and Cyrus became master of the Median Empire about 550. In 546 he toppled Croesus of Lydia from his throne. Next on Cyrus' conquest timetable was Babylon. There the incompetent Belshazzar (Bel-shar-usur) ruled while his father pursued his antiquarian and religious interests at various spots in the empire.

Cyrus took the capital in 539 B.C., and with it went the empire. Cyrus now ruled a vast region extending from the borders of India to the Aegean Sea and from the Caspian Sea to the border of Sinai. The small states of Syria became part of a mighty empire, one of the largest of antiquity.

In contrast with the fearsome rule that Syria endured under the Assyrians and Babylonians, Persian rule was the most enlightened that the area was to enjoy for many years. Cyrus tried to conciliate subject peoples, permitting those deported by the Assyrians and Babylonians to return to their former homes and even aiding them

(as in the case of the Jews) to restore the old sanctuaries. Imperial unity was augmented by an improved road system and postal system (the work of Darius I), a uniform coinage, and an official language—Aramaic. Long the speech of commerce, Aramaic now became the official language of the western provinces. Prosperity was enhanced by the Pax Persica.

Cyrus joined Syria, Phoenicia, and Palestine to Babylonia in one huge satrapy. The satrap Bobryas (or Gubaru, probably the Darius of Dan. 6) officially called the province "Babirush." Over this whole vast stretch of fertile country, Gobryas ruled almost as an independent monarch. But under Darius I (522-486 B.C.), the great organizer of the Persian Empire, "Ebir-nari" (Assyrian for "across the river"), or most of Syria-Palestine, was linked with Cyprus to form the Fifth Satrapy.

In all there were twenty-three satrapies or provinces in the Persian Empire in Darius' day, each ruled by a governor called a satrap, who was a civil, not a military, official. Each satrapy also had a general and a secretary, and all three were authorized to communicate directly with the capital. Within the satrapies, subject nationalities enjoyed a relatively independent position, e.g., the Jews and the Phoenician cities. Thus was created a recipe for empire which included proper amounts of the ingredients of local autonomy, centralized responsibility, and overall control.

Damascus was capital of the Fifth Satrapy, but unfortunately little is known of the city during either the Babylonian or Persian periods. In fact, Damascus played a remarkably small part in the political history of the Levant through the ages. "There is not the dramatic rhythm of greatness and desolation alternating as at Jerusalem and Tyre, but merely a hoary and generally prosperous antiquity, like the steady prosperity of Egypt."[30]

[30]Wilfrid Castle, *Syrian Pageant* (London: Hutchinson & Co. Ltd., 1946), p. 38.

In spite of the humane treatment accorded subject peoples by the Persians, those people were still subjects and could be expected to make a bid for freedom when the opportunity presented itself. Egypt raised the standard of revolt in 358 B.C. and Tripoli did the same in 351. Soon the rest of the Phoenician city-states and Cyprus threw off the Persian yoke. But the uprising was premature, and the flames of freedom were quickly extinguished in Syria. Sidon (Zidon) was destroyed.

However, Persia was about to flounder, and ominous clouds were blowing in from the Greek quarter. Philip of Macedon had been busily subjugating the city-states there and was making preparations to "liberate" the Greek cities in Asia Minor held by Persia. When an assassin's dagger terminated those plans, his eighteen-year-old son Alexander took up the battle-ax.

In 334 B.C. Alexander crossed the Hellespont (Dardanelles) at the head of about 35,000 men and with an empty treasury. Victory over the Persians at the Granicus River won him control of Asia Minor. The following year he again faced the Persians in eastern Asia Minor, on the borders of the Fifth Satrapy. On the shores of the gulf now called Iskenderun, or Alexandretta, the Battle of Issus was fought. Alexander's generalship was never better. The victory restored the morale of his troops and the booty captured enabled him to pay his men for the first time in months.

Alexander was now faced with the choice of pursuing Darius III or marching southward into Syria. He chose the latter in order to cut off the Persian navy from its bases and destroy it. He dispatched a battalion to Damascus while he drove southward along the coast. Damascus, manned by a treacherous governor, yielded up the rich treasures Darius had deposited there. Thereafter it became the seat of authority for occupying forces. Except for Tyre, which required a siege of seven months, the Phoenicians threw in their lot with Alexander. The Fifth Satrapy had become a Greek province.

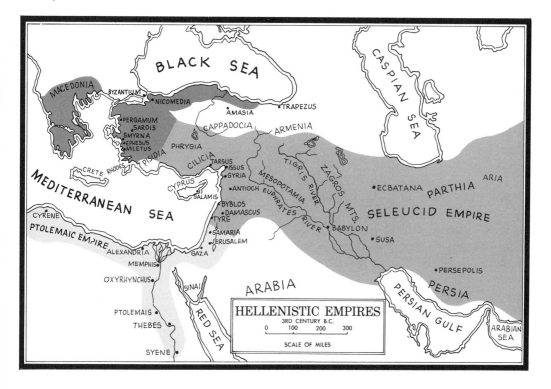

Seleucid Control of Syria

Brought down by a fever at Babylon in 323 B.C., Alexander never had a chance to develop an imperial administration. When he died, he left behind a group of ambitious generals, each of whom sought mastery of the empire Alexander had carved out. From the anarchy which followed, a workable arrangement finally emerged with Ptolemy controlling Egypt, Cyrene, Cyprus, and Palestine, Antigonus ruling Macedonia, and Seleucus founding a dynasty at Babylon in 312. At their height the Seleucids ruled over most of the old Persian Empire except Egypt. Because the Ptolemies needed a fleet to hold their territories, it was necessary for them to have the naval supplies of the Lebanons and Asia Minor. In seeking to control those areas the Ptolemies clashed constantly with the Seleucids.

234. Antiochus IV

Historical review. Before turning to the cultural affairs and the city building activities of the Seleucids, a brief historical statement should prove useful. Seleucus I Nicator (312-280) not only established himself at Babylon but conquered eastern Asia Minor and extended his frontier in the east to the Indus River. But his ambition proved to be his undoing. When he invaded Macedonia, he was assassinated. Seleucus II (246-226) lost almost everything his grandfather had gained. Ptolemy Euergetes I invaded Syria and advanced all the way to the Euphrates and then withdrew because of difficulties at home. Meanwhile, the Parthians successfully revolted a little after 240 and removed Iran from the Seleucid orbit. The Pergamenes were also busy chipping away at Seleucid lands in Asia Minor.

Antiochus III (223-187 B.C.) managed to reconquer Iranian territory and extend Seleucid borders to the Indus once more. In 198 B.C. he defeated Ptolemy and won Palestine and for all his successes won the epithet of "Great." But now Antiochus over-

reached himself. The famous Carthaginian, Hannibal, had come to Syria at the end of the Second Punic War and urged Antiochus to war on the Romans. When Antiochus interfered in Greece to save it from Rome, he met defeat at the hands of the new colossus of the West and in 188 was forced to cede all Seleucid lands west of the Taurus Mountains and pay a huge indemnity. The wealth of Asia Minor was forever lost.

By the time of Antiochus IV Epiphanes (175-163 B.C.), Syria was strong enough once more to take the offensive. Learning that Egypt was preparing for war, Antiochus beat Ptolemy Philometor to the draw and took nearly all of the Delta region except Alexandria. When Rome made Antiochus return home, he turned his attention to more effective Hellenization of his subjects and ignited the Maccabean or Jewish revolt in 168. This eventuated in Jewish independence and further truncation of Seleucid domains.

Meanwhile the Nabataeans were pressing on the southern fringe of the empire. Parthia, Bactria (Bactriana), and adjoining lands were asserting their independence in the east. Arab dynasties set themselves up at Edessa and Emesa (modern Homs). And another native state, Ituraea, established itself in Coele-Syria (El Bika). About 85 B.C. the Nabataeans took Coele-Syria and Damascus. Several of the Phoenician cities were gaining their independence. By 130 the Parthians had expanded their empire to include all the territory from the Euphrates to the Indus. Early in the first century B.C. the ambitious Tigranes of Armenia overran Mesopotamia and by 83 moved into north Syria and Cilicia and in 69 occupied Acre. At this point Rome went into action against the Armenians, chased Tigranes out of Syria, and acknowledged the right of Antiochus XIII to rule at Antioch on the Orontes. Pompey occupied Syria for Rome in 64 B.C., and an era had come to an end.

Cultural affairs. At the head of the Seleucid state reigned the absolute monarch whose bases of power were at least threefold: religious, military, and bureaucratic-ethnic. During the third century B.C., the ruler cult was gradually established as a result of efforts of successive kings. Worshiped first as founders or benefactors of individual cities, the Seleucid kings eventually managed to establish temples for royal worship at the provincial centers and to develop a statewide cult. Ultimately Antiochus IV (175-164) took the epithet "Epiphanes," which means "God manifest." He was not a megalomaniac, as some writers of religious literature assert, but had a political purpose in mind—to strengthen the religious foundations of the kingship at a time when royal power was slipping.

Moreover, Antiochus sought to create an integrated state and to bring the native population into the ruler cult. Up to that time only the Macedonian element and some others in the cities had participated in worship of the royal family. This development explains the unrest in Palestine and the Maccabean revolt which occurred during his reign.

The king had at his disposal a formidable military establishment. The army, at full strength perhaps 70,000 cavalry and foot soldiers, had as its nucleus the phalanx, recruited from Greek and Macedonian settlers. The infantrymen were armed with swords, huge spears, shields, and helmets. Supporting contingents were obtained from non-Greek elements of the population and from mercenaries. These formed the cavalry (to a large extent), and missile (archers, slingers, javelin throwers), and artillery (siege engines) units. Camel and elephant corps also made an effective contribution. Headquarters of the army, the military training schools, and the elephant training depot were located at Apamea. But the camp of the royal guard was located in Antioch. The fleet apparently served primarily the function of troop transport, but the ships were equipped with a metal projection on the prow for ramming the enemy and could effectively destroy opposition in that way. No doubt Phoenicians manned the fleet.

The king was also supported by a numerous bureaucracy which owed its appointment and livelihood to him and by the considerable Macedonian or Greek population in the cities of the realm. The cities were essentially city-states in which the urban center controlled the surrounding rural area and the serfs on its farms. Imperial taxes seem to have been levied on the community as a whole instead of the individual. The native population seems rather apathetically to have supported the Seleucid regime.

Greek and Oriental elements intermingled in the Seleucid state. The king ruled as an Oriental potentate in Oriental splendor, but he and his court spoke Greek. At the center of his army were the Greek phalanx and Greek soldiers. But the military power was rendered effective by native auxiliary units in the infantry, by Phoenician naval squadrons, by Indian elephants and Syrian and Median cavalry. Eating habits, dress, and intellectual diet also mirrored this synthesis of East and West.

Seleucid cities. In an effort to lay solid foundations for their empire, the Seleucid kings built numerous cities throughout the realm. These were planted with care at strategic spots, where they could control river valleys, caravan routes, rich agricultural districts, and other centers of importance. Ethnically they were colonies of Greek and Macedonian soldiers and mercenaries who could dominate the native population. Their wives were supplied partly from native stock, and to these new foundations would gravitate natives who had put on or were willing to put on the externals of Hellenism, as well as traders, artists, scholars, and slaves. Partly out of a desire to build a cultural foundation for the state and partly out of a desire to spread a "superior" culture throughout the realm, the Seleucids established cities as effective missionary centers for the preaching of Hellenism.

These cities were built according to a prepared plan in which streets were laid out in grid or checkerboard fashion, with proper allowance for political, market, and social and recreational centers. Of course these towns were provided with theaters, baths, gymnasia, and other institutions where the individual could express himself as a member of society.

According to Appianus, Seleucus Nicator was responsible for founding at least thirty-three cities: sixteen Antiochs, nine Seleucias, five Laodiceas, and three Apameas.[31] But many of these were not new foundations at all and merely represented a recolonization and renaming of older Semitic towns. Some were probably not genuine cities, i.e., not established with full municipal organization. Four important new foundations in western Syria included Antioch on the Orontes, named after Seleucus' father; Seleucia on the Sea, named after himself; Apamea on the Orontes, named for his wife; and Laodicea on the Sea, named

after his mother.[32] These constituted two pairs of cities with their seaports. Comment on each of these four is in order, with attention being directed to Apamea first.

Apamea dominated the middle Orontes where the valley widens into a swampy basin, into which continual streams flow and produce luxuriant vegetation. It stood on the lower slopes of the eastern hills which open out south of the city, providing easy communication between the Orontes Valley and the East. As has been noted, here was the central office for the Seleucid army, the location of the military schools, the training center for some 500 Indian elephants, and stables for tens of thousands of horses. All around Apamea were settlements of soldiers dependent on this vital city.

Opposite Apamea on one of the few safe anchorages along the rocky Syrian coast was located the port of Laodicea. Communication between the inland city and its port was by road over the intervening mountain ridge. Since passage was difficult at certain times during the year and since Laodicea did not enjoy the advantage of standing on a major commercial route, the city did not enjoy the prosperity of Seleucia, farther north. Laodicea had a rich wine-producing hinterland, however, and enjoyed a brisk trade, especially with Egypt.

Seleucia was built about five miles north of the Orontes River and guarded its mouth. Above this principal harbor of the coast Mount Pieria rises from the sea in a series of ledges. The lower city with the harbor and warehouses stood on a level about twenty feet above the quay. Above the lower city on a much higher shelf perched the upper city. The elevation displayed to best advantage the magnificence of the public buildings and temples of the city and made it a worthy gateway to an affluent kingdom. The sight must have been an impressive one to the Apostle Paul as he

[31]A. H. M. Jones, *The Cities of the Eastern Roman Provinces* (Oxford: At the Clarendon Press, 1937), p. 245.

[32]Dussaud, p. 1.

sailed toward this port of Antioch at the end of his first missionary journey. However, it was not necessary to disembark at Seleucia. The Orontes was navigable as far as Antioch up to the time of the Crusades.

Greatest of all the Seleucid foundations was Antioch on the Orontes, destined to become the third city of the Roman Empire, after Rome and Alexandria. And it was destined to become a great center of Christianity. Antioch was the birthplace of foreign missions; all three of Paul's missionary journeys were launched from there (Acts 13:1-4; 15:35-36; 18:23). Disciples of Jesus were first called "Christians" there (Acts 11:26); and it was among the Antiochians that the question of Gentile relation to the Mosaic law first arose, with the resultant decision at the Jerusalem Council that Gentiles were not under the law (Acts 15).

If Paul and Barnabas chose to sail up the Orontes as they returned from their first missionary journey, they would have had on their left the plain of Seleucia and on their right the base of the sacred Mount Casius (Jebel Akra). As they continued to ascend the river (which fell 300 feet in the some twenty miles between Antioch and its mouth), they would have found themselves in a beautiful gorge, about six miles long, by which the Orontes cut through the coastal range to the sea. Coming out of the gorge, they would have emerged on the plains of Syria; but on their right a spur of Casius still would have hovered, resplendent in its cloak of timber and flowering shrubs, and sending its numerous torrents into the river. At last the mountain chain ends in Mount Silpius, around which the Orontes makes a westward bend coming from the south, hence the two missionaries would have been in the middle of the city. (The Orontes is now approximately 125 feet wide.)

A Hellenistic foundation, Antioch enjoyed all the advantages of scientific city planning that men of that age desired. The

235. Antioch and Mount Stauris, where stood the acropolis of ancient Antioch

area had a healthful climate, an adequate water supply, good drainage, fertile land, and good opportunity for commercial advantage. Moreover, a city located at this spot would be far enough from the sea for protection and close enough for easy communication.

In this part of Syria the limestone is fissured, containing underground caverns and reservoirs in which collects the water that falls during the winter rainy season. Faults in the limestone produce springs which flow all year. Thus numerous springs were available for a new city foundation. Especially was this true of the plateau of Daphne, some five miles southwest of Antioch. This plateau, roughly square in shape and measuring about 2,000 yards on a side, averaged about 300 feet above the level of the city. As a result water from its springs could easily be carried by gravity through aqueducts to the city. In ancient times, five springs served the double function of watering the surface of the Daphne Plateau and supplying water for Antioch.

Antioch enjoyed a benign climate. A regular breeze blew daily from the sea up the Orontes River. This steady stream of fresh cool air was especially welcome during the summer months, when it brought relief from high temperatures. The streets of the city were carefully oriented so the main thoroughfares caught the breeze as it blew up the valley. So pleasant were summers at Antioch that it became a popular

236. Water flowing from the Springs of Daphne

vacation spot for people from Egypt and Palestine, as well as native Syrians.

The neighborhood was rich. A vast open, fertile plain spread to the north of the city, and an abundance of grain, fruits, and vegetables grew there. Good stands of timber were available in nearby forests. Good building stone could be quarried in the adjoining mountains. Plenty of fish could be obtained in the Lake of Antioch, which lay about twelve miles northeast of the city, and in the Mediterranean Sea.

As to commercial advantage, the Orontes Valley at Antioch opened into the plains of north Syria, across which passed the regular land routes from Iran and Mesopotamia to the Mediterranean. So it became a terminus of the caravan route from the East. And as has been said, the Orontes was navigable as far as Antioch. Moreover, the city controlled the north-south road which joined Palestine, Syria, and Asia Minor.

With all of these advantages, the site of Antioch appealed greatly to Hellenistic city planners. Seleucus I founded the city under the northern slopes of Mount Silpius (which rose some 1500 feet above the plain) in May of 300 B.C. The first settlers were Macedonian soldiers and Athenian colonists. The people of Antioch traced the greatness of their city to their Attic origin.[33]

[33]Glanville Downey, *Antioch in the Age of Theodosius the Great* (Norman: University of Oklahoma Press, 1962), p. 12.

As the city expanded, other Greeks came—Aetolians, Cretans, Euboeans. There was a large and flourishing Jewish community too, to whom Seleucus showed great favor. To the original quarter Seleucus later added a second quarter with its own separate wall. Seleucus II and Antiochus III built a third quarter on an island in the Orontes, which no longer appears to be an island because the channel on one side of it has silted up. Apparently the palace was located there. The fourth and last great section of the city was laid out by Antiochus IV Epiphanes on the slopes of Mount Silpius. The fully developed city as Paul would have known it is described in connection with the period of Roman rule.

Seleucus Nicator is also credited with establishing a settlement at Daphne, and the area was particularly developed by Antiochus Epiphanes. The Seleucids erected the famous Temple of Apollo there, as well as many other temples, baths, public buildings, the Olympic stadium, and villas of the wealthy.

The Roman Peace

When Pompey took over Syria in 64 B.C., Seleucid administration had broken down and the area was in a state of chaos. Northern Syria was almost entirely in the hands of Arab chiefs. Damascus had placed itself under the protection of the Nabataean king of Petra. Several princelings had established native principalities of their own. Judaea was torn by civil war. Agriculture and commerce, both by land and sea, were languishing.

Now that the Seleucid kingdom had become the province of Syria, the Romans at once set about restoring order. Damascus became the capital of an administrative unit within which Pompey allowed many free cities and native kings to manage their own affairs. This concession was due to sheer necessity, for Rome could not have governed such a large and heterogeneous tract of country at that time. Therefore the original area of the province of Syria was small. The towns were held responsible for control of their surrounding districts. And the native princes were held responsible for the more remote districts. As the Roman grip tightened, independent or semiautonomous areas were gradually absorbed, and Provincia Syria stretched ever farther to the north, east, and south.

And so the Romans had introduced to Syria the most prosperous era it had ever known—the Roman Peace—and with it some 200 years of almost unbroken quiet. Unruly tribes were pushed back, roads built, trade fostered, and civil government established. Four legions were stationed there to keep order. Never was Syria so effectively ruled, and never was she so populous.

But peace and order did not come immediately. The Romans' descent into Syria had brought them face to face with the Parthians, a formidable power that represented Persia under a new guise. Rome took the offensive against the Parthians in 53 B.C. but met humiliating defeat and the loss of 10,000 soldiers who were carried away into slavery. In 44 B.C. Rome moved the capital of Syria (which from 44 B.C. to A.D. 72 probably included Cilicia) from Damascus to Antioch. Four years later a Parthian force poured across the Euphrates River, defeated the Romans, took Apamea and then Antioch itself, and marched south into Phoenicia, conquering all the towns there except Tyre. The Jews welcomed the Parthians as deliverers, and for three years (40-37 B.C.) the entire area between the Taurus and Sinai was lost to Rome.

In 37 B.C. Roman power surged back, drove the Parthians across the Euphrates, forced the Nabataeans to pay an indemnity, and established Herod the Great on the throne of Judaea (and Samaria). Rome had lost out temporarily in Syria because of the civil wars that brought the end of the Republic. After Augustus' victory at Actium in 31 B.C., a reorganization was effected that brought Syria as well as the rest of the Empire to peace and affluence once more.

Since the frontier province of Syria bordered on the territory of a powerful rival (Parthia), Rome constituted Syria an imperial province. As such it was directly under the control of the emperor, who appointed as governors legates of consular rank for terms of three to five years. A variety of governments presided in local communities. In the Greco-Macedonian colonies the old magistrates continued to rule, associated with a senate and popular assembly. The Greek city-state remained the organization type. In the Phoenician towns the old oligarchic systems continued, as did the tribal and patriarchal administrations in less urbanized areas. Urbanization was an important aspect of Roman policy.

Aramaic was by this time the language of the common man, and Greek the trade language. The Romans planted few colonies, the most important being at Beirut and Baalbek (ancient Heliopolis).

Rome built a chain of garrison posts along the fringe of the desert to protect the more settled areas. Communication was enhanced by a good road system. The great east-west road led from the Mediterranean through Palmyra to the Euphrates River, while the north-south road ran from Damas-

237. The Orontes River at Antioch

238. Early Christian church (St. Peter's) built into a mountainside at Antioch

cus through Hauran, Gilead, Moab, and southward to join the Arabian caravan route. This north-south road followed the King's Highway of the Old Testament (Gen. 14:1-5; Num. 20:17; 21:22). As noted above, four legions were regularly stationed in Syria and could pose as a political as well as a military force. In A.D. 69 these legions made Vespasian emperor. A detachment of the Misenum fleet from Italy was stationed at Seleucia, and the sailors had barracks in the town. This flotilla presumably had the task of searching out pirates in eastern waters.

It is of interest to the Bible student that Quirinius (Cyrenius, Luke 2:2), one of the Roman governors, conducted an accurate census for Syria which became the basis for future taxation. This count was ordered by Augustus and is related to the question of when Christ was born. Historians used to claim that Quirinius was governor of Syria A.D. 6-7 but not when Christ was born. But Ramsay has tried to show that Quirinius was also governor of Syria about 8 B.C. and conceivably a little later than that.[34] Of course it is known that the Gregorian calendar is several years in error—perhaps as much as six or seven. It is off at least four

years because Herod the Great died in the spring of 4 B.C., and Christ was born before that.

The general curve of prosperity continued to rise in Syria during the period of the Roman Peace. Heichelheim estimates that the population may have risen to 7,000,000 early in the second century.[35] Areas of the country which now present a barren appearance were then covered with thriving towns. Fruits, vegetables, and cereals grew in abundance. Advanced methods of fertilization and irrigation were employed. Among chief industries were leather, linen, and wine production. And, as noted elsewhere in this chapter, a chief source of Syrian wealth was the trade that flowed along her busy caravan routes and through her ports.

Thousands of villages studded the Syrian countryside, and the free peasants who inhabited them lived mostly on the produce of their farms and vineyards. Probably these villagers did not make much provision for education or public health. Little Hellenizing or Romanizing influence was brought to bear upon these Semitic people.

But the case was very different with the cities of Syria, which were large and populous and centers of Hellenistic culture. In the sophisticated cities Greek was commonly spoken, at least in public and commercial activities. And, as in other cities of the Roman world, amphitheaters, theaters, baths, and marketplaces attracted the multitudes.

So great was the interest in entertainment in the metropolitan centers of Syria that the province became known throughout the Roman world for its professional performers who organized in regular troupes and hired out for programs at banquets, circuses, and other events. Comments on several of the Syrian cities should prove useful in helping to set the stage for the drama of New Testament history enacted in Syria.

[34]William M. Ramsay, *The Bearing of Recent Discovery on the Trustworthiness of the New Testament* (2d ed.; London: Hodder & Stoughton, 1915), pp. 278-99.

[35]Heichelheim, p. 158.

Antioch. Of course the most prominent of all Syrian cities during the Roman period was Antioch, the capital. Third city of the Empire after Rome and Alexandria, it has frequently been estimated to have sported a population of about a half million during the first century A.D. Though the Jewish community at Antioch was smaller in number than those at Rome and Alexandria, it was large. Metzger estimates that the Jews comprised one-seventh of the population and that during the first Christian century three Jewish settlements existed in Antioch. One was west of the city near Daphne, a second east of the city in the plain of Antioch, and a third in the city proper.[36] Jews enjoyed considerable wealth and prestige there and apparently influenced their pagan neighbors with their monotheistic beliefs to the point that through them many turned from paganism.

The prosperity of Antioch came in part from its political position, in part from the arteries of commerce that flowed through her, and in part from the commodities produced there. Among the luxury goods that one could purchase there were fine leather shoes, perfume, spices, textiles, jewelry, books, and products of goldsmiths and silversmiths, who had held first place among the city's craftsmen ever since its founding.

The ancient critics emphasized the Oriental sensuality of Antioch's citizens wholly devoted to luxury, ease, and licentious pleasure. The pleasure garden of Daphne became the hotbed of every kind of vice and depravity. Juvenal, a Roman satirical poet writing in the second century A.D., scored his society for its decadent morals and complained:

> Obscene Orontes, diving underground,
> Conveys his wealth to Tiber's hungry shores
> And fattens Italy with foreign whores.

But Muller makes something of an apology for the Antiochenes:

> In fairness to Antioch, it was born too late. It never knew independence, never was a genuine Greek *polis*. It was just Greek enough to be sophisticated, satirical in its wit, notoriously critical in spirit, often hostile to its rulers, always turbulent. Having been denied real freedom, its citizens took to license. They exercised their lively wit in ridiculing the traditional virtues of manliness and womanliness, honoring the arts and the vices of luxury. They expressed their civic pride in the magnificence of their games, festivals, and spectacles.[37]

Antioch had schools of rhetoric and eminent sophists who attracted disciples from all over the Mediterranean world, but it had no creative writers or singers of note. In the artistic sphere the city had a leading position only in regard to the theater, and performances there were less strictly dramatic productions than noisy musicals and ballets. The populace was fond of animal hunts and gladiatorial games.

Antiochus IV had celebrated games at Daphne in 195 B.C. before he became king.

239. The Chalice of Antioch

[36]Bruce M. Metzger, "Antioch-on-the-Orontes," *The Biblical Archaeologist,* XI (Dec., 1948), 81.

[37]Herbert J. Muller, *The Loom of History* (New York: Harper & Brothers, 1958), p. 402.

On Augustus' second visit to the city in 20 B.C., he founded local games which in time became the Olympic Games of Antioch, one of the most famous festivals of the Roman world. In July and August of every leap year of the Julian calendar, visitors journeyed to Antioch from all over the Greco-Roman world for these quadrennial games. Lasting for thirty days during the first century A.D. (apparently for forty-five days in later centuries), they offered competition and/or entertainment for everyone: boxing, wrestling, chariot racing, musical competitions, and recitation of tragic passages. Presented regularly at first, the games ceased altogether by the time of Claudius (A.D. 41-54) because embezzlement of funds from the treasury of the games on occasion brought them into disrepute. Claudius re-founded the games in 43/44 and called them "Olympic."[38]

Into this milieu of sensuality and frivolity came Christianity not long after the death of Christ. In Antioch Christian missionaries apparently had little to fear from the attacks of fanatical Jews; the same could not be said of Jerusalem. In the cosmopolitan society of Antioch both classical and Oriental cults were familiar, and new religious ideas were not a novelty. Many, dissatisfied with the traditional pagan cults, were attracted to the Jewish synagogue with its monotheistic and ethical teachings.

At Antioch believers in Jesus were first called "Christians," and here Christians were more opulent than those at Jerusalem

[38]Glanville Downey, *A History of Antioch in Syria* (Princeton: Princeton University Press, 1961), p. 168.

240. Excavations at Antioch

and were therefore able to provide financial resources important for the growth of Christianity. From Antioch all three of Paul's missionary journeys were launched. The fact that believers at Antioch had a fair amount of wealth is further indicated by their sending an offering for relief of the poor in Jerusalem at the time of the severe famine (Acts 11:27-30). Moreover, Antioch's geographical position as the hub of a network of well-established communications fitted it to serve efficiently and fruitfully as a focal point for expansion.

The finding of a chalice at Antioch has been connected with early Christianity there. The chalice is of two parts: a plain inner cup of silver about seven and one-half inches high and an outer gilded silver holder with twelve figures displayed on the outside. Much has been written about the date and interpretation of this piece. The outer cup has been said to represent Christ and His disciples, and the inner cup has even been identified as the Holy Grail, used by Christ at the Last Supper. Dates as early as the first century have been assigned.[39] The present writer is of the opinion that the best which can be said about this chalice is that it is an early piece of Christian art of some century later than the first and that Christ or some of the disciples may be intended by the artistic representations.

By means of historical references and excavations at Antioch, it has been possible to reconstruct some of the main features of the city as it appeared during the New Testament period. In 1931 the Syrian government granted permission to Princeton University and the National Museum of France to excavate at Antioch over a period of six years.

The city, as Paul and Barnabas and other New Testament Christians would have known it, was magnificent indeed. Towering above it on the southeast stood 1500-foot-high Mount Silpius. On the northwest flowed the Orontes. In the east wall stood a heavily fortified gate on top of which Tiberius had placed a stone statue of the she-wolf nursing Romulus and Remus. Inside the gate one found himself on an open roadway thirty feet wide paved with Egyptian granite. All along both sides of this four-and-one-half-mile-long thoroughfare (northeast-southwest) stood covered colonnades, each thirty feet wide. As a result of this construction, a pedestrian could walk the entire length of the city protected from sun and rain. Houses and public buildings could be entered between the columns of the walkway. Statues and bronzes were attached to many of the columns as at Palmyra. Augustus and Tiberius with the assistance of Herod of Judaea built this street with its walks in the period 23 B.C.-A.D. 37.

Side streets intersected the main streets and the more important were colonnaded. Streets were lighted at night, an achievement not matched by any other city of antiquity.[40] Public fountains stood at the corners of the streets, where women and children could get the family water supply. There were numerous squares where children played, shopkeepers sold their wares, philosophers taught, and entertainers performed. In the middle of the city the main thoroughfare opened into a plaza where a striking bronze statue of Tiberius stood, erected by the grateful city for all the emperor's benefactions.

In the river in the northern part of the city lay an island some two miles long by as many wide. There had stood the palaces of the Seleucids, and Roman royal residences had succeeded them. On the island was also a hippodrome with an arena over 1600 feet long, built in the first century. This was one of the largest structures of its type in the Empire.[41]

---

[39]For discussion see H. Harvard Arnason, "The History of the Chalice of Antioch," *The Biblical Archaeologist*, IV (1941), 49-64; V (1942), 10-16; Floyd V. Filson, "Who Are the Figures on the Chalice of Antioch?" *The Biblical Archaeologist*, V (1942), 1-10.

[40]Mommsen, p. 141.
[41]Downey, p. 647.

Along the southeast bank of the river and south of the island was located the original quarter of the city as established by Seleucus Nicator. Here barges discharged cargoes at stone quays. Nearby stood an agora (covering four city blocks) and a temple of Zeus. In this quarter Seleucus erected the famous statue of Tyche, goddess of good fortune, which Seleucus had cast by Eutychides of Sicyon. A symbol of prosperity and good luck, the bronze goddess was draped in a long robe and was seated on a rock representing Mount Silpius. On her head she wore a turreted crown representing the walls of the city. Beneath her feet a figure of a nude youth lay in swimming position, symbolizing the Orontes. In her right hand she held a sheaf of wheat, signifying the material prosperity of the city.

242. A mosaic of the Judgment of Paris, Antioch, second century A.D.

241. A Tyche of Antioch on a silver stater

In the eastern part of the city, against the western slopes of Silpius, was the quarter built by Antiochus IV Epiphanes. Facing his new agora stood his famous council chamber resembling the one at Miletus, as well as the famous temple of Jupiter Capitolinus, the leading Roman deity. During the reign of Tiberius (A.D. 14-37) a great fire destroyed part of this agora, and Tiberius engaged in a sizable rebuilding program, including the redecoration of the temple of Jupiter, which had a ceiling paneled with gold and walls covered with gilded metal plates.[42] In this quarter were located temples of Dionysus and Pan as well. A theater stood on the slope of Mount Silpius.

[42]*Ibid.*, p. 179.

At the southern edge of Antiochus' quarter and just inside the southwest gate of the city was the Jewish section which was established there when the city was founded. Here Titus after the destruction of Jerusalem set up bronze figures that were supposed to represent the cherubim taken from the demolished temple.

From the southwest gate the road ascended to Daphne, five miles away to the southwest. The walk was a beautiful one. A constant succession of orchards and gardens filled with roses and other flowers scented the air. Here were grown the roses for making the perfume for which Antioch was famous. Of course beautiful country houses and villas stood among these gardens. One could pause at inns along the way where, in the shade of vine-covered arbors, he could sip wine or fruit juices cooled in underground cellars.

The pleasure garden of Daphne was ten miles in circumference. It was famous for its laurel trees, old cypresses, flowing and gushing waters, its shining temple of Apollo, and its magnificent festival of the tenth of August. At the center of Daphne was an

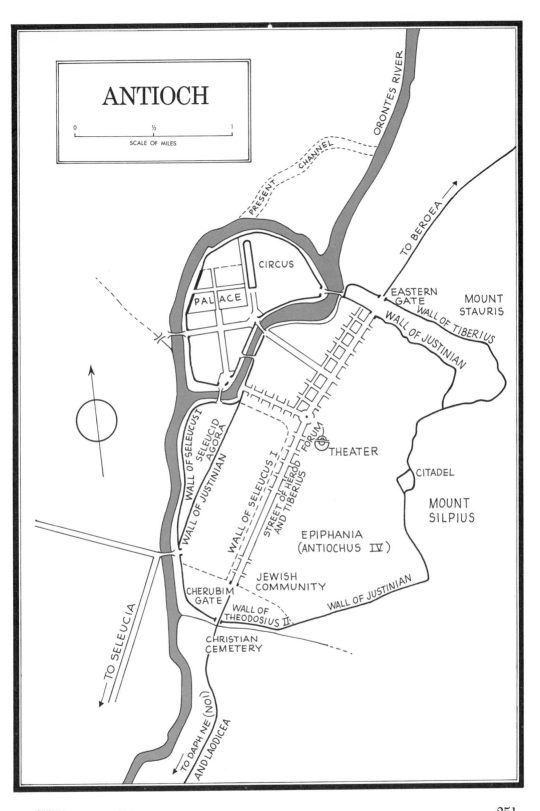

ANTIOCH

0   ½   1
SCALE OF MILES

ORONTES RIVER

PRESENT CHANNEL

TO BEROEA

CIRCUS

PALACE

EASTERN GATE

MOUNT STAURIS

WALL OF TIBERIUS

WALL OF JUSTINIAN

WALL OF SELEUCUS I

SELEUCID AGORA

WALL OF JUSTINIAN

WALL OF SELEUCUS I

STREET OF HEROD AND TIBERIUS

FORUM

THEATER

CITADEL

MOUNT SILPIUS

EPIPHANIA
(ANTIOCHUS IV)

JEWISH COMMUNITY

WALL OF JUSTINIAN

CHERUBIM GATE

WALL OF THEODOSIUS II

TO SELEUCIA

CHRISTIAN CEMETERY

TO DAPHNE (NO) AND LAODICEA

243. Remains of ancient walls atop
Mount Silpius

agora with baths and temples. The streets were laid out on a regular grid plan and were lined with spacious houses. At the south edge of the suburb gushed ever-flowing springs; the temple of Apollo (built by Seleucus Nicator) stood at the foot of the springs. Nearby was the Olympic stadium. Daphne was dedicated to Apollo as Antioch was to Zeus.

The proud city of Antioch was destined to have her share of woes. She suffered from numerous earthquakes, but the worst came in the sixth century A.D. when a reported quarter million are said to have perished.[43] Most of the city was burned by the Persian emperor Chosroes I (Khosrau) in A.D. 540. Justinian rebuilt it, but it never fully regained its greatness. Arabs conquered it in 638, and Crusaders held it for about 200 years during the later Middle Ages. Under Ottoman administration it dwindled to an insignificant town. Today it has a population of some 35,000, and a settlement of Greek Orthodox in this Muslim area is all that is left to remind the modern visitor that this once was the center of Christian missionary activity.

Beroea (modern Aleppo or Haleb). Some fifty miles east of Antioch, between the valley of the Orontes and the Euphrates,

lay Beroea at an altitude of 1220 feet above sea level in a basin surrounded by low, rocky hills. Called "Haleb" in ancient times, the city was the center of a kingdom in the early sixteenth century B.C. when the Hittite Mursilis I swept down through the Taurus passes and took the city. The scene of conflict between the Hittites and Egyptians during the fifteenth century, Haleb fell to Thutmose III of Egypt about 1480 B.C. Later in the fifteenth century the city capitulated to the Hittites, and at the battle of Kadesh a king of Haleb fought on the Hittite side against Ramses II. Haleb was an independent Hittite principality when Shalmaneser III of Assyria conquered it in 853.

Seleucus Nicator (312-280 B.C.) enlarged the city and named it Beroea after the Macedonian city of the same name. It became the chief commercial center of north Syria and during the days of the Sino-Roman world peace (first-second centuries A.D.), Beroea became an important terminus of the silk route from the Yellow Sea to the Mediterranean and she knew considerable prosperity. It is still an important Syrian city with a population of more than 425,000.

Laodicea and Apamea. About fifty miles southwest of Antioch was Laodicea (modern Latakia), a favorite pleasure resort for dignitaries. During the New Testament period it conducted from its excellent harbor a brisk export trade in wines. Exported chiefly to Alexandria, these wines came from the vineyards which stretched inland almost to Apamea. Herod the Great, in an effort to win imperial favor, built an aqueduct for Laodicea and some other cities.

Apamea, Laodicea's sister city inland, had been a considerable city since Seleucid days. Its hinterland was rich in pasturage, and its temple was an important religious center which housed a famous oracle. Dedications to the Baal of Apamea have been found as far west as southern France.[44]

[43]Muller, p. 403.

[44]Hitti, p. 307.

Beloch estimated the population of Apamea to have been as high as 400,000 to 500,000 early in the first century A.D.[45]

Epiphania. Up the Orontes River some twenty-five miles southeast of Apamea stood Epiphania (modern Hama). An early Hittite settlement, Hama became the seat of a local dynasty after the fall of the Hittite Empire and eventually capitulated to the Assyrians (II Kings 18:34; Isa. 11:11). The biblical Hamath, it is frequently mentioned in the Bible as being on the northern boundary of Israel. In the Seleucid period the city received the name "Epiphania" in honor of Antiochus Epiphanes. In the center of a rich agricultural region, the town was dominated by a citadel hill about 130 feet high. Down through the centuries Epiphania-Hama has been an important site and today has a population of about 200,000.

Emesa. Farther up the Orontes, about twenty-five miles south of Epiphania, stood Emesa (modern Homs), which retained its native priest-kings (of the cult of the sun god) throughout the Roman period. The town gained notoriety in the third century A.D. when one of these, Heliogabalus (Elagabalus), became Roman emperor for a brief time. At Emesa the Orontes is some 100 feet broad, and the area has always been fertile, boasting fine gardens and orchards and a good climate. The plain of Emesa was a battleground of warring kings, and about fifteen miles to the southwest was Kadesh, where the Hittites and Egyptians met in the days of Ramses II. This city (c. 85 miles north of Damascus) has maintained a degree of prosperity through the centuries and today has a population of about 325,000.

Heliopolis. Modern Christians are probably much more impressed with the greatness of Baalbek than first century Chris-

tians would have been, for the magnificent complex of temples there was not completed until sometime during the third century.

Baalbek is located on a superb site fifty-one miles east of Beirut at an altitude of 3,850 feet above sea level. On the caravan route linking Damascus, Emesa, and Tyre, it had a fertile hinterland as well as commercial advantages. The site is beautiful too, nestled as it is between the Lebanon and Anti-Liban ranges.

The origins of Baalbek are lost in antiquity. Alouf thinks it probable that Baalbek is to be identified with the Baalath that Solomon built up as a store city and a relay station for his caravans (I Kings 9:17-19). He also thinks that Solomon built there near the end of his reign a temple to Baal to please his concubines.[46] After Solomon's death the Phoenicians beautified the Baalbek temple of Hadad-Baal, their sun god, and thousands from many directions made pilgrimages to the site.

Baalbek means "town of Baal"[47] and seems to have been of Phoenician origin. Because it was considered to be the birthplace of the worship of the sun or of Baal,[48] the site was held in special veneration. The

244. Ritual basin and steps leading to the Temple of Jupiter, Baalbek

[45]Heichelheim, p. 158.

[46]Michel M. Alouf, *History of Baalbek* (20th ed.; Beirut: American Press, 1951), pp. 42-43.
[47]*Ibid.*, p. 38.
[48]*Ibid.*, p. 50.

245. Temple of Bacchus interior, Baalbek

Seleucids called the city "Heliopolis" ("the City of the Sun"), and the Romans identified the Baal of this city with Jupiter and called him "Jupiter Heliopolitanus." When the Romans took over, Augustus planted a Roman colony there and named it "Colonia Julia Augusta Felix Heliopolitana" (c. A.D. 10).

Probably as early as the reign of Augustus, the massive temple complex at Heliopolis was begun. Inscriptions show that the work on the temple of Jupiter was well under way during Nero's reign. And the temple of Bacchus apparently was begun about the middle of the first century A.D. For three centuries construction went on at the site to produce a magnificent complex exhaling a sense of power, size, and glorious magnificence.

A huge substructure (24-42 feet above the ground) was built for the temples to fulfill a psychological function—to render them more imposing by lifting them high above the neighboring landscape. A worshiper would enter the temple complex through a tower-flanked propylaea 165 feet wide and 38 feet deep. He would then pass through a hexagonal court into a great altar court about 350 feet square. On either side of the altar were large stone basins (actually tanks) 68 feet long by 23 feet broad and 2 feet 7 inches high for ritual washing.

246. Temple of Bacchus, Baalbek

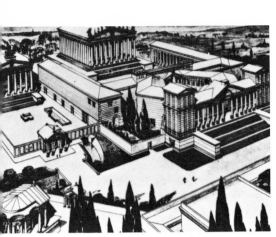

247. Reconstruction of the temple complex, Baalbek

248. Entablature from the Temple of Jupiter, Baalbek

From this court a magnificent stairway led to the temple of Jupiter. Surrounded by a colonnade of fifty-four columns, the cella, or holy of holies, was 290 by 160 feet, over five times as large as that of the Parthenon. Six of the great 100-ton Corinthian columns of the peristyle (colonnade) remain standing. Sixty-five feet high, they are the tallest in the world. Atop the columns is a sixteen-foot entablature ornately decorated with lions' and bulls' heads showing oriental influence.

Adjoining the temple of Jupiter on the south is the temple of Bacchus with a cella 87 by 75 feet, originally surrounded by a peristyle of 46 columns 57 feet high. Beautifully preserved, no better example of a Roman temple interior survives. East of the acropolis was a round temple, rare in Syria, that was probably a temple of Venus, constructed about A.D. 250.

The walls of the temple complex were two miles in circumference. Huge stones appear in this wall, the three largest being about 64 feet long, 14 feet high, and 11 feet thick and each weighing some 1,000 tons. The largest stone of all never made it out of the quarry and may be seen about a mile south of the modern town. It measures 70 by 14 by 13 feet. The busy town that once surrounded the temples at Baalbek has vanished. No attempt to excavate its remains has yet been made. Alouf believes the population of Baalbek must have totaled at least 200,000.[49]

Damascus. Not long after Pentecost, Christianity spread to Damascus, and Saul of Tarsus went there to extirpate the new faith. What the city was like then no one will probably ever know. Damascus is the oldest continuously inhabited large city in the world. It has never lapsed into ruin or been reduced to small town or village status. Because of this, remains of earlier civilizations there cannot be unearthed while the city's life still throbs above them. Large in the New Testament period, Damascus is even bigger today with a population well over a half million.

249. Large stone in the quarry at Baalbek

[49]*Ibid.*, p. 4.

250. East Gate, Damascus

The East Gate, which any visitor to Damascus may see today, probably dates to the Roman times, and the "street called Straight" still follows the course it did in Paul's day. A few stones in the lower courses of the present wall of Damascus date to the Roman period, and houses perch on the walls now as then. No doubt Paul would have been lowered from a window of one of the houses on the wall.

As to where Paul went when he entered Arabia and for exactly what reason he went is not certain. Some have claimed he traveled as far away as Petra, and others have said that he settled in or at some nearby oasis. It seems most reasonable to believe that Paul did not go far from Damascus; at least the biblical narrative does not require that he did. Near Damascus the Syrian Desert runs off to meet the northern section

Damascus figures prominently in the New Testament in connection with the conversion of Saul of Tarsus. It will be remembered that Saul met God on the Damascus Road on the way to persecute Jews who had turned to Christianity (Acts 9:1-8) and that he entered the city through the East Gate and stayed for a while on the street called "Straight." Apparently almost immediately after his conversion Saul went out into Arabia for the better part of three years, subsequently returning to Damascus to preach (Gal. 1:17-18). The object of a plot against his life instigated by Jews who opposed his ministry, Paul escaped over the city wall, being lowered in a basket. According to II Corinthians 11:32, a governor appointed by King Aretas of the Nabataeans ruled Damascus when Paul escaped.

251. "Street Called Straight," Damascus

of the Arabian Peninsula. Paul may have gone into seclusion in some sparsely populated place; but there were cities in Arabia, and there is no reason to suppose he did not visit one of them. He may have gone to "begin a tremendous inner reconstruction of his religious thinking," as someone has suggested. But there is no light on exactly where and why Paul went during this silent period in his life.

253. Houses on the wall, Damascus

252. Roman arch, Damascus

As to Aretas who ruled Damascus at the time of Paul's conversion (II Cor. 11:32), it it is known that Aretas III took control of Damascus after defeating Antiochus II of Seleucia in 85 B.C. and lost it again to the Romans in 64 B.C. Aretas IV (3 B.C.-A.D. 40) would have been the Aretas of Paul's day. It is interesting to note that while Roman coins of Tiberius appear at Damascus until A.D. 34, imperial coins are absent until coins with Nero's image appear again in A.D. 62. Damascus may have been under Nabataean control in the meantime.[50] But the argument from silence is not conclusive.[51]

Apparently Damascus enjoyed increasing prosperity and improved status in the sec-

[50]Finegan, pp. 336-37.
[51]Jean Starcky, "The Nabataeans: A Historical Sketch," *The Biblical Archaeologist,* XVIII (Dec., 1955), 97-100.

ond century. This may have had something to do with Trajan's reduction of Petra and the breaking of Nabataean commercial power in A.D. 105. Damascus depended on its trade and its gardens for its prosperity. But whether or not Damascene prosperity had anything to do with the decline of Petra, the development of Palmyra did.

Palmyra. The oasis of Palmyra is located halfway between the Mediterranean Sea and the Euphrates River at an altitude of 1300 feet. Through it passed the great trade routes to Persia from Phoenicia and from Egypt, Petra, and Arabia. Whether one traveled from Emesa or Damascus to the Euphrates, he would find Palmyra a convenient halfway point on his journey. A clearer idea of Palmyra's position on the caravan routes, from which it derived its very life, is gained from the realization that the city was located 150 miles northeast of Damascus and 190 miles west of the Euphrates. The city lies in the middle of the great Arabian Desert with its mantle of arid sands, from which emerge the unclothed ribs of bare low mountains and projecting scarps. To the west still stand the remains of numerous tower tombs of rich Palmyrene families; some of these towers are seventy feet high. To the east toward the Euphrates stretches a flat waste as far as eye can see.

254. Airview, Temple of Bel, Palmyra

Presumably the Palmyrene trade route began to be regularly utilized not long after 2000 B.C. Assyrian documents speak of Palmyra under its Semitic name of Tadmor before the first millennium B.C. At the beginning of the first millennium B.C., Solomon fortified Tadmor (II Chron. 8:4) and

255. Bust of a man holding a palm leaf symbolizing immortality, Palmyra, second century A.D.

made it a secure outpost through which the wealth of India could be brought to his kingdom. Throughout the classical and Hellenistic periods it must have been a flourishing trading post. However, nothing further is heard about it until Mark Antony tried unsuccessfully to capture it in 38 B.C.

At that time Palmyra was no more than a prosperous oasis village. But Roman commercial policy created the greatness of the site. When Trajan broke the power of Petra and incorporated it into Provincia Arabia in A.D. 106, Palmyra rose to new heights because of its new commercial opportunity. In the stalemate between Parthia and Rome, Palmyra had its chance, serving as a go-between state with its liberty guaranteed by both her neighbors and reaping rich rewards from that position. There the goods of China, India, and Parthia were exchanged for the goods of Rome. Of special interest is the fact that just before World War II beautiful Chinese silks of the first and second centuries A.D. were excavated there—the first evidence in the West for importation from the China of the Han Dynasty.[52]

In the third century Palmyra took the

[52]David M. Robinson, *Baalbek; Palmyra* (New York: J. J. Augustin Publishers, 1946), p. 64.

opportunity provided by the weakness of its Roman protector to build up its own power. Queen Zenobia after A.D. 266 made Palmyra ("city of palms") the capital of a caravan empire. In its heyday the city probably had a population over 30,000 and set up commercial agents in Mesopotamia, Egypt, Spain, Gaul, Italy, and on the Danube.[53]

Palmyra was laid out on a grid plan with the main streets intersecting at right angles. Arches marked the junction of the main with the principal cross streets. Along the ancient caravan route where it passed through the middle of the city was con-

[53]Julian Huxley, *From an Antique Land* (New York: Crown Publishers, Inc., 1954), p. 151.

structed one of the grandest avenues in all Syria. Sixty feet wide, it was once bordered by 375 Corinthian columns of rose-white limestone, each fifty-five feet high. Of these about 150 still stand. On these columns were projecting brackets on which statues were placed.

North of the colonnade lay the chief residential area of the city. Some of the houses were veritable palaces with splendid colonnades around their central courtyards. The great temple of Bel stood in the eastern section of the city. It consisted of an open courtyard over 200 yards square, the whole raised on a masonry base and approached by a splendid staircase which led through

256. Temple of Bel, Palmyra

a formal entrance complex. The court was surrounded on the inside by covered porticoes and within the court was a cella, or holy of holies, an altar, and a libation tank. A discussion of the temple of Bel-shamin, the theater, the great agora (*c.* 90 by 75 yards), and other great ruins of the city would be of much interest to the classical student but is not within the province of the present study.

While Palmyra was adorned with some of its greatest architectural glories during the second century A.D. after it became the financial capital of the Eastern world, it was already a prosperous site in the first century. And some of the greatest structures, such as the temples of Bel and Bel-shamin,

were built by the time followers of Christ were first called "Christians" at Antioch.

＊ ＊ ＊

The modern visitor to such dead cities of Syria as Palmyra may sit in solitude among the ruins and ponder the greatness of these cities and the reasons for their demise. He will be struck by their elegance and evidences of a departed prosperity. But the student of Christianity will be overwhelmed even more by the fact that all across Syria stand ruins of great old Christian churches. Unfortunately today, in this land where Christians were first called "Christians" and where the early church first launched its missionary enterprise, hardly a professing Christian may be found.

Bibliography

ALBRIGHT, WILLIAM F. *Archaeology and the Religion of Israel.* Baltimore: The Johns Hopkins Press, 1946.

ALOUF, MICHEL M. *History of Baalbek.* Beirut: American Press, 20th ed., 1951.

BEVAN, EDWYN R. *The House of Seleucus.* 2 vols. London: Edward Arnold, 1902.

BICKERMAN, E. *Institutions Des Séleucides.* Paris: Paul Geuthner, 1938.

BOUCHIER, E. S. *A Short History of Syria.* Oxford: Basil Blackwell, 1921.

–––. *Syria as a Roman Province.* Oxford: Basil Blackwell, 1916.

CARY, M. *The Geographic Background of Greek and Roman History.* Oxford: At the Clarendon Press, 1949.

CASTLE, WILFRID. *Syrian Pageant.* London: Hutchinson & Co., Ltd., 1946.

DOWNEY, GLANVILLE. *Antioch in the Age of Theodosius the Great.* Norman: University of Oklahoma Press, 1962.

–––. *A History of Antioch in Syria.* Princeton: Princeton University Press, 1961.

DUSSAUD, RENE. *Topographie Historique de la Syrie Antique et Médiévale.* Paris: Paul Geuthner, 1927.

FEDDEN, ROBIN. *Syria.* London: Robert Hale Limited, 1946.

FINEGAN, JACK. *Light from the Ancient Past.* Princeton: Princeton University Press, 2d ed., 1959.

GOODSPEED, EDGAR J. *Paul.* Philadelphia: The John C. Winston Co., 1947.

GURNEY, O. R. *The Hittites.* Harmondsworth, England: Penguin Books, Inc., rev. ed., 1961.

HALLO, WILLIAM W. "From Qarqar to Carchemish: Assyria and Israel in the Light of New Discoveries," *Biblical Archaeologist,* XXIII (1960), 34-61.

HEICHELHEIM, F. M. *Roman Syria,* Vol. IV of *An Economic Survey of Ancient Rome.* Edited by TENNEY FRANK. Baltimore: Johns Hopkins Press, 1938.

HITTI, PHILIP K. *History of Syria.* New York: Macmillan Co., 1951.

HUXLEY, JULIAN. *From an Antique Land.* New York: Crown Publishers, Inc., 1954.

JONES, A. H. M. *The Cities of the Eastern Roman Provinces.* Oxford: At the Clarendon Press, 1937.

JONES, TOM B. *Ancient Civilization.* Chicago: Rand McNally & Co., 1960.

KNOX, JOHN. *Chapters in a Life of Paul.* New York: Abingdon-Cokesbury Press, 1950.

MAZAR, BENJAMIN. "The Aramean Empire and Its Relations with Israel," *Biblical Archaeologist,* XXV (1962), 98-120.

METZGER, BRUCE M. "Antioch-on-the-Orontes," *Biblical Archaeologist,* XI (1948), 69-88.

Mommsen, Theodor. *The Provinces of the Roman Empire from Caesar to Diocletian.* Translated by William P. Dickson. Vol. 2. New York: Charles Scribner's Sons, 1906.

Muller, Herbert J. *The Loom of History.* New York: Harper & Brothers, 1958.

Olmstead, A. T. *History of Palestine and Syria.* New York: Charles Scribner's Sons, 1931.

———. *History of the Persian Empire.* Chicago: University of Chicago Press, 1948.

Paton, Lewis B. *The Early History of Syria and Palestine.* New York: Charles Scribner's Sons, 1901.

Pfeiffer, Charles F. *Ras Shamra and the Bible.* Grand Rapids: Baker Book House, 1962.

Rainey, A. F., "The Kingdom of Ugarit," *Biblical Archaeologist,* XXVIII (1965), 102-25.

Ramsay, William M. *The Bearing of Recent Discovery on the Trustworthiness of the New Testament.* London: Hodder & Stoughton, 2d ed., 1915.

Robinson, David M. *Baalbek; Palmyra.* New York: J. J. Augustin Publishers, 1946.

Smith, George Adam. *Syria and the Holy Land.* New York: George H. Doran Co., 1918.

Starcky, Jean, "The Nabataeans: A Historical Sketch," *Biblical Archaeologist,* XVIII (1955), 84-106.

Stevenson, G. H. *Roman Provincial Administration.* New York: G. E. Stechert & Co., 1939.

Stillwell, Richard (ed.) *Antioch On-the-Orontes.* Princeton: Princeton University Press, 1938.

Unger, Merrill F. *Israel and the Aramaeans of Damascus.* Grand Rapids: Zondervan Publishing House, 1957.

Wiegand, Theodor. *Baalbek.* 3 vols. Berlin: W. de Gruyter & Co., 1921-25 (in German).

Woolley, C. Leonard. *A Forgotten Kingdom.* Harmondsworth, England: Penguin Books, Inc., 1953.

SUSE
PERSEPOLIS

257. A bull capital from one of the columns of the palace at Susa (biblical Shushan)

Biblical Iran

WHEN THE CITY OF JERUSALEM was destroyed by Nebuchadnezzar's armies, the Neo-Babylonian Empire was at its zenith. Within a scant half century its very existence was challenged by the ruler of an obscure Persian province who forged an empire from the states of Media and Persia, conquered Lydia in Asia Minor, and triumphantly entered Babylon itself.

Isaiah had prophesied of this ruler, Cyrus, as the Lord's anointed (44:28; 45:1); it was Cyrus' decree that made possible the return of the exiled Judaeans to their homeland (II Chron. 36:22-23). Under Darius, the second temple in Jerusalem was dedicated in 515 B.C. (Ezra 6:13-18). Ezra the scribe and Nehemiah the statesman brought revival and reform to the life of the Palestinian Jews and rebuilt the walls of Jerusalem while Artaxerxes was on the Persian throne. The story of Esther is concerned with events during the reign of Ahasuerus (Xerxes) which transpired at the Persian capital of Susa (biblical Shushan) when the very life of the Jewish people was threatened. Thus, under Medo-Persian rulers the damage wrought by the Neo-Babylonians was to be at least partially undone.

Geographical Features

"Persia" is the anglicized form of "Parsis," or "Pars," the section of Iran adjacent to the Persian Gulf. Native Persians have always used the term "Iran" to designate their indefinitely bounded country. And this has been the official name of the country since 1935. The modern name "Iran" is derived from the ancient "Ariana," meaning "the country of the Aryans." The Aryans were various Indo-European peoples who settled during prehistoric times in areas north and east of the Persian Gulf.

Geographically "Iran" is an inclusive term referring to the large plateau between the plain of the Tigris on the west and the Indus River valley to the east. On the south it is bounded by the Persian Gulf and the Indian Ocean and on the north by the Caspian Sea and chains of mountains that extend eastward and westward from the south end of the Caspian Sea.

Geographical areas. In the days of the Persian Empire, Iran was divided into geographical and political areas as follows. At the north end of the Persian Gulf was Susiana, with its main center at Susa. North of Susiana in the interior was Media, the chief city of which was Ecbatana (modern Hamadan). Hyrcania (Asterabad) occupied a narrow strip of land south of the Caspian Sea. East of Susiana along the Persian Gulf was Persia with its leading royal cities of Persepolis and Pasargadae.

North of Persia in the interior was Parthia. Gedrosia stretched along the Indian Ocean. It was bounded on the northwest by Drangiana and on the northeast by Arachosia. North of these two regions stretched Aria, and north of that Bactria.

The plateau. The plateau of Iran averages 3,000 to 5,000 feet in altitude. Over one-half of the drainage of the plateau flows inward to form inland lakes and sterile swamps. In its central region lie the great sand and salt deserts of Dasht-i-Lut and Dash-i-Kavir. This continuous desert region stretches northwest to southeast about 800 miles in length and varies from 100 to 200 miles in width.

At the western edge of the plateau rise the Zagros Mountains with several peaks above 10,000 feet. This range is over 600 miles in length and 120 miles in width. It consists of numerous parallel folds enclosing fruitful valleys where wheat, barley, and other grains and fruits grow. South of the Caspian stand the Elburz Mountains, the highest peak of which is Mount Demavend, about sixty miles northeast of Tehran. It is a conical peak 18,934 feet high, which was once volcanic. Demavend is thought to be the Mount Bikni, rich in lapis lazuli,

THE WYCLIFFE HISTORICAL GEOGRAPHY OF BIBLE LANDS

mentioned in Assyrian documents before 800 B.C. as the farthest point to which Aryans were chased by the Assyrian kings. To the northwest, the Iranian Plateau is united by the highlands of Armenia with the mountains of Asia Minor. To the northeast, the plateau is linked by the mountains of Khurasan (or Khorasan) and the Hindu Kush Range to the Himalayas. The total area of the plateau is over one million square miles, more than one-third the size of the forty-eight contiguous United States.

Rainfall. Iran is a country singularly lacking in rainfall. Only on the plain south of the Caspian and on the Elburz Mountains and Zagros Mountains is rainfall abundant. At Resht, precipitation is over 56 inches per year. But south of the Elburz at the national capital of Tehran, the figure drops to 9 inches. Farther south in the interior rainfall is about 2 inches per year. At the head of the Persian Gulf it annually measures about 10 inches.

Resources. Iran is primarily an agricultural and stockbreeding country. The northwestern part of the country, Azerbaijan, has fertile valleys with sufficient rainfall for growing various kinds of grain and fruits and vegetables. Agriculture prospers on the plain between the Caspian Sea and the Elburz Mountains, as it does in the fertile valleys of the mountains of Khurasan. The latter constitute the granary of Iran.

But Iran also possessed rich mineral resources. Its quarries provided marble and its mountain slopes yielded building woods for the Sumerian princes as early as the third millennium B.C. Gold, iron, copper, tin, and lead were exploited early and especially attracted the attention of the Assyrians. Sargon of Akkad was interested in the wealth of the region 1500 years earlier, however. The oil deposits, so important to Iran's economy today, did not of course have any importance for ancient peoples.

Historical Outline

Beginnings. Men appeared in Iran as early as the late Stone Age. By the fifth millennium B.C. numerous tiny Neolithic villages sheltered their agricultural populations. However, a few Neolithic settlements were made in western Iran earlier than that, as postwar discoveries have shown.

During the fourth millennium a painted-pottery culture developed on the plateau, copper gradually came into use for tools, and animals were domesticated (especially the horse). Trade increased. Barley and wheat (indigenous to Iran) were exported to Egypt and Europe. Cultivation of oats spread from Europe into Asia.

At the beginning of the third millennium, Iran experienced a considerable amount of penetration of Western culture but created its own "proto-Elamite" writing and in general absorbed external cultural influences while continuing to export its own culture.

For the Babylonians, civilization ended at the foothills of the Zagros Mountains. Therefore, since people of the plateau left no records during the period, nothing is known of political conditions on the Iranian Plateau during the third millennium.

Something is known of the Elamites, however. They established a dynasty at Susa during the first quarter of the third millennium and constructed a fairly large kingdom. With the rise of Sargon of Akkad during the twenty-fourth century B.C., a conflict broke out between the Semites and Elamites. Ultimately Sargon seems to have absorbed Elam into his empire. Under Sargon's grandson, Naram-Sin, an Elamite revolt erupted, but it was repressed. The Elamites won their independence, however, after the death of Naram-Sin.

During the second millennium B.C., as Iran passed into the Bronze Age, there was considerable military and political activity in the area. A new dynasty rose to power in Elam and invaded Babylonia. Elamites established themselves at Larsa and became masters of Isin, Uruk (Erech), and Babylon. After considerable warfare Hammurabi finally checked this Elamite expansion.

Subsequently the Elamites fell under Kassite control. The Kassites consisted basically of an Asianic element that had been invaded around 2000 B.C. by Indo-Europeans, who formed a military aristocracy among them. The Kassites became a powerful people, dominating the Zagros region and Mesopotamia for about a half millennium and finally disappearing from history about 1175 B.C.

Although the Kassites continued to dominate Mesopotamia, Elam gained independence during the thirteenth century and attained the height of its power about 1200 B.C. Elam won control of the whole Tigris Valley, most of the shore of the Persian Gulf, and the Zagros Range. In fact, all of western Iran fell under Elamite control. However, her power was destined to be short-lived. Nebuchadnezzar I of Babylon about the middle of the twelfth century smashed Elam, which disappeared from history for about three centuries. Babylonia and Assyria now entered on a long conflict.

Entrance of Iranians. About 1000 B.C. the Iranians began to descend on the Iranian Plateau in successive waves. Some came from the northwest via the Caucasus Mountains, and others came from the northeast via Khurasan. These Aryans were blocked from an eastward movement by more powerful Aryans already established in the Indus Valley. They were blocked from a westward movement by the Assyrians and the Kingdom of Urartu (Ararat). The Iranian horsemen and infantry gradually took control of the plateau from the former occupants. As they did so, these new owners constructed fortified towns with double

or triple enclosure walls surrounded by moats.

The Iron Age came to Iran about the same time as the Iranians did. But in addition to the exploitation of metals, the economy was based on agriculture, booty taken in war, and commerce. Since Assyria had no iron mines, she turned to Iran in part for a supply of this metal, so necessary to her war machine. The Assyrians were also interested in the Iranians as a source of horses and because the Iranians posed a threat to Assyria's eastern borders.

Not all Iranian tribes penetrated the Iranian Plateau gradually. From the end of the eighth century B.C., the Cimmerians and Scythians (probably to be equated with Gomer and Ashkenaz, Gen. 10:3) caused serious trouble in northwest Iran. Pouring down over the Caucasus Mountains, these hordes plundered wherever they went. The Cimmerians established themselves on the southern shore of the Black Sea near the mouth of the Halys River (modern Kizil Irmak), from where they attacked the Phrygian kingdom of Asia Minor and brought it to an end. The Scythians established a kingdom in the area of modern Azerbaijan.

Meanwhile the Medes consolidated their holdings in an area south and east of the Scythians. Among their vassals were the Persians. After this consolidation, Khshathrita, king of the Medes, decided to attack Nineveh. But he was attacked by the Scythians, allied with Assyria, and brought under Scythian control in 653 B.C.

Now the Scythians decided to break their alliance with Assyria and attack their former ally. Joined by the Cimmerians, they pillaged Asia Minor, Phoenicia, Syria, and Palestine all the way to the Egyptian border and then fell back toward the Zagros Mountains (cf. Jer. 4:5-31; 5:15-17; 6:1-8, 22-26).

Rise of the Medes. The son and successor of Khshathrita the Mede was Cyaxares.

Even though tributary to the Scythians, he was able to reorganize his forces, introduce contingents of archers and infantry, and borrow cavalry tactics from the Scythians. Ultimately he won a decisive victory over his suzerain. Cyaxares soon made himself master of the western part of the plateau and presumably ruled from a capital at Ecbatana.

Next the Median decided to continue where his father had left off in his attack on Assyria. Meanwhile, Nabopolassar, governor of Babylon, had begun his own war on Assyria. When Nineveh resisted Cyaxares' attack in 615 B.C., the Mede struck northward at Ashur. After his capture of Assyria's ancient capital, he moved southward against Nineveh. This time he effected an alliance with the Babylonians and took the city in 612.

After the demise of Assyria, Cyaxares engaged in a five-year war with Lydia. Peace came between the two powers in 584, sealed by a marriage alliance between Astyages, son of Cyaxares, and the daughter of the Lydian king. The Medes and the Babylonians had divided most of western Asia between them. And it was clear that the Medes had designs on land under Babylonian control. Nebuchadnezzar, son and successor of Nabopolassar, constructed defenses along his northern border to protect himself against such a threat. Later, Nabonidus, last king of the Babylonians, allied himself with Cyrus II of the Persians against the Medes.

Persian power. The rise of the Persians began about 700 B.C. At that time, the Iranian tribe which had settled in Parsumash near the Elamite land of Anshan was ruled by Achaemenes. This founder of the dynasty was succeeded by his son Teispes (675-640), who apparently was brought temporarily under the suzerainty of the Median Khshathrita but became independent once more when the Scythians overcame the Medes. Teispes divided his lands

between two sons: Ariaramnes (640-590) and Cyrus I (640-600). As Cyaxares the Mede expanded his power, he brought the two small Persian kingdoms under his control, the line of Ariaramnes losing their title to the crown. In the other branch of the family, Cambyses I (600-599) succeeded Cyrus I. Nominally he was king of Anshan, but he was actually subordinate to the Median king Astyages, whose daughter Mandane he had married. Their son was Cyrus II, the Great.

When Nabonidus realized the ambitions of Cyrus of Anshan (559-530 B.C.), he made an alliance with him against the Medes. Cyrus quickly defeated the Medes, established the capital of united Iran at Ecbatana, and proceeded westward against Lydia. Croesus of Lydia was defeated in 546, and Cyrus was free to move against Babylon, which he took in 539. After launching the Hebrews and others on pro-

258. Head of a Mede, Persepolis

grams of restoration of their commonwealths and after building a new capital at Pasargadae, Cyrus died in battle in 530 as he fought against enemies in the East. Cambyses II (530-522) annexed Egypt and subsequently went insane. Various provinces tried to become independent during the ensuing period of imperial weakness.

Darius the Great (522-486), a prince of another branch of the Achaemenid line, saved the empire and engaged in a partially successful war against the Greeks. He was also involved in the biblical narrative as the one under whom the second temple was dedicated in 515 B.C. He moved the Persian capital from Pasargadae to Persepolis. Darius' son, Xerxes (486-465), continued the war against the Greeks but ultimately was thoroughly defeated. He was undoubtedly the Ahasuerus who married Esther (Esther 1:1, etc.). Since the narrative took place at Shushan (Susa), it presumably occurred during the winter because Susa was a winter capital of the empire.

Following Xerxes, Artaxerxes I (465-425) ruled the Persian Empire. During his reign Nehemiah (2:1) returned to Jerusalem to rebuild the walls (445 B.C.). After a year of rule by Sogdianus (Secydianus), Artaxerxes' son Darius II (423-405) ruled the empire. Of special significance during his rule was his alliance with Sparta during the Peloponnesian War, a fact which brought the Athenian Empire down in a heap. During the reigns of Artaxerxes II (405-358), Artaxerxes III (358-338), Arses (Xerxes III, 338-336), and Darius III (336-330), the Persian Empire was definitely in a condition of decline. Finally Alexander the Great administered the *coup de grâce*, beginning in 334 B.C.

Alexander and the Seleucids. Although Alexander had been extraordinarily successful in conquering the Persian Empire, he died at Babylon in 323 B.C., before he established an enduring imperial organization and before his son was born. Seleucus, one of his generals, after numerous difficulties managed to conquer the whole of Iran as far as the Indus River and to extend his domains to include most of the old Persian Empire. Seleucus founded a new capital, Seleucia on the Tigris, as well as numerous other Greek towns. These cities became outposts of Hellenic life in Oriental territory, as they were populated by a ruling clique of Greeks and a Hellenized native element.

The Parthian Kingdom. When Seleucus was assassinated in 281 B.C., his son Antiochus I took the reins of government. There-

259. Darius hunting lions, from a cylinder seal

THE WYCLIFFE HISTORICAL GEOGRAPHY OF BIBLE LANDS

260. Griffins from the palace at Susa, probably dating to the reign of Artaxerxes II

after the Seleucid Empire was never at rest and was constantly battling for its very existence. In the middle of the third century B.C., Bactria revolted and became independent. Shortly after, in 248 B.C., Arsaces made himself master of the district of Parthia, southeast of the Caspian Sea. Although Parthia was a small kingdom for several decades, it gradually increased its boundaries. The Arsacids ultimately brought under their control Mesopotamia and most of the northern half of the Iranian Plateau. The southern half of the plateau was divided into a number of minor states, generally dependent on the Arsacids.

The Parthians fought several protracted wars with Rome, beginning in 54 B.C., when Crassus took the field against Parthia. Mesopotamia passed back and forth between the warring powers. Ultimately Rome destroyed Seleucia on the Tigris (A.D. 164) and obtained northwestern Mesopotamia. Subsequent struggles between Rome and Parthia did not seriously change the boundaries.

The Sassanids. After about 400 years of rule the Parthian Empire came to an end in very much the same way as the Median Empire had. In about A.D. 212 Ardashir I, ruler of a small state in Persia, revolted

against his overlord, Artabanus V of Parthia, and by A.D. 224 had brought Artabanus' power to an end. The new Sassanid Empire was a Neo-Persian empire, with Zoroastrian religion and Iranian culture rather than Greek. The Sassanid Empire continued for about four centuries until a long war with the Byzantine Empire so weakened its power that it was not able to withstand the onslaught of Muslim forces, which occupied all of Iran by A.D. 650. Subsequent history of Persia has no connection with the biblical account and need not detain this study. For all practical purposes the history of contemporary Iran began in 1919 with British affirmation of Iran's independence and with the subsequent withdrawal of Russian forces in 1921.

261. Alexander the Great, from a coin

Regional Surveys

Baghdad to Tehran

The road from Baghdad, Iraq, to Tehran, Iran, introduces one to the earliest Iranian history. About fourteen miles west of the border, the traveler comes to a Kurdish town named Qasr i-Shirin at the foot of the Zagros Mountains. It is reputed to have been named for a Christian Armenian princess who languished for her lover while imprisoned in the harem of Khosrau II (Greek Chosroes, A.D. 590-628). Her tragic story was immortalized by the Persian poet Nizami of Gandzha (modern Kirovabad) in 1203. The ruins of the traditional castle of Shirin are northeast of the town. East of Qasr-i-Shirin one enters the Zagros Mountains, which extend southeastward from the Caucasus region between the Black and Caspian seas. The mountains are formed of

a core of granite covered with limestone, and reach heights of 14,000 feet.

Twenty-one miles from Qasr i-Shirin is another Kurdish village, Sar-i-Pul ("bridgehead"), at the entrance to which is a bas-relief showing King Annubanini, prince of the Lullubi tribe, standing with his foot on a fallen enemy. The Lullubi were a warlike people of the Zagros Mountains who are thought to have been ancestors of the Kassites who invaded Mesopotamia about 1500 B.C. Annubanini was a contemporary of the Akkadian ruler Naram-Sin (2320-2284 B.C.).

The relief depicts Annubanini with a long, square-cut beard, a round hat, and a short garment. To the right of the king, who is armed with bow and arrow, stands the goddess Ninni dressed with a high miter and a fringed garment reaching to her feet. She is presenting two kneeling captives to Annubanini, and six more, with hands bound behind them, appear below the king and the goddess. An Akkadian inscription invokes the gods to give Annubanini victory over his enemies. Nearby are stelae of the late Parthian-Sassanian period and a Pahlavi inscription.

Kermanshah. The city of Kermanshah, about 128 miles inside the Iranian border, has a population of about 100,000, mostly Kurds. Its name, meaning "Shah of Kerman," recalls the fact that its founder, Bahram IV (A.D. 389-99) had been governor of the district of Kerman during the reign of his brother and predecessor Shapur III (A.D. 383-388). Kermanshah was probably the location of ancient Cambadene. The Seleucid rulers identified the adjacent Nysa Plain with the swampy birthplace of the god Bacchus. As early as Alexander the Great, the plains east of the city were famed for

262. Annubanini relief

their horses. The climate of the Kermanshah area made it a favorite with the Sassanian rulers of Persia. Excavations were conducted by the French archaeologist Jacques de Morgan north of the modern city late in the nineteenth century.

Luristan. South of Kermanshah is the province of Luristan, named for the Lurs, or "woodsman" people, who inhabited the region. In recent years, thousands of bronze and iron objects from the north of Luristan have enriched private collections and museums in Europe and America. These objects come from tombs, none of which has yet been scientifically excavated, and are sold through antiquities dealers.

There are no permanent settlements in ancient Luristan, for the Lurs seem to have been a nomadic people. The objects discovered at Luristan are nearly all portable: weapons, toilet articles, votive objects, and painted pottery. The Iranian archaeologist Roman Ghirshman suggests that they date from the eighth or seventh century B.C. and that they belonged to an elite clan of warrior horsemen and charioteers who were reluctant to settle on the land, preferring portable goods for that reason.[1] Scythians and Cimmerians from the Caucasus region may have established themselves in Luristan and served as a warrior nucleus for the state of Media, then at the height of its expansion.

Nihawand. Nihawand (Nehavend, "Noah's town") is an ancient town of upper Luristan which was rebuilt by the Seleucids and named Laodicea for the wife of Antiochus III (193 B.C.). In A.D. 640, the Sassanian king Yazdegerd III sought to repulse the Arab invaders of the Iranian Plateau at Nihawand. Yazdegerd's army was utterly routed, however, and Sassanian Iran fell before its Islamic conquerors.

A Jew named Benjamin of Nihawand (c.

263. Darius' inscription appears high on the mountain in right center of the picture.

A.D. 800) was an early leader of the Karaite sect which rejected the traditions of Rabbinic Judaism and insisted on the Scriptures alone as the standard of faith and life. Benjamin wrote in Hebrew and anticipated the work of modern Israeli scholars in working to revive Hebrew as a spoken language.

Tepe Giyan. Excavations at Tepe Giyan, eighteen miles southeast of Nihawand, conducted by Georges Contenau and Roman Ghirshman in 1931/32, have revealed important Chalcolithic remains from the fourth millennium B.C. and Assyrian remains from about 1100 B.C. Ceramic and bronze funerary furnishings were discovered.[2]

Bisitun. Twenty miles east of Kermanshah, on the main highway to Tehran, is the village of Bisitun (Behistun), famed for the nearby bas-relief of Darius I (521-485 B.C.) The boastful king had a record of his exploits engraved 345 feet above a spring and 100 feet above the highest point to which a man can climb. To insure that his inscription would not be defaced by later generations, Darius evidently had the ascent to the inscription sheared off after the work was completed.

In 1835, Henry Rawlinson, a British officer stationed near Bisitun, began the haz-

[1]Ghirshman, *Iran* (Baltimore: Penguin Books), pp. 99, 105.

[2]Contenau and Ghirshman, *Fouilles du Tepe-Giyan* (Paris: The Louvre, 1935).

264. Darius' inscription

ardous task of copying the inscription. Risking his life in the process, he continued until 1847, when the work was completed. To copy the top lines, Rawlinson had to stand on the top step of a ladder, steadying his body with his left arm and holding his notebook in his left hand while writing with his right hand.

In 1904 the British Museum sent L. W. King and R. Campbell Thompson to Bisitun to check Rawlinson's readings by making fresh copies of the inscription. A further study was made in the fall of 1948 when George C. Cameron made fresh copies of the inscription under the auspices of the American Schools of Oriental Research and the University of Michigan.[3]

The top register of the inscription contains a winged disk and twelve figures. Darius is depicted treading on his rival Gaumata, a pretender to the throne. In front of Darius are nine captive rebels. To the right of the relief are four columns of writing in the Elamite language.

The main inscription is given in Persian in five columns directly under and to the right of the relief. To the left of the Persian, on the face of the rock projecting one

inch farther out is the Elamite translation. Above this, projecting out still farther, is the Akkadian (Babylonian) version.

This trilingual inscription unlocked the Assyro-Babylonian system of cuneiform writing in the same way that the Rosetta Stone made possible the decipherment of the Egyptian hieroglyphs. After the Old Persian inscription was deciphered, scholars worked on the hypothesis that the other two texts were but different versions of the same text. Through the labors of Dr. Edward Hincks, rector of a parish church at Killyleagh, County Down, Ireland, and Henry Rawlinson himself, a list of values for cuneiform characters was issued and the key to the decipherment of other inscriptions was made available to the world of scholarship.

The following condensed excerpt from the Bisitun (Behistun) Inscription follows Robert North's *Guide to Biblical Iran:*

> I am Darius [descendant] of Achaemenes, for which reason we are called Achaemenians. By the grace of Ahura-Mazda I am ruler of 23 lands including Babylonia, Sparda [Sardis?], Arabia, Egypt. I put down the rebellions of Gaumata and [8] others in [19] battles . . .

A copy of the Bisitun Inscription was also found at Babylon on black diorite, and an

[3]Cf. W. C. Benedict and Elizabeth von Voightlander, "Darius' Bisitun Inscription, Babylonian Version, Lines 1-29," *Journal of Cuneiform Studies,* X (1956), 1-10.

THE WYCLIFFE HISTORICAL GEOGRAPHY OF BIBLE LANDS

Aramaic papyrus version was discovered among the Jews of Elephantine. Darius evidently spared no effort to tell of his might in the most remote corners of his empire.

Hamadan—Ecbatana. Hamadan, on the site of ancient Ecbatana, is a modern city of about 130,000 population high in the Zagros Mountains of western Iran. Although cold in winter, it has a delightful summer climate, and Cyrus made it his summer capital. The name "Ecbatana" is ultimately derived from the Akkadian "Agamatanu," from *hangmatana*, "gathering place." Ezra 6:2 calls the place Achmetha; there Darius I found the scrolls of Cyrus authorizing the Jews to return to Jerusalem and rebuild their temple. The Apocryphal book of Judith states that King Arphaxad, who ruled the Medes during the time of Nebuchadnezzar, had his capital at Ecbatana (Judith 1:1-14). Antiochus Epiphanes is said to have stopped there after retreating from Persepolis where he had suffered defeat (II Macc. 9:3). The Judith story is fictitious, and there is no serious reason for accepting the statement in II Maccabees, for the more reliable account in I Maccabees (6:4) does not mention Ecbatana.

Ecbatana plays an important part in the Apocryphal legends contained in the Book of Tobit, where we read that the younger Tobit, or Tobias, was guided by the angel Raphael on a journey from Nineveh to collect $30,000 which the elder Tobit, his father, had deposited with Gabel at Rages (Persian Rai, near Tehran). Stopping at Ecbatana, Tobias was entertained at the home of Raguel, his father's brother. Sarah, Raguel's daughter, was marriageable, but her seven husbands had died on their wedding night. Armed with a formula for driving away the demons, Tobias married his charming cousin, and the story ended happily (Tob. 6:1-17).

Cuneiform documents from Tiglath-pileser I (1100 B.C.) mention Ecbatana as a *kar-kassi* ("Kassite town"). The Greek writ-

er Ctesias ascribes the founding of Ecbatana,[4] along with Babylon and other important cities, to Semiramis, a legendary figure who is probably to be identified with Sammu-ramat, described as "lady of the palace" at the time of Adadnirari III (800 B.C.). She was either the king's mother and regent during the early portion of Adadnirari's reign or his wife.

At the northeast sector of Hamadan is the area known as *Sar Qal'a* ("Cliff Castle") where the citadel of Cyrus once stood. Excavations at Sar Qal'a have revealed remains of the walls and foundations of the towers and other parts of the palaces of Median and Achaemenian kings. A gold plate found nearby contains an inscription of Ariaramnes (640-590 B.C.) which is the earliest Achaemenian document, written a century before the time of Cyrus. Southeast of the town is the imposing Sang i-Shir, "stone of the lion," which dates to Achaemenian or Parthian times.

Hamadan also boasts traditional tombs of Esther and Mordecai. The latter may be that of a Jewish physician and prime minister named Mordecai, who was martyred in Tabriz in A.D. 1291. In later years, his tomb may have been erroneously ascribed to the Mordecai of the canonical Esther scroll. The idea of a tomb of Esther may be because of the mistaken idea that an-

265. Modern Ecbatana and excavations
on the mound

[4]*Diodorus*, Books II and III.

cient Susa was located at the site of modern Hamadan. Ernst Herzfeld maintains that a godly woman named Shushan migrated to Hamadan, and that her Esther-like qualities caused her to be called "Shushan-Esther." Her tomb, Herzfeld suggests, is the one now identified as the tomb of the biblical Esther!

The brave, handsome Kurds now occupy the northwestern corner of Iran, northeastern Iraq, parts of eastern Turkey, and Soviet Armenia. Ethnically the Kurds, a nomadic people, engaged largely in sheep-raising and agriculture, are related to the Persians. Carpet-making is their chief industry.

Tell Gomel. Near the present Iraq-Iran frontier of Kurdistan is Tell Gomel ("Camel Hill"), which is the probable site of the Gaugamela where the armies of Alexander the Great defeated Darius III Codomannus in 331 B.C. The battle is often called the Battle of Arbela for the Assyrian town (modern Erbil in Iraq) sixty miles west of Tell Gomel. After his defeat, Darius III fled to Ecbatana, and from there to Bactria, where he was murdered by his cousin Bessus, the local satrap.

Tehran. Seventy miles south of the Caspian, within sight of Mount Demavend, is Tehran, the modern capital of Iran. Although Tehran is first mentioned in A.D. 1220, its suburb Rai (ancient Rages) is the scene of important events in the Apocryphal story of Tobit. Here the young Tobias found $30,000. Traditions vary as to whether Ecbatana or Rages was the place where the lad found his bride. Rages, mentioned by Darius the Great in his Bisitun (Behistun) Inscription, was subsequently rebuilt by Seleucus and named "Europus."

Rages was the largest city of Persia during the Middle Ages, and it acquired additional fame as the birthplace of Harun al-Rashid, the famous caliph of Baghdad (A.D. 766-809). In more recent times, however, it has been eclipsed by Tehran, which has been capital of Iran (Persia) since 1788.

Northern and Eastern Iran

The Caspian. The southern shores of the Caspian Sea form a part of the northern border of Iran, and the name "Caspian" is given to the pre-Iranian indigenous population. The name of the Kassites who left their homes in the mountains of Luristan and dominated Mesopotamia from 1600 to 1200 B.C. may be related to the term "Caspian." But the term may also have been derived from the Greek word for tin, *kassiteros*. Before Median times, a town of Akessaia (Kar-kassi, "Cassite town") was located at or near the site of Ecbatana-Hamadan.

Hyrcania. In ancient times, the southeastern shore of the Caspian Sea was known as "Hyrcania," and the sea itself was known to the Romans as "Mare Hyrcanium (or "Hyrcanum Mare"). The Persian ruler Artaxerxes III (Ochus) (361-338 B.C.), when faced with revolts in Egypt and Phoenicia, deported a sizable number of Jews to Hyrcania (modern Asterabad Province) and Babylonia. It is probable that in this way, "Hyrcanus" became a familiar name among the Jews. When a Jew returned to Palestine from Hyrcania, he would be given the surname "Hyrcanus" ("of Hyrcania"), and this name would be used by subsequent generations. Such is probably the derivation of the name of the famous Hasmonaean ruler John Hyrcanus. The explanation given by Eusebius, that John bore the name because he had conquered Hyrcania, does not account for the fact that many Jews bore the name before John (134-104 B.C.).

Parthia. South of, and at times including, Hyrcania, was the mountainous state of Parthia which had been a part of the Assyrian Empire. This area had been successively ruled by Persia, Alexander the Great, and the Syrian Seleucids. In 250 B.C. the Parthians freed themselves from Seleucid rule and founded their own Parthian state under

Arsaces. During the first century B.C., the Parthians controlled an empire which stretched from the Euphrates River eastward to the Indus River, and from the Oxus River (modern Amu Darya) southward to the Indian Ocean. In 53 B.C. they defeated Crassus and his Roman army at Carrhae (Haran), and for a time they threatened Syria and Asia Minor. They were checked, however, by the Roman general and acting consul Publius Ventidius Bassus (39-38 B.C.), after which the Parthian Empire entered a period of decline which continued until A.D. 226 when Parthia was conquered by Ardashir (Artaxerxes), the founder of the Sassanian Persian dynasty.

From the beginning of Parthian independence (250 B.C.) until it was moved to Ctesiphon (c. 50 B.C.), the Parthian capital was at Hecatompylos ("the city of a hundred gates"). The site is unknown but is probably near modern Damghan, about one hundred eighty miles east of Tehran on the main highway to Meshed.

About fifty miles north of Damghan is the city of Gurgan, formerly known as Asterabad. Mounds nearby have yielded objects of Sumerian ware of the early Lagash type (c. 3000 B.C.). At Shah-Tepe, Swedish archaeologists found artifacts from the Sumerian Uruk Period through the period of Sargon of Akkad.

Northwestern Iran

Tabriz. The modern city of Tabriz, strategically located in Azerbaijan, the northwestern province of Iran, is located on trade routes which lead northward into Russia and westward to Turkey. The name "Azerbaijan" is traceable to ancient Atropatene (Azerbaijan), named for the Persian satrap Atratopes, whom Alexander the Great appointed as governor of Media. The origins of Tabriz itself are obscure. It may go back to Sassanian times but more probably dates from the Arab conquest.

266. The harem, Persepolis

Lake Urmia. West of Tabriz is a shallow salt lake, eighty miles long and twenty-five miles wide known as Lake Urmia (perhaps meaning "salty water"). The city on its western plain, formerly also called "Urmia," is now known as "Rezaieh." There is no certain history of Urmia in pre-Islamic times, but the powerful Kingdom of Van was located in the region between Lake Van (now in Turkey) and Lake Urmia around 2000 B.C. The tribes which formed the Vanic kingdom are the ancestors of later Armenians and Georgians. Irsanians from the east and Thracians from the north were important elements in the Vanic kingdom.

At Geliashin, near the Turko-Iranian frontier, a bilingual inscription was found which mentioned the nearby town of Musasir founded by the people of Urartu. The Urartu people had a flourishing state from the thirteenth to the eighth centuries B.C. They proudly resisted the powerful Assyrians until the eighth century, when Sargon II, by a series of attacks, caused the final demise of Urartu. It was "in the mountains of Urartu" (Anglicized as Ararat) that the biblical ark rested following the flood. Musasir was destroyed by Sargon in 714 B.C., eight years after Samaria fell to the same Assyrian conqueror.

About 900 B.C., a people known as "the Mannai" occupied the region south of Lake Urmia, known as " the Land of Man." An inscription discovered at Tash-Tepe ("stone hill") identifies the site of Mesta, the capital of the Mannai people who vied for power with the Assyrians and the Arartu in the tenth century B.C.

Shiz. About halfway from Urmia to Hamadan, in northwestern Iran, is the city of Shiz (modern Takht-i-Sulaiman), thought to have been the capital of Atropatene. It also bore the name of Gazna. Shiz is one of several legendary birthplaces of Zoroaster and has long been a leading sanctuary in northern Iran. A very old community of magi resided in Shiz and probably functioned there before the time of Zoroaster who himself is thought to have been a magus.

Tehran to Shiraz

Savah and the Magi. The road which winds south 250 miles from Tehran to Isfahan (ancient Aspadana) passes near the village of Savah (Saveh), which has a tenuous claim to the Bible student's interest.

267. The Apadama, or audience hall, Persepolis

THE WYCLIFFE HISTORICAL GEOGRAPHY OF BIBLE LANDS

Some forms of ancient tradition make Savah the home of the wise men who brought gifts to the Child Jesus at Bethlehem. The Bible states that they came from the East, a term which could apply to any area between the Arabian Desert and distant Persia. The magi first appear in history as a Median tribe, skilled in the interpretation of dreams. They served as priests, having the responsibility for all acts of sacrifice.[5] After Cyrus incorporated Media into the Persian Empire, the magi retained their influence; and when the Zoroastrian religion was introduced under Darius, the priesthood of the magi became a part of the new official cult.[6] The Persian magi became experts in astrology, necromancy, and divination. In later years, however, the term "magi" was applied to people of any nation who devoted themselves to the occult sciences. One can read of magi in Chaldea, Egypt, Armenia, Ethiopia, and Gaul.[7] Simon Magus (Acts 8:9-24) and Elymas (Bar-jesus) the sorcerer (Acts 13:6-12) were both magi, and in everyday language, a "magus" came to be regarded as a magician. The Magi who came to Bethlehem, however, are described as wise men in the good sense of the term. In the words of Strabo, they were "zealous observers of justice and virtue."[8]

Most of the church fathers held that the Magi who came to the Infant Jesus were Persians, and a widespread Eastern tradition actually maintained that Zoroaster had prophesied the birth of Christ.[9] It is probable, however, that the wise men described by Matthew came from Arabia rather than Persia. Incense and myrrh which they

268. The Apadama, detail

brought are usually associated with Arabia, which also had significant gold deposits.

Marco Polo took seriously the claim that Savah was the home of the wise men. He stated:

> In Persia there is a city which is called Saba, from whence were the three magi who came to adore Christ in Bethlehem; and the three are buried in that city in a fair sepulchre, and they are all three entire with their beards and hair. One was called Baldasar, the second Gaspar, and the third Melchior. Marco inquired often in that city concerning the three magi, and nobody could tell him anything about them, except that the three magi were buried there in ancient times.[10]

Tepe Siyalk. About midway on the road from Tehran to Isfahan is the Oasis of Kashan, the site of Tepe Siyalk, which was excavated by Roman Ghirshman between 1933 and 1937. Siyalk contained the oldest human settlement to be identified on the Iranian Plateau. Traces of man's first occupation there have been found above virgin soil at the bottom of the mound. The earliest inhabitants found shelter in huts made from branches of trees. Soon, however, a more permanent type of structure

[5]Herodotus, Book I, Chaps. 101, 107, 120, 128, 132; Book VII, Chap. 19.

[6]Strabo, Book XV, Chap. iii, Section 1; Book XVI, Chap. ii, Section 39; and Herodotus, Book VII, Chap. 131.

[7]Pliny, *Natural History*, Book XXV, Chap. v, Section 4; Book XXV, Chap. xcv, Section 1; Book XXX, Chap. i, Section 16.

[8]Strabo, *Geography*, Book XV, Chap. iii, Section 6.

[9]G. Messina, *I Magi a Betlemme e una predizione di Zoroastro* (Rome: Pontifical Biblical Institute, 1933), p. 24.

[10]*The Travels of Marco Polo, the Venetian.* Revised from Marsden's translation, and edited with Introduction by Manuel Komroff (New York: Horace Liveright, 1926), Book I, Chap. 13, pp. 37-38.

developed, and agriculture was added to hunting as a way of life. Bones of domesticated oxen and sheep give evidence that stockbreeding also was practiced by the prehistoric residents of Siyalk.

At Siyalk, Ghirshman was able to trace the development of Iranian pottery from very crude beginnings. During the earliest period, known as Siyalk I, the pottery was black, smoked, and made by hand without the use of a wheel. Later a new red ware appeared with black patches caused by accidents of firing in a primitive oven. Next appeared painted pottery with geometric designs which suggest an imitation of basketwork. The early inhabitants of Siyalk had evidently learned to weave baskets before they developed the ceramic arts, and the basket designs were maintained in the early pots. Baked clay and stone spindle whorls indicate that a textile industry was known at a very early date. There were also stone tools, flint knife blades, sickle blades, polished axes, and scrapers. By the end of the period, small hammered copper objects began to appear. The properties of metal were evidently understood, but the art of casting had not been discovered. The Siyalk civilization dates to the end of the Neolithic age.

During the Siyalk I period, both men and women delighted in adorning themselves with rings, bracelets, and necklaces, and in painting their faces. Along with jewelry, Ghirshman found small pestles and miniature mortars used for the grinding of body paints. The Neolithic artists made use of bone for carving, and tool handles were often decorated with the head of a gazelle or hare. One of the oldest figurines from the Near East is a knife handle representing a man wearing a cap and a loincloth fastened by a belt.

The inhabitants of Siyalk I believed in a life after death, and they buried their dead under the floors of their houses so that the spirit of the deceased could share in the life of the family. Trade with neighboring villages had been developed as early as the Siyalk I community. Shells were imported from the Persian Gulf, six hundred miles away. Itinerant peddlers probably traveled from village to village selling luxury wares such as shells used in jewelry.

The Siyalk II period (fourth millennium B.C.) presents an advance over the earliest settlements. Tools were more refined, and the houses were decorated and improved. Sun-dried bricks were used as building material, and the interiors were decorated with red paint made from a mixture of iron oxide and a fruit juice. Pottery was much improved, some of it being decorated with pictures of birds and animals. Metal became more plentiful. Commerce continued to increase, with barley and wheat, indigenous to Iran, introduced by Iranian traders into both Egypt and Europe.

Siyalk III consists of a large number of superimposed levels covering much of the

269. Painted pottery from Siyalk

history of the site during the fourth millennium B.C. There are evidences of numerous technological advances including rectangular, molded bricks and the potter's wheel. Writing had not yet begun in the Iranian Plateau, but the pictorial representations which came to characterize Iranian ceramic ware may well have contributed to the development of the pictographic Sumerian syllabary which developed in southern Mesopotamia around 3000 B.C.

During the Siyalk III period, copper was smelted and cast, and metals began slowly to supplant stone in the making of tools and weapons. Jewelry became more varied, as carnelian, turquoise, lapis lazuli, and jade were used along with the shell of earlier times. Plain disks with slightly raised borders served as mirrors. Stamp seals were made with geometric, and later, pictorial designs to provide evidence of ownership. During the middle of the fourth millennium B.C., the civilization of northern Mesopotamia (later Assyria) adopted the ceramic tradition of Iran with its chalice shape and painted decoration. The best examples of this come from Siyalk and Hissar.

Excavations indicate a gap of nearly two thousand years at Siyalk. With the beginning of the first millennium B.C., the Indo-European peoples whom we know as Iranians began to penetrate the Iranian Plateau, and Siyalk was again occupied. The Iranians were a pastoral and agricultural people who took pride in the breeding and training of horses. Chariotry and cavalry made possible in large measure their success in battle. At this time Siyalk was occupied by one of the invading princes who built an imposing residence on top of the mound. Then the town, including the houses at the foot of the mound, was surrounded by a wall flanked with towers. Unlike the prehistoric period when the dead were buried under the floors of houses, the new settlers buried their dead in a vast cemetery several yards from the town.

Pottery from Iranian Siyalk depicts fighting men, and a cylinder seal shows a warrior on horseback fighting a monster. Another seal depicts a man, riding in a horse-drawn chariot, shooting an arrow at an animal. Siyalk by this time was a fortified town with local princes who prepared to fight the Assyrians and other Western peoples. Urban life had gained considerable impetus.

Isfahan. Modern Isfahan, in central Iran, is a city of attractively colored houses, spacious balconies, shade trees, flower gardens, and beautifully arched bridges. Although it has no direct biblical interest, both Jews and Christians have been closely associated with Isfahan and its environs. In the seventeenth century when Shah Abbas I the Great maintained his palace there, sixteen thousand Armenian Christians were settled at Julfa (modern Dzhulfa), across the River Araxes (modern Araks) from Isfahan. They were highly regarded because of their skilled workmanship, and Abbas I built churches and brought in missionaries for them. At the height of its prosperity under Abbas I, Isfahan had a population of six hundred thousand, nearly three times its present population. The Jewish settlements of Gayy and Yahudiyya are in the most ancient quarter of Isfahan.

Under the Achaemenian rulers of Persia, Isfahan bore the name "Gaba." Later it was known as "Aspadana" ("having horses as a gift"). It has been a Muslim city since A.D. 640 and has been capital of Persia several times (1051-63; 1072-92; 1590-1722). As early as Aphraat (early fourth century A.D.), Isfahan was the seat of a Christian bishopric. Under Shapur II the Great (A.D. 309-379), Christians were persecuted because the rival Roman Empire had espoused Christianity, and Christians in Persia were suspect.

East of Isfahan, Persia is largely desert with few oases. Lake Hamun (Hamun-i-Helmand, or Lake Helmand) at the Afghanistan border was the center of the ancient state of Drangiana, which Alexander incorporated into his empire. The region is now called "Seistan," apparently from the Saki tribe which gave it the name "Saki-stan." About 130 B.C. the warlike Sakis over-ran Bactria (also Bactriana), the Hellenistic state closest to India, which had been independent of Seleucid rule since about 225 B.C.

Legends grew up in the early church concerning missionary labors of the Apostle Thomas in Parthia and India. According to one of these, Thomas was received by a Greco-Bactrian ruler Gundopharr-Rustam (A.D. 20-65). Ernst Herzfeld, who excavated a mesa within Lake Hamun known as Kuh i-Hwaja ("the Lord's Hill"), is convinced that he has come upon Gundopharr's palace. "Gundopharr" is thought to be the original of the name "Kaspar," one of the traditional wise men.

Shiraz. Shiraz, about three hundred miles south of Isfahan, is the southernmost metropolis in Iran. Situated on a fertile highland plain, it is the metropolis of the Fars (ancient Persis) region, occupying the position that Persepolis held in Achaemenian times. It was not until the seventh century A.D. that Shiraz became an important city. Persia has a long literary tradition, and Shiraz has been linked with most of its great poets. The tombs of Saadi (or Sadi; real name, Muslih-ud-Din) and Hafiz (Shams ud-din Mohammed) are among the important shrines of the city. Northeast of Shiraz stood the proud old Persian capitals of Persepolis and Pasargadae.

Persian Capitals

Pasargadae. Pasargadae, or its variant Parsagada, is a name derived from the Pars, or Fars, tribe which migrated to southwestern Iran from Azerbaijan. Under Cyrus, Pasargadae became the capital of Persia. Its ruins lie fifty-four miles northeast of Persepolis and double that distance from Shiraz. West of the town is a Muslim cemetery, the central tomb of which is called the "Throne of Solomon's Mother." This tomb is considered to be that of Cyrus himself, which was visited by Alexander the Great. According to the Greek historian Arrian (second century A.D.), the tomb bore a Persian inscription which read: "O Man, I am Cyrus the son of Cambyses who founded the Persian Empire and was King of Asia. Grudge me not therefore this monument."[11]

Cyrus built a royal residence at Pasargadae on the spot where tradition says he gained a decisive victory over Astyages the Mede. A trilingual inscription (Old Persian, Akkadian, and Elamite) reads: "I am Cyrus, the King, the Achaemenian." Ghirshman suggests that this inscription dates from the time when he was still a vassal ruler under the Medes. A second trilingual inscription bears the words "great king," suggesting that by this time Cyrus had conquered Media. The great audience chamber of Cyrus' palace is decorated with orthostats showing priests bringing animals for the sacrifice, and genii with the head and claws of eagles. The figures of horses, bulls, and lions surmount the columns.

[11]Arrian, *Anabasis of Alexander*, Book VI, Chap. 29, Section 8.

270. Tomb of Cyrus

271. Persepolis from the
air

North of the Palace of Cyrus is the so-called Palace Harem, which the local guides point out as the tomb of Cambyses, the son of Cyrus. A Persian scholar has recently suggested that this is the real tomb of Cyrus because of its proximity to the palace area and the fact that it is aligned with the axis of the palaces.[12]

Ghirshman notes the composite nature of the art of Pasargadae, "with its Assyrian bulls, Hittite orthostats, its Babylonian polychromy and Egyptian symbols."[13] Yet all agree that the fusion is a happy one and that Pasargadae represents the Iranian spirit at its best.

Persepolis. The first Achaemenian king to move his palace from Pasargadae to Persepolis was Darius the Great who probably began work on his palace-fortress soon after his accession (522 B.C.). From that time on, Persepolis was the principal capital of Achaemenian Persia. The Oriental Institute of the University of Chicago conducted archaeological excavations at Per-

[12]Djavad Zakataly, *L'authentique tombeau de Cyrus* (Tehran: 1954).
[13]*Ibid.*, p. 135.

sepolis under the direction of Ernst Herzfeld (1931-34) and Erich F. Schmidt (1935-39). The palaces and public buildings had been erected on a terrace of masonry some distance from the city proper. The entire city was surrounded by a triple fortification system with one row of towers and walls running over the crest of the mountain.

On the masonry terrace stood the palace of Darius with an entrance hall opening across the entire width of the building. The main hall was fifty feet square, adorned with reliefs proclaiming, "I am Darius, great king, king of kings, king of lands, son of Hystaspes, the Achaemenian, who constructed this palace."

The building now known as the Tripylon was probably the first reception hall in Persepolis. Its stairway reliefs depict rows of dignitaries ascending; and on the eastern gate jambs, Darius I is shown on his throne.

A larger audience hall was the so-called Apadana, begun by Darius I and completed by Xerxes. It was a huge room 195 feet square and surrounded by vestibules on three sides. The wooden roof was supported by seventy-two stone columns, of which thirteen are still standing. Two monumental sculptured stairways were used to approach the building which was on an elevated platform. The reliefs on the eastern stairway, excavated by Herzfeld, are well preserved. They show envoys of twenty-three subject nations bringing New Year's gifts to the Persian emperor.

A third large reception hall is known as "the Hall of One Hundred Columns." It was started by Xerxes and finished by Artaxerxes I. The central unit was larger than the Apadana, being a room 229 feet square. The roof was once supported by one hundred columns. Huge stone bulls flanked the northern portico, and eight stone gateways were ornamented with scenes depicting the victory of the king over the powers of evil.

The impressive Gate of Xerxes stood on the terrace above the stairway leading up from the plain. Colossal bulls guarded the entrance. The accompanying inscription reads, "King Xerxes says: By the grace of Ahura Mazda I constructed this gateway called All-Countries."

A complex of buildings erected largely by Artaxerxes I was called by Schmidt "the treasury" because it contained stone vessels suitable for storing valuables. Alexander the Great seized the valuables from the Persepolis treasury during his victorious march through Persia after the Battle of Gaugamela. Diodorus estimated the treasure at 120,000 silver talents.[14]

[14]Diodorus, Book XVII, Section 71.

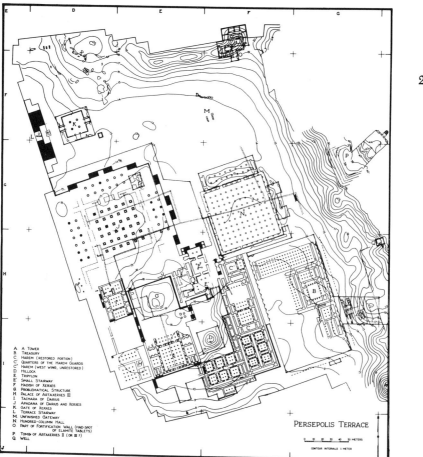

272. Plan of the terrace of Persepolis

A A Tower
B Treasury
C Harem (restored portion)
C' Quarters of the Harem Guards
C" Harem (west wing, unrestored)
D Hillock
E Tripylon
E' Small Stairway
F Hadish of Xerxes
G Problematical Structure
H Palace of Artaxerxes III
I Tachara of Darius
J Apadana of Darius and Xerxes
K Gate of Xerxes
L Terrace Stairway
M Unfinished Gateway
N Hundred-Column Hall
O Part of Fortification Wall (find-spot of Elamite Tablets)
P Tomb of Artaxerxes II (or III ?)
Q Well

PERSEPOLIS TERRACE

CONTOUR INTERVALS 1 METER

THE WYCLIFFE HISTORICAL GEOGRAPHY OF BIBLE LANDS

273. Tombs of the Persian kings, Naksh-i-Rustam

Alexander's treatment of Persepolis has puzzled historians because his usual generosity seems to have left him. The men were slain, the women enslaved, and the property plundered by Alexander's troops. As a climax, the palaces of Persepolis were burned. Did Alexander burn Persepolis in revenge for the burning of Athens by the Persians? Was he persuaded to cast the fatal torch by an evil woman at a drunken feast? Did he repent and vainly order that the fires be extinguished? Accounts vary, and we may never know exactly what happened, but the excavators of Persepolis have uncovered evidence of the horrible conflagration which destroyed the richest city of Achaemenian Persia.

Tombs of kings. A few miles north of Persepolis at Naksh-i-Rustam, the Achaemenian rulers, except for Cyrus, were buried. The name "Naksh-i-Rustam," meaning "Picture of Rustam," was mistakenly given to the site because of a monument which was thought to depict the legendary Persian hero Rustam. Actually, it depicts Shapur I (A.D. 241-272) standing before the god Ahura Mazda. The Tomb of Darius bears a trilingual inscription which boasts: "Says Darius the king: By the favor of Ahura Mazda I am of such a sort that I am a friend to right, I am not a friend to wrong; it is not my desire that the weak man should have wrong done to him by the mighty; nor is that my desire, that the mighty man should have wrong done to him by the weak."[15] To the right and left of the Tomb of Darius are similar tombs for Xerxes, Artaxerxes I, and Darius II.

[15]Roland G. Kent, *Journal of Near Eastern Studies* IV (1945), pp. 39-52.

274. Tomb of Darius, Naksh-i-Rustam

Old Elam

Susa. Susa, the capital of ancient Susiana, had a geographical and historical orientation which differed from the other cities of ancient Iran. It was located about one hundred fifty miles north of the Persian Gulf in the steppe country east of the Tigris River which is in reality a continuation of the southern Mesopotamian plain. The mountains of Luristan begin north of Susa, but the city itself is situated on a low spur of gravel and clay which is naturally raised above normal floods but conveniently situated for exploiting the alluvial plain of the Karun River (Eulaeus, biblical Ulai, Dan. 8:2). For a brief period Susa was known as "Seleucia-on-Eulaeus."

Excavations began at Susa over a century ago when William K. Loftus dug there

in connection with his Warka (Erech) excavation. Although this was the most primitive kind of archaeological work, Loftus proved definitely that he had located the biblical Shushan and established the plan of the Apadana (audience hall).[16] In 1884, Marcel Dieulafoy excavated at the Susa acropolis and sent back to the Louvre the Achaemenian archer frieze and bull capital.

The important name in the archaeology of Susa is the French scholar Jacques de Morgan, who made an archaeological survey of Persia in 1889 and left his position as director of antiquities in Egypt in 1897 to head the Délégation en Perse, which was working at Susa. The large chateau which dominates the site of the Susa excavations was built at that time.

Perhaps the most spectacular discovery in the early years of de Morgan's labors was the diorite stele containing the Code of Hammurabi. The speed with which this text was edited is amazing. The stele was found in three pieces in December 1901 and January 1902, transported to Paris in 1902, and published with transcription and translation by Pere Victor Scheil, a Dominican Assyriologist, in September, 1902. Roland de Mecquenem became architect for the Susa expedition in 1903, and he directed it from 1912 to 1939. His successor (since 1946) has been Professor Roman Ghirshman.

Excavations indicate that Susa was occupied from about 4000 B.C. to A.D. 1200. The earliest settlement left remains about twenty-seven yards beneath the top of the citadel mound. There are two archaic levels, separated by about twelve yards, each with a distinctive type of painted pottery. In the latter part of the fourth millennium B.C., a sizable village was located at Susa. A cemetery contains about two thousand graves. Utensils of copper were in use at this time,

[16]See Loftus, *Travels and Researches in Chaldea and Susiana* (London: James Nisbet and Co., 1857), pp. 287-433.

THE WYCLIFFE HISTORICAL GEOGRAPHY OF BIBLE LANDS

275. Susa from the air

and potters had learned the use of the wheel in making their ceramic ware.

Before 3000 B.C. an undeciphered proto-Elamite type of writing was used at Susa. The script was semipictographic and, although it seems to have originated under Mesopotamian influence, it was distinct in its development. From Susa it penetrated to the heart of the Iranian Plateau and continued in use for many centuries.

Elamite occupation. By the first quarter of the third millennium B.C., Elamites had occupied the plains of Susiana. Elam appears in Genesis 10:22 as a son of Shem. The Semite, Sargon of Akkad, seems to have captured Susa (c. 2360 B.C.), for his stele was excavated there. Shortly afterward, however, Elamites built various installations in the center of the acropolis hill.

The victory stele of Sargon's grandson, Naram-Sin, was discovered at Susa by De Morgan. Naram-Sin had to suppress revolts, and Susa was governed by one of his appointees. Akkadian began to supplant Elamite as the state language, and even Semitic proper names became common. Assimilation, however, was far from complete. A local governor, Puzur-Inshushinak, who had been appointed by Naram-Sin, developed a nationalist movement; and soon Elam embarked on its own policy of con-

quest. On the death of Naram-Sin, Puzur-Inshushinak proclaimed his independence and even invaded Babylonia.

The hill peoples north of Susa took advantage of the weakness of the last kings of the Akkadian dynasty, and about 2180 B.C. the Gutians overran Lower Mesopotamia. A little more than a century later (c. 2070 B.C.), the Sumerian ruler Gudea of Lagash (or Shirpurla) led in a Sumerian renaissance which found its highest expression in the Third Dynasty of Ur. It lasted barely a century, however; then the Elamites sacked the city of Ur. Elamite power was checked by Hammurabi (1728-1686 B.C.) of Babylon.

Kassite domination. From about 1650 to about 1175 B.C., Elam and Babylon alike

276. An archer, from the palace of Susa

277. A bull, from the palace at Susa

Behold, I will break the bow of Elam, the mainstay of their might; and I will bring upon Elam the four winds from the four quarters of heaven; and I will scatter them to all those winds, and there shall be no nation to which those driven out of Elam shall not come. I will terrify Elam before their enemies, and before those who seek their life; I will bring evil upon them, my fierce anger, says the LORD. I will send the sword after them, until I have consumed them; and I will set my throne in Elam, and destroy their king and princes, says the LORD (Jer. 49:35-38, RSV).

Persian domination. In the days of the Achaemenian successors to Cyrus, Susa shared with Persepolis, Ecbatana, and Babylon-Ctesiphon the honors of being a royal city. Nehemiah was at Susa as a palace servant to Artaxerxes I when he received the disturbing report concerning affairs in Jerusalem (Neh. 1:1; 2:1). It was to Susa that Esther was brought in the days of Ahasuerus (Xerxes I), and in the palace there she prevailed upon the king to issue an edict which would permit her people to destroy their enemies.

A tradition dating back to Benjamin of Tudela (A.D. 1170) places the tomb of Daniel in a colorful mosque north of Susa. Actually there is no evidence that Daniel ever personally visited Susa, but the Scriptures state that he was at Susa "in a vision" (Dan. 8:2). Louis Ginzberg in *The Legends of the Jews* (IV, 350) tells of a dissension that erupted among the Jews of Shushan (Susa) because the grave of Daniel was on the side of the city in which the wealthy Jews lived, and the poor citizens who lived on the other side of the river wanted to share in the good fortune that Daniel's grave would bring. It was determined that the bier of Daniel would be moved back and forth on alternate years, until the Persian king had the bier suspended from chains precisely in the middle of the bridge spanning the river!

The history of ancient Persia was never completely lost to the West. On the pages of the Old Testament and in the writings of Greek historians, notably Herodotus, the

were dominated by the Kassites from Luristan. During this period the history of Susa and Elam is obscure. By the twelfth century B.C., however, Elam had reached her golden age. Under Shilhak-Inshushinak (1165-1151 B.C.) and his successors, the numerous sanctuaries at Susa were embellished by trophies of war, including the stone bearing the Code of Hammurabi. The Naram-Sin stele, a statue of the god Marduk, and other trophies also arrived at Susa.

Babylonian and Assyrian domination. With the reign of Nebuchadnezzar I of Babylon, Elam again met serious opposition. Nebuchadnezzar, who ruled at the end of the second millennium B.C. and is to be distinguished from the better-known Nebuchadnezzar II who destroyed Jerusalem in 587/586 B.C., attacked Elam, seized Susa, and restored the statue of Marduk to his temple at Babylon. About 900 B.C. Elam was subjected to a series of Median invasions. The Assyrians Sargon II and Sennacherib both attacked Susa, and Ashurbanipal boasts of its destruction at his hands. In the winter of 596 B.C., the Neo-Babylonian ruler Nebuchadnezzar II attacked Elam in fulfillment of Jeremiah's words:

THE WYCLIFFE HISTORICAL GEOGRAPHY OF BIBLE LANDS

278. Darius seated, with Xerxes standing behind him; from the treasury at Persepolis

Persians emerge as a civilized people who permitted the Jews to return from exile, but who threatened the liberty of the Greek states. The monuments of ancient Iran now permit us to see the Persians as they saw themselves. They emerge as one of the great peoples of ancient times, worthy of study in their own right.

Bibliography

ARBERRY, A. J. (ed.). *The Legacy of Persia.* Oxford: Clarendon Press, 1953.

BERREBY, JEAN-JACQUES. *Le Golfe Persique.* Paris: Payot, 1959.

CONTENAU, G. *La Civilisation de l'Iran.* Paris: Librairie Orientale et Americaine, 1936.

FRYE, RICHARD N. *The Heritage of Persia.* New York: World Publishing Co., 1963.

GHIRSHMAN, R. *Iran.* Baltimore: Penguin Books, 1961.

HERZFELD, ERNST E. *Archaeological History of Iran.* London: Oxford University Press, 1935.

HUART, CLEMENT, and DELAPORTE, LOUIS. *L'Iran Antique.* Paris: Editions Albin Michel, 1952.

MASSE HENRI, GROUSSET, RENE, *et al. La Civilisation Iranienne.* Paris: Payot, 1952.

NORTH, ROBERT. *Guide to Biblical Iran.* Rome: Pontifical Biblical Institute, 1956.

OLMSTEAD, A. T. *History of the Persian Empire.* Chicago: University of Chicago Press, 1948.

ROGERS, ROBERT WILLIAM. *A History of Ancient Persia.* New York: Charles Scribner's Sons, 1929.

VANDEN BERGHE, L. *Archéologie De L'Iran Ancien.* Leiden: E. J. Brill, 1959.

279. The gymnasium at Salamis

Cyprus

A Missionary Journey to Cyprus

Probably the year was A.D. 45. The church at Antioch of Syria was now a thriving church. A year of concentrated effort on the part of Barnabas and Saul had been most fruitful (Acts 11:26). Spiritually responsive, the Christian community at Antioch felt an obligation to share the gospel with others who had not been so fortunate as they, and under the direction of the Holy Spirit, this church sent off the apostles on the first of the most remarkable series of missionary journeys on record. John Mark was their companion (Acts 13:5).[1]

Whether the missionaries took the road to Seleucia, the port of Antioch sixteen miles away, or whether they took a small skiff down the Orontes River and then north five miles along the coast to Seleucia, is not known. At any rate, they reached the port and took passage on a ship bound for Cyprus.

While there were a few ships in the Mediterranean with a regular schedule or prescribed routes, such scheduled ships seem to have been unusual. Generally eastern merchants "tramped" from port to port with whatever cargo seemed to promise the best profits. Probably the ship on which

Barnabas and Saul sailed was the more common "tramp" vessel.

More than likely the time was late spring or early summer when the missionaries set sail for Cyprus. The sailing season in the Mediterranean ran from March to November; and it is reasonable to believe that Barnabas, Saul, and John Mark, who had recently returned from delivering a collection for the poor at Jerusalem (Acts 12:25), would have remained in the holy city until after the Passover. Allowing time for the church at Antioch to receive the report from Jerusalem and prepare to send off the trio, late spring would seem to be the earliest that the group could depart. A sailing date of late summer or fall would have necessitated beginning a trip just before the inclement winter weather; therefore it is unlikely that they would have started so late.

Roman ships. The kind of ship on which the missionary party sailed is not known. The freighters that carried official government cargoes during the first century A.D. were commonly 340 tons; those of Rome's grain fleet ran to 1,200 tons and were sometimes almost 200 feet long. Since there is no indication that this ship carried government cargo, it may well have been smaller than 340 tons. Generally ships of the period carried a square sail, above which was a topsail, and at least a few oars for emergen-

---

[1]Acts does not say that John Mark was "separated unto" the missionary endeavor by the church, as were Barnabas and Saul. John Mark merely accompanied them and apparently was not necessary to the work. His return home from Asia Minor does not seem to have impeded the program of the other two (Acts 13:13).

280. A Roman merchantman

and served as a camouflage. As to speed, merchantmen averaged four to six knots.[2] So the journey between Seleucia and Salamis on Cyprus would have taken about twenty-four hours, with a favorable wind. It is about 80 miles from Seleucia to the eastern tip of Cyprus and another 50 along the southern shore of the Karpas Peninsula to Salamis.[3]

Reason for missionary work. Why Barnabas, Saul, and John Mark went to Cyprus is not hard to discover. Barnabas himself was a native of Cyprus (Acts 4:36) and could be expected to have an interest in the evangelization of his Jewish kinsmen there. Moreover, Jews of Cyprus had been partially responsible for sparking a revival at Antioch (Acts 11:20-21). No doubt the Antiochian church, which had now become quite large, felt an obligation to send Christian workers to Cyprus. Since Barnabas and Saul had accomplished such a remarkable ministry in Antioch (where Barnabas had been sent by the Jerusalem church), it seemed only logical that these men would be entrusted with further evangelistic and supervisory work. Who better could be sent to Cyprus than these experienced leaders—one of whom was a native of the island?

cy or auxiliary work. Some freighters were designed to be driven by sail and rowers together. Merchantmen were fairly beamy: a length to beam ratio of four to one was common. Freighters generally had a cabin aft and above deck—big enough for the captain and his mates. Passengers lived and slept on deck. If they wanted some privacy, they might erect a tentlike shelter. Behind the cabin rose the sternpost, which was generally carried high and finished off in the shape of a goose head.

As to building materials, the planks of the hull were constructed of pine, fir, or cedar, depending on what was available. Inside the ship any kind of wood might be used; fir was preferred for oars because of its light weight. Sails were chiefly made of linen, and ropes of flax, hemp, papyrus, or sometimes leather. Often the underwater surface of the hull was sheathed with sheet lead; in such cases it was the practice to place a layer of tarred fabric between the hull and the lead. Ships were painted in gay fashion with purple, blue, white, yellow, or green—unless they were pirate or reconnaissance vessels, in which case they might use a shade that matched sea water

[2]A knot is a unit of speed equivalent to one nautical mile, or about 6,080 feet, per hour.
[3]One of the finest introductions to a study of seafaring in the Mediterranean in ancient times is Lionel Casson, *The Ancient Mariners* (New York: The Macmillan Co., 1959). See especially pages 215-227 for documentation on the preceding two paragraphs. Perhaps it would be helpful to add that ships of the early Roman Empire were well built and equipped with charts to plot courses, a lead line to test depths, semaphore flags to send messages, a ship's boat (usually pulled behind) for emergencies, an anchor, but not a compass. It was the lack of the compass that dictated a sailing season of March to November in the Mediterranean—along with the fear of winter storms. The point is that in the Mediterranean the skies are clear enough in the summer to permit mariners to sail by sun, stars, and landmarks; these are obscured by overcast winter skies. See *ibid.*, p. 220. Another very helpful book on shipping of the period is Chester G. Starr, *The Roman Imperial Navy 31 B.C.—A.D. 324* (Ithaca, N. Y.: Cornell University Press, 1941).

That the gospel message preceded Barnabas and Saul to Cyprus by some years is evident from such a passage as Acts 11:19, which declares that the persecution arising at the time of the martyrdom of Stephen scattered a number of converts to Cyprus. Stephen's martyrdom occurred shortly after the Pentecost of Acts 2. Perhaps these early Christians on Cyprus appealed to Antioch for help—with the result that Barnabas and Saul went to them.

Magnitude of task. The task of evangelizing the Jews on Cyprus was a substantial one, as is shown by evidence of large numbers of Jews on the island. Apparently the first Jews were brought to Cyprus by Ptolemy Soter, who is reported after the capture of Jerusalem in 320 B.C. to have transported large numbers of them to Egypt and other parts of his dominions.[4] Many more came to the island just before the birth of Christ in hope of employment in the copper mines, which at one time were delegated to Herod the Great.[5] That the number of Jews on Cyprus was large in the middle of the first century A.D. is indicated by events of the early second century. In A.D. 116 a Jewish revolt spread over the eastern Mediterranean world; and according to Dio Cassius, Jews killed 240,000 of their fellow citizens on Cyprus alone.[6] Even if this figure is exaggerated, as is very likely, atrocities of such approximate magnitude would require a considerable Jewish population. In retaliation, imperial forces killed thousands of Jews, and the rest were banished from the island. For centuries thereafter no Jew was allowed on Cyprus.

[4] J. Hackett, *A History of the Orthodox Church of Cyprus* (London: Methuen & Co., 1901), p. 3.

[5] Josephus, *Antiquities of the Jews*, Book XVI, Chap. IV.
[6] Hackett, p. 3.

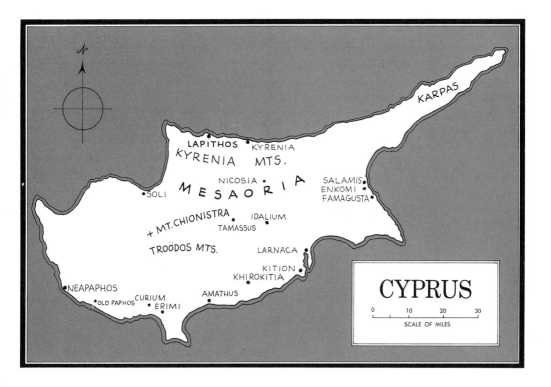

Geographical Features

Location and size. Cyprus is the third largest island of the Mediterranean Sea. Exceeded in size only by Sicily and Sardinia, it has an area of 3,572 square miles. Located in the extreme northeast corner of the Mediterranean, Cyprus can be seen from both Asia Minor and Syria on a clear day. The former distance is about 43 miles and the latter about 60. Between Egypt and Cyprus the distance is about 250 miles. It is therefore easy to see why cultural influences from Asia Minor and Syria were felt on Cyprus long before those of Egypt.

As to shape, Cyprus is sometimes likened to a silhouetted wheelbarrow being pushed along. The long Karpas Peninsula represents the handles, and the Akrotiri Peninsula to the south, the wheels. In ancient times it was compared to a deerskin or bullock's hide spread out on the ground. The tail is represented by the Karpas Peninsula and the legs by four large promontories. The greatest length of the island is 138 miles and the greatest width 60 miles. Subtracting the approximately 40-mile-long Karpas Peninsula, Cyprus averages some 90-100 miles in length. The total coastline is 486 miles.

Mountains. The surface of Cyprus is almost evenly divided between mountain and plain. The mountains divide into two ranges: the Kyrenia, or Northern, Range and the Troodos Range. The gray-pink limestone Kyrenia Range extends along the whole of the northern coast some three miles from the coast and rises from two to three thousand feet. Highest of the several peaks of this range is Akromandra, 3,433 feet in altitude. Conveniently, three gaps pierce this range: Panagra in the west, Kyrenia in the center, and Akanthou in the east. The Kyrenia Range tends to force the moisture from the vapor-laden winds from the north, providing sufficient moisture for the fertile coastal plain. The seaward slopes of the Kyrenia Mountains are profusely covered with trees (especially olive in modern times), shrubs, and flowers; the southern slopes are often bare. Most of the southern half of Cyprus consists of a confusion of steep-sided mountain ridges, arrayed in such tangled profusion that it is almost impossible to discover any backbone or watershed. Several of the peaks of these Troodos Mountains rise more than 4,500 feet. The highest is Chionistra, or Olympus (6,404 feet). White limestone plateaus occupy the area south of the Troodos massif. These fall in steplike fashion as they approach the coast. In places they become sea cliffs, but occasionally they recede to allow coastal plains with quite rich alluvial soil.

The Central Plain. Between the two mountain ranges lies the broad plain of Mesaria, or Mesaoria, some sixty miles long by thirty miles broad. Nicosia, the modern capital of Cyprus, is located in the center of this plain. The granary of the island, this plain also produces substantial quantities of vegetables and fruit. Though now treeless except for a few recently planted trees, Mesaria (Mesaoria) was in ancient times heavily forested. Through this plain flow the two chief rivers of Cyprus—the Pedias (anc. Pediaeus) and Yalias (anc. Idalia)—which dump their waters into the Mediterranean near ancient Salamis on the east coast. During the rainy season these are fairly substantial streams, but they are not navigable during the dry season. Reservoirs now tap most of their water before it reaches the Mediterranean.

Rainfall and climate. Rainfall occurs mainly during the months of December to February, but the amount is not large. The main agricultural areas receive only twelve to sixteen inches per year. Even this amount comes irregularly, and serious droughts occur on the average of every ten years. And since high evaporation involves considerable loss, the supply of water constitutes a serious problem. The visitor to Cyprus becomes aware of how acute the problem is when he reads a sign in his hotel room urging him to inform the management at once of any leaky or defective plumbing in order to conserve water. In recent years British efforts at building dams, expanding irrigation, and initiating reforestation have considerably improved the water supply and the crop production of the island. Perhaps the successful American and Israeli efforts to desalt ocean water inexpensively will in the future make possible an agricultural revolution on Cyprus.

It is easy to guess from what has been said about rainfall that prolonged drizzling from gray skies is rare in Cyprus even during the rainy season—when the sun usually shines for at least some part of every day. The mean temperature of the lowland areas in the coldest months is approximately 50-54 degrees; for the hottest months it ranges from 80 to 84 degrees. The climate is very

healthful, and the death rate is one of the lowest in the world. The growing season roughly corresponds with the rainy season, and crops are harvested by March or April. During the summer and early fall, when there is rarely any rainfall, the fields give an appearance of aridity.

Forests. Forests were once one of the main resources of Cyprus; and her timber, so important for shipbuilding, was much sought after by the ancient imperial powers of the Mediterranean area. Actually, however, more trees were felled for copper and silver smelting than for shipbuilding. Eratosthenes, Greek astronomer and geographer of the third century B.C., talks of the plains as being "formerly full of wood run to riot, choked in fact with undergrowth and uncultivated."[7] The famous cedars have almost disappeared, but there are considerable stands of Aleppo pine and black pine. The main state forests today occupy a good part of the Kyrenia Range, the Karpas Peninsula, and the Troodos mass. State for-

[7]Claude D. Cobbam (trans.), Eratosthenes, *Excerpta Cypria* (Cambridge: At the University Press, 1908), p. 3.

281. An asbestos mine in the eastern Troodos Mountains

ests fill a total of 608 square miles; and private and communally owned forests bring the total to 670 square miles, over 18 percent of the total land area.[8] Under the direction and protective hand of the Forest Department, timber and naval supplies may once again assume an important place in the economy of Cyprus.

Mineral deposits. More important than timber to the economy of Cyprus in antiquity was her production of copper. In fact, so extensive was the island's export of this mineral that copper obtained its name from the name of Cyprus. The English word *copper* is derived from the Greek name of the island, Kypros, through the Latin *cuprum*. Produced as early as the third millennium B.C.,[9] copper has continued to be mined extensively until the present. The Asy from which Thutmose III obtained his copper shortly after 1500 B.C.

[8]Gordon Home, *Cyprus Then and Now* (London: J. M. Dent & Sons, Ltd., 1960), p. 177.
[9]N. G. L. Hammond, *A History of Greece to 322 B.C.* (Oxford: At the Clarendon Press, 1959), p. 25.

is often identified with Cyprus.[10] The island's copper, which was shipped all over the Mediterranean world in ancient times in the form of both ore and ingots, came from the foothills of the Troodos, especially along the southern coast and at Tamassus, southwest of Nicosia. To gain some understanding of the extent of the copper deposits on Cyprus and the extent of trade in the commodity over the millennia, it might be helpful to note that the Cypriot copper exports during the fiscal year ending in 1960 totalled 430,000 long tons.[11]

Though iron was mined on Cyprus in antiquity, the extent is in question. In modern times iron production has far outstripped copper production. Gold and silver were also mined on the island in ancient times. The mining of silver there is thought to account for the large issues of silver coinage in the Ptolemaic Age.[12]

[10]George Hill, *A History of Cyprus* (Cambridge: At the University Press, 1940), I, 9.
[11]Vernon J. Parry, "Cyprus," *Britannica Book of the Year*, 1961, p. 202. Since 1960 political unrest has cut copper production.
[12]Hill, I, 10.

Historical Development

Early Biblical Connections

It is easy to assume after a cursory investigation that Cyprus appears on the stage of the biblical drama only briefly in connection with the first and second missionary journeys of Paul. But deeper probing indicates that such is not the case. In the Old Testament there are several references to biblical Kittim or Chittim (anc. Citium) (e.g., Gen. 10:4; Num. 24:24; Isa. 23:1, 12; Jer. 2:10; Ezek. 27:6; Dan. 11:30). Admittedly this is a word with somewhat general signification, referring to various islands and coasts of the Mediterranean. But the term did have some specific application to Cyprus. The city of Kition (Citium), on the southeast coast of Cyprus and a center of Phoenician influence, gradually

gave its name to the whole of the island. The Phoenicians referred to Cyprians as "Kitti."

The first biblical reference to Kittim is Genesis 10:4, where its association with Javan (Ionia), Elishah (Elis), and Dodanim (Rodanim, Rhodes) seems to point to a Greek connection. It is not necessary to conclude, however, that therefore it could have no connection with Cyprus. The influence on Cyprus has always been largely Greek, and the earliest foreign migration there seems to have come from Asia Minor, where Greek culture appeared very early. Josephus, the famous first century Jewish historian, definitely identified the "Kittim" of Genesis 10:4 as Cyprus.[13] If one identi-

[13]Josephus, *Antiquities of the Jews*, Book I, Chap. VI.

fies the "little horn" of Daniel 11:30 as Antiochus IV Epiphanes (176-164 B.C.) of Syria as many do, he may find in this reference a specific allusion to Cyprus. Daniel prophesied, "Ships of Chittim shall come against him." During Antiochus' reign, Egypt tried unsuccessfully to take Palestine from him, relying quite heavily on her dependency Cyprus for ships and ship timber.

If it be admitted that at least some of the references to Kittim in the Old Testament directly or indirectly concern Cyprus, perhaps the inclusion here of a summary of the early history of the island is justified. Such a history might be justified further as an aid to an understanding of developments in the Near East—especially as they relate to biblical events.

Neolithic Beginnings

The earliest-known occupants of Cyprus appeared about 3700 B.C.[14] and developed a Neolithic[15] culture of a fairly high degree. Their culture has been found at a number of sites located in the foothills of the Kyrenia Mountains, both north and south of the main ridge, and on low hills in the west and south of the island. Since almost all of these sites were located near the sea, Alastos concludes that their inhabitants must have come from overseas;[16] but elsewhere he indicates that their short, stocky build points to anthropological forms distinct from any known contemporaries on the neighboring mainland. He concludes that they probably were of early Helladic (Greek) stock who migrated to Aegean islands, Crete, Rhodes, and Cyprus.[17]

Two of the most important Neolithic sites on Cyprus are Khirokitia, about thirty miles south of Nicosia and about four miles from the sea; and Erimi, near the coast about thirty miles southwest of Khirokitia. The settlement at Khirokitia furnishes the earlier of the two cultures, and its civilization "enters upon history with a fairly developed type of habitation and mode of living."[18] Its dwellings were circular, of the "beehive" type, the lower part of stone which supported a dome of sun-dried mud bricks. The largest of these was thirty-three feet in diameter and may have been a temple or chief's house. The dead were buried under or near their homes. The earliest inhabitants at Khirokitia did not know how to make pottery, and so they used stone vessels and tools of flint and bone. They worshiped stone gods, made necklaces of imported semiprecious stones, and built some of their tables with marble tops. Later they learned to make fairly good-quality pottery and much more impressive stone tools.[19]

The culture of Erimi was more advanced than that of Khirokitia, boasting a magnificent pottery and fairly high quality implements and ornaments. The houses were also circular and built of large unworked stones; each roof was supported from the center.

Cypriot Neolithic culture reached a high peak of development, as has already been indicated. The peoples of the period farmed the land and domesticated the goat, sheep, and pig for food, wool, and hides and may have cultivated the olive and grape vine. They spun wool, worked marble, made ornaments of stone, and produced good-quality pottery. They fished and hunted

[14]A radioactive carbon test made in 1959 on samples from the pre-pottery Neolithic settlement at Khirokitia yielded a date of about the middle of the sixth millennium B.C. (*Cyprus Report for the Year 1959* [London: Her Majesty's Stationery Office, 1960], p. 83). If this becomes generally accepted, it will push back the beginnings of settlement on Cyprus by some 2,000 years and necessitate revision of the dating stated in the various histories of Cyprus, as well as that held in this section.

[15]"Neolithic" means literally "new stone," and the term applies to a culture of which polished stone implements were characteristic. No metal was yet used; there was the domestication of some animals and the development of agriculture. In the earliest Neolithic stages, pottery was not used.

[16]Doros Alastos, *Cyprus in History* (London: Zeno Publishers, 1955), p. 13.

[17]*Ibid.*, p. 17.
[18]*Ibid.*, p. 13.
[19]*Ibid.*, p. 14.

wild Cypriot sheep, boar, deer, and ibex. They conducted sporadic trade—probably almost exclusively with Asia Minor. Their religion seems to have concerned mostly performance of elaborate rituals in connection with burial of the dead, who possibly were thought to guard the living in whose house they were buried. At Khirokitia, at least, human sacrifice may have been practiced.[20]

The Bronze Age

The Bronze Age[21] came to Cyprus rather abruptly about 2700 B.C. Cypriot Neolithic culture declined, but it is not known whether it died naturally or whether it was swamped by a migration of another people who imposed a Bronze Age culture upon it. Although there is some difference of dating, the Bronze Age on Cyprus may be placed at about 2700-1000 B.C. This period is subdivided into three parts: Early Bronze, 2700-2100; Middle Bronze, 2100-1600; and Late Bronze, 1600-1000. The Bronze Age dawned in Cyprus shortly after the beginnings of the Minoan culture on Crete and about the same time as the early Helladic culture on the mainland of Greece. It followed by two or three centuries the unification of upper and lower Egypt into one nation and was contemporary with the Early Dynastic Period in Mesopotamia.

During the Bronze Age Cyprus ceased to have a self-contained civilization. It began to be enfolded by the movements and crosscurrents of the eastern Mediterranean world. But in spite of this, she managed to preserve a high degree of individuality. Probably this was true because Cyprus did not lie astride any of the main lines of communication between east and west or north and south. Nor was Cyprus a route to supremacy or a necessary outpost of defense for one of the great empires or an obstacle to the maintenance of empire. Therefore it did not suffer the same bloody conquests as peoples who lived in strategically important locations. But Cyprus was not immune from conquest or domination. From the Bronze Age on, she became the prey of more powerful neighbors as they attempted to control her valuable resources of copper and timber.

The migration of a foreign element, predominantly from Anatolia, to Cyprus at the beginning of the third millennium B.C. coincided with the mining of the island's rich copper resources. This foreign element seems to have been largely assimilated by the indigenous population, who remained primarily engaged in agriculture. But with the development of the mining industry came other changes. The population grew and concentrated in the eastern half of the island, though settlements were located all over the island. (During the Neolithic Period the population had been located principally in the west.) House plans changed from a circular to a rectangular form, and the dead were now buried in cemeteries and provided with a number of objects for use in the afterlife. The people wore gold and silver jewelry; craftsmanship greatly improved. Foreign influence was seen in the pottery, which was a red polished ware with Anatolian affinities; and outside forces were felt in religion, in connection with which there is evidence of worship of a bull-god and of snakes, and the entrance of the fertility cult. The copper industry was well developed by the end of the Early Bronze Age, as is evidenced by the range of tools and weapons discovered. But pottery was still handmade, and no other craft seems to have kept pace with the advance of metallurgy. Iron was also smelted on Cyprus by the end of the Early Bronze Period, as excavations at Lapithos, on the northwest coast, show.[22]

[20]*Ibid.*, p. 18.

[21]Bronze is an alloy of copper and tin, and a Bronze Age culture is one characterized by the use of bronze implements, utensils, and weapons—at least among the upper classes.

[22]Paul Aström, *The Middle Cypriote Bronze Age* (Lund: Hakan Ohlssons Boktryckeri, 1957), p. 240.

The first centuries of the Bronze Age might be called the Copper Age because copper with almost no tin (not over 2 or 3 percent) was used for implements; but by the middle of the third millennium, true bronze was in common use. The full entrance of the Bronze Age in Cyprus coincided with the great cultural developments at Ur (as revealed by Sir C. Leonard Woolley's excavations there) and with the Pyramid Age in Egypt. Perhaps the first stirrings in Hittite land also came this early.

Middle Bronze Age. During the Middle Bronze Age (c. 2100-1600 B.C.), Cyprus assumed an increasing importance in Mediterranean affairs. At the beginning of the period the Ur III dynasty built its influential commercial empire in Mesopotamia (perhaps contemporary with Abraham); subsequently Hammurabi constructed his empire and formulated his famous code (c. 1700 B.C.). The beginning of the Middle Kingdom, or Middle Empire, of Egypt is to be dated around 2000 B.C. And Hittite beginnings definitely date to within a century or two after 2000. The significant days of the Minoans came during the first half of the second millennium. And during this period Ras Shamra (ancient Ugarit) in Syria became an important commercial center. To it came copper,[23] cheap utilitarian pottery, and perhaps timber from Cyprus. In return there flowed through Ras Shamra to Cyprus pottery from Syria and jewelry and fabrics from Egypt and Ur.

As to what was happening on Cyprus during the Middle Bronze Period, one would gather from what has been said that there was growing prosperity accompanied by an increase in population. With diversification of labor and growth of commerce came the growth of cities—such as the fa-

mous sites of Enkomi, south of Salamis on the east coast, and Amathus on the south coast.[24] The earliest-known Cypriot inscriptions date to the beginning of the Middle Bronze Period. The bull and snake cult, reflecting foreign influence, dominated the religion of this middle period.

As has been indicated, the Middle Bronze Period on Cyprus was contemporary with the rise of Minoan culture on Crete, where several city-states, including Knossos (Cnossus or Gnossus), Phaestus (Phaistos), Mallia, and Tylissos, arose. The Cretans early established centers for the manufacture of very high quality pottery and copper products. With abundant supplies of timber at their disposal, they mastered the art of shipbuilding and became proficient mariners. Fortunately for them, they also developed interstate communications on Crete, building roads, bridges, and harbors. These gave the farmers easy access to the sea and added wine and olive oil to the manufactured goods produced for export. By the eighteenth century B.C., Minoan influence was felt on mainland Greece, the Aegean Islands, Cyprus, Syria, and Egypt. Minoan culture seems to have had considerable influence on Cyprus, and the two in cooperation appear to have cleared the seas around their islands of Carian pirates. They planted a commercial outpost at Ugarit, and after the destruction of the Hyksos Empire many Cypriots settled in Ugarit.

Seemingly there is no reason why Cyprus could not have developed a culture every bit as brilliant as the Minoans'. She had natural resources, including excellent timber, and early developed her copper and shipbuilding industries. She was close to both the Syrian and Asia Minor coasts and

---

[23]*Ibid.*, p. 242. Aström notes that only one Cypriot sword, exported in the Bronze Age, has been found abroad in a known archaeological context (at Ras Shamra), indicating Cyprus mainly exported not weapons but copper ore or ingots.

[24]Extensive excavations on Cyprus were conducted by the Swedish Expedition, 1927-31. Two of the sites at which they worked were Enkomi and Amathus. Einar Gjerstad *et al.*, *The Swedish Cyprus Expedition* (Stockholm: The Swedish Cyprus Expedition, 1934). For Enkomi see I, 467-576; for Amathus see II, 1-142. For a brief note on 1959 excavations at Enkomi, see *Cyprus Report for the Year 1959*.

therefore had access to the highly developed culture of the East. At an early time she seemed destined to great cultural advance.

Alastos has shown that the reason for Cypriot failure to develop a more grandiose culture resulted from foreign domination—that of the Hyksos, who put a stop to the growth of Cypriot culture. After taking Syria, Palestine, and Egypt in the eighteenth century, they spilled over onto Cyprus, probably in the seventeenth century. There they built at least three forts—two on the Karpas Peninsula and a third at Enkomi. The fortress at Enkomi, discovered in 1955, was 210 feet long and had walls up to 40 feet thick. It apparently fell to local inhabitants after a bitter fight shortly after the Egyptians expelled the Hyksos in 1580 B.C.[25] Aström has provided a tabulation of finds of Tell El-Yahudiyeh ware (Hyksos pottery) excavated on Cyprus, showing again the influence of the Hyksos on the island.[26]

Late Bronze Age. During the Late Bronze Age (1600-1000 B.C.), Cyprus became very prosperous as a center of cultural and commercial interchange between East and West. It is commonly suggested that the island came under the control of both the Egyptians and Hittites during the period. This is argued by equating with Cyprus the Asy, Alasiya, or Alasia, appearing in Amarna tablets from Egypt, Hittite tablets from Bogazkoy, and Ras Shamra and Mari literature. Whether or not this identification should be made has been much debated. Those who deny it feel that a full-scale attack on Cyprus would have taxed Egyptian shipping to the limit and therefore seems quite unlikely. Moreover, they cannot believe that a landlocked power like the Hittites could have conquered the island. These opponents of the identification prefer to locate Alasia somewhere in north

Syria. Home has suggested what may be close to the truth—the language of conquest appearing in Near Eastern literature is so grossly exaggerated that a claim to control of Cyprus by either Hittites or Egyptians may mean little more than Cyprus' sending royal presents and engaging in increasing trade relations.[27] At any rate, Egyptian contacts with Cyprus were extensive, as finds in Cypriot tombs indicate. For instance, at Enkomi[28] have been found a scarab of Tiy, queen of Amenhotep III, a silver ring of Amenhotep IV, several scarabs from the time of Ramses III, and a number of other Egyptian objects dating to the Late Bronze Period.[29]

The Late Bronze Age prosperity of Cyprus seems to have been due largely to an influx of Mycenaeans. Having previously consolidated their hold on mainland Greece and having brought the Aegean world within their commercial sphere, the Mycenaeans about 1400 B.C. conquered Crete and destroyed Minoan power. But an amalgamation of Mycenaean and Minoan culture occurred. Mycenaean trading activities constituted a virtual commercial explosion, and their goods reached such faraway ports as England and Denmark. Shortly after the beginning of the fourteenth century their influence became evident on Cyprus, and Achaeans from the Greek mainland must have come to Cyprus in large numbers. With their coming the economy of Cyprus was vitalized, and the islanders produced tremendous quantities of copper and "white slip" and "base ring" pottery for export to centers all over the eastern Mediterranean. When the Canaanites were displaced from Ugarit in the thirteenth cen-

---

[27]Home, p. 18.
[28]Enkomi, which reached its peak of prosperity in the thirteenth century B.C., was surrounded by a great wall, some of whose stones were as much as twelve feet long and weighed sixty tons each. The quarrying and transport of such large stones represent a remarkable achievement. C. F. A. Schaeffer estimates the population to have been 5,000-10,000. See Alastos, p. 31.
[29]Hill, I, 33.

[25]Ibid., pp. 23-24.
[26]Aström, pp. 233 ff.

tury, it became a Cypro-Mycenaean outpost.[30]

Economic and political decline set in on Cyprus at the end of the thirteenth century and continued for some centuries thereafter. The Hittite Empire came to an end about 1200 B.C. Troy was destroyed about the same time or a little earlier. The Egyptian Empire disintegrated about 1100, and the Mycenaean power was brought to an end by Dorian invasions about the same time. International turbulence is never conducive to economic prosperity. The end of the period saw Cyprus rather isolated.

According to Homer's *Odyssey* and other Greek writers, some of the Greek heroes returning from the Battle of Troy settled on Cyprus and established towns there—including such sites as Salamis, Curium, and Nea Paphos. New archaeological evidence from Enkomi (near Salamis) and at Nea Paphos confirms the arrival of Greeks on the island and their building activities there around 1230 B.C. At Enkomi the Mycenaeans apparently built a new town on the site about 1230 B.C.; this was destroyed by the Sea Peoples (Philistines) some thirty years later.[31]

The Iron Age

For some unknown reason—perhaps local resistance or maritime incapability of migratory peoples—Cyprus did not suffer to the extent that mainland Greece, Syria, and Palestine did in the movement of peoples occurring at the end of the Bronze Age.[32] So there was no pronounced break with the past—merely a temporary isolation with an accompanying economic and cultural depression. Soon a new culture emerged—an Iron Age culture, with a metal for making tools and weapons that was superior to bronze. The Cypriots emerged as shipbuilders and a sea power of some consequence. They transported their copper and especially their Cypro-geometric pottery (bearing stiff geometric designs representing a fusion of old Cypriot and Mycenaean types) to many eastern Mediterranean lands. Salamis and Paphos were the most important cities during this period (c. 1050-700 B.C.).

About the middle of the tenth century Phoenician commercial activity became pronounced on Cyprus and contributed greatly to the prosperity of the island. The main Phoenician centers of power were at Kition (Citium) near modern Larnaca on the southern coast and at Idalium (Dali), a few miles inland. Phoenician merchant communities grew up in many other Cypriot towns, but they always remained a foreign element. Whatever is said in general about the identity of Chittim in the Old Testament, it seems that Isaiah (23:1-12) had Cyprus in mind. He refers to a seaport where merchantmen put in on their homeward voyage to Tyre, and where Tyrian refugees found a place of safety. Moreover, in 741 B.C. Hiram II of Tyre had some sort of governor on the island,[33] precisely at the time of the great prophet, who ministered about 740-700 B.C.

How much actual Phoenician migration there was to Cyprus is open to question. But it is clear that from about 925-600 B.C. Cyprus must have been part of a Cypro-Phoenician cultural province. Also, during the same period, trade among Cyprus, Greece, Sardinia, and Etruscan Italy was extensive. Cypriot development was scarcely affected by Assyrian conquests on the mainland.[34]

---

[30]Alastos, p. 29. New evidence of how widespread the trade of Cyprus was during the Late Bronze Era has been turned up by Professor Joseph P. Free in his excavations at Dothan in north central Palestine. He found six Cypriot jars in a tomb at that inland site; these objects dated to the fourteenth and thirteenth centuries B.C. Reported in correspondence with the writer, Nov. 15, 1961.

[31]Discussed by Porphyrios Dikaios, former rector of the Department of Antiquities, Cyprus, at the Oriental Institute of the University of Chicago, March 18, 1964.

[32]But the island was buffeted by hit-and-run attacks.

[33]Home, p. 22.

[34]Judy Birmingham, "The Chronology of Some Early and Middle Iron Age Cypriot Sites," *American Journal of Archaeology*, 67 (January, 1963), 42.

282. A king of Cyprus

The island's great period came during the subsequent century of independence.[35]

Persian and Ptolemaic Control

But Cyprus was not destined to enjoy independence for long. In the future her fortunes would be linked with those of the powerful empires surrounding her. About the middle of the sixth century Egypt conquered Cyprus. When Cambyses II of Persia overcame Egypt in 525 B.C., Cyprus became part of the Persian Empire. In 500 Cyprus joined the Ionian revolt against Persia and fought a glorious but futile attempt to obtain freedom from the colossus of the East. Defeat was not enough. The Cypriots were forced to contribute to the Persian invasion of Greece, and they provided Xerxes with a fleet of 150 ships for the important Battle of Salamis in 480 B.C.

During succeeding decades Cyprus, with its predominantly Greek population, was frequently involved in Greek intrigues against Persia and local efforts to obtain independence from their Persian overlords. One of the most successful of the Cypriot rebellions was engineered by Evagoras, who maintained himself as king of Salamis for thirty-six years (410-374 B.C.). However, the revolutionaries never achieved their aim of freedom from Persia until 333, when Alexander the Great defeated Darius at the Battle of Issus. Rejoicing in this, the Cypriots sent Alexander 120 ships to help him in the siege of Tyre (332).

But Cyprus had little cause for happiness over the successes of Alexander. With his death in 323, conflict over control of his empire arose among his generals. Cyprus was especially desirable to Ptolemy of Egypt for its supply of copper and timber, neither of which Egypt possessed. After almost thirty years of struggle with the Antigonids of Syria, the Ptolemies won

Hardly had the Phoenician city-states reached their height of prosperity when the Assyrians swooped down on the westlands, reducing them to dependencies. Not long after the fall of the Northern Kingdom of Israel to Sargon II (722 B.C.), Cyprus capitulated to the Assyrians. Probably the kings of seven Cypriot city-states surrendered and paid homage without an attack, though Sargon claimed a victory over them and erected a monument (now in Berlin) in Kition (Citium) to commemorate the victory. In 668 B.C. kings of ten Cypriot cities took part in an Assyrian expedition to subdue rebellious Egypt. Shortly thereafter Assyrian domination of Cyprus ended.

[35]Carl Roebuck, *Ionian Trade and Colonization* (New York: Archaeological Institute of America, 1959), p. 65.

Cyprus in 295 and maintained control of the island for some 250 years.

While the Ptolemies were cruel despots, they were energetic rulers who displayed a high degree of administrative ability and interest in scholarly pursuits. Under them Alexandria became the leading intellectual and commercial center of the Mediterranean. Study and experimentation in many branches of science prospered there. Knowledge became a direct concern of the state. And so did economic life, which was scientifically arranged down to minute details. All land was cultivated under a far-reaching supervisory system. The type of plant, quality of seed, agricultural implements, and irrigation machinery were all carefully superintended with a view to increased productivity and prosperity. An efficient bureaucracy made all the decisions.

In Cyprus, administrative control was not quite the same as in Egypt. In Egypt a Greek ruling class subjected a native population; in Cyprus the vast majority of the people were Greek. And in Cyprus the lack of water supply prevented the degree of intense cultivation of land that was possible in Egypt. There was, nevertheless, detailed bureaucratic control of the island under a strategos, or general, who acted as governor. A secretary supervised the administrative machine. Certain local institutions possessed some power, however, and authoritarian tyranny did not exist on the island until the latter part of the period.

One of the most beneficial moves of the first years of Ptolemaic rule on Cyprus (or perhaps a little earlier) was a decree to abolish the petty kingships which had for more than 1200 years dissected the island and hindered its prosperity. The years of peace and affluence of the Ptolemaic era were the greatest the island had ever known. Heightened prosperity brought increased population and the establishment of new cities. And existing cities were beautified with baths, schools, gymnasia, and theaters. The population of the capital, Salamis, has been estimated at 120,000.[36] Eighteen important cities existed at the end of the Ptolemaic era. Greek art flourished, and beautiful sculptures dating to the Ptolemaic period have been found on the island. Main sources of wealth were the shipbuilding industry and the export of timber, grain, wine, and copper. One of the most famous Cypriots of the period was Zeno of Kition (Citium), founder of the Stoic school at Athens. Another was Pyrgoteles, a naval architect.

After the middle of the second century B.C., the Ptolemies made it a practice to call on Rome for arbitration of their dynastic

283. The goddess Poliade, the Hellenistic period

[36]Alastos, p. 89.

squabbles—driving a wedge for Roman imperial expansion in the eastern Mediterranean. These dynastic troubles, accompanied by Roman conquests in the North, increasing piracy on the high seas, and military ambitions of the Ptolemies in the East, brought about financial difficulties on Cyprus during the first century B.C. Cyprus became a separate Ptolemaic kingdom in 80 B.C.

Roman Control

The Romans took over in 58 B.C., claiming a right to the island as heirs named in the last legitimate Ptolemy's will (Ptolemy Alexander II). Moreover, they claimed that the king of Cyprus had given aid to pirates in their raids along the Cilician coast and that the annexation of Cyprus was necessary to future security of the seas. Crassus and Brutus carried out the actual annexation, but Marcus Cato was in charge of the operation. The island was looted on a grand scale. The king's treasures were auctioned off and the money sent to Rome. A brilliant chapter in Cypriot history had come to an end.

Initially Cyprus was made part of the province of Cilicia and was ruled from Tarsus. Rapacity of the early governors was indescribable; and when Cicero, an honest man, became governor in 51 B.C., he could hardly find words strong enough to portray the injustices of his predecessor. Near the beginning of his administration, Cicero received an appeal from Salamis. In 56 B.C. Brutus had made a loan to Salamis, through agents, at 48 percent interest; and when the Salaminians refused to pay, his agents' troops besieged the city councillors in their own senate chamber until five died of hunger. Cicero withdrew troops from the island and reduced the interest to 12 percent; but the matter was never solved during his term of office.

In 47 B.C. Julius Caesar restored Cyprus to the Ptolemies. With the victory of Augustus over the forces of Antony at Actium in 31 and the subsequent suicide of Antony and Cleopatra, the Romans took command once more. Now Cyprus became a province separate from Cilicia. From 27 to 22 B.C. it was administered as an imperial province and ruled by a personal appointee of Augustus. In 22 Augustus turned it over to the senate; thereafter it was governed by an ex-praetor with the title of proconsul. Luke refers to him accurately in the Greek of Acts 13:7 ("deputy" in AV; "proconsul" in RSV).

Not much is known of affairs on Cyprus during the civil wars. But Crassus, Pompey, and Caesar drew heavily on the financial and naval resources of the island. The victory of Augustus led to administrative reorganization and the reintroduction of stable conditions in the eastern Mediterranean. Economic prosperity resulted and continued on Cyprus for a couple of centuries.

Apparently Rome did not markedly disturb the pattern of social and political life as it existed under the Ptolemies. Municipalities possessed self-government in varying degrees, as was true of cities elsewhere in the Empire. For instance, Salamis had a popular assembly, a senate, and a council of elders. Probably officials of many of the cities were appointed by the Romans.

The *Koinon Ton Kyprion*, a sort of representative body acting on behalf of the Greek inhabitants of the island, a carryover from Ptolemaic days, exercised a degree of power. It issued coins, organized festivals and games, and seems to have served as a bulwark of national existence in opposition to Roman encroachment. After A.D. 68 the *Koinon* asserted itself more vigorously. Inscriptions on coins were now in Greek instead of Latin, and occasionally dates on them were on the basis of the local religious year instead of the year of the emperor.[37]

The Romans transferred the capital of

[37]*Ibid.*, p. 104.

Cyprus from Salamis to Paphos, perhaps because it was the port closest to Rome, or because they wished to honor Aphrodite, whose temple was located at Paphos, or because the port at Salamis was beginning to silt up.

Cyprus and the New Testament

When Barnabas and Saul landed on Cyprus in A.D. 45 or 46, it had regained much of the prosperity it lost a century earlier. Strabo, who completed his geography in A.D. 23, says of Cyprus in his day that it was rich in wine and oil, used home-grown wheat, had plenty of copper, and engaged in extensive shipbuilding.[38] The main cities were Salamis, its greatest port and commercial center, and Paphos, its capital.

[38]*Excerpta Cypria*, p. 3.

Salamis

As has been noted, the missionaries landed at Salamis, commonly assumed to be the home of Barnabas, a native of Cyprus. Ancient writers were unanimous in asserting that the city was founded by Teucer, son of Telamon, king of the island of Salamis in Greece. These early accounts state that this founding took place after Teucer was shipwrecked on his way home from the Trojan War. And excavations have

284. The forum at Salamis

285. The beach at Salamis near where Paul and Barnabas landed

shown that a Mycenaean town was built at Enkomi, three miles inland from Salamis about 1230 B.C. This was destroyed by the Sea Peoples (Philistines) about 1200 and rebuilt. An earthquake leveled that town about 1150. Enkomi was again rebuilt but was abandoned about 1100 B.C., after which the inhabitants founded Salamis on the coast. Salamis seems always to have been a characteristically Hellenic town with a predominately Greek population.[39]

Both because of several destructions and rebuildings of Salamis and because of the partial excavation of the site, it is difficult to picture what it looked like in Paul's day. The great limestone forum belongs to the early years of the Roman province (and therefore to Paul's day). The forum covered with its surrounding shops an area of more than three and one-half acres. The open area of the forum, or agora, was some 750 by 180 feet and was surrounded by columns of the Corinthian order about twenty-seven feet high. On a platform at the south end stood a temple dedicated to the Olympian Zeus which was constructed during the lifetime of Augustus. This was probably the largest agora in the Roman colonial empire.[40] At a considerable distance to the

north of the forum are the remains of a complex of baths and a gymnasium (commonly known as "the marble forum"). While most of the construction to be seen there today is second century A.D. or later, there are some remains of earlier Hellenistic baths among the ruins of the later Roman baths.

In 1960, excavation was begun on a theater, located to the south of the baths. This is the largest theater found to date on Cyprus and one of the largest ever discovered in the eastern Mediterranean area. The diameter of the orchestra is about thirty yards as opposed to a diameter of about twenty-three yards for the great and well-known theater at Epidaurus in Greece. In its present state of preservation the theater could hold about one thousand, but its original capacity must have been much larger. The general plan and other evidence suggest it was built in imperial times, but it may have succeeded an earlier theater.[41] One may conclude that there was a theater on the site when Paul and Barnabas arrived.

Salamis suffered a disastrous earthquake in A.D. 76 or 77. In 116, during the Jewish uprising, the city was largely destroyed. After the earthquakes of 332 and 342 (accompanied by a tidal wave) virtually demolished the city, it was rebuilt on a smaller scale by Constantius II and renamed "Constantia."

Population of Cyprus

The potential audience to whom Barnabas and Saul might have ministered on the whole island is usually estimated at about 500,000. Oberhummer, one of the authorities on ancient population, does not feel the facts warrant a higher estimate than 300,000, however.[42] But judging from the usual practice of Paul to preach in the synagogues of the Jews and from the specific reference of Acts 13:5, it seems that the aim of the missionaries was only to

[39]Dikaios lecture cited.
[40]Rupert Guiness, *Historic Cyprus* (London: Methuen & Co., Ltd., 1936), p. 420.

[41]London *Times*, February 22, 1960, p. 10.
[42] Guiness, p. 8.

reach the Jewish element of the population. Of course there would be God-fearers (sympathetic Gentiles) who would form part of the audience. Since Christian witnesses preceded Barnabas and Saul to Cyprus, it may be assumed that there was a small audience ready to listen to them (Acts 11:19).

The Apostolic Journey

After ministry in Salamis, Barnabas, and Saul went through the island to Paphos (Acts 13:6). The passage is better rendered "through the whole island." Probably this means a relatively complete tour of the Jewish communities on Cyprus, involving preaching in the synagogues. How long this mission took is open to conjecture. Ramsay thought at least two months would have been required.[43] Others have estimated that the journey took as much as four months.

The route of the apostolic itinerary is also a matter of speculation. The Romans built a road around the main part of the island. This road ran from Salamis diagonally to Kyrenia in the north, and from there roughly followed the west and south coasts and then back to Salamis. Other roads were constructed in the interior, but their exact routes are not known. It has been variously suggested that Barnabas and Saul went to Paphos by the southern road through Kition (Citium), that they went by the northern road via Soli, and that they crossed the central mountain range to their destination.

Paphos

At any rate, they finally reached Paphos. The Paphos to which they went was Nea Paphos, or "New Paphos," supposed to have been founded by Agapenor, who was wrecked there late in the thirteenth century when returning from the Trojan

[43]William M. Ramsay, *The Church in the Roman Empire Before* A.D. *170* (London: Hodder and Stoughton, 1895), p. 61.

Wars. Gradually New Paphos superseded Old Paphos (modern Kouklia), some ten miles to the southeast. Old Paphos was long famous for the worship of Aphrodite (Agapenor found a temple to her located there when he arrived), who legend declares landed here after her birth among the waves near Cythera.

Nea Paphos, capital of the island during Roman times, was largely destroyed by an earthquake in 15 B.C., after which it was rebuilt largely with funds received from Augustus and renamed "Augusta" in his honor. During the Roman era the city was adorned with magnificent temples and public buildings and was important not only as the capital but as the port for Kouklia and the shrine of Venus, or Aphrodite. Here countless pilgrims landed to visit and worship. Paphos became a great center for the worship of Aphrodite, just as Ephesus was for the worship of Diana.

All the Greek gods were worshiped on Cyprus. But Aphrodite was most widely worshiped—and Apollo second. Because Cyprus was the meeting place of so many peoples, there occurred a fusion of the worship of Aphrodite as practiced among various peoples. The rites included Oriental, Greek, and Roman practices. Aphrodite was the Greek goddess of love, beauty and fertility and was akin to the Phoenician

286. The theater at Salamis

287. "The Birth of Venus" by Botticelli

Astarte, the Babylonian Ishtar, the Anatolian Cybele, and the Roman Venus. Extensive religious prostitution accompanied her rites at Paphos.

Although many legends were told concerning the birth of Aphrodite, the most commonly accepted was that she was born of the foam of the sea, floated in a shell on the waves, and later landed on Cyprus near Paphos. The greatest festival in Cyprus in honor of Aphrodite was the Aphrodisia, held for three days each spring. It was attended by great crowds not only from all parts of Cyprus but also from surrounding countries. During the Aphrodisia a religious procession started at New Paphos and wound its way to Old Paphos, passing through the gardens and sanctuaries of the goddess there.

Temple of Aphrodite. What was believed to be the great Temple of Aphrodite at Old Paphos was investigated by De Cesnola during the last century. He was able to trace the walls of the sanctuary itself and found that it measured 221 feet on the east and west sides and 167 feet on the north and south sides. It was surrounded by an outer wall, which he was not able to trace completely. But on the basis of his discoveries, he concluded that the east and west sides of this enclosure measured 690 feet and the north and south sides 539 feet. The entire structure was built of a kind of blue granite which must have come from Cilicia or Egypt. Between this large structure on the heights (probably visible for many miles at sea) and the shoreline was a smaller temple. De Cesnola thought this was the temple built to commemorate the spot on which the goddess is said to have appeared to the Cyprians for the first time. Here the annual procession stopped to sacrifice before ascending the hill to the sanctuary.[44]

Combining evidence from archaeological investigation on the site, coins, a reference to the temple in Tacitus, and a comparison of this temple with what is known of Phoenician temples, Perrot and Chipiez have put together a description of the worship center.[45] Surrounding the complex was a wall, against the inside of which abutted a covered colonnade designed to protect worshipers or pilgrims from the heat. Within this was an inner court, to which the faithful gained entrance after accomplishing certain rites and paying certain fees. This "holy of holies" was roofless and the deity stood in the center of it, perhaps raised on a pedestal and covered with some sort of canopy. The goddess herself was represented by a conical stone, to which a head and arms may have been attached. In its entirety the structure reflects Phoenician influence. The Phoenicians seem to have built Old Paphos originally.

Like Salamis, Paphos suffered greatly from the earthquake of A.D. 76 or 77. It was virtually destroyed by an earthquake in the fourth century and lay for a long time in ruins.

At Old Paphos there was from ancient times a priestly family, the Cinyradae, the senior member of which was the chief priest of the Temple of Aphrodite. The authority of the chief priest at Old Paphos extended to all Aphrodite temples in Cyprus. Before

[44]Louis P. De Cesnola, *Cyprus: Its Ancient Cities, Tombs, and Temples* (London: John Murray, 1877), pp. 210-13.
[45]Perrot and Chipiez, *History of Art in Phoenicia and Its Dependencies* (London: Chapman and Hall, Ltd., 1885), I, 274-80.

the rule of the Ptolemies he had political and religious authority, but they took his political power away. This family retained its religious authority in Roman times.

Aphrodite worship along with Judaism would have been the chief contender with Christianity for the religious affections of Cypriots. Certainly Barnabas and Saul repeatedly had to meet the opposition of vested interests of Aphrodite as Paul later experienced the antagonism of the vested interests of Diana at Ephesus.

Elymas the sorcerer. The two missionaries met another form of spiritual blight at Paphos—in the person of Elymas the sorcerer or magician. Possibly the proconsul Sergius Paulus, who apparently was a man of high caliber, became disgusted with the immoral excesses of Aphrodite worship and desired some other religious expression. At any rate, Elymas seems to have gained some sort of hearing with or power over the governor. When Sergius Paulus became interested in learning what Saul had to say, Elymas became afraid of losing his prey and attempted to prevent the proconsul's conversion. When the apostle smote the magician with temporary blindness, he performed a miracle that was perhaps the crowning evidence for the governor of the truth of the Christian message. Sergius Paulus believed, and a great victory was won for Christianity (Acts 13:6-12). In passing, it is interesting to observe that Saul is first called Paul in connection with the interview with the governor. This was his first significant Gentile contact and the first use of his Greek name.

288. St. Paul Blinding Elymas and Converting the Roman Proconsul Sergius Paulus as painted by Raphael

Sergius Paulus. Sergius Paulus was proconsul of Cyprus about A.D. 46 to 48. The fact that he held this position is confirmed by an inscription from Paphos, dating to the middle of the first century, which mentions the proconsul Paulus.[46] Other inscriptions have been found which mention "Lucius Sergius Paullus the Younger" and "Sergia Paulla, daughter of Lucius Sergius Paullus." Ramsay thought these individuals were the son and daughter of the proconsul. Ramsay also advanced an argument to demonstrate that Sergius Paulus and his family became Christians.[47] In passing, it should be noted that the Latin spelling of the governor's name would have been rendered

with one *l* while the Greek rendering would have required two.

The early history of Christianity on Cyprus is virtually without records, but its growth is evident. Three bishops (of Paphos, Salamis, and Trimythus) represented Cyprus at the great Council of Nicea in 325.

Of course there have been efforts to fill the literary gap in early Cyprus church history. One of these efforts was the *Acts of Barnabas,* a fifth century work which recounts especially the activities of Barnabas and Mark on their subsequent trip to the island (Acts 15:39). Most of the account is probably unreliable, but possibly its mention of Barnabas' martyrdom and burial at Salamis is factual. Early legend also has it that Paul received thirty-nine strokes of the lash at Paphos, and a column there is pointed out as the place where he was tied to be scourged; but there is no historical evidence for this persecution.

[46]Camden M. Cobern, *New Archeological Discoveries* (9th ed.; New York: Funk & Wagnalls Co., 1929), p. 552.
[47]William M. Ramsay, *The Bearing of Recent Discoveries on the Trustworthiness of the New Testament* (London: Hodder and Stoughton, 1915), pp. 150-72.

Cyprus in the Postbiblical Period

After the first few centuries of the Roman era, Cyprus slipped into economic decline. Natural phenomena were very much to blame. Mention has already been made of the destructive earthquakes at Salamis and Paphos. Drought and famine in the fourth century are said to have lasted thirty-six years and to have largely depopulated the island. From 395 to 1191 Cyprus was under the control of Byzantine emperors; but from the middle of the seventh century and for 300 years, the Arabs attacked intermittently, causing grievous suffering. For instance, Salamis was sacked and the population massacred by the Arabs

in 647. Islamic forces destroyed Paphos in 960.

In 1191 Richard the Lion-Hearted took the island, and a crusader dynasty known as the Lusignans held it until 1489. Subsequently the Venetians controlled Cyprus. Then the Turks conquered it (1571) and held it until 1878, when British administration began. The British lease from Turkey turned to outright annexation in 1915 when she found herself at war with Turkey. Britain held the island until August 16, 1960, when Cyprus became an independent republic.

Bibliography

ALASTOS, DOROS. *Cyprus in History*. London: Zeno Publishers, 1955.

ASTROM, PAUL. *The Middle Cypriote Bronze Age*. Lund: Hakan Ohlssons Boktryckeri, 1957.

A Brief History and Description of Salamis. 3rd. ed. Nicosia: Antiquities Department of the Government of Cyprus, 1959.

CASSON, LIONEL. *The Ancient Mariners*. New York: The Macmillan Co., 1959.

CASSON, STANLEY. *Ancient Cyprus, Its Art and Archaeology*. London: Methuen & Co., Ltd., 1937.

COBERN, CAMDEN M. *New Archeological Discoveries*. 9th ed. New York: Funk & Wagnalls Co., 1929.

Cyprus Report for the Year 1958. London: Her Majesty's Stationery Office, 1959.

Cyprus Report for the Year 1959. London: Her Majesty's Stationery Office, 1960.

DE CESNOLA, LOUIS P. *Cyprus: Its Ancient Cities, Tombs, and Temples*. London: John Murray, 1877.

Excerpta Cypria. Translated by CLAUDE D. COBBAM. Cambridge: At the University Press, 1908.

GJERSTAD, EINAR, *et al. The Swedish Cyprus Expedition*. 3 vols. Stockholm: The Swedish Cyprus Expedition, 1934.

GUINESS, RUPERT. *Historic Cyprus*. London: Methuen & Co., Ltd., 1936.

HACKETT, J. *A History of the Orthodox Church of Cyprus*. London: Methuen & Co., 1901.

HAMMOND, N. G. L. *A History of Greece*. Oxford: At the Clarendon Press, 1959.

HILL, GEORGE. *A History of Cyprus*. 4 vols. Cambridge: At the University Press, 1940-52.

HOME, GORDON. *Cyprus Then and Now*. London: J. M. Dent & Sons, Ltd., 1960.

MANGOIAN, L. & H. A. *The Island of Cyprus*. Nicosia: Mangoian Bros., 1947.

PARRY, VERNON J. "Cyprus," *Britannica Book of the Year*, 1961.

PERROT, GEORGES, and CHIPIEZ, CHARLES. *History of Art in Phoenicia and Its Dependencies*. 2 vols. London: Chapman and Hall, Ltd., 1885.

RAMSAY, WILLIAM M. *The Bearing of Recent Discoveries on the Trustworthiness of the New Testament*. London: Hodder and Stoughton, 1915.

———. *The Church in the Roman Empire Before A.D. 170*. London: Hodder and Stoughton, 1895.

ROEBUCK, CARL. *Ionian Trade and Colonization*. New York: Archaeological Institute of America, 1959.

STARR, CHESTER G. *The Roman Imperial Navy 31 B.C.-A.D. 324*. Ithaca, N. Y.: Cornell University Press, 1941.

289. Teshub, the Hittite weather-god

Asia Minor

CROSSROADS OF CIVILIZATION converged on this important peninsula of the eastern Mediterranean world. At an early time peoples and ideas moved in from the Mesopotamian valley. From this center men migrated to Crete, the Aegean islands, and even the Greek mainland. Waves of Greeks washed onto her shores during the first millennium B.C. During the same millennium Etruscans probably sailed from her western coasts to Italy; Persians swept across her plateaus into Greece; Alexander's hosts conquered her on the way to deal with the Persian king, and his Seleucid successors established flourishing centers there. These cities enjoyed new heights of prosperity under the Roman Peace during the first and second centuries A.D.

Not only was this peninsula important for the flow of population and culture in ancient times; it was also important to the advance of Christianity. The great apostle of Christianity was born at Tarsus and in his missionary activities ranged over the entire length of Asia Minor. Subsequently Peter seems to have preached in the northern and central portions of the peninsula. And the Apostle John spent the last decades of his life ministering in the populous cities of the province of Asia. Altogether at least thirty-five towns, provinces, and islands adjacent to Asia Minor figure in the New Testament narrative.

During the middle ages a flourishing Byzantine Empire was based on the prosperity of Asia Minor. When Constantinople fell to the Turks in 1453, the Ottoman Empire established control over the area along with a considerable portion of the rest of the Near East. Reaching its height in the sixteenth century, the Ottoman Empire declined in subsequent centuries and in the nineteenth century became the "Sick Man of Europe." With the dissolution of the Ottoman Empire after World War I, the history of modern Turkey began. The present cultural level and economic development of the area are far from what they were during the first two centuries of the Christian Era. However, the landscape is still beautiful, the soil is still productive, and signs and sounds of progress are in the air.

311

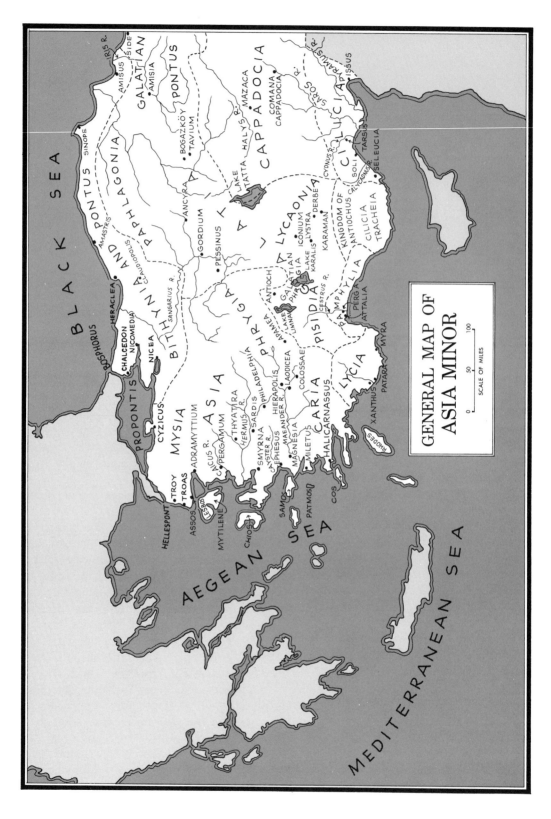

GENERAL MAP OF ASIA MINOR

SCALE OF MILES
0   50   100

THE WYCLIFFE HISTORICAL GEOGRAPHY OF BIBLE LANDS

Geographical Features

Asia Minor is the general geographical term for the peninsula that forms the bulk of modern Turkey. Not in use in classical times, the descriptive seems to have arisen in the fifth century A.D. Anatolia commonly applies to that part of the peninsula west of the Halys River but is frequently used virtually as a synonym for Asia Minor.

Asia Minor is bounded on the north by the Black Sea, on the west by the Aegean and the straits of the Bosporus and Dardanelles, on the south by the Mediterranean Sea, and on the east by a line running northeastward from below the Gulf of Iskenderun to the Euphrates and up that stream to the Coruh (Chorokh) River and then to the Black Sea. The total area of the peninsula approximates 200,000 square miles, equal to that of New England, New York, New Jersey, Pennsylvania, Delaware, Maryland, and West Virginia.

The Central Plateau. The mass of Asia Minor is a plateau 3,000 to 5,000 feet above sea level, tilted down toward the north and west. Extensive and irregular, this plateau is fringed on all sides by higher mountain ranges, but on the west the hills are fewer and less imposing. While the plateau consists largely of rolling upland, it is diversified by highland massifs and numerous sunken basins occupied by lakes and marshes. Although the rivers entering the interior plains from the adjoining mountains in modern times are largely swallowed up in salt lakes and swamps, in New Testament times their waters were used for irrigation and helped to support numerous large cities. The surface of the northern part of the plateau is deeply eroded; in many places there are precipitous valley walls and rugged hillsides.

As a whole the central plateau has slender resources. Because of its enclosed nature, much of the plateau is arid. It supports little plant or animal life and is used for grazing of sheep. It was not until the Hellenistic and Roman periods that town life developed there, and even then the larger towns were strung out along the edge rather than across the heart of the tableland. The middle part of the plateau has never produced an important coordinating center.

The Mountain Ranges. As already noted, the central plateau is surrounded by mountain ranges. The Armenian mountains extend westward and fork near the eastern boundary of the peninsula into two ranges—the Taurus on the south and the mountains of Pontus on the north. The northern rim of mountains rises to about 9,000 feet and the southern to 10,000 feet. Both consist of a series of overlapping ridges which permit only a few narrow and tortuous passages between the coast and the interior. East and northeast of the main Taurus system and parallel to it lies the Anti-Taurus Range.

Along the southeast edge of the plateau for a distance of about 150 miles rise groups of volcanic peaks. At the northeast end of this range stands Mount Erciyas Dagi (ancient Argaeus) at a height of 13,100 feet, the highest point in Asia Minor. Here in western Cappadocia, fertilized by lava dust and supplied with snow waters in summer were fine orchards and the best horse pastures of the Near East, on which a strain of racers for the Roman circus was bred.

From the Phrygian mountains on the west of the central plateau extend mountain ranges—the Temnos, Boz Dag (ancient Tmolus), and Messogis—which delimit respectively the valleys of the Caicus, Gediz (ancient Hermus), and Menderes (ancient Maeander). Since these valleys run east and west, they naturally conduct traffic in those directions. Thus the only open face of Asia Minor is toward the west and northwest, where the plateau ends in a staircase down to a piedmont country. Since the western shore is easily accessible, most invasions of Asia Minor that have had lasting results have been launched from Europe (e.g., Phrygians, Greeks, and Galatians).

As intimated, the mountains of Asia Minor constitute formidable barriers, but there are strategic passes. The most important was, of course, the Cilician Gates north of Tarsus. Two passes made possible routes from Antalya (biblical Attalia) to Laodicea and to Pisidian Antioch or Apamea. Another gave passage between Seleucia in western Cilicia to Karaman (ancient Laranda) in the interior. One other gave access between central Cappadocia and eastern Cilicia.

While the mountains might and did constitute hindrances to communication and transportation, they provided sources of mineral wealth. Since Asia Minor is significant in the biblical narrative during Roman times, only a statement of minerals known and mined then is provided here. The gold of Asia Minor was·depleted by Roman times. A little silver was still mined in Pontus and some in central Cappadocia. Some copper was produced at Chalcedon and in Pontus and Cilicia. How many of the abandoned copper pits all over the country were worked in Roman times is not known. Iron came chiefly from Pontus, Cappadocia, Bithynia, and some from the Troad and possibly Caria. Lead was mined in western Mysia. Zinc seems to have been produced in the Troad and on Mount Tmolus. While various marbles of local importance were quarried, the variegated marble of Docimium was widely exported, as was the white marble of the territory of Cyzicus (modern Kapidagi). The mountains were also important for their timber resources.

Forests of pine, oak, and fir abounded in the mountains of both the north and the south.

The Black Sea Coastlands. The Black Sea coast is generally steep and rocky; an irregular line of highlands rises 6,000 to 7,000 feet within fifteen to twenty miles from the sea. For the most part there is hardly any intervening coastal plain. Rivers of the region generally are short torrents which do not provide access to the interior. Moreover, there are few acceptable harbors. All of these drawbacks, plus the liability to earthquakes, tended to hold back the progress of the area.

The northern seaboard of Asia Minor may be divided into two sections. The eastern section consists of the biblical Pontus and Paphlagonia. A persistent northerly wind keeps the area cool and moderately rainy throughout the entire year. But Trapezus (modern Trabzon or Trebizond), the capital of ancient Pontus, enjoys the weather of a Mediterranean Riviera, screened as it is by the Caucasus Range. The mountains are well clad with ship and carpenter's timber and are provided with deposits of silver and iron, which probably gave rise in Hittite days to the earliest iron industry of Nearer Asia. The inner side of the mountains opened to fertile valleys, and the broad valley of the Lycus River served as a main artery for the Pontic area. Poor harbors were always a drawback. But Sinope (modern Sinop), at the most northerly point on the Black Sea coastline, did become a great maritime center.

The western section of the northern seaboard of Asia Minor consists of ancient Bithynia and Mysia. Here the climate is similar to that of the eastern region. There is not so much mineral wealth; but the mountains stand farther back from the coast, leaving room for good grain and orchard country. And there are better harbors, an especially good one being located at Kapidagi (ancient Cyzicus).

Western Asia Minor. The western fringe of Asia Minor contributed most to the country's history in Greek and Roman days. Its weather is milder than the Greek homeland, and the soil is more fertile. The coastline is highly intricate and broken, with many irregularly shaped islands.

Beginning in the north, the Bosporus is sixteen miles long and on the average one mile wide, though it narrows in places to less than 700 yards. Both banks rise steeply from the waters. The Sea of Marmara is a natural creel for trapping shoals of fish on their annual migration from the Mediterranean to the Black Sea. The Dardanelles is twenty-five miles long and increases in width toward the south, from two-fifths of a mile in the north to four and one-half miles in the south. Because of evaporation in the Mediterranean, a continuous flow of water south from the Black Sea produces a strong current in the Bosporus and Dardanelles. The current is three miles an hour at Istanbul.

As one moves farther south along the Aegean coast, he encounters a series of east-west valleys, which, generally speaking, are broad and flat-bottomed and well furnished with rich alluvial deposits laid by the rivers. But while this deposit makes for very productive valleys when drained and cultivated, it also contributed to the silting up of river mouths and harbors. For instance, the mouth of the Menderes is now several miles west of where it was in Roman times. The site of Miletus, once a focus of naval communication, is entirely cut off from the sea. The harbor of Ephesus is completely filled in. A further disadvantage of this silting is the creation of marshes with their malarial threat.

In biblical times there were four broad river valleys in western Asia Minor: Caicus, Hermus, Cayster, and Maeander. Each provided access to an important hinterland. Pergamum was located in the Caicus. Smyrna, Sardis, and Philadelphia had access to the Hermus. The Cayster flowed north of

290. The Maeander River

Ephesus, and that great city of Diana also tapped the trade of the Maeander, as did Laodicea. In Roman times Miletus also lay on the Maeander.

The towns of western Asia Minor got material for their textile industries from the sheep downs of the Phrygian tableland. Laodicea was known for its black wool, Pergamum for brocades and sheep hides made into parchment, which displaced papyrus as a writing material.

The accidents of geography led to the development of two largely distinct cultures in Asia Minor. The culture of the plateau in the interior was essentially Oriental, while that of the coastal cities was largely Greek or Greco-Roman.

The Mediterranean Coastlands. Along the entire length of the southern seaboard of Asia Minor, the mountains descend steeply to the sea, except in the regions of Pamphylia and eastern Cilicia. Thus the Mediterranean coastlands entered little into ancient history. The southerly winds of the winter season brought sufficient rainfall for a rich forest growth which the Egyptians and many after them coveted for timber resources. Western Cilicia was the most trackless part of the coast and was used as a pirate hideout.

The mountains of southern Asia Minor

are fold ranges, not rift valleys. In the north the western Taurus folds are so closely packed against the plateau of Anatolia that hardly any streams cut their way through the mountains to the sea. Here the mountains are a serious barrier to contact with the interior and roads are few. The main Taurus, reaching 12,000 feet, are much higher than the western Taurus. However, they are not as wide as the western Taurus, and erosion is more active. So a number of narrow and steep river valleys have been cut through the mountain chain at several points. One of these gorges is cut by the Yeziloluk, a tributary of the Cydnus, and forms the famous Cilician Gates.

Eastern Asia Minor. Eastern Asia Minor consists of a series of mountain ranges in the north, falling away into broken plateaus and finally into an undulating plain which continues into north Syria and Iraq.

Climate. The climate of Asia Minor is one of extremes. Parts of the Aegean coastlands never experience frost. In the east snow lies even in the valleys for a third of the year. The Black Sea coastlands have a rainfall which ranges from 25 inches in the west to 100 inches in the east and a mean temperature of 45 degrees for January and 70 degrees for August. The Aegean coastlands have a rainfall of 25 to 30 inches and a mean temperature of 45 degrees for January and 75 degrees in July and August. The Mediterranean coastlands have a rainfall of about 30 inches and a mean temperature of 50 degrees in January and 83 degrees in the summer. The central plateau has about 10 to 17 inches of rainfall; all districts have more than 100 days of frost during the year. The January temperature mean is 30 degrees and the summer mean about 70. In the east the climate is one of the most difficult and inhospitable in the world with hot and dry summers and bitterly cold winters. Rainfall averages 17 to 24 inches, and temperatures of 40 degrees below zero have been recorded in January.

Rivers and Lakes. Several rivers have already been mentioned. Others should be noted. The most important river of the peninsula is the Kizil Irmak (ancient Halys), 600 miles long, which originates in eastern Asia Minor and flows in a great bend to the southwest and finally into the Black Sea through what was Pontus. Unfortunately its gorge is often too narrow to permit it to be an important means of communication into the interior. The Sakarya (ancient Sangarius), 300 miles long, originates in what was ancient Phrygia and makes a great bend to the east and flows into the Black Sea through biblical Bithynia. The Cestrus (c. 80 miles long) was the chief river of Pamphylia. The Calycadnus (c. 150 miles long) drained western Cilicia. And the Cydnus (c. 40 miles long), the Sarus (780 miles long), and the Pyramus (230 miles long) flowed through eastern Cilicia, the latter two originating in the mountains of Cappadocia.

Numerous lakes might be mentioned. The greatest is Tatta, a salt lake in the central plain, some sixty by ten to thirty miles in winter and a mere marsh in the summer drought. A fine freshwater lake is Karalis, southeast of Pisidian Antioch on the road to Lystra. It is about thirty-five miles long and lies at 3,770 feet in altitude. Southwest of Pisidian Antioch is Limnai, thirty miles long, at 2,850 feet in altitude.

Roads. Numerous roads spanned Asia Minor by the days of Paul and John. The great eastern trade route to the Euphrates began at Ephesus and traversed the Maeander Valley, passing through Laodicea, Colossae, Apamea, and then arching north of Pisidian Antioch, and dropping south to Galatian Laodicea and cutting east through Cappadocia.

The trade route from Ephesus to Syria

would have been the same as the former to Apamea and then would have passed through Pisidian Antioch and Iconium and then south through Laranda or southeast through Hyde and then through the Cilician Gates to Tarsus. A fine western road led north from Ephesus through Smyrna, Pergamum, and Adramyttium to Cyzicus. A northern road led west from Byzantium through Nicomedia and Claudiopolis in Bithynia and then arched northward through Pompeiopolis and dipped south to Amisia. Other lesser north-south and east-west routes could be noted.

Historical Developments

Beginnings. On the basis of numerous investigations and excavations in Turkey, Seton Lloyd concludes that human habitation in Anatolia goes back to the beginnings of the Paleolithic period. Four Paleolithic cultures have been reported in stratification in a cave near Antalya in south central Turkey.[1] Signs of habitation of Asia Minor during the Neolithic period are sparse indeed, having been found in earlier years at Mersin (southwest of Tarsus) and Sakjegözü (a considerable distance northeast of Tarsus) and more recently at Hacilar (west of Konya) and Catal Hüyük (southeast of Konya). At the latter site James Melleart has been unearthing a well-developed civilization dating to the seventh millennium B.C.

The Chalcolithic Age. The Chalcolithic (copper stone) age in Asia Minor lasted for a very long time, probably during most of the fifth and fourth millennia B.C. During this period the great plateau of Anatolia seems to have remained unoccupied, the Chalcolithic peoples becoming aware of it only during the last years of their existence. Near the close of the fourth millennium, the lands of Anatolia proper were at last "discovered" and the first farming settlements appeared on the plateau itself and in the Aegean province to the west. But there is no degree of certainty as to the origin of these settlers. Chalcolithic cultures have not yet come to light in Pontic and eastern Anatolia.

The Bronze Age. Probably about 3500 B.C. the Bronze (alloy of copper and tin) age came to Asia Minor.[2] Only in the Cilician Plain was it introduced by newcomers; elsewhere it developed out of the late Chalcolithic culture. Northwestern and central Anatolia became conspicuous for the first time in Anatolian prehistory. While northwestern, central, and southwestern Anatolia possessed considerable mineral resources, the Cilicia and Konya (ancient Iconium) Plains contained some of the richest alluvial soil in the country; and Cilicia controlled an important trade route as well. Metallurgy was so highly developed in Anatolia by the end of the Early Bronze age that this section was the metal market from which much of the metalwork of Assyria and Syria was obtained.[3]

Seemingly the great prosperity of Anatolia during the period 3500 to 2300 B.C. was based largely on the sytematic exploitation of its metal wealth and the ability to market it in many areas of the Middle East. Fully urban communities now arose, prob-

[1]Seton Lloyd, *Early Anatolia* (Harmondsworth, England: Penguin Books, Ltd., 1956), p. 52.

[2]J. Mellaart, *Anatolia c. 4000-2300* B.C. (Cambridge: At the University Press, 1962), p. 45. This is one of the revision fascicles of Volume I of the *Cambridge Ancient History.* The conventional date for the beginning of the Bronze Age in Asia Minor is 3000 or 2750 B.C.
[3]*Ibid.,* p. 10.

ably organized under kings, with a considerable percentage of the population engaged in the metal industry and trade by land and sea. Though its people were illiterate and the cities smaller than those of Egypt and Sumer, Anatolian culture displayed at some of the royal courts there was second to none.[4] Troy, Thermi on the island of Lesbos, Tarsus, Alishar (Alaja) Hüyük, Kültepe, and Poliochni on the island of Lemnos are among the important sites from which our information comes for this period.

Houses of the Early Bronze I period (3500-2800 B.C.), at least in the West, were on the whole rectangular, of a hall-and-porch or megaron type, with several raised platforms which may have been used for sleeping. The hearth was located in the middle of the floor and food was stored in large pots or clay-lined bins sunk in the floor. In some towns houses were grouped in blocks separated by streets and alleys. Generally houses seem to have been of one story and were almost certainly flat-roofed.

Finds of metal objects are comparatively few. All pottery was still made by hand, without the benefit of a pottery wheel; and it was superior to contemporary pottery of Mesopotamia, Egypt, and Syria. A discussion of pottery styles and color of decoration appearing in the various sections of Asia Minor is quite beyond the purpose of this study.

Though the transition from the Early Bronze I period to Early Bronze II (2800-2300 B.C.) was generally peaceful, in the northwest there was considerable destruction which Mellaart feels most likely was produced by an enemy who came from the Thracian coast.[5] During Early Bronze II the main schools of Anatolian metalwork (the northwestern and central) were of local origin, owing little if anything to influences from Mesopotamia, Syria, or Cyprus.[6] Trade was widespread.

[4]*Ibid.*
[5]*Ibid.*, p. 24.
[6]*Ibid.*, p. 26.

Excavations seem to indicate that several kingdoms, large and small, existed in Asia Minor at that time. The rich burials of some of the kings and queens demonstrate their wealth and power, as well as the level of craftsmanship. Alaca Hüyük, east of modern Ankara, was especially productive of richly buried persons.

There is evidence of city planning during this period. A good example is Poliochni on the island of Lemnos, where a main street ran in a north-south direction through the town. Along this street lay a number of blocks or squares, some containing one large house, some containing several houses. A moderate-sized house consisted of a hall and porch with a courtyard and a row of smaller rooms along one of the long sides of the hall. Larger houses simply elaborated on this plan with additional rooms around the hall and court, sometimes with a second courtyard. Typical public buildings included an assembly hall and a huge granary.

Houses in Cilicia were different from those of the West during this period. At Tarsus they were oblong and were entered directly from the street. In the main room was a built-up hearth, and at the rear of the main room a door led into one or two other rooms. Probably these houses had two stories. The hall-and-porch type of house did not become common in the East until after 2300 B.C., when cultural influences from the northwest became strong.

Two Early Bronze Age temples have been found in Asia Minor at Beycesultan in west central Turkey. Measuring forty-five to fifty feet in length, they are of the hall-and-porch plan, with a back room added. Constructed of mud-brick and plastered over, these temples were painted blue. Inside of each was an altar behind which was a screen that sheltered the inner sanctum from the view of worshipers. Numerous storage vessels and bins were found in the sanctuary.

As noted above, the metal industry was

well developed during Early Bronze II. Casting in closed molds, *repoussé* work, metal inlay, sweating and soldering, and techniques of hammering were all known. Considerable use was made of copper, bronze, iron, gold, silver, electrum (an alloy of gold and silver), and lead—all native to Anatolia except the tin used to produce bronze. The large number of weapons and armor found in tombs has led to the belief that the population was quite warlike. Pottery at Troy and Tarsus was made on a pottery wheel during Early Bronze II. Elsewhere in Anatolia it was made by hand.

Early Bronze II was brought to an end about 2300-2200 B.C. by an invasion which was particularly destructive in western and southern Anatolia. There the number of settlements during Early Bronze III (2300-1900 B.C.) was reduced to about a quarter of the number in the previous period.[7] Town after town (e.g., Troy, Tarsus, Poliochni, Beycesultan) was destroyed by burning. Every townsite on the Konya plain shows evidence of conflagration dating to the end of the Early Bronze II period. Subsequently nearly every village there was deserted and never again occupied.

Mellaart has suggested that Luwians from the Balkans moved in at the end of Early Bronze I and effected destruction in western Anatolia, became "Anatolianized" during Early Bronze II, and were joined by fresh groups of destructive Luwians (and probably others) at the end of Early Bronze II.[8] The invaders who came about 2300 B.C. brought to Anatolia a taste for exotic painted pottery (gay colors on light clay) which was quite revolutionary for this country accustomed to plain and burnished ware with decoration that was almost completely limited to simple lines of white paint on a dark background. Seton Lloyd hints that this remarkable change in pottery styles may have something to do with the arrival of Indo-Europeans in Asia

Minor,[9] and Mellaart notes the possibility that Indo-Europeans came to the peninsula in the wake of Luwian invasion about 2300-2200 B.C. But he observes that most Greek scholars feel that the Indo-Europeans did not come so early and that much work still needs to be done on the problem.[10]

At any rate, Indo-Europeans did certainly make their appearance in Asia Minor by the beginning of the Middle Bronze Age (c. 1900). For purposes of organization the Middle Bronze and Late Bronze Ages (covering the period 1900-1200 B.C.) are discussed as a unit here. Troy and the Hittites were the chief powers during the period. But Assyrian influence in the east should not be ignored.

Troy

Throughout the Bronze Age Troy dominated the northwestern part of Asia Minor. Strategically located, it occupied a low ridge some four miles from the Aegean to the west and an equal distance from the Dardanelles to the north. From its vantage point the city controlled traffic through the Straits as well as an important land route.

Although Charles Maclaren identified Turkish Hissarlik as the site of Troy as early as 1822, it was Heinrich Schliemann who fixed the identification and excavated there for seven seasons between 1870 and 1890. Wilhelm Dörpfeld dug there in 1893 and 1894. From 1932 to 1938 a University of Cincinnati team worked there for seven seasons under the leadership of Carl Blegen. Occupational debris covered the hill to a depth of fifty feet and divided into forty-six strata. Archaeologists describe nine main occupational levels at the site.

Troy was first occupied at the beginning of the Early Bronze Age. The earliest settlement was a small fortress some 300 feet across, within which stood a few large

[7]*Ibid.*, p. 46.
[8]*Ibid.*, pp. 47-50.

[9]Lloyd, p. 67.
[10]Mellaart, p. 50.

houses—homes of the ruler and his followers —built of crude brick on stone foundations. Frequently rebuilt, the remains of this complex yielded to the archaeologists copper implements, much pottery (with highly polished surfaces in black, brownish, grayish, or greenish black, and some lighter colors), and many other artifacts. The culture of Troy I influenced or was closely related to that of the eastern shore of the Aegean and the Gallipoli Peninsula across the Dardanelles. By the end of the period, contacts with Greece were considerable; but little evidence of contacts with central Anatolia is yet available.

At the end of Early Bronze I, Troy I came to an end; it was destroyed by fire. The new citadel, increased in diameter to 400 feet, was completely gutted by fire during the invasion at the end of Troy II (end of Early Bronze II). The fire must have completely surprised the inhabitants and must have spread very rapidly because, without exception, the floors were covered with household gear, a considerable quantity of gold ornaments and jewelry, vessels of gold, copper, and bronze, and bronze weapons.[11] These objects demonstrated a great advance in the arts and crafts over Troy I. The pottery wheel was introduced and made possible a greater variety of shapes. Colors of pottery tended to be lighter. Commercial contacts with the Aegean world were more numerous than during Troy I.

Troy III, IV, and V occurred during the Early Bronze III period. There was no discernible cultural break between these cities or between them and Troy II. Troy III covered more ground than Troy II and had a town plan with blocks of houses separated by narrow streets. Exterior house walls were now of stone instead of brick. The fourth settlement at Troy was larger than Troy III, but there was a reversion to building house walls of crude brick. House plans became more complex in Troy V, quality

[11]Carl Blegen, *Troy* (Cambridge: At the University Press, 1961), p. 6.

of construction was improved, and pottery was of better quality too. Throughout the period extensive relations with the West continued. The degree of contact which existed between Troy and central Asia Minor is problematical.

How Troy V met its end is uncertain. But Troy VI marked a considerable break with the past, no doubt resulting from an influx of population connected with the movement of Indo-European peoples that flooded the Aegean world about 1900 B.C. The citadel, now greatly expanded, had a wall some 1800 feet in circumference around the base of the hill which was terraced and covered with freestanding houses. Presumably these houses were occupied by the king's courtiers and favorites, and presumably the palace stood on the summit of the hill. The masonry of many of these structures was carefully dressed and fitted and in some instances almost attained classical Greek excellence. Wooden columns set on shaped stone bases were used in several of these buildings.

Finds of metal objects and pottery at Troy VI indicate extensive external relations with the Aegean world, though some of the commodities may have been produced locally. To date nothing has been found either at Troy or at Hittite sites to indicate that those powers had any contact with each other. But this is merely an argument from silence and is not therefore conclusive.

Troy VI was destroyed by a great upheaval about 1300 B.C.—an upheaval which knocked down the fortification walls and ruined most of the large houses within the citadel. The excavators concluded that an earthquake must have been responsible; there was no evidence of fire. Troy VIIa continued directly upon the cultural foundations of Troy VI. Instead of a smaller number of large freestanding houses within the citadel, there were now more numerous smaller houses packed so close together that many of them had common walls. Each

291. The city walls of
    Troy VI

house had several large storage jars sunk deep beneath the floors with the mouths projecting only slightly above the ground.

While much Mycenaean pottery and some Cypriot ware was imported during this period, a large percentage of the pottery is now of local manufacture. Still there are no identifiable imports from central Anatolia.

Troy VII*a* is now identified as the Troy destroyed by the Achaeans. Certainly this city was completely reduced to ruins by fire that seems to have been of human origin. The crowding of houses within the citadel and the large number of storage jars in private houses indicated preparation for siege. As to exactly when the city fell there is considerable question. A date which has become traditional is 1184 B.C., as calculated by Eratosthenes (third century B.C.). Modern scholars differ considerably in their interpretation of the chronology. Many would put the date of Troy's fall at the hands of the Greeks at about 1200. Blegen suggests that Troy fell about 1250.[12] Such a conclusion would fit the demands of Greek history much better than 1200. By the latter date the Greeks were seemingly

becoming too occupied with the threat of the Dorian invasion to launch an attack on Troy. In accepting an approximate 1200 date for the fall of Troy, Tom Jones[13] thinks that the Phrygians who invaded Asia Minor about that time are much more likely candidates than the Greeks for the honor of having destroyed Troy.

The tradition of Greek destruction of Troy seems too strong to be discounted. Moreover, one can save the day for the view of Greek conquest and the historical accuracy of Homer at this point by accepting the 1250 date for the fall of Troy. At that time the Greeks might still have mustered enough strength to defeat Troy. It is to be noted that Troy VII*b* was built on the ruins of VII*a* without a break in continuity of culture and that it lasted only a generation or two. Then came a very definite break in culture (possibly *c.* 1200). The closest analogy for the pottery introduced at that time was pottery found in Late Bronze Age sites in Hungary,[14] tying the destruction of Troy VII*b* very closely to the Phrygian invasion (from southeastern Europe) which toppled the Hittite Empire.

[12]*Ibid.*, p. 14.

[13]Tom Jones, *Ancient Civilization* (Chicago: Rand McNally & Co., 1960), p. 178.
[14]Blegen, p. 14.

Probably, then, the Greeks destroyed Troy about 1250, after which the city was promptly rebuilt, only to be destroyed by Phrygians about fifty years later. The ancients were right about a Greek destruction of Troy but not about the date of its occurrence.

A town of some importance existed at Hissarlik during the Hellenistic Age. Fortifications and temples dating to that period remain. Ruins of several other buildings at the site date to the early Christian Era. This last city seems to have decayed in the fifth century A.D.

Assyrian Merchant Colonies in the East

As early as 1880 B.C. Assyrian commercial tablets began to appear in eastern Turkey. The source of these was eagerly sought by archaeologists. The Czechoslovakian Bedrich Hrozný in 1925 was finally successful in this quest at Kültepe, near Kayseri almost due north of Adana in central Turkey. He was rewarded with about 1,000 tablets for his efforts. Since 1948 the Turkish archaeologists Tashin and Nimet Özgüç have expended considerable effort at the site and have found several thousand more tablets.

These archives of Assyrian business houses tell an interesting story of an Assyrian merchant colony that flourished at the site between about 1900 and 1800 B.C. This town, ancient Kanesh, was not the only such Assyrian merchant colony in Anatolia, for the tablets tell of six others as yet unidentified, in addition to eight trading stations, likewise unidentified.

Regulating the trading community was the *karum*, a kind of chamber of commerce. It controlled trade with Assyria and served as a tribunal for fixing prices and settling disputes. The colony seems to have been an integral part of the Assyrian state economy, and official messengers maintained regular and effective communications with the homeland.[15] The caravans of donkeys which these traders employed seem to have been extremely free from robbery. Their main cargo imported from Assyria was lead and woven materials; the main export to Assyria was copper. The local princes levied taxes upon the Assyrians and reserved the right to purchase any of their goods.

The Assyrian merchants seem to have been on good terms with the native Anatolians and to have intermarried freely with them. They lived in houses which seem generally to have been of two stories with rooms grouped around an open court or along a corridor. These houses were built of sun-dried brick on foundations of uncut stone and were plastered without and within. Family rooms usually were on the second floor. Burials were commonly made beneath the floor of the houses, and the deceased were provided with numerous funerary gifts. Their business records were arranged on shelves or placed in large jars in a main floor room. Their pottery, called "Cappadocian ware," was painted with intricate designs, and sometimes cups were shaped in the form of bulls' or lions' heads.

Apparently this interesting chapter in Anatolian history came to an end with little warning. The town of Kanesh was destroyed by fire; and the inhabitants departed hastily, leaving the contents of their houses in their proper places—where they remained until the archaeologists uncovered them. We must await further archaeological investigation to determine the extent of this Assyrian influence in eastern Anatolia.

The Hittites

The Bible effectively attests that the Hittites were an ancient people. As early as the Table of Nations, Heth is alluded to as one of the sons of Canaan (Gen. 10:15). The Hittites were involved in the founding

[15]Lloyd, p. 117.

of Jerusalem (Ezek. 16:3). Abraham bought the cave of Machpelah from the sons of Heth (Gen. 23), and Esau married Hittite wives (Gen. 26:34; 36:1-3). Tribal lists include them among the peoples living in Palestine when Abraham arrived and at the time of the conquest (Gen. 15:18-21; Num. 13:29). Two passages refer to "kings of the Hittites" (II Chron. 1:17; II Kings 7:6-7). About a dozen other Old Testament books mention the Hittites on numerous occasions.

Although higher critics doubted the existence of the Hittites because secular history had failed to attest their existence, evidence of their historicity gradually accumulated. Thutmose III of Egypt in the fifteenth century B.C. and Ramses II of Egypt in the thirteenth century B.C. had fought against a people called "Kheta" in Syria, according to Egyptian records. Scholars identified these with the Hittites of the Old Testament. Assyrian records referred to Syria as the "Land of Hatti" after about 1100 B.C.

Over a period of decades travelers and scholars identified archaeological remains in Syria as Hittite. Then similar objects and construction began to turn up in Asia Minor. Finally in 1880 A. H. Sayce read a paper to the Society for Biblical Archaeology in London in which he declared that the Hittites must have occupied much of Asia Minor in ancient times. Subsequently numerous archaeologists made extended surveys in Turkey which tended to confirm Sayce's thesis.

Exploration led to excavation. The British Museum conducted an excavation at Carchemish in Syria in 1879, locating numerous monuments and inscriptions in a Hittite hieroglyphic script. A German team worked at Zinjirli (in Turkey, northeast of ancient Antioch on the Orontes) 1888-92, finding more monuments and inscriptions. Meanwhile the Amarna Letters, discovered in 1887 in Egypt, threw new light on Egypto-Hittite relations. These letters served to indicate the importance of excavations in Anatolia proper. Therefore, in 1906 Hugo Winckler on behalf of the German Oriental Society began to excavate at what proved to be the Hittite capital at Bogazköy, east of Ankara. In addition to monumental remains, he discovered the royal archive there with its some 10,000 tablets written in cuneiform.

Excavations at Bogazköy, interrupted by World War I, were resumed by the Germans under the leadership of K. Bittel in 1931. Interrupted again by war, the excavations at the Hittite capital were reopened by Bittel in 1952. But others were busy with pick and spade in Hittite land. Among the long list of excavations must be included the work of University of Chicago teams at Alishar and Tell Tainat, a Danish team at Hama (ancient Hamath), Sir Leonard Woolley at Tell Atchana, and Hetty Goldman of Bryn Mawr at Tarsus. And under the leadership of Professors Hans Güterbock of the University of Ankara (now of Chicago) and H. T. Bossert of the University of Istanbul, the Turks themselves began to do effective work in Hittite archaeology.

Before a definitive story of the Hittites could be told, their written records had to be translated. Bedrich Hrozný made a beginning in 1915 when he published a sketch of Hittite grammar and showed that its structure was Indo-European. Ferdinand Sommer, Johannes Friedrich, H. Ehelolf,

292. Terrain near Bogazköy

and Albrecht Götze were some of the more important pioneers of decipherment in Germany; and by 1933 they had translated most of the better-preserved Hittite cuneiform historical texts into German. The American E. H. Sturtevant and the Frenchman Louis Delaporte also contributed to the linguistic developments. Hittite hieroglyphic was much harder to decipher. The important names here were the German H. T. Bossert, the American I. J. Gelb, the Czech B. Hrozný, the Swiss Emil Forrer, and the Italian P. Meriggi. Actually a total of eight languages were written in these two scripts, five of which were spoken by peoples of Asia Minor.

Now it remains to sketch the history which the Hittite texts and artifacts can be made to surrender. Something should be said first about the peoples of Asia Minor and their languages. Three of the languages and/or ethnic groups were related to the Indo-European family. The Luwian-speaking peoples probably arrived in Asia Minor at the end of the Early Bronze Age (about 2300 B.C.) and by 1750 controlled much of the southern and western parts of the peninsula. As time passed, they played an increasing role in the Hittite kingdom. Palaic was the language of Pala, commonly placed in Paphlagonia in north central Asia Minor. The official Hittite language itself, in which most of the Hittite texts were written, was referred to in the Bogazköy texts as the "language of Nesha," the Hittite form of Kanesh. These people probably entered the area around Kanesh (Kültepe in east central Asia Minor) during the latter part of the Early Bronze Age and were present in the country during the most flourishing period of the Assyrian merchant colony.

These Indo-European "Kaneshites" mingled freely with the non-Indo-European Hatti (Khatti) of the northeastern part of Asia Minor, and their language gradually replaced that of their predecessors. As can be readily seen, Hatti is linguistically equatable with the English "Hittite." Since the archaeologists had already assigned the name "Hittite" to the Kaneshites, they had to find another term for the "true Hittites." "Khattian," "Khattic," and "Proto-Hittite" have been used to designate this non-Indo-European substratum of the population.

Hittite history. There is some justification for beginning Hittite history earlier (perhaps 1750 B.C. or a little before), but the tendency today is to launch the story of the Hittite kingdom with King Labarnas. (The writer would prefer to date the end of his reign about 1600, though Gurney places it about fifty years earlier.) Says Gurney, "The later Hittite kings liked to trace their descent back to the ancient King Labarnas, and with him therefore Hittite history may be said to begin."[16] At any rate, Hittite history is commonly divided into two distinct periods: the Old Kingdom and the Empire, the latter beginning about 1460 B.C. and ending about 1200 B.C. Actually Hittite power was fairly weak between about 1500 and 1370, when the Mitanni controlled much of the upper Tigris-Euphrates Valley as well as Syria and a portion of Asia Minor.

The conquests of Labarnas were extensive, and his kingdom seems to have reached the limits of expansion attained by the monarchs of the empire period, in the

293. Entrance to the great temple of the lower city, Bogazköy

16O. R. Gurney, *The Hittites* (rev. ed.; Harmondsworth, England, 1961), p. 21.

south and west at least. His son, Hattusilis, moved the capital to Hattusas (Bogazköy). The third king of the Old Kingdom, Mursilis, campaigned along the Euphrates and accomplished the sack of Babylon, bringing Hammurabi's dynasty to an end. W. F. Albright would date this victory to 1550 B.C., but Gurney believes it must have occurred some fifty years earlier.

After Mursilis there was a considerable amount of unrest in Hittite internal affairs, involving palace intrigues and the like. Finally about 1525 Telipinus usurped the throne and proclaimed a law of succession and a number of other rules for the conduct of king and nobles, most of which were observed down to the end of the Empire. Though a degree of internal stability was achieved, Syria and southern and western Asia Minor were lost to the Hittites—who were apparently willing to establish "safe" frontiers.

After the middle of Telipinus' reign, Hittite records cease for about a half century. When the curtain rises again a shadowy figure, Tudhaliyas II, is busy founding a new dynasty in approximately 1460. At about the same time Thutmose III of Egypt was victorious over the Hurrians (Mitanni) and became supreme in Syria. Possibly the Egyptians and Hittites were acting in concert on this occasion. But the Hittites were not destined to reap much benefit from this Hurrian defeat. Around 1400 the Mitanni enjoyed considerable power and brought Hittite power to the verge of collapse.

To Suppiluliumas (1380-1340 B.C.) goes the credit for real establishment of the Hittite Empire. Securing a firm hold on his throne, he proceeded to build the fortifications of Bogazköy. Then he marched off to settle accounts with the Mitanni. Initially repulsed, he was later successful in defeating the Mitanni and taking all of Syria. This was the Amarna Age in Egypt, and Suppiluliumas had nothing to fear from that direction. The great Hittite king also reconquered lands in the south and west

294. The holy of holies of the temple. The statue of the god stood in the stone enclosure at the far end of the room and was flanked by windows that illuminated the image.

that had gained independence during the Hittite period of weakness. A vassal kingdom was set up in Mitanni as protection against the rising power of Assyria, but this proved to be no deterrent to military advance from the east, and soon Assyrians and Hittites were glaring at each other across the Euphrates.

The real enemy of the Hittites lay in the south, however. After a period of preoccupation with internal affairs, the Egyptians under Seti I (Sethos) moved up into Canaan about 1300 B.C. When Ramses II came to the throne approximately a decade later, it became clear that the two powers would soon clash. The Hittite Muwatallis and Ramses met at Kadesh on the Orontes River during 1286/1285. While the Egyptian carved accounts of a great victory there on the temple walls of his homeland, it is quite clear that only by a stroke of good fortune was he kept from annihilation. The Hittites had won at least a partial victory. About fifteen years later, in 1269, a peace pact was concluded between the two powers.

Probably this treaty was a sign of weakness rather than strength. Egyptian power gradually waned during the thirteenth century. Although Hattusilis III (1275-1250)

295. A weathered representation of a King Tudhaliyas carved on the wall of the great outdoor Hittite worship center at Yazilikaya, about two miles from Bogazköy

is open to serious question, but the view has its supporters.[17]

Soon deterioration in the West was accompanied by disaffection in the East. And in the great mass movement of peoples at the eastern end of the Mediterranean world around 1200 B.C., the Hittites were swept from power in Asia Minor and replaced by the Phrygians there. The Hittites themselves fled into Syria where Neo-Hittite kingdoms were to last for no less than five centuries. But these Syrian city-states should be called Hittite only with numerous qualifications. Their script is hieroglyphic rather than cuneiform. Their language is not that of the official records of Bogazköy but is similar to that of the Luwians. Their culture is strongly permeated with Phoenician and Aramaic elements.

If the Hittites' homeland was Asia Minor and if they are not known to have established effective city-states in Syria until the latter part of the second millennium, then it must be asked how this historical evidence may be squared with biblical claims of Hittites in Palestine as early as the days of Abraham. Numerous critics have been quick to assign biblical references to late and inaccurate sources. It does not seem at all necessary to concede to such an allegation, however; and the problems are not all solved even in this fashion.

Let it be remembered that the non-Indo-European peoples who lived in north central Asia Minor before the "Hittites" came were called "Hatti" and spoke a language referred to in the texts as "Hattili." It should be remembered, too, that after the term "Hittite" was used up by historians on the later Indo-European invaders of the area, the "true Hittites" had to be addressed by other terminology. There is nothing to prove that these earlier non-Indo-European Hatti did not live in considerable numbers in Palestine as well as in Asia Minor. The Bible could very easily have reference to

seems in general to have enjoyed peace and prosperity, there is evidence that he had to march against his enemies to the west and that relations with Babylonia were deteriorating. For him to have allowed a worsening of relations with Egypt as well might have been suicidal.

During the reign of his son and successor Tudhaliyas IV (1250-1220 B.C.), the land of Assuwa (largely corresponding with the later Roman province of Asia) was incorporated into the Hittite Empire. But by the end of Tudhaliyas' reign, clouds began to gather on the western horizon. A certain king of Ahhiyawa was one of the Hittite enemies there. Whether or not the name of this enemy principality is to be equated with "Achaean" and to imply that the Greeks were active in the East at that time

[17]For a discussion of the issues involved, see Gurney, pp. 46-58.

these earlier peoples. After all, Heth is classified as a son of Canaan (Gen. 10:15), who was not an Indo-European.

Hittite culture. At the head of the Hittite state stood the king, who was commander-in-chief of the army, supreme judge, and chief priest. While he might delegate his judicial responsibilities, he was expected to perform his other duties in person. There are instances when the king had to leave the front during an important campaign to return home to conduct religious ceremonies. The king was never deified during his lifetime, but there was a cult of the spirits of former kings; and it was said that at his death "he became a god."

The king was advised by a council (which consisted of nobles at least during the later period). A popular assembly (consisting of all warriors) had power to ratify succession to the throne. As the king's power increased, the petty kings of the old feudal political structure were gradually replaced by governors who were members of the royal family.

The social classes were the high-ranking nobles, a middle class of warriors, farmers, and artisans, and a lower class of serfs and slaves. While the base of the economy was agricultural, the exploitation of metals was very important among the Hittites. Copper, lead, silver, and especially iron were among the chief metals worked. The Hittite law code bears striking similarities to Hammurabi's code, even being set up on a case system (e.g., "If a man . . ., then . . . would be his punishment"). But while the Babylonian code stressed retaliation by way of punishment, the Hittite code stressed compensation for the one wronged.

Hittite cities were stone-walled. The most imposing was Hattusas (Bogazköy) the capital, which covered 300 acres. The principal subjects of their stone sculpture, both in the round and in bas-relief, were kings, gods, and other religious representations and warriors. Religious and magical rather than artistic considerations seem to have prompted the sculpture of their massive monuments. The sun goddess and the weather god and his consort were chief among the deities. The cultural indebtedness of the Hittites to the Hurrians and Babylonians was great. From the former they borrowed most of their myths, for instance. From the latter came such things as legal influences and their script.

296. Lion gate, Bogazköy

ASIA MINOR

Phrygians and Lydians

With the collapse of the Hittite Empire not long after 1200 B.C.,[18] Asia Minor entered a dark age about which little is known. This period has commonly been called "Phrygian," a term which many have doubted because they do not find evidence of Phrygian pottery in Asia Minor before about 800 B.C. On the basis of new evidence, however, Goetze believes the Phrygian period there began around 1000 B.C.[19] Eventually the Phrygians, who apparently came from Thrace, seem to have extended their power over nearly all of Asia Minor, refortifying many old Hittite sites. An Assyrian account tells how Tiglath-pileser I (c. 1100 B.C.) routed a "Mushki" army of 20,000 men under five kings which invaded northern Mesopotamia.[20] The Mushki are commonly identified as Phrygians. Some think they may have been natives who joined the Phrygians against the Hittites.

The Phrygians established their capital at

297. A procession of gods at Yazilikaya

[18]Perhaps new evidence will force a lowering of the date of Hittite collapse. Excavations at Bogazköy in 1961 demonstrated that the Hittite Empire was still intact in the early twelfth century B.C. and that the Hittites at that time had command of ships in the eastern Mediterranean. One thousand new tablets were found in the 1961 dig. See Machteld J. Mellink, "Archaeology in Asia Minor," *American Journal of Archaeology,* 67 (Apr., 1963), 176.
[19]Albrecht Goetze, "Hittite and Anatolian Studies," *The Bible and the Ancient Near East,* ed. G. Ernest Wright (Garden City: Doubleday & Co., Inc., 1961), p. 322.
[20]Lloyd, p. 191.

Gordium, fifty-five miles southwest of Ankara, and a second center of power at Yazilikaya about seventy-five miles farther southwest. At the latter, also known as "Midas City," M. A. Gabriel led a French Institute of Archaeology of Istanbul excavation. Occupied from early times, the town had a Phrygian settlement going back to the eighth century B.C. This was destroyed in the sixth century and rebuilt during the fifth or early fourth. The second town lasted to the end of the second century A.D. The upper town or acropolis of "Midas City" measured about 600 yards long and 200 yards wide, while a lower town stretched to the north at the foot of the acropolis. On a hillside to the northwest of the acropolis stood the famous "Tomb of Midas," which was not a tomb at all but a votive monument. Near this structure, which has many inscriptions on it and which honors the mother goddess Cybele, mythical mother of King Midas, was an iron foundry. In the surrounding hills are numerous rock-cut tombs.

Gordium, the Phrygian capital, was excavated by the University of Pennsylvania Museum beginning in 1950. Occupied from the third millennium, it became in the second millennium a Hittite stronghold and was subsequently conquered by Phrygians. The city suffered some destruction when Alexander the Great passed through in 333 B.C., but it was probably the Gallic hordes in the third century B.C. that ruined the city so that it was only a small village in Roman times. In the temple of Zeus on the acropolis was a chariot which legend said had belonged to the founder of the town. An oracle had said that whoever untied the rope which held together the yoke and shaft of the chariot should be ruler of Asia. As the story goes, Alexander the Great simply sliced the knot in two with his sword.

The most enduring contribution of the Phrygians was their worship of the mother goddess, Cybele, a national deity. The chief male deity was her lover-son Attis. Al-

298. The Hittite god Sharma holding King Tudhaliyas IV in his embrace, Yazilikaya

though the Greeks and Romans looked upon her as the mother of the gods, Cybele was for the Phrygians an earth mother, symbol of the union of man, nature, and deity in a single divine life that triumphed over death. Cybele offered no moral teaching to her devotees, but she did extend to them the hope of joining her after death. Her cult spread among the Greek cities because of its affinities with other mystery religions, and Cybele worship had something to do with the rise of Orphism, which spread the idea of immortality among the Greeks.

Shortly before 700 B.C. the Cimmerians poured in from the north and east. A barbarous people whom even the cruel Assyrians called "creatures of hell," the Cimmerians inflicted terrible suffering on the Urartians (northeast of Asia Minor) and then turned on the Phrygians, depriving them of their possessions in eastern Asia Minor. The contemporary King Midas committed suicide. Sargon II of Assyria lost his life fighting the Cimmerians in 705. Early in the seventh century (c. 680) a second Cimmerian invasion finished off the Phrygian kingdom and did away with the last King Midas, the man famous in Greek legend for turning all that he touched into gold.

Lydia, previously a Phrygian dependency, now successfully bore the brunt of the Cimmerian attack and in so doing gained national strength and unity and replaced the weakened Phrygians as the dominant political power in western Asia Minor. For a while, however, there continued to be Phrygian princes at Gordium, and Phrygian culture survived side by side with that of Lydia. But the race of great warriors had become docile subjects and were known to later Greeks as flute players, authors of elegy, and a source of slaves. Aesop was one of these Phrygian slaves. After the fall of Phrygia, the history of central and eastern Asia Minor was always overshadowed or determined by history being made in the west.

This study will return to the Lydians shortly, but to keep the story of Asia Minor in sequence, it is necessary to pause for a moment to notice the Greek immigration. During the Greek Middle Age (1150/1100-800 B.C.), a considerable number of Greeks sailed across the Aegean to the Asia Minor coast and adjacent islands. Greek settlement on Lesbos was no later than 1000 B.C.[21] The Aeolic settlement at Smyrna goes back to about the same time,[22] and Aeolians settled in the Troad at least as early as the eighth century.[23] The Ionian migration to the east central coast of the Aegean and adjacent islands to form ulti-

[21]J. M. Cook, *Greek Settlement in the Eastern Aegean and Asia Minor* (Cambridge: At the University Press, 1961; a fascicle revision of *Cambridge Ancient History*), p. 6.
[22]*Ibid.*, p. 7.
[23]*Ibid.*, p. 9.

299. Lydian walls at Sardis

mately the twelve cities of the Panionic League (including Samos, Chios, Miletus, Ephesus, Colophon, etc.) must also go back to 1000 B.C.[24] Rhodes and Cos were, of course, occupied by Mycenaeans; but Dorian occupation there dates at least as early as 900 B.C.[25] Dorian settlements on the Carian coast at such places as Cnidus and Halicarnassus can be traced at least to the eighth century.[26] Subsequently Greek colonies were planted along the south coast of the Black Sea and at a few places along the Mediterranean coast.

Gyges was the first Lydian king to fight the Cimmerians, but he died in the struggle. Chronological synchronisms indicate that his reign dated between 675 and 650. His successors (Ardys, Sadyattes, Alyattes) managed to overcome many of the Greek city-states along the Asia Minor coast and to expand eastward. Lydian expansion eastward was stopped, however, at the Halys River by the Medes in 585. Subsequently a daughter of Alyattes was married to Astyages, heir to the Median throne. Under Alyattes' son Croesus, who ascended the throne about 560 B.C., the Lydian kingdom reached its height. Croesus was fabulous for his wealth, partly because of the gold washed down by the Pactolus River (modern Baguli), but especially because of the

[24]*Ibid.*, p. 13.
[25]*Ibid.*, p. 19.
[26]*Ibid.*, p. 20.

skill of Lydian artisans and traders and because the great trade route from Assyria to the Aegean crossed his territory. The Lydians are given credit for originating the coinage of money.

The Lydian kings became rather enamored with Greek culture. Alyattes took an Ionian wife, presented two temples to Miletus, and gave gifts to the Delphic oracle. Croesus made rich gifts to all the well-known Greek oracles, contributed heavily to the rebuilding of the temple of Artemis at Ephesus, which the Cimmerians had destroyed, and at his capital, Sardis, maintained a brilliant and cosmopolitan court where Greeks were welcomed.

When Cyrus the Persian began his revolt against his Median overlords, Croesus was duty bound to come to the aid of his Median brother-in-law. In the ensuing struggle, Croesus lost his throne, and the Lydian kingdom came to an end in 546. But Sardis survived its royal master and remained a great city during the Persian, Hellenistic, and Roman periods.

The Persian Period

It is beyond the present purpose to discuss Persian history, but there are two events during the Persian period that are significant for Asia Minor. The first is the Ionian revolt and its aftermath. One of the causes of this struggle was that the Greeks discovered the Persians to be much less philhellenic than the Lydians and much more exacting taskmasters. Moreover, Persian advance in Thrace had scared the Athenians. The uprising began about 499 at Miletus, soon spread to the other Greek towns of the Asia Minor coast, and was supported by Athens and Eretria. Initially the revolutionaries had success and attacked the Persian administrative center of Sardis, sacking and burning it. But ultimately they lost, partly because of Athenian defection. Miletus was leveled by the Persians for her part in the fiasco.

The Persians became more severe than ever with the Greek cities and determined to punish Athens and Eretria. A force sent in 490 B.C. was defeated at Marathon. Before Darius the Great could mount another attack, he died; and it was ten years before Xerxes could try again. He made Sardis his headquarters; and after collecting a huge army and fleet, attacked through northern Greece, carrying the pass at Thermopylae and marching into central Greece. Athens was evacuated.

The Greeks won a signal naval victory at Salamis, however, and in the spring of 479 B.C. they were victorious in a land battle at Plataea. Traditionally, on the same day another great Greek naval victory was won off Mycale. Greek states along the eastern shore of the Aegean were freed from Persia. The Delian League of Greek states organized for war against Persia was gradually transformed into an Athenian empire. Virtually the whole eastern coast of Asia Minor, as well as adjacent islands, was part of the empire.

The second event of significance for Asia Minor history to occur during the Persian period was the revolt of Cyrus the Younger. After the Peloponnesian War was over, Cyrus planned a revolt against his brother Artaxerxes II. At his provincial capital, Sardis, Cyrus collected troops, supposedly to put down tribes in Asia Minor not loyal to Persia. More than 10,000 Greek mercenaries were in the army. In 401 they marched across Asia Minor, through the Cilician Gates, and across northern Syria to the Euphrates and then south toward Babylon. At Cunaxa they defeated Artaxerxes; but Cyrus was killed and the revolt collapsed. After the Greek generals were killed by treachery, Xenophon was chosen to lead the force, which fought its way north to Trapezus (Trabzon) on the Black Sea coast.

During the Peloponnesian War (between Athens and Sparta, 431-404 B.C.), Persia had frequently interfered in Greek affairs. Thus she regained control of the Greek cities of the Asia Minor coast in 386, as a result of the selfish diplomacy of Sparta. But this Persian interference merely kindled greater hatred of the Persians among the Greeks and prepared the way for the Panhellenic war of revenge which Alexander the Great was to initiate in 334 B.C.

Alexander and His Successors

In the spring of that year, Alexander crossed the Hellespont with a force of 34,500. Alexander himself first disembarked near Troy at a spot where tradition said Achilles had landed many centuries earlier. Throwing a spear from his boat to the shore as a token that the land was his by right of conquest, he subsequently made offerings to the great Homeric dead and then joined the main army and advanced against the Persians. The defenders prepared to meet Alexander at the Granicus River in Mysia. Largely a cavalry melee, the battle ended that May sunset with the highways of Asia Minor clear for the invader.

Alexander now marched south to Sardis, the Persian headquarters west of the Taurus; and that strong city surrendered without a blow. Presently in all the Greek cities of the northwestern and central western Asia Minor coast the oligarchies or tyrants friendly to Persia fell and democracies were established in their place. At Ephesus there was an unsavory massacre of the oligarchs. Miletus required a siege. Alexander then ordered the rebuilding of Smyrna, which the Persians had destroyed more than 150 years before. At Halicarnassus the Persians offered determined resistance; the citadel did not fall until the spring of 333.

Meanwhile Alexander's forces occupied the ports of Lycia and Pamphylia and moved into central Asia Minor to establish winter quarters. At Gordium, the old Phrygian capital, he cut the Gordian knot. By the time he left Gordium for the campaign of 333, he had determined to destroy the Persian navy—by occupying the Syrian and Egyptian coasts and depriving the navy of its bases. Alexander made it through the Cilician Gates before the Persians could organize an adequate defense. While Alexander lay violently ill of fever at Tarsus, the Persian army waited for him not far away under the command of Darius himself. In October the Macedonian met Darius on the Plain of Issus at the head of the gulf of the same name. The Persian fled eastward, leaving the door to Syria and Egypt ajar. Alexander elected to follow his previously worked-out plan rather than pursue the enemy. Many of Darius' troops retreated northward to Cappadocia where they posed a continuing threat to Alexander's supply lines.

The rest of the story of Alexander's victories and problems is beyond the scope of a study of Asia Minor. Suffice it to say that he died in Babylon on June 13, 323 B.C. The contest among his generals for his legacy, however, is very much a concern of Asia Minor history. Unfortunately the story of Alexander's successors (the Diadochi) is a very confusing one to follow.

Alexander gave his seal to Perdiccas, who assigned a number of Greek satraps to provinces: Antigonus to Phrygia (where he had ruled since Issus); Ptolemy to Egypt; Eumenes to Cappadocia, Pontus, and Paphlagonia; Lysimachus to Thrace (he later acquired much of Asia Minor); Seleucus to Babylonia (he eventually ruled nearly all Asiatic provinces). When in 306 Antigonus took the title of king, the others quickly did likewise.

At Ipsus in west central Asia Minor in 301, Antigonus was killed by his rivals and Alexander's empire divided four ways. Cassander got Macedonia and Greece; Lysimachus, Thrace and much of Asia Minor;

Ptolemy received Egypt, Cyrenaica, and Palestine; Seleucus got the rest. This arrangement did not stick. In 281 Seleucus defeated Lysimachus and took most of Asia Minor; in 276 Antigonus' grandson, Antigonus Gonatas, became king of Macedon, and his line retained control there for over a century.

Finding themselves in possession of a vast and heterogeneous empire, the Seleucids usually followed the old Persian practices of government. They preserved the old division into more than thirty satrapies, and the satraps enjoyed considerable independence. Moreover, many Persian nobles retained their old estates, and huge temple estates remained intact. In Asia Minor the latter were almost independent countries ruled by Oriental priests. The Seleucids, especially Seleucus I and his son Antiochus I, were active in founding cities. Some were military outposts, and others were designed to act as missionary centers for the spread of the gospel of Hellenism and to act as bonds for cementing the vast heterogeneous empire. In this founding or refounding of cities, Greeks and Jews were usually imported. Many of the cities so established were later centers of Christian missionary activity and are described later in this study.

The Seleucids never did control all of Asia Minor, and they had a remarkable facility for losing what they did have. Seleucus I did not make good his claim to Bithynia, Pontus, and Cappadocia, most of which Alexander had not conquered. Then, soon after the death of Seleucus, the Gauls or Celts invaded Asia Minor from Thrace (278-277 B.C.). Antiochus I (280-261) defeated them near Sardis two years later, and they subsequently located in north Phrygia. In the midst of the confusion brought on by the Celtic invasion and the struggle between Lysimachus and Seleucus I (306-280), Philetaeros set himself up as an independent ruler at Pergamum and founded the Attalid dynasty there. The Pergamenes controlled much of northwest Asia Minor during the third century B.C. and after 190 much of the southwestern part as well. Antiochus I also lost parts of southern and western Asia Minor to Ptolemy II. Although the Seleucids asserted control over part of Cappadocia and Pontus under Antiochus III (223-187), that recovery was ephemeral.

Roman Interference and Control

Antiochus III, still dreaming of reviving Alexander's world empire, had regained lost Seleucid ground in the east, virtually annexed Egypt by marrying his daughter to the king of Egypt, and now turned his attention to Asia Minor. Soon after Philip V of Macedon met defeat at the hands of the Romans in 197 (and was therefore no threat to Syria in the west), Antiochus began to occupy Asia Minor cities held by Egypt. He established his headquarters at Ephesus and laid plans for an attack on Pergamum. Eumenes II of Pergamum decided to seek aid from Rome and never let Rome forget the East. A further complication arose from the arrival of Hannibal at Ephesus in 195. He had escaped from Carthage when his political opponents stirred up Roman suspicion against him there, and he now began to urge Antiochus to take action against Rome. Antiochus was further encouraged to aggression against Rome by the Aetolian League in Greece which urged him to free Greece from Roman oppression.

In 192 Antiochus invaded Thrace and the following year attempted an invasion of Greece. Defeated at Thermopylae, he fled to Ephesus, leaving his army to take care of itself. During 190 the Romans destroyed the Seleucid fleet which Hannibal, a great general but no admiral, had been given to command. Early in January of 189 the Romans and Pergamenes advanced upon

300. Bas-relief from Temple of Artemis at Magnesia, second century B.C., depicting the legendary contest between Greeks and Amazons

301. The Asclepion, or health center, at
Pergamum

Antiochus at Ephesus and defeated him in a fierce battle at Magnesia, southeast of Ephesus on the Maeander River. The Romans spent the summer in a campaign against the Galatians during which they extended their power over most of Asia Minor west of the Taurus Mountains.

According to the peace made in 188 B.C., Antiochus surrendered all Asia Minor west of the Taurus Mountains and Halys River to the Romans; but he kept Cilicia, which he had recently taken from the Ptolemies. He also agreed to pay an indemnity. Rome then handed most of Asia Minor over to Pergamum. Caria and Lycia went to Rhodes, and several Greek cities in Ionia and on the Hellespont were set free.

Eumenes II of Pergamum (197-160 B.C.) was an intelligent and forceful leader who brought his kingdom to the height of her glory. He chose to follow a program of Greek solidarity, according to which he married Stratonice, daughter of Ariarathes IV of Cappadocia (partly Oriental), whom he regarded as a Greek ruling over Asiatics. Another partly Oriental Greek, the king of Bithynia, joined an alliance with Pergamum and Cappadocia. The three in concert defeated the Oriental Pharnaces of Pontus. Eumenes also curried favor with the Achaean League in Greece.

During the latter stages of the Third Macedonian War (172-168 B.C.) Pergamum

and Rhodes aroused Roman suspicion by their intrigues with Macedon. Rome transferred the Galatian territories of Eumenes to a native king and punished Rhodes by taking away Caria and Lycia and by giving Delos to Athens. Rhodian greatness soon declined and was forever gone; and the island kingdom lost the power to suppress piracy in the eastern Mediterranean, a fact which Rome was later to regret. Roman friendship with Pergamum was not permanently destroyed; it was renewed in the days of Attalus II (160-138).

In 133 B.C. Attalus III of Pergamum died leaving no direct heir and having willed his kingdom to the Romans. At this point there was a change in the Roman policy of creating in Asia Minor numerous weak and autonomous states dependent on Rome. Rome turned to annexation, constituting the new territories as Roman provinces. Asia, the first of these provinces, was the old kingdom of Pergamum, virtually as it had come to hand. In spite of the fact that Rome had inherited Asia, it did not come peaceably under Roman control. Aristonicus, who claimed to be a natural son of the king, stirred up a revolt which lasted for three years before combined forces of Rome, the Greek cities, and the kings of Bithynia, Pontus, and Cappadocia could quell it. The pretender's main support seems to have come from the lower classes, predominantly nonurban and non-Greek.

At the end of the revolt, Rome made a settlement which at the same time rewarded the kings who helped her subdue the uprising and which freed her from administrating relatively unsettled areas. Cappadocia received part of Cilicia and perhaps Lycaonia too. Pontus obtained Greater Phrygia (which was soon retracted), and Bithynia apparently got part of Phrygia. The prosperity of Asia was greatly affected by Roman unwillingness to continue the commercial and industrial enterprises of the Attalids and the decision to delegate the taxes of Asia to the Roman knights on five-year terms.

The next event or series of events of significance in Asia Minor history were the Mithridatic wars. Mithridates IV Philopater Philadelphus of Pontus (170-150 B.C.) had formed an alliance with Rome. This was renewed under his successor Mithridates V Euergetes (150-121). Soon after he ascended the throne, he sent warships and a force of soldiers to aid Rome in the Third Carthaginian War. In 133 he responded quickly to the Senate's request for help against the Pergamene claimant Aristonicus. As noted above, this was rewarded by a gift of a district of Phrygia. But later some in Rome had second thoughts about the loss of Phrygian revenue, and Mithridates V lost favor in Rome over an alleged attempt to purchase support among the voters for some favor he wished to obtain.

When Mithridates V was assassinated and left his kingdom to his wife and two young sons, the elder of whom, Mithridates VI, was about eleven, some in Rome thought this was a good time to take back Phrygia. This act aroused the resentment of the young king toward Rome. When Mithridates was about twenty, he began to form a plan for building an empire that would include all of Asia Minor. At this point Greeks of the Crimea sought his help against the Scythians, and within a few years the Crimea had become part of Mithridates' realm. Soon he took Greek cities on the western shore of the Black Sea as well. Then he expanded eastward taking Lesser Armenia. From the latter he obtained iron and silver, from the former large supplies of grain and army recruits.

In order to enter Asia it was necessary for Mithridates to extend his kingdom westward. Therefore, he allied himself with Nicomedes of Bithynia, and the two of them conquered and divided Paphlagonia. Next Mithridates took the part of Galatia that lay between his kingdom and the border of the province of Asia. Rome was wary of all this advance but was busy with Germanic invaders and only remonstrated with Pontus.

Nicomedes was a remarkable man. He was so huge that men marveled at the size of his armor. He was reputed to be able to ride 120 miles in a day and to drive a chariot drawn by sixteen horses. While he could be ruthless and cruel, his tastes were those of an educated Greek rather than a barbarian. He loved music and art, had power as an orator, and his interest in letters and philosophy led him to invite poets and scholars to his court.[27] Unfortunately he knew no way to govern except through terror and violence and therefore failed to win the support of those whom he professed to rescue from tyranny.

A little before 100 B.C. Mithridates attempted to control Cappadocia and in the process crossed swords with Nicomedes of Bithynia, who had been his ally. Both kings made representation to Rome as supporting the proper ruler for the contested throne of Cappadocia, which was virtually a client kingdom of Rome. Rome disallowed the claims of both. Ariobarzanes, a Cappadocian noble, was approved as the new king. Mithridates sought a new alliance, which he found in the person of Tigranes, king of Greater Armenia, who was pursuing the same course of self-aggrandizement as Mithridates. The Pontic king gave his daughter in marriage to Tigranes.

Mithridates tried to bring Cappadocia under his control no less than five times between 112 and 92 B.C., but each time he was forced by Roman interference to withdraw. Then in 91 B.C. he occupied Bithynia and again yielded to Roman demands to withdraw. However, when Roman commissioners encouraged the king of Bithynia to raid Pontic territory and refused Mithridates any satisfaction, he decided to chal-

[27]David Magie, *Roman Rule in Asia Minor* (Princeton: Princeton University Press, 1950), I, 199.

lenge Rome by force of arms. This decision was reached in part because Rome was involved in civil war in Italy.

Mithridates began the struggle late in 89 B.C. Well prepared, the Pontic king had a highly trained army and a fleet of 300 ships. Speedily he overran Bithynia and most of Asia. There, at his orders, the provincials massacred 80,000 Roman tax gatherers, moneylenders, and others who had been oppressing them. In 88 Athens joined his cause, and most of southern Greece followed suit. But Roman armies under the leadership of Sulla ultimately reversed the tide. The peace of 85 required that Mithridates surrender Cappadocia, Bithynia, and Asia and that he pay an indemnity. His kingdom was left intact. Sulla required such a huge indemnity from the rebellious communities that they were saddled with a crushing burden of debt. So extensive was the devastation effected in Hellas that she never fully recovered from it.

Meanwhile piracy had been growing steadily as Rhodes, Syria, and Egypt grew weaker. Moreover, the severity of the Mithridatic wars had driven masses of men of Syrian, Cyprian, and Asia Minor origin into piratical activities. The financial exactions of Sulla greatly aggravated the situation. The pirates made common cause with Mithridates, under whose patronage their operations expanded enormously. Their power eventually made the Mediterranean unnavigable. Rome's efforts to destroy them were ineffectual until Pompey's complete victory.

The Second Mithridatic War (83-81 B.C.) really consisted of a series of raids. Murena, a Roman general left in Asia with two legions, made three sorties into Pontus. During the first two he carried off great plunder and was unopposed by Mithridates who made representations to Rome. When the third raid occurred, Mithridates lost his patience and soundly defeated Murena, devastating much of Cappadocia in the proc-

ess. Rome now agreed to abide by the peace treaty. Meanwhile, by 83, Tigranes had occupied Syria (putting an end to the Seleucid house) and Cilicia and deported hundreds of thousands of people from Cappadocia (which he annexed) to Armenia.

When Nicomedes III of Bithynia died in 74 B.C., he bequeathed his kingdom to Rome. But Mithridates championed the claims of a son of Nicomedes and invaded Bithynia, occupying nearly the entire province. In 73 the Roman Lucullus defeated Mithridates' Aegean fleet and the following year routed his land forces and chased him into exile in Armenia. When Tigranes refused to surrender his father-in-law, Lucullus invaded Armenia. But his troops mutinied because of his strict discipline and because the terms of enlistment of many had expired. At this point Mithridates returned to his kingdom and raised another force while Tigranes made a recovery.

Meanwhile Pompey had been given an extraordinary command to destroy the pirate scourge (67 B.C.) which he succeeded in doing in three months. His victory was more sure because of the mildness he showed to those who submitted, many of whom he used as colonists to revive Mediterranean towns with a declining population. The following year the provinces of Bithynia and Cilicia (which Pompey organized after the victory over the pirates) were transferred to Pompey, along with the conduct of the war against Mithridates and Tigranes. Pompey soon defeated Mithridates who, failing to find refuge with Tigranes this time, sailed for his dependencies north of the Black Sea where his war-weary people revolted and he committed suicide. Tigranes came to terms with Pompey.

Thus the Mithridatic wars came to a close, with Pontus annexed as a Roman province. It is estimated that human casualties during the first war came to a total of 300,000 and during the third war 120,000 on the Pontic side alone.[28] While destruction during the first war occurred over a large area, such damage was restricted during the third war to Bithynia and Pontus.

Pompey's settlement, then, included the annexation of Cilicia and Pontus, which became linked with Bithynia for administrative purposes. Settlement involved as well the confirmation of Tigranes on his throne and the restoration of Ariobarzanes to his throne in Cappadocia (along with a considerable loan for the restoration of his kingdom) and the confirmation of Deiotarus of Galatia in his ancestral kingdom. In addition, several petty dynasts were given or permitted to hold slices of real estate in central Asia Minor. Pompey also endeavored to revive the cities of Asia Minor, drawing up municipal charters which were still operative in the early second century A.D.

Few changes occurred in Asia Minor between 63 B.C. and the outbreak of civil war in 49. The most important was the annexation in 58 of Cyprus, which was joined to the province of Cilicia.

Asia Minor suffered much at the hands of Rome during the Republic. The publicans exacted all they could, not so much through graft connected with tax collecting as through interest collections. The requisitions and fines levied by Pompey and Caesar were heavy, but not nearly so devastating as those exacted by Brutus and Cassius who, armed with senatorial authority to collect the regular revenues, ordered (as a loan) anything else they needed. From Asia they demanded the tribute of ten years to be paid in two. Cassius' demand of 1500 talents from Tarsus, which had favored Caesar, virtually bankrupted the city. Rhodes never recovered from Cassius' collection of 8500 talents there.

Antony's exactions must have reduced most of Asia Minor to the last extremity, but at least he did reward the towns that

[28]T. R. S. Broughton, "Roman Asia," *An Economic Survey of Ancient Rome,* ed. Tenney Frank (Baltimore: Johns Hopkins Press, 1938), IV, 516, 529.

had resisted Brutus and Cassius: Rhodes, Lycia, and Tarsus. To pay his soldiers, he demanded from Asia ten years' tribute in one; but his victims begged him to change his demands to nine years' tribute in two. The client kings seem to have become tributary at this time. What additional burdens fell upon the unhappy peninsula as a result of the Parthian invasion, Antony's Parthian campaign of 36, his Median campaign of 34, and his preparations for the Battle of Actium is not now fully known. These burdens left the client kingdoms and the provinces of the East bare of capital. Octavian found it necessary to cancel all public debts in the provinces of Asia Minor. Under the long period of peace during the first and second centuries, Asia Minor regained her prosperity, some areas enjoying the greatest prosperity they had ever known.

The first major political change in Asia Minor under the Empire came in 25 B.C. when King Amyntas of Galatia died and willed his kingdom to Rome. Augustus decided to annex the territory as the province of Galatia. At that time it included Galatia proper, Pisidia, Isauria, Pamphylia, and parts of Phrygia, Lycaonia, and Cilicia. Several minor shifts of territory, too detailed to consider here, also occurred during Augustus' reign. During the years 6 B.C.-A.D. 2 several small sections of Paphlagonia and Pontus were attached to the northern part of the province of Galatia. Under Tiberius in A.D. 17 Cappadocia was annexed when its king Archelaus died. This left the kingdom of Polemon in eastern Pontus, which was added to Galatia under Nero in A.D. 64. The Lycian League, which Augustus had permitted to remain independent, was annexed by Claudius in A.D. 43 and united to Pamphylia, which was withdrawn from the province of Galatia. Although Caligula (Gaius Caesar, 37-41) reverted in part to reliance upon client kingdoms in Asia Minor, the practice of annexation was resumed under Claudius (41-54). Rome made numerous other shifts of territory during the first century A.D. Most of these need not be considered to obtain a proper understanding of New Testament times. Some that are necessary for such an understanding are discussed at the proper time later in this study.

The Apostle Paul in Asia Minor

Paul's Hometown

After the howling mob had brought about Paul's arrest in Jerusalem, he tried to establish himself with the Roman chiliarch[29] with the proud boast "I am . . . a Jew of Tarsus in Cilicia, a citizen of no mean city" (Acts 21:39). The allegation won him the respect of the chiliarch and the right to address his attackers; Tarsus was one of the great cities of Asia Minor during the first century A.D. But Tarsus was a city in Cilicia; and in order to gain proper understanding of the city, it is necessary first to consider its environs.

Cilicia. Geographically "Cilicia" referred to the area of southeastern Asia Minor between Pamphylia on the west, the Amanus Mountains on the east, Lycaonia and Cappadocia on the north, and the Mediterranean on the south. It had a coastline of about 430 miles, extending from the eastern boundary of Pamphylia to the southern end of the Gulf of Issus. Roughly it was co-extensive with the modern Turkish vilayet of Adana. Politically (in Paul's day at least) Cilicia designated the Roman province which encompassed the eastern part of the geographical area. When Luke spoke of the "sea of Cilicia" (Acts 27:5), he probably had in mind the Mediterranean opposite the entire geographical region. Since Paul used Roman political terminology, he must have applied Cilicia to the Roman province only (e.g., Acts 21:39; 22:3).

Cilicia Tracheia. Cilicia was commonly divided into two territories almost as dissimilar in their physical characteristics as they could be. The western part, Cilicia Tracheia, was a tangled mass of mountains descending abruptly to the sea, with a narrow tract of land along the coast and little or no plain country. The shoreline presented to the sea a convex outline. The mountains of Tracheia were valuable only for their timber (chiefly cedar), and this rugged terrain succeeded effectively in cutting off the inhabitants from much peaceful contact with the rest of the world. The main line of communication skirted the northern edge of the mountains of Tracheia.

In this area a primitive tribal life characterized the interior, while a few small towns existed along the coast as ports of call for coastal trade and depots from which timber could be exported. Other than for its timber resources, Tracheia was of little consequence from prehistoric to Roman times except as a haven for pirates. When the depredations of the eastern Mediterranean pirates became intolerable to the Romans, they assigned to Pompey the task of wiping them out in 67 B.C. That he was successful in Cilicia Tracheia, as elsewhere, is certain; but we do not know what internal arrangements he made in the area.

Tracheia again appears on the stage of history in Mark Antony's days. Part of the territory he granted to Cleopatra as a source of ship timber; members of the Teucrid family continued to rule the rest as client kings. When, after the Battle of Actium, Cleopatra lost control of her lands there, Octavian granted part of Tracheia to Amyntas of Galatia and confirmed the

---

[29]A chiliarch was an officer in charge of 1,000 men, one sixth of a legion at full strength.

Teucrid house in the rest of it. When Amyntas died, the western part of his Cilician domain became part of the province of Galatia. The rest was given to Archelaus of Cappadocia and subsequently passed to his son and in A.D. 38 was granted to Antiochus IV of Commagene who ruled until A.D. 72. Thus, when Paul went north from Tarsus, through the Cilician Gates, and struck out west for Derbe on his second and third missionary journeys, he passed through the northern part of the domains of this client king.

Cilicia Pedias. The eastern part of Cilicia was known as "Cilicia Pedias." Roughly speaking this area was triangular in shape, its apex at the northeast formed by the Amanus and Taurus Mountains. The former ran due south and separated Cilicia from Syria; the latter ran southwest to the sea, cutting off the region from Cappadocia and Lycaonia. The third side of the triangle was the Mediterranean. Three rivers watered Pedias and flowed in a southwesterly direction. On each river a city developed. In the east Mallus rose on the Pyramus (modern Ceyhan); in the center Adana on the Sarus (Seyhan); and in the west Tarsus on the Cydnus. These rivers have changed their courses several times. During the first Christian century they followed much different routes than they now do. In Paul's day the Sarus apparently did not flow into the sea but into a large lagoon. The mouth of the Pyramus was about fifteen miles east of the Sarus, and the Cydnus about nine miles west of the Sarus.[30] While Cilicia Pedias is often called a plain, it actually is not all one plain. In the east the Plain of Issus, where Alexander fought his great battle in 333 B.C., is only a narrow strip around the Gulf of Issus, except at the head of the gulf where it extends eight to ten miles inland. There was also a plain which was coextensive with the upper val-

[30]William M. Ramsay, *The Cities of St. Paul* (London: Hodder and Stoughton, n.d.), p. 100.

302. The Cilician Gates

ley of the Pyramus. But the main plain was the lower valley of the three rivers. This region now contains about 800 square miles of arable land with a strip of dunes and lagoons some two to three miles wide along the coast.

Cilicia Pedias had much in its favor from a geographical standpoint. Its land was fertile and grew cereals of all kinds, and its flax made possible a thriving linen industry. Timber from the nearby mountains moved through Cilician ports. Goats living on the slopes of the Taurus, where snow lies until May, grew magnificent coats used in the famous tentmaking industry of the area. It will be remembered that Paul followed this trade (Acts 18:3). The fact that Pedias was located on one of the great trade routes of the ancient world, the most frequented land route from the East to the Aegean, promoted commerce and industry and contributed to the growth of towns. The trade route coming from the Euphrates over the Amanus Pass and another trade route coming from Antioch in Syria via the Syrian Gates met about fifty miles east of Tarsus, entered the city as a single road, swung north through the Cilician Gates, and led across south central Asia Minor to Ephesus.

About thirty miles north of Tarsus were the Cilician Gates, a narrow gorge which originally was just wide enough to allow passage of the small stream that ran through it. With much effort the Tarsians in early times widened the gorge and built a wagon road up to its approaches and through it. When they did this is uncertain. The route was well known when Xenophon came through in 401 B.C., and the work must actually have been done centuries earlier, perhaps as early as 1000 B.C. At any rate, their industry had put the Tarsians in possession of the one wagon road across the Taurus Mountains. At the Gates (which are about 100 yards in length) the rocks rise steeply on both sides to a height of 500 to 600 feet and the roadbed itself ascends directly to the broad, bare summit of the Taurus Range, here 4300 feet in altitude. With their engineering skill the Romans in imperial times improved on the work that the men of Tarsus had done earlier.

According to tradition the earliest Cilicians were of the same stock as the Phoenicians. They were dominated by the Egyptians and the Hittites and probably were invaded by Aegean peoples in the disturbed period of the twelfth and eleventh centuries. These people were seemingly reinforced by other Greeks in later centuries. During the period of Assyrian control, while Sargon II was on the throne, the area suffered from Phrygian ravages. With the demise of the Assyrian Empire, Cilicia

won her independence and maintained a considerable degree of autonomy under the early Persians. Apparently they won their freedom once more during the latter days of the Persian Empire.

Alexander controlled the area, and after his death the region became debatable ground between the Ptolemies and the Seleucids. Although the Seleucids won out, they did not maintain effective control for long. By the middle of the second century most of the important towns of Cilicia Pedias had won local autonomy and issued a municipal coinage. During the latter part of the second century the Seleucid kingdom was reduced to anarchy. And with the breakdown of Rhodian sea power the Cilician cities suffered greatly at the hands of their piratical neighbors.

At last the pirate menace became so serious that in 102 B.C. Rome organized the province of Cilicia to deal with it. This was merely a chain of coast guard stations along the mountain rim of Asia Minor, and Jones does not think it actually included Cilicia itself.[31] But after Pompey crushed the pirate scourge in 67 B.C., he did organize Cilicia Pedias as a Roman province. At the time he showed great statesmanship, recognizing that much of the piracy of the area was caused by serious economic disorder. Therefore he sought to bring about improved conditions and refounded many towns, in which he settled many of the more respectable of the pirate captives. He organized coastal Cilicia as a group of city-states and recognized a client king in the interior.

Several of the cities of the plain won status as free cities during the civil wars. For instance, Tarsus was freed by Antony and Aegae by Julius Caesar. Though exactions of the period of the civil wars were crippling, the cities of Cilicia regained prosperity under the early Roman Empire.

[31]A. H. M. Jones, *The Cities of the Eastern Roman Provinces* (Oxford: At the Clarendon Press, 1937), p. 202.

But unfortunately they, like so many other cities of the East, dissipated their wealth and energy in feuds and rivalries with each other.

Tarsus. Tarsus was located about ten miles from the Mediterranean at eighty feet above sea level. Normally the oppressive atmosphere of such a place would have been most destructive of vigorous municipal or commercial life. But about two miles north of the city the hills began to rise gently and extended in undulating ridges until they met the Taurus. And about ten miles north of the lowland city a second Tarsus rose. Partly a summer residence, it served a considerable population as a year-round home. The more bracing climate of the upland town provided a means of offsetting the enervating climate of the lower region.

In New Testament times Tarsus lay astride the Cydnus River, which was then navigable by light vessels right up into the middle of the city. However, most ships docked at the harbor, which was five to six miles south of the city. At that point was a spring-fed lake, Rhegma, around all but the south sides of which extended the harbor town and the wharf installations. Great skill and diligence must have been expended on maintaining the channel of the Cydnus and the harbor. In later centuries slackness required an auxiliary channel to reduce flooding. The cut to the east of town (made by Justinian, 527-63) in time became the main bed of the river and remains so today. Tarsians were proud of the Cydnus, which normally was clear as it flowed through the city because its bed to the north was gravel. But south of the city, where the soil is deeper, the water became muddy and took on a yellowish hue. Ramsay thinks the population of the three parts of Tarsus (city proper, hill town, and harbor) reached a half million.[32]

303. The falls on the Cydnus above Tarsus

The origins of Tarsus are shrouded in antiquity, but its history goes back at least to Hittite times when the city was a Hittite stronghold. About 1200 B.C., during the general upheaval in the eastern Mediterranean world, Tarsus suffered considerable destruction, as a burned layer in excavations there demonstrates. Subsequently Greeks settled among the older inhabitants. The first historical reference to Tarsus appears on the Black Obelisk of Shalmaneser (c. 850 B.C.) who claimed to have captured the city. Assyrians do not seem to have remained in power in Cilicia long. During the sixth century a line of native kings arose with the name "Syennesis" prominent among them. These kings were powerful enough to take part in aranging a peace treaty between the Medes and the Lydians.

Under the Persian Empire, the kings of Tarsus seem to have maintained a degree of autonomy for more than a century. But after the city supported the revolt of Cyrus the Younger in 401 B.C. (whether by choice or by force is not clear), the Persians took away what freedom Tarsus had enjoyed. Some of the Greek mercenaries on that occasion plundered the city which Xenophon, leader of the Greek armies in the revolt, described as a "great and prosperous city, a joy of heart."[33] When Alexander the

[32]Ramsay, *The Cities of St. Paul*, p. 97.

[33]Xenophon, *Anabasis*, Book I, Chap. ii, Section 21 ff., p. 79 ff.

304. A Roman arch in Tarsus

Cilicia was then recast, and its cities were reinvigorated. New life was breathed into a country which for centuries had been plunged in Orientalism and ruled by despotism. But, of all the cities, Tarsus was treated most honourably. . . . It now stands forth as the principal city of the whole country, with the fullest rights of self-government and coinage permitted to any town in the Seleucid Empire. The Tarsus of St. Paul dates in a very real sense from the refoundation by Antiochus Epiphanes.

Now at last Tarsus had the status of an autonomous city, choosing its own magistrates and making its own laws, though doubtless subject in all foreign relations to the king.[34]

The Seleucids relied mostly on Greeks and Jews to manage the Oriental peasantry and to lead in the urbanization of their realm. The Greek colonists brought to Tarsus in 171 B.C. seem to have come largely from Argos. A considerable number of Jews probably came about the same time. Ramsay argues that the Jews were at settlement granted citizenship with full burgess rights and that the Jews had a tribe set apart for them as at Alexandria, where the Jews were all enrolled in one tribe.[35] In a tribe of their own, Jews could control their religious rites and relate them to the service of the synagogue. Concludes Ramsay: "No Jew could possibly become a member of an ordinary tribe in a Greek city, because he would have been obliged to participate frequently in a pagan ritual, which even the most degraded of Jews would hardly have faced."[36]

As noted above, when the Romans set up the province of Cilicia just before 100 B.C., this section of the Roman Empire apparently did not include Cilicia Pedias—only Tracheia. Tigranes, king of Armenia, held Tarsus from about 83 until Pompey chased him out and reorganized the East in 65-64, making Tarsus the capital of the newly constructed Cilicia in 64. Not much is known

Great came thundering through the Cilician Gates less than a century later, the retreating Persians set fire to the city. But Alexander's advance guard saved it from destruction.

The coming of Alexander did not accomplish much toward the Hellenization of Tarsus. Soon he died. In the struggle for power that ensued among Alexander's generals, Seleucus ultimately won out in Cilicia. For all the Hellenization the Seleucids generally achieved, they were not successful along that line in Tarsus, where they ruled very much according to the old Persian methods. Free city life on the Greek pattern did not develop under the early Seleucids. But conditions changed after 190 B.C. when Rome won the Battle of Magnesia and took away from Antiochus III of Seleucia most of his Asia Minor domains.

Tarsus and other cities of Cilicia now became frontier towns. And the Seleucid kings were forced to pay more attention to their defenses and to give these subjects greater freedom in order to win their loyalty. During the reign of Antiochus IV Epiphanes (175-164), almost all of the towns of Cilicia began to produce coins as self-governing municipalities. They were also more thoroughly Grecized. Tarsus was given the name "Antioch-on-the-Cydnus." Ramsay well summarizes the situation:

[34]Ramsay, The Cities of St. Paul, p. 165.
[35]Ibid., pp. 174-80. A tribe in a Hellenic or Hellenistic city was commonly a political rather than an ethnic entity. In classical Athens there were ten tribes.
[36]Ibid., p. 176.

THE WYCLIFFE HISTORICAL GEOGRAPHY OF BIBLE LANDS

of Tarsus during the Republican period except that it was the scene of Cicero's activities as governor in 51. Julius Caesar paid a brief visit to the city in 47, and from then on its inhabitants were enthusiastically for the Empire. Cassius forced them in 43 to take his and Brutus' side, but the Tarsians returned to their former loyalty at the first opportunity.

Antony rewarded the city by granting it the status of a free city, permitting Tarsus to be governed by its own laws—along with the right to duty-free import and export trade. Here Antony lived for some time; and here he met Cleopatra (38 B.C.), who sailed up the Cydnus in her luxurious galley right into the middle of the city. Augustus renewed Antony's grants to Tarsus after the Battle of Actium (31 B.C.), when he became master of the Roman world. It seems evident that many citizens of Tarsus received Roman citizenship at the hands of Pompey, Julius Caesar, Antony, and Augustus. Paul's ancestors may have been among them.

A tutor of Augustus in his youth was Athenodorus of the Stoic school at Tarsus. The great philosopher followed his former pupil to Rome in 44 B.C. and remained his adviser there until 15 B.C. In that year he returned to Tarsus invested with extraordinary authority to reform the government. Finding the city seriously misgoverned, he sent the ruling clique into exile and revised the constitution. His successor in A.D. 7 was another philosopher, Nestor, who had risen to a position of imperial trust and who had tutored Augustus' nephew Marcellus from 26 to 23 B.C. Nestor must have held the reins of authority in Tarsus for at least another decade.

The reforms carried out at Tarsus by Athenodorus have significant connection with the Pauline narrative. An oligarchic arrangement was instituted in which the power of the people was curtailed and certain property qualifications required for the

exercise of voting rights. Thus, the burgesses of the city, who enjoyed the franchise and held the right of election, were men of some means. Within this oligarchic body was an inner aristocracy consisting of Roman citizens. So then Paul, in claiming to be a citizen of Tarsus and a Roman citizen, was proclaiming to the world that he was a member of the upper aristocracy of the city.

It is significant that after Paul was beaten in Jerusalem his first words (at a time when the things that matter most are expressed) were that he was a Jew, a citizen of Tarsus, which was "no mean city" (Acts 21:39). He did not claim at that point to be a Roman citizen. As noted earlier, Xenophon, four centuries before Christ, was impressed with the greatness of the city. Its coins called it "Loveliest Greatest Metropolis."

During the first century A.D. Tarsus was the one great city of Cilicia (which until A.D. 72 was joined to Syria for administrative purposes). It was a free city with a fine harbor, and it controlled an important trade route and a rich hinterland. The metropolis had been a self-governing city since about 170 B.C. and was one of the three great eastern university cities, ranking with Alexandria and Athens. But in contrast to its two eastern rivals, Tarsus had the great distinction that its students were largely natives; it did not have to draw extensively from the outside for intellectual greatness. The city's fine scholars were numerous.

305. Tarsus, looking toward the Mediterranean. Farmland covers remains of the ancient city.

306. An area excavated by Goldman at Tarsus

Athenodorus the Stoic was the companion of Cato the Younger; Athenodorus Cananites was tutor and adviser of Augustus; Nestor taught Marcellus and, reportedly, Tiberius; and Antipater was head of a school in Athens. Thus, Tarsus was a city with great economic and cultural attainments.

Here met East and West, Semite and Hellene. Here was born Saul of Tarsus, probably within ten years of the birth of Christ. It is significant that the Jew who was destined to become the apostle to the Gentiles was born here. And it is questionable whether a Palestinian Jew could so effectively have met the Greek on his own level, quoting his own philosophers and alluding on occasion to his athletic contests. Certainly Paul was influenced by his early environment, yet there is no proof that he ever attended the University of Tarsus. He always emphasized his Jewish background without mentioning Greco-Roman influences upon him.

The glory of ancient Tarsus has departed. But its remains do not lie far below the surface. Roman baths were discovered in the middle of the town while the writer was there. Tarsus has not experienced any extensive excavations, however. Even the location of the university is not known. Hetty Goldman's excavations there in 1937 and following years do not seem to have found anything dating closer than 100 years

to Paul. The beautiful Cydnus no longer flows through the center of the city (population now some 40,000). The harbor of Rhegma has silted up. And miles away in open country, bits of the city wall stand in the cotton fields like old teeth.

Pamphylia. The region of Pamphylia consisted of a plain eighty miles long and twenty miles broad at its widest, lying on the southern coast of Asia Minor between the Taurus Mountains and the Mediterranean. It was bordered on the east by Cilicia and on the west by Lycia. The plain was shut in from northern winds but was well watered by springs from the Taurus ranges.

Very likely Dorians came to Pamphylia at the time of the Dorian migrations and mingled with the aborigines. The region was subject successively to Lydia, Persia, Alexander the Great, the Seleucids, Pergamum, and Rome. Pamphylia does not seem to have benefited greatly from civilizing influences and long remained a rough and rather dangerous area. The port of Side is said to have earned its prosperity as the market of Cilician pirates.

About 102 B.C. Rome established the province of "Cilicia" (merely a series of posts along the Pamphylian coast) to deal with the Mediterranean pirates. When Pompey took Cilicia after his tilt with the pirates (67 B.C.), Pamphylia became part of the province of Cilicia and remained such until 36 B.C. when Antony gave it to Amyntas of Galatia. It was probably not detached from Galatia until A.D. 43 when Claudius took away the freedom of the Lycians and added them to the province of Pamphylia. Under Nero the Lycians were freed, and in 69 Pamphylia and Galatia were put under one governor. Vespasian took the Lycians' freedom and reunited Lycia and Pamphylia. In A.D. 74 the Roman province of Pamphylia was extended to include the mountainous area to the north, properly known as Pisidia. Therefore

THE WYCLIFFE HISTORICAL GEOGRAPHY OF BIBLE LANDS

it will be seen that when Paul traversed Pamphylia, it was part of the combined province Lycia-Pamphylia. Besides Perga, the chief cities of Pamphylia were Attalia (c. 12 miles southwest of the metropolis) and Side (more than thirty miles southeast of Perga).

According to his custom, Paul must have been concerned for the Jews of Pamphylia. That there were some Jews in Pamphylia is demonstrated by the fact that representatives from the province were present in Jerusalem on the day of Pentecost (Acts 2:10). Although introduced by Paul and Barnabas, Christianity was slow in being established there.

The First Missionary Journey

Perga. After Paul and his party embarked at Paphos on Cyprus, they headed for the Asia Minor coast, 180 miles away (Acts 13:13). Sailing up the Cestrus River, they docked at Perga, or rather at its port, five miles from the city. Perga itself lay eight miles inland at a junction of a small stream with the Cestrus and was a very ancient place when the apostolic company arrived.

The founding of the city probably dates back to the beginning of the first millennium B.C., though the story of its establishment is not known. The earliest city was built on the 160-foot-high acropolis. But as Perga grew during the Persian period, it expanded to the south of the acropolis and was a considerable town when Alexander the Great arrived. The Macedonian used Perga as a base for conquest of the interior of Asia Minor. After the conqueror's death and the dismemberment of his empire, the Seleucids took over the area. Set free from the Seleucids in 188, the city became part of the Pergamene kingdom and passed to Rome in 133 B.C.

Perga was an important place during im-perial times. Inscriptions on contemporary coins reveal that it was called the metropolis of Pamphylia. The city minted its own coins over a very long period of time—from the second century B.C. to A.D. 276. It was a great center for the worship of Artemis, which like the Ephesian Artemis (or Diana) was more Asiatic than Greek. In her honor an annual festival was held, and vast crowds assembled. On Pergan coins she was sometimes represented as the Greek Artemis, the huntress, but more often in the Asiatic way as a pillar of stone with the top rounded or carved to represent a head. Where the great temple to Artemis was located at Perga is not yet known with certainty.

Considerable ruins can still be seen at Perga, where Turkish archaeologists have been working since 1955. At the present stage of investigation, it is not possible to determine to any great extent exactly what the city was like in Paul's day. It is known that the walls of the lower city roughly formed a rectangle in Hellenistic times and were probably built by the Seleucids in the third century B.C. These walls were in use during the Roman period and still stand in places to a height of approximately forty feet. They were reinforced with square bastions.

Within this rectangular enclosure a main colonnaded way ran north and south and led up to the acropolis and was intersected by another street running east and west at the foot of the acropolis. In the southern part of the city at the Hellenistic gate and to the east of the colonnaded way, lay the town agora which was square and faced with shops on all four sides. Beyond this one cannot go in describing the town Paul would have known. The ruins within the walls have as yet received little attention.

Roman walls, probably built after Paul's day, were erected to enclose an irregular area south of the Hellenistic town. The triumphal gateway into this enclosure was built in Nero's day, as was the gymnasium on the lower slopes of the acropolis.[37] The semicircular theater, which was built on a slope southwest of the town, held some 12,000 persons. Near it stood the horseshoe-shaped stadium, which was 768 feet long and had a track 111 feet wide. Its seating capacity was about the same as that of the theater. Both of these structures and other ruins of the Roman period probably dated to either the later first or the early second century A.D.[38] It should be noted, however, that theaters built in eastern towns during the Roman period frequently were constructed on the same site as earlier Greek theaters and sometimes merely constituted an enlargement of them.

Pisidia. From Perga Paul desired to go inland to Antioch. In order to do so, he had to pass through Pisidia. This district was about 120 miles long (east-west) and

[37]Broughton, p. 729.
[38]*Ibid.*, p. 784.

fifty miles wide and was entirely filled by ranges of the Taurus. It had always been a wild country infested by brigands. Alexander the Great had had to fight his way through them as he tried to conquer the interior of Asia Minor. Augustus, about 25 B.C., determined to reduce these bandits by establishing a chain of posts which included Antioch and Lystra on the northern side. Apparently the Romans felt they had achieved their aim by A.D. 74 when Pisidia was linked to the Pamphylian plain in the province of Pamphylia. Formerly Pisidia had been treated as part of Galatia.

But the area of Pisidia was still very dangerous when Paul came through on his first missionary journey. It is thought that Paul had the journey through Pisidia in mind when he made his autobiographical comment about "perils of robbers" in II Corinthians 11:26. It is often suggested too that the dangers in further missionary activity to the north of Perga caused John Mark to turn back and for this reason Paul refused

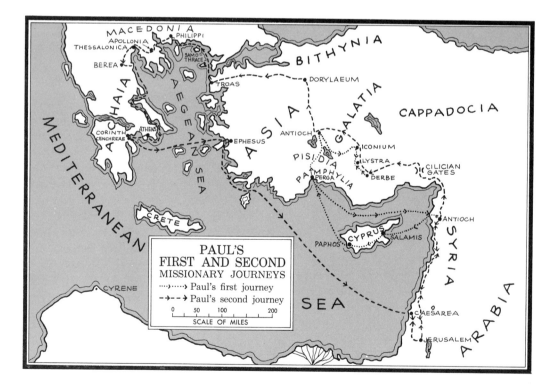

PAUL'S
FIRST AND SECOND
MISSIONARY JOURNEYS
····→······→ Paul's first journey
-→-- → Paul's second journey
0   50   100   200
SCALE OF MILES

to take the young man with him on his second missionary journey (Acts 13:13; 15:37-39). Of course there is no way of knowing whether either supposition is correct.

Antioch. At any rate, Paul and Barnabas made the 100-mile trek north to Antioch. Very likely they took the route which followed one of the tributaries of the Cestrus to Adada and thence went north. Perhaps the altitude of some 3600 feet at Antioch was welcome to Paul, if indeed he contracted malaria in the fever-infested plain of Pamphylia as has been suggested. It would seem that Paul was ill when he reached the interior (Gal. 4:13-14).

Antioch was not a city of Pisidia but lay on the north side of that district in Phrygia when Paul came through on his first missionary journey. Ramsay observes that the accurate and full geographical description of Antioch at that time would have been "a Phrygian city on the side of Pisidia." But the convenient way of alluding to it came to be "Pisidian Antioch" to distinguish it from the Antioch on the Maeander River. Only as the term "Pisidia" became widened in inclusiveness did "Antioch of Pisidia" receive universal acceptance. This latter title for the town found its way into some of the later, inferior biblical manuscripts and appears in the King James Version. But the better manuscripts read correctly "Pisidian Antioch."[39] Thus Luke's language is seen again to correlate minutely with contemporary conditions.

Perhaps it may be asked why Paul went to Antioch at all. The answer seems fairly obvious when one considers Paul's strategy of missions and the nature of Antioch. Paul worked longest in fairly large and strategic centers where there was a mobile population, centers which could act as springboards for the rapid spread of the gospel. Corinth and Ephesus illustrate this procedure. Antioch was a main stop on the great eastern trade route from Ephesus to the Euphrates. It was a city which had been established by the Seleucids for Hellenization of the district and utilized by the Romans as a chief center for the pacification of southern Galatia. Moreover, it was situated in a fertile valley at the natural center of its district.

Antioch stood just to the west of the Anthios River (which flowed southwest into Lake Limnai), on a roughly rectangular plateau some two miles in circumference. The plateau sloped upward to the east, where there was a sharp drop to the Anthios, about 200 feet below. At the western end the plateau is only about fifty feet above the plain. The natural configuration of the site made it a strong fortress, a great asset in so unruly a region. The ordinary water supply was by means of an aqueduct which brought water from a spring in the mountains six or seven miles to the north of the city. During most of its course the aqueduct was underground, but for the last mile it marched across the landscape on great arches, twenty of which still remain. Though this source might easily have been cut, water in sufficient amounts was also available from the Anthios. Just to the east of the Anthios rose a range of hills, on one of which stood the great sanctuary of the god Men.

Whether or not there was a Phrygian fortress at or near Antioch is uncertain. Probably the town was originally a temple village on the vast estates of the god Men located in the area. About 280 B.C. or a little earlier, Seleucus Nicator founded the city, naming it after his father, Antiochus, and using as the main population element Greeks from Magnesia on the Maeander River. This Antioch, one of the more than sixteen Seleucus founded, was designed to strengthen his hold on native tribes and to spread Hellenistic culture in this Phrygian area.

[39]William M. Ramsay, *The Church in the Roman Empire Before* A.D. *170* (4th ed.; London: Hodder and Stoughton, 1895), p. 26.

When Antiochus III was expelled from Asia Minor as a result of his defeat at Magnesia, Antioch became an independent city in 189 B.C. and seems to have remained such until Mark Antony gave it to Amyntas, last king of Galatia. When on his death in 25 B.C. Amyntas willed his kingdom to Rome, the city passed with the rest of the province into Roman hands. Soon after the province of Galatia was organized, the Romans constituted Antioch a Roman colony and settled it with veterans of the Fifth Legion (the Gallic) and apparently of the Seventh also.[40]

The new colony was officially called "Colonia Caesarea," but the old name was so strong that by the end of the first century "Antiocheia" began to appear with the official name. Apparently much of the land used by the Roman colony had been confiscated from the temple of Men by Amyntas. Thus the temple lost its political significance but remained religiously important.[41]

Colonia Caesarea was the most important of a chain of military colonies founded by Augustus to control the wild tribes of Pisidia and Pamphylia. It was the administrative center of the southern half of the province of Galatia. By now it had become quite cosmopolitan. There were some Phrygians. To these Seleucus had added Greeks. He and his successors had settled thousands of Jews in the cities of Phrygia,[42] and no doubt many of these found their way into Antioch because the Jewish element there was strong when Paul arrived (Acts 13:50).

Finally, Romans had come in to dominate the social and political structure. Every effort was exerted to make the new colony as Roman as possible. When Paul went to bed in Pisidian Antioch, he heard the night watch give their commands in Latin. The appearance of the city itself also gave the impression that a little bit of Rome had been flung down on this hillside in Asia Minor. The city was prosperous during the Roman and Byzantine periods but apparently was completely destroyed by the Arabs about A.D. 713.

As the 1924 University of Michigan excavations have shown,[43] life at Antioch in Paul's day centered around two paved squares, the Square of Tiberius and the Square of Augustus. The former was at a lower level, and scattered around on its 3,000 square feet of paving stones were many incised circles or rectangles on which the Romans in their idle hours could play all kinds of games. From the lower square, twelve steps some seventy feet long led into the Square of Augustus through a magnificent triple-arched gateway. The facade of this propylaea was faced with two pairs of Corinthian columns which flanked two enormous reliefs of Pisidian captives (representing Augustus' victories on land) and had a frieze with tritons, Neptune, dolphins, and other marine symbols (commemorating Augustus' victories on the sea, especially at Actium).

At the east end of the Square of Augustus a semicircle was cut out of the native rock, before which rose a two-story colonnade with Doric columns below and Ionic above. In front of the center of the semicircle stood a Roman temple, the base of which was cut out of native rock and the superstructure built of white marble. It had a portico of four Corinthian columns across the front. The frieze of this temple, apparently dedicated to the god Men and to Augustus, consisted of beautifully executed bulls' heads (the symbol of Men) bound together with garlands of all sorts of leaves and fruits.

What the rest of the city was like the excavators were not able to determine. The

---

[40]Magie, I, 457.

[41]Broughton, IV, 643.

[42]Josephus, *Antiquities of the Jews*, Book XII, Chap. iii.

[43]David M. Robinson, "A Preliminary Report on the Excavations at Pisidian Antioch and at Sizma," *American Journal of Archaeology*, XXVIII (October, 1924), 435-44.

squares were at least partly faced with shops and houses. The water system was superb. Everywhere in the excavations terra-cotta pipes were found. On the northern, western, and southern sides of the town substantial fortifications were built. On the east side, where the plateau dropped sharply to the Anthios, defenses do not seem to have been so necessary.

Near Antioch was the great sanctuary of Men on a mountain spur some 5500 feet in altitude.[44] The sacred precinct measured 137 by 230 feet (inside measurement) and was surrounded by a five-and-one-half-foot wall. The structure was built of dark limestone veined with white, of which the hills in the neighborhood are composed. A great part of the existing wall is covered on the exterior with sculptured dedications. Apparently this sacred precinct was open to the sky and the structure within (sixty-six by forty-one feet) was a great altar to the deity which was approached by steps on the west.

On the northern slopes of the hill are remains of buildings which have been identified as houses for the numerous sacred personnel attached to the temple. Similar remains exist on the south and west slopes as well. To the north of the sacred enclosure in a hollow on the mountaintop stood a semicircular structure which has been thought to be a theater or possibly a stadium with only one end constructed. It measures 113 feet wide and 130 feet deep. Statue bases lined the sacred way adjacent to it. Possibly this is the stadium where the annual gymnastic contests in honor of the god Men were held.[45]

Men was the chief god of Antioch. He commonly appears on the city's coins as a standing, fully draped figure with a Phrygian high-pointed cap on his head. In his outstretched left hand he holds a figure

representing victory, and he rests his left arm on a column to help bear the weight. In his right hand he holds a long scepter, and behind his shoulders appear the horns of a cescent moon. Variously called "Dionysius," "Apollo," and "Asklepius" by the ancients, he must have been thought of as the giver of wine, the giver of prophecy (or the sun god), and the great physician. In short he was the Anatolian supreme god.[46]

One of the more interesting of the inscriptions found at Antioch was one discovered and interpreted by Sir William Ramsay. Dedicated to Lucius Sergius Paullus the Younger, it was studied by Ramsay in conjunction with another published earlier, in which Sergia Paulla was mentioned. He tried to show that Sergia Paulla and Lucius Sergius Paullus were daughter and son of the Proconsul Sergius Paulus of Cyprus (Acts 13:7). Ramsay thought further that the inscription about the daughter suggests she may have been a Christian and trained her children in the Christian faith.[47] Ramsay has had numerous followers who have accepted his conclusions. He explained the difference in spelling by saying that the spelling of the Latin name is always *Paullus* but the Greek *Paulos*.

As was their custom, Paul and Barnabas preached first to the Jews in Antioch. By the second sabbath the Gentiles of the community readily heard the missionaries. Apparently the evangelization was rapid and effective, and many converts were made, because Acts 13:49 states that the whole area had heard the Christian gospel. At this juncture the Jews of the city determined to expel the apostle. Since they were living in a Roman colony, his opponents

[44]For a discussion of the site see Margaret M. Hardie, "The Shrine of Men Askaenos at Pisidian Antioch," *Journal of Hellenic Studies*, XXIII (1912), 111-50.

[45]Broughton, p. 788.

[46]Ramsay, *Cities of St. Paul*, pp. 285-87.

[47]See William M. Ramsay, *The Bearing of Recent Discovery on the Trustworthiness of the New Testament* (2nd ed.; London: Hodder & Stoughton, 1915), pp. 150-72; Camden M. Cobern, *The New Archeological Discoveries* (9th ed.; New York: Funk & Wagnalls, 1929), pp. 538-40; Egbert C. Hudson, "The Principal Family at Pisidian Antioch," *Journal of Near Eastern Studies*, XV (Apr., 1956), 103-7.

did not try riot tactics. Nor did they try to arraign him before Roman courts on a fraudulent charge. Rather they decided to take the indirect approach, to enlist the "devout and honourable women," no doubt the proselytes of the synagogue, in a campaign to persuade their Roman husbands to get rid of the "blasphemous visitors."

Iconium. Paul and Barnabas were expelled from Antioch and traveled southeastward to Iconium at the western edge of the vast central plains of Asia Minor. Almost certainly the missionary pair took the Royal Road about eighteen miles south to Neapolis. After about another eighteen miles, at the north end of Lake Karalis, they left the Royal Road and traveled almost due east to Iconium (modern Konya). The total distance was about eighty miles.[48]

Iconium stood on a level plateau about 3400 feet above sea level. Approximately six miles west of the city mountains rose to a height of 5000 to 6000 feet. From them a stream flowed down into the city, and other smaller streams flowed into the surrounding region, making the land around into a great garden. On the north and south, hills rose at a distance of ten to twelve miles from the city. To the east lay the plains of Lycaonia.

Although Iconium was unsuited for defense, a site such as this with an ever-flowing natural supply of water and fertile soil was a center of human life among arid plateaus. Unfortunately the supply of water pouring into the plains is not so well regulated and properly distributed now as in ancient times, and much of it is at present left to stagnate in marshes.

During the first century, Iconium controlled the fertile district around it for some 200 square miles.[49] The population was, of course, scattered in numerous villages, the ruins of which have never been carefully or exhaustively studied by modern explorers. These villages were just fragments of the central city, each having its chief officer or "first man." The free inhabitants were not villagers but citizens of the chief city where they enjoyed political rights.

The origins of Iconium are hidden in the immemorial recesses of antiquity. A local Phrygian tradition pushes the beginnings of the city "before the flood." What that means is a question that need not detain this study. Iconium was, of course, part of the Persian Empire. Later, perhaps during the third century under Seleucid control, it came to be recognized as the chief city of Lycaonia. After the Roman victory at Magnesia in 190 B.C., when most of Asia Minor was taken from the Seleucids, Iconium was assigned to Pergamum. But the Pergamenes never seem to have actually controlled it, and the city probably soon passed under the power of the Galatai. The Pontic kings took over about 130 to 125 B.C., and the city was set free after the Roman defeat of Mithridates.

Possibly it was in 63 B.C. that a tetrarchy of Lycaonia was formed, containing fourteen cities; Iconium was the capital. In 39 B.C. Mark Antony gave this city to King Polemon but three years later transferred it to King Amyntas of Galatia. When Amyntas died in 25 B.C., Iconium was incorporated in the Roman Empire as part of the province of Galatia. Jews were settled in Iconium by the Seleucids during the third century, but they apparently did not become influential until the Roman period.

How and when Iconium was transformed from an Oriental town to a Hellenic self-governing city is unknown. But transformed it was. And when Paul and Barnabas came through on their first missionary journey, it was still a Greek city, in which the powers of the state were exercised by the demos, the Greek assembly of all citizens. It was not yet a Roman colony, in which the body

[48]See Ramsay, *Church in the Roman Empire,* pp. 27-36, for a discussion of the route. The distance he gives is by road over actual terrain, rather than sixty miles in a direct line, as most books give it.

[49]Ramsay, *Cities of St. Paul,* p. 340.

of coloni in assembly would have ruled. That would come during Hadrian's reign (A.D. 117-138). Thus, as Morton observes, the approach of the Jews in discrediting the effective ministry of Paul in this town was not to try to influence the leading citizens indirectly as at Antioch. "The most effective way to expel the apostles was obviously to create a public argument, to rouse the whole city against them, and then sit back and allow democracy to do its worst."[50] When a plot against the lives of the missionaries was discovered, they left for Lystra. This action should not be construed as cowardice. Events at Lystra would demonstrate the qualities of which Paul and Barnabas were made.

Luke observed that when the missionaries left Iconium for Lystra and Derbe they crossed over the line from Phrygia into Lycaonia (Acts 14:6). This long created a problem for Bible students because many ancient authorities who wrote from the Roman provincial point of view assigned Iconium to Lycaonia. Ramsay has demonstrated, however, that many of these ancient authorities had not been carefully read and that the most authoritative of them called it a city of Phrygia. Ramsay has shown further from inscriptions he found at Iconium that the city was so completely Phrygian that even leading citizens were using the Phrygian language on inscriptions as late as A.D. 150 to 250.[51] Perhaps, as Ramsay has suggested, Luke mentioned this particular frontier because when Paul and Barnabas crossed it they were safe for the moment. They were now under a new jurisdiction.

Lystra. The hurried flight of Paul and Barnabas brought them in one day to Lystra, about eighteen miles southwest of Iconium. An American Professor J. R. Sitlington Sterret in 1885 identified the site as

[50]H. V. Morton, *In the Steps of Paul* (New York: Dodd, Mead & Co., 1936), p. 214.
[51]Ramsay, *Bearing of Recent Discovery*, p. 58.

307. Mound of Lystra

lying a mile northwest of Khatyn-Serai. Positive identification was accomplished by means of an inscribed altar still standing, on which appeared the name of the city and the indication that it had been a Roman colony. Support of the testimony of the altar stone came from coins found at the site.

Lystra was founded as a Roman colony by Augustus, probably in 6 B.C., for the purpose of training and regulating the mountain tribes on the southern frontier of the province of Galatia. It seems to have been a place of some importance under the early emperors, but during the last quarter of the first century it sank back into the insignificance of a small provincial town. It was not on a main commercial route, and its purpose as a military outpost had been achieved. The area had been subdued.

The city stood on a small, elongated hill in the center of a valley abundantly supplied with water by two streams. Lystra possessed a considerable territory of fertile soil in the valley, as well as a tract of low hilly ground. The site was off the main roads, and its seclusion marked it out as a small rustic town, where the people and customs would be quite provincial. It is to be noted that the inhabitants addressed Paul not in Greek but in the "speech of Lycaonia" (Acts 14:11). Moreover, there do not even seem to have been enough Jews in the place to build a synagogue. The relative seclusion of Lystra has been compared with that of Berea; at both towns Paul sought to wait out a storm of opposition.

Initially the missionaries were very well received. Luke reported that the healing of a lame man by Paul led the native population to hail the pair as gods, identifying Barnabas as Zeus (Jupiter) and Paul as Hermes (Mercury) (Acts 14:8-12). The implication seems to be that Barnabas was much the older of the two and had a dignified bearing. Paul was addressed as Hermes, the messenger of the gods, because he did most of the speaking. It has also been suggested that Paul's being addressed as Hermes indicates he must have been a virile-looking, gracious, and attractive youth. Inscriptions show that Zeus and Hermes were especially coupled in the worship of the Lycaonians. Apparently the worship of these two deities represented an essentially native cult under a thin Greek disguise.

In spite of their protestation against being considered as gods, Paul and Barnabas were still hailed as such by the natives. They seem to have had considerable success in preaching the Christian gospel, however. At length Jews came down from Iconium and caused trouble for the evangelists. Ramsay suggests that the Jews who came to Lystra were middle men who were speculating in the approaching harvest and that the time of the stoning of Paul was August.[52]

At any rate, the Jews came and stirred up the fickle multitude to turn against Paul and to stone him and leave him for dead. But his followers cared for him, and he left with Barnabas for a second refuge, Derbe. This time the pair seem to have been unmolested in their religious endeavors.

Derbe. Ever since Sir William Ramsay identified Derbe with Gudelisin (c. 1890),

some forty miles southeast of Lystra, this view has been traditional. But in 1957 an inscription was found at Kerti Hüyük, which seemed to fix that site definitely as ancient Derbe.[53] In 1962 a second inscription was found at Kerti Hüyük, demonstrating almost beyond doubt that the mound was ancient Derbe.[54] In terms of location, Gudelisin is about thirty miles west of the modern Turkish town of Karaman (sixty-six miles by road southeast of Konya), and Kerti Hüyük is some fifteen miles northwest of Karaman. This new identification requires a whole new study of the history and geography of Derbe, which has not as yet been made.

Paul and Barnabas apparently had a fruitful ministry at Derbe, where they must have remained for some time. Since Derbe was near the Galatian frontier, it was only logical for them to refrain from going much farther east. At length they retraced their steps and passed once more through Lystra, Iconium, and Antioch, establishing churches among the converts made earlier. Ramsay suggests that this return route was possible because by this time new magistrates had been installed in office in the three cities.[55] It may also be observed that trouble was not so likely to occur from a quiet organization of churches as from extensive evangelistic outreach.

Perga and Attalia. Paul had not preached at Perga (modern Murtana) before he headed for the interior of Asia Minor. Now he determined to do so, apparently without effect. So he headed for the seacoast town of Attalia (modern Antalya) about twelve miles southwest of Perga.

[52]Ramsay, *The Church in the Roman Empire,* p. 69.

[53]Jack Finegan, *Light from the Ancient Past* (2nd ed.; Princeton: Princeton University Press, 1959), p. 343.

[54]Reported on by Prof. Bastian Van Elderen at the Wheaton College Archaeology Conference, October 15, 1962. Dr. Van Elderen was given permission by Turkish officials to publish the inscription.

[55]William M. Ramsay, *St. Paul the Traveller and the Roman Citizen* (8th ed.; London: Hodder and Stoughton, 1905), p. 120.

Attalia had the most important harbor of the coastal belt of old Pamphylia, which was largely a steep cliff on the seashore. Along the coast on both sides of the town the mountains soar up in tier after amber-colored tier, woods-green and olive-green, clothed in a forest of leaves, the sea sweeping their feet. To the north of the city is a fertile plain. Attalians shipped timber from the Taurus to Egypt and Phoenicia, and Attalia had developed into a big and rich commercial city in Paul's day.

Although there certainly must have been inhabitants of the place much earlier, Attalus II of Pergamum (159-138 B.C.) receives credit for having founded Attalia. Certainly the Pergamenes did not effectively control the place, which became a center of pirate activity and passed to Rome with the defeat of the Mediterranean pirates by Pompey. The town was mulcted of its territory for complicity with the pirates, and these lands were probably utilized by Augustus for settling veterans. Attalia grew rich again by the time Paul and Barnabas arrived. It was the richest town of the area during Byzantine times, and during the Seljuk period it was the headquarters of the Seljuk Mediterranean fleet.

The chief god of Attalia was Zeus, as at Pergamum. But Athena and Apollo were also worshiped. Since the modern town covers the ancient site, almost nothing of the Roman period can be detected; so little is known concerning what the place was like in the middle of the first century A.D. The most prominent monument surviving from classical times is Hadrian's gate, erected on the occasion of his visit to the city in A.D. 130.

Paul and Barnabas apparently did not try to preach in this port but merely sought passage for Antioch. Back in Syria, they faced a controversy over whether or not their numerous Gentile converts should be forced to keep the Mosaic law. The Council of Jerusalem was called to settle the matter.

The Second Missionary Journey

The Council of Jerusalem was over (Acts 15:1-35). The mother church had taken its stand. Gentile Christians were not to be required to keep the law of Moses, and a record of the decision was sent to Antioch in the hands of Barnabas and Paul, Judas Barsabas, and Silas. Having delivered their message, Paul and Barnabas stayed in Antioch for a while preaching and teaching. Then they decided to embark on another missionary journey to "visit our brethren in every city where we have preached the word of the Lord, and see how they do" (Acts 15:36). Barnabas wanted to take John Mark along, but Paul was opposed; so the two parted company, Barnabas taking Mark to Cyprus, and Paul choosing Silas and setting out for Asia Minor.

This time Paul went through Syria and Cilicia and then came to Derbe and Lystra (Acts 15:41—16:1). Obviously this means that he went by land from Antioch into the province of Cilicia. The road led north out of Antioch and crossed the Amanus Mountains (modern Alma Dag) at the Syrian Gates. The Amanus, a short offshoot sent southward by the Tauric system, separated the provinces of Syria and Cilicia at an altitude of 5,000 feet. The Syrian Gates (Beilan Pass) at an altitude of 2400 feet was the practicable route through the Amanus. About thirty-eight miles north of Antioch lay Alexandretta (modern Iskenderun). From there the road curved around the Bay of Issus to the town of Issus twenty miles away. Here Alexander the Great won a great battle against Persian forces in October, 333 B.C.

From Issus the road led inland, crossed the Pyramus and Sarus rivers, and passed through Adana (c. 125 miles from Antioch) and Tarsus (c. 150 miles away). The Acts narrative does not record a visit by Paul to his hometown on this occasion, but it is almost certain that he did go there because the main road led past Tarsus and to the Cilician Gates. Going north from Tarsus Paul passed through the Cilician Gates about thirty miles away. The road now ran in a northwesterly direction and about 170 miles farther ran down the main street of Iconium.

But Paul and Silas made stops south of Iconium at Derbe and Lystra. At the latter Paul met Timothy and made him a part of the apostolic company. The young man already had a good testimony in his own and nearby communities, and he was to serve Paul faithfully until the end of his days (see II Timothy).

Now a geographic problem arises that has engendered considerable discussion. In Acts 16:6 the statement is made in the King James Version that the apostolic company went "throughout Phrygia and the region of Galatia." What does this mean? It should be useful first to comment on Phrygia, then on Galatia, and then to draw some conclusions.

Phrygia. The Phrygians moved across the Hellespont from what is now European Turkey about 1200 B.C. and gradually spread over Asia Minor, destroying Hittite rule in many areas. They established a kingdom with considerable power governed from Gordium, some distance to the west of modern Ankara. Gradually other powers encroached upon their territory in Asia Minor—Greeks in the west, Bithynians in the northwest, Assyrians in the east. Shortly after 700 B.C. the Cimmerians, a Thracian people, destroyed the Phrygian kingdom but later passed out of existence. During the Lydian period there was a Phyrgian revival, but these people experienced decline under Persian rule.

About 275 B.C. the eastern part of Phrygia came under the control of Celtic invaders from the Danubian area and was renamed "Galatia." At approximately the same time the Pergamene kingdom took over western

Phrygia, which was their undisputed possession after the Roman victory at Magnesia in 190 B.C. expelled the Seleucid kings from Asia Minor and forced the Celts to settle in Galatia. When the Pergamene kingdom became the province of Asia in 133 B.C., most of Phrygia came under control of Rome.

By that time Phrygia in a narrower sense was considered to be that interior tableland of Asia Minor (c. 3,000-5,000 feet) roughly bordered by the Sangarius River (modern Sakarya) on the north and northeast, the upper Hermus River on the west, and the upper Maeander River on the south and southwest, and Galatia on the east. It was a region best suited to grazing. Most of the area of Phrygia in Paul's day was part of the province of Asia, but a small portion of it lay in the province of Galatia. Iconium and Antioch (of Pisidia) were cities of Galatian Phrygia.

Galatia. "Galatia," derived from "Galatai," was the Greek name for the Gauls, or Celts, who invaded Asia Minor in 278-277 B.C. at the invitation of Nicomedes of Bithynia. After much raiding and plundering, the Gauls were finally penned in an area between the Sangarius and Halys rivers in north central Asia Minor by Attalus I of Pergamum about 230 B.C. For the next forty years they continued to harass their neighbors. After the battle of Magnesia in 190, Rome sent forces to subdue them. They remained loyal to Rome during the Mithridatic wars, and after 64 B.C. they were a client state of Rome.

At that time the territory was organized on the Celtic tribal basis; and three tribes occupied separate areas with their respective capitals at Pessinus, Ancyra (modern Ankara), and Tavium. From 44 B.C. Galatia was under one ruler only. Four years later Mark Antony conferred Galatian domains on Castor and gave Amyntas a kingdom comprising Pisidic Phrygia and Pisidia generally. In 36 B.C. Castor's kingdom was given to Amyntas, also additional territory in subsequent years. His government was so effective in pacifying the area that when he died in 25 B.C. and bequeathed his kingdom to Rome, he left it in such a state that Rome incorporated it into the Empire as the province of Galatia.

The province of Galatia then included, besides Galatia proper, parts of Phrygia, Lycaonia, Pisidia, and Pamphylia. It remained in this form until about A.D. 72 when additional increases in its territory were made. The two principal cities of the province of Galatia were Ancyra (the metropolis) and Pisidian Antioch. Actually the history of Galatia is extremely complicated, both before and after Roman control. A good source of information on the subject is Sir William M. Ramsay's *A Historical Commentary on St. Paul's Epistle to the Galatians.* In width the Galatian province varied from 100 to 175 miles; it was some 250 miles north and south.

It may be readily seen that "Galatia" could refer either in an ethnic sense to a territory in north central Asia Minor or in a political sense to the province of Galatia. The questions often arise as to the sense in which Luke and Paul used the term and to whom Paul wrote when he penned the epistle to the Galatians. Paul, proud of his Roman citizenship, always used the provincial names of the areas under Roman control, never the territorial, except as the two were identical in significance. Paul used the term "Galatia" only three times: in I Corinthians 16:1, Galatians 1:2, and II Timothy 4:10, all of which certainly must refer to the Roman province. Peter must have used the term in the same sense in I Peter 1:1, because the other four areas he addresses in the same verse were adjacent Roman provinces.

Now what of Luke's use of the term "Galatia"? He does not use either "Galatia" or "Galatians" but only the adjective "Galatic" or "Galatian." Following Ramsay, Sou-

308. Temple of Hadrian, Ephesus

ter argues that Acts 16:6 should be translated "the Phrygo-Galatic region," which no doubt referred to that section of the province of Galatia known as Phrygia Galatica, containing Pisidian Antioch and Iconium. He further argues that in Acts 18:23 the Greek may be translated either "the Galatico-Phrygian region" or "the Galatian region and Phrygia" (preferably the latter), the Galatian region including Derbe and Lystra, and the Phrygian, Iconium, and Pisidian Antioch.[56]

Ramsay also notes that Acts 16:6 must be looked upon as connected with Acts 15:36 and 16:1-2, verses 2 to 5 being considered as somewhat parenthetical.[57] The apostle purposed to visit churches he had previously founded in Derbe, Lystra, Iconium, and Antioch. After he had visited these towns Luke said, "When they had gone throughout the Phrygo-Galatic region . . ." (Acts 16:6). Obviously there is no room here for the idea that Paul on this journey circled far north through the old ethnic area of Galatia. The writer does not personally feel there is much support for the north Galatian theory, in regard to Paul's either having

[56]A. Souter, "Galatia," *Dictionary of the Bible,* ed. James Hastings, rev. ed. F. C. Grant and H. G. Rowley (New York: Charles Scribner's Sons, 1963), p. 311; Ramsay, *The Church in the Roman Empire,* pp. 75-89.
[57]Ramsay, *St. Paul the Traveller and the Roman Citizen,* p. 77.

visited the area or writing his epistle to the people of it.[58]

Where Paul and Silas went from Pisidian Antioch is uncertain. They may have taken the main east-west trade route through Colossae and Laodicea, out the Maeander Valley to Ephesus and north along the coast to Mysia. Or they may have gone northwest on the main road through Phrygia and then west to Pergamum and from there north to Mysia. At any rate, they were forbidden by the Holy Spirit from preaching in Asia and Bithynia (Acts 16:6). So they passed through Mysia and came to the port town of Troas.

Mysia was a district of northwest Asia Minor south of the Propontis (modern Marmara) and Hellespont. Its boundaries were never carefully defined. After being part of the dominions of Persia and Alexander,

it came under the control of Pergamum and thus of Rome, forming part of the province of Asia in 133 B.C. Mysia is mentioned only in Acts 16:7 in the Bible. Assos and Troas, both of which Paul visited, lay within its bounds. The greater part of Mysia is mountainous, being traversed by northwest branches of the Taurus Range; the main branches were Mount Ida and Mount Temnus. Most of its rivers were small and not navigable.

When Paul arrived at Troas, he received the vision of the man from Macedonia (Acts 16:9-11) and decided to heed the call to do missionary work in Greece. The rest of the second missionary journey, which is treated in detail in the section on Greece, took the apostolic company to Greek shores. Since Troas was the beginning of that venture and was itself a very much Hellenized city, it is discussed in connection with Paul's ministry in Greece.

[58]*Ibid.*; Henry C. Thiessen, *Introduction to the New Testament* (Grand Rapids: Wm. B. Eerdmans Publishing Co., 1943), pp. 214-16.

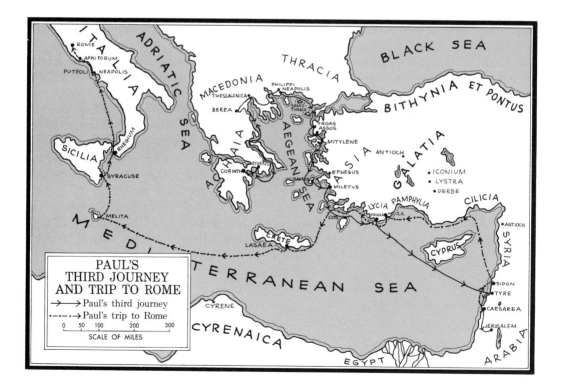

PAUL'S
THIRD JOURNEY
AND TRIP TO ROME
→ Paul's third journey
-·-·→ Paul's trip to Rome
0 50 100   200   300
SCALE OF MILES

THE WYCLIFFE HISTORICAL GEOGRAPHY OF BIBLE LANDS

The Third Missionary Journey

Luke does not tell us how long Paul remained at Antioch at the end of the second missionary journey. At length Paul decided to make a third visit to the cities of the Galatic region and Phrygia (Acts 18:23). No doubt he took the same route he followed at the beginning of the second journey—through the Syrian Gates, Tarsus, and the Cilician Gates. The "Galatic region" is a general term which could cover the portion of Galatia where Derbe, Lystra, Iconium, and Pisidian Antioch were located. The region also included Galatian Phrygia, adjacent to which was Asian Phrygia. So it would be a simple matter for him to move from one area of Phrygia to the other and to pass "through the upper coasts" (better, "the higher districts") to Ephesus (Acts 19:1).

Ramsay observes that during the first century the terms "High Phrygia" and "Low Phrygia" (referring to the elevation of land) had specific distinction, the former designating the mountain country just west of Pisidian Antioch and equatable here with "the higher districts." The main trade route to Ephesus traversed Low Phrygia and the Lycus and Maeander valleys. The shorter hill road, practicable for foot passengers but not for wheeled vehicles, ran more or less due west from Pisidian Antioch and came into Ephesus north of the Messogis Range.[59]

Ephesus. Paul's real destination on the third missionary journey was Ephesus, and he apparently wished to arrive there with all reasonable speed. This was not his first contact with the city. On his return trip to Jerusalem at the end of the second missionary journey, he had stopped at Ephesus briefly and had even ministered in the synagogue there (Acts 18:19). Perhaps on that occasion he had recognized the strategic

309. Church of St. John, Ephesus

value of evangelistic endeavors in this important city and had made plans to return at an early date. Ephesus was at that time one of the greatest cities of the Roman world.

Broughton estimates the population conservatively at more than 200,000.[60] MacKendrick reports that the excavators calculate its peak population to have been 500,000.[61] The importance of the city was at least threefold when Paul arrived: political, economic, and religious. It had become the *de facto* capital of the province, and the Roman governor resided there. Its economic prowess lay in the fact that Ephesus stood astride the great route to the interior up the Maeander and Lycus valleys and the great north-south road through Smyrna, Pergamum, Adramyttium, and Cyzicus on the Propontis Sea and had access to the Aegean by way of the Cayster River. Religiously, Ephesus was a leading center for the worship of Diana, or Artemis.

The importance of Ephesus as a crossroads of civilization held the apostle there for two years and three months according to Acts 19:8 and 10 and three years according to Acts 20:31. The discrepancy is easily explained by reference to the Roman method of computing time. Any part of a year was reckoned as a year. Thus, considering

[59]Ramsay, *St. Paul the Traveller and the Roman Citizen*, p. 94.

[60]Broughton, p. 816.
[61]Paul MacKendrick, *The Greek Stones Speak* (New York: St. Martin's Press, 1962), p. 420.

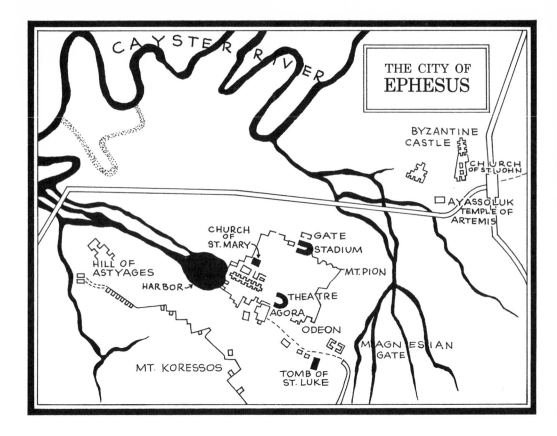

The City of
EPHESUS

two years and three months to be the correct figure, Paul could have spent four months there the first year, twelve the second, and eleven the third; and according to the prevailing method of computation, he would have been there three years.

Ephesus also attracted the ministry of other New Testament figures: Tychicus (Eph. 6:21), Timothy (I Tim. 1:3), John Mark (I Peter 5:13), and John the Apostle (Rev. 1:11; 2:1).

Ephesus was already an ancient city when the apostle arrived. By about the middle of the second millennium B.C., settlers of Asiatic origin inhabited the site. During the eleventh century, Athenians arrived and gradually assimilated the older population, founding one of the twelve cities of the Ionian Confederation. The city of this period occupied an area along the lower slopes of Mount Coressus at the

southwest of the later city complex. The temple of Artemis lay about a mile to the north. During this period Ephesus maintained itself against the Cimmerians and the Lydians.

About 560 B.C., however, Croesus of Lydia finally managed to conquer Ephesus and forced the inhabitants to take up their abode on the plain near the temple of Artemis, with whom the old mother goddess of the Asians had been identified. Soon thereafter Cyrus the Great took over. Ephesus was involved in the abortive Ionian revolt of 499 but was ultimately freed from Persia and joined the Delian League in 479. Ephesus revolted against Athenian control in 415 B.C. and presently sided with Sparta. For about a century the history of the city is quite complicated and need not detain us here.

After brief control by Alexander the

Great, Ephesus passed under the suzerainty of Lysimachus, one of his generals, who about 286 B.C. refounded the city once more in the valley between Mounts Pion and Coressus. Shaped like a bent bow, with Mount Pion at its eastern end and the Hill of Astyages at the western end, the lower town and its port were surrounded by a wall some five miles long. The town was called "Arsinoe" after its builder's wife.

Ephesus was involved in the power struggle between Macedonia, Seleucia, and Egypt. In 196 B.C. Antiochus landed at Ephesus and controlled the city briefly, but his defeat at Magnesia in 190 freed the city from Syria. Then the Roman conquerors gave it to Pergamum. When Attalus III willed his kingdom to Rome in 133, Ephesus became part of the province of Asia.

During the Republic rapacious tax collectors and moneylenders descended like vultures on the rich province of Asia and especially on Ephesus which had become the leading port. Therefore when Mithridates invaded Ionia in 88 B.C., Ephesus and other towns gladly received him, participated in the massacre of Romans living there, and threw down the statues and monuments they had erected. Later the Ephesians changed sides and murdered Mithridates' general. Rome punished the province with heavy fines. Later Brutus and Cassius exacted tremendous tribute from Ephesus to aid their cause. Mark Antony did likewise. Ephesian prosperity was virtually ruined.

Under the Empire, Ephesus enjoyed a long period of peace and prosperity. Augustus saw to it that the extreme exactions of Republican days ceased, and he began a number of structures in the city. Tiberius continued his predecessor's policy; and when the destructive earthquake of A.D. 17 occurred, he helped to restore Ephesus. About the same time Strabo wrote that the prosperity of the city was increasing daily. Early in the second century A.D., Hadrian

did considerable building there, as did Antoninus Pius (138-161).

However, by the middle of the third century, signs of decay had appeared. In A.D. 263 Goths raided the city and caused great destruction at the temple of Diana. By the fourth century the port was silting up fast. Since Christianity was now the official religion, the great temples were dismantled, their marble used for other buildings. During the first half of the sixth century, when the great Justinian was emperor, the town of Ephesus was moved once more, this time to the area around the Church of St. John to the north of the famous temple of Artemis. The site was heavily fortified and the population of the area gradually moved behind the city walls. By the tenth century the prosperous city of Roman times was completely deserted and invaded by marshes.

In order to picture Ephesus as Paul and John would have known it, it will be necessary first to comment briefly on the geography of the area and then to describe the city as archaeology has revealed it.

Ephesus stood at the entrance to one of the four clefts in the hills of west central Asia Minor. It was along these valleys that the roads across the central plateau of Asia Minor passed. (Other great cities standing at the entrance to clefts into the interior were Pergamum, Smyrna, and Miletus.) Chief of these four routes ran up the Mae-

310. Ruins of the Magnesian Gate, Ephesus

ander and Lycus valleys to Apamea and eastward. Miletus and Ephesus both contested for mastery of the trade flowing over this route. The latter won out because the track across the hills from the main road to Ephesus was shorter than the road to Miletus and because this track was over a pass over 600 feet high. As already noted, Ephesus was also on the great north-south road of western Asia Minor and was on the main sea route from Rome to the east.

In his researches J. T. Wood demonstrated that Ephesus was approximately four miles from the sea and that the shoreline was therefore approximately the same in apostolic times as it is today.[62] Its inland harbor was connected with the Cayster River, which wound through the plain to the north of the city. The harbor was kept large enough and deep enough only by constant dredging; and when the empire declined and efforts to maintain the harbor slackened, it silted up entirely. As

[62]Merrill M. Parvis, "Archaeology and St. Paul's Journeys in Greek Lands, Part IV—Ephesus," *The Biblical Archaeologist,* VIII (Sept., 1945), 62-63.

to the configuration of the land, the hill of Astyages stood directly west of the harbor, Mount Coressus to the south of it. Mount Pion towered over the harbor at its eastern end; and to the northeast, across the fertile plain, stood the little hill of Ayassoluk, which has always been a religious center. Below its southwest slope was the magnificent temple to Diana, or Artemis. In later centuries on the hill itself stood the great Church of St. John (supposedly built over the apostle's tomb) which is now being restored.

The archaeological history of Ephesus began on May 2, 1863, when the British architect, John Turtle Wood, started his search for the Temple of Diana. He dug seventy-five trial pits the first year, without success. Year after year Wood continued his excavations at the site. Finally, while clearing the theater, he came upon an inscription which indicated that when the images of the goddess were carried from the temple to the theater, the procession was to enter the city by the Magnesian Gate. Wood found the magnificent triple-

311. Plan of the Temple of Diana, Ephesus. From I. H. Grinnell, *Greek Temples,* Metropolitan Museum of Art

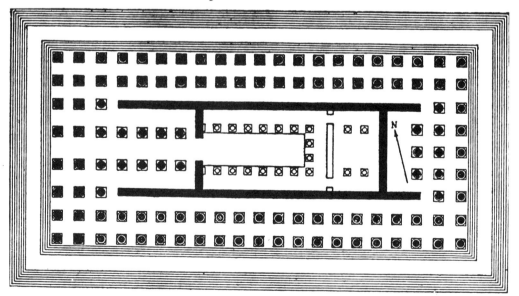

arched gateway and the thirty-five-foot-wide road paved with marble which led from it. Following this sacred road for more than a mile northeast of the city, he came to the boundary wall of the sacred precincts on May 2, six years to the day after beginning his quest. But he did not actually discover the ruins of the temple itself until December 31, 1869. These he found at a depth of over twenty feet. He worked five more years at the temple site.

The work at the temple was carried forward by D. G. Hogarth (1904-5), who found a magnificent foundation deposit of hundreds of objects—jewelry, figurines of the goddess, and the like. In the meantime the Austrian Archaeological Institute began work there in November, 1897 and excavated continuously for sixteen years. The Austrians, in part subsidized by Rockefeller money, worked there again (1926-35) under the direction of Josef Keil. Keil resumed excavation there in 1954 and continued until his death in 1959. Since then F. Miltner has been directing the project. It has been the Austrians' task to uncover the city proper, and they have done a magnificent job on the Roman period. Ephesus now very definitely has that edited look which archaeology brings to ruins.

A great many of the structures that the archaeologists have uncovered at Ephesus date to the prosperous days of the second century A.D. or to some other period with no biblical relevance and therefore are not mentioned here. Several, however, hold special interest for the New Testament student.

Since the devotees of Artemis (Diana) came into such violent conflict with Christianity at Ephesus and since the goddess' temple there was one of the wonders of the ancient world, it seems logical to begin our story of the archaeological remains with this structure. Hogarth in his work at the site was able to distinguish five phases of the temple. The earliest of these, dated by

312. Ruins of the Temple of Diana at Ephesus

coins from the foundation deposit, was not constructed earlier than 600 B.C.[63] Construction of the latest, now known as the Hellenistic temple, was begun probably before 350 B.C. and continued until 334 B.C., when Alexander the Great arrived. The conqueror offered to pay the costs of completion if his name were inscribed upon it, but he was refused. This was the temple Paul and John saw; it was destroyed by the Goths in A.D. 262.

The temple platform was 239 feet wide by 418 feet long. A flight of ten steps led up to the pavement of the platform and three more to the pavement of the peristyle (colonnade around the temple). The temple itself was 180 feet wide and 377 feet long, and the roof was supported by 117 sixty-foot columns. These columns were six feet in diameter and thirty-six of them were sculptured at the base with life-size figures. Praxiteles and Scopas are believed to have done some of the sculpture of the temple. White, blue, red, and yellow marble, as well as gold, were used to decorate the structure. The cella or holy of holies was seventy feet wide and apparently open to the sky. In it was the altar, twenty feet square, behind which the statue of Artemis no doubt stood. Several writers have indicated that this image may have been carved

[63]MacKendrick, p. 316, notes that this correction in chronology was not made until 1951.

313. Sculptured column base from the
Temple of Diana

matic, and musical contests. Ephesus was proud of her position as "temple-keeper" of Diana (Acts 19:35, "worshipper"), a boast which has been found on inscriptions excavated there. The temple treasury acted as a bank in which deposits were made by cities, kings, and private persons.

A structure mentioned specifically in connection with Paul's ministry in Ephesus is the great theater (Acts 19:29). It was situated on the western slopes of Mount Pion and looked west toward the harbor. Measuring some 495 feet in diameter, the theater held about 25,000 persons. The cavea of the theater was divided into three bands of twenty-two rows of seats each, and twelve stairways divided the cavea into huge wedge-shaped sections. The orchestra measured eighty by thirty-seven feet. Behind the orchestra stood a stage eighty feet long and twenty feet deep, supported by twenty-six round pillars and ten square ones. While it antedated Paul's time, the theater was rebuilt between the reigns of Claudius (34-41) and Trajan (98-117).

From a large meteorite. This they deduce in part from the reference that the "image . . . fell down from Jupiter" (Acts 19:35).

"Artemis" is the Greek name for the Roman goddess Diana who had been equated with the Asia Minor Cybele, the mother goddess. As worshiped in Ephesus the goddess was a considerably Orientalized deity, adored as the mother of life and the nourisher of all creatures of the earth, air, and sea. Her statue was a many-breasted figure, rather than the gracefully draped Greek or Roman figure. A recent suggestion is that the "many breasts" are ostrich eggs, also a symbol of fertility. Hundreds, if not thousands, of priests were connected with her ritual in Ephesus. Many of these had cells within the temple area. A multitude of priestesses were also dedicated to prostitution in the temple service. The Artemision (March-April) was the sacred month especially devoted to the worship of the goddess. The religious festivals held during this month included athletic, dra-

From the theater the Arcadian Way, 1735 feet long, led to the harbor. This marble-paved street thirty-six feet in width was lined on both sides by a colonnade behind which were shops. At both ends of the street were monumental gateways. While this street, in the form the excavators found it, dates long after the days of Paul and John, certainly there was a fairly sumptuous street on the site in their time. As one walked from the theater to the harbor, he passed the Roman agora on his right. Not yet contemplated during Paul's ministry, it was completed before John's death.

The marble street which ran in front of the theater was probably taking its final form in Paul's day, however. And the Hellenistic agora near the southwest corner of the theater was also probably in its final form when he was there. A total of 360 feet square, it was lined with porticoes behind which were small shops. At the time of this writing, the central part of the agora is still not excavated, nor are most of the shops. But Miltner found shops of the silversmiths there.[64]

North of the theater lay the stadium. Soundings demonstrate that a small stadium existed on the site in the third century B.C., but that it was rebuilt during the days of Nero. The prytaneum, or town hall stood on the street between the Hellenistic agora and the Magnesian Gate at the southeast of the city. It stood there as early as the third century B.C. but was considerably rebuilt during the Augustan period.

While most of the other structures excavated at Ephesus date to the second and third centuries or later, John must have observed a considerable spurt of building activity there during Domitian's reign (A.D. 81-96). A temple was built to the emperor at that time and a great complex of baths and gymnasia was built to the north of the road between the theater and harbor.

314. Statue of Ephesian Diana in the museum at Ephesus

[64]*Ibid.*, p. 422.

Before this discussion of Ephesus is terminated, several items mentioned in the New Testament narrative deserve comment. As was his custom in the towns where he went to preach, Paul went first to the synagogue at Ephesus, where he presented the Christian message (Acts 19:8). When he got nowhere with the Jews, he turned to the Gentiles. According to Josephus, the Syrian ruler Antiochus II (261-247 B.C.) granted citizenship to the Jews of Ionia (including Ephesus). When the Ionians tried to deprive them of citizenship rights in the first century B.C., Rome protected them, as did the Ephesian officials.[65] It is thought that the Jewish quarter at Ephesus was at the northern outskirts of the city, but this has not been proved. Their synagogue has not been found[66]

As Christianity spread in the city, its converts determined to make public demonstration of the fact they had forsaken their old ways. To do so they consigned books (scrolls) of magical formulas and incantations to a huge bonfire. The heap of books was valued at 50,000 pieces of silver (Acts 19:19). This biblical allusion is quite in keeping with what is known of life at Ephesus, where such literature was so common that it came to be known in the Roman world as "Ephesian Writings." Even some of the Jews became involved in exorcism at Ephesus. A formula similar to the one mentioned in Acts—"We adjure you by Jesus" (Acts 19:13)—has been found in Egyptian papyri: "I adjure you . . . by this god."[67]

The expenditure of 50,000 pieces of silver for magical books indicates that Ephesus was a place of great wealth. Literary sources attest to the fact. Her commercial and political position further support it. Likewise, Ephesian possession of surround-

[65]Josephus, *Antiquities of the Jews,* Book XII, Chap. iii, Section 2; Book XIV, Chap. x, Section 25.
[66]Floyd V. Filson, "Ephesus and the New Testament," *The Biblical Archaeologist,* VIII (Sept., 1945), 78.
[67]*Ibid.*, p. 79.

ing towns and farmlands would have greatly bolstered her economy, as would the
stature of her Artemis cult in the Roman
world.

Luke alluded to the craft of Demetrius
the silversmith who made silver shrines for
Diana and stirred up his compatriots when
their business was in danger (Acts 19:23-
27). An inscription has been found at Ephesus which mentions a Demetrius and indicates that he was a very influential citizen
of the community. Hicks dates the inscription A.D. 50-60 and thinks it may have reference to Paul's great opponent. Ramsay
prefers to date the inscription slightly
later.[68]

Demetrius is said to have been the leader

315. "Diana the Huntress" shows the
difference between the Ephesian and
Greek concepts of Diana

[68]Cobern, p. 482.

of a guild of silversmiths that made shrines
for Diana. No doubt what is meant is miniature replicas of the temple of Diana for the
pilgrims who came to Ephesus. Numerous
replicas in terra-cotta and marble have been
found but none of silver. This has led some
to doubt the accuracy of the New Testament narrative. But as Ramsay has pointed
out, these shrines were probably presented
as votive offerings at the temple, rather
than carried away from the city. Therefore
one should not expect to find them at widely scattered places. Moreover, the number
of votive offerings in various materials must
have grown so great at the temple that the
priests had to clean house from time to
time. Silver shrines they would have melted
down; less expensive ones they would have
destroyed. Not only would priests have
destroyed them; less reverent hands would
readily have made off with them for their
intrinsic value.[69] It should also be remembered that an argument from silence in this
instance is not proof of error. The great
villas of Ephesus remain unexcavated.

The "chiefs of Asia" (Greek, "Asiarchs,"
Acts 19:31) are well known from the inscriptions. These men were chosen from
the chief families of Asia and were provincial rather than municipal officers. They
led the rites of the emperor cult observed
by the league of cities in the province and
were expected to give handsomely from
their own estates to put on games and celebrations in connection with the emperor
worship. Since these "high priests of Asia"
held office for only one year, there would
have been several in Ephesus at the time of
the riot who deserved the honorific title,
just as ex-governors are called "governor"
out of courtesy.

Presiding at the assembly in the theater
was the town clerk (Acts 19:35), who we
know from the inscriptions was the dominant figure in the political life of the city.
He chaired meetings of the assembly,
helped draft decrees to be submitted to it,

[69]Ramsay, *Church in the Roman Empire*, p. 134.

sealed such decrees with the public seal, and had charge of money bequeathed to the people. The office was held in rotation by the city's leading citizens. The clerk's social prestige plus his political power insured ready attention on the part of the crowd, especially since he had let them yell themselves hoarse for two hours and came to the rostrum at a point when they were ready to listen to responsible leadership. The crowd was especially ready to listen when he reminded them that this irresponsible action put the city in jeopardy of losing its privileges of local autonomy. Rome took freedom from towns whose native officials could not maintain order.

After the riot caused by the silversmiths at Ephesus had subsided, Paul decided to leave the city. No doubt it was the fall of the year.[70] Traveling across Macedonia, he settled down in Achaia (probably Corinth) for three months (Acts 20:3) and then determined to return to Syria. When a plot against his life was discovered, Paul thought it wiser to take a less direct route eastward. Journeying through Macedonia once more, he sailed from Philippi to Troas.[71]

Troas. There the apostolic company spent a week. There too occurred the somewhat amusing incident of a young man falling asleep as the long-winded apostle spoke. Falling out of a third floor window, the young fellow was taken up for dead but was restored by Paul—seemingly by an act of healing (Acts 20:6-12). After being up all night and subjected to all the strain and confusion of the evening hours, Paul set out on foot in the morning for Assos, about thirty miles away. What stamina he must have had! He could have sailed south with the rest of his party but for some reason decided not to do so.

[70]He spent three months in Achaia (or Achaea) after leaving Ephesus and probably spent a like amount of time traveling elsewhere. His aim was to reach Jerusalem by Pentecost of the next spring (Acts 20:16).
[71]This site is discussed in the chapter on Greece, p. 449.

316. The badly ruined theater at Ephesus

Assos. Assos stood on a volcanic hill some 700 feet in altitude. Since it was located on the Gulf of Adramyttium and faced south toward Lesbos, it is not at all surprising that it was founded by Aeolians of Lesbos (Mytilene) about 900 B.C. This virtually impregnable site rose in steep cliffs sheer from the sea. Its sides were covered with both natural and artificial terraces.

Assos was successively a part of the Lydian Kingdom, the Persian Empire, Alexander's empire, the kingdom of Pergamum, and the Roman Empire. Aristotle taught there for three years (348-345 B.C.), and Cleanthes the Stoic philosopher was born there.

An American Archaeological Institute team explored and excavated at Assos from 1881 to 1883. Upon the terraces of the hill they found such public buildings as the gymnasium, the treasury, the baths, the marketplace, and the theater. The marketplace (agora) was nearly rectangular in shape, and along its north and south sides were long stoas of typically Pergamene form. (See Fig. 319.) Around the base of the hill stood a Hellenistic wall about two miles in length and thirty feet high. A second wall at the site dated to the Byzantine period. On the summit of the acropolis stood a Doric temple which the excavators assigned to the fifth century B.C. but which many others feel dated a century earlier.

317. The great theater looking toward the stage

Rüstem Duyuran, assistant director of the Archaeological Museum of Istanbul, says of this, "Nowhere else in Anatolia do we find another temple of the archaic period with the architraves and metopes decorated so richly with sphinx, centaurs, and such mythological creatures, and with animals, as lion and boar."[72] The harbor from which Paul sailed to Mitylene (Mytilene) has since silted up and is covered with gardens. Modern inhabitants have constructed an artificial harbor at its side.

Island journey. Paul's journey through the coastal islands off Asia Minor must have been most scenic those spring days. Instead of being clothed with the brown mantle they wore much of the year, they shone like emeralds, green with growing wheat, fruits, vegetables, and shrubs and trees of various kinds. Benefiting from seasonal rains, the mountain torrents coursed through the pine woods to the sea.

Mitylene, Lesbos. After a sea voyage of some forty miles, the apostolic party dropped anchor at Mitylene, chief city of the island of Lesbos. Located on the southeast part of the island, Mitylene was settled by Aeolians who claimed to have migrated from Boeotia before 1000 B.C. and whose nobles traced their descent from Agamem-

[72]Rüstem Duyuran, *The Ancient Cities of Western Anatolia* (Ankara: Turkish Press, n.d. [since 1948]), pp. 22-23.

non, who captured the place during the Trojan War. These early Greeks settled down on a small offshore island. With growth in population, the town spread to include a portion of Lesbos proper. The two parts of the city were connected by bridges. Harbors were constructed on the north and south of the city, and one could pass from one to the other via the channel between the smaller island and Lesbos. The northern harbor was protected by a breakwater. Although the two islands are now linked by the silting up of the channel between them, they were still separate in Paul's day, as is attested by references in Strabo (contemporary with Christ) and Pausanias (2d century A.D.).

Located some seven to ten miles from the Asia Minor coast, Lesbos is about forty-three miles long and about twenty-eight miles wide. Roughly triangular, it is indented by two bays in the south and has an area of 623 square miles. Its surface is rugged, the highest mountain being Olympus, about 3100 feet high. Despite the nature of the terrain, the country is fertile in olives, wine, and grain. Its position near the old trade route between the Hellespont and points south and east made Lesbos and her capital an important center at all times.

As Lesbos expanded her commercial activity, she established colonies in Thrace and the Troad and participated in the settlement of Naucratis in Egypt. Her great century was the seventh century B.C., during which her commercial power was extensive and her cultural development considerable. This was the century of the musician Terpander, the dithyrambist Arion, and the lyric poets Alcaeus and Sappho. The greatest political leader of the century was Pittacus, who for his wise administration won a place among the Seven Sages of Greece. The historian Hellanicus was a Lesbian of the fifth century B.C. and the philosopher Theopharastus a Lesbian of the third century.

After the fall of Lydia, Lesbos became subject to Persia. She participated in the ill-fated Ionian revolt of 499-493. Later freed from Persia she became a member of the Delian League (Athenian Empire). In spite of the fact that she enjoyed a privileged status in the league, Mitylene led a revolt against Athens in 428 B.C. Defeated by Athens, she lost her fleet, fortifications, and much of her land and was brought to the verge of destruction. Released from the Athenian Empire at the end of the Peloponnesian War (404), she joined the Second Athenian Alliance in 377 and remained a loyal member for its duration. Mitylene supported Athens in her struggle with Macedonia.

Lesbos and its capital fell under the sway of Alexander the Great and successively under Antigonus, Lysimachus, and the rule of the Ptolemies. When Rome took over, the island became a favorite resort area for Roman aristocrats. Tacitus described it as a "noble and pleasant island." Though occupied during 88 to 79 B.C. by Mithridates, it was restored to Rome by Pompey, who granted Mitylene status as a free city within the province of Asia. It enjoyed this privilege when Paul arrived, though it was later suspended by Vespasian and restored by Hadrian.

Chios (modern Khios). The next stop on the apostolic itinerary, a day later, was near the island of Chios. Luke says, "We came the following day over against Chios" (Acts 20:15). Some interpret this statement to mean that the ship was becalmed there. Others feel that because of a dark moon the ship lay at anchor on the Asian coast opposite the island until daybreak would facilitate further sailing.

As Paul approached from the northeast, the bold yellow mountains of Chios formed a striking outline against the blue sky. Straight ahead the channel between the island and the mainland narrowed to five miles, and this was blocked by a group of small islands.

Chios itself, shaped like a bow aimed at the Asia Minor coast, stretched thirty-two miles along the starboard side of the ship. Its width varies from eight to eighteen miles. Some 110 miles in circumference, Chios has a surface of 350 to 400 square miles. While the north end of the island is mountainous (highest altitude, 4,255 feet) with steep coasts, there are four plains (mostly in the south) with very fertile soil. In spite of the fact that there is no real watercourse on the island, luxuriant vegetation is made possible by numerous springs. The place was renowned in antiquity for its wine, figs, wheat, and gum mastic. The last was obtained from the lentiscus tree by making incisions in the branches from which a sort of resin would flow and form a gum. This still constitutes an important element of the economy of the place.

The chief city, located in the southeastern part of the island and bearing the same name as the island, was founded on the finest harbor of the eastern seaboard of the Aegean. Eighty ships could anchor in her roadstead.

Colonized by Ionians from Euboea, Chios early became highly prosperous. Schools of artists working in metal and stone flourished there, and the island had a distinguished literary tradition. It was perhaps the lead-

318. Unexcavated shops along one side of the agora at Ephesus

319. An inscribed lintel mentioning Augustus Caesar in the agora at Ephesus

ing contender for the honor of being the birthplace of Homer.

Incorporated in the Persian Empire under Cyrus, Chios fought heroically against her overlord during the Ionian revolt. Crushing the revolt, the Persians burned the cities and temples of the island and carried off her most beautiful girls. During the fifth century B.C. Chios joined the Delian League (Athenian Alliance) and remained loyal until 413. For her insurrection she suffered terribly at the hands of the Athenians who ultimately recaptured the entire island. During the fourth century Chios joined the Second Athenian Alliance and revolted successfully only a few years before conquest by Alexander the Great. Independent during the early Hellenistic era, she allied with Rome during the second century and was virtually depopulated by the sack of 86 B.C., carried out by Mithridates in his temporarily successful contest with Rome.

The Roman general Sulla restored the Chians to their homes and bestowed on them the rights of a free city, which implied that there was local autonomy and in certain respects the privilege of being governed according to native law, while many of their neighboring cities in the province of Asia were governed according to Roman law. Chian efforts to regain prosperity were interrupted by a violent earthquake during the reign of Tiberius. The Roman emperor helped in the rehabilitation, and a reasonable degree of prosperity had been attained by the time Paul sailed by.

Samos. Sailing in a southeasterly direction from Chios, the apostolic company on the next day headed for the northern shore of the island of Samos. The coast was rocky, precipitous, and thickly wooded. The party veered east and sailed through the channel between Samos and the mainland, here only about a mile in width. Rising above them on the left was Mount Mycale. They dropped anchor in the harbor of the town of Samos at the southeastern edge of the island.

Apparently the ship stopped every evening. The reason lay in the wind which at that time of the year generally blows from the north, beginning at an early hour in the morning and dying away in the afternoon. At sunset there is a dead calm; a gentle southerly wind blows during the night.

Samos is twenty-seven miles long and fourteen at its greatest width. A little over 100 miles in circumference, the island has an area of about 180 square miles. A continuation of the Mycale Ridge cuts across Samos and gives it a rugged, picturesque appearance. The highest elevation is in the west, where Mount Kerkis stands at an altitude of 4,725 feet. There are several small plains on the southern part of the island which are remarkably fertile and largely covered with vineyards.

Samos was colonized by Ionians during the century before 1000 B.C. and the settlers early became distinguished mariners and merchants. Samos established colonies of her own in numerous places, including Thrace, Egypt, Libya, Cilicia, Sicily, and perhaps southern Italy. Her sailors were probably the first Greeks to reach the Strait of Gibraltar. Important Samian industries in classical times were metalwork and woolen production.

Samos became an important center of Ionian luxury, art, and science. The sixth century B.C. was her greatest. She was the home of notable architects, sculptors, gem engravers, moralists, and poets (including Aesop). The greatest of all Samians, Pythagoras, migrated to southern Italy. The tyrant Polycrates (c. 535-522) was her great political leader. A friend and contemporary of Pisistratus of Athens, Polycrates cut a subterranean aqueduct right through the mountain on which the citadel of the town was placed, built the great temple of Hera, and in other ways made the city significant. The Samian navy ruled the waves around her island from her new deep-sea harbor and blockaded mainland subjects of Persia.

After the death of Polycrates by treachery, the Persians conquered Samos and partly depopulated it. The Samians had largely recovered by 499 B.C. when they joined the general Ionian revolt. At a criti-

cal moment during the sea battle off Lade in 494, the Samians deserted, probably because of jealousy of Miletus, dooming the Ionian cause. They redeemed themselves, however, at the Greek victory of Mycale in 479.

Samos held a privileged status in the first Athenian confederacy until 441, when revolt brought them degradation to tributary rank. Thereafter Samos was one of the most loyal dependencies of Athens, serving for a time as the home of the democracy (411) and winning the Athenian franchise during the last stages of the Peloponnesian War. Thereafter it was occupied by Sparta, then Persia, and later recovered by Athens (365). After the death of Alexander, Samos was for a time controlled in turn by Egypt and Syria. During the Hellenistic age it was eclipsed by Rhodian sea power and wealth.

Made a part of the Roman province of Asia, Samos entertained Augustus during the winter after the Battle of Actium (31 B.C.) and in 17 B.C. was made a free city by Augustus, a position which it retained until the days of Vespasian. There were many Jewish residents on the island; Herod visited there and bestowed numerous benefits on the Samians. Samos seems to have enjoyed a fairly high degree of prosperity during the entire New Testament period.

If Paul had had a little longer to spend at Samos, he might have walked the two-mile sacred way westward from the city to the great temple of Hera (Juno). Though the early temple had been destroyed about 517 B.C., it was rebuilt shortly thereafter. However, the edifice was never completely finished (i.e., some of the columns were not fluted, etc.). Cicero and Strabo recorded their visits to this religious center during the first century B.C. German excavations[73] at the site reveal that the temple measured 368 by 178 feet, that it was of the Ionic or-

320. The great marble main street of Ephesus, lined with statue bases and columns

[73]F. H. Marshall, *Discovery in Greek Lands* (Cambridge: At the University Press, 1920), pp. 84-85.

der, and that it had 132 columns in all—a triple row of eight at each end and a double row of twenty-four on each long side, together with ten in the front chamber of the temple. Herodotus called this "the greatest temple of all those we know." When this temple is compared with the Parthenon at Athens (228 by 101 feet) and the Temple of Zeus at Olympia (slightly smaller than the Parthenon), one may be inclined to think Herodotus was right.

Considerable remains of the ancient wall of Samos may also still be seen. Some of these ruins stand to a height of eighteen feet and are ten to twelve feet thick. In the higher part of town, portions of the theater survive. Little remains of the ancient city itself, which Herodotus says was the greatest of cities, Hellenic or barbarian, while under Polycrates.

Trogyllium. After leaving Samos Paul "tarried at Trogyllium" (Acts 20:15), according to the Authorized Version. The principal manuscripts (Aleph, A, B, C) omit these words but D includes them. Possibly the latter was founded on a tradition that survived in the church of Asia and gives a detail which is highly probable. The promontory of Trogyllium juts out from the mainland opposite Samos, and it is entirely possible that Paul's ship was becalmed in the lee of the promontory. Close by was an island bearing the same name, and at

321. The Pergamene stoa at Athens built by Attalus II during the second century B.C.

the end of the promontory an anchorage still called St. Paul's port.

Miletus. At any rate, the apostle sailed on to Miletus (twenty-three miles from Trogyllium), which he reached the following day. On the way he passed the site of the battle of Mycale (479 B.C.) and moved through waters where the great battle of Lade had been fought in 494. In fact, the island of Lade protected the main harbor of Miletus.

Miletus lay on the southern shore of the Latonian Gulf, which penetrated Caria south of Mycale. Paul stopped there and sent a messenger to Ephesus to summon the elders to Miletus. No doubt the messenger sailed the twelve miles north across the gulf to Priene and traveled another twenty-five miles by land to Ephesus. This sending of a messenger, waiting for the Ephesian elders, and the subsequent conference must have taken several days (Acts 20:15-38). Meanwhile Paul had a chance to look around Miletus. When the apostle arrived at Miletus, it was an important city with a population of something like 100,000.[74] But its most illustrious days had occurred several centuries earlier.

The origins of Miletus are lost in the haze of legend and the mists of time. Probably about 1100 B.C. Ionians from Athens seized the city, which during subsequent centuries became a great commercial and cultural center. One of her most famous commodities was wool. Her ships sailed to every part of the Mediterranean and even into the Atlantic. She is said to have founded some seventy-five colonies in the eighth, seventh, and sixth centuries on the Black Sea and its approaches and in Egypt. Her greatest century was the sixth; and some of her greatest sons included the philosophers Thales, Anaximander, and Anaximines, and the chronicler and cartographer Hecataeus.

Maintaining a running contest with Lydia for some time, Miletus finally fell to her

[74]Broughton, p. 813.

neighbor in the days of Croesus (who took all Ionia) but apparently maintained a privileged status. This position she seems to have held in 564 B.C. when Lydia fell to Cyrus and when the Greek cities of the coast came under his control. In 499 Miletus led the Ionian revolt against Persia. After the naval disaster at Lade, Miletus was destroyed, her inhabitants were killed or sent into slavery, and the temple at Didyma was burned.

During the fifth century Miletus rose once more and became a member of the Delian League. Fifth century greats were Hippodamus, the city planner who laid out the Piraeus at Athens, and the poet Timotheus. Revolting against Athens in 412 B.C., the city merely fell under control of Persia and subsequently to Alexander the Great. Hellenistic monarchs—the Seleucids, Antigonids, Ptolemies, and Pergamenes—successively held the city and erected impressive buildings there. Miletus became a part of the Roman province of Asia in 129 B.C. and thereafter tended to live on past glories. During Paul's day she was unimportant by comparison. The trade of the Maeander River valley now flowed through Ephesus, and Ephesus shared with Smyrna the trade that traversed the great road from interior Asia Minor.

The Miletus which Paul saw was not the city which once had been the intellectual center of Ionian Asia Minor; that had been destroyed by the Persians. Rather, he witnessed the metropolis which had been designed in the fifth century B.C. and which had since been much added to by Hellenistic and Roman rulers.

It is assumed that Paul was on a small freighter and that he docked at the Lion's Port, the commercial port of Miletus on the north side of town. Flanked by two huge stone lions, this port could be protected by closing off the mouth with chains. As the apostle disembarked on a marble-paved

322. An aqueduct and Byzantine church, Miletus

quayside, he saw to his left one of the largest temples of the city, dedicated to Apollo Delphinion. Built during Hellenistic times, this consisted of a mere enclosure surrounded by porticoes. In part this structure served as a public archive.

To the right of the temple stood a monumental gateway that opened on a street which led into the heart of the city. As Paul walked down this street, to his right lay the northern marketplace (agora) surrounded by a Doric colonnade and numerous shops. To his left stood baths and a gymnasium.

Now the short street came to an end in a square, on the east of which was a Doric temple to Esculapius. To the west (Paul's right) was the bouleuterion or hall of the assembly of the city council. This structure, apparently built in the days of Antiochus IV Epiphanes (c. 170 B.C.), was rectangular on the outside and was fitted inside with a semicircle of seats rising in tiers. This building held 500 people. Actually the council house was a complex consisting of the chamber proper and a square surrounded by a portico and entered by a monumental gateway and having an altar in the center. Wedged in between the council house and the agora to the north of it, a small temple stood. It was dedicated to the worship of Rome and Augustus.

To the south the square opened into the

great south agora of the city which could vie with any in the ancient world for size. It covered some 33,000 square yards, embracing sixteen city blocks. Like the northern agora (which was the more ancient of the two) the southern was surrounded with a Doric colonnade.

If the apostle had taken a street at the west end of the Lion's Port instead of the east end, he would have found himself on the main north-south thoroughfare of Miletus. It would have led him past the theater and the stadium with its adjacent temple of Athena, all of which would have been on his right. Smaller in Paul's day, both the theater and stadium were subsequently enlarged, the former to hold some 30,000 people. Paul would have passed numerous blocks of houses too before he reached the town gate, just beyond which was the cemetery.

323. Sculpture from the Temple of Apollo at Didyma

If Paul had passed through the southern gate, he would have found himself on the sacred way that led ten miles south to Didyma (within the territory of Miletus) where stood the great temple of Apollo. This ancient temple was destroyed by the Persians in 494 B.C. but was subsequently rebuilt. But the builders planned too big, and the structure never was completely finished. Measuring 163 by 341 feet on the ground plan, the temple had sixty-foot-high columns.

After his conference with the Ephesian elders, Paul sailed away from Miletus. He returned again briefly, probably after release from his first Roman imprisonment, and was forced to leave Trophimus there ill (II Tim. 4:20).

Gradually during succeeding centuries the waters of the Maeander River silted up the Latonian Gulf, and Miletus is now five miles from the sea, while the former island of Lade, which helped to make the largest harbor of the town, is a hill rising in the alluvial plain. The area has become in large part a malarial swamp, and much of the ancient city is now under water.

In spite of these difficulties, Theodor Weigand led a German team to the site in 1899 and continued season after season to lay bare the city which fifth century B.C. leaders planned and which Paul saw. German excavators also worked at Didyma, beginning in 1906. Many seasons of excavation were later conducted at Miletus between World Wars I and II and after World War II. Professor G. Kleiner worked there in the fall of 1961, investigating again the theater hill, the north market, the bouleuterion, and some of the second century A.D. villas (with their lovely mosaics) on the plateau. For up-to-date annual surveys of archaeological work at Miletus or other sites in Asia Minor, one can read the excellent reports in the *American Journal of Archaeology* by Machteld J. Mellink.

Cos. The next stop on the apostolic itinerary, probably about a day out of Miletus, was Cos, on an island by the same name. Cos was a long, narrow island oriented east and west. About twenty-three miles long, it had a circumference of sixty-five miles and consisted of an area of 111 square miles. It was divided into three parts or regions: an abrupt limestone ridge along the eastern half of the southern coast, a rugged penin-

324. Harbor at Cos

the great Hippocrates (*c.* 460-377 B.C.), the father of medicine, first used to cure his patients.

The sanctuary of Asclepius (the god of healing) was excavated by Rudolf Herzog of Tübingen University 1898 to 1907. He uncovered a sanctuary on three terraces set in a sacred grove of cypresses about two miles from town. The topmost terrace had a Doric temple built of white island marble surrounded on three sides by a U-shaped portico with its open side facing the lower terraces and dating about 160 B.C. The middle terrace dated about 280 B.C. and supported a great altar faced by a small temple and other structures. The lowest terrace had a U-shaped portico with its open side facing the one on the top level. Dated about 350 to 250 B.C., the stoa contained rooms where the patients slept.[75]

When an earthquake nearly devastated the city of Cos in 1933, the Italians, who then controlled the island, availed them-

sula at the west end, and along the northern coast a central lowland of fertile soil which produced an excellent quality of grapes. The harbor was at the eastern end of the island. Mount Oromedon, a landmark for navigators, rose in the middle of the island.

Cos was settled by Greeks as early as the fifteenth century B.C. During the fifth century the city-state joined the Delian League and suffered considerable destruction during the Peloponnesian War (431-404). A member of the Second Athenian Alliance, it revolted successfully against Athens in 354. Coming under the control of Alexander, Cos subsequently oscillated between Macedon, Syria, and Egypt to find its greatest glory as a literary center under the protection of the Ptolemies, when it was the home of such greats as the poet Philetas. In the second century Cos was loyal to Rome even before it became a part of the province of Asia. Claudius, influenced by his Coan physician, Xenophon, made Cos a free city and conferred immunity from taxation upon it in A.D. 53.

Cos was one of the most beautiful ports of the ancient world and no doubt was most famous as a health resort and as the site of the first school of scientific medicine and the sanctuary of Asclepius (Esculapius). The island had a healthy climate and hot ferrous- and sulphur-bearing springs which

325. Relief of Asclepius from Epidaurus

[75]MacKendrick, p. 380.

selves of the opportunity to excavate the ancient city. They found a planned Hellenistic town with main cross streets, a stadium, and a surrounding wall; and they found evidence of occupation at the site as early as Mycenaean times. At the lower level of the sanctuary the excavators uncovered Roman baths which utilized the healing waters of the island's springs and which (by inscriptions) dated to Nero's reign (and thus to the time of Paul's ministry).

Rhodes. A regular port of call for the small ships coasting the Aegean, Rhodes was the next stop of Paul and his associates. As they sailed up to the double harbor, they probably were struck with wonder at the sight of the great colossus which guarded the entrance. This great statue of the sun god stood to a height of about 105 feet and was recognized as one of the seven wonders of the ancient world.[76] A hollow casting of bronze on an iron armature, the colossus was filled with blocks of stone.[77] In his left hand the image held a javelin with the blunt end resting on the ground. In his right hand he held a torch aloft, and on his head he

326. St. Paul's Harbor, Rhodes

[76]The Colossus of Rhodes seems somewhat puny compared with the Statue of Liberty, which is 151 feet high and which with its pedestal stands to a height of 305 feet.

[77]Shakespeare notwithstanding, there seems to be no basis for concluding that the statue's legs straddled the harbor entrance. In such a case the straddle of the legs would have had to be 400 yards. No doubt it stood on a stone base with the legs together.

wore a crown adorned with sunrays protruding somewhat in the fashion of the American Statue of Liberty. Dedicated about 290 B.C., the statue was broken off at the knees by an earthquake about 225 B.C., restored by the Romans, and demolished by the Arabs during the seventh century A.D.

Rising from the harbor, the city was constructed in the form of an amphitheater against the surrounding hillsides, and it was protected by strong walls and towers. The acropolis rose at the southwest extremity of the city. On it stood two temples (one dedicated to Athena), a stadium, a theater, a gymnasium, and other structures.

Perhaps Paul could have said with the Roman geographer Strabo, who was there not long before him, that Rhodes was the most splendid city known to him in respect of harbors, streets, walls, and public buildings, all of which were adorned with a profusion of works of art, both painting and sculpture. In spite of the fact that under Roman rule Rhodes kept a modicum of prosperity and boasted no small distinction as a beautiful city and center of higher education, it was no longer at its height when Paul came.

Largest of the Dodecanese Islands (about 45 miles long by 22 wide and covering an area of 545 square miles), Rhodes had a long history. Many believe that the "Dodanim" of Genesis 10:4 and I Chronicles 1:7 should read "Rodanim" instead and that the reference is to Rhodes. The Minoan culture maintained itself there, as archaeological remains indicate. The "Dorian invasion" resulted on Rhodes in the establishment of three towns: Lindus (modern Lindos), Ialysus, and Camirus (all three in the Pentapolis). In subsequent centuries the island founded colonies in Spain, Italy, Sicily, and Asia Minor.

During the fifth century, Rhodes was a member of the Athenian Empire but revolted against Athens in 412 B.C. The war with Athens led to union of the three cities on the island into one state with a new federal capital of Rhodes (408). Early in the fourth century, Rhodes fell into the hands of the Athenians again and subsequently was controlled by Alexander the Great. After Alexander's death, Rhodes won her freedom again, and her really great period of history began.

Rhodian prosperity always came mainly from the carrying trade. Her commercial activities received great impetus from the conquests of Alexander the Great, which gave unrestricted access to Egypt, Cyprus, and Phoenicia; and in the third century she became the richest of the Greek city-states. A center of exchange and capital, Rhodes was naturally the enemy of piracy and for a long time effectively checked it on the high seas.

By her appeal to Rome (along with Pergamum) for help against Syria and Macedonia (201 B.C.), Rhodes was largely responsible for the first major intervention of Rome in eastern affairs. She cooperated with Rome in subsequent wars against Syria and Macedonia and was rewarded with territory in Caria and Lycia. Rhodes achieved her height of prosperity during the first part of the second century B.C. When Rome thought Rhodian actions too equivocal during the Third Macedonian War, she took away the Carian and Lycian territory and made Delos a free port (167 B.C.). This competition plus a probable increase in piracy ruined Rhodes. She later became an ally of Rome on unfavorable terms. However, she remained a free city even down to the Apostle Paul's time and retained her fine harbors, public buildings, and other indications of a past glory.

Patara. In Paul's desire to reach Jerusalem by Pentecost, he next sailed to Patara. Since the prevailing winds in this part of the Mediterranean are from the west, ships sailing from the Aegean or Italy to Phoenicia or Egypt would often risk the voyage straight across the sea from Patara, rather

than taking the slow coastal route along the southern shores of Asia Minor. Apparently the apostle embarked on the more daring course at this time (Acts 21:2). It was her position on the maritime routes rather than the value of her hinterland that gave wealth and prominence to Patara during the first century A.D. Though the city lay on the coast of Lycia only seven or eight miles southeast of the mouth of the Xanthus (modern Koca) River and though the valley of this river is the best part of Lycia, Patara's location in relation to the Xanthus was of relative unimportance compared with her relation to international trade and passenger routes.

Lycia was not definitely colonized by Greeks in early times, and not until the third century B.C., under Ptolemaic rule, did the natives of the area abandon their native tongue for Greek. Thought to be of Phoenician origin with a later infusion of Dorians, Patara was enlarged by Ptolemy Philadelphus of Egypt. The chief Lycian god was identified with Apollo, who had a celebrated oracle at Patara—second only in renown to that of Delphi. Since the oracle spoke only during the six winter months, Paul would not have known of any revelations given during his visit there.

Patara has not yet been excavated, so the ancient city is not well known. To be seen at present are a theater (dating to the reign of Antoninus Pius), a ruined temple, town walls of considerable extent, and open sarcophagi outside the walls. Within the walls are remains of temples, altars, and statue bases; and fragments of sculpture in profusion lie about ruined and mutilated. The location of the harbor is still apparent, but the area is at present a swamp, choked with sand and bushes.

To Palestine and back to Myra. The apostolic company reached Jerusalem safely, but the success of the trip was quite in contrast with the treatment Paul was to suffer at the hands of Jews and Romans in the center of Judaism. The story, recorded in Acts 21:10–26:32, is quite beyond the intent of this study. At length, more than two years after Paul left the coast of Asia Minor, he was back again. But this time he was in the custody of a Roman centurion who had the responsibility of bringing him to Rome for trial before Caesar.

The westerly winds which favored the voyage from Patara or Myra to Tyre made the return voyage from Tyre to Myra an impossibility. The regular course for ships from Palestine or Phoenicia was northward past the east end of Cyprus and thence along the Asia Minor coast. Then, by means of ocean currents and land winds which blew off the coast, they made their way westward toward Myra. The voyage from Caesarea to Myra might be done in as short a time as ten days, but recorded trips over that route took as long as twenty days. Ships of the Roman grain fleet (on one of which Paul probably sailed) might take the same route if the winds required, but normally they sailed directly from Alexandria to Myra on the Lycian coast, from there westward across the Aegean north of Crete, through the Ionian Sea, and then up the western coast of Italy.

In Greek times Patara surpassed Myra, but in Roman times Myra, forty miles east of Patara, became the chief seaport of Lycia. It grew especially as a result of the Alexandrian grain trade with Italy. Though Myra was located two and one-half miles up the Andracus River from the coast, the same name was often applied to its harbor, Andriaca. There are splendid ruins at Myra, but they have never been systematically excavated. There are remains of a theater 355 feet in diameter, one of the largest and best built in Asia Minor, several public buildings, and numerous inscribed tombs. Exactly what the town was like when Paul stopped there cannot now be determined.

Other Pauline Cities

Three additional cities of Asia Minor figure in the Pauline narrative: Colossae, Hierapolis, and Laodicea (Col. 2:1; 4:13-16). The last of these is more important as one of the seven cities which John addressed in the Revelation, but it is more conveniently discussed here along with its sister cities of the Lycus Valley. Of the three sites, Colossae figures more prominently in the New Testament narrative because an entire epistle was addressed to the church there. But apparently Paul considered that the Colossian epistle was pertinent to the Laodiceans as well because he urged that it be read in their churches (Col. 4:16).

It is commonly assumed that Paul never visited these Lycus cities, and such references as Colossians 1:4, 7-8; 2:1 are cited to prove it. However, it seems best to conclude that the apostle more than likely did visit one or more of these Phrygian cities. He might possibly have done so on his second missionary journey (Acts 16:6). The natural route for him to have taken on that occasion was from Syria, through the Cilician Gates, then to Derbe, Lystra, Iconium, Antioch of Pisidia, Apamea, Colossae, Laodicea, and down the Maeander River to Ephesus. The statement of Colossians 2:1 need not compel a student to believe that Paul knew none of the Christians at Colossae personally, though nearly all of them may have been converts made later by someone else. At any rate, he could have visited the Lycus cities on one of his journeys.

The best way to introduce these Lycus cities to the modern student is to take him on a journey up the Maeander River (modern Menderes) from its mouth near Miletus. (The Maeander Valley was the route followed by the eastern trade route between Ephesus and the Euphrates in Roman times.) As one travels inland, the broad and fertile Maeander Valley becomes narrower; and about seventy-five miles from its mouth, near one of the ancient Antiochs, the foothills compress the valley to a width of about a mile. Approximately twenty-five miles farther on, the Maeander makes a sharp turn northward. At the bend it is joined by the Lycus, one of its principal tributaries. The traveler is now in the open Lycus Valley.

Roughly triangular in form, the plain of the Lycus (which runs from southeast to northwest) is about twenty-four miles long. At its widest the plain is six miles. It is hemmed in on all sides by highlands which on the south ascend to Mount Cadmus (8,250 feet) and the Salbacus Mountains (7,590 feet) and which on the west form part of the Messogis Range that stretches from interior Anatolia out to Mycale. The Lycus Valley is on the edge of the steppeland; to the east is the lonely sheep country.

Laodicea. About twelve miles southeast of the junction of the Lycus with the Maeander stood ancient Laodicea. This city was situated on the long spur of a hill between the narrow valleys of the small rivers Asopus (on the west) and Cadmus (on the east), which emptied their waters into the Lycus. Laodicea stood at an altitude of about 850 feet approximately three miles south of the Lycus. By Roman road the distance from Ephesus was some 100 miles.[78] The great road[79] from the coast to the interior of Asia Minor passed right through the middle of the city, making it an important center of trade and communication.

[78]Sir William M. Ramsay, *The Historical Geography of Asia Minor* (London: John Murray, 1890), p. 164. Ramsay has done a remarkable job of evaluating the ancient sources on Roman roads and distances between towns. His computations for the biblical sites of the province of Asia may be found on pages 164-68 of the above book.

[79]This road, extending from Ephesus to Magnesia, Tralleis, Antiochea (Antioch), Laodicea, and Apamea, a distance of about 158 miles, was built by Manius Aquilius, *c.* 130 B.C. Ramsay, *The Historical Geography of Asia Minor,* p. 164.

327. Looking out the gate of Laodicea toward Hierapolis

Exactly when the first settlers came to Laodicea is not known, but it was called successively in ancient times "Diospolis" and "Rhoas." Antiochus II, who ruled Seleucia 261-246 B.C., refounded the city and named it after his wife, Laodice. When the Romans defeated the Seleucids in 190 B.C., they assigned Laodicea to their ally Eumenes of Pergamum. When the Pergamene kingdom was willed to the Roman state in 133 B.C., Laodicea became Roman territory and part of the province of Asia. Mithridates, king of Pontus, besieged the city in 88 B.C. and held it until 84, when the Romans returned. Thereafter Roman rule was on the whole favorable to Laodicean prosperity.

The city's wealth came from its favorable location on the great east-west commercial route across Asia Minor and especially from its production of a very fine quality of world-famous black, glossy wool. Whether this wool came from a breed of black sheep or whether the fabric was dyed is not known with certainty. The city was also a center of banking; Cicero was one of the more famous men of the Roman world to cash drafts there. Furthermore, the establishment of a celebrated school of medicine in connection with the temple of the Phrygian god Men Karou, thirteen miles west of Laodicea, contributed to the importance of the area. Actually the school of medicine was located in Laodicea itself. Ramsay notes that a market was held under the auspices of the god somewhere near the temple and that people of the valley met and traded there with strangers from a distance.[80] The prosperity of Laodicea is well attested by the fact that the rebuilding of the city after the devastating earthquakes in the reigns of Tiberius and Nero was accomplished without proffered imperial or provincial aid.

Almost every phase of John's condemnation of the Laodiceans in Revelation 3:14-19 has been related by commentators to some phase of the city's character or activity. The apostle condemns them for being neither cold nor hot but lukewarm. Ramsay described the people there as follows: "There are no extremes, and hardly any very strongly marked features . . . ever pliable and accommodating, full of the spirit of compromise."[81] Others have seen in this mention of lukewarmness an allusion to the condition of the water supply which was brought by a six-mile aqueduct from the south. The water either came from hot springs and was cooled to lukewarm or came from a cooler source and warmed up in the aqueduct on the way.

In Revelation 3:17 the Laodiceans were scored for their trust in their riches. The following verse tells those who were noted for their beautiful black cloth to seek white raiment (symbolic of spiritual cleansing). Likewise they were told to anoint themselves with (spiritual) eye salve that they might really see. No doubt this is an allusion to the "Phrygian powder" used as a medicine for the eyes—a treatment which seems to have come through Laodicea into general use among the Greeks. This was mentioned with respect as early as Aristotle's day. Laodicean ointment for treating the ears also became renowned.

There were many Jewish inhabitants of Laodicea, and this may well explain the early spread of Christianity in the area.[82] Apparently the church there was not founded by Paul but may have been established by Epaphras (Col. 4:12-13). It early became the chief bishopric of Phrygia.

The identification of the "epistle from Laodicea" (Col. 4:16) which the Colossians were encouraged to read has given rise to much discussion. Some have held that it was written by Laodiceans, others that it was written by Paul from Laodicea, yet others that it was an epistle written by Paul to the Laodiceans and subsequently lost. An additional view which many accept is that the reference here is to the canonical Ephesians. The words "at Ephesus" in Ephesians 1:1 do not appear in the best manuscripts, and many have held that this epistle was a circular letter or perhaps designed originally for consumption by the Laodiceans.[83]

Laodicea continued prosperous during Roman and Byzantine times, but it was badly damaged by the Seljuk Turks who captured it in A.D. 1094. The Byzantines recaptured it three years later and held it until the end of the thirteenth century. After that it continued to decline and finally became uninhabited. In recent centuries the ruins, which cover hundreds of acres, have served as a stone quarry for surrounding villages. This practice has continued until the present so that some ruins which were fairly extensive a century ago have now largely disappeared.

In spite of this it is possible to make some general comments on the nature of the site during the first century A.D. The city was approximately square with the corners ori-

---

[80]Sir William M. Ramsay, *The Letters to the Seven Churches of Asia* (New York: A. C. Armstrong & Son, 1905), p. 417.
[81]*Ibid.*, pp. 422-23.

[82]Ramsay notes the evaluation of a tax document for 62 B.C., which seems to give evidence of 7,500 adult Jewish freemen in the district in that year. To this figure must be added women and children. *Ibid.*, p. 420.
[83]For a discussion of this position see John Rutherfurd, "Laodiceans, Epistle to the," *International Standard Bible Encyclopedia*, III, 1837-39.

ented toward the points of the compass. Covering about a square mile, the city was surrounded with walls dating to Hellenistic times. The great aqueduct came into Laodicea at about the middle of the southwest wall. The Ephesus gate pierced the northwest wall, and a road led from it across a bridge over the Asopus River. At the north corner of the city stood the acropolis and at its feet the gate which led to Hierapolis.

Against the southwest wall stood an amphitheatric stadium, so-called because both ends were semicircular and because rows of seats ran continuously around the whole circumference. The proper Greek stadium had only one end rounded. Buildings of this type are sometimes found in Asia Minor and are indiscriminately called "stadiums" and "amphitheaters." This structure was 900 feet long in the arena, had an axis line approximately northwest to southeast, and was dedicated in the latter part of A.D. 79 after news of the death of Vespasian had been received (according to the dedicatory inscription). Next to the stadium on the east was a building commonly thought to be a gymnasium, probably constructed A.D. 123-24.

There are three theaters inside the walls of Laodicea: a small one just north of the stadium, a middle-sized one near the Hierapolis gate, and a larger one along the northeast wall. The dates of these are unknown. Few temples have yet been found; possibly they were purposely destroyed by Christians as paganism declined. A small Ionic temple has been found some 230 yards southwest of the second theater. Remains of other buildings dot the site, but they have not yet been positively identified.

Fortunately Asia Minor archaeology is beginning to come into its own. Laodicea is among the ancient cities there receiving attention. An expedition to the site has now been organized by Laval University, Quebec. The director is Professor Jean des Gagniers, who conducted campaigns there

in 1961 and 1962. A survey of the site has been made; some streets and buildings are in the process of being cleared. A sounding revealed a colonnade of Hellenistic or early Roman date. Several fragments of sculpture and a number of inscriptions have been found. Scholars await with interest more definitive study of the town and detailed publication of the findings.

Hierapolis. As one strolled out through the north gate of ancient Laodicea, he could see the white cliffs of Hierapolis, six miles away, gleaming in the sunshine. The water from the hot springs of the place has tumbled over the cliffs from earliest times, depositing its heavy content of carbonates, sodium, and chlorides of calcium in its wake. Though from a distance the cliff is blinding white, one can see on closer inspection that it is streaked with yellow and black and gives the appearance of a frozen waterfall.

"The holy city" (*hiera polis*) was situated on a shelf about 1100 feet above sea level and 150 to 300 feet above the plain. The terrace which the city covered was about a mile and a third long and some 300 yards wide. It stood on the north side of the Lycus while Laodicea was on the south.

Like other Hellenistic cities, Hierapolis gives evidence of having been laid out all at one time. It had a main street running the

328. Hierapolis, appearing as a frozen waterfall

length of the city (southeast to northwest). On either side were covered sidewalks, and cross streets intersected it at right angles. Remains of two theaters may still be seen there—a smaller Hellenistic and a larger Roman structure. The Roman theater stands on the side of the hill at the eastern edge of the city. The front width is more than 325 feet and the orchestra measures about sixty-five feet in diameter. It is one of the most impressive archaeological remains in all Asia Minor.[84]

At the west end of the city stood the baths, which covered a large area. Some of the arches are still standing with a width of as much as fifty-two feet. Next to the baths are the remains of what appears to be a gymnasium. And nearby is a structure that has been called a statuary hall because it is believed that the niches in the walls held statues of the emperors. Archaeologists have dated some of these buildings to about A.D. 100. The great necropolis lay outside the north gate of the city.[85] In 1887 a German team under the leadership of Karl Humann investigated the remains on the ground at Hierapolis. Professor Paolo Verzone has led a corps of excavators at Hierapolis in recent years. In 1957 and 1958 he made a new survey of the city area and necropolis and studied a monumental city gate, and other buildings. He had reason to believe that the gate was of the first century A.D. In 1961 and 1962 he worked at the theater, the necropolis, the baths, and some private homes, and excavated and tried to restore an inscribed gateway.

Hierapolis seems to have been of Lydian origin. Little is known of its history during the Greek and Roman periods. Apparently after the battle of Magnesia in 190 B.C. (when Antiochus lost Asia Minor), this town was placed at the disposal of Eumenes II (197-159) and became part of his kingdom. He is thought to have refounded it. When Pergamum became Roman territory in 133 B.C., Hierapolis took her place as one of the towns of the province of Asia. Mithridates, king of Pontus, took the city in 88 B.C. and held it for four years. The city was destroyed by an earthquake in A.D. 17 during the reign of Augustus and had begun to regain its prosperity when it was again extensively destroyed by earthquake in A.D. 60, during the reign of Nero.

No doubt Epaphras conducted his ministry of church establishment there before the second earthquake (Col. 4:12-13), but whether one holds that the Colossian letter arrived before or after that catastrophe depends on the interpretation of the chronology of Paul's life and ministry. Hierapolis gradually struggled to its feet again and seems to have regained a measure of prosperity by the end of the century. Its great centuries of prosperity were the second and third. It was a flourishing episcopal see during Byzantine times; but sometime during the Middle Ages the city was ruined and finally deserted.

Tradition has it that Philip the Evangelist preached there during the latter part of his life. Later the church father Papias lived there. But possibly the most famous man Hierapolis produced was Epictetus, though he probably did not owe much to the education provided by his native city. A slave in Rome, he was freed by his master and taught philosophy in the capital until he was expelled from the city with the other philosophers by Domitian in A.D. 90.

The acceptance of Christianity in Hierapolis may have some connection with the large number of Jews in the place, settled there by one of the Hellenistic kings. The inscriptions attest to their power in the city. They were organized in trade guilds: the purple-dyers, the carpet-makers, and possibly others.[86] In regard to dyeing, it may

[84]Sherman E. Johnson, "Laodicea and Its Neighbors," *The Biblical Archaeologist*, XIII (Feb., 1950), 13-14.
[85]*Ibid.*, p. 14.

[86]Ramsay, *The Letters to the Seven Churches*, p. 421.

be noted that the hot springs of Hierapolis, rich in alum, were especially useful in the dyeing process.

But Judaism and Christianity were minority religions at Hierapolis, probably until Byzantine times. Hierapolis means "holy city" (though it is thought to have taken its name from a mythical Amazon queen Hiera), and it lived up to its name. No doubt the hot springs of the area were sacred to nature divinities, as was a cave filled with deadly fumes. This cave was called the "Plutonium" or "Charonion." It has been thought that a priest or priestess sat upon a stool deep in the Plutonium and when under the influence of the vapors uttered prophecies of value to those who sought them. One of the temples of the town was dedicated to Apollo, as was a temple near the Plutonium. Cybele, the mother goddess, was especially worshiped, along with Pluto, Men, Isis, and the imperial cult.

Colossae. The third of the Lycus Valley cities, Colossae, lay near the upper end of the valley about eleven miles east and a little south of Laodicea. At Colossae the valley narrowed to approximately two miles, and the city was overshadowed by great mountain heights. Colossae itself stood at an altitude of 1150 feet; Mount Cadmus towered above it some three miles to the south at an altitude of 8,013 feet. The streams which watered the Colossae area coursed down the sides of Cadmus. The fortified acropolis of the city lay on the south bank of the Lycus, but buildings and tombs stretched out on the north bank.

Colossae was once a great city of Phrygia. According to Herodotus it was an important city when Xerxes came through it in 481 B.C. According to Xenophon it was still important in 401 B.C. when Cyrus the Younger marched through. The rise of Hierapolis and especially Laodicea brought crippling competition to the older town, and it gradually dwindled, occupying a comparatively insignificant status by New Testament times. In its better days it had been an important center for the wool and dye industries. Its specialty was woolen goods of Colossene red. The surrounding countryside produced sheep that were known for the softness of their wool.

Epaphras, a member of Paul's missionary team, seems to have been chiefly responsible for the evangelization of Colossae as well as Laodicea and Hierapolis (Col. 4:12-13). But it is clear from the epistle that Paul wrote to the Colossian church that Christianity there had a severe contest with aspects of paganism, Judaism, and asceticism. Among the deities worshiped there during the Roman Period were Isis and Serapis, Helios, Demeter, and Artemis, in addition to the native Phrygian god Men.

Though Colossae later achieved the status of a bishopric, the city was deserted sometime between A.D. 600 and 700. Large blocks of stone, foundations of buildings, column fragments, and remains of a theater may still be seen, though the site has been largely rifled by inhabitants of nearby villages. It is still possible, however, that a systematic excavation there would be quite satisfying.

The Apostle Peter and Asia Minor

The Apostle Peter wrote to "sojourners of the dispersion in [preferred reading] Pontus, Galatia, Cappadocia, Asia, and Bithynia" (I Peter 1:1). Note that the provinces named include all of Asia Minor north of the Taurus Range and that the persons addressed were not Jews only nor even Christian Jews but Christians in general, as the contents of the epistle bear out.

Peter is not certainly known to have preached in the areas he addressed. Since the New Testament narrative is almost completely silent about him after his imprisonment by Herod, it is not known what he may have done or where he may have gone. Possibly he simply wrote to Christians in Asia Minor to encourage them, but it seems more likely to the writer that some ministry there established a contact and concern which led Peter to write to his children in the faith.

Where Peter was when he wrote has occasioned considerable discussion. He said he was in Babylon (I Peter 5:13). Some have argued that he meant literally the famous Babylon on the Euphrates (so Erasmus, Calvin, Alford, and others). But a much larger number of scholars have considered Babylon to be used here symbolically of Rome. John followed this practice in the Revelation, and writers of the second century and following did also. Whether or not Peter did as early as about A.D. 65 may be open to question.

The peculiar order in which the provinces are named in Peter's address has also received scholarly attention. An explanation which many have followed was advanced by F. J. A. Hort.[87] He says the reason for the order lies in the route followed by the messenger who brought the letter (perhaps in so many distinct copies) to the central cities of the various provinces. Some have suggested that the order in which the provinces are named favors the Babylonian origin of the epistle. Others suggest that the bearer of the letter sailed from Rome, landed at some port on the Black Sea, possibly Sinope (modern Sinop) in Pontus, traveled through the provinces named, took ship again at some Bithynian port, and sailed to Rome.

If the latter is true, the apostolic messenger may have landed at Sinope or Amisus (modern Samsun) in Pontus, dropped south to Ancyra (Ankara) in Galatia, traveled southeast to such a place as Archelais (modern Akserai) in western Cappadocia, moved westward from there on the east-west trade route to Ephesus, journeyed by road north to Cyzicus, taken ship to Nicomedia (modern Izmit) in Bithynia, and then sailed to Rome. All this is of course hypothetical, but it is a reasonable reconstruction. At any rate the provinces are discussed here in the order Peter introduces them.

Pontus. Pontus was originally an area along the southern shore of the Black Sea bordered on the west by the Halys River (modern Kizil Irmak), on the east and southeast by Armenia, on the south by Cappadocia, and on the southwest by Galatia. The area varied according to the political fortunes of its rulers. Along the Black Sea is a beautiful and well-watered but narrow coastland, with wider plains at the mouths of the Halys and Iris rivers, which provided the main lines of drainage and communication. Backing the coastal plain is a noble series of mountain ranges running parallel to the coast. The mountain valleys were fertile and productive of olives and other fruits, nuts, grains, and good pasturelands. The mountains themselves were clad with forests of beach, pine, oak, and fir which were exported to the forestless

[87]*Ibid.*, p. 183.

countries of the Mediterranean and used for local construction of ships. But the greatest wealth of the mountains lay in the mineral deposits of iron, copper, silver, and alum.

Under the Mithridatic line Amasia (modern Amasya) on the Iris River was the capital (and was later important as the birthplace of Strabo). Amisus, west of the Iris on the coast, possessed a large part of the coastal plain and controlled the easiest road to the plateau. Sinope to the west, the most northerly point in Asia Minor, had the best harbor on the Black Sea and was beautifully walled and adorned with public buildings in Peter's day. Amastris in western Pontus also had a good harbor, a good supply of timber, and numerous ships. Trapezus (Trabzon, or Trebizond), in the east gained immensely in importance during Nero's Armenian campaigns and maintained that position as the nearest port of supply for armies on the frontier. Nicopolis, Neocaesarea, and Sebastea are among other important towns of the region.

No doubt the Hittites occupied towns in the region of Pontus, but they only held uneasy control over the area at best. During the first half of the first millennium B.C., Greek colonists established themselves all along the southern shore of the Black Sea and in Pontus settled at such places as Sinope, Amisus, and Trapezus. (It was near Trapezus that Xenophon and his famous 10,000 reached the sea in 400 B.C.)

When the Persians established themselves in Asia Minor in 546 B.C., Pontus was joined to the empire and ruled by a dynasty of satraps, who managed to gain their independence a little before 350 B.C. and to maintain it during the Macedonian Period. As a result of the confusion following the death of Alexander the Great, Mithridates II was able to carve out for himself a fair-sized kingdom east of the Halys River (c. 300-280). In concert with Nicomedes of

Bithynia, he succeeded in quieting the Galatians (Gauls, i.e., Celts) in Phrygia. The Mithridatic dynasty lasted until 63 B.C. when for all practical purposes it was brought to an end by Pompey. During those centuries the area of Pontus varied with the strength of the individual kings, but it was generally on the increase.

The greatest of the Mithridatic line was Mithridates VI. He made an alliance with his son-in-law Tigranes of Armenia and then attacked Roman forces in Asia Minor. The first war (89-85) began with striking Pontic successes but ended with Mithridates contained once more within the original bounds of his kingdom. The second war (83-81) was little more than a series of three raids. The third war began in 74; and after initial Pontic advances, the Roman Lucullus took Mithridates' capital by siege, scattered his army, and drove him from the country. Finally Pompey, appointed in 66 B.C., utterly destroyed Mithridates' power, and the aged king died by suicide in the Crimea (63 B.C.).

Mithridates' kingdom was incorporated into the Roman Empire under the name "Pontus" and constituted half of the combined province Bithynia-Pontus. During the civil wars, Pharnaces II, a son of Mithridates VI, was able to establish himself as ruler over his father's kingdom. But his success was short-lived; he was defeated by Caesar in 47 B.C. While Mark Antony was ruling in the East he reestablished a narrowed kingdom of Pontus alongside the Roman province and gave it in 36 B.C. to Polemon, who founded a dynasty that ruled the kingdom until A.D. 63. This was a client kingdom on the order of that of Herod the Great in Judaea. In A.D. 63 Polemon's kingdom (Pontus Polemoniacus) was brought to an end. Part of it was added to the province of Cappadocia (and remained so until Diocletian) and part of it to Galatia (Pontus Galaticus).

In early Pontus, society was essentially feudal, some of the villages and territorial units being ruled by the nobility and some by the priests as part of large temple estates. Some of the mountainous regions were for a long time uncivilized tribal territories. The kings apparently brought priests and nobility under effective control but did little to develop cities. To the end of the Roman Empire, Pontus kept much of its native character. The cities were artificial constructions; the feudal aristocracy remained important. In the eastern part the natives were only slightly touched by Hellenistic civilization.

During the first century A.D. the name "Pontus" had at least two significations: client kingdom and Roman province. No doubt the Roman province is in view in I Peter 1:1 and Acts 18:2, where Aquila is said to have been a native of the place. It is interesting to note that an inscription has been found which refers to an Aquila at Sinope. Perhaps the Pontic Jews who were present in Jerusalem on the Day of Pentecost (Acts 2:9) were likewise from the province, though they might also have been from the kingdom (Pontus Polemoniacus).

How Christianity was established in Pontus is not known. Possibly some natives of the place were converted on the Day of Pentecost. Perhaps some Christians from the west Asian coast settled at Sinope or Amastris. At any rate by the beginning of the second century, Christianity was widespread there. Pliny the Younger, who governed the province 111-13, inquired of the Emperor Trajan how to treat Christians there (in respect to persecution) and indicated that they were to be found among men and women of all ages and rank and in town and country. However, the Christianization of the inland districts of Pontus did not begin until about the middle of the third century.

Galatia. Galatia has already been discussed in connection with Paul's ministry in Asia Minor.

Cappadocia. In early classical times Cappadocia was thought of as the whole inland district of eastern Asia Minor extending from the Taurus Mountains to the Black Sea. But during the latter days of the Persian Empire, the area was divided into two administrative districts called Cappadocia and Pontus. So Cappadocia has come to be defined as that area of east central Asia Minor bounded by the Euphrates River on the east, the Taurus Mountains on the south, Pontus and Galatia on the north and northwest, and Lake Tatta on the west.

Cappadocia covered some 250 miles east and west and about 150 miles north and south. The eastern portion is traversed by the Anti-Taurus Mountains. The rest of the country consists of a great rolling plateau about 3,000 feet in altitude. Almost treeless in the west, the plains provide pasture for flocks of sheep. Rising from the plains in the central and western parts of the area are detached groups or masses of volcanic mountains, the highest of which is Argaeus (Erciyas Dagi, over 13,000 feet). The ranges of the Taurus and Anti-Taurus are for the most part well watered and well timbered. The severe winter climate limits agricultural production to hardy cereals and sheep. The Roman emperors kept studs of racehorses there. Quartz, salt, and silver mines were found in the province.

The chief rivers of Cappadocia were the Halys, which flowed north, and the Sarus (Seyhan) and Pyramus (Ceyhan), which flowed south through Cilicia. The chief cities, according to Strabo, were Caesarea Mazaca (modern Kayseri), the capital of the Roman province in central Cappadocia, and Tyana in the southwest. Archelais, a Roman colony in the western part of the province on the vital east-west trade road, was also a place of some importance during the Empire period.

Cappadocia seems first to have had some historical significance early in the second millennium B.C. when the Assyrian merchant colonies were established there. Later in the millennium the Hittites controlled the area. It next figured in international affairs during the Persian Period, when an Iranian nobility with feudal dominion over considerable districts established itself. Besides these estates of the nobles large areas were owned by the temples and ruled by priests. The ordinary people lived in villages on land owned by nobles or temples. This socioeconomic structure lasted many centuries.

For a while Cappadocians ruled there more or less independently as tributary to Persia. Later this freedom was destroyed, to be regained once more under Ariarathes I, a contemporary of Alexander the Great. The conqueror was content to accept tributary acknowledgment of the Cappadocian without entering his territory.

Ariarathes' line was interrupted by Eumenes I of Pergamum, but it later returned to power. Under the fourth Ariarathes, Cappadocia came into relations with Rome. After the battle of Magnesia in 190 B.C., he and his successors adopted a pro-Roman policy. Cappadocia was devastated by Tigranes the Great of Armenia during the Mithridatic wars, but it was restored by Pompey who gave the king large loans for reconstruction. During the civil wars Cappadocia sided first with Pompey, then with Caesar, then with Antony and then against him. Antony replaced the Ariobarzanes dynasty, which by that time controlled the throne, with Archelaus Sisines.

When the latter lost the favor of Rome, Tiberius annexed Cappadocia in A.D. 17; and it remained a procuratorial province until A.D. 70. In that year Vespasian united to it Armenia Minor and formed a large and important frontier province, governed by an ex-consul. Afterward the province received various accessions of territory.

Efforts of the later kings and of the Roman rulers of Cappadocia to achieve Hellenization and urbanization in the area were not greatly successful. Urbanization was never fully developed in Cappadocia; and with the economic decline in the Empire during the later second and third centuries, large imperial estates grew up there. The area subsequently became part of the Byzantine Empire and suffered greatly from Arab encroachment, passing into Muslim hands in the eleventh century.

As to religion, Cappadocia boasted several famous pagan temples. The most celebrated was at Comana, where the goddess Ma was served by 6,000 priestesses. At Venasa a male god equatable with Zeus was served by over 3,000 devotees. Jews were settled in the kingdom by the middle of the second century B.C., as is implied in I Maccabees 15:22, where a letter on their behalf is addressed by the Roman senate to King Ariarathes. Jews from Cappadocia were present at Jerusalem on the Day of Pentecost (Acts 2:9). The address of I Peter 1:1 demonstrates that Christianity had taken root there by shortly after the middle of the first century. During the fourth century the Christian church there was especially served by the three great Cappadocians: Basil the Great (Basilius), Gregory of Nyssa, and Gregory of Nazianzus.

Asia. Asia, one of the finest jewels in the imperial crown, came to the Empire without the expenditure of blood. Attalus III of Pergamum had willed his domains to the senate and the Roman people; and on his death in 133 B.C., his legacy was constituted, virtually as it came, into the province of Asia. Including Ionia, Mysia, Lydia, Caria, and western Phrygia (approximately the western third of Asia Minor), the province remained geographically intact until it was broken up by Diocletian. It was, however, reorganized by Sulla in 84 B.C.

When Asia came into the Roman Empire, it was the most highly urbanized of all the provinces. Mommsen gives as 500 the total of urban communities existing there at the time.[88] But none of these completely dominated the others as Antioch in Syria and Alexandria in Egypt dominated the other towns in their provinces. Pergamum was the residence of the Attalids and seat of the diet and therefore the proper metropolis. Ephesus was the *de facto* capital and location of the governor's residence and the public records. Smyrna was in constant rivalry with Ephesus, calling itself on coins "the first in greatness and beauty." Sardis strove after the same honorary right. Many other important cities could be noted, and great rivalry existed among a number of them. This competition may ultimately have had much to do with the decline of Asian municipalities because it caused them to overextend themselves financially.

The traditional forms of democratic polity were in general retained in the Hellenistic cities of Asia. Magistrates continued to be chosen by the burgesses; but everywhere the determining influence was placed in the hands of the wealthy, and no free play was allowed to the pleasure of the multitude. Having established oligarchic systems of government in the municipalities, Rome left them very largely to manage their own affairs. She was content to extract from them certain taxes and to exercise a limited degree of jurisdiction, principally in foreign affairs and in cases affecting Roman citizenship.

Asia suffered terribly under its "tax farmers" during the period of the Republic, under Mithridates, under Sulla's indemnity and the rapacious moneylenders who helped the provincials raise the sum, and under Pompey as a result of his levy of ship money to support the fleet designed to destroy the pirates. Whatever degree of prosperity was left was almost obliterated during the civil wars.

Under the Principate and settled conditions, prosperity returned. The finances of the province had been so disordered by the civil wars that Augustus resorted to the extreme expedient of striking off all claims to debt. Other evidence of a new imperial attitude came in A.D. 17. When an earthquake in that year destroyed twelve cities of Asia, the emperor sent immediate aid. For instance, Sardis received ten million sesterces and remission of all contributions to the public or the imperial treasury for five years. Apparently by the time of Titus the province had regained a prosperity surpassing her condition in pre-Roman times.[89] Her highest prosperity came under the Antonine emperors in the following century. Broughton estimates that the population of Asia reached 4,600,000 during the second century.[90] A steady growth in urbanization, promoted by the emperors, accompanied rising prosperity. Most of the remaining tribal communities were urbanized during the Principate, and by the end of the second century, tribal organization seems to have been almost eliminated. But because of the haphazard way in which they had grown, cities (really city-states) varied greatly in size. Ephesus and Rhodes acquired enormous territories. In some areas cities were sparse and ruled large territories; in others they were thickly clustered, each ruling a tiny territory. Pliny gave the number of communities in the province in his day as 282.[91] The Romans on the whole left unchanged the kaleidoscopic variety of the old city constitutions. The Greek city with its characteristic institutions and its ideal of life flowered a second time.

Although the imperial government was more beneficent in its attitude toward Asia

[88]Theodor Mommsen, *The History of Rome: The Provinces from Caesar to Diocletian Part I,* trans. William P. Dickson (New York: Charles Scribner's Sons, 1906), p. 355.

[89]J. Keil, *Cambridge Ancient History* (Cambridge: The University Press, 1936), XI, 583.
[90]Broughton, IV, 815.
[91]Jones, *Cities of the Eastern Provinces,* p. 95.

under the Empire than under the Republic, the prosperity of the province was not primarily the work of a government of superior insight and energetic activity. Asia was basically rich. Cereals were cultivated to some extent almost everywhere. The island wines were renowned and a number of Lydian and Carian wines were favored. Fruits and nuts were produced in most regions. Timber was adequate. Pastoral wealth was great and varied. Although the gold and silver deposits were largely exhausted by the Imperial period, lead and other metals were mined. The province was rich in fine marbles and excellent building stone. Her merchants were enterprising, and the larger towns boasted a multitude of artisans and a large manufacturing population. Great cities like Ephesus and Smyrna benefited from their domination of trade which flowed along the Hermus and Maeander river routes into the interior of Asia Minor.

The pre-Roman history of Asia coincides with that of Asia Minor in general and has been told earlier in this chapter. Its history under Rome is to a large degree the history of its individual cities, much of which is detailed in connection with the ministry of the Apostles Paul and John in Asia Minor. The wealth and culture of the province did not begin with the Roman period but were centuries old when Rome came on the scene. Prosperous days also lay ahead under Byzantine leadership.

Jews were numerous in Asia. Some of them were present in Jerusalem on the Day of Pentecost (Acts 2:9). The story of the advance of Christianity among both the Jews and the Gentiles of Asia occupies several chapters in Acts and receives considerable attention in this volume.

Bithynia. The term "Bithynia" originally applied only to the peninsula of Chalcedon, but it gradually extended eastward to Heraclea and south to the Mysian Olympus. It was bordered on the north by the Black Sea and on the west by the Propontis and the Thracian Bosporus. The west coast was indented by two deep inlets, the Gulf of Astacus (modern Izmit) and the Gulf of Cius.

The greater part of the land surface was occupied by mountains, the highest of which was Mount Olympus on the south (7,600 feet). However, Bithynia had districts of great fertility near the seacoast, as well as productive interior valleys. Bithynia produced good timber, excellent pasturage, and a variety of fruits and grain and possessed fine marble quarries. The main river was the Sangarius (modern Sakarya) which bisected the country, flowing from south to north into the Black Sea. The placement of mountains and valleys in the district permitted rather easy communication.

The Bithynians were of Thracian origin and long kept their tribal identity among the people about them. But Croesus incorporated them into the Lydian monarchy; and when Cyrus toppled Lydian power in 546, they fell within the Persian Empire. They preserved a measure of autonomy under the Persians. Before Alexander launched his successful attack on the Persians, the Bithynians declared their independence from their overlords.

Zipoetus (Zipoetes) founded a dynasty of Thracian stock in 297 B.C. and transmitted his power to his son who assumed the title of king as Nicomedes I in 278 B.C. The latter founded Nicomedia which soon became an important city.

Nicomedes I and his successors Prusias I, Prusias II, and Nicomedes II by a combination of aggressive policies and judicious alliances (especially with the Galatians, whom they invited into Asia in 279), greatly expanded their domain. They founded cities, fostered trade, and advanced the cause of Hellenism within their realm. They lost some territory to Pergamum during the second century, but they generally maintained their power. The last king, Nicomedes IV, was unable to maintain himself, especially in the face of the Mithridatic disturbances. After being restored to his throne by the Romans, he bequeathed his kingdom to Rome at his death in 74 B.C.

Bithynia now became a Roman province. Pompey apparently divided the land of the province among the cities for convenience in maintaining order and collecting taxes. For administrative purposes Bithynia was generally united with Pontus under one governor. In the early Empire it was treated as a senatorial province, but in A.D. 165 it was taken over by the emperor.

Paul and Silas wanted to preach in Bithynia, but they were prevented by the Spirit from doing so (Acts 16:7). How Christianity was established there is not known, but apparently believers in considerable numbers were to be found in the province by the time of Peter's later years. As already noted in commenting on Pontus, Christians were numerous in Bithynia-Pontus by A.D. 110. The area played a significant part in the history of the church in later centuries. The first ecumenical council was held at Nicea (modern Nice, 325); another was held at Chalcedon (451).

Diocletian was later to establish his capital at Nicomedia, and Bithynia shared the fortunes and misfortunes of Constantinople for another millennium.

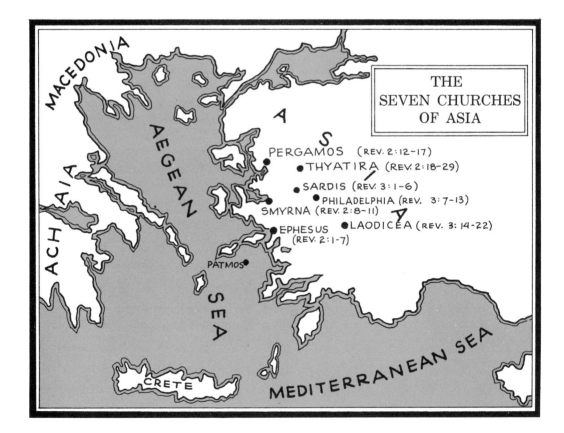

THE WYCLIFFE HISTORICAL GEOGRAPHY OF BIBLE LANDS

The Apostle John and Asia Minor

Tradition almost universally represents the Apostle John as spending his last years at Ephesus. While he was there, he seems to have become a sort of "bishop of the see of Asia." The ring of authority evidenced in II and III John is certainly apostolic if not episcopal. He addressed himself to seven churches of Asia in a rather forceful way in the book of Revelation. Whether he wrote Revelation on the Isle of Patmos or subsequently in Ephesus will probably never be known. At Ephesus the apostle also probably wrote his Gospel. The date of John's move to Ephesus from Jerusalem is a matter of some conjecture. Possibly he went just before the fall of Jerusalem in A.D. 70, or possibly just afterward.

Ephesus, John's headquarters in Asia, has already been discussed in conjunction with Paul's third missionary journey. Laodicea was treated along with the other Lycus Valley towns. Five other cities addressed in the Revelation remain to be considered.

Why seven cities? Why John should have addressed only seven cities and these particular seven in the Revelation is a question that has led to considerable discussion. Many more cities than these had received the gospel and had established churches by the time the Revelation was written. Perhaps Sir William Ramsay has provided the most useful treatment of the subject.

Ramsay concluded, first of all, that these cities were addressed because they had already achieved preeminence among the churches of Asia. More specifically, he noted that the first three (Ephesus, Smyrna, Pergamum) were the greatest cities of the province, always claiming to be "First of Asia." Sardis and Laodicea were each at the head of a conventus (governmental district for legal purposes). But a very real problem occurs in trying to account for Thyatira and Philadelphia, second-rate cities. The former was in the conventus of Pergamum and the latter in that of Sardis. Ramsay finally concluded that these cities rose to prominence because of their location. All seven stood on the important circular road that brought together the most populous and prosperous part of Asia, the west central region.[92] The order in which they lay on the Roman road is precisely the order in which they are addressed in Revelation 2–3.

Distances Between the Cities. It should be useful at this point to note the distances of these cities from each other on the Roman highway system. A few of the figures given here differ considerably from those appearing in some of the guides the author has seen. This is true partly because some writers have given distances "as the crow flies," which is a very unrealistic approach for a reader who wants to know how long it may have taken these churches to communicate with each other.[93] Others simply were not in possession of the most reliable records.

329. View of modern Izmir from Mount Pagus

[92]Ramsay, *The Letters to the Seven Churches*, pp. 178, 181-83.
[93]For rates of speed on Roman roads, see section on Italy, p. 536.

In the writer's opinion, Sir William Ramsay is the best authority on this subject. He has critically evaluated the accounts in Roman writers of the road system of Asia and the distances between towns and produced convincing conclusions. Moreover, the writer has checked the mileage between most of these towns while traveling in the area and found it to tally quite closely with Ramsay's conclusions. In this connection it must be noted that modern roads do not always follow the route of the ancient roads.

The distances according to Ramsay run as follows (figures are given in Roman miles with approximations of English miles in parentheses): Ephesus to Smyrna, 45 (41.5); Smyrna to Pergamum, 70 (64.5); Pergamum to Thyatira, 48 (44); Thyatira to Sardis, 36 (33); Sardis to Philadelphia, 28 (26); Philadelphia to Laodicea, 51 (47); Laodicea to Ephesus, 107 (98.5).[94]

330. Upper level of the agora, Izmir

[94]Ramsay, *The Historical Geography of Asia Minor*, pp. 164-68.

Smyrna. As one travels north from Ephesus, the first of the seven cities of the Revelation which he visits is Smyrna, modern Izmir. The city which John addressed was located in the same spot as the modern city, at the southeast edge of the Gulf of Smyrna. (Old Smyrna was located at the northeast end of the gulf.) Smyrna was a beautiful city. Located beside the beautiful Aegean Sea, it possessed a good harbor—a double one in fact. The outer harbor was a portion of the gulf which served as a mooring ground; the inner harbor, now silted in and occupied by bazaars, had a narrow entrance that could be blocked by a chain.

The city itself curved around the edge of the bay at the base of 525-foot Mount Pagus, its splendid acropolis. Its streets were excellently paved and were drawn at right angles. One of them was known as the "Street of Gold" and ran from west to east, curving around the lower slopes of Pagus. This famous street was lined with especially impressive buildings, and at each end was a temple. Probably the temple of Zeus stood at the western end and the temple of the mother goddess Cybele Sipylene (patroness of the city) at the eastern end. The city had several squares and porticoes, a public library, numerous temples, and other public buildings.

While Smyrna contested with Ephesus and Pergamum for the rank of "First of Asia," some of her coins defined her rank as "First of Asia in beauty and size." Her prestige was also enhanced by her claim to have been the birthplace of Homer. About the time of Christ, the theater of the city (located on a slope of Mount Pagus fronting the gulf) could have held 20,000, and the total population has been estimated at about 100,000.[95] The population probably reached twice that number in the second century.[96]

Smyrna's wealth was derived from her commerce, for which she was excellently lo-

[95]Duyuran, p. 74.
[96]Broughton, p. 816.

cated. Not only did she have a fine harbor but she had access to the trade of the Hermus Valley (which river flowed into the Gulf of Smyrna) and competed with Miletus and Ephesus for the trade of the Maeander Valley. Throughout the Roman period the city was famous for its wealth and was a center of learning, especially in science and medicine.

The earliest settlement beside the Gulf of Smyrna goes back to the third millennium B.C. However, the first Greek community there dates to just before 1000 B.C. At that time Aeolians came in from the islands of the Aegean, especially Lesbos. Traditionally the town was founded by an Amazon who gave the town her own name. About 700 B.C. Ephesus and Colophon conquered Smyrna, and it became a member of the Ionian Confederacy. Approximately a century later Alyattes of Lydia captured the city and destroyed it. For three to four hundred years the city did not exist as an organized entity. Small villages were scattered around the plain and surrounding hills.

Alexander the Great had planned to restore the city but did not succeed. His successors Antigonus and Lysimachus executed his plan about 290 B.C. The city they founded was located on the southeast shore of the gulf some two to three miles from the earlier site, which had been on the northeast shore. The object of the change was to obtain a good harbor and a convenient location for tapping the trade route to the interior.

When the conflict arose between Rome and Seleucia at the beginning of the second century B.C., Smyrna sided with Rome and in 195 B.C. built a temple to the deified Rome. Smyrna also fought on the side of Rome in the war with Mithridates. With the inauguration of the Empire, a new period of prosperity dawned for Smyrna. The city was granted important privileges by Tiberius; these were confirmed by later

331. Lower level of the agora, Izmir

emperors. When the city was virtually destroyed by an earthquake in A.D. 178, Marcus Aurelius rebuilt it at the request of his friend, the orator Aelius Aristides, who then lived there.

Thus the city which John addressed is almost beyond recovery. The excavations conducted at the site have centered on the agora of Marcus Aurelius and Old Smyrna, neither of which tells anything about the first century A.D. Few remains may be seen on the acropolis. Lower courses of walls there date back to Hellenistic times. Since the modern city covers the ancient, it is not likely that sufficient work can be done there to recover the plan of New Testament Smyrna.

In spite of the earthquakes and other vicissitudes that Smyrna has suffered through the centuries, the city has continued to prosper and is today probably larger than it was in the Apostle John's day. At that time it may have had a population of close to 200,000.

Numerous interesting allusions to Smyrna's history may be discovered in John's message to the church there; his letter was wholly commendatory. Christians there suffered greatly at the hands of the Jews (Rev. 2:9-10). These Christians probably were themselves converted Jews. It was Jewish

332. Sculpture of the god Poseidon (god
of the sea), Izmir

Pergamum. The third church which John addressed stood in the city of Pergamum, capital of Asia. Situated on a hill about 1,000 feet high, Pergamum commanded the fertile valley of the Caicus River, in the south of the district of Mysia. The city was located about three miles north of the Caicus and about eighteen miles from the ocean opposite the island of Lesbos. Pergamum communicated with the sea via the Caicus, which was navigable for small native craft. From the city a highway ran to the interior of Asia Minor almost to the border of the province of Asia. Pergamum was also located on the important north-south road which ran from Ephesus to Cyzicus on the Propontis or Sea of Marmara.

Although Pergamum must have been inhabited from early times, extant literature does not mention the city before Xenophon (401 B.C.). There are various traditions that it was originally settled by Arcadia or Epidaurus, and many Greeks were there when Xenophon visited it. Its real history began in the third century B.C. under the Attalid dynasty, when it became the capital of a Hellenistic kingdom of considerable importance. Lysimachus, one of the generals of Alexander the Great, chose this fortress of considerable strength as a depository for his treasure, reputedly totaling 9,000 talents of gold, and selected Philetaeros as its keeper. At first loyal, the steward revolted and declared himself independent in 283 B.C. Lysimachus had other troubles and could not give full attention to this insubordination.

Philetaeros was able to transmit control over the principality to his nephew, Eumenes, who ruled 263-241 B.C. and was succeeded by his cousin Attalus (241-197). After a victory over the Gauls, Attalus I (Soter) assumed the title of king. Attalus advocated the interests of Rome against Philip of Macedon and in conjunction with the Rhodian fleet rendered important service to Rome. Attalus was succeeded by his

Christians rather than pagan converts whom national Jews hated so violently. Ramsay suggests[97] that the word *faithful* (Rev. 2:10) would have a special appeal to people of Smyrna because they had been known for their faithfulness to Rome over a period of three centuries.

Ramsay believed that the promise of a "crown of life" (Rev. 2:10) would also have had added meaning for Smyrnean readers. The "crown of Smyrna" was a phrase familiar to the natives of the city, and it probably arose from the appearance of the hill Pagus topped with stately public buildings and covered on its slopes with other structures of the town.[98] The promise was given that she would wear not only a mere crown of buildings and towers but a *crown of life.*

[97]Ramsay, *The Letters to the Seven Churches,* p. 275.
[98]*Ibid.,* pp. 256, 275.

THE WYCLIFFE HISTORICAL GEOGRAPHY OF BIBLE LANDS

son Eumenes II (197-159) who, after the defeat of Antiochus (190), received from Rome all of western Asia Minor. Eumenes was followed by his son Attalus II (159-138) and by Attalus III (138-133), who willed his kingdom to Rome. The son of Attalus III, Aristonicus, contested the will but was defeated by Rome, and the Attalid kingdom was effectively organized as the province of Asia in 129 with Pergamum as its capital.

Although Pergamum possessed the constitution of a Greek city-state under the Attalids, the king assumed wide powers of interference. The monarchs ruled directly the native population of the surrounding countryside. And as their domain expanded, they controlled it increasingly in the fashion of Hellenistic kings, relying on a Greek bureaucracy and a predominantly Greek semiprofessional army. The Pergamene kings owed their power of expansion to their skillful managing of the country's natural wealth, which included silver mines, a surplus from agriculture (wheat), stock breeding, and the dependent industries of woolen textiles and parchment.[99]

It was mainly the first Attalus who amassed the wealth for which the dynasty became proverbial. Eumenes II was a liberal patron of the arts and sciences, and Pergamum was mainly indebted to him for its embellishment. He built new city walls, decorated the great altar of Zeus with magnificent bas-reliefs, constructed a theater on the acropolis, as well as a temple to Athena, a palace, and a library. The library, second only to that of Alexandria, contained some 200,000 books and pictures in four massive halls. Readers could sit on stone seats in the library gardens and enjoy well-executed statuary. This library was later given to

Cleopatra by Antony and largely transferred to Alexandria by the Romans.

While the Attalids were not great founders of cities like the other Hellenistic kings, they made Pergamum one of the greatest and most beautiful of all Greek cities. An excellent example of Hellenistic town-planning, Pergamum was laid out in terraces on a hillside, culminating in the palace and fortifications of the acropolis. The city was renowned for its school of sculpture.

As already noted, Pergamum was the political capital of Asia under the Romans. This fact, coupled with its prestige, its commercial activities, and its religious power contributed to Pergamene prosperity during the early centuries of the Christian Era. A large new section of the city developed at the foot of the hill during the second century A.D. especially. The hill on which the old city stood now became the acropolis.

One of the most important structures of the lower city was the Asclepion or health resort dedicated to the god Asclepius. Dating back to Hellenistic times, Pergamum was at its height during the second century A.D. when the physician Galen practiced there and when the orator and rhetorician Aelius Aristides lectured in its theater. Here the sick, who often came from great distances, underwent treatment by suggestion, sun and water baths, music, prayer, and interpretation of dreams.

333. The theater of the Asclepion, Pergamum

[99]Parchment, made from sheepskin or goatskin, gets its name from Pergamum (through the Latin *Pergamenus,* "of or belonging to Pergamum") and was allegedly invented by Eumenes II, founder of the library.

At its height in the second century Pergamum boasted a population of about 200,000, if one can accept Broughton's calculation.[100] Probably it was not too much smaller during John's day.

Pergamum is one of the most completely excavated of ancient cities. First visiting the city in 1864, the German architect Karl Humann established his headquarters there in 1868, thus beginning an excavation that was to develop over a span of ninety years and that was to be approximately 60 percent completed by 1962. The first major triumph of the German excavators was the location of the great altar of Zeus with its remarkable sculptures, probably built by Eumenes early in the second century B.C. The rectangular foundations of the altar were 125 by 115 feet. The altar rested on a great horseshoe-shaped plinth thirty feet high, approached by twenty-eight 60-foot steps on the western side. These steps led through an Ionic colonnade into a square court where the altar proper stood.

The three outer sides of the monument were sculptured with scenes of struggle between gods and giants (the former defeating the latter in a struggle symbolic of the conflict between civilization and barbarism) and scenes representing the defeat

334. The altar of Zeus

[100] Broughton, p. 813.

335. The palace area

of the Gauls by King Eumenes. The famous frieze was eight feet high and was placed eight feet above the base of the podium. Another frieze ran around the three inner sides of the altar court on the upper level. This sculpture depicted events from the life of the legendary hero Telephus, son of Hercules, traditional founder of the city. Only the Parthenon frieze exceeds in length that of the altar of Zeus at Pergamum, which was about 400 feet long. The altar of Zeus was carried off to Berlin and installed in a Pergamum museum there. Hidden during the Second World War, it has since been restored in a museum in East Berlin.

The altar of Zeus was only one of numerous beautiful structures that stood on the acropolis at Pergamum in John's day. Altogether there were no less than five palaces with mosaic floors in black, white, green, and red; walls painted in yellow, blue, rose, and red; and wall paintings of fruit, flowers. and birds as in the Villa of Livia near Rome.

At the foot of the acropolis stood the lower agora dating to the reign of Eumenes II, measuring 210 by 110 feet. Surrounding the paved court were Doric porticoes giving entrance to the shops. Up the hill from the lower agora lay a gymnasium on three terraces. This complex of buildings was constructed over several centuries, at least from the second century B.C. to the second century A.D.. Next to the gymnasium stood the marble temple of Hera built in the second century B.C. Above the gymnasium and to the west of it was the temple of Demeter built in the third century B.C.

Continuing up the slope and about in the middle of it, one came to the upper agora. Like the lower one it was surrounded by Doric porticoes. Next to this stood the great altar of Zeus, above which in turn stood the temple of Athena, built at the very end of the fourth century B.C. Appropriately enough this was surrounded on three sides by the great U-shaped library, a structure of two stories. Its lower gallery was faced by a portico of the Doric order and the upper Ionic.

Against the side of the hill adjacent to the temple of Athena lay the theater of the acropolis, one of the five at Pergamum. This was one of the steepest and most spectacular theaters of antiquity, as anyone who has climbed this one and others can testify. Constructed about 170 B.C., the theater contains eighty rows of seats spread out at a height of 165 feet. It could seat about 15,000. On the level of the stage of the theater, at the bottom of the hill, stood a temple to Dionysus which was built during the Hellenistic period. Before the temple stood an altar, to the rear of which twenty-five steps led up to the gigantic portico of the temple with its six Ionic columns.

At the very top of the acropolis stood an arsenal, probably built about 200 B.C. It was well stocked with catapult balls and had a storage area that could hold enough grain for 1,000 men for a year.[101]

Prior to World War II attention was for some years centered on the lower town. Modern Bergama was found to overlay the Roman city. Its streets and alleys follow the ancient ones, as digging trenches for the modern water system has demonstrated.[102] And since 1951 much work has

336. The gymnasium

been done on the Asklepion, which in part has been reconstructed. This great healing center, as mentioned above, dated back to Hellenistic times and was important in John's day. But its greatest days came during the second century A.D., and some of the buildings there date from that century. Many other structures of the city could be commented on, but they were built long after the New Testament era closed and therefore have value for classical rather than biblical studies.

References in John's missive to Pergamum demand some attention before one can turn to a study of Thyatira. He spoke of "Satan's throne" being in Pergamum and of Satan dwelling there (Rev. 2:13). At least three suggestions have been made as to what the apostle meant. Some have thought that he referred to heathen worship in general. Among the numerous deities worshiped at Pergamum were Zeus, Athena, Asclepius, Dionysus, and Demeter.

Others have thought that the imperial cult was implied. Three temples were dedicated to emperor worship at Pergamum, and it would have been easy to think of Satan enthroned there instead of the true Deity. Certainly in the capital of Asia, the state religion would have been more thoroughly promoted than elsewhere. The fact that the martyrdom of Antipas is men-

[101]MacKendrick, p. 353.
[102]Ibid., p. 354.

337. Temple of Athena

tioned in the same verse as "Satan's throne" may give some support to this view. If John was sent to Patmos for refusal to worship the emperor, he may well have chosen such vicious language for a place where the emperor was worshiped.

It is tempting, however, to suggest that John had specifically in mind the great altar of Zeus, which was one of the wonders of the ancient world and an object of pride to Pergamene citizens.

John referred to two errors that had crept into the church at Pergamum: the doctrine of Balaam and the doctrine of the Nicolaitans. The former apparently had to do with Christians marrying pagans and thus defiling their separation to God (Num. 31:15-16; 22:5; 23:8). The latter held that heathen ceremonies meant nothing since pagan deities did not exist anyway and that Christians were therefore at liberty to join in idolatrous feasts in order to maintain their social position and to justify their loyalty in the sight of the law.

Thyatira. As one traveled east from Pergamum up the valley of the Caicus River in ancient times, he came after about twenty-five miles to the town of Germa. Nearby the road turned southeast and ran down a long valley which connected the Caicus and the Hermus valleys. Down this main valley flowed a stream which poured

its waters into the Hermus River. Thyatira stood on the east bank of this stream in a fertile plain about 330 feet in altitude. Its citadel or acropolis was built on very slightly rising ground. Since its location was not strong, it was never a fortress—only a military post.

Thyatira's location on a main road meant that it would always be an important trading center. So while it was destroyed several times, it was destined always to be rebuilt. During Roman times, Thyatira was a great trading city, its height of prosperity coming about the end of the first century A.D.

In connection with this commercial activity, there is evidence of more trade guilds there than in any other Asian city. Included among them were wool workers, linen workers, tailors, dyers, leatherworkers, tanners, and bronzesmiths. Lydia, a seller of purple from Thyatira, probably represented her guild at Philippi (Acts 16:14). And the purple which she sold was probably made in the region of Thyatira, which produced the well-known "turkey-red." This was obtained from the madder root, which grows in abundance around Thyatira. The bronze work of the city was also very excellent.

In addition to its commercial importance, Thyatira was also a station on the imperial post road from Brundisium and Dyrrhachium across Macedonia to Thessalonica, Neapolis (port of Philippi), Troas, Adra-

338. The theater

THE WYCLIFFE HISTORICAL GEOGRAPHY OF BIBLE LANDS

myttium, Pergamum, Philadelphia, and then across Asia Minor to Tarsus, Syrian Antioch, Caesarea in Palestine, and Alexandria in Egypt.

Old Lydian in origin, Thyatira was refounded by Seleucus Nicator who reportedly named it "Thygatira" or "Thyatira" on being informed that a daughter (Greek, *thygater*) had been born to him. Earlier it had been called "Pelopia," "Euhippa," and "Semiramis." At first a Seleucid outpost against Macedonia, Thyatira became a Pergamene outpost after the defeat of Antiochus at Magnesia in 190. When the

340. Ruins at Thyatira

339. Modern Bergama and the basilica

Pergamene kingdom became the Roman province of Asia in 133 B.C., Thyatira passed directly under control of Rome. As already noted, the city enjoyed a considerable amount of prosperity when John addressed the church there.

The apostle condemned "that woman Jezebel" (Rev. 2:20), which some have interpreted to be a literal prophetess living in Thyatira at the end of the first century A.D. But it seems best to treat the name symbolically to refer to the teaching of a lax attitude toward pagan customs and practices and conformity to the pagan social milieu of the day. No doubt the trade guilds of the city had their patron deities which all members were expected to honor. And all phases of contemporary society—music, sports, or politics—were so linked to pagan ritual that accommodation to paganism was very tempting to those who wished to remain completely acceptable members of society. But Christianity would have disappeared if it had not stood out in opposition to the popular beliefs and customs of the day.

Christianity must have come to Thyatira early; perhaps the city was evangelized from Ephesus. Probably the new faith spread first among the Jews of the community. Seleucus I, the founder of the city, is known to have shown special favor to Jews and to have made them citizens of cities he founded in Asia; he was likely responsible for bringing Jews to Thyatira.

Actually very little is known about the city in ancient or medieval times. No excavation has been undertaken, and almost no ruins are obvious in the vicinity. The modern town of Akhisar (some 25,000 population) which occupies the site makes exploration or excavation there difficult.

Sardis. Sardis is not as much of a historical blank as her northern neighbor. She was more important during several periods of history, and excavation there is gradually restoring a picture of the ancient city. Sardis dominated the region of the Hermus

341. Temple of Artemis with acropolis of Sardis in the background

River (modern Gediz) and its tributaries, the broadest and most fertile of all the river basins of Asia Minor. She commanded the great trade and military road from the Aegean islands into the interior of the peninsula.

To the south of the Hermus River rises the Tmolus Range (modern Boz Dag, 6,200 feet), which extends like an arm from the Anatolian Plateau. From the Tmolus stretches a series of hills which form a transition to the valley below. On one of these hills, over 1,000 feet above the Hermus and about five miles south of the river, stood early Sardis. Like the other hills of the region, this site forms a small elongated plateau with steep sides and is connected by a narrow ridge with the northern foothills of the Tmolus. In fact, the hill on which Sardis perched had almost perpendicular sides except on the south. Even this approach is none too easy, and the city was virtually impregnable.[103]

As Sardis grew it spread out along the western slopes to the Pactolus River (which flows north into the Hermus), and the hill on which the first city was built became the acropolis. Later Sardis expanded northward into the valley of the Hermus, where

[103]The modern visitor to the acropolis at Sardis finds it hard to visualize what this site was like in the days of the Lydian kings because constant erosion has worn away the plateau at the top so that little now remains of the upper plateau on which the city stood.

ruins of great structures of the Roman period may be seen.

Greek legend has it that the fabulous wealth of the Lydians came from the gold-bearing sands of the Pactolus River. While some have cast doubt on the gold-producing nature of the river in ancient times, it is quite certain that King Croesus and others found wealth in this way. But certainly all of Lydian wealth did not come in the form of bullion washed down by the river. Sardis stood in a fertile and carefully cultivated area and benefited immensely from her position on the trade and communication routes. Lydian artisans were also highly skilled.

Lydians probably occupied the region of Sardis during the latter part of the second millennium B.C. Whether they founded the city or took over an existing town is unknown. At least the site first achieved greatness as the capital of the Lydian Kingdom. With the demise of the Phrygian Kingdom near the beginning of the seventh century B.C., the Lydians conquered Phrygian territory and the Greek cities of Ionia except Miletus. Ultimately they came to rule all of Asia Minor west of the Halys River. The Lydian Kingdom reached her height during the first half of the sixth century B.C. but came to an end with the death of Croesus and the successes of Cyrus the Persian in 546.

Sardis now became the chief town of a Persian satrapy (equivalent to a province). As such it was a prime object of Greek attack during the Ionian revolt. In 499 the Greeks marched up the Cayster Valley, delivered a surprise attack on Sardis, burned the buildings of the city to the ground, and destroyed the famous temple of the Lydian goddess Cybele.

Quickly rebuilt, Sardis served as headquarters for Xerxes during the winter before his campaign against Greece. Almost a century later Cyrus assembled forces there for the revolt against his brother Artaxerxes (401 B.C.). Sardis was an important city when it surrendered to Alexander the Great in 334 B.C. When Alexander died, a struggle ensued among his generals for control of his empire. For a while Antigonus controlled Sardis, then the Seleucids took over and ruled there until 190 B.C. Rome bestowed the city on the king of Pergamum after defeating Antiochus in that year. When the Pergamene kingdom became the province of Asia in 133 B.C., Sardis came under direct control of Rome.

After the terrible earthquake of A.D. 17, the Emperor Tiberius rebuilt the city and the senate remitted the city's taxes for five years. The grateful inhabitants erected a temple to Tiberius. Shortly thereafter Rome made a *conventus juridicus* with Sardis, by which the city became one of the centers of the Roman judicial administration in Asia. Although Sardis never regained the political power it had had in the days of the Lydian kings, the city enjoyed great prosperity during the second and third centuries A.D. It continued to be a wealthy city down to the end of the Byzantine Empire. The Turks took possession in the eleventh century, and in 1402 the city was thoroughly destroyed by Tamerlane and never rebuilt.

In an effort to recover a picture of life at ancient Sardis, two major archaeological campaigns have been launched there. In 1910, Howard Crosby Butler of Princeton began to work there on behalf of the American Society for the Excavation of Sardis. His efforts were chiefly centered on the great Temple of Artemis to the west of the acropolis, and he opened more than 1,000 graves in the so-called "Cemetery Hill" along the west bank of the Pactolus. This dig was halted by World War I.

In 1957 the Fogg Art Museum of Harvard, Cornell University, and the American Schools of Oriental Research began a joint

excavation at Sardis, made possible in part by a grant from the Bollingen Foundation. George M. A. Hanfmann of Harvard has been the director. Periodic reports on progress at the site may be found in the *Bulletin* of the American Schools of Oriental Research and the annual survey of "Archaeology in Asia Minor" in the *American Journal of Archaeology*. This expedition has worked at numerous locations in the area—the Temple of Artemis, the necropolis, the acropolis, along the Pactolus, and on Roman and Byzantine ruins in the plain north of the acropolis.

Unfortunately it is not yet possible to point to much at Sardis that John's readers would have known. Of course the Lydian and Hellenistic remains date much earlier and the Byzantine much later. Most of the large Roman structures probably date to the second or third centuries A.D., when the city knew a high degree of prosperity—though the dates of all these buildings have not yet been determined. To the north of the acropolis is located a stadium over 230 yards long; by its side are the remains of a theater. Perhaps a city plan will emerge after further seasons of excavation.

The great Temple of Artemis (that is, the Asiatic Artemis, the mother goddess)

342. Ionic capital, Temple of Artemis

was perhaps the most imposing structure of Sardis in John's day. Located to the west of the acropolis, it measured 160 by 300 feet and covered some 5,000 square yards. Though begun in the days of Alexander the Great, it was never finished. Most of its 65-foot Ionic columns (once 78 in all) are unfluted. Some of the columns rest on rough pedestals; no doubt these were intended to be carved like those of Ephesus. The temple had twenty columns on each of the long sides and eight columns at each of the ends. The cella or main cult chamber on the east end was divided by two rows of six columns. At the west end was the treasure chamber. The capitals show a variety of form; some of the columns have richly decorated bases. Beneath the cella were discovered the foundations of the temple built by Croesus in the sixth century B.C.

344. Marble court in the "House of Bronzes," Sardis

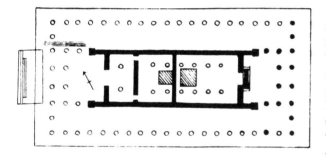

343. Plan of the Temple of Artemis

Philadelphia. From the Hermus Valley and Sardis a long valley runs up southeast into the flank of the central plateau. Down this valley runs the river Cogamus to join the Hermus. And up the valley runs a road, the best means of making the ascent from the Hermus Valley (500 feet in altitude) to the main plateau (c. 3,000 feet in this area). This was the route by which trade and communication were maintained between Smyrna and northwest Asia Minor and Phrygia and the east. Furthermore, the imperial post road of the first century A.D.,

which came from Rome via Troas, Adramyttium (modern Edremit), Pergamum, and Sardis, passed through this valley (and Philadelphia) on its way to the east.

In the Cogamus Valley, some twenty-six miles from Sardis (c. 100 miles from Smyrna) by Roman road stood Philadelphia. The city was located at about 800 feet in altitude on a broad hill which slopes up gently from the valley toward the Tmolus Mountains. The hill is not far south of the Cogamus River and is separated from the Tmolus mass so that it could be made a very strong fortress. The strength of its fortifications was to be proved in several terrible sieges by Muslim forces in later centuries. Northeast of the city lay a great vine-growing district, which contributed greatly to its prosperity.

A Lydian town may have existed on the site of Philadelphia as long ago as the beginning of the first millennium B.C. But the real establishment of the city dates from the Pergamene period. After 189 B.C., when Pergamum gained control of the area, a group of Macedonians was settled there, probably during the reign of Attalus II Philadelphus (159-138). The new foundation was named in honor of Attalus, who had been given the epithet "Philadelphus" ("brother lover") because of his loyalty to his brother.

Ramsay concluded that Philadelphia was established to become a center for consolidating and educating the central regions of the Pergamene Kingdom—a center for the spread of Greco-Asiatic civilization. The city was a successful teacher and was in part responsible for the fact that Lydian ceased to be spoken in Lydia by A.D. 19, and Greek took over.[104]

The same severe earthquake that destroyed Sardis and ten other cities of the western part of Asia Minor in A.D. 17 also destroyed Philadelphia. The earthquake was more demoralizing at Philadelphia than at the other cities hit at that time because tremors continued over an extended period of time. These shocks produced such a state of panic that many were afraid to return to buildings in the city and lived outside in huts. The writer has found reference to another quake there in A.D. 23 but has not been able to document the claim.

To assist Philadelphia in its plight, the Emperor Tiberius gave a large donation for its reconstruction. In gratitude the city voluntarily changed its name to Neocaisarea ("New Caesar"). But later in the century during the reign of Vespasian (A.D. 70-79), it took the name of "Flavia," a name which continued to be used along with Philadelphia during the second and third centuries.

During those same centuries Philadelphia continued to increase in prosperity and under Caracalla (Bassianus, or Marcus Aurelius Antoninus, A.D. 211-17) was awarded the title "Neokoros," or "Temple Warden." This means that a provincial temple of the imperial cult was built there at the time. During the Byzantine period the prosperity and importance of Philadelphia increased even more until the city was destroyed by Islamic attacks.

Approached by a poor road from Sardis, the present-day insignificant town of Alase-hir (some 9,000 population) with its winding streets presents a poor contrast to the prosperous Philadelphia of Roman days. A visitor may see a few ruins of Byzantine walls and churches, but there is almost no evidence of the city of John's day. Without an excavation of the site it is impossible to recreate a view of the city as the apostle knew it.

Several items in the Revelation passage addressed to Philadelphia have been viewed by commentators to have special significance to residents of the city. The divine challenge was "I have set before thee an open door" (Rev. 3:8). Thus a divine mission was introduced to a city which had from the beginning been a missionary city. For some 250 years it had been preaching the gospel of Hellenism and Greek culture to the surrounding area. Now it was encouraged to preach the gospel of Jesus Christ to that same region.

The church there had "a little strength" (Rev. 3:8). Some have tried to apply this to the fact that Philadelphia had been destroyed by earthquake and therefore was not of great significance when John wrote. However, the city was quickly rebuilt after A.D. 17. Probably the reference has to do instead with the church there, which seems to have been small and struggling and to have remained so for a long time. In time

345. Roman or Byzantine lead water pipes being excavated at Sardis

[104]Ramsay, *The Letters to the Seven Churches*, pp. 391-92.

346. A pillar of the Church of St. John rises above a modern roof in Philadelphia.

Philadelphia came to be known as "Little Athens" because of the considerable attention there to the worship of pagan deities.

God through the apostle also promised these Christians a new name: "I will write upon him the name of my God" (Rev. 3:12). The city had been renamed twice during the first century A.D., and in both instances the imperial cult must have been established. At least this was true in the days of Tiberius. Now a truly divine name was to be bestowed upon all believers in the true God. The promise to keep these believers from the "hour of trial" would according to some commentators have had a special appeal to those who lived on the edge of an earthquake belt and stood in dread of terrible suffering at the hands of the forces of nature.

The Isle of Patmos. According to Revelation 1:9 the Apostle John received his revelation on the Isle of Patmos. Whether he wrote the book there or at Ephesus after his release from exile is a matter of conjecture. Tradition has it (Irenaeus, Eusebius, Jerome, and others) that the apostle was exiled there during the fourteenth year of Domitian's reign (A.D. 95) and was released during the reign of Nerva (A.D. 96) about eighteen months later.

Patmos is one of the Sporades Islands about twenty-eight miles south-southwest of the island of Samos and about the same distance from the coast of Asia Minor. Its length is about eight miles, its greatest width six miles, and it covers an area of approximately twenty-two square miles. The island has been described as a horse's head and neck with the nose pointing eastward, or as similar to a crescent with the horns facing eastward.

The harbor of Patmos, which opens eastward, divides the island into two almost equal parts which are connected by a narrow isthmus. The ancient town was at the north of this isthmus; the modern town stands at its southern end. Today the southern half of the island belongs to the monks, and the northern part to the civil community. About a half mile up the hill from the modern town is a cave where John is supposed to have received his visions. About a mile farther is the Monastery of St. John, built in the eleventh century.

The soil of Patmos is volcanic and barren. Red and gray rocks which frequently break into quaint pinnacles flank the Patmos coasts. The interior consists of three main masses of volcanic hills, the highest point of which is about 900 feet. Patmos depends

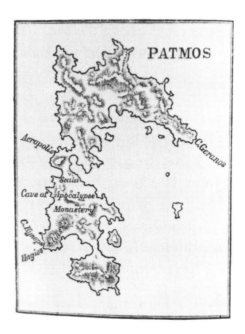

THE WYCLIFFE HISTORICAL GEOGRAPHY OF BIBLE LANDS

on a few wells and numerous cisterns for its water supply, which is roughly sufficient.

If John had the freedom of the island, which is likely, he could have seen some wonderful panoramas from its heights. The greater part of the irregular island would have lain at his feet. Away to the north would have appeared the peaks of the island of Samos and the promontory of Mycale, to the south the island of Leros. To the southwest in the open expanse of the Aegean could have been seen Amorgas Island and the distant volcano of Santorin. To the northwest lay Icaria (modern Ikaria), and numerous other islands clustered on the horizon.

Frequent suggestions are made concerning the influence of John's surroundings on him as he composed the Revelation (and he probably wrote at least part of it on Patmos). Henry M. Field comments:

And is it too much to say that the Book of Revelation is a different book, written on an island, on the seashore, from what it would have been if written, like the Book of Job, amid Arabian deserts? All its imagery is of the sea. As the Apostle walked along the shore of Patmos when the waters were still and reflected as in a mirror the blue of the heavens, they furnished a not unworthy symbol of "the sea of glass, like unto crystal, which was before the throne." Again he stood upon the cliff, his white hair streaming in the wind, and saw the clouds rolling up on the horizon, the flashes from which lighted up at once the dark heavens above and the angry sea below, and these were images to him of judgments that were coming on the earth. And when he speaks of One "whose voice was as the sound of many waters," the very expression is an echo of the deep.[105]

The earliest inhabitants of Patmos seem to have been Dorians. These were probably followed by Ionian immigrants. In the Roman period the island was one of the many places of exile for political prisoners. On the height occupied by the ancient city may be seen the remains of ancient fortifications and walls on both its southern and northern sides. But no one has cared much about the nature of Patmos in classical times; the island is chiefly noted for its ecclesiastical significance.

⁕   ⁕   ⁕   ⁕   ⁕

According to Revelation 1:19 the Voice John heard on Patmos commanded, "Write the things which thou hast seen, and the things which are, and the things which shall be hereafter." While John devoted much of his book to the "things which shall be hereafter," he had abundant time while on Patmos to think about the past, about his days spent with the Master, about early apostolic efforts at church establishment, and about the present with the church attacked by heresy within and persecuted by civil authorities without.

No doubt he had a sense of satisfaction as he looked back on achievement. No doubt he also had grave apprehensions about the future of the church. He saw numerous danger signs in the churches of Asia and scored them in his letters to the seven churches (Rev. 2–3).

[105]*The Greek Islands and Turkey After the War* (New York: Charles Scribner's Sons, 1885), p. 42.

Bibliography

BEAN, GEORGE E. *Aegean Turkey*. London: Ernest Benn Ltd., 1966.

BLEGEN, CARL W. *Troy*. Cambridge: At the University Press, 1961.

BROUGHTON, T. R. S. "Roman Asia," *An Economic Survey of Ancient Rome*. Edited by TENNEY FRANK. Vol. IV. Baltimore: Johns Hopkins Press, 1938.

BUTLER, HOWARD CROSBY. *Sardis*. Leyden: E. J. Brill, Ltd., Vol. I, 1922; Vol. II, 1925.

CADOUX, CECIL J. *Ancient Smyrna*. Oxford: B. Blackwell, 1938.

CARY, M. *The Geographic Background of Greek and Roman History*. Oxford: At the Clarendon Press, 1949.

CARY, M., *et al.* (ed.). *The Oxford Classical Dictionary*. Oxford: At the Clarendon Press, 1949.

CERAM, C. W. *The Secret of the Hittites*. Translated by RICHARD and CLARA WINSTON. New York: Alfred A. Knopf, 1956.

COBERN, CAMDEN M. *The New Archeological Discoveries*. 9th ed. New York: Funk & Wagnalls Co., 1929.

COOK, J. M. *Greek Settlements in the Eastern Aegean and Asia Minor*. Cambridge: At the University Press, 1961.

DUNHAM, ADELAIDE G. *The History of Miletus*. London: University of London Press, 1915.

DUYURAN, RUSTEM. *The Ancient Cities of Western Anatolia*. Istanbul: Turkish Press, n. d. (since 1948).

FIELD, HENRY M. *The Greek Islands and Turkey After the War*. New York: Charles Scribner's Sons, 1885.

FILSON, FLOYD V. "Ephesus and the New Testament," *Biblical Archaeologist*, VIII (Sept., 1945), 73-80.

FINEGAN, JACK. *Light from the Ancient Past*. 2d ed. Princeton: Princeton University Press, 1959.

FISHER, W. B. *The Middle East*. London: Methuen & Co., Ltd., 1950.

GARDNER, ERNEST A. *Greece and the Aegean*. London: George G. Harap & Co., Ltd., 1933.

GOETZE, ALBRECHT. "Hittite and Anatolian Studies," *The Bible and the Ancient Near East*. Edited by G. ERNEST WRIGHT. Garden City: Doubleday & Co., Inc., 1961.

GOODSPEED, EDGAR J. *Paul*. Philadelphia: The John Winston Co., 1947.

GURNEY, O. R. *Anatolia c. 1750-1600 B.C.* Cambridge: At the University Press, 1962.

———. *The Hittites*. Revised ed. Harmondsworth, England: Penguin Books, Inc., 1961.

HARDIE, MARGARET M. "The Shrine of Men Askaenos at Pisidian Antioch," *Journal of Hellenic Studies*, XXXII (1912), 111-50.

HROZNY, BEDRICH. *Ancient History of Western Asia, India and Crete*. New York: Philosophical Library, Inc., 1953.

HUDSON, EGBERT C. "The Principal Family at Pisidian Antioch," *Journal of Near Eastern Studies*, XV (Apr., 1957), 103-7.

JOHNSON, SHERMAN E. "Laodicea and Its Neighbors," *Biblical Archaeologist*, XIII (Feb., 1950), 1-18.

JONES, A. H. M. *The Cities of the Eastern Roman Provinces*. Oxford: At the Clarendon Press, 1937.

JONES, TOM B. *Ancient Civilization*. Chicago: Rand McNally & Co., 1960.

KEIL, JOSEF. *Ephesos: Ein Führer Durch Die Ruinenstätte und ihre Geschichte*. Vienna: Austrian Archaeological Institute, 1957.

LLOYD, SETON. *Early Anatolia*. Harmondsworth, England: Penguin Books, Inc., 1956.

MacKENDRICK, PAUL. *The Greek Stones Speak*. New York: St. Martin's Press, 1962.

MAGIE, DAVID. *Roman Rule in Asia Minor*. 2 vols. Princeton: Princeton University Press, 1950.

MARSHALL, F. H. *Discovery in Greek Lands*. Cambridge: At the University Press, 1920.

MELLAART, J. *Anatolia c. 4000-2300 B.C.* Cambridge: At the University Press, 1962.

MELLINK, MACHTELD J. "Archaeology in Asia Minor," *American Journal of Archaeology*, 62 (Apr., 1963), 173-90.

MORTON, H. V. *In the Steps of St. Paul*. New York: Dodd, Mead & Co., 1936.

MULLER, HERBERT J. *The Loom of History*. New York: Harper & Bros., 1958.

ORGA, IRFAN. *The Caravan Moves On*. London: Secker & Warburg, 1958.

PARVIS, MERRILL M. "Archaeology and St. Paul's Journeys in Greek Lands, Part IV—Ephesus," *Biblical Archaeologist*, VIII (Sept., 1945), 61-73.

RAMSAY, WILLIAM H. *The Bearing of Recent Discovery on the Trustworthiness of the New Testament*. 2nd ed. London: Hodder and Stoughton, 1915.

———. *The Church in the Roman Empire Before A.D. 170*. 4th ed. London: Hodder and Stoughton, 1895.

———. *The Cities and Bishoprics of Phrygia.* 2 vols. Oxford: At the Clarendon Press, 1895.

———. *The Cities of St. Paul.* London: Hodder and Stoughton, n.d.

———. *A Historical Commentary on St. Paul's Epistle to the Galatians.* New York: G. P. Putnam's Sons, 1900.

———. *The Historical Geography of Asia Minor.* London: John Murray, 1890.

———. *The Letters to the Seven Churches of Asia.* New York: A. C. Armstrong & Son, 1905.

———. "Roads and Travel in the New Testament," *A Dictionary of the Bible.* Edited by JAMES HASTINGS. Extra Vol., 1904.

———. *St. Paul the Traveller and the Roman Citizen.* 8th ed. London: Hodder and Stoughton, 1905.

ROBINSON, DAVID M. "A Preliminary Report on the Excavations at Pisidian Antioch and at Sizma," *American Journal of Archaeology,* 28 (Oct., 1924), 435-44.

SMITH, WILLIAM (ed.). *A Dictionary of Greek and Roman Geography.* 2 vols. London: John Murray, 1873.

STARK, FREYA. *The Lycian Shore.* New York: Harcourt, Brace & Co., 1956.

SWAIN, JOSEPH WARD. *The Ancient World.* 2 vols. New York: Harper & Bros., 1950.

TOZER, HENRY F. *The Islands of the Aegean.* Oxford: At the Clarendon Press, 1890.

ZEHREN, Erich. *The Crescent and the Bull.* Translated by JAMES CLEUGH. London: Sidgwick & Jackson, 1962.

347. The Acropolis and ruins along the Lechaeon Road, ancient Corinth

Greece

GREECE MEANS MANY THINGS to many people. To some it means the repository of ancient culture and the birthplace of philosophy, science, sculpture, and classical literature. To others it means a place where one many establish a nostalgic link with the past as he gazes at the lion gate at Mycenae, walks the battlefield at Marathon, climbs the steps to the Acropolis at Athens, or enjoys a dramatic production in the beautiful theater at Epidaurus.

To yet others Greece is a symbol of independence, whether one thinks of the struggles of the ancient city-states with Persia or Philip of Macedon, the fight for independence from Turkey in the last century in which Lord Byron lost his life, the heroic war against Mussolini, or the bitter postwar struggle against Communists from over the Bulgarian border.

To the Bible student, however, Greece is something more. It is the scene of evangelistic activities of the Apostle Paul and the first European country in which the Christian message was preached. In this land the Christian visitor can still stand by the river at Philippi where Paul spoke at the Jewish prayer meeting, on Mars Hill where he addressed the Areopagus Court, and on an excavated section of the ancient Egnatian Way—the highway across Macedonia which Paul traveled from Neapolis to Thessalonica.

Geographical Features

The Boundaries of Greece. Just as Greece has a variety of appeals, so also its geographical bounds have been variously placed. In classical times Greece or Hellas was the southern projection of the Balkan Peninsula, stretching south from Thessaly and Epirus, and including the Ionian and Aegean islands. Covering approximately 30,000 square miles, this Greece was about the size of Scotland or Maine.

Subsequently, as Macedonia was Hellenized, it came to be considered part of the Greek world. Those who include Macedonia as part of Greece have in mind an area covering some 50,000 square miles, comparable to that of England or Alabama. Probably Crete should also be included as part of the Greek world, raising the total by 3,200 square miles, thus constituting an area about the size of Florida or Wisconsin. Modern Greece comprises much of ancient Macedonia and Thrace, the Greek peninsula, Crete, and the islands of the Aegean—about 51,000 square miles.

The Hellas of the days of the Apostle Paul (when the biblical narrative becomes most involved with the area) was very differently constituted. Crete was a Roman

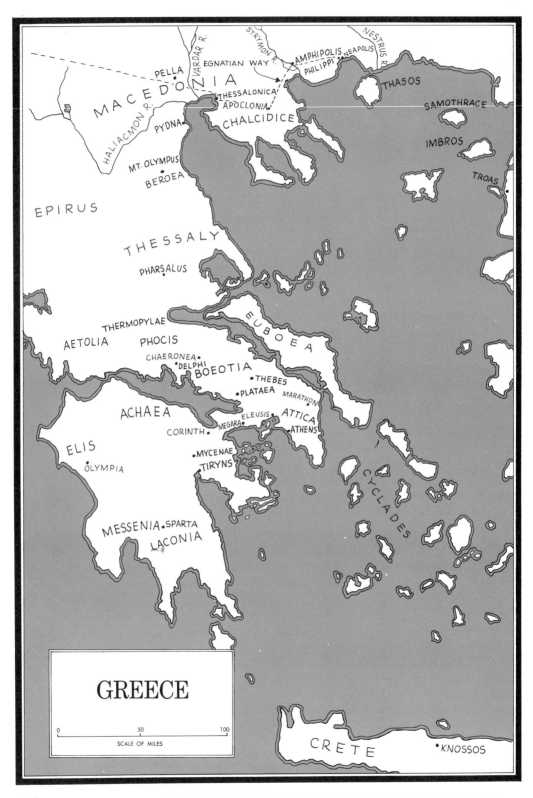

GREECE

0   50   100

SCALE OF MILES

province by itself. The Asia Minor coast and the adjacent islands comprised part of the province of Asia. The province of Thrace occupied eastern Greece. Macedonia and northern Greece were incorporated into the province of Macedonia. The rest of the peninsula and a number of Aegean islands formed the province of Achaea. At one point Luke described the last two of the above-mentioned provinces as Macedonia and Greece (Acts 20:1-2), perhaps a carry-over of the old idea that Macedonians were not really Greeks.

In line with the Roman division, the portions of greater Hellas discussed in this chapter are Macedonia, Achaea, Crete, and some of the islands of the western Aegean. The Greek communities which were part of the province of Asia are discussed in the chapter on Asia Minor.

The mountains. Dominant in the life of any Greek were the mountains and the sea. Mountains covered two-thirds to three-fourths of the land surface, leaving not more than 25 percent of cultivable soil. No other country of the Mediterranean area presents a more tumbled surface than Greece; so while the mountains of Greece are not especially high, one is seldom ever out of sight of them.

Mount Olympus, the highest (located in the northeastern corner of the peninsula), is only about 9,600 feet, and few of the others are over 8,000 feet. Those that are include Mount Pindus (8,500 feet), Mount Ida in Crete (8,200 feet), and Mount Parnassus (8,060 feet). Thus it is obvious that the capacity of Greek mountains for holding snow is limited, and the constancy of water supply is thereby curtailed.

Although the placement of mountains in Greece is chaotic, there is a degree of symmetry. The Magnesian Range extended south from Olympus in eastern Greece; the Pindus Range lay between Thessaly (Thessalia) and Epirus in central Greece; and the Epirus Range stretched along the west-

ern coast. These were crossed by other ridges, dividing the country into a vast checkerboard of tiny valleys, few of which are more than a dozen miles long and more than half as wide. Often the mountain passes between these valleys are 3,000 feet or more in altitude and buried in snow at least part of the winter.

With communications so hampered, a provincialism developed in Greece such as has probably existed in no other historically important area of the world. Moreover, it was the mountain barriers that contributed much to the city-state development of ancient Greece. Though periodic efforts were made to overcome this suicidal division, none was really successful until Macedonia, Rome, and other powers exerted an external pressure for unity.

Rivers. Down from the mountainsides coursed the rivers of Greece. They were mostly non-navigable winter and spring torrents whose floods drowned the arable land. In summer their dry beds served as highways for travelers. These raging torrents washed soil away from the hillsides during the rainy season. During the dry season some of them formed stagnant pools, breeding mosquitoes. Therefore, the rivers were a positive hindrance to Greece, eroding the land, forming breeding places for malarial mosquitoes, silting the mouths of rivers so their harbors were impracticable, and impeding travel. During floods these rivers were difficult to cross for either man or animal; bridges were almost an impossibility for streams that varied from a few feet in width to more than five hundred feet with the seasons. Moreover, these streams were too muddy to serve as a water supply for men or animals. The larger rivers were the Peneus (Salambria) in Thessaly (c. 125 miles long), the Achelous in western Greece (100 miles long), the Arachthus (Arakhthos) in Epirus (80 miles long), and the Alpheus in the western Peloponnesus (75 miles long); but some of the smaller ones were more prominent in song and story.

The sea. While the mountains dominated the landscape of Greece and also affected her politics, economy, and climate, the sea was also a major factor in Greek life. Although the mountains almost closed Greece to the European continent, she was accessible on her seafronts. The coast is so deeply indented that Greece has the longest coastline in proportion to enclosed area of all important historical regions. With a coast of 2,600 miles, it exceeds Italy's (2,150 miles) and that of the Iberian Peninsula (2,300), though its land area is only one-third of the former and one-sixth of the latter. As a result, nowhere in central or southern Greece can a person travel more than forty miles from the sea.

The many indentations afforded numerous harbors. When men sailed the Aegean, they were never out of sight of land on a clear day until they moved south of Crete into the eastern Mediterranean. "An observer on the promontory of Sunium at the tip of Attica may take in at a glance the cluster of the Cyclades as far as Melos, as though he were reading a map. . . . Navigation in the Aegean is thus reduced to the simplicity of a ferry service."[1]

So the Greeks, unable to wrest a living from the rocky farms, became a seafaring people. Learning from all the peoples with whom they came in contact, they cross-fertilized the whole Mediterranean area. It is significant for the history of Hellas that her best ports and many of her valleys lay on the east coast. Therefore her eastern areas received civilizing influences from the Orient first. In contrast, Italy faced west and was slowed in receiving eastern culture.

It is easy, however, to overemphasize the place of the sea in Greek economic life.

The mountains adjacent to many of the city-states did not produce good ship timber and sometimes were literally a barrier between the inhabitants and the sea. Moreover, the Aegean waters are too clear and too devoid of plant life to support large schools of fish. And overseas trade was not vital in the early days when most of the communities of Greece were self-sufficient.

Then, too, the seas around Greece are typically Mediterranean. In winter the Adriatic Sea is a storm center; gusty north winds plague the northern Aegean. The surrounding seas remained closed to all Greeks in winter and to some Greeks most of the time. Sheer cliffs line a good part of the Greek coast. The Thessalians and Boeotians always remained landsmen. The inhabitants of Corinth and Megara were the only peoples of the Peloponnesus or of the area around the Corinthian Gulf to have much of an overseas trade. Sparta only broke out of her landlocked condition for a period during and after her great war with Athens, when she built a navy with the help of Persia. Even the peoples of the Aegean Islands were not seafarers continually.

It should be remembered that the Greeks have always been primarily rural and agricultural. As late as the end of the nineteenth century, 70 percent of them still lived in rural areas. The lack of soil forced them to terrace the hillsides and plant grapevines, olive trees, and whatever else they could produce on some very unpromising land. The stony nature of the soil also often forced them to raise barley and millet rather than wheat. Pasturelands were more suited to the raising of sheep and goats than cattle. Most of their wheat was imported.

Climate. The climate of Greece is mild and has not changed appreciably in at least the last 2,000 years. Northern Greece has a climate similar to that of the Continent with a fair amount of snow, while southern

[1]M. Cary, *The Geographic Background of Greek and Roman History* (Oxford: At the Clarendon Press, 1949), pp. 46-47.

Greece has a climate more Mediterranean in nature. Cold winds, however, bring snow even to Athens in winter. There are two seasons: rainy or winter (October to April) and dry or summer (May to September). The winters are rather boisterous but not devoid of sunshine. Rainfall is fairly heavy, measuring forty inches in the west and slightly less in the east. In the summers there is little precipitation. This period of drought lasts for two months in the North and four months in the Peloponnesus. The hot summer sun is tempered by sea breezes in most places, but some of the cup-shaped valleys are effectively isolated from this relief by the surrounding mountains. In such places summer weather is equal to that of the tropics. For instance, at Larissa in the Thessalian Basin July has a mean temperature of 90 degrees.

Natural resources. "To Hellas poverty has always been a foster sister,"[2] Herodotus well observed. It is certainly remarkable that this minor poverty-stricken people was able to soar above its environment and

[2] Ancient Greece presented a greater impression of prosperity than some of the terrain today. Hillsides terraced and covered with a mantle of trees were less subject to erosion than they have been since. Many rocky slopes in Greece once had a thin topsoil on them.

produce great cultural achievements. Something has already been said about the poor quality and small amount of arable soil in Greece. While in most ancient times there was a considerable amount of timber, by the fifth century B.C. Greece was no longer able to supply her needs and had to import.

Neither did she have much in the way of minerals. Silver and lead were mined in Attica, iron and copper in Euboea and Laconia, and a little gold on the islands of Siphnos and Thasos. Most of the ancient minefields are now exhausted. Some fields that do exist were never exploited in antiquity. There were considerable supplies of potters' clay, especially at Athens and Corinth. Greece also had plenty of good building stone and was famous for her marble.

The finest of the white marbles were quarried in the Cyclades and on Mount Pentelicus in Attica. While Pentelic marble had a smooth grain, the ancient Greeks preferred the marble of Paros, which was more translucent, for sculpture. The only colored marbles of Greece quarried extensively in ancient times were the white and green *cipollino* of Euboea, much desired by the Roman emperors, and the *verde antico* (old green) of northern Thessaly.

Significant Areas of Greece

Since the history of ancient Greece was to a large extent the history of its particular districts, some of the chief areas of Greece require further comment. Only a very general statement is made here. Additional details appear in connection with Paul's ministry in Greece.

Macedonia. At the north of Hellas lay Macedonia. Since its boundaries varied over the centuries and since during much

of the country's history the exact boundaries are not known, it is hard indeed to describe its exact size. The kingdom was, however, always located at the northeast corner of the Aegean; and Pella (24 miles northwest of Thessalonica) was the capital during most of its history. Under Philip II (359-336 B.C.) Macedonia came to include Thrace and to dominate all of Greece. Under Alexander the Great it conquered the entire Persian Empire.

348. The Strymon River at Amphipolis

finally the Nestos Plain. The fertility of these plains has enabled the Greeks to export wheat for the last several years—a considerable achievement for such a rocky country.

Thessaly. Moving south from Old Macedonia proper (as distinct from the province of Macedonia), one comes next to Thessaly. This region has been likened to a "boxlike compartment with an almost level floor and four upright sides." Hemmed in by the Pindus Range on the west, Mount Olympus on the northeast, and other lesser mountains on the north, east, and south, the Thessalians were virtually cut off from the sea. This situation, compounded by the dangerous wind currents along the coast and a broad and fertile interior plain, contributed toward making the inhabitants of the area landsmen.

The Peneus River drained the basin, which, as has already been noted, is oppressively hot in the summer, because cooling sea breezes are blocked by the mountains. The inhabitants of Thessaly were not historically important. This region is a good example of the fact that Greek city-states did not develop for more reasons than simply because of geographical barriers. In this basin (about the size of Connecticut) there were no natural barriers to union, and yet the communities of this area achieved no durable political union until Macedonia and Rome forced it upon them.

When Macedonia became a Roman province in 148 B.C., and throughout most of the first century A.D., the boundaries of the territory were quite well fixed. The Macedonia in which Paul ministered had a borderline which stretched from a point near the Nestos River in eastern Greece to the Adriatic at approximately the latitude of Tiranë (Tirana), modern capital of Albania, then south to the northern border of Epirus, which it skirted to its southern end and turned eastward to the Gulf of Volos (ancient Pagasaeus). Therefore it may be seen that the province included not only most of the northern part of modern Greece but also portions of Bulgaria and Yugoslavia and about half of Albania.

While Macedonia was very mountainous, it also had some fertile plains along the northern rim of the Aegean. Four great rivers (west to east, the Haliacmon [Vistritsa], Vardar, Strymon and Nestos) of the "European" type (which flow all year instead of drying up in the summer) break through the coastal ridges to the sea and deposit around their mouths rich alluvial plains. In the west, the Haliacmon and Vardar plains have been joined at least since the fifth century B.C. Moving east, one comes to the Strymonic Plain which is the most fertile plain of the north Aegean area. Next comes the Philippian Plain and

Epirus. A very mountainous territory in northwestern Greece, Epirus had no important political contacts with the rest of Hellas until the days of King Pyrrhus (d. 272 B.C.), who united the kingdom and aided the southern Italian cities in their war against Rome. The rocky coast has no good harbors, but the interior mountains provided large supplies of timber; and an abundance of rainfall (fifty-two inches a year) contributed to the agricultural pro-

THE WYCLIFFE HISTORICAL GEOGRAPHY OF BIBLE LANDS

ductivity of the small valleys, where many cattle were also raised. Constituted a Roman province in 146 B.C., Epirus was about four-fifths the size of Connecticut.

Boeotia. South of Thessaly lies Boeotia, which reproduces on a smaller scale some of the features of Thessaly. Like Thessaly it is a river basin (the Cephisus) encased in mountains which keep its inhabitants from the sea and which bring to it sultry summers and raw winters. Thebes, its main city, was in the southern part of Boeotia. While Thebes figured often in Greek history, it was mostly on the receiving end of blows struck for conquest. It did, however, achieve a brief hegemony in Greece under Epaminondas (371-362 B.C.).

Euboea. Across the Gulf of Euboea from Boeotia lay the island for which the gulf was named. About ninety miles long, it came to within 100 yards of the mainland at Chalcis. Never politically important, it did have resources of copper and iron that were desired in ancient times but which were exhausted by the Roman period. The Romans, however, appreciated the white and green marble of the southern part of the island.

Phocis. West of Boeotia stretched the territory of Phocis. Dominated as it was by Mount Callidromus on the north and 8,060-foot Parnassus on the south, the area had few resources and little land of value except along the Cephisus River, which flowed between the two mountain ranges. The chief importance of Phocis historically is that Delphi (Delphoi) was located within her borders, six miles north of the Corinthian Gulf. Seat of an important oracle and temple of Apollo at least as early as the seventh century, Delphi received pilgrims from all over Greece. She was enriched, too, as numerous city-states sent their votive gifts and erected shrines there. The Pythian Games, in honor of Apollo, were held at Delphi every four years.

Aetolia. West of Phocis lay Aetolia, a very mountainous and isolated territory inhabited by a backward group of tribes that did not come to the fore until the formation of the Aetolian League about 275 B.C. At its height this military confederation controlled most of central Greece. The territory became part of the Roman province of Achaea, created in 146 B.C.

Attica. Southeast of Boeotia lies the peninsula of Attica. Though very significant for the history of civilization, this small territory comprises only about 1,000 square miles and is approximately the size of Rhode Island. The peninsula is roughly triangular in shape and measures some forty miles east and west and a like distance north and south. No spot in Attica is more than twenty-five miles in a straight line from Athens.

Those who are enamored with the greatness of this area often are unaware of its drawbacks. It is the driest region of Greece with an annual rainfall of only sixteen inches. Only about one-fourth of its soil is arable, and part of that will raise nothing but olives. On the credit side of the ledger are a coast where the mountains leave room for easy landing places, excellent clay beds for pottery manufacture, the famous marble of Mount Pentelicus, and the lead and silver mines of Laurium in the south of the peninsula (exhausted by the time of the Christian Era).

349. Modern Athens with Lycabettus rising in the midst

Athens gradually became the true center of all of life in Attica. At the center of Athens stood her citadel on the Acropolis, an isolated hill about five miles from the coast and three to four hundred feet above the town. It has an almost vertical drop on all sides but the west. After about 500 B.C. the great port of Athens was developed at Piraeus. Another important town of Attica was Eleusis, a religious center fourteen miles northwest of Athens.

The Peloponnesus. Moving southwest of Athens, one crosses the Isthmus of Corinth and enters the Peloponnesus. This peninsula, shaped like a mulberry leaf, has actually been an island since the Corinth Canal was finished in A.D. 1893. Slightly smaller than New Hampshire, the Peloponnesus had several important districts, six of which are noted here. The Peloponnesus formed the larger part of the Roman province of Achaea, organized in 146 B.C.

Occupying the northeast corner of the Peloponnesus was the city-state of Corinth, which never did control a large territory. Blessed with considerable deposits of white and cream-colored clay, Corinth developed the most prolific ceramic industry of early Greece, but after about 550-525 B.C. lost out to Athenian competition in the field.

More important to the development of Corinth, however, was her geographical position. Located a mile and a half south of the Isthmus of Corinth, she commanded this four-mile-wide neck of land, as well as its eastern port of Cenchreae (Cenchrea, Acts 18:18) and its western port of Lechaeum. In New Testament as well as classical times, a large amount of shipping passed through Greek waters, and the trip around the southern tip of Greece was not only long but extremely dangerous. Therefore it became customary to transport goods across the Isthmus of Corinth, a saving of more than 150 miles. Smaller ships were pulled across the Isthmus on a tramway; larger ones were unloaded and their cargoes reloaded on the other side. Short stretches of this tramway can still be seen. Corinth served as the capital of the Roman province of Achaea.

South of Corinth lay Argolis, the coasts of which were almost continuously rockbound and the interior of which was a tangled mass of low mountains. While this area was dominated in classical times by Argos, its significance in history lies in the fact that the important site of Mycenae was located here. Standing astride the main road between Corinth and Argos, it not only controlled communications in that area but came to dominate politically or economically much of the eastern Mediterranean world.

Across the top of the Peloponnesus stretched Achaea, which occupied a narrow fertile coastland. In this territory twelve cities formed a religious confederacy, meeting in Poseidon's sanctuary at Helice. From this developed the politically important Achaean League of Hellenistic times.

To the southwest of Achaea lay Elis, occupying a wide piedmont terrace at the western edge of Arcadia. The area had the best cattle pastures of the Peloponnesus and produced flax as well. Its significance in Greek history arose from the fact that the great Panhellenic sanctuary of Olympia was located there. The local population

350. Area of the old port of Cenchreae

was entrusted with the stewardship of the Olympic Games.

The two southern districts of the Peloponnesus were Laconia and Messenia. Each consisted of a fertile plain framed in a horseshoe of mountains fronting on a sea gulf. The more significant of these plains historically was the Laconian, where Sparta was located. Laconia was watered by an abundance of streams from the Taygetus Range (c. 8,000 feet) on the west. Most important of these was the Eurotas River, along the banks of which Sparta lay. Since this area could support a considerable population, it was not so necessary for the Spartans, as it was for the Athenians, to engage in commercial and political adventure. In this matter Sparta was fortunate because her natural hindrances to overseas commerce were great. Her ports were not good, and sailing at the southern tip of the Peloponnesus was difficut and dangerous. Although the pass into Messenia was through a difficult gorge which reached a height of 4,500 feet and which was impassable in midwinter, the valiant Spartans managed to conquer and control their neighbors. The development of the Spartan state is described subsequently in this work.

The Cyclades. A group of about 220 islands with a total area of only slightly more than 1,000 square miles, extends from the tip of Attica in a southeasterly direction. These are known as the Cyclades and were so called by the Greeks because they formed a circle or cluster (*kyklos*) around the sacred Island of Delos, seat of the Delean League (of which Athens was the chief member). Geologically they represent a submerged mountain chain with their tops protruding above water level. While these islands are mountainous, they are quite productive agriculturally. Their mineral deposits have not as yet been fully exploited. Through the millennia the Cyclades have been subject to the more powerful states in the area. In New Testament times they were part of the Roman province of Achaea.

Crete. Crete is the southernmost and largest of the Greek islands. It is the fourth largest island in the Mediterranean (Sicily, Sardinia, and Cyprus being larger). Located sixty miles south of Cape Malea in the Peloponnesus and 110 miles west of Cape Krio in Asia Minor (with Rhodes and other islands between it and Cape Krio), its location made inevitable its use as a seedbed and distributing center for the cultures of the Near East from the fourth to the first millennia B.C.

Comprising an area of 3,200 square miles (about half the size of New Jersey), Crete is of elongated form—160 miles from east to west and 6 to 35 miles from north to south. While the northern coast is deeply indented and provides a good natural harbor at least at Suda at the western end of the island, the southern coast is less indented. In the southern part of the island, the mountains often appear to rise from the sea.

In the center of the southern coast is Cape Lithinos, the southernmost point of the island. Immediately to the east of that is the small bay of Kali Limenes, or Fair Havens, where the ship carrying Paul took refuge (Acts 27:8). A little less than twenty-five miles southwest of Cape Lithinos lies the rocky, treeless isle of Clauda (modern Gavdos) which Paul's ship passed as it began to fight the storm which eventually blew it to Malta (Acts 27:16). While the history of Crete is discussed subsequently, it may be helpful to mention here that it was a separate Roman province when Paul passed it and when Titus ministered there, having been conquered by Rome 68/67 B.C.

If one flies along the coast of Crete, he gets the impression that the island is a solid mass of mountains. On closer examination, however, he discovers that the mountains divide into four principal groups which between them do cover most of the

351. Storage jars in the palace of Knossos

in some of the higher regions. Numerous caves exist in these mountains, one of the most important to the Greeks being the Dictaean Cave in Lasithi, the legendary birthplace of Zeus. Several small rivers flow both to the north and south shores of Crete.

Southeast of Mount Ida lies the Messara Plain, largest on the island, extending about thirty-seven miles in length and ten miles in breadth. One of the richest plains in Greece, it no doubt supplied the wine and olive oil for the huge storage jars found in the palaces at Knossos (Cnossus or Gnossus) and Phaistos (Phaestus), the chief cities in the north and south of Crete, respectively. Probably the Messara also furnished orchard produce which served as a chief staple in the early trade of Cretan merchants. In several places on Crete there are level upland basins which furnish good pasturage for flocks and herds during the summer months.

island. In the West are the White Mountains, which reach an altitude of almost 8,000 feet; in the center is the ancient Mount Ida (modern Psiloriti) 8,200 feet high; in the middle of the eastern half of the island rise the Lasithi to a height of 7,200 feet; and at the east end the Sitia Mountains only 4,800 feet high. Many of these peaks are covered with snow the greater part of the year. Forests which once covered the mountains and which were much valued for ship timber have for the most part disappeared, and the slopes are now desolate wastes. Cypress still grows

The rainy season on Crete lasts from October to March and the dry season from April to September, when almost no rain falls. Total rainfall for an average year is about twenty inches. At Candia (Heraklion), near ancient Knossos, the mean temperatures vary from 51 degrees in January to 79 degrees in August.

Peoples of Greece

The earliest ages. Though Paleolithic remains have been found in Greece, there is no pattern of human settlement to be described from those remains. Such a pattern, however, does begin to emerge with the Neolithic period. Neolithic settlements, which are now beginning to appear in various parts of Greece,[3] may probably be dated as early as the fifth millennium B.C.,

certainly as early as the fourth.[4] These pre-pottery cultures in which cultivation of foodstuffs, domestication of animals, and the construction of huts in regular village sites occurred are considered to have received at least an initial impetus from Mesopotamian developments.

Whether this influence came primarily

[3]Examples are Nea Nikomedeia (33 miles west of Thessalonica), Sesklo in Thessaly, Nea Makri in Attica, Corinth, the island of Melos, and Knossos.

[4]New discoveries at Nea Nikomedeia, however, appear to date to the seventh millennium B.C. See *Illustrated London News*, April 11, 1964, and April 18, 1964.

THE WYCLIFFE HISTORICAL GEOGRAPHY OF BIBLE LANDS

from the south, the east, or the north is open to question, but quite certainly it came through Asia Minor. The thrust that came from the north probably moved in an arc from Asia Minor around the top of the Aegean. While there were some contacts between peoples of Greece and those of the Bulgarian region, there was probably no considerable Alpine influence upon Greece at this early time. Again, there is some question whether the cultural influences appearing in Greece during Neolithic times came as a result of migration of peoples or simply transmission of ideas. The weight of scholarship at present favors the former.

While the ethnic composition consisted primarily of Mediterranean stock,[5] the skeletal remains in various Neolithic sites show that the people were not entirely Mediterranean but consisted of a variety of human types.[6] The ethnic composition of the Neolithic period does not seem to have changed appreciably during the Early Bronze Age (down to c. 2000 B.C.).

Indo-European invasion. At the beginning of the Middle Bronze Age (c. 2000 B.C.), a shock hit Greece that was destined ultimately to bring about considerable change. Coming probably from the north, Indo-European peoples moved into the peninsula, disrupting the older civilization that had been built up there. While they modified much of what they found, the culturally inferior invaders also adopted much. Ultimately, however, they did impose their language on the Mediterranean peoples of the peninsula. The invasion of Greece by these Achaeans was only part of a wider movement which threw Kassites into Mesopotamia, Hittites into Asia Minor, and perhaps Hyksos into Egypt.

In thinking about these Indo-European peoples, it is well to observe that they were a conglomeration of humanity who had come to share a common language and certain cultural characteristics. Starr's observation is quite in order: "A man who spoke an Indo-European language did not necessarily share with his comrades one particular structure of body or color of hair and eyes; and his blood stream did not carry any specific outlook on life or aesthetic point of view."[7]

The Minoan peoples of Crete did not suffer greatly from the invasion which upset the mainland but continued to develop to new cultural heights under Near Eastern tutelage and as a result of internal impetus. Around 1600 B.C. when the mainland had achieved an adjustment between the old and new cultures, the Minoans became the educators of Hellas. After about 1400 B.C. the Mycenaean peoples of the mainland established their hegemony in Greece.

A second Indo-European invasion. As the Mycenaean civilization began to disintegrate during the thirteenth century, a new threat came from the north. Around 1200 B.C. another invasion of Indo-European peoples descended into the peninsula, laying waste cities everywhere and causing a definite break in civilization. Introducing a "dark age," these people are commonly called "Dorians" and are thought to have come from Epirus and other Balkan areas, such as Yugoslavia. Whether the Dorians spoke Greek before moving south or whether they adopted it subsequently has not been absolutely proved. That they brought any very significant cultural developments with them may be questioned. Starr feels that their greatest contribution was to free Greece from the Minoan and Mycenaean conventions thereby permitting a new culture to emerge from native roots.[8]

[5]A branch of the white race, they were short, slender, dark people of the same physical type as found in North Africa, Spain, and Italy.
[6]Chester G. Starr, *The Origins of Greek Civilization 1100-650* B.C. (New York: Alfred A. Knopf, 1961), p. 18.

[7]*Ibid.*, p. 34.
[8]*Ibid.*, pp. 73-74, 78.

New cultural emergence. When the lights came on again at the end of the dark ages about 800 B.C., Greeks were speaking three main dialects: Aeolic, Ionic, and Doric. These were spoken in geographical bands which stretched roughly across north, central, and south Hellas, respectively. Aeolic was found in northwestern Asia Minor, Thessaly, and Boeotia; Ionic in west central Asia Minor, the Cyclades, and Attica; Doric in Rhodes, Crete, and the Peloponnesus. However, the pattern was not so regular as that in other states of the Greek Peninsula.

It must be remembered that these are dialects of one language and that the terms do not necessarily carry with them any greatly differentiated racial or cultural patterns. The peoples of the Aegean Basin were Indo-European by the end of the second millennium B.C., and as sons of Hellas had one language (with many dialects), a common religion, and a bond in their great athletic events. But they were also sons of their own city-states to which they pledged fierce loyalty to the point of committing "national" suicide.

The History of Greece

The re-creation of the story of early Hellas began with the fabulous Heinrich Schliemann (1822-1890), Homeric fundamentalist, who believed in the literal truth of Homer's *Iliad*. Having dedicated his life to making a fortune and learning several languages in order to prove the accuracy of Homer, he finally began to excavate at the site of Troy in 1870 in his forty-ninth year. Successful there, six years later he started to work at Mycenae on mainland Greece. In November, 1876, he sent a telegram to the king of Greece announcing that he had discovered the body of Agamemnon.

The romance was continued by Arthur Evans who, as an act of faith, purchased the hillock of Knossos in Crete in the 1890's and, in 1900, when political conditions became more stable, began to excavate. His strong faith was richly rewarded. Others also made their archaeological contributions. In 1953 Michael Ventris and John Chadwick announced the successful decipherment of Linear B (a script found on numerous tablets in Mycenaean sites), which would enable historians to form a clearer picture of early Greek civilization. As a result of the work of these and many

others, it is now possible to describe the flowering of early Greek culture and to establish the fact that the greatness of Greece during the Classical Age came late indeed.

The Glory of the Minoans

Historical developments. The civilization which Evans found at Knossos was called Minoan because this was the capital of the legendary King Minos. But of course the brilliant culture that has been associated with early Crete did not appear full-blown as Athena was said to have sprung fully armed from the head of Zeus. This culture developed over a period of many centuries. Evans himself found a Neolithic stratum 23 to 26 feet in depth at the bottom of the Knossos excavation. Crete was first occupied by 4000 B.C. by migrants who seem to have come from Asia Minor and who were of Mediterranean stock. Minoan history proper is commonly divided into Early, Middle, and Late periods, and each of these three periods is subdivided.

The Early Minoan period may be dated

352. A reconstructed entrance to the palace at Knossos

3000-2100 B.C. During this millennium Cretan cultures were not particularly different from or superior to those of the rest of the Aegean. About the middle of the period new waves of migrants from Asia Minor settled in the Cyclades and in east and central Crete, and then the Bronze Age came to Crete. Within a couple of centuries bronze was in common use for weapons and tools, the olive had been introduced, and longhorn cattle were imported. The indoor hearth which the migrants brought with them was abandoned in the warmer climate of Crete. The Cretan house as a collection of rooms around an open court became characteristic. Trade relations with Egypt grew increasingly common. During the last centuries of the millennium Cretan culture began to coalesce.

With the Middle Minoan (2100-1600 B.C.) and Late Minoan I (1600-1500/1450 B.C.) periods, Cretan culture attained extraordinary achievements. However, these attainments were not developed in a vacuum. Here was an example of what could happen when early Aegean culture made contact with the highly advanced cultures of the Orient. While some elements came from Egypt and others from Asia, all such cultural borrowings were assimilated by the genius of the Cretan people and transmuted into an individual art. For instance, the Cretan palace was architecturally unlike the buildings of any other land. The masterpieces of painting on its walls, with all of their evidence of enjoyment of life, contrasted remarkably with contemporary Egyptian preoccupation with another world and the pompous arrogance of later Mesopotamian art.

The first palaces on a grand scale appeared at Knossos and elsewhere on the island at the beginning of the Middle Minoan period. During Middle Minoan II (1900-1700 B.C.) came a flowering of Cretan culture. This was the age of the famous eggshell ware with walls as thin as Haviland china. The cartwheel arrived from Asia, and the first stone-paved roads in Europe were constructed on the island, connecting Knossos and Phaistos, and protected by guard-posts. The center of power moved from eastern to north central Crete, which suggests that trade was becoming more oriented to the Greek mainland. Although there were several cities on the island at the time, Knossos and Phaistos seem to have dominated Crete during the period.

Setting off the Middle Minoan III period were two severe earthquakes which occurred in 1700 and 1600 B.C. During the century, palaces at Knossos, Phaistos, and elsewhere were rebuilt on a grander scale. From local hieroglyphic scripts developed a linear script—which has become known as Linear A.[9] It was syllabic in nature and written from left to right. Life became more luxurious on the island as trade developed with Byblos and Ugarit in Syria and with the Cyclades, through whose market at Melos goods reached the Greek mainland. Their chief exports were wine, olive oil, metal products, and their magnificent pottery, which has been found in Egypt, Syria, Greece, and Italy.

Crete attained her greatest prosperity during the Late Minoan I and II periods (1600-1400 B.C.). After the great earthquake of about 1600 B.C., the palaces at Knossos and Phaistos were again rebuilt along even grander lines than before. At first there was not complete political unity of the island, but that was achieved about 1500 B.C. when Knossos became supreme. During these two centuries Minoan trade with Egypt (then in its Empire period) was extensive, though it seems to have declined somewhat with Ugarit and Byblos. One of the wall paintings in the tomb of Rekhmire, grand vizier of Thutmose III of Egypt, shows foreigners with gifts who, judged by

their dress and the nature of their gifts, may have been Minoans. Part of the accompanying inscription is "the coming in peace of the Great Ones of Keftiu and of the Isles in the midst of the sea."[10] Keftiu may have been Crete; she was queen among the isles of the sea. Cyprus felt the impact of trade with Crete too.

But the Aegean area became something of an economic province of the Minoans. Minoan colonies were planted on Rhodes and at Miletus; Minoan trading stations were probably established on the Greek mainland; and the Cyclades passed strongly under Cretan control. It is too much to claim that Crete exercised a naval control over the Aegean during this period. Chester Starr has scored this commonly held view as impossible of proof logically, archaeologically, or historically.[11]

As has now been confirmed by the decipherment of the Linear B script,[12] sometime between 1500 and 1400 B.C. Knossos

[9]Gordon thinks that Linear A is linguistically based on West Semitic of the Phoenician type; Cyrus H. Gordon, "Minoica," *Journal of Near Eastern Studies*, XXI (July, 1962), 210.

[10]N. G. L. Hammond, *A History of Greece to 322 B.C.* (Oxford: At the Clarendon Press, 1959), p. 32.

[11]Chester G. Starr, "The Myth of the Minoan Thalassocracy," *Historia*, 1955, pp. 282-91.

[12]Some 3,000 inscriptions in Linear B now exist, having been excavated in palaces at Knossos and on the Greek mainland at such places as Mycenae, Pylos, and Tiryns. Michael Ventris and John Chadwick were primarily responsible for its decipherment. See M. Ventris and J. Chadwick, *Documents in Mycenaean Greek* (Cambridge: Cambridge University Press, 1956). It appears that this script, found exclusively at palaces, was used only by the ruling class—very largely for keeping palace records and the like. At least no literary compositions written in Linear B have yet come to light.

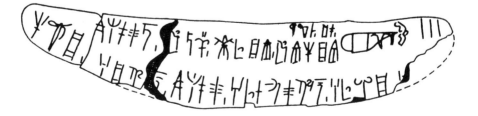

353. A Linear B tablet

came under the control of the Mycenaean Greeks on the mainland. Possibly this was achieved by a marriage alliance of the ruling houses at Mycenae and Knossos. Linear B, which is definitely Greek, replaced the older Minoan Linear A (from which it borrowed heavily) as the script of Knossos. Linear B also became the script of the Mycenaean mainland, whereas Crete outside of its chief city retained the use of Linear A.

Many other cultural changes occurred. For instance, mainland themes were introduced into the pottery of Crete; henceforth, far greater attention was paid to warlike representations in the art of the island. The Mycenaeans changed the system of numerical notation and probably of weights and measures. Presumably Mycenaean influence also led to the introduction of the throne room into the palace at Knossos at this time. It seems quite clear that during her period of Mycenaean political and cultural domination Knossos continued to control Crete.

On a spring day about the year 1400 B.C., the unfortified palace at Knossos was sacked and burned. About the same time the other leading cities of Crete suffered the same fate. The occasion is unknown. Some have speculated that rebellion by Cretans against the rule of Knossos and Mycenae sparked an uprising. In rebuttal, it has been argued that such an extensive destruction throughout the island would probably not have resulted. Others have suggested that a new invasion from the mainland worked the destruction. On the theory that the Mycenaeans already controlled the island, this view does not seem plausible. Moreover, no Mycenization of Crete followed this destruction. It should be remembered, however, that never was all of the Greek mainland dominated by one power during the Mycenaean period; a rival of the dynasty controlling Knossos could have attacked. Yet others have proposed the view that piratical sea raids of

354. The queen's bathroom in the Palace at Knossos

other powers of the eastern Mediterranean were responsible for the catastrophe. Whoever the culprit was, Minoan supremacy in the Aegean ended.

During the great days of Mycenaean power (1400-1200 B.C.) Crete continued to prosper. She did not suffer the extensive catastrophe which befell the mainland during the Dorian invasion, after 1200 B.C. There was, however, quite a contrast between the ordered unity of the Minoan days and the political chaos of the later period, when principal towns of the island tended to neutralize one another and piracy became a common pursuit of the islanders or a monster to afflict the formerly prosperous communities.

Crete has often been considered the home of the Philistines, who made their way to Palestine about 1200 B.C. after being repelled from Egypt by Ramses III.[13] Scripture itself speaks of Caphtor as the Philistine homeland (Jer. 47:4; Amos 9:7). Caphtor (or Caphtorim) is also mentioned in Genesis 10:14 and Deuteronomy 2:23. A variant, Caphthorim, appears in I Chron-

[13]It must be observed that Scripture speaks of the presence of Philistines in Palestine as early as the days of Abraham (Gen. 21:34), but that problem is not within the purview of this chapter. It may be noted, however, that there is nothing to prove that an earlier migration of Philistines did not come to Palestine from the Aegean or eastern Mediterranean many centuries before the known migration of the twelfth century.

icles 1:12. The question is whether Caphtor and Crete are identified with one another. The present knowledge of ancient
Near Eastern developments does not permit a final decision, though many scholars
are convinced that Crete and Caphtor are
to be identified. While this factor may have
no conclusive bearing on the question, it is
interesting to note that the translators of
the Greek Septuagint translated Caphtor by
the Greek name Cappadocia, located in
east central Asia Minor.

In assessing questions of this kind, it is
well to remember that a potpourri of humanity spilled over the whole eastern Mediterranean world at the end of the thirteenth
century B.C., toppling the Mycenaean kingdoms, devastating the remnants of the Hittite Empire in Asia Minor, testing the
strength of Egyptian Empire defenses, and
invading Palestine. To determine the ethnic and geographical origins of each of
these peoples constitutes a Herculean task
indeed.

Minoan culture. Before turning to historical developments on the Greek mainland, something must be said about non-
political aspects of Minoan life. Minoan
civilization rested on an agricultural base.
Building on that, the populace developed
extensive industry and trade during the
second millennium.

The finest monument to their prosperity
is the great palace at Knossos. (However,
the palaces at Phaistos and Mallia should
not be ignored.) Covering between five and
six acres, this rambling structure consists of
a vast collection of rooms arranged around
open courts. Built of stone, brick, and
wood, it had fine state entrances with spacious staircases and state halls, in addition
to private quarters and extensive storerooms. Pavements, foundations, and some
walls were built of stone; upper parts of
walls were generally of brick; lintels and
columns were of wood, and columns tap-
ered downward instead of upward. Parts

of the structure were four stories high.
More than a mere royal residence, the palace served as an administrative headquarters, and as a storehouse, factory, arsenal,
and artistic center.

One of the most impressive features of
the palace was the many wall frescoes,
which were quite remarkable for spontane-
ity, creativity, and sensitivity to natural
beauty. Some of the loveliest include a
monkey gathering saffron in a meadow
filled with crocuses, a bluebird amid rocks

355. The snake-goddess, Knossos

and roses, and a cat creeping among the rushes toward an unsuspecting pheasant. These frescoes are even more remarkable when one realizes that they were painted while the plaster was still wet and therefore had to be completed within a few hours. The fact that Minoan artists could execute an entire painting in so short a time is a great tribute to their skill.

Judging from the themes portrayed in their art, one concludes that the Minoans were a people who loved the beauty of nature and were not warlike. Their subjects were people, social gatherings at court, animals, plants, trees, flying fish, and religious motifs. In contrast with contemporary Egypt and Assyria in later centuries, they did not have any interest in pompous military representations.

The importance of religion in the state and in private life is attested to by the position of the pillared shrine in the central court of the palace at Knossos. There were also numerous sanctuaries in mountain caves. The king himself was probably a high priest and was very possibly worshiped as a divine being in a manner similar to the Pharaohs of Egypt. But the Minoan king was not a haughty master like the Egyptian Pharaoh. His throne was a simple chair of gypsum, and a stone bench for his courtiers lined the throne room. Buttressed as it was by religious, economic, and military sanctions, the king's power must have been great, however, and virtually dictatorial during the last century of the Minoan kingdom.

At the center of Minoan religion was the worship of a female deity clothed in Minoan dress, with sacred serpents entwined around her arms. Exactly what this goddess represented is not definitely known. The idea that she was a mother goddess, a fertility deity, is concluded on the basis of comparison with known cults of Asia Minor in later centuries. The characteristic male deity is represented as a young boy.

356. Fifty-four gold dress attachments from Knossos, 1700-1500 B.C.

Minoans were longheaded, narrow-faced, and short, the men averaging five feet two inches and the women four feet eleven inches. Men commonly wore shorts or kilts and sandals, but the women chose more elaborate costumes: low-necked dresses with full skirts, ruffled or flounced. Men were beardless, perhaps as a result of Egyptian influence. Men and women seem to have mingled rather freely at athletic events and religious festivals, possibly indicating that the Minoans gave their women freedom and dignity above that of any other Near Eastern people.

The common people of Crete lived in one- or two-story houses with no windows on the ground floor. Such windows as existed appeared in the second story; houses received their light and ventilation from the open court upon which the rooms faced. There seems to have been a reasonably prosperous middle class of farmers, artisans, and traders, which contrasted with the two-class structure of contemporary Egypt.

The Power of the Mycenaeans

Historical developments. While the Minoans were developing their culture on their island of Crete, cultural advancement occurred less rapidly on the Greek main-

357. Remains of the palace at Tiryns

land. To distinguish it from Minoan culture, that of the mainland is called Helladic (after the ancient name for Greece, Hellas); and it is divided into three periods of historical development: Early Helladic (2500-1900 B.C.), Middle Helladic (1900-1600 B.C.), and Late Helladic (1600-1200 B.C.).

About 2500 B.C. Greece emerged from the Neolithic into the Bronze Age under the impetus of a new wave of settlers. Coming by sea, probably from Asia Minor, they settled in east and central Greece and preferred sites on or near the coast. Meanwhile Macedonia and most of Thessaly retained a Neolithic culture. As noted earlier, the first Greeks or Indo-Europeans arrived in the peninsula around 2000-1900 B.C., at which time the Middle Bronze Age (1900-1600 B.C.) began.

The Mycenaean Age really began about 1600 B.C. (as did the Late Bronze Age) and was coextensive with the Late Helladic period. This was a time when kings, who apparently tried to ape the Oriental monarchies, managed to extend their dominions over considerable stretches of countryside. Building their palace complexes at such sites as Mycenae and Tiryns in the northeast Peloponnesus and Pylos in the southwest Peloponnesus, they produced in them masses of pottery, bronze weapons, and other commodities which they marketed

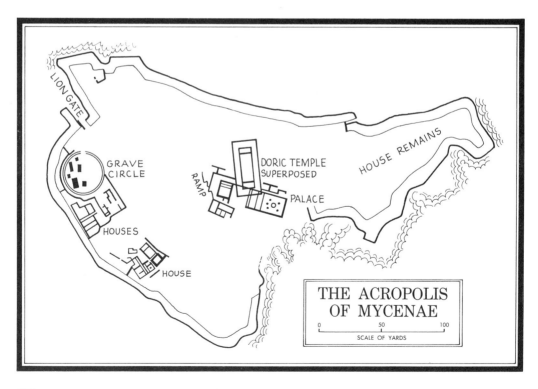

THE ACROPOLIS OF MYCENAE

0   50   100

SCALE OF YARDS

358. The Lion Gate,
    Mycenae

extensively in the Mediterranean world. They also exacted taxes from peasants on the surrounding lands as an additional source of wealth.

These palaces, then, were heavily fortified centers in which kings lived with a number of artisans and members of their bureaucracy and in which they kept their accumulated treasure. The palace centers were not true cities, for the bulk of the population seems to have lived in villages nearby.

Mycenaean traders and explorers ranged far with their wares searching for various metals. From Mycenaean objects appearing in excavations elsewhere and foreign objects coming to light at Mycenaean sites, it may be concluded that these intrepid adventurers established contacts in Sicily, southern Italy, the upper Danube region, along the northern shore of the Aegean, the western shores of Asia Minor and the Syrian coast, the Cyclades, and Egypt. Occasionally they went beyond commercial activities and established colonies—in such places as Rhodes, the Asia Minor coast, perhaps at Tarentum in southern Italy, and elsewhere.

The civilization called "Mycenaean," which developed at the palace centers of the Peloponnesus and Boeotia, was given its name in honor of Mycenae, where it was originally discovered by Schliemann. By no means all of Hellas participated in the Mycenaean development. Macedonia, Epirus, Thessaly, and other sections of Greece retained much of the earlier culture of the Middle Bronze Age.

While a description of any or all of the known centers of Mycenaean culture is tempting to the historian, attention is directed here only to the best known of them all—Mycenae, traditional home of Agamemnon, leader of the Greeks in the Trojan War. Actually, however, the palaces are best preserved at Pylos and Tiryns. At the former site is the "Palace of Nestor," named for another participant in the Trojan War. Here one may still see the remains of sixty rooms.

The acropolis of Mycenae enjoyed an enviable location. Situated about ten miles from the sea, it was reasonably safe from pirate attacks. The acropolis stood 912 feet high and was isolated by two steep ravines, on the north and south. The site dominated the main road and thus the trade between Argos and Corinth and central Greece. The wall around the acropolis forms an irregular triangle, measuring 656 feet at the base and 984 feet on the sides. Most of the wall, varying in thickness from 10 to 46 feet and standing to a height of 55 feet, was built of huge undressed stones. But at the corners and around the gateways, the blocks are squared and arranged in horizontal layers. The main gate, the famous Gate of the Lions, is in the northwest corner of the wall. Measuring about ten feet in width and slightly over ten feet in height, it is topped by a great lintel over fifteen feet long, which is in turn surmounted by a triangular slab on which is carved two lionesses (protectresses of the palace) standing face to face on their hind legs; between them stands a column.

Just inside the Lion Gate on the right is a royal grave circle almost ninety feet in diameter. In this enclosure, ringed by a double row of stone slabs, were found nineteen skeletons. Buried there around 1550-1500 B.C., the male skeletons were accompanied by masks and breastplates of gold, swords, daggers, gold and silver drinking cups, gold signet rings, and vessels of metal, stone, and clay; the female skeletons were accompanied by gold frontlets, toilet boxes, and jewelry. The graves were marked by stelae, on some of which horse-drawn chariots were represented. These chariots and scenes of war and hunting portrayed on

359. Royal grave circle, inside the walls at Mycenae

artifacts within the tombs definitely show a mainland influence rather than Minoan. This grave area was originally outside the walls but was brought within them during a later expansion about 1400 B.C. In 1952, a second grave circle (dating before 1600 B.C.) was found outside the walls of Mycenae. It was likewise almost ninety feet in diameter and also contained many rare *objets d'art* but no precious metals.

From the Lion Gate to the palace led the royal way, a ramp for chariots proceeding to the palace. Twenty-two steps led up from this ramp to an anteroom, which in turn led into the throne room. Adjacent to the throne room was an open courtyard about fifty by forty feet. To the east of this stood the megaron, or great hall, measuring about forty-two by forty feet. The rest of the two-story structure has slid into the ravine.

As to decoration of the palace, the stuccoed floors were laid out in colored checkerboard squares, and the walls were adorned with frescoes in the Minoan style. A great painted fireplace stood in the center of the megaron. Water for the acropolis area was supplied by great cisterns (the largest of which was 26 by 13 by 15 feet deep) and by the Perseia spring.

After 1500 B.C. great tholoi, or beehive tombs, were built in the surrounding hillsides. The most famous of these is the so-called Treasury of Atreus, or Tomb of Agamemnon, or Tomb of the Lioness, across the road from the Lion Gate. An inclined unroofed passageway led down to the entrance of it. A doorway about 18 feet high and 9 feet wide led into the circular chamber, shaped like a beehive, over 43 feet high and almost 47 feet in diameter. The great lintel over the door is 28 feet long, 10 feet thick and 4 feet high and is estimated to weigh 120 tons. Above that is a triangular area with sides measuring about 10 feet. Probably a carved stone block once filled the gap.

The dome of the tomb was formed of 33

rings of stone blocks curved in their inner surface and arranged in corbels and capped with a round slab which formed the lid. The interior originally was decorated with bronze rosettes at the fourth ring of masonry. On the right of this "beehive" was a chamber about 20 feet wide, 28 feet deep, and 20 feet high. Many of these unusual tombs have been found at Mycenae, Pylos, and elsewhere in Greece.

That Mycenae continued to be inhabited in the classical period is attested both by history and archaeology. For instance, Mycenae sent 80 men to the battle of Thermopylae and 200 to the battle of Plataea. Foundations of a Doric temple were in the seventh century B.C. superimposed on the Mycenaean palace. Hellenistic walls may be seen on the acropolis, as well as remains of houses of post-Mycenaean construction.

Mycenaean civilization. Mycenaean civilization has been described as basically Minoan with the addition of certain northern or Indo-European elements introduced by the Greeks. The material remains unearthed in such places as the grave circle at Mycenae show a high development in metal working and pottery production, reflecting Minoan influence and perhaps a Minoan hand. But the artistic motifs show northern influence, with a preference for war and hunting scenes and with bearded men, as opposed to the smooth-shaven Minoans with their interest in nature scenes. Mycenaean houses and palaces had as their chief element the megaron, or great hall, with its fireplace, whereas Minoan structures were generally collections of rooms surrounding open courts. Mycenaean clothes were heavier and more voluminous than those worn by Minoans. Mycenaean chariots were heavier than those of the Minoans, their body armor more extensive, their weapons more numerous, and their fortifications more formidable. Minoan cities were unwalled.

360. Remains of the palace at Mycenae

Stripped of their poetic additions, the legends of the period reveal a hard, brutal, and violent society in which piracy and murder were not uncommon. In this troubled age the guardian of trade was the sword. While Mycenaean culture developed under the tutelage of the Minoans after 1600 B.C., it was more or less on its own after 1400, when the Cretan palaces were destroyed. During its later stages, art and other aspects of culture showed a noticeable decline.

As to religion of the period, although the tablets mention priests and priestesses, no Mycenaean temples are known. And other than Zeus, Hera, Poseidon, Athena, and Hermes, no deities can be identified with certainty.

Fall of Mycenaean civilization. The Mycenaean world almost literally came apart at the seams. But as in all periods of stress, outside forces were also tugging at the fabric of civilization and eventually tore it to shreds. There seems to have been serious internal stress among the Mycenaean states. Thebes was destroyed about 1350 B.C. by Mycenae. After about 1250 B.C., Mycenae, Tiryns, Pylos, and Athens were strengthening their defenses, whether against unrest at home or attack from abroad is not known.

Meanwhile Mycenaean markets must have shriveled with the unrest in the eastern Mediterranean. An irruption of Indo-European peoples hit the Egyptian coast about 1230 B.C. and again shortly after 1190. Many great trading centers on the coasts of Palestine, Syria, and Cyprus were sacked around 1200. Raiders delivered blows to the Hittites which sent them reeling about 1225 and destroyed their empire early in the twelfth century. Troy was destroyed around 1240 or perhaps earlier, presumably by the Mycenaean chiefs described in Homer's *Iliad*, and was subsequently occupied by Phrygians. Between 1200 and 1150 invasions from the north wiped out the Mycenaean political and economic systems built around the kings and their palaces.

Their greatness continued in ancient times only in the shadowy historical memory of Greek legend (later embodied in Homer). Today the memory of Mycenaean greatness is perpetuated in such places as the Mycenaean room in the National Museum, Athens, and the archaeological shrines which dot the landscape of the Peloponnesus. The invasion responsible for the destruction of the Mycenaeans and the subsequent break in civilization is commonly known as the Dorian invasion. But it should be remembered that groups speaking other Greek dialects were arriving about the same time. Moreover, the Dorians themselves were no "pure" race and picked up other ethnic elements as they pushed through Greece.

The Dark Ages

From about 1150 B.C. to 850 or 800 B.C. Greece passed through what is known as the Dark Ages or the Middle Ages. The period may be called a dark era either because so little is known about it or because the light of culture burned very low. Three general observations may be made about the events of these three centuries.

First, there was the death of the old order. There was probably a sharp decline in population. Economic and social life sank to a primitive level. Craftsmanship became cruder, and sculpture almost disappeared. Commerce passed from the Greeks to the Phoenicians. It will be remembered that the tenth century B.C. encompasses the era of Hiram of Tyre and Solomon of Israel, who carried on joint maritime exploits.

Second, this was an age of movement and confusion. Peoples who moved into Greece kept on moving southward into the peninsula and the Peloponnesus, southeastward into the Cyclades, and eastward to the coast of Asia Minor. Third, a new order emerged with an Iron Age culture. In place of the larger Mycenaean kingdoms arose small barbaric states with a local patriotism so strong as to prevent the unity of Greece in the classical period. Greek city-states on the Asia Minor coast developed earlier and prospered more than the communities of the Greek mainland because of trade with the interior and contact with older cultures of the Orient.

361. Tomb of Agamemnon at Mycenae

THE WYCLIFFE HISTORICAL GEOGRAPHY OF BIBLE LANDS

The Formative Age (850 or 800-500) [14]

Why these small city-states arose during the Dark Ages, developed more fully during the Formative Age, and came to their zenith during the subsequent Classical Age is a matter of considerable discussion and debate. As previously indicated, the configuration of Greece is given a large share of the credit. But that is not the whole story. The Mycenaean kingdoms had managed to slice off larger chunks of real estate than most of the city-states. Moreover, there was between many of the city-states, e. g., Corinth and Sicyon, no physical barrier to hinder unification. Some of the most mountainous parts of Greece (Arcadia and Aetolia) did not develop city-states at all or at least not until very late. They used instead something like the canton system.

There was also something in the unsettled conditions of the times to explain the formation of city-states. Groups of people, related or unrelated, tended to band together for defense, especially around high places, such as the Acropolis of Athens or Corinth. Then geographical conditions, economic self-sufficiency, and especially a fierce local loyalty kept several city-states from uniting.

In his *Republic* Plato expressed the view that an ideal city should have about 5,000 citizens. Actually, many had less than that, and three (Syracuse and Acragas [Agrigentum] in Sicily and Athens) had more than 20,000. At the height of her glory, Athens had a population of some 250,000 to 350,000, including men, women, and children as well as resident aliens and slaves. As to area, it has already been noted that Athens controlled about 1,000 square miles in the homeland of Attica, Sparta (including Messenia) controlled 3,200 square miles, and Corinth 330 square miles.

Characteristic of the ninth and eighth centuries was the Homeric[15] type of king-

362. Interior of Agamemnon's tomb

[14]In a view of history which looks upon the Classical Era as the zenith of Greek development, the centuries prior to it are commonly considered to be a formative age. Without debating the rightness of such a period name, it is used here as a convenience—with the realization that every age of history is to some extent a formative age.

[15]Homer probably lived and wrote about 850 B.C. somewhere along the Asia Minor coast, perhaps at Chios or Smyrna. His great epics, the *Iliad* and the *Odyssey*, were composed by weaving together many source materials into effective and enduring dramatic accounts. The historical setting of the poems seems to be that of the Mycenaean Age (the time of the Trojan War), but the economic, political, and social organization is that of Homer's own day.

ship. Although the king was commander-in-chief of the army, high priest, arbiter of disputes, and general head of state, he was no Oriental autocrat. He enjoyed as much authority as his forcefulness of personality, military prowess, and wealth could gain for him. Moreover, his office seems to have had some religious sanction attached to it, and his subjects were bound to him by an oath of allegiance—at least in wartime. The kingship was not hereditary in one family, though a son might succeed his father in office; rather, it was bestowed on a candidate possessing greatest power and prestige on the death of his predecessor. In a very real sense, the king was a noble among peers.

The power of the king was conditioned by the existence of a council and assembly. The council was made up of the nobles or elders or clan heads of the city-state. The council met on the call of the king, whenever some important business arose; it had no formal vote. Seniority determined who should speak first, and in the discussions that followed it would soon be obvious to the king what the consensus of opinion was. He was not obligated to follow the wishes of the council, but he was in no position to ignore their wishes constantly. The assembly probably consisted of men capable of bearing arms in defense of the state. It was normally summoned by the king. Not really a legislative body, it served as a means of sounding public opinion and obtaining approval for a given course of action, and it presumably approved the choice of a new king.

During the eighth century there was an evolution from monarchy to the age of nobles. This came by gradual limitation of the king's power, while the nobles jealously guarded the traditional rights of their families. The seventh century, then, was the age of nobles—at least the first half of it.

By the middle of the century a new force arose to challenge the nobles' power. The price of iron, and thus of iron weapons, be-gan to fall, coincidental with a recognition that heavily armed infantry was superior to the old cavalry and chariotry units of the nobility. In addition, a nascent commerce made possible new sources of income. Since it was the practice of ancient states to depend on their warriors to provide their own armor, and since it was expected that those who contributed most to the protection of the state should have the most to say about ruling it, this new aristocracy began to demand more voice in government. It is important to observe that with the rise in trade came the urbanization of much of central and eastern Greece.

The sixth century B.C. has often been characterized as the age of tyrants. These men were called tyrants because they won power in defiance of law and ruled without legal restraint. They commonly rose to power because of some social or economic imbalance in the state which produced a crisis.

There is sufficient data to prove that they were not mere cruel despots but often were men of considerably progressive and constructive statesmanship. For instance, Periander of Corinth encouraged commerce and letters. Pisistratus of Athens encouraged commerce, manufacturing, art, music, drama, and literature. And they often enforced laws against injustice, stopped oppression of the masses, and confiscated large estates and divided them among the landless. By bending the upper classes to their iron rule, they helped to establish a reign of law and make future constitutional government possible.

During the classical period of the fifth and fourth centuries oligarchy and democracy were characteristic. As time went on, the nobles and the wealthy classes tended to merge to form a government in which political rights were determined by property qualifications, regardless of pedigree. In Athens, a democracy of sorts came into being, and that form of government spilled over into some of her imperial possessions;

but democracy was never very much at home in the ancient Greek world. It should be observed that while the foregoing description of the pattern of political evolution in the various city-states serves as a useful generalization, the development was not everywhere the same, nor did it come everywhere at the same pace.

Colonization. While there was an evolution in the political and social structure at home, the city-states were expanding abroad. There was a tremendous colonization movement during the Formative Age. This was to a degree merely a continuation of the earlier migrations, but special forces continued to impel Greeks to settle all along the Asia Minor coast, and also in Cyprus, Egypt, Libya, Sicily and Italy, France, Spain, and along the Black Sea.

The Greeks were a maritime people, and it would be natural for them to establish outposts along the sea-lanes. Presumably they realized a definite economic advantage in the settling of colonies as sources of raw materials and markets for goods. Also, colonization was to some extent a result of social discontent and overpopulation.

This widespread movement of Greeks brought with it a massive dissemination of Greek language and culture. On this early foundation Alexander the Great and his successors were to build effectively in later centuries. So when the Romans later took over the East, they were not able to Latinize it. A Greco-Roman culture developed throughout the Mediterranean world and greatly facilitated the spread of Christianity when it came upon the world scene. Thus Paul could address his message in Greek to the whole Mediterranean world. His letters and other New Testament books could become the common possession of all literate persons of the Empire. And the Old Testament in Greek (the Septuagint) served as the Bible of the early church everywhere.

The Greater Greek States of the Formative Age

The city-states which were most important during the Formative Age were Argos, Aegina, Corinth, Megara, Sicyon, Chalcis, Thebes, Sparta, and Athens. Argos was strong in the eighth and seventh centuries. During the following century, the rise of Sparta and Corinth brought a decline of Argos. Aegina, Corinth, Megara, Sicyon, and Chalcis owed their importance to trade. Thebes was great because she was the chief power of Boeotia and established authority over the other cities of the plain. Athens and Sparta were especially significant to the history of Greece and to the history of civilization and therefore require more extended comment here. Other city-states receive greater attention elsewhere in this chapter.

Sparta. Down in the south central Peloponnesus, along the Eurotas River, lay five Dorian villages which about 750 B.C. united to form the Spartan state. About the same time there was an aristocratic revolution in which the power of the state passed from the kings to the aristocracy. Not long afterward, Sparta seems to have conquered all of Laconia. Then, about 700, she conquered neighboring Messenia to the west. Sparta surpassed all of her neighbors in wealth and power. The fact that she possessed a considerable amount of good farmland made overseas expansion unnecessary. This was fortunate for Sparta, for she had no good natural harbors. Nevertheless she conducted trade abroad. Egyptian and Oriental commerce is implied in certain archaeological finds in the area. In the earlier years of her history Sparta enjoyed the cultural advantages common to much of the rest of Greece. Her sculptors worked in stone and wood, and her builders constructed some fine buildings—notably the council building and the Temple to Athena at Sparta. Such poets as Alcman and Terpander settled in the capital.

But then, about 650 B.C. the smoldering fires of liberty broke into open flame in Messenia. At approximately the same time, the value of heavy armed infantry became apparent; and those sufficiently wealthy to provide themselves with such armor sought and won political power. After a long and bitter conflict, Sparta crushed the rebellion and organized a form of government and society to prevent future challenges to Spartan power.

363. Athena

Socially there were three classes. At the bottom of the social structure were the Helots or serfs who belonged to the state and were assigned to work Spartan lands. Some were descendants of the old Achaean population, and others were degraded to serfdom by debt. They could not be sold, transferred, or freed except by action of the state. The middle class were the Perioeci, or business class, who lived in cities around Spartan lands and in garrison towns along the coast. They had some local autonomy but no political rights.

The Spartiates or equals were the upper class and the rulers of the state. They alone had full citizenship and full political rights. Completely at the disposal of the state, they were not permitted to do manual labor or to engage in business. At birth it was decided which infants should live and be reared. Boys were hardened physically and morally by exposure and necessity, and during almost all of their adult lives men were subject to the call of the state for military duty. Women, too, were trained to be healthy and hardy.

Politically, Sparta had four institutions. A dual kingship was hereditary in two families. Originally the kings enjoyed supreme power, which they gradually lost to the magistrates and the council. Actually they executed orders of the other three agencies of government and presided over religious rites. The five ephors were elected, probably annually, by the assembly. They had power to summon the council and the assembly, and presided over them. They were judges in civil matters, supervised the training of youth and the behavior of citizens, and periodically they expelled all foreigners who could not justify their presence in the country. The council consisted of the two kings and twenty-eight nobles over sixty years of age and constituted the real power in the State. Chosen for life, they tried criminal cases and originated all legislation. All citizens were members of the

THE WYCLIFFE HISTORICAL GEOGRAPHY OF BIBLE LANDS

popular assembly, which was a passive body that acted on measures submitted to it by the council and elected ephors and members of the council.

The total result of the political and social system of Sparta was to produce an oligarchy organized in such a way as to prevent change and a state which has often been called a "city-state in arms." It was not until the middle of the third century B.C. that the Helots were freed and a democratic revolution occurred.

The foreign policy of Sparta was effected through the medium of the Peloponnesian League. Organized before the end of the sixth century, it was not a federal organization, nor was it in complete subjection to Sparta. Rather, it was a permanent offensive and defensive alliance under Spartan leadership. It had no regular tribute. Decisions of the assembly were binding on all members and none could secede. However, all of the states had local autonomy and could go to war with each other.

Athens. Although Athens was an important center in Greece during the Mycenaean era, she lost much of her early power and prestige during the Dorian invasion and the Dark Ages. And she was certainly not one of the more progressive Greek states in 750 B.C.[16] For centuries Athens remained a backward little country town with little interest in trade.

During the seventh century important changes occurred in the legal and political structure of the state. The power of the monarchy was broken and an aristocracy established in its place. The political instrument of the aristocracy was the Council of the Areopagus which annually elected an archon, who was the chief executive officer in charge of civic activities and chief judicial official. Six thesmothetai presided over the courts and assisted the archon. The old basileus (king) became the priest

in charge of religious functions of state. During the latter part of the century, in 621 B.C., Draco codified the laws of Athens and therefore brought more order into the legal processes. However, it was a harsh code and did little to alleviate popular discontent.

This discontent arose largely because of the agrarian problems of the state. The land, which was incapable of supporting the entire population, was concentrated in the hands of a few people; and a large segment of the once free population had been reduced to serfdom. Some had even been sold abroad as slaves. The threat of civil war was met by giving Solon, an aristocrat trusted by the common people, the authority to make sweeping economic, political, and social changes.

Perhaps such a happy arrangement would not have been effected except for the fact that trouble between clans prevented the upper class from maintaining a solid front against the lower classes. Moreover, Megara was exerting military pressure on Athens at this point; and there was a need for a larger number of free citizens to fill the ranks of the Athenian army.

In order to meet the immediate problem of the early sixth century, Solon put through a reform known as a *seisachtheia*, or "disburdenment," which freed the peasants who had become slaves because of their debts and forbade debt slavery in the future. Then he proceeded to change the direction of the economy of Attica. Solon encouraged the settlement of foreign artisans at Athens, the teaching of trades by fathers to their sons, and the production of commodities for export. Development of the Athenian olive oil and pottery making industries dates to this time. (Attica had the finest deposits of ceramic clay in Greece.)

Solon is also credited with having rated the citizen classes according to income to determine their relative participation in government. Of the four classes established at

[16]Tom B. Jones, *Ancient Civilization* (Chicago: Rand McNally & Co., 1960), p. 193.

this time, the upper two were eligible for the magistracies, the third could be elected as minor officials, and the fourth—landless men—could not hold office. The citizen assembly was revived and strengthened, and it obtained the right of electing officers and magistrates and became sovereign in the area of legislation. More than likely the Areopagus Court presented the slate of business to the assembly.

Within a generation it became clear that the Solonian program was not an adequate solution for the ills of Attica. Clan groups continued to dominate society; the poor and landless were still in a precarious economic position; and the new group of artisans sought a place in the governmental sun. This fracturing of the socio-political organism made possible the tyranny of the Pisistratid family during the last half of the sixth century. This tyranny may be described as a benevolent despotism designed to solve the economic problems that beset Attica.

Pisistratus and his sons broke the power of the landed aristocracy and confiscated the land of exiled clan chieftains and divided it among the landless or those with insufficient holdings to support a family. They also encouraged the industrial and commercial development of the state and broke down the traditional Athenian policy of isolation. They engaged in a deliberate attempt to urbanize Athens to make it the center of Attica, to establish a state coinage, and to enhance the city with public works. Pisistratus began the construction of the great Temple of Zeus in the southeastern part of the city and a monumental gateway to the acropolis. He also built up the Panathenaic festival in honor of Athena—for commercial as well as religious reasons.

In the struggle that followed the expulsion of the tyranny from Athens, Cleisthenes rose to power and in 508 B.C. was given authority, like Solon, legally to reform the government. He became the real founder of Athenian democracy. First he divided

Attica into demes or townships, of which there were less than 200. All residents were enrolled in their local deme, and this enrollment was the basis of citizenship in the state. Adjacent demes were combined into thirty trittyes, and these in turn were organized into ten tribes. In order to destroy the old sectionalism, Cleisthenes formed each tribe by combining an urban, a rural, and a coastal trittyes. Each of the ten tribes furnished a contingent for the army and elected its own general; voting in the assembly was also by tribes.

Then Cleisthenes set up a new council of 500—fifty from each tribe; and the representatives of the tribes took turns acting as a committee of the whole for thirty-six-day periods. The council prepared the business for the assembly and developed functions that reduced the power of the magistrates.

364. Attic vase from late sixth century B.C.

The Persian threat. While Athens and Sparta were becoming the leading powers in Hellas, the rest of the world was not standing still. In the West, Rome had revolted against her Etruscan overlords by 500 B.C.; and Carthage was becoming an increasingly significant power. In the East, Croesus of Lydia had conquered all of the Greek cities in Asia Minor except Miletus by 550. Four years later Cyrus of Persia toppled the Lydian kingdom and inherited her Greek possessions along the Asia Minor coast. Those Greeks were forced to pay heavier tribute and their freedom-loving inhabitants became cogs in an imperial machine.

After Cyrus destroyed the Babylonian Empire in 539 B.C., his successors began to eye Greek possessions across the Hellespont. In 512 Darius crossed the Hellespont and conquered the Thracian coast, posing a threat to European Greece. For Athens the advance meant loss of outposts to guard approaches to the Hellespont and the Black Sea trade as well as the loss of revenue from mines owned by the Pisistratids in the north Aegean. Relations between the Persians and Greeks were strained by two further conditions. The Spartans had been allies of Croesus; and Hippias, last of the Athenian tyrants, had fled to Persia when expelled by the Athenians about 510. When the Persians requested that Hippias be restored to power, they had been granted less than diplomatic courtesy.

The immediate cause for the Greco-Persian War was an uprising of the Asiatic Greeks in 499 B.C. Led by Aristagoras of Miletus and supported by Athens and Eretria (in Euboea), the revolt was initially successful. All of Greek Asia Minor burst into flames of revolution, and the Persian center of Sardis was destroyed. But soon the Persians regained their composure; Athens and Eretria forsook their allies; and the Persians quelled the revolt, destroying

365. Greek ship of the fifth century B.C.

Miletus and selling the survivors into slavery. Thus a leading center of the arts and humanities passed temporarily out of existence with a great loss to Hellenic culture.

In 492 B. C. as soon as Asia Minor was secured, the Persians again went into action. The purpose of the campaign was twofold: to reconquer Thrace and to punish Athens and Eretria. The first aim was easily accomplished, but the second was thwarted because the fleet was destroyed by a storm in the north Aegean.

Two years later the Persians were ready to go into action once more. This time they determined to attack directly across the Aegean with a force which Herodotus said consisted of 600 ships. They besieged Eretria and Attica at the same time. With a Persian army occupying the plain of Marathon, the Athenians were not free to go to the aid of their compatriots to the north. When the Persians had destroyed Eretria, they moved southward in force. Hippias, the former tyrant of Athens, guided the Persian troops.[17]

The plain of Marathon is about five miles long and two miles deep. At its northern and southern ends lie marshes, and the plain itself is bisected by the Charadra River. From the plain's northern extremity the Cynosura (Kynosura) promontory extends a mile into the Aegean, forming an anchorage sheltered from the north and

[17]Herodotus, *History,* Book VI, Section 102.

east. The battle took place in the southern part of the plain. The Persians were flanked on the right by the river, on the left by the southern marsh; at their backs was the sea. The Greeks had the benefit of descending from a higher position.

Most of the Persians remained on board ship waiting for their troops to destroy the Athenians. It was planned that then the victorious Persian army would march on Athens by land, while the fleet sailed around Attica to attack the unwalled city by sea. Tradition has it that 10,000 Athenian and Plataean infantrymen defeated a force twice as large, inflicting 6,400 casualties and sustaining 192. Then an Athenian Olympic runner dashed the twenty-two miles to Athens, falling dead at the outskirts as he gasped, "Rejoice, we conquer!" Modern historians tend to reduce the numbers of the men involved and the number of casualties inflicted. The truth is that it is not really known exactly how many were involved. It is certain, however, that the Athenians won a signal victory, made a forced march during the night (variously thought to be August 10, September 12, or September 21), and appeared at the shore to greet the Persian hosts when they arrived at the port of Phalerum the next morning. The Persians sailed away, having had enough. Greece was awarded a ten-year respite from attack.

The conflict with Persia was characterized by disunity of the Greeks, lack of persistence by the Persians, and heroism of the Greek soldiers and sailors. In Greece prior to Marathon, Sparta was perfecting her military machine and achieving greater dominance of the Peloponnesus; she overcame Argos in 494 B.C. At Athens, Themistocles was in control and in 493-492 B.C. began to develop port facilities for naval squadrons at Piraeus. The new democracy was developing a small but strong citizen army. After Marathon, Themistocles persuaded the people to invest the proceeds of a new rich vein of silver discovered at

Laurium in south Attica in the Athenian navy.

Between 490 and 480 B.C. the Persians did not attack. They were occupied with a revolt in Egypt, and Darius died in 486. Finally, in the spring of 480, Xerxes began his march through Thrace and Macedonia. The Greeks (the Peloponnesian League under the leadership of Sparta) had devised a plan of sorts, but it was by no means an effective united effort. Their first stand was at the vale of Tempe, just south of Olympus on the northern border of Thessaly. There the Greek flank was turned because the Persian fleet was able to sail in behind their position.

The next stand was at Thermopylae. Here in central Greece the chance of defeating the Persians was good. The pass was only about forty-five feet wide between

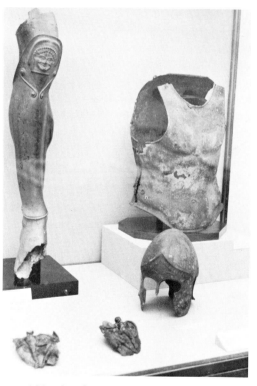

366. Greek armor of the fifth century B.C.

the mountains and the Malian Gulf.[18] Although the army might be outflanked by naval forces as at Tempe, the Greek navy could and did control the Gulf. Leonidas and his Spartans fought bravely, but a traitor showed the Persians a secret pass through the mountains. The Greeks were defeated, and the Persians came pouring into Boeotia and Attica; Athens was easily taken, but the populace had been evacuated.

The Peloponnesian generals were determined to hold the line at the Isthmus of Corinth, but Themistocles fought against the abandonment of Athens, Aegina, Salamis, and Megara, and even threatened to withdraw and colonize in the West. Ultimately he was able to lure the Persian fleet into the narrow strait between the island of Salamis and the mainland of Attica and there to precipitate a naval battle in which the small, swift Greek warships destroyed the Persian navy. The Persian army withdrew to winter in Boeotia, and Xerxes left Greece.

The Athenians returned home, and they spurned offers of Persian benefits. In the spring of 479 B.C., the Athenians found it necessary to evacuate their city again. Finally Sparta grew worried that the Athenians could not stand the strain much longer and gathered a huge allied force, which virtually annihilated the Persian army at Plataea, nine miles south of Thebes. Meanwhile insurrection was brewing in the Greek cities of Asia Minor. A Greek fleet was enticed to come over, and it won a great naval victory at Mycale near Miletus, traditionally on the same day as the battle of Plataea. Within a year many of the Greek cities on the Asia Minor coast were free, and the European side of the Hellespont was recaptured. At the same time the western Greeks were winning a struggle with the Carthaginians, whose fleet they completely destroyed in 474.

[18]In modern times deposits of the Sphercheius River have spilled out into the Malian Gulf and have widened the pass breadth to 1½-3 miles.

Rise of Athenian Empire. The Greeks were free—but for what? It soon became clear that no continuing cooperation would follow on the heels of the Panhellenic cooperation in the war against Persia. The Hellenic League had been dominated by Sparta during the war. With her military outlook she had been able to provide good leadership. Now Pausanias, hero of Plataea, began to antagonize some of the Greek states with his overbearing attitude. Moreover, the isolationist home government of Sparta was not in sympathy with the policy of continued aggression against the Persians advocated by Pausanias. At this point, in 478 B.C., under the leadership of Themistocles Athens proposed a confederacy known as the Delian League.

367. Athenian four-drachma piece of the Athenian Empire

The Delian League was so-called because its treasury and administrative center were located on the sacred island of Delos. Among the stipulations of the league were these important provisions: 1. Each ally was to contribute ships or money for the common cause. 2. Athens was to make the assessments and act as collector. 3. No state might withdraw from the league without the consent of all. 4. There was to be an annual congress of deputies in which each state had an equal vote; this congress was to meet under Athenian leadership.

368. Pericles

cles was exiled and the conservatives ruled for nine years. The democratic element regained power in 462, and the following year Pericles gained the reins of government, to hold them until his death in 429. The period is sometimes called the "Age of Pericles," sometimes the "Golden Age of Athens."

Pericles was a direct heir of Themistocles—an enemy of Sparta and a democrat. He sought to build up a land empire in central Greece to match the maritime empire Athens already possessed. Temporarily he was successful in attaining his goal, but in the process he incurred the enmity of Sparta and involved himself in warfare with a large number of the Greek states. At the same time his interference with Persian affairs in Egypt and Cyprus led to war with the colossus of the East, resulting in a loss of 250 ships and control of the sea as well. In 449 he was forced to make peace with the Persians and five years later arranged a thirty-year truce with Sparta. All he had accomplished was to weaken Athens and arouse the suspicion and enmity of the other Greek states.

Closer to home, Pericles gradually transformed the Delian League into an Athenian Empire. In the face of danger of Persian confiscation, the treasury was moved from Delos to Athens in 454 B.C., and the council of the league ceased to meet in 439. As a further protective measure, the two long walls were built between Athens and Piraeus. Completed in 456, they were four and one-half miles long, twelve feet thick and thirty feet high; and they guaranteed access of Athens to her port and thus to the sea—as long as her fleet kept the sea-lanes open. It should be remembered that Themistocles had previously built walls around Athens and Piraeus.

In political affairs, Pericles succeeded in instituting a fully developed democracy. Before his day the power of the archon had been weakened and the office of strategos, or general, was made the most powerful

The league started well, with just assessments and continued success against the Persians, whom they were able to drive from almost all Ionian cities in Asia Minor by 468. But gradually the league was turned into an Athenian empire; an increasing number of states were reduced to subject status and forced to enact democratic constitutions.

Meanwhile, politics in Athens turned into a duel between the conservative pro-Spartan faction and the democratic, anti-Spartan faction. Themistocles led the latter, Cimon the former. In 471 Themisto-

office in the state; Pericles was elected to this post thirty times. About 460 B.C. the Areopagus Court was stripped of most of its political power and retained control only over religious matters. About a decade later pay for public office was instituted; so it was no longer necessary for a man to be wealthy to hold office. Ultimately all state servants were remunerated—including men in the army and navy.

In spite of the losses during the early years of Pericles' rule, Athens was wealthy. The maritime empire was intact, and the income was immense. Pericles determined to beautify the city and especially to develop the Acropolis as a fitting symbol of the greatness of Athens and a suitable home for her patron goddess. Hippodamus of Miletus, the great city planner, was engaged to lay out the port city of Piraeus. Phidias, the master sculptor, was appointed to oversee the construction of the Parthenon and otherwise to beautify the Acropolis.

The Age of Pericles was a time of flowering for culture. Contemporary with Pericles were several of the greatest literary figures of all time, though they produced some of their best work before or after his day. Herodotus, the "father of history,"[19] of Halicarnassus, an Athenian dependency, knew Pericles and lived in Athens for a time. Thucydides of Athens, the first scientific historian, was over thirty years old when Pericles died. The great dramatists, Aeschylus, Sophocles, and Euripides all wrote tragedies during his period of rule. And Aristophanes, the great comedy writer, was coming to maturity when Pericles died. A number of the early philosophers were also known to him, including Anaxagoras, who taught for many years at Athens and died one year after Pericles. Greatest of the philosophers of the time, however, was Socrates whose highest honors were earned during the thirty years after Pericles' death.

The Peloponnesian War. The thirty-year truce which Pericles arranged with Sparta was recognized as just that—a truce. Both sides knew that a showdown could not be postponed forever. Ever since the days immediately after the Battle of Salamis, fuel had been periodically added to the fire of contention between the two powers that would in a sense turn into a funeral pyre for independence of the city-state. Pericles' efforts to construct a land empire in central Greece had lost friends and had inclined several states to look to Sparta for help. And Athens' high-handedness with

369. Euripides

[19]R. H. Pfeiffer asserts that the author of the early source of the Old Testament books of Samuel was the father of history "in a much truer sense than Herodotus a half millennium later" (Pfeiffer, *Introduction to the Old Testament* [New York: Harper and Brothers, 1941], p. 357). It should be remembered, however, that Pfeiffer, a liberal scholar, does not accept the Mosaic authorship of the Pentateuch. Accepting the definition that history is an interpreted record of the past and holding the theologically conservative position, one might claim that Moses was the "father of history" centuries before the writer of Samuel.

many of her dependencies led some to intrigue with Sparta; this was especially pronounced after the Peloponnesian War started.

In addition to this basic animosity, there was a specific cause of the war. Corinth was having a tiff with one of her colonies, Corcyra (Corfu), an island in the Adriatic Sea. At the height of the struggle, Corcyra appealed to Athens for help. Although realizing the danger, the Athenians decided to answer the appeal. Corcyra was an important naval power and could be used to outflank the commerce and naval potential of Corinth. The economic struggle between Athens and Corinth had led up to this explosive situation, and now Corinth demanded that the Peloponnesian Congress act. Sparta had tried to remain aloof from the struggle but was no longer able to do so. An ultimatum was sent to Athens, which was not met; and the long-awaited explosion occurred.

The strategy adopted by Pericles was to fight a defensive war, withdrawing the population of Attica, at least the western part of it, within the powerful fortifications around Athens and the Piraeus and depending on the fleet to keep food supplies at an adequate level. Meanwhile, Athenian warships were to make commando raids along Peloponnesian shores and gradually bring the anti-Athenian alliance to its knees. This policy was unpopular with the wealthy, who were unwilling to see their estates in Attica ravaged, and with the military, who wanted action.

During the first year of the war, all went about as Pericles had planned. But he had reckoned without the effects of population congestion, water pollution, and Leeuwenhoek's "little beasties." A plague ravaged the city in 430 and 429 B.C., became virulent again in the winter of 427 and 426, and lasted through 426. It wiped out one-third of Athens' first-line troops and an unnumbered host from the rest of the population,

including Pericles himself.[20] Probably something like a third of the total population was lost.[21] After several more years of inconclusive battle, the Athenian conservative leader Nicias arranged a peace treaty in 421, which called for a fifty-year truce with Sparta.

But Alcibiades, Pericles' nephew, saw no future for himself in this peaceful, conservative arrangement and began to scheme for renewal of the war. He influenced an Athenian alliance with four states of the northern Peloponnesus. These were attacked and defeated by Sparta in 418 B.C., leaving a residue of bitterness both among the Athenian allies (whom Athens failed to support) and the Spartans, who considered the Athenian alliance a warlike act.

Soon thereafter, in 415 B.C., an embassy arrived at Athens from Segesta in Sicily with a request for help against Syracuse. Involvement appealed to the Athenians, and especially Alcibiades, because success would give the Athenians control of the grain supply of Corinth and possession of the triangular trade in the West. Therefore an expedition was launched. But hardly had it started when Alcibiades was recalled to stand trial in Athens for impiety. Without an able commander, the whole project became a great fiasco. Athens lost more than 200 warships and their complement of seamen, some 40,000 recruited from subject states, plus many thousands of cavalrymen and infantry; and an enormous amount of money, weapons, and materials.[22]

Alcibiades escaped to Sparta on the way home for trial and persuaded the Spartans to renew the struggle in 413 B.C. Meanwhile, the Athenians were feverishly trying to rebuild the navy and prepare for future attacks. By 411 the Spartans had become disenchanted with Alcibiades, and he went to Asia Minor, where he began to intrigue

[20]Hammond, p. 351.
[21]*Ibid.*, p. 369.
[22]*Ibid.*, p. 400.

with the Persians. He persuaded them that it was not to their best interests to have the Spartans achieve a victory in the Greek world; instead they should keep the Greeks fighting among themselves. Thus he won help for Athens, enabling her to win victories for three years. Then Persia switched sides and came to the aid of the Spartans, who with Persian fleets were able to bring Athens to her knees in 404. As the price of peace, Athens lost her empire, her navy, and her fortifications, and was forced to accept an oligarchic government on the order of Sparta's.

Continued Persian interference. Lysander of Sparta was now in control in Greece. States that began to rejoice in freedom from Athens were surprised to discover that they were under a far more exacting master. Soon the Greeks found themselves at war with Persia. Some 13,000 mercenaries from various Greek states hired themselves out to Cyrus the Younger, who tried to unseat his brother Artaxerxes II, ruler of the Persian Empire. After Cyrus was killed in battle, the famous retreat of the 10,000 Greeks under Xenophon (401-399 B.C.) occurred, described in his *Anabasis*. Spartan support of the rebellion of Cyrus and later entanglement in a rebellion of Ionian cities in Asia Minor against the Persians involved the Spartans in war against Persia.

Continuing her policy of fomenting strife in Greece, Persia incited Corinth, Athens, Argos, and Thebes to revolt against Sparta. She sent Persian money and ships, and some of these ships under command of the Athenian admiral Conon sailed to Athens in 393 B.C. and rebuilt the walls with Persian money and labor. Five years later Persia and Sparta signed a peace treaty which assigned most of the Greek cities in Asia Minor to Persia and a few to Athens.

The treaty seemed also to herald a new Persian policy. Up to that time she had espoused a policy of pitting one Greek state against another. Now she seemed interested in making the strongest Greek state her executor. Sparta was predominant, then, from 387 to 371 B.C. With a relatively free hand in Greece, she had built up an empire by 379.

Meanwhile, Athens was climbing back to a place of prominence once more. In 377 B.C. she organized the second Athenian confederacy and by 374 had over seventy states in it. But Thebes was also pulling herself together and, under Epaminondas, disastrously defeated the Spartans at the battle of Leuctra (371 B.C.) and was predominant in Greece until 362.

During the fourth century a number of great figures connected with the cultural history of Greece made their contributions —all of whom were connected with Athens for at least part of their lives. Plato (428-347 B.C.) founded his Academy in Athens about 387. Borrowing from his teacher Socrates the dialogue form of writing, he employed it in his famous *Republic* and his *Laws*, both of which enunciated his conception of the ideal state. Aristotle (384-322 B.C.) was a student in Plato's Academy, tutor of Alexander the Great, and founder of the Lyceum in Athens. His interests were broad, and he wrote on logic, metaphysics, natural history, ethics, rhetoric, aesthetics, and political science. In his *Politics* he, like Plato, saw the city-state as the chief form of government and scored democracy for its inadequacies.

Two great orators are also representative of the century: Isocrates (436-338 B.C.) and Demosthenes (384-322). The former was Panhellenic and favored a confederation of Greek states. He ultimately turned to Philip II of Macedon to unite the Greeks by force. Demosthenes looked backward to the days of the independent city-state and called the Athenians to effective warfare against Philip. Xenophon (430-350) is best remembered for his historical writings, the *Anabasis* and the *Hellenica* (which was intended to be a supplement to Thucydides'

Peloponnesian War), although Xenophon wrote many other pieces.

Rise of Macedon

The accidents of history had changed. It was no longer possible for the petty city-states of Greece to enjoy the luxury of destroying each other without the danger of external conquest. Persian interference during the later fifth and early fourth centuries had demonstrated that fact. Now Macedon loomed on the northern horizon. Soon the colossus of Rome would rise in the West. The city-states were now second-rate powers with an uncertain future.

370. Coin of Philip II of Macedon

Macedonia had had a slow development in the fourth century from a peasant state to a military state, from a purely rural to a more urbanized state. Philip II (359-336 B.C.) played the most important part in her development. A curious combination of savagery and Hellenic culture, he was determined to weld an effective power. Within two years he cleared the land of invaders and pretenders and began formation of the finest army the world had yet known. He drew men into his army from the turbulent vassal states and instilled them with a spirit of nationalism. In 357 he took the area on his eastern frontier and a year later began the conquest of Greece.

Athens, one of Philip's most formidable opponents, was galvanized to action against him by the *Philippics* of Demosthenes, greatest orator of all time. Finally Philip crushed a combined Athenian and Theban force at Chaeronea in 338 B.C. and then overran the Peloponnesus. A year later he summoned all the states south of Thermopylae to send delegates to a federal council at Corinth to organize a Hellenic League against Persia. All complied but Sparta. Before Philip could execute his plan of warfare against Persia he was murdered; and his son Alexander the Great assumed the reins of government at the age of twenty.

Alexander the Great. Alexander promptly set his house in order in Macedonia. When Thebes, led by a false rumor of his death, revolted, he swept down upon that city and destroyed it. By the spring of 334 B.C., he was ready for his invasion of the Persian Empire and the institution of the Panhellenic war of revenge against the colossus of the East. Crossing the Hellespont with only about 35,000 men, he won a signal victory at the Granicus River which opened all of Asia Minor to him. There is a real question as to what Alexander's objectives were when he began his conquests; probably they were not too grandiose. But they apparently mushroomed with his phenomenal success.

One victory led to another until the entire Persian Empire was won. In 333 B.C., a victory at Issus in Cilicia opened Syria to Alexander. He spent the following year securing the Syrian coast and occupying Egypt, where he founded the city of Alexandria. Having protected the rear of his army and having taken control of the Persian fleet by conquering its bases, Alexander marched off in hot pursuit of the hosts of Darius. He caught up with them and

THE WYCLIFFE HISTORICAL GEOGRAPHY OF BIBLE LANDS

defeated them at Gaugamela, southeast of Nineveh, in October of 331. In the next four months Alexander gained possession of Babylon, Susa (biblical Shushan), and Persepolis.

Meanwhile Darius was encamped at Ecbatana in Media. When Alexander set out after him in the spring of 330 B.C., Darius fled northeast toward Bactria (or Bactriana). In swift pursuit, Alexander covered four hundred miles in eleven days —only to come upon the corpse of his prey, who had been slain by one of the Persian provincial governors. Alexander was now king of Persia. But rather than consolidating his conquests, he tried to conquer India. After initial successes in the Indus Valley, he was unable to persuade his war-weary troops to go farther. While planning further conquests, Alexander fell ill of a fever (perhaps malaria) and died at Babylon in June of 323.

Exactly what Alexander had in mind as a master plan for his empire—its organization and integration—is not known. In recent years C. A. Robinson and W. W. Tarn have spun out a very elevated thesis concerning Alexander's aims. As Tarn puts the thesis, it has three closely interconnected facets or aspects.

> The first is that God is the common Father of mankind, which may be called the brotherhood of man. The second is Alexander's dream of the various races of mankind, so far as known to him, becoming of one mind together and living in unity and concord, which may be called the unity of mankind. And the third, also part of his dream, is that the various peoples of his Empire might be partners in the realm rather than subjects.[23]

Research on this thesis will show that it is based primarily on statements in Plutarch, the interpolation of which has been somewhat strained. The thesis has had little acceptance among historians. It seems that the reputedly high-flung ideas and statements of the conqueror (the discussion of

[23]W. W. Tarn, *Alexander the Great* (Cambridge: Cambridge University Press, 1950), II, 400.

which is not necessary here) did not reflect any emancipated sociological viewpoint on his part.

The reputed Alexandrian statements concerning brotherhood and partnership in the realm were directed only to the Persians—not to Egyptians, Syrians, and others. An appeal to the Persians was particularly timely because Alexander needed Persian troops and Persian loyalty. And while he offered to share the administration with them, he had no intention of relinquishing the top spot, which he himself occupied.

Moreover, the establishment of Greek cities in Alexander's day seems to have been more for the regulation of commerce and the control of the empire than to promote fusion of peoples, as has been claimed. It is very hard to distinguish Alexander's own arrangements for city building from the later Seleucid and Ptolemaic arrangements.

Successors of Alexander

For about fifty years after the death of Alexander, his empire was torn by the efforts of his ambitious generals to become supreme. They united under the titular headship of Alexander's half-witted brother Philip and Alexander's posthumous son, both of whom were killed by 310 B.C. Eventually the empire was divided into three large states and a number of smaller ones.

Ptolemy managed to establish himself in Egypt and in 306 B.C. took the title of king. His kingdom came to include Egypt, Cyrene, Cyprus, and Palestine. His line ruled Egypt until 30 B.C., when the suicide of Cleopatra brought the dynasty to an end; then Rome took over there.

Another of Alexander's generals was Seleucus. After many difficulties he established a dynasty at Babylon in 312 B.C. His descendants were known as the Seleucids, and in their days of greatness they controlled almost all of the Persian Empire except Egypt. But dynastic quarrels and external pressures weakened their kingdom and reduced its territory so that by 64 B.C., when Seleucia fell before Rome, it consisted of little more than northern Syria.

Confusion reigned in Macedon after the death of Alexander, as one general after another tried to secure the throne. Finally Antigonus Gonatas, grandson of the great Antigonus of Alexander's entourage, secured control over Macedon and established his dynasty there; it lasted until the Roman conquest. To a large degree Antigonus won the throne of Macedon by defeating in 277 B.C. a horde of Gauls that had moved into Greece. Macedonia was a strong military monarchy in which the rulers were generals who were recognized as kings by consent of the army. Unlike the Ptolemies and Seleucids, the Antigonids made no claim to divinity. The state was financed by income from the royal domains, forests, and mines, and from customs duties.

The great period of these three Hellenistic kingdoms was approximately 275 to 200 B.C. During those decades large urban centers were developed in the eastern Mediterranean world, and a flourishing culture was disseminated from them. It is not within the purview of this chapter to discuss this new cultural continuum and its expression at such great centers as Alexandria, Pergamum, Antioch on the Orontes, and Seleucia on the Tigris. That description appears in the chapters on Asia Minor, Syria, and Egypt.

While most of the great cultural developments of the Hellenistic world occurred outside the boundaries of Greece, it maintained its philosophical importance. At Athens, Epicurus set up his school in 306 B.C. This taught a materialistic philosophy which viewed the world as a soulless mechanism. Atoms flying through space met to create life and flying apart caused death. This world view stated that there was no such thing as existence after death—at least not conscious existence. Therefore one was to live for the present and seek a life of greatest happiness in the present. This life of happiness consisted not in sensual pleasure but in an escape into the gentle, quiet world of the intellect, symbolized by the garden in which Epicurus taught. If there were gods, they lived by themselves and had nothing to do with men. Thus fear of divine beings and prayer to them were useless.

Contemporary with Epicureanism was Stoicism. The founder of the movement, Zeno, a Phoenician from Cyprus, began to teach in Athens in 302 B.C. The Stoics believed that a divine fire, a world soul, animated all of matter. This being had established a perfect, unalterable, universal law for the universe. Whatever happened, therefore, had to be endured as part of the divine plan. And the divine spark in the individual, the soul, was constantly engaged in an effort to overcome the flesh. Moreover, since all men had this divine spark within, all men were brothers; therefore men had obligations to their fellowmen. Upon death the individual would rejoin the world soul in a rather hazy continued existence.

While certain intellectuals were interested in Epicureanism, Stoicism, or other contemporary philosophies, most people still worshiped the old gods, and a large number turned to the Mystery Religions during the Hellenistic Age. In the mysteries men sought a more personal faith that would bring them into immediate contact with deity and a faith that would offer a more emotional experience than the worship of the old gods or involvement in the newer philosophies.

Each of the Mystery Religions was centered about a god who died and was resurrected. Each had a ritual through which the initiate was made to participate in the experience of the god and rendered a candidate for immortality. Each guaranteed its devotees an ultimate escape from the miserable world about him into an immortal afterlife. They were called "mysteries" because they aimed by secret and mysterious ritual to achieve the fusion of the worshiper and a divine savior. The chief mysteries were the Eleusinian of Greece (described later), Cybele of Asia Minor, Isis and Osiris of Egypt, and Mithraism of Persia.

Christianity is often classified as one of the Mystery Religions. It does bear numerous similarities to them.[24] However, it is not really one of them. Probably the main differences lie in the facts that at the center of Christianity is a historical rather than a mythical person and that the Christian faith demands a distinctive way of life subsequent to an experience of "contact with deity." After the candidate went through the stages of initiation at Eleusis, for instance, he had no obligation to live in any particular way, according to any particular code of ethics. He merely had to observe strict secrecy concerning the ritual in which he had participated.

As far as political affairs were concerned, Macedonian control was in no sense complete in Greece. Macedonian garrisons were stationed in Athens, Chalcis, and Corinth; but in central Greece and the Peloponnesus the Achaean and Aetolian leagues exercised considerable power. A backward people during the classical period of Greek history, the Aetolians of central western Greece had joined their villages into a league before 350 B.C. And at its height during the third century, in alliance with Macedon, this league controlled central Greece from sea to sea.

The Achaean League, organized about 275 B.C., was composed of some of the small states along the southern shore of the Gulf of Corinth. It became important after 250 under the leadership of Aratus of Sicyon and expanded to incorporate the whole northern Peloponnesus. During the first part of the third century, the Aetolians

[24]For a discussion of religious backgrounds of the New Testament see J. Gresham Machen, *The Origin of Paul's Religion* (New York: The Macmillan Co., 1921), Chap. VI.

were friendly with Macedon and the Achaeans were not.

The picture changed about 230 B.C. when a temporary revival of Spartan power frightened the Achaeans and led them to call for Macedonian help. This alliance outflanked the Aetolians who feared that Macedonian interference would endanger Aetolian independence. This fear led the Aetolians ultimately to link their fortunes with Rome against Macedon. Rome's involvement in Greek and Eastern affairs ultimately resulted in Roman control of the whole area.

Roman Conquest of Greece

Greek interference in Roman affairs began early in the third century B.C. when Pyrrhus of Epirus brought over an army to help the Greek cities of southern Italy in their contest with Rome. Although Pyrrhus lost the flower of his army in conflict with the Romans, he was not destroyed and returned to Greece in 275 B.C. to involve himself in an initially victorious war with Antigonus Gonatas of Macedonia. When Pyrrhus was killed in battle in 272, Epirus entered a cycle of almost continuous decline in prestige and progressive loss of territory; and a Roman punitive expedition to Greece was unnecessary at that time.

Rome did not find it necessary to send troops eastward until after the First Punic War. Greek cities of southern Italy, now allied with Rome, suffered from the depredations of the Illyrians, who lived along the coast of modern Yugoslavia and "elevated piracy to the dignity of a national profession." After a victory over the Illyrians in 229 B.C., the Romans established a certain Demetrius as ruler over the territory. He proved to be a rather intractable puppet and soon outdid the Illyrians in acts of piracy. When Rome defeated him in 219 B.C., he fled to Macedon where he constantly urged an anti-Roman policy.

This groundwork laid by Demetrius was to bear fruit during the Second Punic War, when in 215 B.C. Philip V of Macedon allied himself with Hannibal of Carthage against the Romans. Hardly had Philip made the alliance when civil war erupted in Greece. At this point Rome entered into an alliance with the Aetolians and their allies, including Sparta and Pergamum, and sought to confine Philip to Macedonia.

After an inconclusive war, both Rome and Macedon were eager for peace—the former to be free for action against Carthage, and the latter to try a hand in the political arena of the Hellenistic monarchies of the East. Philip's activities there brought open conflict with Pergamum and Rhodes. The Aetolians, deciding to renew attacks on Macedonia, sent to Rome in 206 B.C. asking for aid. A few months later Pergamum and Rhodes appealed to Rome for help.

Neither the Roman assembly nor senate wanted war. The long struggle with Hannibal had consumed their energies. But a group of bellicose senators managed to maneuver the Romans into war against Macedon in 200 B.C. Of course Rome was successful, but not without overcoming serious difficulties. At the conclusion of the war in 196, the victorious Flamininus announced the freedom of all Greek cities from Macedonia. He made this proclamation at the Isthmian Games at Corinth. Macedonia was disarmed and forced to pay an indemnity, and Flamininus established pro-Roman and aristocratic governments in several Greek cities.

Romans who thought peace had been achieved were in for a rude awakening. Antiochus III of Syria was nibbling away at Egyptian possessions in Syria and along the Asia Minor coast. Advance around Ephesus alarmed Eumenes of Pergamum, who sought aid from Rome. Meanwhile, Hannibal had escaped from Carthage and was nagging Antiochus into an anti-Roman policy. And the Aetolians, deeply hurt because they had not shared the spoils of war in the victory over Macedon, were stirring up Greeks against Rome and looking to Antiochus for aid. When Antiochus invaded Thrace in 191 B.C., Rome was forced to act.

The success was all with Rome. Antiochus lost all of Asia Minor except Cilicia. Pergamum and Rhodes expanded their influence there. In Greece, Macedon was rewarded for her loyalty and Aetolia punished with the loss of territory and the obligation to pay an indemnity.

This peace of 188 B.C. was not destined to bring settled conditions to the Near East or to Greece. While the Orient was restive, Greece had troubles peculiarly Hellenic. The city-states, "freed" by the Romans, engaged in the liberty of anarchy, as they struggled with one another and as factions within them struggled for supremacy.

Philip V of Macedon sulked in the wings, remaining loyal to Rome until his death but building up his country for his son Perseus, who intrigued with the Achaean League and other states of Greece against Rome in an effort to bring order out of chaos. Rome was not permitted to forget Greek affairs because representatives of one city or another were constantly shuttling back and forth to Rome seeking aid against their neighbors. To add to the confusion, Eumenes of Pergamum denounced Perseus to Rome.

A series of these aggravations finally led Rome to send legions against Macedonia once more. The war began in 171 and ended with the battle of Pydna in 168, after which Rome divided Macedonia into four independent republics and imposed an annual indemnity. The Achaean League was compelled to send 1,000 hostages to Rome, among whom was the celebrated historian Polybius. And Epirus suffered the destruction of seventy towns and the sale of 150,000 citizens into slavery.

After 168 B.C. Greece slowly declined into economic and spiritual bankruptcy. However, the Greeks were not so completely broken in spirit that they were unable to attempt another bid for independence from Rome. When the 300 Achaean hostages who were still living returned to Greece in 151, old wounds were reopened. About the same time a pretender named Andriscus appeared in Macedonia, claiming to be the son of Perseus, the last king of the country. After initial difficulties, the Romans were able to destroy his army of 20,000 and restore their power in Macedonia.

Fires of insurrection were still smoldering in Greece, and they broke into leaping flames in 147 B.C. when a border dispute between Sparta and the Achaean League ignited a popular uprising. Slaves were freed and armed; aristocrats were murdered; and the poor made a bid for a better life. Roman legions swooped down from Macedonia, destroyed Corinth (chief city of the league), and sold its inhabitants into slavery (146 B.C.). Greece was cowed by this act of atrocity.

In 148 B.C. Macedonia became a Roman province in the sense that from this time a Roman governor was regularly in charge. The four republics remained as local organizations and continued to have their assemblies. The status of the rest of Greece is somewhat uncertain. But it appears that Greece was largely under Roman control and that this control was generally exercised through the governor of Macedonia. The Achaean League was apparently broken up, at least temporarily. The Romans probably did not greatly interfere with other loyal leagues and towns.

In succeeding decades, however, Rome gradually established governments of her own choosing in a number of the cities of Greece. Most of Greece was still free, though some cities paid tribute; and the practical value of that freedom had been much reduced. It seems that the rights of free cities depended somewhat upon the good pleasure of the governors and the dictates of the Roman senate.

Greece Under the Roman Republic

Greece suffered terribly in the century between 146 and 30 B.C. The hardships brought on by the revolt of Andriscus in Macedonia were compounded during a subsequent revolt of a second pretender and a long series of raids and invasions by neighboring tribes. In 88 these raids merged with the first of the Mithridatic wars, which were to plague the Greek area for four years. Mithridates VI of Pontus in Asia Minor occupied several centers in eastern, central, and southern Greece. Considerable destruction was wrought in the country by the Pontic armies and Sulla's Roman legions. Sulla levied heavy war taxes on Greece and systematically destroyed the Piraeus to punish Athens for throwing in her lot with Pontus.

The rout of Mithridates did not bring lasting peace to Macedonia or Greece. Raids of neighboring tribes continued into Macedonian territory, and pirate raids increased with the decline of Rhodes; and taxes were levied for the support of further Roman wars against Mithridates. The land was racked again by the opposing armies of Pompey and Caesar. The final defeat of Pompey came in Greece at Pharsalus in 48 B.C. It was six years later that Brutus and Cassius collected their forces near Philippi for a last stand against Octavian. This campaign cost Macedonia and eastern Greece heavily.

The deciding battle between the forces of Octavian and Antony was fought at Actium in western Greece in 31 B.C. The hardships caused by the stationing of the forces of Antony and Cleopatra in Greece for one year require little imagination or development. And when Antony's communications began to be cut, he seems to have laid hands on all available supplies and to have impressed Greeks for all kinds of service. Especially burdensome was the galley service. When Octavian became emperor, all of Greece was suffering from exhaustion and depopulation.

The Roman Imperial Period

Augustus' efforts to bring order out of chaos in the empire involved a provincial reorganization in Greece. In 27 B.C., Achaea and Macedonia were made separate provinces under the control of the senate. The former included nearly all of Greece proper, including Thessaly and most of the Epirus. Macedonia encompassed Macedonia proper, northern Epirus, and a little of northern Greece. These provinces fluctuated between senatorial and imperial control. Tiberius brought these provinces under his control; Claudius gave them back to the senate. Nero declared Achaea free and immune from tribute. A little later, Vespasian revoked this privilege. And under either Hadrian or Antoninus Pius in the early part of the second century, another provincial reorganization was effected, in which Achaea was greatly reduced in size—the western part formed into a new province of Epirus with Thessaly falling under the control of Macedonia.

In Augustus' organization and throughout the first century A.D., much of the area of Greece was free from the direct domination of the Roman governor of Achaea stationed in Corinth. The towns of Greece most distinguished by material importance and by great memories were set free. Some of the better known were Athens, Sparta, Pharsalus, and Plataea. Several of the old leagues continued too, e.g., the Boeotian and Achaean leagues. There were free cities in Macedonia also. Thessalonica and Amphipolis are examples in point. But while the old freedoms were outwardly maintained, they became increasingly meaningless as Rome chipped away at them and found ways to circumvent the forms of Greek independence.

While it is true that Greece suffered greatly during the first century B.C., she experienced a return of a degree of prosperity in the following century. Some of the most pessimistic statements on Greece in the Imperial Period were made by individuals not fully in possession of the facts or by those writing early in the Empire when conditions were worse. Therefore, these references must be carefully evaluated by those who would construct an accurate picture of Greece during the New Testament period.

What seems to have been the case is that there were fewer flourishing cities than formerly; this may have been owing to the fact that Rome followed a practice of assigning smaller towns and considerable tracts of land to larger cities for their support. In several areas, such as Boeotia, there seems to have been agricultural prosperity in spite of the decay of cities. This trend of the Roman period is particularly noticeable in the Peloponnesus, where urban life was largely concentrated along the coast, with the interior given over to agriculture and herding. A high point in the economic recovery of Greece appears to have been achieved during the first part of the second century.

Corinth (rebuilt by Julius Caesar) was the great commercial emporium of Greece during the Empire. As such she could easily make her own way. Thessalonica was also a bustling port and governmental center. Athens lived largely on her past. As a center of learning and art and a city with an illustrious history, she attracted many visitors and benefactions from emperors and wealthy patrons. But while the handouts were great and she must be considered something of a parasite, Attica was not without products to export. For instance, her marble and olive oil were widely marketed. Yet, her revenues were insufficient. Hadrian gave the city a large sum of money and arranged that she be provided with annual supplies of grain.

The Apostle Paul in Greece

Although Greece slowly ascended the ladder of prosperity once more during the Roman Imperial Period, she was still quite poor in the middle of the first century A.D., when she entered the biblical narrative. Corinth and Thessalonica were bustling ports, but Greeks in the famous old centers of Athens and Sparta had to look backward to days of greatness. Alexander's capital at Pella was also in a state of decline. While it is possible that the average Greek lived a more secure and prosperous life under the Pax Romana (Roman peace) than he had during the Hellenistic and Classical times, most of the chief arteries of commerce now bypassed the country; and her share of the world's economic pie was considerably smaller. The Greek world of Pericles was considerably different from that of Paul.

During his second missionary journey through Asia Minor, Paul sensed some divine compulsion to refrain from preaching. When he reached the port of Troas, this compulsion was still upon him (Acts 16:6-8). But while there, he received an urgent plea to carry the gospel to Macedonia. According to the Acts narrative, this call was extended to him in a vision by a man from Macedonia (Acts 16:9). The apostle seems to have eagerly embraced this opportunity and apparently left promptly for Europe. "The man from Macedonia" has raised considerable discussion. Ramsay argues cogently for identifying him with Luke.[25] Whether or not he is right, it is interesting to note that immediately after Paul's vision, Luke joined Paul on the journey to Macedonia; probably the two first became acquainted at Troas.[26]

Troas. Troas lay about ten miles south of the western end of the Dardanelles (ancient Hellespont) and thus about ten miles south of the site of ancient Troy. It is obvious, therefore, that Troy and Troas are not to be confused, as often happens. Originally called "Alexandria Troas," the town came to be referred to simply as Troas. In Paul's day the town had an excellent harbor and was a thriving port. Today the harbor has silted in, and the site is deserted. Ruins of a wall six miles in circumference, a theater, and an aqueduct stand as mute testimony to former prosperity. Probably most of the stone for construction was quarried from the ruins of ancient Troy.

Tenedos and Imbros. As the missionaries sailed for Europe, they were never out of sight of land. On the first day they passed the little island of Tenedos (modern Bozcaada), well known from the account of the Trojan War; then they passed the larger island of Imroz, or Imbros. In keeping with the custom of small Aegean sailing ships of anchoring for the night at a convenient island or port, Paul's ship spent the night at Samothrace (Samothracia), fourteen miles farther on toward the Greek coast (Acts 16:11). From Samothrace one can see the mainland of Macedonia and Mount Athos at the end of the nearest of the three peninsulas of Chalcidice to the southwest.

Samothrace. Samothrace is a small island of only sixty-eight square miles that had no harbor, only an anchorage, and even this is dangerous in winter because of the north winds and currents from the Dardanelles.

[25]William M. Ramsay, *St. Paul the Traveller and the Roman Citizen* (8th ed.; London: Hodder and Stoughton, 1905), pp. 198-205.
[26]Acts 16:10 says, "We endeavoured to go into Macedonia." This is Luke's unobtrusive way of telling his readers when he joins the Pauline company. Three sections of the book indicate that Luke (author of Acts) was a companion of the apostle: 16:10-17; 20:5—21:18; 27:1—28:16.

The island is traversed from east to west by a chain of bare granite mountains, the highest peak of which is 5,200 feet, highest point on any of the Aegean islands.

Samothrace owed its importance in ancient times to the existence there of a shrine of the Cabiri, an obscure mystery cult whose protection was often sought against the perils of the sea. Numerous important personages of antiquity visited the shrine. Philip of Macedon and his wife Olympias were initiated there. Most important structures of the place were built by Arsinoe Philadelphus and her brother during the first half of the third century B.C.

Today the island is best known for the "Victory of Samothrace," now in the Louvre in Paris. Found in 1863, this winged figure was erected at the shrine by Demetrius Poliorcetes of Macedonia to commemorate a naval victory over the Egyptians at Cyprus in 306 B.C. Several archaeological expeditions have been sent to the island and have systematically studied the very dilapidated antiquities, which include two temples, a theater, a long stoa, and other structures.

On to Neapolis. The next day the apostolic company started for the Macedonian mainland. As they neared shore, on their right the brown, turbid waters of the Nestos River could be seen gushing far out at sea —in marked contrast to the beautiful blue Aegean. On the left were the pyramidal heights of Thasos, an island which protected the bay; on the far side of the bay rose Neapolis, seaport of Philippi.

Neapolis. Neapolis was beautifully situated on a promontory which stretched out into the bay and had a harbor on either side. The harbor on the west was especially suitable for anchorage and it was there that the galleys of Brutus and Cassius were moored during the battle of Philippi in 42 B.C. In the past there was some question whether the modern Kavalla occupied the same site as ancient Neapolis, but this has now been quite conclusively demonstrated. During the early centuries of the Christian Era the town was known as "Christopolis," doubtless in commemoration of Paul's visits. More than likely the apostle stopped there during each of his several visits to Philippi.

Exactly when Neapolis was founded is not certain, but it is generally thought to have been settled by inhabitants of the nearby island of Thasos. Subsequently it was a member of both the Athenian Empire and the later Athenian Confederacy. Some have thought that it was refounded by the Athenians. During the fourth century it passed under the control of Philip of Macedon and at the time of Paul was part of the Roman province of Macedonia and of the Roman colony at Philippi. Since the town has been continuously occupied,

371. Victory of Samothrace

there is little to be seen that dates back to the Roman Imperial period. Commonly when diggings in the area go very far below the surface, Greek and Roman artifacts are found. And one may see remains of a Roman aqueduct and of the ancient acropolis.

To Philippi. Apparently the missionaries had no plan to evangelize at Neapolis, because they turned inland along the much-traveled road to Philippi, some thirteen miles away (Acts 16:12). The road ascended the Symbolon Hills, which reach a height of 500 feet and descend into the plain of Philippi. This plain is bounded on all sides by mountains or hills. On the west rises Mount Pangaeus; on the east a spur of Mount Orbelos with a conical shape. Philippi was located at the foot of this spur. In addition, the plain was bordered along the northern edge by forests and on the south by a marshy area (now drained), formed because the Symbolon Hills created a too formidable barrier for waters from the nearby mountains to make their escape to the sea.

Philippi. Philippi was founded by Philip II of Macedon in 360 B.C. and replaced the former Thracian settlement of Crenides. It was significant to the Macedonian as the chief mining center in the Pangaeus gold fields, which provided him with revenue for his gold currency, the support of his army, and the bribery of his enemies. These important mines seem to have been largely exhausted by the time Macedonia passed into Roman hands.

After the battle of Pydna in 168 B.C., all of Macedonia came under the control of Rome and was divided into four regions. Philippi was in the first of these. The town appears to have declined greatly under Roman occupation, as a result of both the depletion of the mines and the depredations of the civil wars of the first century B.C. She must have suffered especially during

372. Neapolis

the great battle of 42 B.C., fought on the plain of Philippi, in which Octavian and Antony defeated Brutus and Cassius.

After this battle a colony of Roman veterans was settled on the site, which was renamed "Colonia Julia Philippensis" in honor of the victory of the cause of Julius Caesar (Acts 16:12). After the battle of Actium in 31 B.C., Octavian constituted the city as a colony for defeated partisans of Antony evicted from Italy, and he changed the name to "Colonia Augusta Julia Philippensis." The territory of the colony included the port of Neapolis. As a colony Philippi enjoyed many political and economic privileges, including the *Ius Italicum*, which exempted it from imperial taxes. Colonies were a little bit of Italy set down on foreign shores, and their government was closely patterned after that of the municipalities of Italy. As the Acts narrative suggests, inhabitants of such colonies were very proud of their privileged position.

Paul and his associates (including Silas, Timothy, and Luke) probably came to Philippi before the end of A.D. 50. How long they stayed is open to question, but it has been suggested with some basis that they ministered there for as long as two months. Perhaps on the first Sabbath the apostolic company went out by a riverside to attend a prayer meeting held by the Jews of the place (Acts 16:13). Apparently

373. Possible site of the prayer meeting Paul attended at Philippi

there were very few Jews living in Philippi because if there had been ten heads of families there they would have been obligated to build a synagogue. The fact that the group met outside the city probably indicates that they were well beyond the pomerium, or sacred area, within which foreign deities were not permitted.

Excavations at Philippi have revealed the remains of an archway at the western entrance to the town. This is thought to date to the time of Paul.[27] Through this archway, the road led to the only real river of the place—the Gangites (the Gangas or Angites). And the prayer meeting which Paul attended probably was held where the road and the river intersected. Simply an outlet of the Philippi Lake into Lake Tahinos some thirty miles to the east, the Gangites is still deep and swift with clear, sweet water. It is ten to fifteen feet deep and maintains a regular breadth of about forty feet.

Paul's ministry on this occasion seems to have been almost immediately successful, for a certain businesswoman by the name of Lydia, a seller of purple cloth, was converted along with her whole household (Acts 16:14-15). She immediately opened her guest rooms to the evangelists. Subse-

[27]Jack Finegan, *Light from the Ancient Past* (2d ed.; Princeton: Princeton University Press, 1959), p. 351.

quently a demented slave girl who served her masters as something of a fortune-teller was restored to normalcy by the apostle. Her masters, seeing that their source of gain had vanished, stirred up a riot against Paul, falsely charging that he was spreading social teachings that would destroy the citizens' Roman way of life. They dragged Paul and Silas into the agora or marketplace and accused the missionaries before the magistrates. These magistrates are called *stratēgoi* by Luke, a Hellenistic title to render the untranslatable *duoviri*—the two chief officials of a Roman municipality that corresponded to the consuls of the period of the Republic.

The agora where the judgment scene took place has been completely excavated by the French School at Athens (1914-38) and by Greek archaeologists since World War II. A rectangular area about 300 feet long and 150 feet wide, it was bounded by porticoes, temple facades, and other public buildings. There is evidence that the city's prison was also located adjacent to the forum, but where is not known. There does not seem to be much support for identifying a prison some distance away (now shown to tourists) as the place where Paul and Silas were incarcerated. Along one edge of the agora ran the Egnatian Way, the main highway across Greece, which unequally bisected

374. Agora at Philippi

THE WYCLIFFE HISTORICAL GEOGRAPHY OF BIBLE LANDS

the city. At the northern end of the agora stood a rectangular podium with steps leading up to it on either side. This was apparently the place where magistrates dispensed justice. Unfortunately for the modern student of the New Testament period, the agora area was much rebuilt during the reign of Marcus Aurelius in the second century A.D. It seems, however, that the general plan of the area that can be studied there today is essentially the same as it was in Paul's day.

376. Basilica B across the Agora at Philippi

375. Theater at Philippi

The acropolis of the town towers above the agora of Philippi on its north side. Over 1,000 feet high, it affords an excellent view of the Philippian Plain. On the eastern slope of the acropolis one may see the remains of a Greek theater which some have estimated to have seated 50,000 people. The structure was certainly at its prime during Paul's visits there.[28] Near the theater was the Temple of Silvanus and a temple to Egyptian gods (Serapis, etc.), both constructed early in the first century A.D.

Remains of Christian churches are also coming to light at Philippi. The most spectacular of these lies just south of the agora. Known as Basilica B, this structure dates to the sixth century; it was a huge vaulted

edifice with a dome. None of the churches now known as a result of excavations at Philippi dates before about A.D. 400.

As the magistrates rendered their judgment at the north end of the agora, they commanded that Paul and Silas be beaten and cast into prison, ordering the jailer to keep them securely (Acts 16:22-24). The story of the subsequent earthquake which opened the prison doors, the conversion of the jailer and his family, and the decision of the magistrates to let Paul and Silas go is familiar to most Sunday school students.

What is probably not so familiar is the distinctly Roman element in the Acts account and in the later epistle to the Philippians. When the magistrates gave the order to release Paul and Silas, the former decided not to let the officials off so easily. He complained that they as Roman citizens had the right to be tried properly before the courts and that they should not have been beaten when they had not been sentenced by the court. Then he demanded that the magistrates themselves come and release the missionaries from prison. Greatly disturbed over the whole affair, the officials did so (Acts 16:36-39). Perhaps Paul had tried to make it clear that he was a Roman citizen during the mob scene of the previous day, but no one paid any attention to him or, possibly, did not hear him in the din and confusion.

[28]Paul E. Davies, "The Macedonian Scene of Paul's Journeys," *The Biblical Archaeologist,* XXVI (Sept., 1963), 100.

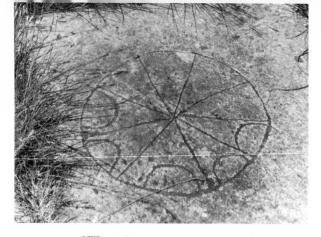

377. A Roman game cut into the pavement of the Agora at Philippi

Elements of interest to Romans are numerous in the epistle to the Philippians, written during Paul's Roman imprisonment to thank them for a gift and to stop some sort of quarrel among them. To those proud of their citizenship, he spoke of a superior citizenship in a spiritual commonwealth (Phil. 3:20; *conversation* in AV). To those accustomed to marching in step he addressed an appeal that they should walk in step (literal Greek of Phil. 3:16) and in unity of purpose instead of allowing the ranks of the church to be rent with dissension. Those walking out of step (literal Greek of 3:18) and living in a confused way religiously were compared by Paul to enemies of Christ. To those proud of their military connections he commented that through his imprisonment in Rome the gospel had been preached to the whole Praetorian Guard, the crack troops of the Empire (literal Greek of Phil. 1:13). Again, he appealed to the military-minded by calling one of the faithful members of their church a fellow soldier (Phil. 2:25). To those interested in feats of bodily prowess and success in war, he made a number of appeals in the choice of verbs and figures of speech (e.g., "stand fast" and "striving," 1:27; the figure of the race in Phil. 3:14).

Soon after Paul's release from prison, he left Philippi, but he left Luke behind, as is clear from the fact that the "we" phrase-ology, always used when Luke accompanied Paul, abruptly ceased. The narrative is described in the third person until Paul left Philippi on his last journey to Jerusalem, some five years later (Acts 20:6). If Luke remained at Philippi during the entire interim, there would be some explanation for the solid establishment of the church there and its peculiar interest in helping Paul over the years. This church more than any other is singled out for its gifts toward the apostle's support. They sent him at least four gifts (II Cor. 8:3-4; II Cor. 11:8-9; Phil. 4:10-14, 15-16). It seems that Paul visited the city on his third missionary journey (Acts 19:22; 20:1) and again between his first and second imprisonments (I Tim. 1:3).[29]

So then, the town of Philippi was extremely significant for world history. Here Christianity first entered Europe. This faith was to affect the development of the Continent from that day to this—whether in connection with the conquests of the "universal church" during the Middle Ages, the conflicts of the Reformation Era, or the impetus given to empire building in the nineteenth century by missionaries who urged assumption of the "white man's burden." On the Plain of Philippi in 42 B.C. the battle was fought which decided to a large degree that the Roman Republic should be an empire. And in this area Philip of Macedon annually extracted from the earth precious metals valued at 1,000 talents for the construction of a military machine which Alexander the Great used to conquer the East.

The Egnatian Way. When Paul left Philippi by the Crenides (or west) Gate, he struck out on the Egnatian Way for Thessalonica. This paved road some fifteen feet wide was the great military highway which connected Illyria, Macedonia, and Thrace. Scholars are almost totally in the

[29]The present writer holds the view that Paul was released from his first Roman imprisonment and made a fourth missionary journey.

378. A section of the Egnatian Way near Philippi

Plain, the most fertile plain of the north Aegean area. The great Strymon River which flows through it is on an average 100 feet broad and 6 to 9 feet deep with a current of about four miles per hour. It is fordable at most times of the year except when in strong flood, and its bottom is mostly firm though sandy.

Amphipolis. A few miles north of the Aegean, the Strymon emerges from Lake Tahinos, through which it flows on its way to the sea. On leaving the lake, the Strymon winds in a horseshoe around the western side of a terraced hill on which Amphipolis was built. Thus the town was protected on three sides by the river. On the east a protecting wall was built. Located three miles from the sea, Amphipolis was served by its seaport Eion.

The position of Amphipolis was one of the most important in this part of Greece. It stood in a pass which cuts through the mountains bordering the Strymonic Gulf and commanded the only easy communication from the coast of that gulf into the great Macedonian plains. In ancient times it was important because it controlled the western approach to the gold and silver mines and timber stands of Mount Pangaeus. Those natural resources meant much to the prosperity of the town, which declined when the veins of ore gave out.

Aristagoras of Miletus attempted to colo-

dark with regard to its origin, but it must have been built shortly after the formation of the province of Macedonia in 148 B.C. The road started at two points on the Adriatic coast—Dyrrachium (Albanian Durrës) and Aulon (modern Vlona). These two branches merged inland and continued as a single road all the way to Byzantium (Istanbul), a distance of 535 Roman miles (a Roman mile is 1,614.6 yards). On such a road one would probably travel about 17 Roman miles per day on foot and would probably drive a vehicle about 4 Roman miles per hour for an average of 25 Roman miles per day.

As Paul and his associates traveled westward, they passed between mountains most of the way. Near Amphipolis, their next stop (32 Roman miles from Philippi), the foothills dropped away into the Strymonic

379. Amphipolis

nize the site of Amphipolis, but his settlement was destroyed in 497 B.C. The Athenians also tried to colonize there, but their colony was destroyed in 465. Finally Athens established a successful colony in 437. The town surrendered to Sparta in 425. Two years later Athens tried to recover it but failed. After the Peace of Nicias in 421, Amphipolis became independent and defeated Athenian attempts to resubjugate her in 416 and 368. Philip of Macedon took the town in 358 and annexed it to his domain. Thereafter Amphipolis was part of Macedonia until 168 when the Romans made it the capital of the first of the four districts into which they divided Macedonia (the same district in which Philippi was also located).

Since the extensive ruins of neither the acropolis nor lower city of Amphipolis have been carefully examined or excavated, it is difficult to picture what the place was like when Paul passed through; and that is apparently all he did. Christianity seems to

380. The Lion of Amphipolis

have reached Amphipolis later from Philippi or Thessalonica. One striking landmark along the road in Paul's day has been discovered and properly mounted once more. The "Lion of Amphipolis," erected in the early part of the fourth century B.C. to commemorate some unknown victory, again stands as a silent sentinel along the road.

Apollonia. Continuing westward along the Via Egnatia, the apostolic company found themselves skirting the seacoast for some ten miles. To their right, mountains closely hugged the shore. Then the road struck inland south of Lake Bolbe (Volve) to Apollonia, another of the more important stops on the Egnatian Road, 22 Roman miles from Amphipolis (Acts 17:1). The name of the ancient town seems to be preserved in the modern Pollina. Though the town probably existed as early as the fifth century B.C., very little is known of its history or of the nature of the site during the first century A.D. Practically no formal exploration has been conducted there.

Apparently having no intention of ministering extensively at any town short of Thessalonica, Paul led his companions farther westward along the Egnatian Way. As they traveled across the Chalcidice (that land shaped like a bird's foot with three claws extending into the north Aegean), the road continued to follow the southern shore of Lake Bolbe. Leaving that lake behind, the road soon brought the missionary party to the south shore of another lake, the Coronea. As was true of the route ever since they left Apollonia, mountains hemmed in the Egnatian Way on their left. Nearing Thessalonica (36 Roman miles from Apollonia), the road ascended the foothills of the Cortiates Mountains and dropped down into the city of Thessalonica.

Thessalonica (or Thessaloniki). The city lay on the Gulf of Thessalonica, the largest gulf indenting the Balkan Peninsula, and rose at the end of the bay in amphitheater form, on the slopes of the foothills of the Cortiates Mountains. On the east and west sides of the city, ravines ascend from the shore and converge toward the highest point, on which the citadel stood. The port, which is an open roadstead sheltered by Chalcidice, was and still is convenient for large ships. In the fifth century B.C., the Gulf of Thessalonica was perhaps twice as large as at present. As a result of the silting action of the Vardar (or Axios) River, the western portion of the gulf was gradually filled in. By Paul's day silting action had enclosed the western area so that it was a large lake which has since silted up. This silting action created marshy areas which have bred malarial mosquitoes, plaguing the city until very recent times.

Mount Olympus stands in clear view from the upper streets of the city, rising 9,600 feet above the sea. In ancient times its glittering snow-covered dome was thought to be the throne before which Zeus gathered in council the deities of Greece. Dense forests at the mountain's base concealed the Pierian Spring, beside which the Muses were reputedly born and Orpheus first saw the light.

In early times there were various small villages in the area of Thessalonica. A town on the present site was called "Therme," from which the Thermaic Gulf received its name. In 315 B.C. Cassander grouped together the villagers of the area and founded the city of Thessalonica, which he named in honor of his wife, the daughter of Philip and stepsister of Alexander the Great. Apparently the town served as a Macedonian naval station.

When Macedonia capitulated to Rome in 168 B.C. and the kingdom was divided into four parts, Thessalonica became the administrative center for the second district. In 148, when the province of Macedonia was formed, Thessalonica became the capital. During the civil wars of the first century B.C., it was the headquarters of the Pompeian party and the senate and later

381. The Egnatian Way in Thessalonica

took the side of Antony and Octavian against Brutus and Cassius. By virtue of the latter action, it was made a free city. It had its own city council and was ruled by politarchs, according to the New Testament narrative (Acts 17:6). This fact used to be doubted because such a name was unknown from other sources. But numerous inscriptions have turned up in the area confirming the accuracy of the New Testament.

Thessalonica was an important city in Paul's day. The population has been estimated at about 200,000. Besides serving as the capital of the province of Macedonia, it was the main stop on the Egnatian Way, a naval base, and an important commercial port. With overland caravans thronging its hostelries, with its harbor filled with ships' bottoms from overseas, with old salts, Roman officials, and thousands of Jewish merchants rubbing shoulders in its streets, Thessalonica presented a very cosmopolitan picture. It is very suggestive that the Jewish opponents of Paul should have called Paul and his co-workers "world-topplers" (Acts 17:6).

This cosmopolitanism apparently appealed to Paul. Judging from the fact that he spent so long a time at great centers like Corinth and Ephesus and sought to minister at other large centers with great moving populations, it would seem that

382. The harbor of Thessalonica

Paul's strategy was to use these cities as springboards for the propagation of the gospel. Individuals converted in them would move all over the Roman world and would rapidly spread the Christian message. The fact that he could greet so many persons by name in the Roman church (Rom. 16), doubtless acquaintances from other places who had moved to the capital, is proof of the effectiveness of this program. Probably some of these acquaintances led the group of friends who came to meet the apostle at Appii Forum and Three Taverns when he was on his way to Rome for trial (Acts 28:15). It should be remembered, however, that in general Paul also ministered in cities that had fairly large Jewish populations and that it was his custom to preach first to the Jews wherever he went. When they rejected his message, he then turned to Gentiles.

That there was a fairly large Jewish population in Thessalonica may be seen from the fact that so great a number of Greeks had become "God seekers" or converts to Judaism. Of these a "great multitude" (Acts 17:4) were won over to Christianity. Moreover, the ease with which the Jews of Thessalonica marshaled the city crowd against Paul and Silas (Acts 17:5) indicates that their numbers were either large or at least influential.

As usual, Paul began his ministry among the Jews of Thessalonica, preaching to them in their synagogue for three Sabbaths (Acts 17:2). It need not be concluded, however, that Paul remained in the city for so short a time. The success of Paul's labor among Gentiles indicates an extended ministry outside the synagogue. A stay of longer than three weeks would certainly have been required for the Philippians to collect and send two gifts to the apostle while he was in Thessalonica (Phil. 4:16).

As already indicated, Paul's ministry in Thessalonica was extremely successful. Many of the Jews, taking exception to his message, stirred up a riot against him. The mob attacked the house of Jason, Paul's host, but the apostle was away at the time. So they dragged Jason and some fellow Christians to the politarchs, with the accusation of sedition: "These all do contrary to the decrees of Caesar, saying that there is another king, one Jesus" (Acts 17:7). The politarchs required the suspects to post bond for good behavior, and then they freed the Christians. Though greatly disturbed because of the tumult, the rulers were apparently bent on justice and legal protection of Paul and his companions. The inability of free cities to keep order raised a threat of Roman interference.

Paul and Silas now seemed to be a liability to the young church; besides, their lives were in danger. So the Thessalonian believers decided to send the pair to Beroea (modern Veroia). The persecution leveled against Paul and Silas was continued against the church in the city. Within a few months, while Paul was ministering at Corinth, he found it necessary to write to encourage the Thessalonians to bear up under persecution (I Thess. 2:14; 3:2-4). The Thessalonians had also become involved in erroneous teachings on the Lord's coming and were neglecting everyday business. A little later Paul was compelled to send a second epistle to Thessalonica to correct some beliefs concerning the second coming.

Little detailed information can be produced on the Thessalonica of Paul's day. No excavations on a large scale have been attempted, owing chiefly to the cost of demolishing the overlying buildings of the modern city. The main street of the lower city is still the Egnatian Way, which follows the ancient route. At the western extremity stood an arch until A.D. 1876. Known as the Vardar Gate, it possibly was built long before Paul arrived. It was erected by the people in honor of Octavian and Antony and in memory of the battle of Philippi. Constructed of large blocks of marble, it had on its outside face two bas-reliefs of a Roman wearing the toga and standing before a house. The inscription on this arch, which mentions the politarchs, is now in the British Museum. The Arch of Galerius, which still stands at the east end of the street, was built about A.D. 305 and therefore has no connection with the New Testament period. The same is true of the several well-preserved Byzantine churches of the town. The wall of the acropolis dates to the Medieval period but its rests on foundations of Greek times and incorporates many ancient blocks bearing inscriptions.

Because of its location, Thessalonica has remained an important city throughout the Christian Era. It was the second metropolis to Constantinople in the Byzantine Empire, and in spite of all its sufferings it has always arisen from the ashes. Today greater Thessalonica has a population of almost 400,000.

Beroea. Leaving Thessalonica, Paul and Silas traveled westward on the Egnatian Way for about twenty miles. Then, shortly after crossing the bridge over the Axios River, they turned southwest on a side road to Beroea. Thirty miles later they arrived at their destination. On this leg of their journey the terrain had been much different from what they had previously experienced. This time almost their entire journey had been across plains. The town of Beroea it-

383. Arch of Galerius, Thessalonica

self was located at an altitude of 600 feet on the tableland of the eastern mountains of the Varmion chain. The area is well supplied with gushing springs and fertile farmland.

Although Beroea existed for several centuries prior to the New Testament period, the date of its founding is uncertain. Without doubt it was a thriving community in the fourth century B.C. After surrendering to Rome, it became a part of the third of the four regions into which Macedonia was divided. Pompey spent the winter of 49-48 B.C. there in preparation for the battle of Pharsalus. The Jewish community seems to have been established about the time of Christ. The town, which is much smaller today than in New Testament times, possesses considerable remains of antiquity, but they have not really been explored. A few remains of the ancient walls may be seen, but the inhabitants still carry away the stones.

Paul found the Beroean Jews even more receptive to the Christian message than the Jews of Thessalonica. Many of them were converted, as were numerous Greeks, including some of fairly high social class (Acts 17:12). When word of this success reached the Thessalonian Jews, they sent rabble-rousers to Beroea to stir up trouble. The Beroean church then sent Paul away by sea (by what route is not known) and

384. A street scene in Berea

conducted him safely to Athens. Paul's stay at Beroea must have been brief[30] but effective.

Silas and Timothy remained behind, but Paul sent word with his escorts to request them to come as soon as possible (Acts 17:15). Since Timothy suddenly reappears in the biblical narrative, it seems that he had been left behind at Philippi and now had come directly from that town to Beroea. Apparently too Silas and Timothy came to Athens promptly on receipt of the summons from Paul. But some emergency or concern must have led him to send them away again —Timothy to Thessalonica (I Thess. 3:1-3) and Silas probably to Philippi. Both of them rejoined him at Corinth (Acts 18:5).

The chronicling of these scurryings back and forth should serve to allow the reader to peep behind the curtain to see a little more of the feverish between-acts activity that must have characterized Paul's effort to evangelize, establish churches in, and maintain contact with many of the centers of the eastern Mediterranean. This review also serves to underscore the relative ease and frequency of travel in the Roman world of Nero and Paul.

Athens. As Paul landed at the Piraeus and made his way into Athens (*c.* 5 miles away), he must have had much the same

feelings as a postwar guest of an impoverished London gentleman. The great house is still intact, though there is some destruction around the grounds; the beautiful old furniture is still in place; the coat of arms still hangs over the mantel. But the rugs are threadbare. Few servants circulate about the place. It grows increasingly hard to keep up appearances. And the conversation often turns to a better day long since gone.

Vestiges of the destruction wrought by Sulla in 86 B.C. probably still remained. Certainly the effects were still felt. Sulla had burned the arsenals and shipbuilding yards and leveled the city walls. Athens' importance as a commercial and political center was gone. It was now a "quiet" university town, respected for its learning, its arts, and its past prestige. The young Roman elite were especially impressed by the city's beautiful monuments and the brilliance of her schools of rhetoricians.

Mommsen characterized Athens during the first century A.D. as financially and morally ruined. While it should have been prosperous and could have been with the peace and prosperity of the period, it was not. With the increasing poverty went begging and street riots. Mommsen believed that the decline of Athens was largely the fault of her government and held that the free towns of Greece were incapable of ruling themselves. By doing them a favor and giving them their freedom, the Romans had permitted them to destroy themselves. With their increasing bankruptcy, the Roman government was ultimately forced to intervene and appoint correctors, extraordinary commissioners "for the correction of evils prevailing in free towns."[31]

Perhaps Mommsen has made an important point, but it should be remembered that Athenian silver resources had been exhausted by the beginning of the Roman Im-

[30]Ramsay believes Paul spent several months in Beroea. Cf. *op. cit.*, p. 234.

[31]William P. Dickson (trans.), Theodor Mommsen's *The Provinces of the Roman Empire from Caesar to Diocletian* (New York: Charles Scribner's Sons, 1906), I, 300-303.

perial Period; Athens no longer controlled an empire; and great rival centers such as Corinth, Ephesus, Antioch, and Alexandria had cut into the Athenian share of the economic and cultural pie of the Mediterranean world.

In spite of the decline of the imperial city, it remained outwardly beautiful. Her acropolis, agora, and other public centers remained intact. And the despoiling of much of her most exquisite statuary did not come until A.D. 64 (after Paul's visit), when Nero sought art pieces to beautify the Rome he was rebuilding.[32] Foreigners expended considerable sums on public buildings there during the first century, some of them having been built before Paul arrived.

For instance, about the time of the birth of Christ the Temple of Roma and Augustus was erected on the Acropolis and the Roman Agora constructed near the Athenian Agora. Claudius, not Caligula as some have claimed, built the upper part of the

[32]Paul Graindor, *Athènes De Tibère A Trajan* (Cairo: Imprimerie Misr, Société Anonyme Egyptienne, 1931), pp. 14-15.

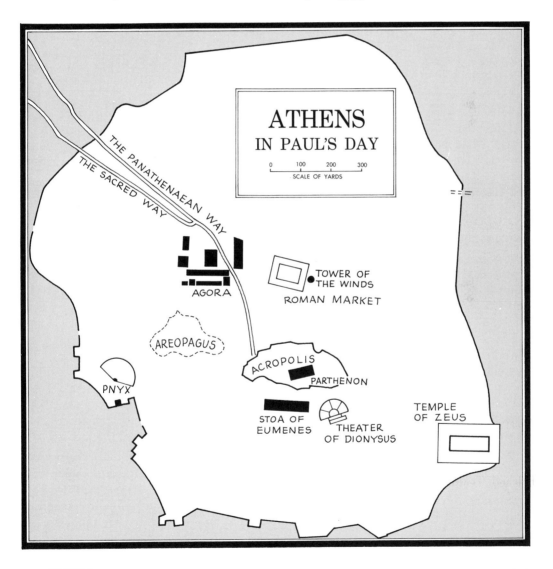

ATHENS
IN PAUL'S DAY

0   100   200   300
SCALE OF YARDS

THE PANATHENAEAN WAY
THE SACRED WAY

AGORA

TOWER OF THE WINDS
ROMAN MARKET

AREOPAGUS

PNYX

ACROPOLIS
PARTHENON

STOA OF EUMENES

THEATER OF DIONYSUS

TEMPLE OF ZEUS

Roman stairway of the Acropolis.[33] Many of the greatest structures erected with funds from abroad were built later, however—in the first half of the second century —by Trajan, Hadrian, and Herodes Atticus. Perhaps it should be added that for all the benefits bestowed, the Athenians became obsequious emperor worshipers.

Not only could the apostle still see the beautiful structures of ancient Athens; he could enjoy her wonderful climate and her gorgeous scenery. The mean temperature is 63 degrees, the maximum of 99 degrees in July and the minimum of 31 degrees in January. The summer heat is moderated by the sea breezes or the cool northerly winds from the mountains. On the average there are only three days a year that are overcast all day. Observations over a period of 24 years at Athens give on the average 179 clear days when the sun is never hid, 157 bright days when the sun may be hid for a half hour or so, 26 cloudy days, and 3 days when the sun is not seen at all.[34]

If Paul had stood on the 340-foot hill of the Nymphs (where an observatory now stands) at the west wall, he would have been in an excellent position to orient himself to the landscape. Some 500 yards in front of him and slightly to the left would have been the Agora. Sharply to his right would have stood the Pnyx, a roughly shaped theater where the assembly met. A little to his right would have been the bare-topped rocky Areopagus, 377 feet high. Towering above the Areopagus was the Acropolis (512 feet high), capped with its incomparable collection of temples. Behind that and out of sight was the great unfinished Temple of Zeus. Far off in the distance to his right stretched the Hymettus Range (3,370 feet high). If it was evening, its barren western flank was colored a flaming purple by the reflected rays of the setting sun. Apparently this beautiful sight

had led the poet Pindar to describe Athens as the "violet-crowned city."

To his left in the near distance the sharply pointed Lycabettus (1,112 feet high) thrust its top above pine-clad slopes. Almost behind that, ten miles away, arose the conical form of Mount Pentelicus (3,640 feet), whose green slopes were dotted with gleaming white mounds from the marble quarries. From the foot of Pentelicus, the Cephisus River flowed to the north of Athens, and coming from the Hymettus, the Ilissus River skirted the city on the southwest. Between Pentelicus and Hymettus there is an opening in the mountains leading out toward the Plain of Marathon.

Paul probably traversed the five miles from the Piraeus to Athens on the road just north of the long walls and entered by the Dipylon Gate at the northwest corner of the city. Just outside the gate the road passed through a large cemetery which held graves dating from the eleventh century B.C. to Roman times. In this cemetery a number of Jewish gravestones were found. Inside the Dipylon Paul would have found himself on a long avenue leading to the Agora—the political, commercial, and social center of the city. In this northwest section of Athens were the potters' quarters. From the Agora Paul could have gone directly eastward to the Roman marketplace, south to the Areopagus, or southeast to the Acropolis.

Oscar Broneer is quite convinced that Paul spent part of his time sight-seeing in Athens. He feels that the full force of the Greek of Acts 17:23a demands "going about and examining objects of religious devotion."[35] Ramsay translates the passage "As I went through the city surveying the monuments of your religion."[36] If Paul went sight-seeing in Athens, a few of the more

[33]*Ibid.*, p. 11.
[34]Doremus A. Hayes, *Greek Culture and the Greek Testament* (New York: Abingdon Press, 1925), p. 14.

[35]Oscar Broneer, "Athens, 'City of Idol Worship,'" *The Biblical Archaeologist*, XXI (Feb., 1958), 3.
[36]Ramsay, p. 237.

385. Temple of Jupiter, Athens

significant things he saw should be considered. A discussion of the Areopagus and the Agora comes later in connection with Paul's ministry in Athens.

One of the most colossal religious structures of this "city of idol worship" was the Temple of Olympian Zeus or Jupiter Olympus, located not far to the southeast of the Acropolis. Unfinished and roofless in Paul's day, it was completed by Hadrian. Fifteen of its gigantic columns are still standing. The temple was begun by Pisistratus of Athens in 515 B.C. Antiochus IV Epiphanes of Syria resumed the work during his reign (175-164 B.C.). Hadrian finished it and consecrated it in A.D. 131-32.

The structure had 104 Corinthian columns of Pentelic marble 56 feet high and 5 feet 7 inches in diameter at the base. These were arranged in two rows on the sides and three rows at the ends and rested on a foundation 354 feet long and 135 feet broad. The height was over 90 feet. The image of Zeus was made of gold and ivory. This temple was one of the four largest in the Roman world. Of its three rivals, the best known to Bible students is the Temple of Diana at Ephesus.

If Paul carried on his religious disputations daily in the Athenian Agora (Acts 17:17), he certainly must have visited the Roman Agora adjacent to it on the east. This marketplace was a large rectangular area 367 by 315 feet, enclosed by a high wall of stone. It was lined with shops. The interior open courtyard, measuring 269 by 187 feet, was paved with marble and surrounded with an Ionic colonnade, upon which the shops opened. The main entrance, on the northwest side, still stands. This consists of four fluted Doric columns 26 feet high and 4 feet in diameter, capped

386. The Roman Agora, or market, at Athens

by a gable surmounted by a statue of Lucius Caesar, grandson of Augustus. This entrance also bears an inscription to the effect that the Agora was erected with a donation from Julius Caesar and Augustus. Another inscription on this entrance, by Hadrian, stipulates regulations for the sale of oil. Apparently this was primarily a wine and oil market.

On the southeast side of the Roman Agora stood a most unusual structure popularly known as the Tower of the Winds. An octagonal structure of Pentelic marble, it stood 42 feet high and 26 feet in diameter. On its roof stood a weather vane in the form of a bronze triton pointing with a wand at the personifications of the prevailing winds as portrayed in the reliefs below the cornice. These eight reliefs bear inscriptions giving their names. For instance, Caecias, the boisterous northeast wind, is bearded and warmly clad and carries a vessel containing what seems to be hailstones; Apeliotes, the mild and rainy east wind, is a youth with a bundle of grain and fruits. This tower was also equipped with a hydraulic clock and sundials so an individual could tell time by it in fair or cloudy weather.

Over on the other side of town, due west of the Acropolis, was the Pnyx—a place with which many significant memories were already associated in Paul's day. This is

where the Athenian assembly met during the days of Athens' glory. In this sort of rustic theater (230 feet deep and 395 feet broad) on the northeast slope of the hill facing the Acropolis, such greats as Aristides, Themistocles, and Pericles had addressed the citizens of the "violet-crowned" city. After the Theater of Dionysus was built in stone during the latter half of the fourth century B.C., the assembly preferred to meet there.

Greatest of all the tourist attractions in Athens—in Paul's day and ours—is the Acropolis. No effort was spared to make it the crown of Athens and her empire. The southern slope of the Acropolis supported structures which were almost as important as some of those on the sacred hill. At the southeast corner stood the Odeion of Pericles, which was built in 445 B.C. Burned by one of Mithridates' generals in 86 B.C., it was restored some twenty-five years later by the king of Cappadocia. It was con-

387. The Tower of the Winds

sidered the most beautiful concert hall of the Greek world. In it were performed the cantatas of the Dionysian festivals, and rehearsals were conducted there for the dramas held in the theater. Its surviving architectural members are so few that reconstruction has been problematical.

Walking westward along the south slope of the Acropolis, one comes next to the Theater of Dionysus where a great festival was celebrated every spring (March-April) in honor of the god Dionysus. Out of the dancing and singing of these festivals developed the dramatic forms of tragedy and comedy. Although Dionysiac celebrations were first carried on in the Agora, they were enacted on this site from about 500 B.C. Here the plays of Aeschylus, Sophocles, Euripides, and Aristophanes were acted. Originally in wood, construction of the theater in stone was completed by Lycurgus about 330 B.C. It is estimated that the seats could hold some 17,000 spectators, but on occasion many more attended.

In front of the whole south slope of the Acropolis, extending westward from the theater, Eumenes II, king of Pergamum (197-159 B.C.), had built a great stoa or portico 535 feet long and 58 feet wide.

388. The Theater of Dionysus

Designed to serve as a shelter for the theater audience, it was faced with a two-story Doric colonnade with sixty-four columns on each story. Behind this, on the slope of the Acropolis, several small temples were located. And at the west end of the stoa the Odeion of Herodes Atticus was to be built during the second century A.D.

The entrance to the Acropolis looked quite different in Paul's day from the way it looked when it was ultimately completed and from the impression that the modern visitor receives. The two pylons flanking the Roman entrance and jutting out seven-

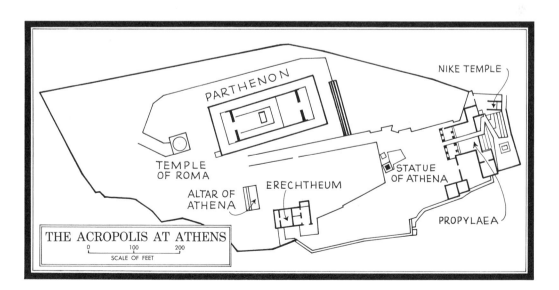

THE ACROPOLIS AT ATHENS

teen feet from it were built at a much later date, perhaps in the reign of Septimius Severus, about A.D. 200. In fact the whole monumental stairway, the upper part of which was built by Claudius, was a Roman addition. The Greeks preferred a system of ramps or slopes which would break the architectural lines.

Entering by a path a little above the lower Roman entrance, Paul would have passed below the exquisite little Ionic Temple of Athena Nike (victory). The parapet around it was sculptured with figures of victories in a variety of poses. And beside the temple was the triple figure of Hekate, awesome queen of the underworld.

Before the apostle on the left stood the Agrippa monument, a statue mounted on a chariot drawn by four horses atop a thirty-nine-foot rectangular pedestal of marble. There is reason to believe that this originally was erected by Eumenes of Pergamum in the second century B.C.

Passing next through the impressive ornamental gateway called the Propylaea, Paul gazed upon the colossal bronze figure of Athena Promachos (the goddess who fights in front), made by Phidias from spoils taken from the Persians at Marathon. Continuing along the sacred way, Paul saw a temple of Artemis on his right. The Parthenon was in full view. But the main entrance was on the east, so the apostle continued on the sacred way. He noticed, how-

390. Entrance to the Acropolis at Athens in classical times

ever, that on the west pediment was portrayed in statuary the quarrel between Athena and Poseidon for possession of Attica while the other gods and heroes looked on. On his left was the Erechtheum, temple of Athena Polias (of the city) and Poseidon-Erechtheus with its beautiful porch of the maidens (caryatids). The main part of this structure is a rectangle 78 feet long by 42 feet wide with an Ionic colonnade at either end standing 25 feet in height. The porch, with its six maidens whose heads support the roof, extends from the southwest corner of the temple.

Next on the left was the great Altar of Athena. Behind that stood the sanctuary of Zeus Polias (protector of the city). As the sacred way turned toward the eastern entrance of the Parthenon, the apostle saw on his left a circular structure surrounded by nine Ionic columns which housed the altar of Roma and Augustus. This was built between 27 and 14 B.C.

At last the apostle reached the main entrance of the magnificent Parthenon. Begun in 447, it was dedicated to the goddess Athena in 438, when Athens was at the height of her glory. Pericles was the political chief, and supervision of the work was entrusted to the great sculptor Phidias. What an impressive sight it was for the apostle, who lamented that so much effort and expense had been devoted to the worship of a deity that did not exist.

389. Entrance to the Acropolis at Athens today

The great marble structure measured at its base 238 feet in length and 111 feet in width. Its encircling row of 46 fluted Doric columns (17 on each side and 8 on each end) stood to a height of 34 feet, each column having a diameter of six feet at the base. The top of the pediment rose to a height of 65 feet. And the pediment was filled with sculptures of the important gods of Greece. In the center of the group was Zeus, from whose head Athena sprang fully armed. Encircling the entire structure above the colonnade was the Doric frieze. Divided into 92 panels, this frieze consisted of groups of sculptures depicting legendary and mythological stories dear to the hearts of the Greeks. On the east end Paul found himself looking up at scenes from the struggle between the gods and the giants.

Looking between the columns of the peristyle, the Apostle saw another frieze near the roof, known as the Ionic frieze. It completely encircled the building with a continuous series of sculptures 524 feet in length. The approximately 600 figures of this frieze included men, women, and animals that participated in the Panathenaic Procession, formed every year to carry a new robe to Athena in proper state.

Peering through the tremendous bronze doors into the sanctuary, Paul saw the great gold and ivory image of Athena, one of the greatest works of Phidias. The fleshy parts were carved ivory and the rest consisted of plates of gold suspended on a framework of cedar wood. The room was surrounded by a two-story Doric colonnade and measured 98 feet long, 63 feet wide, and 43 feet high. The west room, or treasury, Paul did not see, but he was told that in the center of it were four great Ionic columns arranged in a rectangle and extending from the floor to the ceiling. The room was 44 feet long and 63 feet wide.

Walking around the outside of the temple, the apostle noticed the perfect form of the structure. He was told that there was not a straight line in the building and that the columns bowed slightly inward at the top to avoid optical illusions of sagging lines or crooked columns. Moreover, the upper part of the friezes was cut deeper than the lower to cause optical equalization. His attention was also called to a row of significant statuary along the south wall of the Acropolis adjacent to the Parthenon. These were figures of Gauls and Amazons in defeat, dedicated by King Attalus of Pergamum some two centuries earlier.

As Paul turned to leave the Acropolis, he noticed that the walk was bordered with numerous statues of gods and famous men, many of which were votive offerings to the gods. In fact, wherever he went in Athens

391. The Erechtheum

392. The Porch of the Maidens

393. The Parthenon reconstructed in Nashville, Tennessee, viewed from the east

he was impressed with the many altars to the gods, statues of them, and other evidences of the religiosity of the people.

Of course the apostle did more than sight-seeing in Athens. Though he had come primarily to wait for conditions to quiet down in Beroea and Thessalonica and had no plans for an extended ministry in Athens, he nevertheless did conduct some

394. The Parthenon as it appears today, from the west

evangelistic ministry there. As was customary elsewhere, he went first to the Jews, reasoning with them in their synagogue concerning acceptance of the Christian message (Acts 17:17). Where the synagogue was located is not known. But a stone slab excavated in the eastern section of Athens bearing Psalm 118:20 might have been incorporated in such a building as a synagogue.

Not restricting himself to religious discussion with Jews, Paul reasoned daily with chance comers to the Agora (Acts 17:17). Ramsay believes that this "reasoning" was according to the Socratic style of discussion characteristic of the city and cites this as an example of Paul's ability to be "all things to all men."[37] Thanks particularly to the excavations of the American School of Classical Studies at Athens during the years 1931-40 and since 1946, it is now possible

[37]Ramsay, p. 237.

to see quite clearly what the Agora was like in Paul's day.

Let us pretend that he entered the area at the southeast corner, on the road leading from the Acropolis (the Panathenaean Way). At the entrance on his left stood the mint of Athens, dating from the second half of the fifth century B.C. Here the famous "owls" of Athens were coined, which provided the standard coinage of the eastern Mediterranean for nearly two centuries. Across the alley from it to the west was a fountain house, the earliest in the Agora. Sprawling out northeast of that lay the commercial agora. Constructed in the second century B.C., it included south, east, and middle stoas facing an open market area. The south stoa consisted of a single wide aisle with Doric columns along its

395. Horsemen in the Panathenaic Procession, from the Ionic frieze of the Parthenon

north side; its back wall acted as a retaining wall against higher ground to the south.

The east stoa connected the south and middle stoas, thus screening the commer-

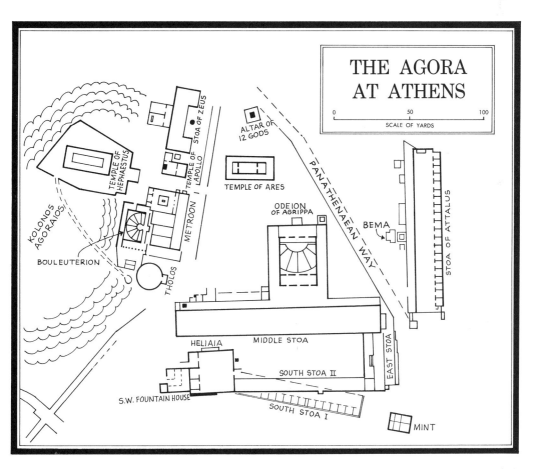

396. The east room of the Parthenon, where Athena's statue stood

cial agora from the Panathenaean Way. Facing in two directions, it had colonnades on both east and west sides. Since the ground level was so much lower on the west side, the architect divided the stoa down the middle with a solid wall and set the eastern half over a yard higher than the western. Access to the commercial agora was gained by means of a broad stairway leading through this stoa to the lower level. The middle stoa also faced both southward on the commercial agora and on the larger area to the north. This middle stoa was the largest structure in the Agora; it was about 450 feet long and, like the south and east stoas, was faced with unfluted Doric columns. At the end of the south stoa was the Heliaia, largest of the law courts at Athens, dating originally to the sixth century B.C. To the right of its entrance a water clock was erected in the fourth century. Next to the Heliaia was the southwest fountain house.

Having passed through the commercial agora, the apostle was now at the southwest corner of the Agora on the road leading in from the Areopagus. On the west side of the Agora, to his left, was the important political center of ancient Athens. First came the circular Tholos, the office and dining room of the prytany, a committee of the city council. Built about 470 B.C., this building was the real headquarters of the Athenian government.

The full Council of Five Hundred met in the Bouleuterion a few feet away off the road. This building, constructed in the form of a theater with raised banks of seats, was set against a steep hillside, called Kolonos Agoraios. Continuing along the road, the apostle next passed the Metroon, built in the second century B.C. Consisting of four rooms sharing a single colonnade facing the Agora, this structure housed the state archives and the sanctuary of the mother of the gods. Across the road from

397. The Athenian Agora from the west

this, to the apostle's right, was a fenced enclosure surrounding a long base, on which statues of the tribal heroes of Attica are thought to have been located. The base of these statues served as a public bulletin board.

Between the Metroon and the Temple of Apollo to the north is a wide passageway that provided access to the Temple of Hephaestus (god of the forge) and Athena on the Kolonos Agoraios. This temple (one of the best preserved of all Greek temples) is entirely constructed of Pentelic marble, except for the lowest of the three steps which lead up to it. It is 104 feet long, 45 feet wide, and 34 feet high. The Doric colonnade consists of six columns at the ends and thirteen on the sides. Within its cella stood cult statues of Athena and Hephaestus. On the east pediment, above the entrance, were sculptures representing the labors of Hercules. A formal garden surrounded the temple (built a few years before the Parthenon), and plants were set out in flower pots which were sunk into the rock and carefully spaced. Just north of the temple on the hill was a Hellenistic building thought by some to have been a state arsenal.

Back on the level of the Agora again, the apostle next would have passed the fourth century Temple of Apollo Patroos, reputed father of the Athenians. Inside the temple he is represented as a musician dressed in long robes and holding a lyre in his hand. In a tiny shrine at the side of the Temple of Apollo, Zeus Phratrios and Athena Phratria were worshiped as ancestral gods of Athenian family groups. Across the road to the apostle's right was the Temple of Ares, the god of war, whom the Romans called Mars.

North of the Temple of Apollo was the Stoa of Zeus, a large U-shaped structure with the wings jutting toward the Agora. In front of the structure stood a colossal statue of Zeus the Deliverer. The walls of this stoa are painted with various religious subjects, including an assembly of the

398. The Tholos

Twelve Gods. Various administrative offices may be found here. Socrates is known to have discussed philosophy with his friends here.

Across the north of the Agora stood the Painted Stoa. So-called for a series of battle scenes painted on its walls (including Troy, Athenians vs. Amazons, Marathon, etc.). It was a haunt of philosophers in the fourth and third centuries B.C. Here Zeno, founder of the Stoic school, held academic court.

The apostle now turned onto the Panathenaean Way, which led diagonally across the Agora to the southeast. As soon as he did so, he passed the Altar of the Twelve Gods. This was considered the very center of Athens from which distances to outside points were measured. After passing the Temple of Ares (already mentioned), he stood alongside the Odeion, or music hall, of Agrippa, originally entered from the terrace of the Middle Stoa. Built about 15 B.C., it had a seating capacity of approximately 1,000.

All along the east side of the Agora, to the apostle's left, stretched the magnificent Stoa of Attalus. Attalus built this stoa for the Athenians about 150 B.C. It was some 385 feet long and 64 feet wide and was faced by a two-story colonnade of 45 columns, Doric at the base and Ionic at the top. The second story was reached by stairs at either end. Shops lined the back wall of the structure. This beautiful stoa has been rebuilt by the excavators and serves today as the Agora Museum. In front of it stood the Bema, or public rostrum, where officials could address citizens gathered in the square. In addition to those already mentioned, the apostle noted numerous monuments and altars scattered around the Agora, which demonstrated the religiosity of the people.

At length the teachings of Paul began to disturb the philosophers. Perhaps some had heard secondhand and in garbled fashion what he was preaching; no doubt others had caught phrases directly from his mouth as they moved about in the Agora. In this cosmopolitan city of learning they had often come in contact with religious teachings from all over the known world. However, this religion was different; it taught resurrection for the believer and a hope for the life to come. The Epicureans with their atomistic view believed that the atoms constituting the soul of man simply flew apart at death and joined some other form of matter. The Stoics believed that the human soul became part of the universal soul in a very impersonal sense. Both of these views were far from the teachings of Paul.

They called him a "babbler" (AV; Greek *spermológos*). Ramsay seeks to give the proper understanding of the Greek term by means of a kind of word study:

399. The state archives of Athens

400. The Temple of Hephaestus

. . . a worthless fellow of low class and vulgar habits, with the insinuation that he lives at the expense of others, like those disreputable persons who hang round the markets and the quays in order to pick up anything that falls from the loads that are carried about. Hence, as a term in social slang, it connotes absolute vulgarity and inability to rise above the most contemptible standard of life and conduct; it is often connected with slave life, for the *Spermológos* was near the type of the slave and below the level of the free man; and there clings to it the suggestion of picking up refuse and scraps, and in literature of plagiarism without the capacity to use correctly. . . . Probably the nearest and most instructive parallel in modern English life to *Spermológos* is "Bounder," allowing for the difference between England and Athens. In both there lies the idea of one who is "out of the swim," out of the inner circle, one who lacks that thorough knowledge and practice in the rules of the game that mould the whole character and make it one's nature to act in the proper way and play the game fair.[38]

Then these philosophers laid hands on Paul—an indication that they (educated men, who are usually more restrained) were greatly disturbed indeed. And they brought him "unto Areopagus" (Acts 17:19). The question immediately arises as to how the word *Areopagus* is to be understood. Some have taken the word merely to signify the Council of the Areopagus. They hold that this meeting could have taken place wherever the Council met. The ancient meeting place was on the Areopagus Hill (Mars

[38]*Ibid.*, pp. 242-43.

Hill, Acts 17:22). By Paul's day they also met on occasion in a stoa at the north end of the Agora. Some scholars feel that the circumstances of Acts 17 seem to fit an Agora scene better than the hill.

Others believe, however, that while this meeting could have taken place in the Agora, it actually did occur on the Areopagus. This writer holds that the meeting was held on the hill. Oscar Broneer makes a strong argument for that conclusion in his observation that in Acts 17:19 *epi* with the accusative means "up to" Areopagus.[39] The result is, then, that Areopagus in Acts 17 refers both to the council and its place of meeting. In verse 19 the primary reference seems to be to the hill; in verse 22 it clearly applies to the council. The King James translation "in the midst of Mars' hill" (v. 22) is an impossible rendition of the Greek; the passage must be rendered "in the midst of the Areopagus"—referring to the council. This verse may be coupled with verse 33: "he went forth from the midst of them."

As already indicated, the Areopagus was located just to the west of the Acropolis and in plain view of it. There are at least two explanations of the meaning of "Areopagus." The one derives it from *pagos*, "hill," and Ares, god of war, and alludes to the legend that the first case tried on the hill involved a charge of murder against Ares. The other explanation is that the name means "hill of the Arai [curses]," because according to another legend the first trial on the hill was that of Orestes who had been hounded by the Furies for the murder of his mother.

The hill itself is 377 feet high. A rocky eminence, it rises gradually to its highest point on the south and east. Sixteen worn steps cut into the rock lead to the summit. Rough rock-hewn benches forming three sides of a square were carved from the rock on top of the hill. There were also two special stones on which the prosecutor and defendant stood. Provided he knows Greek, the modern visitor to the Areopagus can

401. The Areopagus

read Paul's sermon to the Areopagus on a bronze plaque affixed to the hill on the right of the stairs.

The question next arises as to why Paul should have been taken before the Areopagus Council at all. Something has already been said about the place of the Areopagus in Athenian life. It will be remembered that it once held a place of supreme importance in the political and religious affairs of the state. During the period of the democracy in the fifth century, it lost its political power and became largely a criminal court. In Roman times it was charged mainly with religious and educational affairs. Ramsay concludes that the Areopagus had power to appoint or invite lecturers at Athens and to exercise some general control over the lecturers in the interests of public order and morality. The scene described in Acts 17:18 seems to indicate that recognized lecturers had power to take a strange lecturer before the council. This authority of appointing lecturers existed at least as early as Cicero's day because he induced the Areopagus to pass a decree inviting Cratippus, a Peripatetic philosopher, to become a lecturer at Athens. What such a privilege entailed is not known.[40] At any rate, the appearance before the Areopagus does not seem to have been a formal trial, because it did not conclude with any sort of verdict.

[39]Broneer, p. 27.

[40]Ramsay, pp. 246-47.

Some mocked, and others expressed interest in hearing him again (Acts 17:32).

In his appearance on Mars Hill, Paul showed an acquaintance with Greco-Roman culture, which he tried to use to make contact with his hearers. It has also been suggested that the speech indicates that he may have addressed the group in the flowery New Alexandrian Rhetoric, which was a favorite among the educated classes of the day. He showed, too, that he had been greatly impressed by the religiosity of the Athenians, as reflected by the multitude of altars and other religious monuments he had seen all over the city. He observed that they even had an altar to an "unknown god," erected just to make sure they had not omitted any possible gods from their worship. This was the god that Paul claimed to be preaching to them. Although remains of no such altar have been found at Athens, Apollonius of Tyana reports having seen one (or more) there later in the century. Pausanias saw one there in the middle of the second century, and one was discovered in 1909 at Pergamum in Asia Minor.[41]

Paul's ministry at Athens has been declared a failure by some. It may be asked, however, whether one has failed if he did not set out to do anything special in the first place. It is to be remembered that Paul was very largely marking time while waiting for trouble to die down in Macedonia and while waiting for Silas and Timothy. Moreover, he did have several converts in Athens, including Dionysius, one of the members of the Council of the Areopagus (Acts 17:34).

Whether or not Paul was disappointed over the reception of his message in Athens may be open to question. Many commentators have felt that he was. Finegan[42] and Broneer[43] have concluded that he learned from his Athenian experience that it was foolishness to try to meet the wisdom of the

402. Altar to an Unknown God

world with the wisdom of men. Rather he should meet it with the power of God. In support they note such verses as I Corinthians 1:1-3, 19, 21, 25, 27. The point is that in Corinth, Paul's tactics changed completely; and he never again sought to impress his hearers with human learning. Perhaps a word of warning should be injected here. Even if Paul did change his whole way of approach at Corinth, this is no indication that thereafter he put a premium on ignorance or believed that ministers of the Christian gospel should be intellectually unprepared for their tasks. He always benefited from his own superior education in the performance of his ministry, and his success was due in part to his education—both Hebrew and Hellenic.

At any rate, Paul determined to move from the intellectual center of Greece to Corinth, her commercial center. He probably walked the sixty-mile distance because by this time he was quite low on funds. And by the time he reached Corinth, his resources were so exhausted that he went back to tent-making. When Silas and Timothy arrived at Corinth from Macedonia, however, presumably with an offering from Philippi (or Thessalonica or Berea or all three), Paul was able once more to "hold to the Word" (preferred reading for

[41]Finegan, pp. 356-57.
[42]*Ibid.*, p. 358.
[43]Broneer, p. 28.

"pressed in the spirit" of Acts 18:5). He then was able to give up secular employment and to concentrate on preaching the gospel.

As the apostle left Athens, he probably took the Street of the Panathenaea which led diagonally across the Agora toward the Dipylon Gate. As he neared the north end of the Agora, he may have paused by the Altar of the Twelve Gods, beyond which rose the colossal statue of Zeus, to pray for the conversion of this pagan center. Possibly Dionysius was at the office of the Areopagus in the Royal Stoa across the street, and there was a chance for a last farewell. As he reached the Dipylon Gate, he almost certainly took the Sacred Way that led to Eleusis, fourteen miles away. If he was disturbed by the extent to which Athens was given to idolatry, he was now in for another shock; for this road was bordered by altars, chapels, and tombs.

In about three miles Paul crossed the bridge over the first branch of the Cephisus River. A couple of blocks down the road on his right stood a temple of Demeter, at which pilgrimages to Eleusis stopped. About a half mile farther another bridge crossed the second branch of the Cephisus. After about two more miles the road began to ascend the slope of Mount Aegaleos. Much of the way the road was about fifteen feet wide and was paved. Now it is sometimes as narrow as eight feet and is cut in rock. At a point about six miles from Athens the Sacred Way reached its greatest altitude, about 625 feet. Here the apostle may have turned around for a last and most impressive glance at the "violet-crowned city." On the height above him (1,535 feet) Xerxes had sat watching the defeat of his fleet by the Greeks in the Battle of Salamis in 480 B.C. Before the apostle lay the Bay of Eleusis a little over a mile away. At the bay the road turns north. In a plain bordering the sea, it passes two sacred lakes and finally reaches Eleusis. Having now walked fourteen miles,

Paul probably decided to spend the night at Eleusis.

Eleusis. Before Paul went to bed, he might have tried to find out something about the famous Eleusinian Mysteries, the most famous of the Greek Mysteries. Since he was not an initiate, he would have had a difficult time learning anything. He would have found the sanctuary on the east slope of the Acropolis. It was surrounded by a wall about twenty-five feet high, over which one could see only the roofs of buildings. A temple of Artemis stood outside the entrance. Paul could not have seen that there was a double wall on the entrance side between which was a long inner courtyard.

The entrance through the second wall into the inner enclosure was an elaborate monumental gateway donated by a friend of Cicero, Appius Claudius Pulcher, about 50 B.C. If Paul could have passed through this monumental gate and ascended the Sacred Way, paved with white marble, he would have seen two caves on his right. Before the larger stood a sanctuary of Pluto. The cave represented the entrance into Hades. Farther on he would have passed a megaron-type temple of Demeter. And finally the Sacred Way led to the northeast entrance of the Telesterion (sanctuary or initiation room) of the Mysteries. This was a large covered building 168 by 177 feet backed against the rock. There were two doors on each of the three free sides. The timber roof was carried by six rows of six columns each at a height of twenty feet. These must have greatly impeded the vision of spectators who sat on banks of stone seats around the four sides.

As he stood there on the outside of the wall, Paul could not know that the gospel would not be immediately successful in bringing down this fortress. It was to have a brilliant period of prosperity under Hadrian and Antoninus Pius in the second century. Alaric the Visigoth sacked it in

A.D. 395. And finally Theodosius II (401-50) banned the Mysteries.

If the apostle could not have found out much about the sanctuary at Eleusis, he could find out less about the religious practices connected with it. Initiates would not, of course, divulge the secrets of the cult. Paul knew that the Mysteries involved worship of Demeter and her daughter Kore. According to legend, Hades, god of the underworld, had snatched away Kore (Persephone); and in her great sorrow and searching for her daughter, Demeter had come to Eleusis. After having received hospitality, she had revealed her secret rites to the people of the place. Paul also knew that Demeter was a sister of Zeus and goddess of agriculture.

While in Athens he had learned that on the thirteenth of Boedromion (parts of our September and October) some of the socially elite young men marched out to Eleusis and returned to Athens the next day with some religious objects. On the fifteenth there was a gathering of the catechumens to hear an address by the current cult leader. On the following day the candidates for initiation went to the seashore for ceremonial purification rites and returned to offer sacrifices to the goddess. On the seventeenth of Boedromion there was a great sacrifice with prayers for Athens and the cities of the other delegates participating. The next day was a day of rest for most, and there was opportunity for latecomers to be prepared for initiation.

On the nineteenth of Boedromion a great religious procession started along the sacred way bearing the "fair young god" Iacchus, probably the youthful Dionysus. Arriving at Eleusis, they held a midnight celebration under the stars. The twentieth of the month was spent in resting, fasting, purification, and sacrifice. As to what went on inside of the sanctuary, Paul could not have found out. The whole ceremony lasted for nine days.

From various bits of information, it now appears that initiation included a kind of passion play, probably centering about the sufferings of the goddess. Then there seems to have been a revelation of sacred cult objects and, among other things, the celebration of a sort of holy communion involving a barley drink and certain foods. In this initiation service (little is known of the details) the initiate supposedly established mystic contact with the mother and daughter. And by an act of faith he regarded himself certain of blessing at the hands of Demeter and Kore in the next life because he had established friendship with the pair in this life. Both the sacred pageant and the viewing of sacred objects presumably took place in the Telesterion.[44]

Megara. The next day Paul started out for Corinth once more. The road followed the coast of the Saronic Gulf. For several miles hills crowded close to the shore and then receded to make room for the Megaran Plain. About fifteen miles from Eleusis the apostle came upon the ancient town of Megara, perched atop two hills and occupying their slopes as well. The eastern hill is a little under 900 feet in height; the western hill is about 950 feet. Enjoying an illustrious history, Megara retained only a shadow of its former greatness in Paul's day.

With ports on both the Saronic and Corinthian gulfs, the city-state had become an important commercial center as early as the eighth century B.C. Along with its commerce on the Black Sea and in Sicily, Megara had established colonies in those areas. It had also controlled Salamis, which it lost to Athens about 570 B.C. Megara's commerce was ruined during the Peloponnesian War, and it suffered severely during the civil war of 48 B.C. However, it was still a place of some importance during the

[44]Both the ritual and the structures at Eleusis are discussed authoritatively and thoroughly by George E. Mylonas, *Eleusis and the Eleusinian Mysteries* (Princeton: Princeton University Press, 1961).

first century A.D. The apostle probably spent the night there.

The Isthmian journey. West of Megara the road hugged tightly the shore of the Saronic Gulf as it skirted the Geraneia Ridge (c. 4,450 feet high). About six miles from Megara the apostle passed under the dangerous precipices of the famous Scironian rocks. Here travelers had to pick their way on a track along the face of the cliff for six miles at a height of 600 to 700 feet. At points the road was perilously poised on the edge of a cliff. Later Hadrian provided a safer road. Gliding along in comfort in a car or bus on the highway between Athens and Corinth, today's tourist little suspects the difficulties of travel experienced by the ancients in this area. After walking for about sixteen miles, Paul came to the town of Crommyon, an ancient possession of Corinth. Perhaps he spent the night there. It was impossible to travel the additional fifteen to twenty miles that day in order to reach Corinth.

The next day the apostle began the last part of his journey to the great commercial emporium of Greece and one of the greatest of the eastern Mediterranean. No doubt excitement rose as he neared his chosen center of ministry. Would there be ready reception for his ministry there? If so, would there be great public opposition stirred up by Jews or others as had been the case at so many other places? He would soon know.

About seven miles from Corinth Paul came to the narrowest point of the Isthmus; a section that is about four miles wide. Here, just southwest of the present Corinth Canal, a tramway was built upon which small ships could be transported between the Saronic and Corinthian gulfs. Larger ships frequently unloaded their cargoes at one of Corinth's ports and arranged for them to be picked up by another freighter

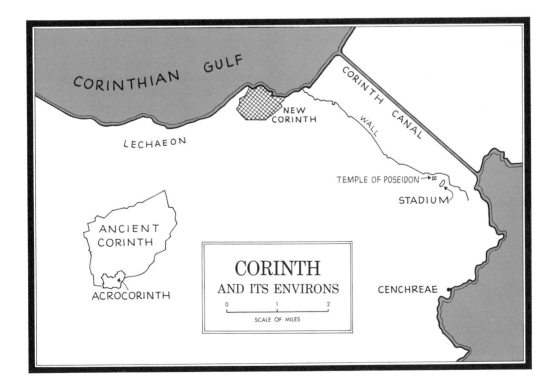

CORINTH
AND ITS ENVIRONS

403. Corinth Canal

at the other port. The geographical situation is this. The voyage around the southern tip of the Peloponnesus was dangerous and some 200 miles farther than it would have been for a ship crossing the isthmus. So in early times Corinth had developed the tramway across the isthmus, between the port of Cenchraea on the Saronic Gulf and the port of Lechaeon on the Corinthian Gulf. It was her geographical position that gave Corinth her reason for existence.

Long before Paul's day thought had been given to cutting a canal through the isthmus. It is reported that as far back as the days of Periander of Corinth (c. 600 B.C.) the question of the feasibility of a Corinthian canal had been raised. Among the Romans, Julius Caesar considered it. Caligula sent an engineer to work on the project. A few years after Paul arrived, Nero actually began the excavation. But it was not until 1893 that the canal was actually completed. Its four-mile bed is 75 feet wide and the water 26 feet deep. The cut is 260 feet deep at the highest rise of the terrain of the isthmus.

As Paul crossed over the ship tramway, there loomed before him a wall. This he learned was the Isthmian Wall. Originally constructed in 480 B.C. to repel the Persians, it had subsequently been rebuilt to meet other threats. But now that the Romans

had established the Pax Romana, it had fallen into disrepair. Paul noticed that the wall had towers about every 300 feet and that it rose to a height of about 25 feet in places.

Passing through the gate in the wall, the apostle probably noticed a considerable amount of activity to his right. He was likely told that some repairs were being made on the stadium where the Isthmian Games were held in honor of Poseidon. Paul no doubt thought that if he were still there when the games started,[45] this would be a good place to meet people from all over the Mediterranean world to present the Christian message to them.

Walking southwest, Paul passed stone quarries on his right. After a couple of miles he passed through the great necropolis of ancient Corinth. Soon the highway joined the Cenchraea-Corinth road. Another stone quarry was at the junction. Paul turned right and after about two miles found himself passing through the Cenchraea gate into the city.

Corinth. Although the city to which Paul came had been built on a new foundation, the history of Corinth was very ancient indeed. The earliest settlers came in the fifth or sixth millennium B.C., attracted perhaps by the abundance of springwater, nearness to the sea, the easily defensible site, and the fertility of the Corinthian plain. About 3000 B.C. an influx of migrants brought with them the knowledge of the use of metals and introduced the Bronze Age. Shortly after 2000 B.C. an invasion of Indo-European peoples laid the site in ruins; and it remained thus for most of the second millennium, although settlements existed elsewhere in Corinthia. Perhaps there was more occupation of the area of Corinth during this millennium than is known. At present only about 1 percent of

[45]Oscar Broneer, "The Apostle Paul and the Isthmian Games," *The Biblical Archaeologist*, XXV (Feb., 1962), 20. Broneer believes that Paul was there during one of these athletic festivals.

the site has been excavated.[46] The Homeric poems allude to Corinth as a dependency of Mycenae at the time of the Trojan War. If this is an accurate historical reference and not merely a reflection of the times of the writer, there must have been a fair-sized town there in the latter part of the second millennium.

Corinth of the classical period was really established with the Dorian invasion. About 1000 B.C. these Greek people settled at the foot of Acrocorinth. Occupying a place of safety, they also controlled the main overland trade route between the Peloponnesus and central Greece, as well as the Isthmian route. The city early came to a height of prosperity. This is demonstrated by the fact that in the eighth century she colonized Syracuse on Sicily and the Island of Corcyra along the eastern shore of the Adriatic Sea. Under the tyrants Cypselus (655-625 B.C.) and Periander (625-585 B.C.) the town achieved a new peak of prosperity as great energy was expended on commercial and industrial development. Corinthian pottery and bronzes were exported widely over the Mediterranean. About the middle of the fifth century the city's fortunes declined as a result of effective competition of Athenian industrial production. During the days of her independence, Corinth controlled about 248 square miles of territory in the northern part of the Peloponnesus, approximately one-fourth the size of Attica.[47]

During the Persian Wars Corinth served as Greek headquarters. Contingents of her army fought at Thermopylae and Plataea; her navy participated in the Battle of Salamis. In 459 B.C. Corinth made war on Athens and was worsted. The subsequent defection of the Corinthian colony, Corcyra, and its alliance with Athens led Corinth to instigate the Peloponnesian War against Athens (431-404). Later Corinth rebelled

against the domineering attitude of Sparta and made common cause with Athens, Argos, and Thebes in the Corinthian War (395-387).

Although the city lost her independence with the rise of Macedon, she was the most populous and most prosperous city of mainland Greece during the period 350-250 B.C. Thereafter, as the chief member of the Achaean League, she clashed with Rome. Finally Rome destroyed Corinth in 146 B.C., killed the adult male population, and sent the women and children into slavery. It is generally believed that the city was virtually uninhabited for a century, but there are indications (and excavations may give supporting evidence) that there was at least a small settlement there.

At any rate, Julius Caesar refounded the city in 44 B.C., largely with freedmen, perhaps many of them descended from slaves taken at the second century destruction. The growth of Corinth was rapid, and possibly by the time of Paul—certainly there-

404. The Acropolis of Corinth

[46]Rhys Carpenter, *Ancient Corinth*, rev. by Robert L. Scranton (6th ed.; Athens: American School of Classical Studies, 1960), p. 11.
[47]J. G. O'Neill, *Ancient Corinth: Part I* (Baltimore: The Johns Hopkins Press, 1930), p. 2.

after—it became the largest and most flourishing center in southern Greece. In addition to its commercial achievements, it was the capital of the Roman province of Achaea. The writer has seen population estimates for Corinth at its peak which range from 100,000 all the way to 700,000. Certainly the higher figure is much too large, but it is really impossible to determine the exact figure with any degree of accuracy.

As to its later history, Corinth was burned by Alaric the Goth in A.D. 395. When rebuilt it turned away from its classical, pagan culture toward Christian ways. Destroyed by an earthquake in 521, the city was rebuilt and enjoyed considerable prosperity under Justinian. Its final period of prosperity was brought to an end by a Norman sacking in 1147. It has suffered various catastrophes since. After the earthquake of 1858 obliterated the old town, the inhabitants moved to a new site on the Corinthian Gulf—a tremendous boon to the excavators. As late as 1930 this new town was largely destroyed by earthquake.

It now remains to ask what sort of place

ASKLEPION

THEATER

LACHAEON ROAD

ODEION

TEMPLE OF APOLLO

THE AGORA

ACROCORINTH

CORINTH

Corinth was when Paul arrived and what sort of a ministry he had in it. As to the city's physical situation, it has already been noted that Corinth controlled the trade routes between the Peloponnesus and central Greece and across the Isthmus of Corinth. In this connection, she had built a tramway across the Isthmus and was served by ports on the Saronic and Corinthian gulfs. She administered the Isthmian Games, thereby serving as a religious, athletic, and cohesive center in Hellas. The city itself lay about a mile and one-half south of the Corinthian Gulf on the north side of its acropolis at an altitude of about 400 feet. The Acropolis towered about 1,500 feet over the city to an altitude of 1,886 feet. From its peak on a clear day the Acropolis at Athens can be plainly seen.

The city and its acropolis were enclosed by a wall over six miles in circumference. A number of large towers were spaced along this wall. In the north central part of town, about equidistant from the east and west walls (about a mile from each) was the Agora, nerve center of the metropolis. Outside the walls in the surrounding plain stretched grain fields, olive groves, vineyards, and other agricultural holdings of the city.

As to the nonphysical aspects of Corinth, several generalizations need to be made. It was a new city—less than 100 years old when Paul visited it. This means that a social structure with an aristocracy possessing illustrious genealogies had not had time to develop. Probably the social and economic structure was more fluid than at most other centers in Greece. Many of those possessing wealth were the *nouveaux riches*, with all of the attendant inadequacies of that class. Since Corinth had not had time to develop a native culture, the culture it had was imitative and, as a result of the overweening economic interests of the community, was only a shallow veneer.

Much of the population was mobile (sailors, businessmen, government officials,

405. The Lechaeon Road at the Agora of Corinth

et al.) and was therefore cut off from the inhibitions of a settled society. To make matters worse, religious prostitution was commonly practiced in connection with the temples of the city. For instance, 1,000 priestesses of the Temple of Aphrodite on the Acropolis were employed in religious prostitution.[48] From the social mobility and the evils of religious practices there arose a general corruption of society. "Corinthian morals" became a byword even in the pagan Roman world. It is no wonder that Paul had so much to say about the sacredness of the body in his first Corinthian letter. And if he wrote the epistle to the Romans from Corinth (as is commonly believed), he had plenty of reason for condemning the unmentionable practices alluded to in Romans 1. The conditions which Paul and the Christian gospel faced in Corinth should give pause to the modern preacher who laments the moral corruption of his own day and feels that his task is almost impossible in such a context. Conditions in Corinth were far worse. The message and power of the gospel are the same in the twentieth century as they were in the first.

As was customary in Paul's ministry, he went first to the Jews of Corinth, reasoning "in the synagogue every sabbath" (Acts 18:4). It is now thought that this syna-

[48]Broneer, "Corinth, Center of St. Paul's Missionary Work in Greece," *The Biblical Archaeologist*, XIV (Dec., 1951), 87.

406. The Bema of Corinth

gogue was located east of the Lechaeon Road and just north of the Agora. In 1898 a large block of stone bearing the words "Synagogue of the Hebrews" was found on the Lechaeon Road near the foot of the marble steps leading to the marketplace. This has been identified as the lintel of a synagogue. Finegan believes that it may date to the time of Paul; and he feels that since the residential district was here, the house of Titus Justus could have been "next door" (Acts 18:7).[49] To the present no existing foundation has been convincingly associated with the lintel. Others, including Oscar Broneer[50] and William A. McDonald,[51] hold that the lintel may date as much as three or four centuries after Paul's visit. Even if the lintel is dated to a later century, there is nothing to prevent a later synagogue from standing on the same site as the one of Paul's day.

The Jews of Corinth took exception to the Christian message, as they had in such places as Lystra and Thessalonica, and stirred up some sort of mob action against Paul. They brought him before Gallio with insinuations that he had broken the law (Acts 18:12-13). Gallio is called the "deputy [anthupatou, proconsul] of Achaia"

[49]Finegan, pp. 361-62.
[50]Broneer, "Corinth," p. 88.
[51]William A. McDonald, "Archaeology and St. Paul's Journeys in Greek Lands, Part III—Corinth," The Biblical Archaeologist, V (Sept., 1942), 41.

quite accurately by Luke the historian. As the governor of a senatorial province, Gallio would correctly have been called "proconsul." The Roman Gallio (like Festus later on in Jerusalem) had no interest in judging questions of Jewish law and dismissed the case brought against Paul (Acts 18:14-17; cf. Acts 25:10-27). It is interesting to note that this Gallio was the elder brother of the philosopher Seneca.[52]

The time of Gallio's rule, and thus of Paul's ministry in Corinth, is fairly well fixed by an inscription discovered at Delphi a few miles to the north of Corinth. This inscription mentions correspondence between the Emperor Claudius and Gallio, proconsul of Achaea, and may confidently be dated to the first half of the year A.D. 52. More than likely Gallio took office about the middle of 51. It may be inferred from the Greek of Acts 18:12 that he heard Paul's case shortly after taking office. Also the apostle had been there eighteen months at the time (Acts 18:11). It may therefore be concluded that Paul arrived in Corinth early in A.D. 50.[53] This inscription is the most important single contribution to establishing the Pauline chronology.

The place where Paul was arraigned before Gallio was quite certainly the bema or rostra in the great Agora. This center of Corinthian life was almost 700 feet east and west and about 300 feet north and south. Following the natural configuration of the land, the southern section was about thirteen feet higher than the northern part. At the dividing line of the two levels was a row of low buildings flanking the rostra, which served as a speaker's stand for public addresses and a judgment seat for magistrates.

Originally covered with ornately carved marble, the bema is now in a poorly preserved condition. Officials reached the bema from the south, where the ground was

[52]Finegan, p. 362.
[53]Ibid., pp. 362-63. See also Jack Finegan, Handbook of Biblical Chronology (Princeton, N.J.: Princeton University Press, 1964), pp. 316-22.

nearly level with the floor of the monument. Those who appeared to present their cases or to be judged stood on the lower northern level. While they waited their turn, they might sit on marble benches in waiting rooms on either side of the bema on the lower level.

As Paul waited for his case to be heard, he sat and looked around at the great marble-paved Agora. Towering above the Agora on the northwest, on a rocky terrace of its own, was the Temple of Apollo. Built during the sixth century B.C., it was not destroyed by the Romans in the terror of 146 B.C. The temple measured 174 feet long by 69 feet wide, and the 38 columns of its peristyle stood almost 24 feet in height. These fluted Doric columns were more impressive than many in Greece because they were made of single blocks of stone instead of being built up with drums of stone.

Lowering his gaze, the apostle let his eye run along the northwest shops westward. At the end of those shops stood a monumental gateway straddling the road which ran northwest to Sicyon. On the west side of the Agora he saw another row of shops. (The Roman temples whose ruins the modern visitor may see in front of these shops were built later.) To the east of the northwest shops stood a two-story arcade, which was joined on the east by a beautiful monumental gateway leading to the Lechaeon Road, a limestone-paved thoroughfare forty feet wide and closed to wheeled traffic. East of the Lechaeon Road was the Peirene Fountain, an important source of water for the city. It supplied as much as 3,000 gallons per hour, and its adjacent reservoirs held 100,000 to 120,000 gallons.[54] Along the east side of the Agora lay a large basilica of the Augustan period. Corinthian columns surrounded a large interior court and supported a raised clerestory. The side aisles were covered with shed roofs.

Out of sight to the south Paul could hear the hammering of stonecutters. This sound

[54]Carpenter, p. 28.

came from the great south stoa which stretched across almost the entire south side of the Agora. About 500 feet long, it was probably the largest secular structure in Greece proper.[55] When it was originally built in the fourth century B.C., it consisted of a double colonnade facing thirty-three small shops. All of these except two had a well in them, connected with a water channel which in turn was connected to the Peirene Fountain. These were apparently wine shops, each with its private cooler. Other perishables were sold there as well. When the Romans rebuilt the city, they restored the stoa but during the first half of the first century A.D. proceeded to convert many of the shops to other uses. Thus the hammering Paul heard came from these projects. About two-thirds of them were converted by the end of Nero's reign. Taking their place were the office of the director of the Isthmian Games, the office of the governor, and the city council chamber. From the middle of the stoa, the road led away eastward to Cenchreae.

Most of the shops for the sale of meat and other foodstuffs remained in the south stoa in Paul's day. In one of them an inscription "Lucius the butcher" was found. Since it was customary for Greeks and Romans to group shops selling a certain type of goods, the Corinthian meat market of Paul's day may have been located here.[56] Also, an in-

407. The Temple of Apollo, Corinth

[55]Ibid., p. 51.
[56]McDonald, p. 44.

scription found in one of these calls the shop a *macellum*, the Latin equivalent of the Greek *makellon*, used in I Corinthians 10:25 and translated "shambles" in the King James Version.[57] Perhaps what Paul was trying to tell his readers, then, was to ask no questions about meats sold in these shops on the south side of the Agora. The Corinthian believers were not to be held responsible if meats offered to idols had been sold by the temples to legitimate businessmen there.

Another interesting inscription with a possible bearing on the New Testament turned up in the excavations at Corinth. It concerns Erastus, an aedile (a Roman municipal official) of the city who laid a pavement at his own expense. Paul in writing to the Romans from Corinth sent greetings from a "chamberlain" (Greek, *oikonomos*) or steward by this name (Rom. 16:23). Erastus is also referred to in II Timothy 4:20 and Acts 19:22. A Roman aedile and a Greek *oikonomos* would both have been commissioners of streets and public buildings. Perhaps the Erastus of this inscription may be equated with the person of the same name mentioned in the New Testament.[58]

This inscription was found in a pavement near the theater of Corinth which was built

408. The Peirene Fountain

[57]Finegan, p. 361.
[58]McDonald, p. 46; Carpenter, p. 74.

in the fifth century B.C. and rebuilt by the Romans. The theater held some 18,000 during the Greek period. Its capacity in Paul's day was no doubt greater, but it is impossible to give an accurate estimate. Another important structure that Paul might have seen was the Asclepion, the nearest ancient equivalent for a general hospital, with the accompanying Fountain of Lerna, just inside the northern city wall. This was an ideal location for a healing establishment, situated as it was on the edge of the plateau where it could benefit from the sea breezes and its proximity to fresh water.

When Paul had come across the isthmus to Corinth, he had passed the location of the Isthmian Games. The following year, in April and May of A.D. 51, while he was still in Corinth, the biennial games would have been held.[59] Paul probably saw these and in his first epistle to the Corinthians he was probably alluding to this important event in the life of the people (I Cor. 9:24-27). Perhaps the opportunity of preaching to the large crowds gathering for the event led Paul to go to Corinth in the first place.

The origin of the Isthmian Games is lost in antiquity. But it is known that they were administered by Corinth until the city was destroyed in 146 B.C. Thereafter they were administered by Sicyon until the refounding of Corinth. The competitors came chiefly from Corinth, Aegina, Thebes, Athens, and some of the islands of the Aegean. The festival lasted several days. Beginning with a sacrifice to Poseidon, it included athletic, equestrian, and musical competitions, and perhaps also a regatta. There were separate competitions for men, youths, and boys.

The athletic events included footraces of 200 and 800 yards, races in armor, throwing the discus and javelin, two-horse chariot racing, the Pentathlon (running, jumping, discus and javelin throwing, and wres-

[59]Broneer, "The Apostle Paul and the Isthmian Games," p. 20.

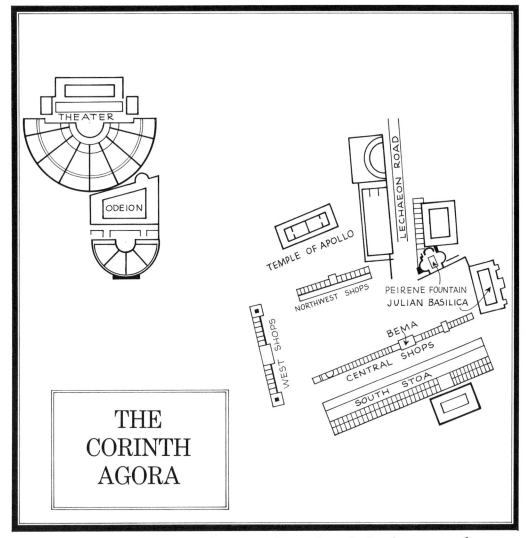

THEATER

ODEION

LECHAEON ROAD

TEMPLE OF APOLLO

NORTHWEST SHOPS

PEIRENE FOUNTAIN
JULIAN BASILICA

WEST SHOPS

BEMA

CENTRAL SHOPS

SOUTH STOA

THE
CORINTH
AGORA

tling), and the Pankration (a combination of boxing and wrestling).[60] Ministers who paint glowing pictures of the Isthmian Games in their sermons on Paul or I Corinthians often do not realize how corrupt and degraded Greek athletics were during Paul's lifetime, and they were nowhere more degraded than at the Isthmia.[61] Pro-

fessionalism had taken over; there was plenty of quackery in training and dieting. ". . . the gymnasia, instead of producing healthy, useful citizens, had become schools of idleness and immorality; from a physical and military point of view the whole nation had degenerated."[62] The victor's crown seems to have been withered wild celery during the first century A.D.,[63] a corruptible crown indeed (I Cor. 9:25). Judging from the available accounts of what went on at the Isthmian Games, one gets the impres-

[60]It is not claimed that this list is complete. It is very difficult to determine exactly what events occurred during the first century A.D., when the great athletic festivals of Greece were in a state of decline.
[61]E. Norman Gardiner, *Greek Athletic Sports and Festivals* (London: Macmillan and Co., Limited, 1910), p. 218.

[62]*Ibid.*, p. 164.
[63]Broneer, "The Apostle Paul and the Isthmian Games," p. 17.

409. The South Stoa, Corinth

sion they were more like "old home week" than a serious religious and athletic event. Philosophers parried intellectual blows; their students wrangled. Magicians showed off their stunts. Fortune-tellers preyed on a gullible and superstitious public. Hucksters hawked their wares among the assembled throngs.

The area given over to the Isthmian games was about six miles from Corinth, just south of the east end of the Corinth Canal. In recent years the area has been quite thoroughly investigated and largely excavated. The three main structures at the site are the Temple of Poseidon, the stadium, and the theater. The temple was surrounded by an irregular wall flanked by towers at intervals of about thirty-three feet. Originally constructed in the seventh century, the temple was ravaged by fire and was rebuilt about 470 B.C. Heavily damaged by fire in 390 B.C., it was restored and stood until the mid-sixth century A.D. Inside were colossal statues of Poseidon, lord of the sea, and the goddess Amphitrite, joint ruler of the sea. Near the temple was an impressive altar to Poseidon.

The stadium was located to the southeast of the sanctuary. This great structure, 650 feet long, was seated with marble. From the temple to the stadium stretched an avenue lined with pine trees and statues of victorious athletes. About fifty yards northeast

of the sanctuary of Poseidon was the theater, which was built in the fifth or fourth century B.C. There Flamininus in 196 B.C. declared the freedom of the Greeks. In A.D. 66 Nero staged a repeat performance when on his famous concert tour of Greece. And there many other musical and dramatic events were conducted.

Very likely the Isthmian Games occurred prior to Paul's arraignment before Gallio. And after his acquittal he remained in Corinth "yet a good while" (Acts 18:18). It is not known how long a time is implied, but he may have stayed in Corinth as late as the beginning of A.D. 52, or possibly he left before the sailing season closed in the late fall of 51. Whatever the exact time of his departure, he set out on the road from the southern end of the Agora to Cenchreae (Acts 18:18), taking Aquila and Priscilla with him, and embarked for Antioch. On the way he stopped briefly in Ephesus, where he left his traveling companions and hastened on to Antioch with the fervent hope of reaching Jerusalem in time for the Passover (Acts 18:21).

Two or three years later, while Paul was ministering in Ephesus (I Cor. 16:8-9), he wrote two epistles to Corinth. The first was apparently occasioned by the coming of Stephanus, Fortunatus, and Achaicus (I Cor. 16:17) from the Corinthian church with a letter asking counsel from the apostle. Much of the epistle seems to have been an answer to that letter (7:25; 8:1; 12:1; 16:1; 16:12). The apostle also received information on problems in the Corinthian church from Apollos (16:12) and the household of Chloe (1:11).

In I Corinthians, Paul dealt with five issues—all involved in the problem of relating Christianity to Corinthian culture. First, he rebuked the spirit of factionalism, which arose because some of them were impressed with Apollos' rhetorical ability; others followed the strictly Jewish way; a third group claimed to be followers of Paul; yet others said they were merely followers of Christ

(I Cor. 1:12). Second, Paul dealt with problems of sexual morality; third, with the question of eating food offered to idols; fourth, with disorders in public worship; and last, with the doctrine of resurrection from the dead, which a Greco-Roman community had very great difficulty accepting. While the first letter seems to have made some impact, it did not end the factional strife in Corinth. This was one of the main themes of II Corinthians.

* * *

Although Christianity had its troubles in first century Greece and was to be perse-cuted sporadically there until the early fourth century A.D., it ultimately became the official religion of the area. The many Byzantine churches with their famous old mosaics still to be seen in the country are a testimony to the extent of the official support given to Christianity during later centuries. In spite of the long Muslim occupation of Greece, Islam never won the people there as it did in North Africa and the Near East. With the establishment of the modern state of Greece, the Orthodox church has once more assumed the position of guardian over the spiritual affairs of the people.

Bibliography

ANDERSON, WILLIAM J., and SPIERS, R. PHENE. *The Architecture of Ancient Greece*. Revised by WILLIAM B. DINSMOOR. London: B. T. Batsford, 1927.

BOLKESTEIN, H. *Economic Life in Greece's Golden Age*. Revised and annotated by E. J. JONKERS. Leiden: E. J. Brill, 1958.

BOTSFORD, GEORGE W., and ROBINSON, CHARLES A. *Hellenic History*. 4th ed. New York: Macmillan Co., 1956.

BRONEER, OSCAR. "The Apostle Paul and the Isthmian Games," *Biblical Archaeologist*, XXV (1962), 2-31.

———. "Athens, City of Idol Worship," *Biblical Archaeologist*, XXI (1958), 2-28.

———. "Corinth, Center of St. Paul's Missionary Work in Greece," *Biblical Archaeologist*, XIV (1951), 78-96.

CARPENTER, RHYS. *Ancient Corinth*. Revised by ROBERT L. SCRANTON and others. 6th ed. Athens: American School of Classical Studies at Athens, 1960.

CARY, M. *The Geographic Background of Greek and Roman History*. Oxford: Clarendon Press, 1949.

———. *A History of the Greek World from 323 to 146 B.C.* 2d ed. London: Methuen & Co., Ltd., 1951.

CARY, M., *et al.* (ed.). *The Oxford Classical Dictionary*. Oxford: Clarendon Press, 1949.

CASSON, STANLEY. *Macedonia, Thrace and Illyria*. London: Oxford University Press, 1926.

COUCH, H. N. *Classical Civilization: Greece*. New York: Prentice-Hall, Inc., 1951.

DAVIES, PAUL E. "The Macedonian Scene of Paul's Journeys," *Biblical Archaeologist*, XXVI (1963), 91-106.

DINSMOOR, WILLIAM B. *The Architecture of Ancient Greece*. 3d ed. revised. London: B. T. Batsford Ltd., 1950.

FINEGAN, JACK. *Light from the Ancient Past*. 2d ed. Princeton: Princeton University Press, 1959.

FINLEY, M. I. *The World of Odysseus*. New York: Meridian Books, Inc., 1959.

GARDINER, E. NORMAN. *Greek Athletic Sports and Festivals*. London: Macmillan and Co., Limited, 1910.

GORDON, CYRUS. "Minoica," *Journal of Near Eastern Studies*, XXI (1962), 207-10.

GRAHAM, JAMES WALTER. *The Palaces of Crete*. Princeton: Princeton University Press, 1962.

GRAINDOR, PAUL. *Athènes De Tibère A Trajan*. Cairo: Imprimerie Misr, Société Anonyme Egyptienne, 1931.

GUTHRIE, W. K. C. *The Religion and Mythology of the Greeks*. Cambridge: University Press, 1961.

HAMMOND, N. G. L. *A History of Greece to 322 B.C.* Oxford: Clarendon Press, 1959.

HAYES, DOREMUS A. *Greek Culture and the Greek Testament*. New York: Abingdon Press, 1925.

HIGNETT, C. *A History of the Athenian Constitution to the End of the Fifth Century* B.C. Oxford: Clarendon Press, 1952.

HUXLEY, G. L. *Early Sparta*. Cambridge: Harvard University Press, 1962.

JONES, A. H. M. *The Greek City*. Oxford: Clarendon Press, 1940.

JONES, TOM B. *Ancient Civilization*. Chicago: Rand McNally & Co., 1960.

KINSEY, ROBERT S. *With Paul in Greece*. Nashville: Parthenon Press, 1957.

KITTO, H. D. F. *The Greeks*. Harmondsworth, England: Penguin Books, Inc., 1951.

LAISTNER, M. L. W. *A History of the Greek World from 479 to 323 B.C.* 2d ed. London: Methuen & Co., Ltd., 1947.

LANG, MABEL, and ELIOT, C. W. J. *The Athenian Agora*. Athens: American School of Classical Studies, 1954.

LARSEN, J. A. O. "Roman Greece," *An Economic Survey of Ancient Rome*. Edited by TENNEY FRANK. Vol. IV. Baltimore: Johns Hopkins Press, 1938.

LAWRENCE, A. W. *Greek Architecture*. Harmondsworth, England: Penguin Books, Inc., 1957.

MCDONALD, WILLIAM A. "Archaeology and St. Paul's Journeys in Greek Lands," *Biblical Archaeologist*, III (1940), 18-24.

———. "Archaeology and St. Paul's Journeys in Greek Lands, Part II: Athens," *Biblical Archaeologist*, IV (1941), 1-10.

———. "Archaeology and St. Paul's Journeys in Greek Lands, Part III: Corinth," *Biblical Archaeologist*, V (1942), 36-48.

MACKENDRICK, PAUL. *The Greek Stones Speak*. New York: St. Martin's Press, 1962.

METZGER, HENRI. *St. Paul's Journeys in the Greek Orient*. New York: Philosophical Library, 1955.

MOMMSEN, THEODOR. *The Provinces of the Roman Empire from Caesar to Diocletian*. Translated by WILLIAM P. DICKSON. Vol. I. New York: Charles Scribner's Sons, 1906.

MYLONAS, GEORGE E. *Eleusis and the Eleusinian Mysteries*. Princeton: Princeton University Press, 1961.

———. *Ancient Mycenae*. Princeton: Princeton University Press, 1957.

MYRES, JOHN L. *Geographical History in Greek Lands*. Oxford: Clarendon Press, 1953.

O'NEILL, J. G. *Ancient Corinth: Part I*. Baltimore: Johns Hopkins Press, 1930.

OOST, STEWART I. *Roman Policy in Epirus and Acarnania in the Age of the Roman Conquest of Greece*. Dallas: SMU Press, 1954.

RAMSAY, WILLIAM M. *St. Paul the Traveller and the Roman Citizen*. 8th ed. London: Hodder and Stoughton, 1905.

ROBERTSON, D. S. *A Handbook of Greek and Roman Architecture*. Cambridge: University Press, 1929.

ROEBUCK, CARL. *The World of Ancient Times*. New York: Charles Scribner's Sons, 1966.

SCRAMUZZA, VINCENT M., and MACKENDRICK, PAUL L. *The Ancient World*. New York: Henry Holt & Co., 1958.

SHERWIN-WHITE, A. N. *Roman Society and Law in the New Testament*. Oxford: Clarendon Press, 1963.

SMITH, WILLIAM (ed.). *A Dictionary of Greek and Roman Geography*. 2 vols. London: John Murray, 1873.

STARR, CHESTER G. *A History of the Ancient World*. New York: Oxford University Press, 1965.

———. "The Myth of the Minoan Thalassocracy," *Historia*, 1955, pp. 282-91.

———. *The Origins of Greek Civilization 1100-650 B.C.* New York: Alfred A. Knopf, 1961.

SWAIN, JOSEPH W. *The Ancient World*. Vol. II. New York: Harper & Brothers, 1950.

TARN, W. W. *Alexander the Great*. 2 vols. Cambridge: Cambridge University Press, 1950.

THIESSEN, HENRY CLARENCE. *Introduction to the New Testament*. Grand Rapids: Wm. B. Eerdmans Pub. Co., 1943.

WELLER, CHARLES H. *Athens and Its Monuments*. New York: Macmillan Co., 1913.

WYCHERLEY, R. E. *How the Greeks Built Cities*. 2d ed. London: Macmillan & Co., Ltd., 1962.

410. Augustus Caesar

Italy

WHEN PAUL LANDED at Puteoli (modern Pozzuoli) and traveled north along the Appian Way to Rome, he was headed for the city that had for decades dominated the Mediterranean world. To say, as some carelessly do, that Rome dominated the then-known world during New Testament times is quite erroneous. The Romans knew of many lands beyond their borders in Europe, Africa, and Asia, which they either did not choose to conquer or were not able to subdue. And the Empire did not reach its greatest extent until A.D. 117. The statement in Luke 2:1 that the decree was issued that all the *world* should be taxed (the decree that sent Joseph and Mary to Bethlehem) of course meant the Roman world. The Romans were under no illusion about world control. However, they did sufficiently control the Mediterranean and its environs to call it *mare nostrum* (our sea).

Geography of Italy

Slashing diagonally across the center of the Mediterranean, Italy is strategically located for control of that sea. When she had annexed Sicily, Italy was in a position to dominate the east-west sea-lanes. Not only is it significant that the peninsula is centrally located in the Mediterranean basin, but it was important for the development of the Roman Empire that nature had brought certain forces to bear to constitute that basin as a unified area. The homogeneous character of the basin is manifested in a similar climate, a likeness of geological structure, and a similar distinctive type of vegetation. Moreover, the Mediterranean lands, while sharing a common seafront, are rather clearly separated from their hinterlands by an almost unbroken ring of mountains and deserts. The modern student, influenced by the differing religious and political ideologies in conflict there and the impact of the world power struggle on the area, loses sight of the factors which were so significant in unifying the Mediterranean world in antiquity. Roman arms made the Mediterranean a Roman lake, surrounded on all sides by Roman territory. The sea (some 2,300 miles from east to west), not the lands around it, was the center of the Empire. The sea routes were the arteries through which the trade of the Empire flowed. Mediterranean ports were the chief cities of the Roman world.

While Italy was strategically located for controlling the Mediterranean, Rome was strategically located for controlling the peninsula of Italy. Situated in the center of the peninsula, she could meet her enemies one by one and could prevent them from effectively uniting against her. If such

ITALY

SCALE OF MILES

THE WYCLIFFE HISTORICAL GEOGRAPHY OF BIBLE LANDS

a combination should be formed, she could move against it with the advantage of a central base and short lines of communication. Early in her career of expansion, Rome developed the practice of building military roads to all parts of her domain. Moreover, Rome was located at the lowest point of the Tiber River where firm abutments for a bridge could be found. So Rome controlled the main line of communication along the western and more populous side of the peninsula. As is well known, Rome was built on seven hills.[1] None of these exceeded two hundred feet above sea level, but they rose for the most part in steep slopes above the surrounding valleys and at some points formed sheer cliffs towering over these valleys. The Tiber flowed past and later through the city and was navigable for the fifteen-mile distance between the coast and the capital. Ships docked at the foot of the Aventine Hill. Her days as a leading center of trade did not come until the reign of Claudius, however, when her port of Ostia was developed. Even then, most of the trade consisted of imports.

The area of Italy comprises some 90,000 square miles, a little less than that of Oregon. It divides into two regions: the continental on the north and the peninsular on the south. The northern region is some 320 miles east and west and about 70 north and south; the boot-shaped peninsula stretches some 700 miles toward the continent of Africa and is never more than 125 miles wide. In the toe and the heel of the "boot," the peninsula is only about 25 miles wide.

Mountains. Mountains dominate much of the landscape of Italy. The Alps form an irregular 1,200-mile arc across the north. While they arise rather abruptly on the Italian side and impede expansion, they slope more gently on the European side

[1]Capitoline, Palatine, Aventine, Caelian, Esquiline, Viminal, Quirinal. Eventually it expanded onto other hills, including the Pincio and Janiculum.

411. The Tiber River and Fabrician Bridge

and did not prevent migration into Italy. The Apennines extend the full length of the peninsula in a bow-shaped range about 800 miles long and 25 to 85 miles wide. Since the average height of these mountains is only about 4,000 feet and since the passes through them are not generally difficult, they did not pose the problem to the unification of the country that the mountains of Greece did. The Apennines approach closely to the Adriatic Sea, permitting little more than a coastal road in many places along the eastern coast, while on the west they leave room for arable lands which are carved up into plains by spurs extending from the main Apennine Range. Therefore, Italy faced west. Because she did, the flow of culture from the more highly developed civilizations of the East was slowed in its journey to her shores. Along the west coast of the peninsula, both north and south of the Tiber and on adjacent islands, are extinct volcanoes. Active since ancient times have been Vesuvius, Stromboli, and Etna.

Rivers. Several rivers originate in the mountains of Italy. Longest of these is the Po, which rises in the western Alps and flows eastward for 360 miles to the Adriatic Sea. This alone of the Italian rivers can be classified as navigable. Along the Adriatic, rushing mountain torrents punctuate the rocky coastline. Flowing into the

Tyrrhenian Sea and navigable by small craft are the Volturno, the Liri (Liris), the Tiber, and the Arno rivers. Not only did the rivers of Italy fail to give the desired highway to much of the land but they presented a special health problem. The sill at the Straits of Gibraltar breaks the force of the ocean tides flowing into the Mediterranean; and this lack of brisk tidal movement prevents a daily scouring of the coasts. Consequently, the accumulation of silt at the river mouths creates marshy areas that serve as breeding spots for malarial mosquitoes. Both in ancient and modern times Italy has suffered much from this dread disease.

Harbors. As can be readily seen, the silting up of the river mouths prevented Italian rivers from providing much in the way of harbor facilities. So extensive was this silting that in the days of the Emperor Claudius (A.D. 41-54), it was necessary to make a new cut for the discharge of the Tiber into the sea. Moreover, throughout a coastal length of over 2,000 miles, Italy has few deep bays or good harbors. Almost all of those that do exist are located on the southern and western shores. The chief harbor on the Adriatic was Brundisium, far down on the heel of Italy; to the south was Tarentum (Taranto) on the gulf of that name; on the west was Puteoli (Pozzuoli) on the Bay of Naples. Genoa and Lunae Portus (La Spezia) became important only in late Roman times. Ostia, which assumed importance as the port of Rome during the first century A.D., was a man-made harbor.

Climate. The climate of Italy differs in the northern and southern regions. The Po Valley climate is similar to the continental climate of central Europe, with marked differences between summer and winter temperatures and clearly defined periods of spring and fall. There are frequent winter snows, copious spring and fall rains, and moderate rains in the summer. The climate of peninsular Italy conforms more closely to the Mediterranean type with boisterous rain-washed winters, during which the Apennines lie heavily mantled with snow, and summers of deficient rain. On most of the peninsula the drought extends over three or four months; at Rome· it is of two months' duration. Land and sea breezes temper the heat. In general, the climate of the west and south coasts is subtropical. It is now generally believed that the climate of Italy has not changed since classical times.

Plains. A further word must be said about the plains of Italy. The large, level and fertile Po Valley was the best grainland, but it was never an important source of supply for Rome. Since bulky goods had to be transported by water, Romans found it cheaper to obtain their food supply from a closer source. The distance from the mouth of the Po to Rome is longer than that from Sicily or North Africa and very little shorter than that from Egypt. Etruria is rough and broken by stone and better suited for pasture than for cultivation. Latium and Campania are small; their rich but shallow surface soil was soon exhausted, leaving a volcanic subsoil better for orchards and vineyards than for grain. But Campania was for long the chief granary of peninsular Italy and produced large amounts of fruits and vegetables.

412. Greek and Roman agricultural tools

Resources. Italy's primary source of wealth was always agricultural and pastoral. As some of the grain-producing soil became exhausted, farmers turned more to viniculture and pastoral pursuits. In fact, the name "Italia" was derived from the Oscan word *vitelliu,* meaning "calf-land." There were also notable mineral resources in ancient times, especially the copper and iron beds of Etruria and Elba. The marble quarries of Carrara in Liguria were first exploited in the last days of the Republic. There was limestone for building purposes; the best was travertine from Tibur (Tivoli) near Rome. Large stands of timber still covered the mountainous areas and some of the lowlands in the first centuries of the Christian Era. Italy also had abundant supplies of good clay for pottery, bricks, and tile.

The Peoples of Italy

Exactly when the first men arrived in Italy and where they came from is not known with certainty at present. Nor is it important for this study to be concerned with such questions. In fact, there is no evidence to connect the culture of these early men with what followed. Probably about 5000 B.C. a Neolithic, or New Stone Age, culture was introduced by migrants who apparently came from North Africa. Moving northward, some of them entered northwest Italy via the Straits of Gibraltar, Spain, and France; others moved into Sicily. These people belonged to the Mediterranean branch of the Caucasian race and were characterized by dark complexion, dark hair, narrow head, and medium to short stature. They have remained dominant in Italy to the present, assimilating both the Alpine and Nordic peoples introduced by subsequent migrations.

It seems that these people mastered some of the basic techniques of constructing and sailing small seaworthy vessels and were thereby enabled to move into Sicily, Italy, Sardinia, and Corsica. They also learned how to domesticate pigs, sheep, and cattle; they engaged in agricultural pursuits and settled in rudimentary village communities. As with other Neolithic peoples, their weapons and implements were of polished stone.

Much later than was true of Greece and the Near East, the Bronze Age came to Italy about 2000 B.C. Although it may be that a knowledge of working in copper and bronze (an alloy of copper and tin) first came to southern Italy from Cyprus via the Aegean area, the Bronze Age peoples migrated to the Po Valley from the north. Some of these were known as the Palafitte, who probably came from the vicinity of modern Switzerland. These people (partly Indo-European and partly native stock) received their name from the Italian *palafitta* (meaning "row of stakes or piles") because they built their villages on piles over the north Italian lakes.

Probably about 1500 B.C. another Indo-European people moved into northern Italy, seemingly coming around the northern end of the Adriatic from Greece. Known as Terramare people, they were so designated because of the black earth of their house walls. They developed a fairly high civilization, domesticating a number of animals, cultivating several crops, and producing commodities in bronze, wood, and cloth. Current evidence indicates that neither the Palafitte nor Terramare peoples moved south into the peninsula. The Bronze Age culture in central and southern Italy was an outgrowth of the Neolithic and copper-stone (Chalcolithic) developments there, given impetus by contacts with the eastern shores of the Adriatic and Sicily, where Mycenean Greeks peddled their wares.

About 1000 B.C. another wave of Indo-European people came into Italy, settling in the Po Valley and in the north and central parts of the peninsula, bringing the Iron Age with them. They are called Villanovans because their culture was first found at the site of Villanova, five miles from modern Bologna. In their irregular villages of round huts, these people used swords, spears, and axes of iron; clothing of wool; and helmets, shields, body armor, and utensils of bronze, the working of which was now greatly improved. The Iron Age culture of the southern half of the peninsula probably developed not so much from immigration as from trade contacts with the Aegean and Balkan areas.

Within a few generations the population of Italy had become largely Italic. Various Italic tribes, the Umbrians (north central peninsula), Sabellians or Samnites (south central peninsula), and the Latins (central Italy around Rome), were among the most important. The latter ultimately were to occupy the center of the stage of history. They formed the nucleus of Roman stock; their language developed into classical Latin; and their geographical position and innate abilities enabled them to become masters of the peninsula.

About 800 B.C. three other peoples made their way to Italy: the Carthaginians, the Etruscans, and the Greeks. The Carthaginians were Semites from the Phoenician coastlands. Settling mostly in North Africa, they also moved into Sicily, where they were later to come into conflict with the Romans.

The Etruscans were more directly concerned with Roman or Latin development. Exactly why, when, and how they came are matters of considerable controversy. Probably they came from western Asia Minor by sea in relatively small numbers, beginning about 800 B.C. or perhaps a little earlier. Gradually, by superior military prowess, they conquered the natives and formed the ruling class in a new society characterized by urbanization and an economy based on commerce, superior craftsmanship in metalworking, and agriculture. From about 700 to 400 B.C. they were the most important people in Italy. At the height of their power, they controlled the western coastal region from Campania to Etruria, as well as most of the Po Valley.

The Greeks moved into the peninsula about 775 B.C. or a little later. Establishing themselves at most of the good harbors of southern Italy and eastern Sicily, they influenced the culture of the area greatly. They taught the people to write and made an impact on their pottery making and other crafts. In the third century the Romans came face to face with them, and through them were more fully introduced to the ways of Hellenization, with which they first had become acquainted under Etruscan domination.

Latecomers to Italy were the Celts, or that branch of Celts known as Gauls. During the fifth century they were pushed from their homeland in the upper Danubian region by Germanic peoples farther north. Swarming over the Alps, they defeated the Etruscans and occupied much of the Po Valley. A barbarous people who supported themselves by cattle raising and primitive agriculture, they nevertheless showed considerable skill and artistic ability in metalworking, their chief industry. Something is said later of their place in Roman history.

History of Rome and the Empire

Roman Beginnings

As almost every schoolboy knows, Rome traditionally was founded in 753 B.C. by Romulus. Son of the god Mars and the daughter of a king of Alba Longa in Latium, Romulus established the city on the Palatine Hill. Modern research demonstrates that this, as well as other legends of the origin of the city, is almost devoid of any shred of historical value. Archaeological investigations have shown that a village of primitive settlers existed on the Aventine Hill from very early times, that in the tenth century a colony of Latins established themselves on the twenty-five acre flat-topped Palatine Hill, and that during succeeding generations several other Latin villages were founded on adjacent hills.

The historical legends preserved in the writings of Livy, Vergil, Plutarch, and others present a Rome ruled by seven kings between 773 and 509 B.C., the traditional date of overthrow of the monarchy and establishment of the Republic. The first four kings (Romulus, Numa Pompilius, Tullus Hostilius, and Ancus Marcius) were Latin or Sabine, and the last three (Tarquinius Priscus, Servius Tullius, and Tarquinius Superbus) were Etruscan. These legends seem to contain a degree of truth. It is certain that Rome was ruled by kings in the early days and that the Tarquins ruled during the latter days of the monarchy.

While *Roma Aeterna* was gradually occupying her hills along the Tiber, the Etruscans were expanding their holdings in Italy. Apparently coming by sea, they established a number of city-states along the coast of Etruria by the seventh century B.C. and during the seventh century seized Rome and most of Latium. During the following century they moved into Campania and the Po Valley and were at their height a little before 500 B.C. In addition to their landhold-

413. An Etruscan woman, seventh century B.C.

ings along the whole west coast of Italy and in the Po region, the Etruscans were an effective sea power, ably contesting with the Greeks and Carthaginians for control of the western Mediterranean. Formidable warriors and possessors of superior weapons, the Etruscans also built massive walls and fortifications around their cities. They became the ruling aristocracy in a society which they effectively marshaled.

Although the Etruscans were important to the urbanization of Italy, they were un-

414. A Gorgon's head, Etruscan, seventh century B.C.

able to achieve an effective political unity. A collection of cities and their colonies held together by commercial, religious, and cultural ties, they were politically and militarily incapable of meeting their foes with a united front. After their territory was split by the revolt of Rome and after their navy was severely defeated by the Greeks of Syracuse in 474 B.C., they became increasingly vulnerable to Roman offensives on their southern flank and Celtic pressures in the Po Valley.

The Etruscans took control in Rome about 600 B.C. or shortly thereafter, and they did much for the development of the city. They were responsible for the urbanization of Rome, for the training of an efficient army, for the introduction of many crafts, for promoting economic advancement in general, for the improving of Roman cultural life, and in short, for making Rome the leading state in Latium. Moreover, under the Etruscans, Roman territory expanded from about 60 square miles to some 350, and her population from 10,000 to more than ten times as many.[2] The Etruscans also brought to

[2]Fritz M. Heichelheim and Cedric A. Yeo, *A History of the Roman People* (Englewood Cliffs, N. J.: Prentice-Hall, Inc., 1962), p. 58.

Rome such typically "Roman" items as the purple-embroidered toga, the eagle-headed scepter, and the use of the fasces (bundles of rods enclosing a double-edged ax—see the 1916-1945 American dime) as a symbol of political power. Last, they introduced to Roman religion the worship of the triad of Jupiter, Juno, and Minerva and the practice of divination.

Rome under the monarchy was ruled by a king-council-assembly type of government. The king, who was commander of the army as well as judge and priest, had immense power, especially in the Etruscan period. Neither quite hereditary nor elective, the monarchal candidate was chosen by the senate and approved by the popular assembly. The senate was the king's council. According to tradition, Romulus appointed a senate of 100 to assist him in government. Whenever it began, the Senate certainly consisted of the leaders of Roman society; and the number increased to 300 by the end of the monarchy or the beginning of the Republic. As men of wealth and prestige in the community, the senators exercised considerable influence over the king. But the resolutions they passed were not binding on the monarch; nor did they have the force of law in the state. The king, however, could not afford to flout their wishes consistently. In addition to the power of *consultum*, the senate had, as already indicated, the right to nominate candidates for king.

The popular assembly (*comitia curiata*) was composed of all citizens capable of bearing arms. They voted by *curiae* (a political subdivision), which seemingly consisted of groups of related families organized for religious, political, and military purposes. Supposedly the assembly was the sovereign power in the state, but whatever power it had was largely passive. It met on call of the king, listened to debates held before it, and voted on issues submitted to it. It was present at the king's inauguration, and its members swore an oath of loyalty to him and participated in religious festivals at which the monarch presided. Whatever the political incapacity of the assembly, wise kings were careful not to ignore it, and they used its meetings as a propaganda platform to win support for their policies.

The Republic

Roman tradition concocted a glorious patriotic tale of origins of the Republic. The story recounts the tyranny of Tarquinius Superbus, a violent revolution against the monarchy, and successful expulsion of the king and the Etruscans, against whom the Romans fought with remarkable valor. Almost immediately thereafter a republic was established under the rule of two consuls and a firmly entrenched Latin nobility. All of this is supposed to have occurred in the year 509 or 508 B.C. There is a considerable amount of dispute among scholars as to how much of this story to accept.

It has become traditional to date the fall of the monarchy and Etruscan rule over Rome about 509/508 B.C. and to posit that this change was revolutionary. Moreover, most scholars have put the beginnings of the Republican form of government at about this time. Those who dispute this traditional view feel that the transition from the monarchy to the Republic was evolutionary rather than revolutionary, that the rule of consuls and other elected officials came as a result of trial and error over a number of decades, and that Etruscan power over Rome disintegrated in connection with their general economic and military decline early in the fifth century. However one works out the details, the present state of knowledge seems to require belief that the constitution of the Republic came about through a long and complicated process.

Unification of the Peninsula

Struggle with Etruscans. About 500 B.C. Rome began a struggle with the Etruscans that was to last some two centuries. At about the same time must be dated the beginning of the Republic, during which Rome managed to dominate the entire Italian peninsula, to expand on three continents, and to democratize her constitution to some extent. One must not be misled, however, into thinking that Rome ever really wanted a democracy or that she achieved such a form of government. As has been said, apparently all the Romans were interested in was a "government of law rather than of men."

Early in their struggle with the Etruscans, the Latins of Rome made a league with nearby Latin tribes against the common enemy. This league fell under the domination of Rome. The provisions of this alliance were extremely significant for the future development of Rome and the Emprie. In addition to the expected arrangements concerning equal responsibility for providing troops in wartime and equal privileges in dividing spoil taken, there were important provisions relating to peacetime rights. Citizens of every city in the league had the right to own property, to trade, and to enjoy the rights of the law in every other city of the league. Moreover, rights of intermarriage were guaranteed by the treaty. Therefore, if a Roman married a woman from a nearby Latin town, his children would enjoy full Roman citizenship and could vote in Rome if they moved there. In this way a bond of union was established that would serve as a pattern for the ultimate establishment of an Italian nationalism and imperial citizenship.

During the fifth century, Rome and the Latins were busy securing the borders of Latium against frequent attacks of the Italian tribes (of the Sabellian group). At the end of the century Rome fought a war to the death with Veii, an important Etruscan citadel a dozen miles north of Rome. At Veii's fall, Rome almost doubled her territory. During this war Rome learned that the maintenance of an effective force for siege purposes demanded the payment of troops and the establishment of a professional army. Here were the real beginnings of Roman military power.

Gallic threat. Hardly had Rome beaten the Veientes when sudden disaster swept down on them from the north. The Gauls, having dispossessed the Etruscans in the Po Valley, broke into Etruria and Latium on a massive plundering expedition. Fierce, reckless warriors, the Gauls were able to break the ranks of even the disciplined Roman soldiers. While the remains of the Roman army holed up in the ruined fortifications of Veii, the rest of the population of Rome fled to nearby towns. The Gauls descended like vultures on the unoccupied city, thoroughly plundering it. It was at this time (*c.* 390 B.C.) that the records of early Rome were destroyed, a fact which has led to much uncertainty in the reconstruction of the city's early history. Not interested in the annexation of Roman territory, the Gauls accepted a ransom, collected their souvenirs, and went home. Gaulic raiders again moved into the peninsula subsequently, although they did not come as far south as Rome. A show of Roman might sent them home on the double in 349 B.C., and the Romans concluded a peace treaty with them in 331.

Latin League in rebellion. Meanwhile, Rome was having more serious trouble closer to home. Taking advantage of Rome's weakness, conquered Etruscan and Italic cities revolted. Some of the Latin towns, fearing loss of their independence, broke their alliance with Rome. Rome was eventually successful on every front. First she toppled the resistance of the Italic towns. By 350 B.C. she had soundly defeated the Etruscans. By 340 the whole Latin League

was in arms against Rome and had made an alliance with some of the cities of Campania. During the subsequent Latin War, Rome first succeeded in detaching the Campanian cities from their Latin alliance and secured with them a very favorable peace. Three of them, including the important town of Capua, received the Roman private rights enjoyed by the Latin cities (but not the right of franchise). Then Rome defeated the Latin League and dissolved it. Several of the Latin cities were incorporated into the Roman state with full citizenship rights. The rest were returned to their position as Latin allies. While they retained the rights of trade and intermarriage with Rome, they lost the privilege of exercising those rights with each other.

Roman conquest was not planned. Every time the Romans made a new conquest, their frontiers faced a new enemy. There was no logical stopping place until the Romans controlled the entire peninsula. By that time they faced new enemies beyond their shores and conquered them. The process continued until they had mastered the entire Mediterranean world and penetrated some distance into the interior. It should be added that sometimes Rome became involved in areas beyond her frontiers because some power appealed to her for armed intervention or to arbitrate a dispute.

Samnite attacks. One of the main reasons why the Campanian cities joined the Roman Republic was that they were periodically plagued by attacks of Samnite bands as they made sorties from their Apennine homeland. Not having sufficient land for expansion in their mountain fastnesses, the Samnites sought new homes among the rich acres of Campanian farmland. Rome found the task of defense against the Samnites to be costly indeed. She fought two long and bitter wars with them: 326-304, 298-290 B.C.

To institute the first war, the Romans began their famous highway system. The first part of the Appian Way was laid in 312 B.C. and was completed as far as Capua in its initial stage. The Samnites were only slightly inferior to Rome in population size, and they were more adept at the kind of warfare that the rugged terrain demanded —at least in the early years of the war. At the end of the first war, which was bitterly fought, the Samnites retained nearly all of their territory in central Italy; but Rome was much stronger, having made several new allies during those years.

The second Samnite war was not to be won easily, however. The Samnites made joint cause with disaffected Etruscan cities of Etruria and with the Gauls, who had once more grown restless and were making sorties from their base in the Po Valley. After hard fighting, Rome brought the Samnites to their knees in 290 B.C. Part of their land was added to the Roman public domain, and the Samnites became Roman allies. Rome now controlled the central part of the peninsula. But war was not over. Costly defeats stood between the Romans and their ultimate victory over the Etruscans and Gauls. When it finally came (in 280), Rome had annexed a considerable tract of Gallic territory in northwest Italy and forced Etruscan cities to resume their alliance with her.

Struggle with the Greeks. Hardly had the Romans concluded peace in the North when war clouds blew in from the South. During the latter half of the fourth century, Greek cities in southern Italy suffered increasing attacks from the mountain peoples of that area. Tarentum, located on a gulf by the same name in the instep of the boot of Italy, was the largest and most powerful of the Greek cities and assumed a position of leader and protector of those cities. She was aided in this effort by mercenaries from Greece. Jealous of her own leadership over the other Greek cities,

Tarentum had extracted treaties from Rome in 334 and 303 B.C. which guaranteed that Roman ships would not enter the Gulf of Tarentum. In 282 Rome answered the appeal of Thurii in the upper part of the toe of Italy for help against attackers from the mountains. Winning a land battle, the Roman army left garrisons at Thurii and at Locri and Rhegium (in the toe of Italy), all of which had now allied themselves with Rome and received Roman protection. Tarentum was disturbed that her sphere of influence had been invaded. And when Roman warships entered the Bay of Tarentum, she attacked posthaste, sinking the ships.

The two powers were now at war. Tarentum counted on the help of the mountain peoples of south Italy and, more especially, on some 25,000 Greek troops from Epirus under the expert generalship of Pyrrhus. The forces of Pyrrhus included 3,000 cavalry, 2,000 archers, and 20 war elephants—a sort of armored tank of the times. Pyrrhus won the first engagement in 280—with losses so heavy as to originate the expression "a Pyrrhic victory." The Greeks were now able to move up into Latium itself. Pyrrhus won another hard-fought battle in 279 B.C., he himself being wounded. At a strategic moment, when Rome had entered into negotiations with the Greeks, Carthage threw in her weight on the side of Rome in an effort to keep Pyrrhus out of Sicily. But the Greek army decided to answer an appeal of Sicilian Greeks anyway and soon virtually drove the Carthaginians from the island. As Pyrrhus attempted to return to Italy, he lost part of his fleet to the Carthaginians. When he was subsequently defeated by the Romans, he decided to take most of his army back to Greece, where chances now seemed good for conquering Macedonia. Soon Tarentum and other Greek cities of southern Italy were subjugated and became Roman allies. After sporadic fighting elsewhere in Italy, Rome became mistress of the entire peninsula by 265.

Political Developments

As Rome conquered the peninsula, she developed a program of organizing and controlling the area. In general it may be said that this was a system of confederation. At the center was Rome and its surrounding territory where the citizen body, divided into thirty-five tribes, possessed full rights of every type. Then there were Latin and Italian allies, bound to Rome by treaty. The Latin allies enjoyed the privilege of intermarriage with Romans, the right of trade with Rome, the protection of Roman law, the right of inheriting property and, if they moved to Rome, the chance of voting as full citizens.

The Italian allies did not enjoy the rights of trade, marriage, and protection of Roman law which the Latin allies possessed. But they did benefit, along with the Latin allies, from a new peace, security, and prosperity in Italy and exercised the prerogatives of government in their own communities, where a large measure of local autonomy existed. Both of these categories of allies were responsible for supplying troops or ships to the Roman military establishment.

In addition there were both Roman and Latin colonies established at strategic points throughout Italy. Roman colonies possessed full citizenship rights while Latin colonies possessed rights other than suffrage.

Constitutional changes. It is to be expected that a change from a monarchy to a republic and the expansion and internal development of Rome would bring about significant changes in the constitution. In the executive branch of the government, six groups of officials existed in 265 B.C. All of these were elected annually except the last. Chiefs of state were the two consuls who also served as generals of the army. During periods of crisis a dictator might be chosen to rule for a six-month period.

Quaestors supervised finance; aediles administered public welfare. The rex (king) now presided over religious affairs. Tribunes had the responsibility of protecting plebians, or commoners. Censors, elected every five years for an eighteen-month term, took the census, supervised public morals, and arranged for important public construction.

In the judicial branch were the praetors—one to supervise legal affairs of Romans and another to try cases of non-Romans carrying on business in the city.

In the legislative branch of the government, there were now three popular assemblies in addition to the senate. The power of the old Assembly of the *Curiae* had dwindled to mere formality involving the right to install magistrates after their election. The Assembly of the Centuries, based on an organization of society according to ability to provide armor in time of war, elected consuls, praetors, and censors, declared war, and voted on laws submitted to it. The Assembly of the Tribes elected tribunes and quaestors and voted on laws presented by tribunes or consuls. It was perhaps the most important lawmaking body in the state. The Senate possessed the power of consultation with consuls, who were reluctant to act contrary to the senate's advice. This body also initiated and formulated legislation submitted to the assemblies. Senators served for life and were appointed by the consuls—who came mostly from certain patrician families. A consul automatically became a senator at the end of his term of office.

Social conflicts. The changes in the Roman constitution between 500 and 265 B.C. were accompanied by and often caused by conflicts on the social scene. The patrician nobility held strong control over social, economic, and political affairs of state. Gradually the commoners (plebians) were able to force the patricians to relax that hold. It should not be concluded, however, that the plebians consisted only of the poor masses. Among them was quite a social gradation: there were the rural and urban poor, the merchants, the craftsmen, and the laborers.

The first great political victory of the plebians came about 471 B.C. At that time the Assembly of the Tribes won the right to pass laws binding on the plebians. About the same time they elected the first tribunes, who had the power of protecting any plebian against an act of some magistrate being enforced against him. A century later the consulate—and therefore the senate—was opened to plebians. By the Ogulnian Law of 300, all offices were opened to commoners. And in 287, by virtue of the Hortensian Law, legislation passed by the Assembly of the Tribes became binding on all without consent of the senate.

About twenty years after the plebs won the right to pass legislation binding on themselves, they reaped a judicial victory. The Valerio-Horatian Laws of 451-449 B.C. provided for codification of the Twelve Tables of the law and made legal provisions, previously known only to the nobility, available to all. Once familiar with these provisions, commoners had more adequate recourse to the law.

Some five years later the plebs obtained the right to marry into the patrician class. Subsequently society was grouped in three classes: the Optimates (landed aristocracy); the Equites (those with money wealth); and the Populares (the poorer classes). Supposedly the plebs won an economic victory in the passage of the Licinian-Sextian Laws (367-362 B.C.); but this legislation, designed to limit the amount of land a man might hold, was never effective. Soon these statutes were dead.

The Punic Wars

The Romans had hardly completed the conquest of peninsular Italy when they became embroiled in a series of foreign wars with Carthage. The immediate cause of these wars was an appeal from Messana (Messina) in Sicily. The background for the appeal was this. The Carthaginians occupied the western part of Sicily; Greek colonists held the eastern part. Chief of the Greek cities was Syracuse, located in the southeastern part of the island. A considerable number of Campanian mercenaries had contracted to serve in the army of the king of Syracuse and later defected and shut themselves up in the town of Messana, just across the straits from the toe of Italy. Fearing certain defeat by Syracuse, the Messanians looked to Carthage for help. The latter, eager to give any assistance that would prevent Syracusan expansion, sent a garrison to Messana.

At this point the Messanians decided they did not want to be ruled by Carthage and sought alliance with Rome. Roman intervention might lead to a costly war with Carthage. Although the Senate recognized that Carthaginian control of Messana would put this North Africa power in a position to dominate the narrow sea-lanes[3] between Sicily and Italy and endanger the Italian mainland, they were loath to answer the appeal. Therefore, the Senate sent the request to one of the popular assemblies, probably the centuriate. Though warweary, the people were persuaded by their leaders to accept Messanian alliance, thereby beginning a devastating war to the death between the two great powers of the western Mediterranean.

Of course the causes of the Punic Wars involved more than the Messanian issue. As indicated, there was the weighty question of who was to control Sicily. Again, there was a basic racial difference between the two peoples. Rome was Indo-European, and Carthage Semitic, having been colonized by Phoenicia. Furthermore, the two

[3]The straits were about one mile wide in ancient times, but today they have widened to about two miles.

powers were beginning to develop an economic and national rivalry in the western basin of the Mediterranean. It seemed only a question of time before they locked horns.

The First Punic War. So it was that the Roman people entered rather carelessly into the conflict with Carthage in 264 B.C. The First Punic War was fought very largely for the control of Sicily and was waged principally on the sea. At the beginning of the war, Carthage was a naval power, but Rome was not. In constructing her navy, Rome, however, was not without resources; her Greek naval allies of southern Italy supplied her with ships already built and furnished her with the knowledge of shipbuilding and with crews for new ships under construction. Rome developed and made effective use of the quinquereme (a warship with five banks of oars) during the conflict.

The Roman method of fighting involved simply a transferal of land warfare to the sea. To aid them in this transfer, they employed the corvus principle, which involved the use of a gangplank with grappling hooks on it. When a Roman ship came close enough to a Carthaginian man-of-war, it simply lowered this gangplank. The two ships were locked together by the huge grappling hooks, and Roman soldiers poured onto the enemy ship and captured it. This transfer of land fighting to the sea remained essentially the same until the days of the Spanish Armada in A.D. 1588.

After a hard-fought struggle, Rome won the first Punic conflict in 241 B.C. It has been estimated that her losses were about 500 ships and 200,000 men. In the terms of the peace treaty, she won a large indemnity, Sicily, and some smaller islands. During the next few years, contrary to the terms of the treaty, Rome took Corsica and Sardinia. In retaliation, Carthage expanded into Spain. Meanwhile, Rome finally defeated the Celts and pushed her boundaries

to the Alps. She also brought to terms the Illyrian pirates, who were operating from the coasts of modern Yugoslavia.

Second Punic War. It soon became clear that the peace of 241 B.C. was merely a truce. The western Mediterranean apparently was not big enough for the two powers. So war started again in 218. The immediate issue involved Saguntum (Sagunto) in Spain. Carthaginian expansion northward had been limited to the Ebro River in Spain. Saguntum was a Roman ally south of the river. Tensions around the Spanish town developed to the point that Carthage attacked it in 218. Consequences of great magnitude awaited both belligerents.

Rome's strategy was to send an army to Spain to detain the great Hannibal there, while she prepared an army for an African campaign. Since she controlled the seas (Carthage had never rebuilt her fleet), Rome thought she could effectively take the offensive. However, she planned without the genius of Hannibal, who determined to cross the Pyrenees Mountains, cut through southern Gaul, traverse the Alps, and invade Italy. The Carthaginian general counted heavily on Celtic and Italian defections to enable him to destroy the Roman confederation and bring Rome to her knees. Hannibal made the difficult crossing—but at the cost of some 40 percent of his forces and nearly all his war elephants. He arrived with about 20,000 infantry and 6,000 cavalry. Though worn out, the Carthaginians administered a resounding defeat to the Romans south of the Alps and moved into winter quarters in the Po Valley, where they increased their forces to about 50,000 by the spring of 217.

In battle after battle Hannibal defeated Roman armies sent against him. Most disastrous for the Romans was the Battle of Cannae in 216 B.C. On that occasion the Romans were thoroughly defeated, losing perhaps 40,000 men (some put the figure much higher). Only 10,000 escaped. Several Roman allies now defected to the enemy, including Capua and Syracuse. Worse still, Philip V of Macedon made an alliance with Hannibal.

But Rome was undaunted. She raised new armies and continued the struggle. She besieged and retook one by one the defecting allies. She made an alliance with Greece and Pergamum to keep Philip occupied in the East. Meanwhile, after initial defeats, armies sent to Spain were able to take the country for Rome, robbing Carthage of much wealth and a base of operations. Moreover, Hasdrubal, Hannibal's brother, was defeated in northern Italy after crossing the Alps and was therefore prevented from bringing relief to the famous Carthaginian.

Despite all this, Hannibal remained undefeated. But finally, in 204 the Roman general Scipio crossed over into Africa and won victories that caused Carthage to sue for peace. With a preliminary peace treaty drawn up and the war nearly over, Hannibal embarked for home, having maintained himself in enemy territory for almost fifteen years and having effected great destruction in Italy. On the return of Hannibal, Carthage received a transfusion of valor and confidence which caused her to break the truce and prepare for a last major battle with Rome. It took place at Zama in North Africa in 202. The two skilled generals, Hannibal and Scipio, pitted all their skill against each other. Hannibal might have won if all the men under his command had played their parts. At the crucial moment, a contingent of Carthaginian mercenaries mutinied.

Scipio's triumph was complete. By terms of the peace treaty, Rome was granted a huge reparation and Spain. The Carthaginian army and navy were disbanded. In spite of her apparent triumph, Rome never quite recovered from the ravages of Hannibal's fifteen years in Italy. Thousands of small farmers lost their livestock, their farm buildings, and their homes. After the war they sold out to the large landholders. The virility of the lower middle class in Italy was greatly affected. Many moved to Rome where they constituted part of the unemployed mob depending on the largess of the state.

Third Punic War. The end of Carthage was not yet. During the next fifty years she achieved a certain amount of recovery through her raising of olives and grapes and successful mercantile activity. Finally Rome waged another war against her (149-146 B.C.) and utterly destroyed the city. The land controlled by the once proud metropolis became the province of Africa.

Conquest of the East

A significant international effect of the Punic Wars was to involve Rome in affairs of the Hellenistic East. This involvement led ultimately to Roman control of the eastern basin of the Mediterranean.

By way of background, it should be remembered that Pyrrhus of Epirus had provided effective help for the Greeks of southern Italy in their struggle against Rome early in the third century. Between the First and Second Punic Wars, Rome found it necessary to protect her shores against Illyrian pirates. Her activity in the East at that time led to favorable relations with Aetolian and Achaean leagues in Greece and to the hostility of Macedon. During the Second Punic War, Philip V of Macedon made an alliance with Hannibal, so Rome had been involved in warfare in the East for some ten years at that time (215-205 B.C.). During those years Rome's command of the sea made it difficult for Philip to bring effective aid to Hannibal in Italy. Moreover, Rome's allies in the East—the

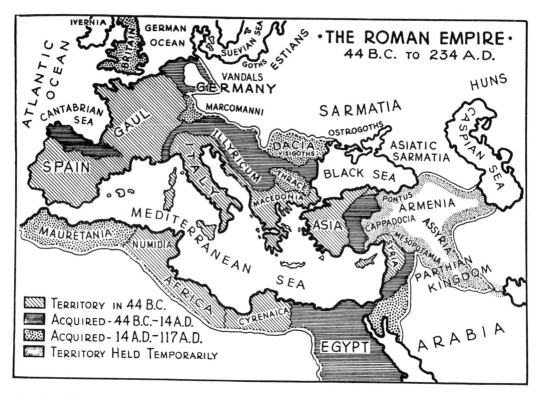

·THE ROMAN EMPIRE·
44 B.C. TO 234 A.D.

- Territory in 44 B.C.
- Acquired—44 B.C.–14 A.D.
- Acquired—14 A.D.–117 A.D.
- Territory Held Temporarily

Aetolian League: Athens, Sparta, and Pergamum—kept Macedon and the Achaean League so busy that it was unnecessary for Rome to become very directly involved. Philip was forced to make peace with the Roman senate in 205.

Rome seemed quite content to let the East alone as long as a healthy balance of power was maintained between Egypt, the Seleucid power of Syria and Asia Minor, and Macedonia. She grew uneasy when that balance of power was threatened, because a dominant power in the eastern Mediterranean might prove to be a foe stronger than Rome could handle. Such a situation was developing near the end of the Second Punic War. In 203 B.C. an infant came to the throne of Egypt, and Seleucia and Macedonia began to get expansionist ideas. Egypt and the Aetolian League appealed to Rome; subsequently Rhodes and Pergamum did also.

Rome thought that quick action would prevent the Seleucids and Macedonians from combining forces and thereby would preserve the balance of power and at the same time win the friendship of Rhodes, Egypt, and the Greek cities. Therefore Rome issued an ultimatum to Philip to cease attacking Egypt and the Greek cities, but he refused. Rome entered the conflict. Making little headway at first, the Romans finally won a decisive victory. Philip now sued for peace, but Rome wanted a complete victory. Finally Rome saw the value of a buffer state in Greece and made peace. She demanded an indemnity from Macedonia, the dissolution of the Macedonian navy, the autonomy of all Greek states that had been dominated by Philip, and an alliance between Philip and Rome. Thus· ended the Second Macedonian War, 200-196.

While Rome was busy with Philip, the Seleucid Antiochus III conquered Palestine, Ephesus, and other Greek cities held by the Ptolemies. By 195 B.C. Antiochus had crossed the Hellespont (Dardanelles) into

THE WYCLIFFE HISTORICAL GEOGRAPHY OF BIBLE LANDS

Europe and had begun the conquest of Thrace. In passing, it might be interesting to observe that Hannibal of Carthage was now in the service of Antiochus. Having aroused the suspicions of the Romans by his political activities in Carthage, Hannibal fled to the court of the Seleucids. When the Seleucids were defeated and forced by the peace terms to give up Hannibal, the famous general fled again and ultimately committed suicide. As the Syrians moved farther into Greece, Rome issued an ultimatum demanding that they turn back. The result of this demand was the establishment of spheres of influence. Rome was not to interfere in Asia Minor, and Antiochus was to stay out of Greece.

The arrangement was quite satisfactory until the Aetolians staged a revolt against Rome and tried to set up alliances, calling upon Antiochus for help. Then began the Third Macedonian War (192-189 B.C.), sometimes called an Asiatic war. At the battle of Thermopylae in 191, the Romans drove Antiochus from Greece and the following year at Magnesia brought the Syrian to his knees, forcing him to pay an indemnity, to surrender his navy, and to give up most of Asia Minor. Rome did not annex this territory but followed her old policy of curbing the strong and strengthening the weak, leaving a group of mutually jealous states to check each other.

The Greek world remained outwardly quiet for about two decades, but there was much agitation under the surface. The Greek states were very discontent at finding themselves subject allies of Rome. Finally Perseus of Macedon resolved to free his country from Rome's dictation. Inheriting an army of 30,000 and a reasonably full treasury, he exhibited unwarranted confidence. A Roman ultimatum to come to terms was refused and war broke out in 171 B.C. For some two years the Romans "muddled through," but in 168 the Battle of Pydna ended the kingdom of Macedon. The country was divided into four states under Roman direction. Other Greek states were dealt with sternly. Rome took 1,000 hostages from the Achaean League, among them the great Polybius. These hostages were important for the process of Hellenization at Rome.

But Rome was still not ready to assume the responsibility of foreign government. She made an occasional display of force but was not ready to annex territory and make it part of her empire. Twenty years later this situation was to change. In 149 B.C. there was another Macedonian rebellion, which was crushed after initial successes by the rebels. During the following year Rome organized the country as a Roman province. However, troubles in Greece were not yet over; rebellion erupted among states of the Achaean League in 147. Of course the rebels were no match for Roman legions. The League was disbanded, and Corinth was made a terrible object lesson. In 146 it was sacked and burned. It will be remembered that Carthage was destroyed in the same year—both under the stern new policies of Cato.

A Century of Revolution

A nation always purchases an empire at an enormous price. The cost to Rome of acquisition of lands abroad was frightful indeed and was most effectively related to the tragedy of the Second Punic War. During the fifteen years that Hannibal stalked the Italian countryside, it was often impossible for the citizen assemblies to meet. The senate gradually assumed the powers of the purse, of handling foreign affairs, and of exercising the normal legislative functions of state. Because of these developments, the constitutional balance was upset.

Also, Hannibal's living off the countryside had ruined a large percentage of the class of citizen farmers. Unable to restock their pilfered farms, they had sold their holdings to wealthy landlords who worked their estates largely with slave labor or who converted the land to the raising of sheep or olives or grapes, which required less help. This gradual depopulation of the countryside reduced considerably the number of men from whom military levies could be drawn. Moreover, those who left the farms generally drifted to Rome where they swelled the unemployed mass that was such a burden to the state.

All of the small farmers of Italy who left their lands did not do so because of the depredations of Hannibal, however. Many men, finding it necessary to be away from home for years at a time in military service, mortgaged their property heavily to support their families and finally went bankrupt. Too, they often found farm life rather prosaic after life in service. Also, the slow gains won from the soil required much more patience than the fast gains through booty available to the successful soldier.

Another problem which Rome faced as a result of imperialism was class conflict. The middle class which was rising before the wars was greatly benefited by the wars because of the peculiar way in which Rome attempted to supply her wartime needs. Rather than attempting to supply the military directly, the government contracted with private concerns to deliver goods to

415. The Senate House, or Curia, in the Roman Forum

the army and navy. The rising middle class also became rich by exploiting the provinces. This new class of men with money wealth (Equites) soon contested with the old aristocracy with wealth in lands (Optimates) for political power, which the latter then effectively held.

In acquiring an empire, Rome had found a new and unhealthy basis for her economy. She was now living largely from the exploitation of the Empire. Benefits from such exploitation went into the pockets of the Optimates and the Equites, not the common people. And an increasing percentage of Rome's labor force consisted of slaves taken in war. These competed with the free labor force, to the detriment of the latter. On occasion slave rebellions threatened the very peace and safety of the state. A number of such revolts occurred in the years just prior to 133 B.C.

Revolts of other kinds occurred during those years too. Especially fierce were the rebellions in Spain 154-133 B.C. Roman reverses there made Tiberius Gracchus determined to return the Italian peasants to their land and thereby provide new military strength for the state by restoring a basic source of manpower. More concerning this subject will be discussed later.

Yet another area where Rome experienced rising tension in 133 was in relations with the Italian allies. Rome used these allies but did not give them booty. Their citizenship rights were limited. And the Equites kept allied merchants from the profits of war.

In these times of stress the Senate failed to give the necessary leadership to the state. Accepting privileges without the corresponding responsibilities, this body failed to discover a satisfactory solution to the problems that threatened to bring the Republic down in a heap. The senatorial class were bitterly opposed to any changes of the existing order that would affect their position in government and society. So adamant was their stand and so rapidly did the problems increase that revolution seemed inevitable. Senatorial opponents often were not much less selfish or less responsible in their statesmanship, and it must be borne in mind that much of the leadership for the reform movements came from the senatorial class.

The Gracchi. The lid blew off the political caldron in 133 B.C. In that year Tiberius Sempronius Gracchus, newly elected tribune, submitted to the Assembly of the Tribes a land law designed to limit the estates of the wealthy. The head of a house might own as much as 350 acres, and two sons might possess an equal amount, for a total of 700 acres for a household. Initially, Tiberius seems to have been concerned about restoring the peasants to their land in order to provide a source of military manpower and to solve some of the food problem of Italy. While Italians had traditionally grown grain, owners of the large estates raised cattle, sheep, olives, and grapes; and there was now an actual shortage of food in Rome.

There was nothing particularly new or revolutionary about a land bill. Rome had had such for centuries. But this bill challenged the social and economic position of the Optimates, and it forecast a change in the political control which the Senate had enjoyed since the days of the Second Punic War. Putting legislation through the Assembly of the Tribes was something of a revolution in itself. Worse than that, Tiberius introduced an unconstitutional election of recall when his fellow tribune threatened to veto the land bill, at the instigation of the Senate. When the recall failed, Tiberius simply overrode the veto.

Now the Senate threatened to render the land reform ineffective by failing to appropriate sufficient funds for its operation. At that juncture, Attalus III (Philometor), King of Pergamum, conveniently died and left his kingdom (the province of Asia) to the Roman people. Tiberius proposed to use Attalus' treasury to finance his program, thereby challenging the Senate's power of the purse. However, Tiberius' term of office was ending. When he stood for an unprecedented second term, the Senate provoked a riot in which he was assassinated.

After the death of Tiberius, his younger brother Gaius continued active on the agrarian commission. In 124 B.C., on return from a quaestorship in Sardinia, Gaius offered himself for the tribunate, with the hope of making the land distribution program more effective. More politically astute than Tiberius, he tried to organize a political party, composed of political "outs"— Equites and Populares. He converted the tribuneship, previously an agency of the Senate, into an instrument of almost absolute power. His example was followed by others in the future, notably Julius Caesar, who rose to power through the tribunate.

He appealed to the Equites by making them jurymen to try senators who misgoverned provinces, by indemnifying them for war losses sustained while executing state contracts, and by giving them the right to contract for tax collection in the wealthy province of Asia. He appealed to the Populares with a program of cheap grain and an increase of acreage available in the land distribution program. The grain made available inexpensively to the Roman masses at this time was later given to them, and the dole was continued until the fall of Rome. Gaius attempted to placate the senators by declaring off limits for land distribution certain areas where their holdings were most extensive.

Although Tiberius had been unsuccessful at reelection, Gaius did manage a second term. But during his second term he made a dual proposal which was very dangerous to his political career: citizenship for the Latin allies and promotion of Italian allies to status of Latin allies. Whether he was a courageous statesman risking his life on a piece of enlightened legislation, as some historians claim, or whether he turned to the Latins for support as he saw his political clientele being divided by his opponents, is something of a question. At any rate, he made the proposal, and the Senate determined to rid itself of him. Passing a decree of martial law, a senatorial posse routed and killed some 250 Gracchans and executed thousands more after farcical trials. Thus ended the period of hero reformers. Apparently Rome's problems were not to be solved by legislative means. Men who dominated the political scene during subsequent decades were dictators.

Marius. The first of these dictators was Marius. He was one of the few politicians of the period to come from a class other than the senatorial nobility. An equestrian, he rose to fame through a military career. After service in the cavalry in Spain, he held the office of tribune in 119 B.C., of praetor in 116, and of propraetor in Spain in 115. He next appeared during the Jugurthine War in North Africa (111-105). Dissatisfaction in Rome with the progress of the war led a coalition of Equites and Populares to elect Marius to the consulship for the year 107 and thus to the command of the troops in Africa.

In recruiting troops for the Jugurthine War, Marius broke all precedents by accepting as volunteers all who were physically fit, regardless of property qualifications. He created a professional long-term army for which men volunteered for sixteen to twenty years. He introduced improvements in weapons and organization and developed an army with a loyalty often greater to its commander than to the state. From now on, Rome was faced with the problems of a personal army in the state and the provision of rewards for veterans when they were mustered out of service.

With his new army behind him, Marius prosecuted the war with vigor. As this war and other threats plaguing the state required more than a one-year consulship, Marius was elected for an unprecedented

seven-term consulship, in a day when a ten-year interval was supposed to elapse between consulships. These many reelections came as a result of a menace from north European tribes along the Alpine border and the fear of a repetition of the Gallic sack of Rome in 390. Marius' success was phenomenal. The invaders were virtually annihilated.

Having won his victories and served his consulships, Marius dropped out of sight for several years. Although he had the power to become a dictator, he refused to use his army to attain that position.

Civil War. While Marius was in retirement, Marcus Livius Drusus the Younger, an idealistic senator who had been elected tribune, attempted a reform program, including citizenship for Italians. He did not try to stir the proverbial hornet's nest but attempted to avoid the civil war which would certainly come if Rome failed to let the Italians have their way. For his efforts he was stabbed by an unknown assailant.

Almost immediately the flames of rebellion swept like a prairie fire from the Gulf of Tarentum to the Po. The insurgents established a confederacy they called "Italia," with a government modeled on that of Rome. The Latin allies remained loyal, as did a number of municipalities and rural areas throughout Italy. But the two-year war (90-88 B.C.) was a bloody one, especially because so many veterans of Roman wars fought in the rebel army, and the havoc created must have approximated that of the Second Punic War in many communities.

Although Rome commanded the seas and could bring in troops and supplies from the provinces, what really broke the rebellion was the *lex Julia*, which conferred citizenship on all Latins and Italians still loyal to Rome and to those who would at once lay down their arms. Subsequent legislation granted full citizenship to all free persons living south of the Po River.

The Mithridatic War. As Italy counted her dead and set her house in order after the civil war, a new threat loomed in the East. Mithridates VI, the Great, king of Pontus in Asia Minor, took the offensive and swept all Roman opposition before him. As he advanced into the province of Asia, the inhabitants welcomed the chance to make the Romans pay for their forty years of oppression. The whole province rebelled, slaughtering (on order of Mithridates) some 75,000 Italians in one day (mostly tax agents, moneylenders, and merchants), according to some. Next Mithridates advanced into Greece, taking most of the southern part of the country and massacring the merchant and slave-trading population of Delos. The island never recovered.

Two generals were particularly eager for the appointment to the Mithridatic command: Marius and Sulla. Marius wanted to recover his lost popularity, and Sulla desired a road to power and fame. The Senate awarded the command to Sulla. All might have gone well, if it had not been for the actions of a tribune named Rufus who managed to force passage in the Assembly of the Tribes of an omnibus bill which replaced Sulla with Marius in the command against Mithridates.

Sulla returned to Rome at the head of an army and instituted a reign of terror. Marius escaped to Africa. Hardly had Sulla made an about-face when a consul, Cinna, annulled the Sullan laws and recalled Marius from Africa. Marius, enraged at the treatment he had received after having been the savior of the state, roamed the streets of the capital, striking down nobles and senators he hated. After arranging election to the consulship, he fell ill and died in a few days.

Sulla proceeded to the East this time, postponing the squaring of accounts with his enemies in the capital. Marching east from Epirus (Epeiros), he defeated a Pontic force sent against him. Then he invaded Attica and besieged Athens, which held out for several months. When it did fall, his soldiers killed every tenth Athenian, looted the town and destroyed the docks and harbor installations at the Piraeus (Peiraieus). Next he defeated a force of 100,000 sent against him in eastern Greece by Mithridates.

Crossing the Hellespont, Sulla had to fight little to persuade Mithridates that the end had come. Sulla, eager to return to Rome to deal with his enemies there, offered the softest terms of any Roman victor: the surrender of conquests in Asia Minor, the payment of an indemnity, and the relinquishment of eighty warships. The cities of Asia did not fare so well. Forced to pay a huge indemnity for the slaughter of the Italians and to provide quarters and pay for the upkeep of Sulla's troops during the winter of 85/84, they fell victims to a crushing burden of debt.

When Sulla landed in Italy, he brought with him some 35,000 men, more loyal to himself than to the state. Among those who subsequently joined his forces were Pompey (Pompeius) and Crassus, who will soon be heard from again. His opponents proved incapable of turning him back, and he entered Rome in 82. Proclaimed dictator with authority to revise the constitution, he ordered a bloodbath which in many ways surpassed the worst days of the French Revolution. Shortly after he entered Rome, he tortured to death 6,000 captives from the army that had opposed his entry into Rome. Thousands of others were exiled or had their property confiscated, many of them only for the crime of possessing property which Sulla needed to reward his veterans. Among those killed were 90 senators and 2,600 Equites.

Next Sulla revised the constitution. He increased the Senate by 300, adding many from the equestrian class; reformed the courts, initiating trial by jury in many instances where it did not exist; established an orderly progression of office-holding, establishing minimum age limits for each office; and reorganized the provinces. He designed his whole program to restore to power the senatorial class, which by now had completely lost its control of the state and had proved itself incapable of ruling in the past as it would in the future. Having accomplished his aims, Sulla retired to private life in 78 B.C. and died soon thereafter. Before the ashes of his funeral pyre had cooled, forces were at work to demolish the house of cards he had erected.

Pompey. From this time on it became increasingly clear that the Senate could not control affairs and that the important man in Rome was the man with the army. And the important man with the army in the 70's and 60's was Pompey. Having been a general in the army of Sulla, he was one of the military leaders called on by the state to suppress the rebellion of Marcus Aemilius Lepidus in 78 B.C. When he subsequently refused to disband his army and demanded to be sent to Spain to quell the revolt of Quintus Sertorius there, the Senate reluctantly granted his wish. Although he was not the best general on the field, he had the best public relations staff. When the war was over, the populace believed he was the real victor. On his way home from Spain, he was able to share in the glory of Marcus Crassus' victory over the slave revolt of Spartacus in southern Italy. Pompey and Crassus shared the consulate for the year 70 and both thereafter retired from public life.

Pompey did not have long to wait for a new assignment. Pirates were racing all over the Mediterranean with hundreds of fast ships. They stormed dozens of cities around the Mediterranean, including coastal cities in Italy itself, destroyed a large Roman fleet, and prevented much of the grain supply from reaching the capital. With their food prices skyrocketing and food increasingly scarce, the people of Rome determined to clear the seas. To this

end the Gabinian Law was put through the Assembly of the Tribes in spite of senatorial opposition. It provided for a fleet of 500 ships, an infantry force of 120,000 men, and power superior to that of the provincial governors over a strip of territory fifty miles wide around the entire Mediterranean. This command, bestowed upon Pompey, was to last for three years. He completed the task in about three months.

Meanwhile, Rome was fighting another fierce war with Mithridates VI of Pontus in Asia Minor. After rather brilliant initial victories, Lucius Licinius Lucullus was not able to lead the Roman forces to ultimate victory. "Like a buzzard come to enjoy another's kill," Pompey, already in the East with a large army, was appointed to succeed Lucullus. Pompey vigorously prosecuted the war during the years 66-62 B.C. He conquered Asia Minor and pacified it, dividing it into the provinces familiar to the student of the New Testament; he brought Syria into the Empire in 64 B.C. and Palestine the following year. When Pompey landed at Brundisium (modern Brindisi) in 62, he disbanded his army rather than attempting to become ruler of the Empire by force. As soon as he did so, he lost his bargaining power with the Senate, which was opposed to the political settlement he had made in the East. Thus his veterans went without the grant of homesteads that they expected at the time of mustering out.

While Pompey was engaged in his conquests, two new figures came in from the wings and began to stride across the Roman stage: Marcus Licinius Crassus and Gaius Julius Caesar. Their political alignment was with the radical popular element and to some extent with the Equites. Their advance was somewhat impeded by Cicero, who defended the interests of Pompey. Cicero earned much of his fame by quashing two conspiracies against the state by Cataline, who seems to have been connected in some way with Crassus. Cicero then tried to effect an alignment between the senators and the Equites in order to give proper direction to the politics of the state. His efforts were never successful.

Three against the state. In 60 B.C., the interests of Pompey, Crassus, and Caesar all seemed to coincide. At least, all of them wanted something, and none by himself was strong enough to get what he wanted. Caesar, returning from a governorship in Farther Spain, sought a consulship, commission, and army to conquer new lands for Rome. Crassus was interested in a modification of contracts which he and some of his friends had made with the government for the collection of taxes in the province of Asia. Harvests had been particularly bad there, and the Equites stood to lose heavily. As has been stated, Pompey wanted a recognition of his political settlement in the East and land for his veterans. The three made an informal agreement to pool their resources—an arrangement known as the First Triumvirate. Caesar was to be elected consul and was to push through legislation to satisfy the needs of all. He did just that.

Crassus and his friends got their rebate. Pompey got his eastern settlement approved and land for his veterans. Caesar won the proconsulship of Gaul for five years, and the right to raise and lead an army into battle in the conquest of this very rich province. Cicero was banished because of his opposition to Caesar and Crassus.

While Caesar was off in Gaul winning battles, the political situation in Rome deteriorated rapidly. Pompey and Crassus began to quarrel. With the Triumvirate about to collapse, Caesar called for its renewal in 55 B.C. The terms of the new agreement dictated that Pompey and Crassus should stand for the consulship in 55, that Pompey should thereafter be governor of the two Spains and Cyrenaica for five years with six legions, that Crassus for an equal period should be governor of Syria with the

416. The Forum of Julius Caesar

right to wage war against Parthia, and that Caesar's proconsulship should be renewed for another five years. Apparently what happened was that both Crassus and Pompey became increasingly disturbed over Caesar's military successes and demanded positions in the state wherein they could also command armies with which to protect themselves.

The story of Caesar's brilliant campaigns in Gaul, the revolts of subjugated peoples, and his ultimate victory, need not detain this study. Neither is it necessary to go into the details of his invasion of Britain. Suffice it to say that he did conquer Gaul, ended the Gallic danger to Rome, and provided Italy with another market. Moreover, Caesar's conquest of the area is important to the history of western civilization because the effective beginnings of the Romanization of Gaul were to lead ultimately to a cultural difference between France and Germany that has been disastrous in modern history.

The Triumvirate began to disintegrate. In the spring of 53 B.C. Crassus was killed in battle against the Parthians. Pompey had for some time been blowing hot and cold toward the Senate and toward Caesar and Crassus. As an impossibly vain man, it seems that he could not bear to be anything but first. As Caesar's star rose, Pompey became more difficult. Although he had renewed his governorship of Spain for five years, he had never gone there. In the breakdown of civil government in Rome in 52, Pompey obtained a third consulship—this time without a colleague—and thereby ruled as a virtual dictator. Determined to check Caesar's rise to power, he demanded that all military personnel in Italy take their oath to him personally and obtained from the Senate a third five-year proconsulship in Spain.

Supporters of Caesar and Pompey parried legal blows in the Senate. Finally, on December 1, 50 B.C., that body voted to strip Caesar of his command in Gaul. Subsequently a motion was passed calling for Pompey to step down. A short time afterward the Senate declared Caesar a public enemy and proclaimed martial law.

On hearing of the Senate's action, Caesar decided to act without further delay. Crossing the Rubicon River, which separated Italy from Cisalpine Gaul, he provoked a civil war. Pompey, of course, was the only leader in Italy capable of opposing him. Caesar had few troops, but he counted on speed and surprise tactics to win the day. Pompey had not yet been able to mobilize his troops; and some that he had under arms had fought with Caesar and might possibly desert to his side. With lightning thrusts Caesar took the entire peninsula; Pompey escaped with his army to Greece. The task before Caesar would have made a lesser man quail. His opponent had forces in Spain, had tremendous resources in the East, and controlled the sea.

In setting the Italian house in order, Caesar apparently won over few senators, but he did win the support of the rising Equites; and this backing was to stand loyally behind the Empire when it was established. His efforts to draw Cicero into his entourage were disappointing. Having established control of Italy, Caesar led an army overland to Spain and subdued the Iberian Peninsula in forty days. But the victory was not without hard-fought and almost disastrous battles.

Meanwhile, Pompey was amassing a large force in Greece for the invasion of Italy. Again counting on the value of speed and the element of surprise, Caesar managed to slip past Pompey's naval patrols on the night of January 4, 48 B.C., and land his troops in western Greece. Although later reinforced by Mark Antony, he lost initial battles to Pompey. At Pharsalus (Pharsalos) the story was different. Outnumbered more than two to one, Caesar won a tremendous victory by using tactics that Hannibal developed at Zama in Africa. Pompey fled. As he landed in Egypt, a Roman living there assassinated him. Caesar arrived three days later.

Caesar alone. Caesar wintered in Egypt, conquering the kingdom for Rome and marrying Cleopatra, which he could do under Macedonian or Ptolemaic law but not Roman, for the Romans did not permit bigamy. Returning to Italy the next year, he was confronted with the task of considerable economic and political reform before he could embark for Africa to destroy the last pocket of resistance. There, at Thapsus, in Tunisia (Tunis), Caesar again outgeneraled his opposition and became the undisputed master of the Roman world. Subsequent rebellions of Pompey's sympathizers in Spain need not detain this discussion.

Caesar was now faced with reconstruction of the Roman state. For this he had sufficient power. From 48 B.C. on, he was steadily a consul. In 46 he was named dictator for ten years and the following year dictator for life. In 45 he was also made censor and given the power and inviolability of a tribune.

As Caesar began to reform the government, he stood peculiarly alone. He did have a few of the old nobility, such as the Julians and Claudians, on his side; but the great families of the last century of the Republic were conspicuously absent from his train. The bulk of his following was the new middle class. So he made deliberate use of men with talent, rather than men with family connections. Mark Antony illustrates this procedure. Subsequent rulers would follow him in this practice.

The overall effect of Caesar's reforms was to start Rome toward true imperial organization and to stake out paths in which later emperors would walk. The importance of Rome and the Roman Senate was gradually reduced. To begin with, the Senate was increased from 600 to 900. A large percentage came from the equestrian class. Some came from Gaul. Meanwhile, a process of development had been evolving in the Italian towns whereby these municipalities were achieving a political and social structure similar to that of the capital. Caesar's Julian Municipal Law was something of a culmination of that process. The burghers of the "downstate" towns were satisfied to participate in their local senates and aspired less to membership in the Roman Senate.

As a second aspect of his reforms Caesar conferred full Roman citizenship on many cities of Spain and Gaul, and Latin rights on others. In a further effort to Romanize the Mediterranean world and at the same time to relieve the problem of the poor in Italy, he established numerous colonies of Roman citizens in the Empire. Third, he rebuilt strategically important Carthage and Corinth. Fourth, as dictator he could control the provincial governors and bring an end to the confusion and corruption of the previous century. This objective was not fully accomplished until the days of Augustus, however. Fifth, Caesar improved the administration of Rome by increasing the number of magistrates and reforming the lawcourts. Sixth, one of his most enduring acts was the reform of the calendar, which, after that, had a year of 365¼ days. He proposed other changes,

such as a census of the Empire and a codification of Roman law, but these were not carried out. This list is by no means complete, but it shows that Julius Caesar was more than merely the conqueror of Gaul, the writer of a famous work on the Gallic wars, and a character immortalized by Shakespeare.

Demise of the Republic. But Caesar did not have a chance to pursue his statesmanlike program. As almost every schoolboy knows, he was struck down by the knives of assassins on the Ides of March (March 15), 44 B.C. The conspiracy involved a combination of supporters of Pompey, jealous members of his own camp, and Republicans opposed to dictatorship. While he had not destroyed the forms of the Republic, he had sapped the life out of them. Elections had become empty political acts because Caesar had determined their results in advance. For many the sacrifice of the old Republican political structure for an apparent achievement of peace and security in the Empire was too costly.

Unfortunately for Caesar's conspirators, they had not come to terms ahead of time with Caesar's supporters: with Lepidus, the master of the horse, who gained control of the army; with Mark Antony, who got Caesar's money and his papers; and with Octavius, Caesar's grandnephew and adopted heir. The last-mentioned, then eighteen, was waiting in Epirus to join Caesar in prosecuting the Parthian War. On receiving the news, he came to Rome with his friend Agrippa. During the suc-

417. Municipal government buildings in the Forum of Pompeii

ceeding months there was a jockeying for power by these three and Brutus and Cassius, the leaders of Caesar's assassins.

Finally Antony, Octavius, and Lepidus formed the Second Triumvirate. This one was not as informal as the first had been but was recognized by the Senate. Before the triumvirs took office on January 1, 43 B.C., they engaged in a cold-blooded proscription in which some 2,000 senators and Equites lost their lives. As in the case of Sulla's proscription, many were executed merely to get their property. Some, however, were political enemies of the triumvirs. Most distinguished of the expendables was Cicero. After squelching all opposition in Italy, the triumvirs set out to dispose of Brutus and Cassius, who had been ransacking the treasuries of eastern provinces to raise a formidable military force. The story of the defeat and death of the two assassins on the plains of Philippi in the fall of 42 has become one of the best-known events of military history, thanks to the pen of William Shakespeare.

418. Coins of Brutus (left) and Mark Antony

With their Republican enemies eliminated, the triumvirs started to dispose of each other. Lepidus, weakest of the three, was the first casualty. The other two shunted him off to the province of Africa. Antony was much better off than Octavian for the moment; he had control of the entire East and the provinces of Gaul. Octavian was not even undisputed master of Italy, and he was plagued by Sextus Pompey, who enjoyed naval superiority over much of the Mediterranean, as well as Sicily and Sardinia. He was able to harass the grain supplies of Italy and incite considerable unrest in the peninsula.

Before long, Gaul came over to Octavius, and in 40 B.C. the triumvirs arranged a peace with Pompey. Later, with the help of Antony, Octavius managed to destroy Pompey and to become more fully master of the West. Meanwhile, Antony was busy fighting the Parthians and enjoying the feminine graces of Cleopatra. Octavius' hope was to bide his time and effectively propagandize the areas under his control.

Of great value to his propaganda machine were Roman fears of the loss to the Empire of the rich kingdoms of the East and/or the threat of a divided empire. Then there was Roman dislike of an Oriental queen and Roman revulsion against Orientalization of the government. Octavius' greatest propaganda victory came as a result of the publication of Antony's will. Whether it was real or forged is another question. One of Antony's supporters defected to Octavius and reported that his will had been deposited with the vestal virgins in Rome. Octavius promptly found it and read it to the Senate. Supposedly it confirmed the disposition of eastern lands to the children of Cleopatra and acknowledged Caesarion, her son, as the true son and successor of Julius Caesar. A shudder swept across Italy, and Octavius capitalized on it by fomenting opposition to Antony.

Both antagonists headed toward the final showdown in 32 B.C. Antony gathered his forces at Ephesus and sailed for Greece, taking up battle stations at Actium on the Ambracian Gulf in northwestern Greece. Octavius massed his forces across the Adriatic Sea. When Octavius' troops attacked on September 2, 31 B.C., their victory was complete. Antony's ships were too heavy and slow, and the morale of his troops was low. When in the middle of the battle Cleopatra broke away with several

THE WYCLIFFE HISTORICAL GEOGRAPHY OF BIBLE LANDS

ships and the treasure, Antony panicked and followed her to Egypt. There Octavius pursued them the following year. After a brief battle Antony committed suicide and Cleopatra followed suit a few days later. Octavius had conquered Egypt for Rome and was undisputed master of the Empire. He had established his claim to the political inheritance of Julius Caesar.

The Empire

Augustus. In the late summer of 29 B.C., Octavius returned to Rome in triumph. His victory ended a century of civil war. With the cessation of hostilities, the great *Pax Romana* (Roman Peace) began; and the gates of the Temple of Janus at the northeast end of the Forum clanged shut. Closed only when the land was at peace, these gates had been shut only four times before the Christian Era. This peace was to last for about two centuries. Everywhere Augustus was hailed as the savior of the Empire and founder of a new golden age. And he spared no effort to make that hope a reality. Piracy virtually disappeared from the high seas. Brigandage markedly declined on land. He brought a general stability to the frontiers. Because of settled conditions, commerce flourished throughout the Empire.

During the year 28 B.C., Augustus conducted something of a sociopolitical reformation. He purged from the Senate some 200 unworthies who had come there under the administration of the triumvirs, and he established property qualifications for senatorials and equestrians.

In a very dramatic move, Augustus appeared before the Senate on January 30, 27 B.C., surrendered the extraordinary powers which he had exercised during the civil war, and handed the commonwealth back to the Senate and Roman people, retaining the consulship which he had enjoyed continuously since 33. But the Senate did not

419. Augustus

want the responsibility of governing the state; nor did they quite know what to do with it. They first delegated to Augustus proconsular power for ten years (later renewed) over the provinces of Spain, Gaul, and Syria. Since these were the provinces where most of the troops were stationed, this power gave him command of the real power in the state, the army. Three days later they conferred upon him the title of "Augustus," meaning "the revered or respected one."

During subsequent years the Senate conferred many other powers on Augustus. He was never a dictator but princeps (first citizen) of the Empire. His proconsular power gave him control over the army and an authority superior to that of governors of the provinces; his office of *pontifex maximus* gave him power over the religion of the state; as *princeps senatus* (president of the Senate) he was in a position to direct the affairs of that body; his tribunician power gave him control over the assembly.

As the first citizen of the Empire, Augustus exercised actual control over all phases of government. But he tried to operate within the framework of a dyarchy in which he cooperated with the Senate in running the government of Rome and the Empire. Elections of Roman magistrates continued. By monopolizing what amounted to a spoils system, he was able to manipulate the social and political structure of the state. While men rose to places of prominence through the army or the magistracies, he had final control over their advancement to the highest positions. Those whom he wished to reward he admitted to senatorial rank. As chief executive, he created boards or commissions to dispense governmental functions. He also organized a sort of cabinet or council to aid him in shaping policies. As early as 27 B.C., he secured appointment of a committee of the Senate to work with him in preparing an agenda for meetings of the Senate. Later this became a sort of cabinet, consisting of other topflight administrators outside the Senate. He also could issue executive edicts; these became more and more important with successive emperors and gradually replaced the legislative functions of the Senate and became an important source of judicial principles.

420. Tomb of Augustus, Rome

Just as Augustus shared the administration of Rome with the Senate, so he also shared the rule of the provinces with them. In general, senatorial provinces (such as Sicily) were those most thoroughly Romanized and, therefore, needed only a few local police or militia to keep order. Imperial provinces, on the other hand, required legionary forces to keep order. Since the emperor commanded the troops, such provinces were assigned to him. Especially did subjugation of the warlike and restless peoples of the newly conquered provinces along the Rhine and Danube frontiers necessitate a show of military force.

A study of the history of the period will demonstrate that the division of these provinces between Senate and emperor was not fixed. As provinces became settled, they were turned over to the Senate; and occasionally the emperor took control of one that needed a demonstration of Roman might. The Senate appointed governors of the senatorial provinces and the emperor of the imperial provinces.

In the former, office usually lasted for one year; in the latter, term of service depended on ability or the emperor's need for the services of the governor elsewhere. In all provinces, governors and other officials received a salary in Augustus' day, thereby removing one of the great causes of extortion during the days of the Republic.

In addition to these two classes of provinces, a number of client kingdoms existed within the Empire. While the foreign relations of these principalities were controlled by Rome, they enjoyed a great deal of local autonomy. Judaea and Galatia, among others, fell in this category in Augustus' day; before the end of his reign he transformed them into provinces. Egypt was in a special category, treated as a private possession of the emperor, very important to him as a source of wealth and a supply of grain.

At home, Augustus turned his attention to problems that the Senate had never been successful in handling during the days of the Republic. To provide adequate police protection for the capital, he organized three cohorts of 1,500 men each. For general administrative purposes, he divided Rome into fourteen districts and in turn subdivided these into 265 precincts. After trying other ineffective measures to solve the problem of fighting fires, he organized a corps of 7,000 men to serve as a fire brigade and as night police. This force was divided into 1,000-man cohorts, each cohort serving two of the fourteen districts. To solve the problem of the grain supply and the needs of the large number on public dole (some 200,000 or more), the Senate turned over to Augustus the responsibility of maintaining the grain fleet and obtaining adequate grain stores—from Egypt and elsewhere.

Of special interest to Bible students is Augustus' census-taking activities. Censuses were nothing new to Rome, for they had been taken regularly at five-year intervals for centuries. But now that Rome had an empire, was free from civil strife, and had a ruler who wanted to set in order the administrative machinery, empirewide censuses were in order. Augustus tallied up the citizen roster in 28 B.C., 8 B.C., and A.D. 14. Exactly how far beyond the boundaries of Italy the census-takers operated in 28 is not clear.

There must have been a degree of irregularity in the Empire—at least in the early days of Augustus when the emperor was getting administrative details organized. For instance, censuses were taken in Gaul in 27 and 13 B.C. In Egypt they were apparently taken at fourteen-year intervals for some centuries thereafter. A record exists of a census in Egypt during the year A.D. 20. Assuming that the fourteen-year cycle was followed, a census could have occurred there about 8 B.C.

According to Luke 2:2, the imperial cen-

421. Forum of Augustus with Temple of Mars

sus was first taken in Palestine at the time of Christ's birth. It is known that the Gregorian calendar (the one now in use) is several years in error. For instance, Herod the Great, who ruled Judaea at the time of Christ's birth, died in 4 B.C. Christ may well have been born a couple of years or more before that. On the basis of this and other evidence, it is possible to push the date of the birth of Christ back to 6 or 7 or possibly even the end of 8 B.C.

Population estimates based on the imperial census and other evidence vary greatly, but some useful approximations can be noted. Italy in Augustus' day probably had about 14,000,000 people; by the end of Nero's reign the figure probably reached 20,000,000. The city of Rome is usually thought to have had a population of something like 1,000,000 in the days of Nero, although some place the figure as low as 750,000 and others considerably over a million.

A discovery of an inscription, reported in

422. Forum of Augustus reconstructed, model by I. Gismondi

keeping it loyal. There was always the way of military subjection. But neither Augustus nor his successors chose that method. The usual number of legionnaires kept under arms during the first century was 150,000, of which about one third was stationed along the Rhine, another third along the Danube, and the remaining scattered in Syria, Egypt, and Africa. Clearly the troops were primarily for protecting the frontiers. Other ways of keeping the Empire in line were through a process of extension of Roman citizenship, through ruler worship, and through creation of urban centers as means of controlling the countryside. All of these paths Augustus followed.

423. Livia, wife of Augustus

424. A sesterce of Augustus

the *American Journal of Archaeology* a number of years ago, supposedly set the population of the city of Rome at 4,100,000 in the year that Augustus died.[4] The writer has not been able to discover further reference to this inscription or to learn its exact phraseology, but it does seem highly exaggerated. It hardly seems likely that the capital in those days sheltered close to one-third of the population of Italy. There was at the time an active and prosperous life in the Italian municipalities and no great shift of population from them to the capital. The population of the Empire as a whole during the first century was probably about 80,000,000.

It was one thing for Augustus to work out an administration of the Empire. It was quite another problem to devise means of

[4]A news note in the *American Journal of Archaeology*, 45 (1941), 438.

Augustus tried to create an Italian nation out of the Empire through the above-mentioned urbanization and extension of Roman citizenship. Much of the East was already urbanized with a culture different from that of Rome. In the West the population lived mainly in tribal communities. As Augustus' successors followed his lead, the entire Empire was urbanized within a couple of centuries. Moreover, in A.D. 212 all freemen of the Empire were granted citizenship.

During the latter days of the Republic, colonies of Roman citizens, civilians and veterans, were settled in various places of the Empire; this policy was continued and augmented. Other municipalities, as they became Romanized, were granted full citizenship. Yet other communities had Latin rights (of trade and intermarriage with Rome). A fourth category consisted merely of native communities without rights.

There was a regular process of promoting these towns to higher categories. Naturally, since Roman citizenship carried with it legal and political rights and since it opened the way to important careers, it was highly prized. The process of voluntary Romanization was steady as natives in the provinces imitated the language, religion, and customs of the citizens in their presence.

A second means which Augustus used to maintain support for his regime was through the ruler cult. This concept had at its background the god-king ideal of the ancient Near East, and the efforts of the successors of Alexander the Great in Egypt and Seleucid territories to link worship of the ruler with loyalty to the state. During his rise to power Augustus had arranged the deification of Julius Caesar in an effort to win the loyalty of his troops. The eastern provinces were quick to seek permission to worship the living ruler, whom many hailed as a divine savior responsible for the peace, prosperity, and security of the Empire. (Many had already deified Julius Caesar and Mark Antony.)

Traces of Augustus worship can be seen in the East as early as 29 B.C., when Nicaea, Ephesus, Pergamum, and Nicomedia erected temples to him and the goddess Roma. Soon thereafter Herod the Great built temples to Augustus at Caesarea and Samaria. Emperor worship was not at home in the West and was established there more slowly. In 12 B.C. an altar to Augustus was erected in Gaul near the modern city of Lyons (ancient Lugdunum), in order to prevent revolt there. Augustus himself erected a temple to the divine Julius in the Forum. And in each of the 265 precincts of Rome he set up shrines dedicated to the genius of Augustus—the divine spirit that watched over his fortunes. Gradually the ruler cult was established; by A.D. 100 the whole Empire was blanketed with ruler cult establishments.

While emperors encouraged this worship, they did not demand it until the days of Domitian, at the end of the first century. Emperor worship unified patriotism and worship and made support of the state a religious duty. It created a very serious problem for Christians, for refusal to worship the emperor and the goddess Roma constituted treason. Treason has never been lightly handled by the state. Thus the persecution of Christians came about. The harassment waxed and waned until Constantine declared Christianity a legal religion early in the fourth century.

One of the chief difficulties of Augustus' administration was how to arrange for a successor. Theoretically, since the Senate had conferred his powers on him, those powers reverted to the Senate on his death. But with the reconstruction of the state by Augustus, it was impossible for the Senate to take over again. In solving this problem, Augustus chose the plan of selecting his successor, adopting him as his heir, and associating his heir with him in a coregency.

425. Remains of the Temple of Julius Caesar in the Roman Forum, supposedly built on the site where Caesar was assassinated

Thereby an orderly succession would be assured, with the Senate later ratifying the successor.

This became the solution used by Augustus' successors during the next two centuries of the principate. From 14 to 68 the Julio-Claudian line held the reins of government; from 69 to 96 the Flavians; and after them what are known as the five good emperors (Nerva, Trajan, Hadrian, Antoninus Pius, and Marcus Aurelius), who broke the dynastic principle but continued the fiction of a line by adopting their successors.

During the next two centuries, the political arrangements which Augustus inaugurated were generally continued. There was, however, a gradual usurpation of senatorial and assembly rights and a decline in the value of elections. Eventually the functions of the magistrates were assumed by individuals appointed by the princeps.

Although there were times when the state was in danger of losing its civilian character and becoming a military monarchy, that did not happen until after 180. So the first two centuries of the Christian Era were for Rome a time of peace and prosperity and political stability.

Tiberius. Before his death, Augustus adopted Tiberius (a stepson by his third wife) as his son and associated Tiberius with himself in ruling the State. Upon his death in A.D. 14, the Senate and assembly voted Augustus' powers and prerogatives upon his successor. The new emperor was by birth a member of the Claudian family, by adoption a member of the Julian family. Therefore, in him these two great houses were united and from this Julio-Claudian line came the first four successors of Augustus in the principate.

Tiberius (who ruled A.D. 14-37) had become embittered and suspicious during the years of mistreatment at the hands of Augustus (Tiberius had not been Augustus' first choice as his successor), and his personality caused him much trouble with the

426. Tiberius

Senate and the people of Rome. Finally, Tiberius grew tired of this friction and retired to Capri in A.D. 26 (the year he appointed Pilate procurator of Judaea), leaving the rule of Rome to the commander of the Praetorian Guard. While Tiberius did not get along well with the Senate and while his economy in expenditures of the public funds won him unpopularity with the city mob, he was a blessing to the provincials, to whose welfare he directed particular attention. Of prime significance for the Christian movement is the fact that Christ was crucified during Tiberius' reign.

Caligula. The next ruler was Gaius Caesar Caligula (37-41), grandson of Augustus' daughter Julia. After the stern and efficient rule of Tiberius, the lavishness of Caligula's public entertainments, his donations, his reduction of taxes, and his pardoning of political offenders imprisoned by Tiberius, brought him great popularity.

THE WYCLIFFE HISTORICAL GEOGRAPHY OF BIBLE LANDS

But as a result of a serious illness, he seems to have become mentally deranged. He attempted to establish a full Oriental monarchy and forced senators to kiss his feet in homage. Then he had a temple erected to himself out of public funds and appointed his favorite horse as high priest of his cult. His extravagance in giving public entertainments soon exhausted the full treasury which Tiberius had left.

In order to obtain new funds, he resorted to new taxes and confiscations, and used treason laws as a means of seizing money and property. Caligula therefore incurred the wrath of many of the most prominent members of government and society. A plot against his life, carried out by a member of the Praetorian Guard, was successful on January 24, A.D. 41.

Caligula had alienated not only the Romans but the Jews as well. Their monotheistic beliefs prevented them from worshiping images of the princeps, and his statues were forcibly erected in the synagogues in Alexandria. Before the order to set up his statue in the temple in Jerusalem could be carried out, news of the Emperor's death arrived.

Claudius. In the Senate's enthusiasm over the death of the tyrant, it began to entertain heady ideas of restoring the Republic. However, the senators failed to realize how completely the reins of government had been removed from their hands. Some soldiers of the Praetorian Guard (the flower of the army, 9,000 strong, stationed on the outskirts of Rome), while they were plundering the palace after the murder of Caligula, saw two feet sticking out from under a curtain. They belonged to Claudius, Caligula's uncle. The frightened captive evidently feared that the governmental purge would include him too. But the soldiers took him to the Praetorian camp, where he was hailed as emperor. The transaction involved a handsome bribe for each member of the Guard. The Senate had

no choice but to confer the imperial powers upon Claudius.

Claudius was plagued all his life by a deformed and somewhat incapacitated body—some say as a result of a birth injury; others, as a result of poliomyelitis. This incapacity had turned him into a student and something of a recluse. His enemies have presented him as a much more grotesque figure than he probably was. They have also seen him as under the domination of members of his household rather than the real leader of the state. Whatever the real situation, it seems that the Emperor Claudius provided a high quality of administration for the Empire. He adjusted tax burdens and inaugurated an extensive

427. Claudius

program of public works. This involved building new aqueducts, roads, and canals; swamp drainage; and especially the development of Ostia as a harbor for Rome.

In foreign policy, Claudius followed more in the train of Julius than Augustus. He annexed Thrace and spread Roman influence around much of the Black Sea. In the Near East he reestablished the Roman protectorate over Armenia and restored Judaea to its position as an imperial province after its brief experience as a client kingdom under Herod Agrippa I (41-44).

Britain was invaded and conquered in the years 43 and following. While Julius Caesar had invaded the island long before, he had never added it to the Empire. Exactly why Claudius determined to undertake this conquest is uncertain. There were appeals to Rome by British tribes for help against other tribes of the island; there was a threat to the peace and security of Gaul by British tribes; but probably of most importance was an exaggerated estimate of the resources of the island. Claudius extended Roman citizenship in the provinces and advanced the process of urbanization there.

At home Claudius, like Augustus, tried to give a large share of the responsibility of the state to the Senate and returned to that body some powers it had lost under Tiberius and Caligula. And he introduced Gallic members into the Senate. On the other hand, he dealt the Senate a mortal blow in his effective organization of the departments of government (treasury department, justice department, records department, etc.), each with a head who was a member of the imperial cabinet—an organization composed largely of freedmen loyal to the emperor.

Whether or not Claudius was dominated by his freedmen and adulterous women in his governmental policies, he was dominated by his second wife to the point that he adopted Nero, her son by a previous marriage, as his son and successor, in preference to his own natural son. Subse-

quently Nero married Claudius' daughter Octavia and succeeded to the imperial chair when Claudius died in 54. Reportedly Claudius was poisoned.

Apparently Claudius had some trouble with the Jews in Rome. Suetonius (c. A.D. 75-160), made this statement in his *Life of Claudius*: "Since the Jews were continually making disturbances at the instigation of Chrestus, he [Claudius] expelled them from Rome."[5] This is a corroboration of Luke's statement in Acts 18:2: "Claudius had commanded all Jews to depart from Rome."

428. Nero

Nero. Nero was the last of the Julio-Claudians. Coming to the imperial chair at sixteen, he was during the first five years of his rule largely dominated by his mother, Agrippina, and the very capable heads of the executive departments of government which had been instituted by Claudius. Chief of this circle of leaders was Nero's tutor, the Stoic philosopher Seneca—greatest of the literary figures of the Julio-Claudian period. During these early years, administration of the Empire was generally efficient and peaceful, and prosperity continued. In fact, the Empire as a whole was not seriously affected by Nero's inade-

[5]Suetonius, "Life of Claudius," *The Twelve Caesars*, Chap. XXV, Section 4.

THE WYCLIFFE HISTORICAL GEOGRAPHY OF BIBLE LANDS

quacies until the rebellion at the end of his life.

As Nero grew into manhood, he attempted to assert his independence; in so doing he clashed with his domineering mother. This conflict, involving as it did the threats of his mother, led Nero to fear plots against the throne. This fear, coupled with the ambitions of his mistress, Poppaea Sabina, proved to be his undoing. Ultimately his mother, his wife, and his stepbrother Germanicus (son of Claudius) were all disposed of. Increasingly Nero's rule became a reign of terror as plots against the throne were ruthlessly tracked down.

One hot July night in 64, fire broke out in Rome in the slums east of the Circus Maximus and burned with unabated force for nine days, gutting more than half of the city. No effort to check it succeeded. Even Nero's palace lay a charred mass, with all of its priceless art treasures forever lost to posterity. In spite of the emperor's measures to alleviate the sufferings of the homeless, he could not allay the people's suspicion that he started the fire in order to have the glory of rebuilding Rome along grander lines. Rebuild it he did, and he spared no expense in the process. In the middle of the new capital he built his great Golden House, which with its gardens and lakes covered 120 acres.

According to Tacitus,[6] Nero tried to lay the blame for this holocaust on Christians in order to divert suspicion from himself. This view has been generally accepted. Moreover, it has commonly been asserted that Nero was actually to blame for the fire. On the other hand, some have doubted that Nero persecuted Christians or that he blamed the fire on them. For instance, Heichelheim and Yeo[7] observe that none of the contemporary writers mention the Neronian persecution and that Suetonius mentions the Neronian persecution without relating it to the fire. Tacitus, it should be observed, wrote about A.D. 120 and Suetonius about 150.

What is the modern student to think of all this? To begin with, no one will probably ever know whether or not Nero had anything to do with starting the fire; very likely he did not. Second, apparently by Nero's day, Christians were considered to be enemies of society. Increasingly numerous, they strongly opposed many social and religious practices that acted as something of a cement for the pagan society of which they were a part. Therefore, they could be regarded as enemies of that society. In such a hostile atmosphere it was possible to charge them with incendiarism. Third, it seems that the testimonies of Tacitus and Suetonius are reliable and that a very severe persecution of Christians did occur in Rome, instigated by Nero and related to the charge of incendiarism, and that it began in the latter part of 64 and lasted until 66 when Nero went abroad. Ramsay has given a helpful and detailed discussion of the whole question.[8]

In 66 Nero embarked on a grand concert tour of Greece. Having pursued his musical interests for many years, he now invaded the land of the muses, accompanied by numerous musicians, actors, and soldiers. He won hundreds of prizes for his singing and acting. Whether or not he had much real ability modern students will probably never know. The judges at any contest awarded first prize to another at the peril of their lives.

While Nero "fiddled," or rather sang and played his cithara, Rome not only burned but plots against his rule thickened in back rooms at the Senate, in barrooms around the city—and especially in barracks on the frontiers. Nero made the fatal mistake of not paying enough attention to the troops which were, after all, the basis of the emperor's

<hr>

[6]Tacitus, *The Annals*, Chap. XV, Section 44.
[7]Heichelheim and Yeo, pp. 326-27.

[8]William M. Ramsay, *The Church in the Roman Empire Before* A.D. *170* (4th ed.; London: Hodder and Stoughton, 1895), pp. 226-51.

power. Not only did he finally allow their pay to fall in arrears because of worsening financial conditions but he had not even bothered to become acquainted with the commanders. Worse, the full effects of long-term service of men at one location on the frontier were now being felt. Men in the ranks became more attached to their commander than to the emperor or the state. They were willing to fight to raise their officers to the imperial chair.

Civil War. Not long after Nero's return from Greece, a rebellion broke out in Gaul and spread to Rome, where it was supported by the Praetorian Guard and the Senate. Nero fled from the capital and committed suicide. Whether or not he was really insane, as some writers have implied, is open to question. His intense interest in music and drama need not be considered as evidence of his madness. His suspicious nature may in part be attributed to his conflicts with his mother and the resultant insecurity of his office. Some of his executions or exiles were more for the purpose of obtaining funds for such projects as the rebuilding of Rome than for the thwarting of plots. A few of the contemporary writers who endeavored to discredit him did so because of his Hellenistic or Oriental or other non-Roman tendencies in his political and cultural pursuits.

With Nero, the last of the Julio-Claudians, removed from the scene, with armies on the frontiers determined to advance their particular candidates for the imperial chair, and with the Praetorian Guard interfering in affairs closer home, Rome was in for trouble. The year 68/69 is sometimes known as the year of the four emperors. The first, Galba, who had been governor of Hither Spain, was able to buy the support of the Praetorian Guard, and the Senate followed their lead.

Galba ruled during the latter part of 68, but the lukewarm support of the Praetorians

and his failure to win support of the Rhine legions were his undoing. Otho (a former husband of Nero's wife Poppaea) next bought the support of the Guard, which slew Galba. Otho ruled from January to April 69, then was defeated by the legions from the Rhine, and committed suicide. The victorious army set up their commander, Vitellius, who lasted from April to December.

At that point the army of the East went into action under Vespasian. The Danubian legions soon declared for him too. Next the fleet sided with Vespasian. But hard battles were fought in Italy before the incumbent, Vitellius, was slain and Vespasian was recognized as emperor. In this way was inaugurated a dynasty which was to last through three imperial administrations.

Vespasian. Vespasian's rule (69-79) was faced with numerous problems. The entire Empire was in a disheveled state after the civil wars. Rebellions were still in progress in Germany, Gaul, and Judaea. Finances were in disarray; his political position was not effectively established. However, the new emperor met the challenges. He had served in eight different provinces in various capacities and knew the Empire better than most of those who occupied its highest office.

The rebellions were all suppressed in 70. Perhaps the most fiercely fought was the insurrection in Judaea, which had begun in

429. A bronze coin of Vespasian, inscribed "Judaea Capta," commemorating the capture of Jerusalem and Judaea. A palm tree, symbol of Judaea, is flanked by mourning Jew and Jewess.

66. Friction existed between the Jews and Hellenized inhabitants of the cities of Palestine. The Jews also opposed the pressure of Roman taxation. But the greatest cause of the rebellion lay in the monotheistic religion of the Jews which would naturally be opposed to Greco-Roman polytheism and which identified national loyalty and uncompromising devotion to religion.

Vespasian was battering the Jewish rebels when he made his bid for power in 69. He had conquered the countryside and was ready to begin the siege of Jerusalem when he left for Rome. The conquest of the capital he left to his son Titus. After a protracted siege Titus destroyed the city and temple, slaughtered many thousands, and sold many more into slavery. To commemorate this victory, Titus erected a triumphal arch adjacent to the forum in Rome. One of the reliefs of this arch shows plunder from the temple, including the golden candelabra and the silver trumpets.

Next Vespasian reformed the army by developing legions and auxiliary troops of men of mixed nationalities, instead of recruiting them from the frontier regions in which they served. In this way their loyalty would not likely be accorded a given area in its struggle against the state. He also sought legionary enlistment in the provinces, thereby contributing to the broader policy of Romanizing the provinces. This process of Romanization and urbanization he effectively pushed, extending the benefits of citizenship to many communities and enrolling senatorial members from Spain and Gaul.

To insure greater stability of the frontiers, he established extensive fortifications, strengthened defense lines, extended conquests in Britain, and came to terms with the Parthians in the East.

At home, Vespasian treated the senate with respect but not in any sense as an equal partner. They obviously had less power now than earlier in the principate. Part of this decline resulted from an ex-

430. Arch of Titus in the Roman Forum

pansion of the civil service, which now was largely managed by equestrians rather than freedmen.

Vespasian showed tremendous ability in the fiscal affairs of the Empire. Frugality, good business procedures, and sufficient control over the bureaucracy to prevent embezzlement—all contributed to his success. Of special importance was the fact that he had such firm control over the military that he did not have to bribe them to do what he wanted.

Though thrifty, Vespasian managed to find large sums for construction of defenses in the provinces and for public buildings and education in the capital. His most famous structure, which he was not able to finish, was the great Colosseum, built on the site of one of the lakes on the grounds of Nero's palace. On the whole he used much restraint in the treatment of his opposition in the Senate and the city of Rome. For some time he even allowed the Cynics and Stoics to continue their open-air tirades against him, but finally banished them from the city.

Titus. Before he died in A.D. 79, Vespasian had so effectively linked his son Titus with him in the government that there was smooth transition to the new administration. Titus lasted only twenty-six months and died with the goodwill of the populace and the Senate. He showed great moderation in the treatment of political enemies and promoted the general welfare. He delighted the public with his splendid games and shows, and on the occasion of the dedication of the Colosseum held a festival of 100 days' duration. Three major catastrophes marred his reign. In August of 79 Mount Vesuvius erupted, burying Pompeii, Herculaneum, and Stabiae. Then a plague descended on Campania. And in Rome another great fire burned for three days, destroying thousands of homes and several important public structures, including the Pantheon.

Domitian. Titus was succeeded by his younger brother Domitian (81-96), who was received without opposition by the Praetorian Guard and the Senate. Very soon he won the undying hostility of the Senate by his autocratic ways, which indicated his intention of absolute dictatorship. After A.D. 86 he seems to have required officials of his household to address him as "Lord and God." After the rebellion of Saturninus, legate of Upper Germany, during the winter of 88/89, Domitian grew increasingly suspicious and inaugurated something of a reign of terror in Rome. Many prominent persons were executed on trumped-up charges of treason, others on the ground of "atheism."

Among the latter were some notable converts to Judaism or Christianity. A persecution of Christians broke out in the Empire about 90. Actually, it was originally

431. Relief from Arch of Titus showing seven-branch lampstand, the ark and trumpets being carried off from the Temple by Titus

directed against Jews who refused to pay a tax to Jupiter Capitolinus. Being associated with Judaism in the minds of many, Christians also suffered during this persecution. Domitian generally enforced emperor worship. Upon refusal to participate, Christians were charged with treason. Some were martyred, some dispossessed of property, and others banished. It was during this persecution that the Apostle John was exiled to the Isle of Patmos, where he received the vision of the Revelation.

But Domitian cannot be dismissed as a mere tyrant. In Rome he was an able administrator and built extensively in an effort to erase the scars left by the great fire of 80. His finest public structure was the Temple of Jupiter on the Capitoline Hill, with columns of Greek marble, gold-plated doors, and a roof overlaid with gold leaf. He kept the populace happy with bread and games and the soldiers content with higher pay. He pushed Romanization in the provinces and saw to it that they were governed by men of ability, with the result that they flourished under his rule. Along the frontiers he built numerous fortresses and garrison camps; and after costly battles in Dacia, he managed to stabilize the situation there. Roman territory in Britain was increased.

While Domitian had his abilities and demonstrated them, he is more often remembered for his tyranny and his reign of terror. Ultimately it seemed that no one was safe. His wife Domitia, believing she was to be the next victim, conspired with two members of the Praetorian Guard and others. When the emperor fell a victim to the assassin's dagger on September 16, 96, his memory was cursed by the exultant senate. Nerva, who followed him, was the first of the group known as the five good emperors.[9]

[9]In keeping with the general plan of this work, the history of an area is not carried in detail beyond the end of the first century, about which time the Revelation, last book of the New Testament to be composed, was written.

432. Titus

Demise of the empire. In the first decades of the second century A.D. there were wars which added territory north of the Danube and in the Mesopotamian valley and brought the Empire to its largest extent in 117, but these conflicts did not upset the general peace and security.

Toward the end of the second century, the principate was on the way out. The economic base of the municipalities began to show increasing signs of strain; this was coupled with the militarization of the state. The latter situation was largely the fault of Lucius Septimius Severus (193-211), who was put into power by the army of the Danube and felt that he had to favor the army. He increased its size and improved its conditions of service and discharge benefits. From this time on, officers moved di-

433. The Colosseum today

rectly into important positions in the civil service on retirement from army life. The effects of this militarization were soon felt.

The years 235-283 constituted a period of anarchy, of barrack-room emperors, many of whom bought their position from the armies. Some forty of them were put forward by the armies during those years. At last Diocletian established order out of confusion and effected a reorganization of the state, the details of which are not particularly relative to this study. His reorganization was not very effective because civil war started again at the end of his reign. Peace was restored when Constantine established himself as sole ruler and moved the capital of the Empire to Constantinople.

During the decades just before Diocletian took office, barbarian tribes moved against the northern frontiers of the Empire, especially in the Danubian region.

Some of these had been permitted to move into the Empire and to settle along the frontiers where they would serve as a buffer against other barbarians. Before these tribes were completely Romanized, a new wave of barbarian infiltration began in the fourth century during the days of Constantine. This was too much of a strain for the Empire, and it began to disintegrate into semibarbarian states. Although Rome was no longer the seat of power after A.D. 476, the Empire continued on in the East, with its capital at Constantinople, until 1453.[10]

[10]This historical treatment is somewhat elongated and seemingly throws this work out of balance. However, it is inserted here because it provides historical background for the New Testament period, since the Roman Empire at that time controlled the whole Mediterranean world. Moreover, this survey provides a wider historical context for several of the other sections of this book: Greece, Asia Minor, Cyprus, Phoenicia, Syria, Palestine, and Egypt.

434. The Colosseum reconstructed

The Apostle Paul in Italy

The Italy Paul visited was fully enjoying the *Pax Romana* and had not yet reached the height of her prosperity. Her most magnificent structures had not yet been built and the limits of her territorial expansion had not been reached. Moreover, cracks had not yet begun to appear in the hull of the ship of state, and there were no evident signs that the ship would one day break apart and sink. Romans were still quite confident, and their rule of the Empire was still effective. As will be recalled, the Apostle Paul was brought to Italy because he had appealed to Caesar for the adjudication of a case which had not been satisfactorily handled in Palestine. On the way he had been shipwrecked at Malta.

After three months in Malta,[11] Paul and

[11] The island where Paul was shipwrecked is called "Melita" in Acts 28:1, Authorized Version. Although some have claimed in the past that an island in the Adriatic Sea was where the apostle really landed, it now seems beyond all reasonable doubt that the African Melita (Malta) is the correct identification.

Malta is an arid, rocky islet 58 miles south of Sicily, 149 miles south of the European mainland, and 180 miles north of Cape Bon in Tunisia. A little over 17 miles long, 9 miles wide, and 60 miles in circumference, it is the chief island of the Maltese group—which also includes Gozo and Comino Islands. The island of Malta with its 95 square miles of land is of limestone formation with thin but fertile soil. Agriculture is its chief occupation, but uncertain rainfall makes farming a rather risky business. With an average rainfall of 21 inches per year, it actually has a rainfall which varies from 12 to 27 inches; and periods of drought have extended over three years. There are no rivers or rivulets on the island. Springs flow, but the largest part of the water supply is pumped from strata just above sea level. The climate is temperate and

435. Interior of the Colosseum

his companions boarded ship for Italy (Acts 28:11). Very likely the month was March.[12] The year may have been 59.[13] The vessel on which they traveled, "a ship of Alexandria," was almost certainly one of the large ships of the grain fleet supplying Rome. Some of these ships must have been approximately as large as modern merchantmen. The grain ship on which Paul sailed to Malta carried 276 passengers besides its cargo of wheat (Acts 27:37). The ship on which Josephus came to Italy later in the century had a passenger list of 600.[14] A grain ship on which Lucian of Antioch sailed late in the second century was 180 feet in length and 45 feet in breadth. Smith estimates the tonnage of that ship at between eleven and twelve hundred tons.[15] By comparison, Columbus' three ships had a combined tonnage of about 200, and a combined crew of about 90.

Ancient ships were sailed mainly by one large sail on a single mast. The leverage of this one large sail on a single mast exercised a tremendous disruptive power on the hull of the vessel. Sometimes there was a topsail above the mainsail. Also, there might be one or more small storm sails which could be substituted for the great sail when the wind was too strong. In addition, there was frequently a small sail on the bow.

healthful for the greater part of the year, with a mean annual temperature of 64.5 degrees. There are no high mountains on the island; the Bingemma Range rises 726 feet. Sheer cliffs 400 feet in height are seen along the southwest coast.

The occupation of Malta dates to Neolithic times. It was inhabited by Phoenicians in St. Paul's day. Luke calls the people *barbaroi* (Acts 28:2), which tallies with the testimony of Diodorus Siculus that they were Phoenicians, neither Hellenized nor Romanized. Exactly when the Phoenicians came is a matter of some debate. Perhaps they visited the island as early as 1000 B.C., but they did not found colonies there before approximately the seventh century B.C. Interesting Phoenician remains may still be seen on the island. Carthaginians came in the sixth century. Apparently the high stage of manufacturing and commercial prosperity attained in Carthaginian times continued under the Romans, who captured the Maltese group from Carthage in 218 B.C.

Ruins of palaces and dwellings of the Roman period indicate a high degree of civilization and wealth. After the fall of the western part of the Roman Empire, Byzantium continued to hold the island, which was finally overrun by Muslims in A.D. 870. The British conquered it in 1800 and have constructed an important naval base there. It became the "world's most bombed spot" in World War II, suffering more than 1200 air raids. The present capital is Valletta, and the population of the island is some 330,000. Malta became an independent country within the Commonwealth of Nations September 21, 1964.

On his voyage to Rome, Paul was shipwrecked on the island after two weeks in a storm (Acts 27: 43) and stayed there three months until favorable sailing weather (Acts 28:11). The traditional place of the landing is eight miles north of the present capital. James Smith argues from a detailed comparison of the account in Acts with the topography of the area that the traditional site is the actual one (*The Voyage and Shipwreck of St. Paul* [4th ed.; London: Longmans, Green, and Co., 1880], pp. 129-47).

Soon after the shipwrecked party landed, Paul was attacked by a poisonous snake. The fact that the only species of snakes on the island today are

nonvenomous means nothing. Malta has been stripped of its woods since New Testament times, and the populace would tend to destroy poisonous snakes during the intervening 1900 years.

The castaways were hosted by Publius, apparently the Roman governor of the island, whose father was healed in answer to the apostle's prayers (Acts 28:7-8). Tradition has it that the island was evangelized at this time, that Publius was one of the converts, and that he became the first Christian bishop of Malta.

[12]The closed season in the Mediterranean was November 10 to March 10.

[13]Paul apparently appeared before Festus shortly after the latter took office, probably in 58. The apostle would then have been sent to Rome late in the same year. After wintering in Malta, he would have resumed his journey in 59. There are many problems involved in establishing the Pauline chronology. On the basis of a different calculation, the apostle may have come to Rome in 61.

[14]Josephus' *Life*, Section 3.

[15]Smith, pp. 188-90.

THE WYCLIFFE HISTORICAL GEOGRAPHY OF BIBLE LANDS

436. A street scene in Pompeii

Syracuse. After leaving Malta, Paul's ship next docked at Syracuse, about 100 miles away. Located on the east coast of Sicily, Syracuse was the principal city of the island. Originally a Corinthian colony founded in the eighth century B.C., Syracuse became one of the most magnificent Greek states. Its ancient power was well demonstrated by its conquest of the great Athenian expedition of 415 B.C. At the end of the First Punic War in 241 B.C., Syracuse fell with the rest of Sicily to the Romans. During the Second Punic War it sided with Carthage; and Rome was forced to conquer it, which she did in 212. The city was thoroughly plundered and tremendous booty was taken.

From that time it sank into the condition of an ordinary Roman provincial town. Sicily suffered terribly during the Roman civil wars of the last part of the first century B.C. Syracuse was so decayed that Augustus tried to restore it by sending a Roman colony there in 21 B.C. Strabo, writing around the time of Christ, described the whole island of Sicily as in a state of decay, some of the cities having disappeared and others declining. The interior to a large extent was given over to grazing and horse breeding. Whether Syracuse regained its old prosperity during the first century A.D. is uncertain. But it did continue to be one

of the most important cities of Sicily throughout the Roman Empire. It was destroyed by the Muslims in A.D. 878 and never recovered the greatness it once enjoyed. Today it is located in one of the most economically depressed sections of Italy.

Paul's ship lay at anchor here for three days on his way to Rome. Nothing is said about his doing any preaching in the city. The ship was waiting for favorable winds and needed to be ready to sail at any moment, so there were no shore leaves. It seems that Christianity spread to Sicily from the mainland at a later time.

Numerous proud structures would have met the eye of the apostle if he had been able to roam the streets of Syracuse. For instance, Augustus had built a great amphitheater there. The city boasted the largest ancient theater in Sicily—about 440 feet in diameter. From the fifth century B.C. dated an imposing Greek fortress, a temple to Athena 160 by 70 feet, and an even larger one to Apollo.[16]

Rhegium. From Syracuse the grain ship sailed northeastward to Rhegium (modern Reggio). The King James Version says the sailors "fetched a compass" (Acts 28: 13). The New English Bible says they "sailed round." Commentators have some-

437. Part of Domitian's palace on the Palatine

[16]Camden M. Cobern, *The New Archeological Discoveries* (9th ed.; New York: Funk & Wagnalls Co., 1929), pp. 557-58.

times suggested that the ship actually sailed around the island. The Greek *perielthontes* is difficult; but James Smith, a practical yachtsman, provides a satisfactory explanation. To him the term signifies that the wind was so unfavorable that the ship could not run a straight course but had to tack, running out northeastward toward Italy and then back to the Sicilian coast.[17] J. B. Phillips, in *The New Testament in Modern English*, supports this viewpoint with his translation "from there we tacked round to Rhegium."

Rhegium was close to the narrowest point of the Straits of Messina, separating Sicily and Italy, just opposite the Sicilian town of Messana (formerly Zancle). The actual point of crossing from Sicily was at Columna, six miles or more north of Rhegium. The straits were very dangerous in ancient times—more so than now. Some miles north of Rhegium was the dangerous rock Scylla (Scilla) and north of Messana was the whirlpool of Charybdis (Galofalo). Ships often had to lie at Rhegium waiting for a suitable wind so that they might avoid these dangers and also navigate the periodically swift currents in the straits. As a result, Castor and Pollux, the patrons and protectors of sailors, were much worshiped at Rhegium and were represented on its coins. Mariners of the ships that put in there often discharged their vows to the

439. Gladiator's bronze helmet, second century A.D.

twin gods in the town. It will be remembered that the ship on which Paul traveled sailed under the sign of Castor and Pollux (Acts 28:11).

Rhegium, a Greek town founded by Chalcis about 720 B.C., was destroyed by Syracuse in 387, and the inhabitants were sold as slaves. Rebuilt, it was destroyed again between 280 and 270 by Campanian troops. When her army captured it, Rome gave the town back to the remnant of its former population. From that time on, the town was allied with Rome and successfully withstood attacks by Rome's enemies, including Hannibal. The inhabitants received Roman citizenship in 88 B.C. at the end of the social war. Despite frequent earthquakes, it remained a populous Greek-speaking city throughout imperial times. The ship in which Paul sailed from Malta to Puteoli (Pozzuoli) lay for a day in the harbor of Rhegium, waiting for a south

438. Trajan, who brought the Roman Empire to its greatest extent, built a new forum near the Roman Forum.

[17]Smith, p. 156.

wind. The Rhegium to Puteoli run, a distance of 180 miles, probably took about twenty-six hours (Acts 28:13).

Puteoli. Puteoli was the great commercial port of Italy, located on what is now called the Bay of Naples. The name is of doubtful origin but is attributed either to the putrid odor of the sulphurous springs close by or to the wells (*putei*) of the place. A colony of the nearby Greek town of Cumae, to which it served as a port, Puteoli was in existence at least by the sixth century B.C. During and after the Second Punic War it rose to a high degree of commercial importance, which it subsequently retained.

Puteoli became the chief port of Rome, though it was 150 miles away. It won that distinction because of the safety of its harbor and the inhospitality of the coast near Rome. Although Claudius created an artificial harbor at Ostia (near Rome), Puteoli's trade had not markedly declined in the days of Nero. But the southern port decayed rapidly early in the second century after Trajan made the harbor at Ostia adequate. The city never recovered from the Barbarian invasions of A.D. 410, 455, and 545.

While a great part of the goods handled at Puteoli were Alexandrian grain supplies for Rome, that was only one branch of its extensive commerce. The iron of Elba, after being smelted in Populonium (Populonia) was brought to Puteoli for manufacture into a variety of implements and formed an important element in the brisk trade with Africa and Spain. The port also profited from an extensive copper and bronze industry. Campanian bronze was used all over Europe in the form of utensils and weapons. Work in gold also went on there, as did production of Surrentine pottery (a red ware).

Campania was also famous for its wines, and it produced olive oil and perfumes from its rose gardens. Luxury goods from the

440. L. Septimius Severns built a triumphal arch at the west end of the Roman Forum.

Orient formed an important part of the trade of Puteoli in value, though not in bulk. Trade with Tyre was of such importance that the Tyrians had a merchant colony there. Several merchants of Berytus (Beirut) also lived at Puteoli. Travelers from the East frequently landed there; the disembarkation of Paul and that of Cicero before him are cases in point. The neighborhood of Puteoli became a favorite resort of the Roman upper classes; many of them had villas there.

As already indicated, Puteoli had an excellent port. It was well sheltered by its natural situation and was further protected by an extensive mole or pier thrown out into the bay at least 418 yards. This pier may date from the time of Augustus. Extensive docks were constructed to care for the city's widespread maritime interests. A great boon for construction of dock works was the fact that the city had a good supply of volcanic sand which formed a mortar or cement of extreme hardness and durability and was also waterproof.

Into this bustling port of some 100,000 came the Apostle Paul, probably on one of the first grain ships to dock that spring. The smoke of Mount Vesuvius is something he did not see as his ship glided across the Gulf of Puteoli. The volcano was at that time a harmless-looking mountain whose

441. "The situation of the ship [Paul's] on the fifteenth morning," painted by H. Smartly

southern slopes were covered with vines. Less than twenty years were to elapse before the lava flowed and hot cinders fell on that terrible August night in A.D. 79.

There seems to have been a Jewish colony at Puteoli,[18] and this may possibly account for the presence of Christians in the town. At any rate, believers there desired Paul to stay with them for a week (Acts 28:14). Exactly how this was possible when the apostle was a prisoner is not quite clear.

Some of the ruins of the ancient mole, at which Paul must have landed, are still to be seen. How many of the other archaeological remains (including baths, aqueducts, villas, and the like) date to the middle of the first century is not clear. The great amphitheater, which was not too much smaller than the Colosseum, was certainly built after Nero's day. The second amphitheater was already in existence during Augustus' reign.[19] This was no mean structure, measuring 426 by 312 feet. In it Nero entertained Tiridates, king of Armenia, with shows of gladiatorial combats and wild beast fights.

The Roman roads. From Puteoli, the apostolic company took the tomb-lined Via Consularis to Capua (20 miles away),

where it joined the main line of the Appian Way. The distance from Puteoli to Rome was 155 Roman miles or 142 English miles (a Roman mile was 1,614.6 yards). From Capua to Rome was considered to be a journey of five days for an active traveler. Ramsay concluded that travelers on foot seem to have accomplished 16 to 20 miles a day on an average Roman road, the ordinary rate being about 17. Travelers driving wagons or other vehicles moved at the rate of 4 Roman miles an hour or about 25 Roman miles a day. The imperial post could travel as fast as 50 miles a day.[20] Whether Paul and his companions walked or rode we have no way of knowing.

Rome took great pride in her road system which she flung in every direction from the capital throughout Italy and the Empire. In those days it was literally true that all roads led to Rome. Initially designed as military highways, they served also as arteries for commerce. Special officials of praetorian or even of consular rank were entrusted with the maintenance of the roads. And at important points permanent military guards in special guardhouses were stationed. These guards had responsibility not only for care of the roads but even more for keeping the roads and the public in the region around safe from robbers.

Rome not only exercised great care in the maintenance of her roads but she built them to last. Some modern roads in Italy and elsewhere in the Mediterranean world are merely blacktopped Roman roads. Naturally the type of construction varied with expected traffic, terrain, and available materials. Mountain roads might be only five to six feet wide (with wider places for passing) and surfaced with gravel, while the main roads were fifteen to twenty feet wide and paved with stone.

When constructing an important road, Roman engineers dug a trench the full

[18]Josephus, *Antiquities of the Jews*, Book XVIII, Chap. VI.
[19]G. T. Rivoira, *Roman Architecture*, trans. G. M. Rushforth (Oxford: At the Clarendon Press, 1925), p. 91.

[20]William M. Ramsay, "Roads and Travel in the New Testament," *A Dictionary of the Bible*, ed. by James Hastings (New York: Charles Scribner's Sons, 1904), Extra Volume, pp. 386-87.

THE WYCLIFFE HISTORICAL GEOGRAPHY OF BIBLE LANDS

width of the road four to five feet deep. The roadbed was then built up with successive layers of large and small stone and rammed gravel. The surface paving was made of large carefully fitted stone (without the use of mortar or metal), about a foot thick and a foot and a half across. Generally the roads were straight, going over hills rather than around them. Therefore, slopes might be steep; 10 percent grades were common. Where roads crossed streams, stone bridges were usually built, resting on a series of arches based on piers of masonry. Some Roman bridges are still in use.

The Appian Way, the principal road to southern Italy, was begun in 312 B.C. as a military road by the famous censor Appius Claudius Caecus and ultimately was extended to Tarentum and Brundisium. Paving of the road was begun in 295 B.C. and was certainly completed by Gracchan times. Its width was about eighteen feet, wide enough for two wagons to pass abreast; and it was paved with basaltic lava (silex).

As on the other great roads, inns, taverns, and places of refreshment existed in abundance along the Appian Way. Little is known about them and the little that is known gives no favorable picture. The inns seem to have been little removed in character from houses of prostitution. The Antonine Itinerary lists eight main stations on the Appian Way between Capua and Rome, two of which are mentioned in Luke's narrative—Appii Forum and Tres Tabernae (Three Taverns).

Appii Forum. When Christians in Rome received word that Paul was coming, they came as far south as Appii Forum and Three Taverns to meet him (Acts 28:15). Appii Forum, apparently named for the builder of the Appian Way, was located forty-three Roman miles from Rome, in the middle of the Pontine Marshes. A canal ran alongside the road from here to the sixty-second milestone, and it was used chiefly at night for conveying passengers in barges towed by mules. Horace (65-8 B.C.), not long before the birth of Christ, told of his experience of spending the night at Appii Forum. Apparently conditions did not change much before Paul's arrival.

Horace said that the water was so bad it made him sick. And when night descended, a "hideous clatter" arose as the bargemen along the canal prepared to move their human cargo downstream. Then there was the confusion of stuffing 300 passengers on one barge and collecting their fares. All hope of sleep fled because of croaking bullfrogs, buzzing mosquitoes, and the singing of drunken bargemen and passengers. And so the hours of a romantic Italian evening wore on.[21]

Three Taverns. Ten Roman miles closer to Rome was Three Taverns (Tres Tabernae). The location of this place, long in doubt, has now been determined with some degree of certainty at a point near the beginning of the Pontine Marshes, about three miles from modern Cisterna. The Latin *tabernae* signifies booths, huts, or shops of various kinds. Here it probably denotes inns for travelers. From Tres Tabernae the apostolic party traveled the seventeen miles to Aricia and then moved along the last sixteen miles between Aricia and Rome.

442. The Appian Way near Rome

[21]Horace, *Satires*, Chap. I, Section 5, p. 87.

The last leg of the journey. About eleven miles from the capital was the ancient village of Bovillae. Here was the center of the ancestor cult of the Julian family, and here Augustus' body lay for a night on its way to Rome. Tiberius reconstructed the shrine, in which the statue of the deified Augustus was placed. He also instituted games in the nearby circus, a few of the arches of which may still be seen among the vineyards. Probably most of the way between Bovillae and Rome was lined with tombs. Since Roman law forbade burial of the dead inside the city, it became the practice to build tombs along the principal roads. By the time of Nero, tombs extended for many miles along the main roads, especially the Appian Way.

Some three miles from the Porta Capena, which led through the old Servian Wall and into the main part of the city, Paul would have passed the famous Claudian aqueduct, though it was obscured from his view by the contour of the land. This great water channel rested on 110-foot arches which strode across the landscape to bring water to Rome from a distance of forty-five miles. Begun by Caligula in A.D. 38 and completed by Claudius in 52, it brought a total of nearly 50,000,000 gallons of water per day to the city.[22] There were at least seven other aqueducts supplying the capital in Nero's day.

With the Claudian aqueduct far off to his right over the hill, the tomb of Caecilia Metella stood almost in front of Paul to the right of the road. The woman for whom the tomb was built was the wife of a certain M. Crassus, presumably the son of the triumvir of the same name, who had shared power in Rome with Julius Caesar and Pompey. Some have thought Caecilia was the wife of the triumvir himself, but decorations of the tomb seem to date it to the beginning of the Augustan period. The tomb is a huge drum of concrete on a square base. Faced with travertine, it is sixty feet in its outside diameter. The roof probably originally consisted of a conical vault. In the Middle Ages the tomb was transformed into a fortress and the crenellation (battlements) added around the top. The elegant frieze of ox heads and leaves remains as a memento of its former grandeur.

About a mile farther down the road was the Campus Rediculi, where, according to Pliny the Elder, a pet crow of Tiberius was buried.[23] A little beyond that, still on the right, were the columbaria (burial vaults) of the slaves and freedmen of Livia, wife of Augustus. A mile farther down the road, again on the apostle's right, would have been a celebrated temple of Mars, god of war. And about a half mile beyond stood the third century B.C. tomb of the celebrated Scipio family. After another five or six blocks, Paul found himself at the Porta Capena, the gate through the old Servian Wall into the main part of the city. This wall, built during the first half of the fourth century B.C., was deep within the city of the first century A.D. No longer needed for defense, the wall had been allowed to fall into decay.

Arrival in Rome. It is hard to imagine what the Apostle Paul's thoughts may have

443. Tomb of Caecilia Metella

[22]Samuel B. Platner, *A Topographical Dictionary of Ancient Rome*, completed and revised by Thomas Ashby (London: Oxford University Press, 1929), p. 22.

[23]Thomas Ashby, *The Roman Campagna in Classical Times* (New York: The Macmillan Co., 1927), p. 178.

been as he stood there at the Porta Capena. If he had been a poor provincial from rural Palestine, one might picture him as over-awed with the great metropolis. But such was not the case. Paul had been born in the proud city of Tarsus. His missionary activities had taken him to most of the important cities of the East—to Antioch, Ephesus, Corinth, Athens, Thessalonica, and Jerusalem. Certainly he did not come with the curiosity of a tourist or the acquisitiveness of a businessman. No doubt there was some trepidation as he realized that the moment when he would stand trial for his life was drawing closer. And probably there was the enthusiasm of an evangelist who longed for a means of winning some in this strategic center to faith in the Lord Jesus.

The Circus Maximus. As the apostolic company passed through the gate, before them stood the great Circus Maximus, and overhanging it on the right were the palaces of the Caesars on the Palatine Hill. As a modern visitor to Rome strolls across the great grassy area where once stood the Circus Maximus and glances up at the massive ruined substructures of the imperial palaces, he has a hard time visualizing the sight which greeted the apostle's eyes.

Between the parallel slopes of the Aventine and Palatine lay a valley some 600 yards long and 150 yards broad. Here the great circus had evolved through a process of repeated destruction and rebuilding. And it was destined to be almost completely rebuilt by Nero after the fire of 64.

In Paul's day the total length of the circus was about 600 yards and the total width not over 200 yards. The width was achieved by building out over the streets on the north and south sides. The size of the arena was

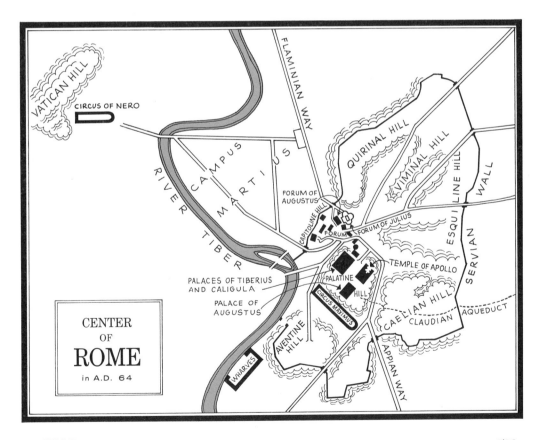

about 570 yards long by about 85 yards wide. In the middle of it stood the spina (the central barrier around which chariots raced), 345 yards in length. On the spina were fountains, statues of dignitaries, an obelisk from Egypt, and bronze dolphins and large egg-shaped blocks of wood to help spectators keep track of the number of laps run in a given race.

At the west end were the twelve *carceres* or starting places for chariots. These were set on a curve so the distance was the same from each to the starting line, and they were closed by rope barriers which were dropped simultaneously at the start. The east end of the circus was curved, with a gate in the center. A raised platform surrounded the arena, on which chairs of high officials were placed. From this platform rose three tiers of seats, the lower of stone and the upper and perhaps the middle of wood. Estimates of seating capacity vary greatly, but perhaps 200,000 is not far from wrong. The exterior consisted of a three-story arcade with engaged columns, like the Colosseum, and all was covered with marble.

The circus was by no means the only place a Roman could go to be entertained in Paul's day. There were also amphitheaters, theaters, and baths. It was the emperor who took the lead in building most of the structures for public entertainment, and it was usually he who paid for the entertainment provided in these structures once they were finished.

445. The Circus Maximus reconstructed, viewed from the west end. The palaces of the Caesars on the Palatine Hill rise on the left.

Palaces of the emperors. As already noted the palaces of the emperors stood on the Palatine Hill overlooking the Circus Maximus. Today virtually all one can see on the Palatine is great masses of brickwork with arched roofs. In Paul's day these structures were all encased in marble. On the Palatine Hill Augustus, Tiberius, and Claudius had all built their palaces, which eventually covered the hill.

Connected with the palace of Augustus (more modest than the rest) was a beautiful temple of Apollo built of white marble and surrounded by porticoes with columns of yellow marble. Of the images within, of Apollo, Latona, and Artemis, the first was sculptured by Scopas. This temple lasted throughout the imperial period.

The location of neither the temple nor Augustus' palace can be identified with certainty today. But one can still see part of the house of Livia, Augustus' wife, with its wall paintings that are reminiscent of those to be seen at Pompeii. On the northwest part of the hill, Tiberius built his palace, the site of which is today almost covered by the Farnese Gardens. Only a little of the southern and western sides of the palace can be seen, and little is known of it. Caligula extended the palace of Tiberius toward the Forum, and it seems that there were stairs leading from the palace down into the Forum in Paul's day. At that time too there were temples to Jupiter and Magna Mater (Cybele) on the Palatine.

444. The Circus Maximus from the east end

The entire Palatine was modified by new buildings of Domitian, who demolished earlier buildings of the whole central part of the hill. The palace of his day consisted of two great complexes of rooms, each surrounding an open courtyard. One of these complexes is known as the *Domus Flavia* and the other, the *Domus Augustana*. Adjacent was the "stadium," which was probably used for minor games or entertainments; it was not big enough for chariot racing.

Although Nero is probably responsible for some of the construction on the Palatine, he built his palace on the Esquiline, northeast of where the Colosseum now stands. The palace was destroyed by the great fire of 64. It was not in the palace but in one of the public buildings in the Forum that Paul would appear before Nero.

446. Remains of the palace of Tiberius

Appeal to Caesar. But Paul was not destined to be granted a hearing for a long time. After a stay of two whole years in the capital, his case still had not been adjudicated (Acts 28:30). Reasons for the delay can only be conjectured. Perhaps there was a large backlog of cases; perhaps the court did not meet often to deal with cases of this type; conceivably the prosecution failed to present its case; possibly the settlement of such cases depended on the whim of the emperor. At any rate, there was a delay; and meanwhile the apostle lived "at his

447. The palaces of the Caesars from the Circus Maximus

own expense," the preferred translation of "his own hired house" (Acts 28:30).

There Paul was in Rome. He had appealed to Caesar; exactly why is not clear, but reasons may be found. In the first place, he may have been afraid that authorities in Judaea would keep him in prison indefinitely with the hope of obtaining handsome bribes (Acts 24:26) and that the only way to escape was to appeal to Caesar and in this way be guaranteed a hearing of his case. Second, he may have felt that to submit to another trial in Judaea would result in his ultimate conviction and execution. Festus, the new procurator, apparently was interested in buying the goodwill of the Jews by tokens of this sort (Acts 24:27). Then too the Jews seemed rather determined to destroy him (Acts 23:12). Third, Paul may have actually felt that an appeal to Caesar would win him an opportunity to go to Italy to engage in missionary work and that he could reasonably hope for acquittal in the pagan capital on the mere charge of propagating the Jewish religion.

Whatever the reason, Paul had appealed; and Festus, after discussing the case with his council, decided to send him to Rome (Acts 25:10-12). He delivered him and other prisoners to Julius, "a centurion of Augustus' band" (Acts 27:1). Probably by this we are to understand that Julius was

448. Remains of a fountain and pool in
the Domus Flavia

captain of a cohort of the Praetorian Guard
responsible for communication service between the emperor and his provincial armies and authorities. When he arrived in
Rome, Paul was delivered to the "captain
of the guard" (Acts 28:16), which Sherwin-
White understands to be the head of the
organizational command of the Praetorian
Guard.[24]

The opportunity for provincials to appeal
to Caesar presumably arose early in Augustus' reign. When he appeared before the
Senate in 27 B.C. to turn over control of the
state, that venerable body conferred upon
Augustus the proconsular imperium, by
which he had full authority to rule the imperial provinces. Generally speaking, imperial provinces were those not fully Romanized and therefore requiring a body of
soldiers to keep order. Senatorial provinces on the other hand were pacified and
did not require troops. Gradually Caesar
became the supreme court for provincials
in imperial provinces. Since Judaea was
ruled directly by the emperor through his
procurators,[25] appeals would early have
been sent from there.

[24]A. N. Sherwin-White, *Roman Society and Roman Law in the New Testament* (Oxford: At the
Clarendon Press, 1963), p. 110.
[25]The first procurator, Coponius, was appointed
in A.D. 6 when Herod Archelaus was deposed. Procurators then ruled Judaea continuously until the
fall of Jerusalem except for the brief reign of Herod
Agrippa I (41-44).

Subsequently, in 23 B.C., the Senate conferred upon Augustus the *maius*, or greater,
imperium, which gave him the right to interfere in any province. Thus all provincials
came to look upon the emperor as the final
court of appeal. What began with Augustus was continued to an increasing degree
under successive rulers.

When the emperor acted as judge, he
called a council of about a half dozen of
his advisers to consult with him on how to
deal with the case at hand. Usually the
Praetorian prefect (commander of the Praetorian Guard, who might be almost a second ruler, as was Sejanus during Tiberius'
reign) judged *vice principis*. And probably in the case of lesser individuals like Paul,
the Praetorian prefect handled the entire
case as president of the emperor's court,

449. A marble floor in the Domus Flavia

without consulting his superior. Certainly
it was impossible for the emperor to handle all of the maze of detail which called
for his attention; and during periods when
the chief executive was out of the city,
much work had to be deputized. Seemingly under Nero the trial of capital cases on
appeal was delegated to other persons and
the sentences were confirmed by him afterward.[26] It is probable then that Paul never
appeared before Nero at all.

[26]Sherwin-White, p. 111.

THE WYCLIFFE HISTORICAL GEOGRAPHY OF BIBLE LANDS

Appearance of Rome. So Paul had appealed, and now he waited for his case to be heard. In what part of the city he was confined is not known, and how much freedom he had to move about is not known. If he had gone for a walk in Rome, he would not have found it to be very impressive. True, the city had its palaces, some fine temples, recreational establishments, and the like. And there were parks (perhaps as much as one-eighth of the city was reserved for this purpose) and homes of the wealthy.

But in much of the old city the streets were narrow, steep, and crooked—often not more than ten feet wide. They were frequently littered with garbage and were unlighted at night—quite in contrast to the well-illuminated Antioch from which the apostle's missionary journeys had been launched. In the poorer sections of the city, wooden tenement houses (*insulae*) rose to a height of as many as six stories, each one covering a block. Often these were poorly constructed, and sometimes they collapsed. Running water from the aqueducts was available only on the first floors. Light and heat were inadequate. These huge tinderboxes provided abundant fuel when the fire of Rome roared through the city in 64.

The wider streets, the great baths, and many of the finest buildings of Rome were to come during the rebuilding after the fire and as Rome with her imperial income was able to finance more beautiful and imposing structures in later centuries. Though reportedly Augustus had bragged that he had found Rome a city of brick and left it a city of marble, there was much lacking when Paul arrived close to a half century later.

The Forum area. At last the day for Paul's trial came; exactly when it was we do not know. More than likely it occurred in the Basilica Julia at the southwest end of the Forum. There is no way of knowing from

450. The stadium of Domitian

which direction Paul came to the Forum. For the purposes of this study, let us suppose it was from the east. Let us remember that the Roman Forum no longer served as the scene for as much business as it had in the days of the Republic. To the northwest Julius had begun a new forum of his own. Augustus had finished it and added one of his own alongside that of Julius'. After Paul's day, Vespasian, Domitian, Nerva, and Trajan would continue the expansion.

As Paul came into the Forum[27] area down the Sacred Way from the east, the first building he would have passed was the house of the vestal virgins. He might have observed that the house was rather large for a sisterhood of only six priestesses. But such an objection is erased with the observation that the vestals were held in high esteem and that their house was chosen by private citizens and by the state as a safe deposit for documents.

Adjacent to this house was the Temple of Vesta. Vesta was the goddess of the hearth and was considered the patron of the fire that symbolized the perpetuity of the state. It was the responsibility of the priestesses

[27]It is very difficult for the modern visitor to Rome to visualize the Forum as Paul knew it because of the constant rebuilding carried on subsequently. Many of the ruins to be seen are of buildings dating to the rebuilding by Septimius Severus (193-211).

451. A coin of Agrippa II (Acts 25:13–26:32)

to maintain this sacred fire and to renew it each year on March 1, the first day of the Roman year.

Just in front of the Temple of Vesta was the Regia, official residence of the Pontifex Maximus, head of the religion of the State and repository of the acts of the college of pontiffs concerning the religious life of Rome and the sacred law. As Paul continued westward, he passed the Temple of Caesar, or the Temple of the Divine Julius, which is supposed to have stood on the very site where the dictator's body was burned on a pyre improvised by the crowds after Mark Antony's famous speech.

When the apostle came to the corner of the Temple of Caesar, the Sacred Way turned left and passed in front of the temple and led straight to the steps of the Temple of Castor and Pollux, which became the sanctuary of horsemen. As Paul faced this temple with its eleven Corinthian columns about thirty-eight feet high (three of which may be seen today), to his left was the Arch of Augustus.

Now the Sacred Way turned right, and Paul found himself alongside the Basilica Julia at last. Straight before him in the center of the Forum stood the Rostra, where orators made public speeches. At one corner of the Rostra was the *miliarum aureum,*

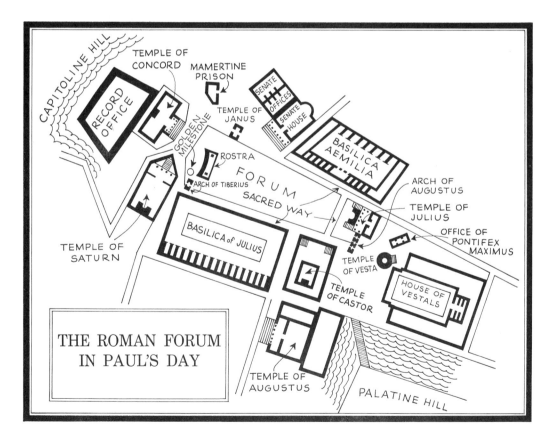

THE ROMAN FORUM IN PAUL'S DAY

452. Remains of the Temple of Vesta

Lucius Caesar, his two young grandsons. The structure was 312 feet long by 156 feet wide[28] with a great center hall measuring 234 by 85 feet. The latter was surrounded on all sides by a double row of brick pillars, faced with marble, which formed aisles that were vaulted and stuccoed. Above the aisles were galleries.

The central hall was covered with a wooden roof, which rose above the roof of the side aisles on a clerestory. Through this light was admitted into the great hall. The floor was paved with slabs of marble, colored in the central court and white in the aisles. The structure was abundantly beautified with sculpture, mostly in the form of freestanding statues.

or golden milestone, a marble column covered with gilt bronze, on which the distances from Rome to the principal towns of Italy and the Empire were marked. Next to the golden milestone stood the Arch of Tiberius. Behind that a portion of the Temple of Saturn was visible; and beyond, at the edge of the Capitoline Hill was the Temple of Concord, behind which rose the Public Record Office.

If Paul had made a half-turn to the right and looked across the Forum, he would have faced the Basilica Aemilia, a great commercial center about 300 by 80 feet, especially used for money changing. Next to that stood the Senate House and the Senate Office Building, and in front of the latter the small Temple of Janus.

But Paul's concern was the Basilica Julia. This great structure was probably begun in 54 B.C. and completed by Augustus. It burned down soon thereafter, but was rebuilt and enlarged by Augustus and dedicated in A.D. 12 in the names of Gaius and

453. Columns of the Temple of Castor and Pollux

[28]Authorities differ slightly on the measurements of this building and its parts. The figures given here are from Pietro Romanelli, *The Roman Forum* (Rome: Instituto Poligrafico Dello Stato, 1959), p. 36.

454. Basilica Julia today, right foreground

The Julian Basilica was the seat of the tribunal of the *Centumviri*, who judged civil cases, especially inheritance disputes. Therefore, large and curious crowds frequented the place. Like crowds which gathered in Pilate's judgment hall and along the edge of the Forum at Philippi and elsewhere in the Roman world, they carved diagrams of games on the floor and amused themselves while public business was conducted.

Release of Paul? The conviction that Paul left the emperor's court a free man has found growing support among Bible students; the present writer holds to that view.[29] To begin with, the charges of in-

---

[29]While Sherwin-White does not hold that there is any necessity to conclude that Paul was released, he notes that emperors might cancel outstanding cases on the judicial docket to shorten the list of cases in arrears or engage in acts of clemency. He notes that there were numerous known acts of clemency during the first five years of Nero's reign, encouraged by his tutor Seneca. Sherwin-White, p. 119.

fraction of Jewish law brought against Paul would not have been serious in the eyes of a Roman. Apparently the case against him was not strong anyway. In this connection Acts 26:32 is quite revealing: "Then said Agrippa unto Festus, This man might have been set at liberty, if he had not appealed unto Caesar." Moreover, when the apostle arrived in Rome, he learned from Jews there that no documents from his opposition had reached the Jews of Rome (Acts 28:21). If his prosecutors did not carry the case to Rome, Paul might have won by default.

Second, the attitude of the apostle while in prison was that he would be released (cf. Philemon 22; Phil. 1:25-26; 2:23-24). He had also planned to go to Spain, where he had not gone before his imprisonment (Rom. 15:24, 28). Early church writers indicate that Paul did go to Spain and that his ministry there came after his first Ro-

455. Basilica Julia reconstructed

man imprisonment, that he was imprisoned a second time in Rome and martyred.[30]

Third, there are several other biblical references which may indicate a fourth missionary journey. Two are considered here. In II Timothy 4:20, Paul mentions that he left Trophimus sick at Miletus. This could not have been an occurrence of Paul's last journey to Jerusalem, because Trophimus was not left behind (Acts 20:4; 21:29), nor of the journey to Rome, because he did not touch at Miletus then. This seems to presuppose another voyage.

Again, according to the King James Version, shortly before his death Paul sent Crescens to Galatia (II Tim. 4:10). Several manuscripts (admittedly not the most valuable) read "Gaul" instead of "Galatia." On the supposition that Paul had been to Spain and probably traveled through Gaul on the way during a fourth missionary journey, it

would be natural for him to send a fellow worker to Gaul.

If Paul made a fourth missionary journey, he probably went first to Spain and then to the East once more. Very likely he spent some time in Crete winning converts—therefore the need for sending Titus there to organize the church on the island and for penning an epistle to him there later.

456. Temple of Saturn and the Public Record Office today

[30]Clement, *Epistle to the Corinthians,* chap. v; Eusebius, *Ecclesiastical History,* ii, 22; and the Muratori Canon.

Probably he was arrested in Asia, possibly at Ephesus. He had left books, parchments, and clothes at Troas expecting to return for them. The particular wrong which Phygellus, Hermogenes, and Alexander had done him in Asia may have been misrepresenting him to the authorities and securing his arrest (II Tim. 1:15; 4:14).

Rome again. This second arrest would have occurred after the fire of Rome, when Christians could no longer enjoy the freedom they once had. It is not necessary to hold, however, that Paul was arrested because of his faith. Some of his enemies may have hauled him into the courts on false charges—perhaps devised by the men he berated in the references just noted.

When Paul arrived in Rome the second time, perhaps about 66, the city had a very different appearance than during his earlier visit. The fire had made possible some extensive changes. Many streets had been widened and straightened, the Circus Maximus had been rebuilt and embellished, and many other public structures had been built or rebuilt. Much still lay in ruins. Nero had reserved the entire center of the city for his grand new palace, which justly deserved the name *Domus Aurea*, or "Golden House."

Built between 64 and 68, the entire complex covered 125 acres, which reached from the Palatine Hill, across the Forum and the Velia as far as the Oppian Hill. Besides the palace, the grounds included parks, groves, pastures, a zoo, and a lake. It was a kind of first century Versailles in the center of an earlier teeming metropolis. Later emperors did their best to destroy the memory of this monstrosity of Nero. The Flavians filled in the lake and built the Colosseum on it; Trajan built his baths on top of the palace on the Oppian Hill. These and others built temples and other public buildings over the monumental approach to the grounds along one side of the Forum.

Since 1907, when the German archaeolo-

457. West end of the Forum reconstructed

THE WYCLIFFE HISTORICAL GEOGRAPHY OF BIBLE LANDS

458. A false window in Nero's Golden House

scapes, impressionistically painted, attempt the illusion of the out-of-doors.[31]

The Mamertine. Tradition has it that during his second imprisonment Paul was detained in the Mamertine Prison in Rome. The name *Mamertinus* is postclassical; during the Empire the place was known simply as the *Carcer*. This was the ancient state prison of Rome at the foot of the Capitoline Hill. It was used as a place of detention, not of penal servitude, although executions

gist F. Weege wormed his way through a hole in the wall of the Baths of Trajan and began to explore the *Domus Aurea*, modern archaeologists have been working on the site. So far eighty-eight rooms of the palace complex have been worked on; there is much more to be done at the site. It is quite unnecessary to describe the palace in detail. It is absolutely fantastic and requires an extended on-the-spot examination to appreciate the magnitude of the place. A description of one room should suffice.

Room 70 is a vaulted corridor 227 feet long . . . painted sky-blue. . . . Seabeasts, candelabra, and arabesques, sphinxes with shrubs growing out of their backs, griffins, centaurs, acanthus-leaves, Cupids, gorgons' heads, lions' heads with rings in their mouths, dolphins holding horns of plenty, winged horses, eagles, tritons, swags of flowers make up the riotous decor. In recesses in the walls, landscapes and sea-

459. Entrance to the Mamertine Prison

[31]Paul MacKendrick, *The Mute Stones Speak* (New York: St. Martin's Press, 1960), pp. 190-92.

occurred there. The upper room is a vaulted trapezoid, the sides varying in length from eleven to sixteen feet.

Below it was a subterranean chamber, originally accessible only by a hole in the roof. This Tullianum was nearly twenty-one feet in diameter and, according to Sallust, twelve feet high.[32] All who wrote of the place described it with horror. Sallust (86-34 B.C.) described it as "exceeding dark, unsavory, and able to craze any man's senses."[33] Under such circumstances the apostle would indeed have felt the need of the cloak and the books he had left behind at Troas (II Tim. 4:13).

[32]Platner, pp. 99-100.
[33]Sallust, *Conspiracy of Cataline*, p. 55.

As Paul wrote Second Timothy, he had none of the optimism expressed in his earlier letters, when he expected release. He had obtained a preliminary hearing, and it had been a dismal failure (II Tim. 4:16). Though he found himself in dire circumstances, he delivered what sometimes has been called his valedictory, for he was about to "graduate." "For I am now ready to be offered, and the time of my departure is at hand. I have fought a good fight, I have finished my course, I have kept the faith: Henceforth there is laid up for me a crown of righteousness, which the Lord, the righteous judge, shall give me at that day: and not to me only, but unto all them also that love his appearing" (II Tim. 4:6-8).

Bibliography

ANDERSON, WILLIAM J., and SPIERS, R. PHENE. *The Architecture of Ancient Rome.* Revised by THOMAS ASHBY. London: B. T. Batsford, 1927.

ASHBY, THOMAS. *The Roman Campagna in Classical Times.* New York: Macmillan Co., 1927.

BOAK, ARTHUR E. R. *A History of Rome to 565 A. D.* 5th ed. New York: Macmillan Co., 1965.

BOETHIUS, AXEL. *The Golden House of Nero.* Ann Arbor: University of Michigan Press, 1961.

BUCKLAND, W. W. *A Text-Book of Roman Law from Augustus to Justinian.* Cambridge: Cambridge University Press, 1921.

CARCOPINO, J. *Daily Life in Ancient Rome.* New Haven: Yale University Press, 1941.

COBERN, CAMDEN M. *The New Archeological Discoveries.* 9th ed. New York: Funk & Wagnalls Co., 1929.

DILL, SAMUEL. *Roman Society from Nero to Marcus Aurelius.* New York: Meridian Books, 1956.

FINEGAN, JACK. *Light from the Ancient Past.* 2d ed. Princeton: Princeton University Press, 1959.

FRIEDLANDER, LUDWIG. *Roman Life and Manners Under the Early Empire.* Translated by J. H. FREESE and LEONARD A. MAGNUS. 3 vols. London: George Routledge & Sons, Ltd., 1936.

HAMMOND, M. *The Augustan Principate in Theory and Practice During the Julio-Claudian Period.* Cambridge, Mass.: Harvard University Press, 1933.

HEICHELHEIM, FRITZ M., and YEO, CEDRIC A. *History of the Roman People.* Englewood Cliffs, N. J.: Prentice-Hall, Inc., 1962.

HENDERSON, BERNARD. *Five Roman Emperors.* Cambridge: Cambridge University Press, 1927.

JONES, TOM B. *Ancient Civilization.* Chicago: Rand McNally & Co., 1960.

MACKENDRICK, PAUL. *The Mute Stones Speak.* New York: St. Martin's Press, 1960.

MACKINNON, ALBERT G. *The Rome of Saint Paul.* Philadelphia: John C. Winston Co., 1930.

MAIURI, AMEDEO. *Pompeii.* Rome: Instituto Poligrafico Dello Stato, 1959.

MARSH, F. B. *The Founding of the Roman Empire.* 2d ed. New York: Oxford University Press, 1927.

NASH, ERNEST. *Roman Towns.* New York: J. J. Augustin, 1944.

PALLOTTINO, M. *The Etruscans.* Harmondsworth, England: Penguin Books, Inc., 1955.

PARKER, H. M. D. *A History of the Roman World from A.D. 138 to 337.* London: Methuen & Co., Ltd., 1935.

PLATNER, SAMUEL B. *A Topographical Dictionary of Ancient Rome.* Completed and Revised by THOMAS ASHBY. London: Oxford University Press, 1929.

RAMSAY, WILLIAM M. *The Church in the Roman Empire Before A.D. 170.* 4th ed. London: Hodder and Stoughton, 1895.

————. "Roads and Travel in the New Testament," *A Dictionary of the Bible.* Edited by JAMES HASTINGS. Extra Vol., 1904.

RIVOIRA, G. T. *Roman Architecture.* Translated by G. M. RUSHFORTH. Oxford: At the Clarendon Press, 1925.

ROBERTSON, D. M. *A Handbook of Greek and Roman Architecture.* Cambridge: Cambridge University Press, 1929.

ROEBUCK, CARL. *The World of Ancient Times.* New York: Charles Scribner's Sons, 1966.

ROMANELLI, PIETRO. *The Palatine.* 2d ed. Rome: Istituto Poligrafico Dello Stato, 1956.

————. *The Roman Forum.* 3d ed. Rome: Instituto Poligrafico Dello Stato, 1959.

ROSTOVTSEV, MIKHAIL. *The Social and Economic History of the Roman Empire.* Oxford: At the Clarendon Press, 1926.

SALMON, E. T. *A History of the Roman World 30 B.C.-A.D. 138.* 2d rev. ed. London: Methuen & Co., Ltd., 1950.

SCULLARD, H. H. *From the Gracchi to Nero.* London: Methuen & Co., Ltd., 1959.

————. *Roman Politics 220-150 B.C.* Oxford: At the Clarendon Press, 1951.

SHERWIN-WHITE, A. N. *The Roman Citizenship.* Oxford: At the Clarendon Press, 1939.

————. *Roman Society and Roman Law in the New Testament.* Oxford: At the Clarendon Press, 1963.

SMITH, JAMES. *The Voyage and Shipwreck of St. Paul.* 4th ed. London: Longmans, Green, and Co., 1880.

SMITH, WILLIAM (ed.). *A Dictionary of Greek and Roman Geography.* 2 vols. London: John Murray, 1873.

STARR, CHESTER G. *A History of the Ancient World.* New York: Oxford University Press, 1965.

————. *The Roman Imperial Navy.* Ithaca: Cornell University Press, 1954.

SWAIN, JOSEPH WARD. *The Ancient World.* Vol. 2. New York: Harper & Brothers, 1950.

SYME, R. *The Roman Revolution.* Oxford: Oxford University Press, 1939.

TUCKER, T. G. *Life in the Roman World of Nero and St. Paul.* New York: Macmillan Co., 1911.

WALTERS, H. B. *The Art of the Romans.* London: Methuen & Co., Ltd., 1928.

WHEELER, MORTIMER. *Rome Beyond the Imperial Frontiers.* Harmondsworth, England Penguin Books. Inc., 1955.

General Index

Ain Tabgha, 135; *see also* Bethsaida
Akhenaton, 96, 100, 119; *see also* Akhnaton, Amenhotep, and Ikhnaton
Akhetetaton, 75, 76, 82; *see also* el 'Amarna, Tell
Akhisar, 397
Akhnaton, 76, 77, 82; *see also* Amenhotep IV
Akhsas, Tell, 169; *see also* Succoth
Akkad, 3, 13, 215, 275; *see also* Accad and Agade
city of, 22
dynasty of, 15
Akkadian
language, 41, 280
Period, old, 632
Akkadians, 18, 223
Akra, Jebel, 218, 243. See Casius, Mount
Akrotiri Peninsula, 292
Alaca Hüyük, 318
Alalakh, 42, 226-28, 233. See Atchana, Tell
Alasiya (Alasia), 298
Alastos, Doros, 295, 298, 299, 301, 309
Albright, William Foxwell, 110, 115, 123, 145, 146, 151, 181, 199, 206, 207, 213, 260, 325
Aleppo, 43, 220, 222, 226-28, 233, 236, 252
pine and cyprus of, 188
see also Beroea or Haleb or Yamkhad
Alexander the Great, 7, 9, 54, 55, 61, 98, 107, 122, 187, 196, 209-11, 239, 240, 268, 270, 274, 275, 280, 282, 283, 300, 311, 328, 331, 332, 339, 340, 342, 344-46, 353, 359, 361, 365, 367-69, 371, 373, 375, 383, 385, 387, 391, 392, 399, 400, 441-43, 449, 454, 457, 548
successors of, 443-45; *see also* Ptolemies and Seleucids
Alexandretta, 217, 223, 353
Gulf of, 239
see also Iskenderon
Alexandria, 72, 243, 247, 252, 342, 376, 393, 397, 444, 461, 523
hepostadium, 62
library, 61, 62
lighthouse, 62; *see also* Pharos
Serapeum, 62
Alishar, 323
Alma Dag, 215; *see also* Amanus
Alma Dag Mountains, 353
Alma Dag River, 187
Al Mina. See Poseideion
Alphabet, Hebrew, 207
Altar of the Twelve Gods (Athens), 471, 475
Alyattes, 330, 391
Amalekites, 90, 92, 147, 173

Amanus Mountains, 21, 187, 188, 192, 215, 218, 338, 339, 353; *see also* Alma Dag
Amarna Age, 33, 100, 114, 194, 197, 230, 325
Amarna Letters, 42, 76, 108, 110, 119, 122, 123, 130, 131, 137, 139, 154, 155, 194, 228, 229, 298
Amarna, tombs of, 76-77
Amasa, 148
Amastris, 383, 384
Amasya, 383
Amaziah of Judah, 112, 236
Ambracian Gulf, 516
Amel-Marduk, 28
Amenemhet I, 57, 71, 81, 82
Amenemhet III, 72
Amenhotep I, 81, 193
Amenhotep II, 82, 118, 131, 193, 194
Amenhotep III, 82, 115, 194, 228, 229, 298
Amenhotep IV, 33, 42, 76, 82, 119, 194, 228, 229, 298; *see also* Akhnaton
American School of Classical Studies at Athens, 468
American Schools of Oriental Research, Drew University, 11, 43, 123, 139, 145, 151, 171, 272, 399
American Society for the Excavation of Sardis, 399
Amisia, 317
Amisus, 283, 382; *see also* Samsun
Amman, 168, 176, 177, 179; *see also* Rabbah (Rabbath-Ammon)
Ammon, 232
nation of, 232
oasis of, 61
Ammonites, 169, 175, 176, 177
Amon, god, 80-83
priesthood of, 83
Amor, god, 221; *see* Amurrû
Amorgas Island, 403
Amorites, 41, 43, 96, 113, 190, 194, 195, 221-24
kings, 111
Amos, the prophet, 104, 145, 171, 181
Amphipolis, 448, 455, 456
lion of, 456
Amu Darya, 275; *see also* Oxus River
Amun, temple of, 65, 118, 123
Amurrû, land of, 217, 221, 222; *see also* Syria
Amurrû, god, 221; *see also* Amor, god
Amyntas, 337, 339, 344, 348, 350, 354, 355
Anatolia, 21, 24, 296, 313, 316, 317, 319, 320, 322, 323, 366, 377
plateau, 398
southern, 319

strongholds, 42
tablelands, 1
western, 319
Ancyra, 354, 355, 382; *see also* Ankara
Anderson, William J., 487, 550
Andracus River, 376
Ankara, 318, 323, 354, 382
University of, 323
see also Ancyra
Anshan, 238, 267
Antakya, 217; *see also* Antioch of Syria
Antalya, 314, 317, 353; *see also* Attalia
Anthios River, 347
Antigonids, 300, 371
Antigonus I, 240, 332, 367, 391, 399, 444
Antigonus II Gonatas, 332, 444-45
Anti-Liban Mountains, 166, 188, 218, 219, 253; *see also* Anti-Lebanon Mountains
Antioch (Antiochea) of Pisidia (Asia Minor), 212, 314, 317, 323, 347, 348, 349, 350, 351, 355-57, 376, 377; *see also* Apamea
Lake of, 244
Antioch, of Syria, 217, 233, 241-43, 245, 247-52, 260, 289, 291, 340, 353, 357, 386, 397, 444, 461, 486, 532, 539, 543; *see also* Antakya
map of, 251
Olympic games, 247
Antiochus, 347
Antiochus I, 268, 332, 333, 347
Antiochus II, 257, 363, 377
Antiochus III (the Great), 107, 240, 244, 271, 333, 342, 348, 359, 380, 393, 399, 446, 506, 507
Antiochus IV (Epiphanes), 59, 98, 158, 240, 241, 247, 250, 253, 273, 295, 339, 342, 371, 463
Antiochus V, (Eupator), 59
Antiochus XIII, 241
Antipas, Christian martyr, 395
Antipas, Herod, 133, 167
Antipater, associate of Cato, 212, 344
Antipater, the Idumaean, 104, 181
Antipatris (Antipatria), 104. See Aphek
Anti-Taurus, mountains, 187, 313, 384
Antoninus, Marcus Aurelius, 401; *see also* Caracalla or Bassianus
Antoninus Pius, 359, 375, 448, 475, 522
Antony, Mark, 62, 258, 302, 337, 338, 340, 343, 344, 348, 350, 354, 359, 383, 385, 393, 447, 451, 457, 459, 514, 515-17, 544

Apamea, 215, 241, 242, 245, 252, 253, 316, 317, 360, 376, 378; *see also* Latakia
Apennine Mountains, 493, 500
Aphrodite, goddess, 63, 225, 305-6
temple of, 174, 481
'Apiru, 137
Apis, 208
bull, emblem of Ptah, 66
sepulcher of, 67
Apocrypha, 273, 274
Apollo, 63, 85, 207, 244, 252, 305, 353, 375, 381, 413, 471, 483, 486, 540
Apollo Delphinion, temple of, 371
Apollo Patroos, temple of, 471
Apollonia, 456
Apollonius, 57, 212, 474
Apollos (early Christian, I Cor. 16:12), 486
Appian Way, 491, 501, 537
Appianus, 242
Appii Forum, 537, 458
Apries, 55; *see also* Haphra
'Aqaba (Akaba), 174
Gulf of, 88, 91, 95, 99, 172, 179, 180, 218, 220
Aquila, 384, 486
'Araba, 166, 171, 172, 181; *see also* Arabah
Arabah, the, 91, 92; *see also* Dead Sea, valley of
Arabia, 106, 201, 202, 224, 232, 257, 272, 277; *see also* Yemen
central, 180
northwestern, 91
southern, 179
Arabia Petraea, province of, 180, 258
Arabian Desert, 1, 175, 220, 277
Arabian Peninsula, 13, 173, 257
Arabic language, 221
Arabic period (Shiloh), 143
Negeb, 174
Arabs, 51, 99, 308, 348, 374, 385
of Abu Ghosh, 112
Marsh, 5
Nabataean, 162, 172, 180, 181
Arachosia, 264
Arachthus, 409
Arad, 173
Aradus, 193, 212, 228. *See also* Arwad or Arvad
Arakhthos. *See* Arachthus
Aram, 2
Aramaeans, 43, 195, 231, 233
merchants, 209
states, 25
Aramaic language, 221, 238, 245
Ararat; *see also* Armenia and Urartu
kingdom of, 3, 233, 236, 276
Mount, 1
Ar'areh, Khirbet, 173; *see also* Aroer

Araxes, river, 279
Arbela, battle of, 7, 274; *see also* Erbil
Arcadia, 392, 414, 429
Archelais, 382, 384
Archelaus, 337, 339
Areopagus, 407, 433, 434, 437, 462-63, 470, 472-73, 475; *see also* Mars Hill
Ares, god, 473
temple of, 471
see also Mars, god
Aretas III, 256, 257
Aretas IV, 257
Argaeus, Mount, 384
Argolis, 414
Argos, 342, 414, 426, 431, 436, 441, 479
Aria, 264
Ariaramnes, 267, 273
Ariarathes I, 385
Ariarathes IV, 334
Ariobarzanes, 335, 337, 385
'Arish, Wadi, El, 88, 90; *see also* Brook of Egypt
Aristides, Aelius, 391, 464
Armageddon, 120
Armenia, 1, 2, 3, 218, 241, 277, 335, 336, 342, 382, 383, 385, 524, 536
mountains of, 1, 313
plateau of, 265
Soviet, 274
see also Urartu and Ararat
Armenians, 275
Armenoid, 192, 249
Arnason, H. Harvard, 249
Arno River, 494
Arnon River, 95, 175, 178; *see also* Hesa, Wadi
Aroer, 173; *see also* Ar'areh, Khirbet
Arpachiya, 10
Arphaxad, 273
Arrapkha, 42
Arrian, 279, 280
Arsaces, 269, 275
Arsacids, 269
Arses (Xerxes III), 268
Arsinoe, 87, 359; *see* Ephesus
Artabanus V, 269
Artaxerxes I, 263, 268, 282, 283, 286, 399
Artaxerxes II, 268, 331, 441
Artaxerxes III, 268, 274
Artemis, goddess, 225, 345, 361, 362, 540
temple of, 177, 358, 360, 399, 466, 475
see also Diana of Cybele
Artemision, 362
Arvad, 187, 193, 194, 203, 205, 228
city of, 185
see also Aradus or Arwad
Arwad, 193, 228; *see* Aradus or Arvad
Asa, 113, 148, 152, 234
Ascalon, 105, 197; *see also* Ashkelon
Asclepion (Corinth), 484

Asclepion (Pergamum), 393
Asclepius, 207
sanctuary of, 373, 393, 395
see also Esculapius
Ashby, Thomas, 538, 550
Ashdod, 105, 107-8; *see* Azotus or Esdud
Asher, Ben, 128
Asher
plain of, 100, 101, 116
tribe of, 101, 126, 129
Ashera, 225
Asherah, 123
Ashirat, goddess, 221
Ashkelon, 108, 197; *see also* Ascalon
Ashkenaz, 266
Ashtaroth, goddess, 124, 169, 175, 207
see also Astarte
Ashur, 3, 9, 32-39, 43, 237, 267
Ashurbanipal, 25, 35, 66, 83, 84, 205, 286
Ashurnasirpal II, 7, 33, 35, 38, 203, 204
Ashur-uballit I, 33
Ashuruballit II, 237
Asia, 1, 2
western, 33, 38, 126
Province of, 326, 336, 368, 369, 370, 371, 373, 378, 382, 384-87, 389, 392, 409, 509, 548
Asia Minor, 24, 33, 43, 101, 192, 194, 210, 215, 218, 229, 233, 240, 244, 263, 265, 266, 275, 292, 294, 296, 297, 311-405, 409, 415, 417, 418, 419, 422, 423, 424, 425, 428, 429, 431, 435, 437, 438, 440, 441, 442, 444, 445, 446, 447, 449, 474, 496, 506, 511, 512, 530
Black Sea coastlands, 314
Bronze Age, 317-19
late, 321
Byzantine period, 353, 365
central plateau, 313
Chalcolithic age, 317
city-states, 239
climate, 316
earliest inhabitants, 317
early Bronze Age, 324
eastern, 316
geographical features, 313-17
Greek, 435
Greek immigration, 329
Hellenistic period, 313, 315, 321, 379
historical developments, 316-38
Hittites, 322-27
John, the Apostle, 389-403
Macedonian period, 383
map of, 312
Mediterranean coastland, 315
mountain ranges, 313-14
Neolithic period, 317
New Testament period, 313
Paleolithic period, 317

Paul, the Apostle, 338-81
  first missionary journey,
    345-53
  second missionary journey,
    353-56
  third missionary journey,
    357-76
Persian period, 330-31
Peter, the Apostle, 382-88
Phrygians and Lydians, 328-
  30
rivers and lakes, 316
roads, 316-17
Roman interference and con-
  trol, 333-38
Roman period, 313, 315, 338,
  353, 361, 379, 391
Seven Churches, map of, 388
western, 315-16
Askar, El, 142; see also Sychar
Asmar, Tell, 14; see also Eshnunna
Asnapper, 35
Asopus River, 377, 379
Aspadana, 276; see also Isfahan
Assembly of the Centuries, 502
Assembly of the Tribes, 502-3,
  509, 511, 512
Asshur, 28, 36, 38
Asshur-nadin-shum, 25
Assos, 356, 365
Assyria, 25, 66, 108, 109, 114,
  120, 131, 140, 196, 203,
  228, 233, 234, 236, 266,
  267, 279, 317, 325, 329,
  330, 423
  empire of, 1, 2, 7, 25, 33-35,
    55, 186, 208, 236, 274, 340
  rainfall in hill country, 5
  strength of, 217
  law code, 32, 33
  map of, 34
Assyrians, 43, 51, 97, 118, 126,
  141, 157, 188, 203-5, 206,
  215, 217, 223, 233, 235,
  238, 276, 299, 300, 319,
  322, 324, 328, 354, 385
Assyrian-Babylonian language
  (Akkadian), 221
Astacus, Gulf of, 387
Astarte, goddess, 125, 225, 306
Astartus, 199
Asterabad, 263, 274, 275; see
  also Hyrcania
Aström, Paul, 296-98, 309
Astyages, 238, 267, 280, 330
  Hill of, 359, 360
Aswan, 47, 54, 57, 65, 74, 85-
  87; see also Syene
Aswan Dam, 84, 88
Asy, 294, 298
Asyut, 77-78; see also Lycopolis
Atbara River, 49
Atchana, Tell, 226, 323. See
  Alalakh
Athaliah, 189
Athena, goddess, 353, 374, 395,
  427, 466, 467, 471
Athena, temple of, 372, 395,
  432, 466, 533

Athenian Alliance, Second, 367,
  373
Athenian Confederacy, 450
Athenian democracy, 434
Athenian Empire, 268, 367, 374,
  437-39, 450
Athenians, 330, 358, 368, 415,
  533
Athenodorus Cananites, the
  Stoic, 343, 344
Athens, 283, 301, 330, 331, 334,
  336, 343, 344, 367, 369,
  370, 374, 407, 410, 411,
  413, 414, 415, 427, 428,
  429, 430, 431, 433, 434,
  435, 436, 437, 438, 439,
  440, 441, 442, 445, 447,
  448, 449, 452, 456, 460-77,
  479, 481, 484, 506, 511
  colonists from Syria, 244
  Dionysus, theater of, 464
  Golden Age of, 438-39
  map of, 461
  Piraeus, the, 371
Athirat (Ashera), 225
Athos, Mount, 449
Atlantic Ocean, 370
Aton, 76, 82
Atreus, treasury of, 426
Atropatene, 275, 276; see also
  Azerbaijan
Attalia, 314, 345, 352, 353; see
  also Antalya
Attalids, 333, 386, 393
Attalus I, 354, 392, 467
Attalus II, 334, 353, 393, 400,
  471
Attalus III, 334, 359, 385, 393,
  509
Attalus, stoa of, 471-72
Attica, 410, 411, 413, 414, 415,
  416, 418, 429, 433, 434,
  435, 436, 437, 440, 448,
  471, 479, 511
Attis, 328
Atum, god, 59
Augustan period (Corinth-
  Greece), 483
Augustana, Domus, 541
Augustus, Caesar, 62, 103, 107,
  135, 141, 245, 246, 248,
  249, 254, 302, 304, 337,
  342, 343, 344, 346, 348,
  351, 353, 369, 371, 380,
  386, 448, 461, 464, 515,
  517-22, 533, 535, 536, 538,
  540, 541, 542, 543, 545
  palace of, 540
Auranitis, 219; see also Bashan
  or Hauran, plateau
Aurelius, Marcus, 391, 453
Avaris, 57, 60
Avdat (Abde), 174
Aventine Hill, 493, 497, 539
Awaj River, 219; see also Phar-
  par River
Axios River, 457; see also Var-
  dar
Ayassoluk, 360
Azekah, 110, 113, 114, 116

Azerbaijan, 266, 275, 280; see
  also Atropatene
Aziru, 195
Azotus, 107; see also Ashdod or
  Esdud

B

Baal, 96, 100, 123, 139, 207,
  225, 253
  of Apames, 252
  Phoenician worship of, 139,
    185, 205
  prophets of, 100
  temple of, 230, 253
  see also Hadad
Baal-berith (El-Berith), 137
Baal, king of Tyre, 205
Baal-zephon, 89; see also Ras
  Qasrun
Baalat, temple of, 191; see also
  Baalath, god
Baalath, god, 207
Baalbek, 218, 245, 253-55; see
  also Heliopolis
Baasha, 142, 152, 234
Babel (Hebrew, Bab-el), 2, 21
  tower of, 22
  see also Babylon
Babylonia, 3, 7, 12, 14, 40, 41,
  54, 66, 98, 103, 111, 113,
  157, 170, 181, 186, 215,
  223, 236, 237, 238, 240,
  263, 267, 272, 274, 285,
  286, 325, 326, 327, 331,
  332, 382, 443
  armies of, 114
  city, 3, 43, 47, 268
  empire, 1, 2, 47, 237, 435
  map of, 23, 28
  environs of, 21-32
  Ishtar Gate, 28, 31; see also
    Ishtar Gate
Babylon
  map of, 29
  power of, 196
  the procession way, 31
Bacchus, god, 270
  temple of, 255
Bactria (Bactriana), 240, 264,
  269, 280, 443
Badezorus, 199
Baghdad, 5, 9, 13, 14, 30, 31,
  174, 270, 274
  modern, 2, 3, 6, 21
Baikie, James, 59, 71, 72, 93
Balaam, doctrine of, 396
Balata, Tell, 138; see also Shechem
Baldasar, 277
Balearic Islands, 206
Balfour Declaration, the, 99
Balkan
  area, 417, 496
  peninsula, 407
  people, 319
Banias, Nahr, 166
  village of, 166
Banquet Stele, 35

Barada River, 177, 219; *see also* Abana or Chrysorrhoas
Barak, 116, 132
Barbarian invasions, Italy, 535
Barbarus, 65
Bargylus Mountains, 218; *see also* Nusayriyah Mountains
Barnabas, 212, 243, 249, 289, 290, 291, 303, 304, 305, 307, 308, 345, 347, 349, 350, 350-53, 351
Bartholomew, 130
Bashan, 175, 217, 219, 235
    hills of 168
    plains of, 175
    see also Batanaea or Auranitis or Haura
Basra, 5, 14; *see also* Busra
Bassianus, 401; *see also* Caracalla or Marcus Aurelius Antoninus
Basta, Tell, 56; *see also* Bubastis
Batanaea, 175; *see also* Bashan
Bedouins, 55, 89, 172, 221, 231
Beersheba, 88, 92, 95, 106, 144, 147, 172, 173
Behistun, 271; *see also* Bisitun
Beilan Pass, 218, 353; *see also* Syrian Gates
Beirut, 185, 187; *see also* Berytus and Biruta, 188, 190, 195, 245, 253, 535
    Plain of, 185
Beisan, 124, 169, 224; *see also* Beit-Shean
Beitin, 146; *see also* Bethel
Beit Mirsim, Tell, 110
Beit-Shean, 126; *see also* Bethshean
Bel, temple of, 259
Beleagarus, 199
Belshazzar, 29, 238
Bel-shemanni, 29
Bema, 472
Benedict, W. C., 272
Benhadad I, 232, 234
Benhadad II, 140, 204, 235
Benjamin
    rule of, 148
    territory of, 152
    tribe of, 41, 144, 151, 152
Benjamin of Tudela, 286
Beqa, El, 188, 237
Berea, 352, 474
Bergama, 395; *see also* Pergamum
Berlin, 300
Berlin, East, museum, 394
Beroea, 252, 458-60, 468; *see also* Aleppo or Haleb
Berytus, 187, 212, 535; *see also* Biruta and Beirut
Besharreh, 188
Bethany, 159
Beth-arabah, 162
Beth-eglaim, 107
Bethel, 111, 135, 144-46, 148, 170; *see also* Beitun
Beth-horon
    lower, 111
    upper, 111

Bethlehem, 160, 277, 491
Bethsaida, 135, 167; *see also* Ain Tabgha
Bethshalem, 154; *see also* Jerusalem
Bethshean (also Beit-Shean), 116, 124-26; *see also* Scythopolis
Beth-shemesh, 65, 109, 110-12; *see also* On or Hermonthis
Beycesultan, 318, 319
Bickerman, E., 260
Bikni, Mount, 264
Birket Iarun, 70
Birs Nimrud, mound of, 32; *see also* Borsippa, ancient
Biruta, 187; *see also* Berytus and Beirut
Bisitun, 271-72
    inscription, 274
    see also Behistun
Bithynia, 314, 316, 317, 332, 334, 335, 336, 337, 354, 356, 382, 383, 387, 388
Bittel, K., 323
Bitter Lakes, 57, 89
Black Sea, 39, 270, 313, 314, 315, 316, 330, 331, 335, 336, 370, 382, 383, 384, 387, 476, 524
    coastlands, 314
    trade, 435
Blanchegarde, 112; *see also* Tibnah or Tell es-safi
Blegen, Carl W., 319-21, 404
Bliss, Frederick Jones, 112, 181
Boak, Arthur E. R., 550, 551
Boeotia, 366, 413, 418, 425, 431, 437, 448
    people of, 410
Boethius, Axel, 550, 551
Bogazköy, 323, 325-28; *see also* Hattusas
Book of the Dead, the, 48
Borsippa, 32; *see also* Birs Nimrud
Bosporus, 313, 315
    thracian, 387
Botsford, George W., 487, 488
Botta, Paul Emile, 36, 39
Bouchier, E. S., 213, 260
Bozcaada, 449; *see also* Tenedos
Boz Dag, 313, 398; *see also* Tmolus Range
Bozrah, 181; *see also* El Buseira
Braidwood, Robert J., 6, 8, 9, 44
Breasted, James A., 1, 87, 93, 118, 191, 213
Britain, 99, 308, 524, 529, 532
British Museum, 10, 14, 114, 323, 459
British School of Archaeology, 10, 65
    in Iraq, 35
    in Jerusalem, 100, 140
Broneer, Oscar, 462, 473, 474, 478, 481, 484, 487, 488
Bronze Age, 112, 142, 146, 317, 424, 478, 495
    early, 153, 417

late, 107, 108, 110, 115, 131, 132, 139, 169, 321, 424
middle, 105, 107, 132, 139, 143, 145, 338, 417, 424, 425
Brook of Egypt, 88; *see also* Arish, Wadi El
Broughton, T. R. S., 337, 346, 349, 357, 370, 386, 394, 404
Brundisium, 396, 494, 512, 537; *see also* Brindisi
Brutus, 302, 337, 343, 359, 447, 450, 451, 457, 516
Bubastis, 55, 56; *see also* Pibeseth or Tell Basta
Budge, E. Wallis, 36, 48
Burckhardt, J. R., 180
Burrows, Millar, 228
Busiris, 64, 79
Busra, 14; *see also* Basra
Butler, Howard Crosby, 399, 404
Buto, 64
Byblos, 41, 54, 187, 189, 190, 192, 194-98, 203, 208, 210, 212, 222, 225, 229, 420; *see also* Gebal or Jubayl
    alphabet, 206-7
    inhabitants of, 204, 205
    travelers, 190
Byzantine
    churches, 459, 487
    emperors, 308
    empire, 98, 269, 311, 378, 380, 385, 399, 459
    period, 124, 126, 174, 354, 365, 385, 401
    ruins, 399
Byzantium, 317, 455, 532

C

Cadiz, 206; *see also* Gades or Gadir
Cadmus, Mount, 377, 381
Caecias, 464
Caelian, 493
Caesar, Augustus, 541; *see also* Augustus, Caesar
Caesar, Gaius, 337
Caesar, Julius, 62, 302, 337, 340, 343, 383, 385, 386, 448, 451, 464, 478, 479, 509, 512, 513, 514, 515, 516, 517, 521, 524, 541
Caesar, Lucius, 464
Caesar, temple of, 544
Caesarea, 99, 101, 103, 104, 164, 166, 376, 397, 521
Caesarea, Colonia, 348; *see also* Antioch (Asia Minor)
Caesarea, Mazaca, 384
Caesarea Philippi, 166
Caesarion, 516
Caicus
    Valley of, 313, 315
    River, 392, 396

Cairo, 48, 50, 55, 64, 65, 67, 68, 80, 174, 191
    modern, 47
    museum, 58, 65, 76
Calah, 3, 35, 36; see also Kalakh and Nimrud
Caleb, 161, 173
Calendar
    Gregorian, 246, 519
    Sumerian, 6
Caligula, 337, 461, 522, 524, 538, 540, 545; see also Gaius Caesar
Callaway, Joseph A., 146
Callidromus, Mount, 413
Callimachus, 62
Calneh, 2
Calycadnus, 316
Cambyses I, 267, 280
Cambyses II, 66, 83, 84, 268, 286, 300
Cameron, George C., 272
Campania, 494, 496, 497, 500, 503, 528, 535
Cana, 130
Canaan, 1, 14, 88, 90, 91, 92, 96, 100, 106, 114, 137, 180, 189, 224, 322, 325, 327
    allies of, 116
    city-states, 225
    culture and religion, 230
    language, 221
Canaanites, 92, 96, 105, 115, 118, 123, 130, 189, 224, 298
    of Shechem, 135
Canaanites, Athenodorus. See Athenodorus Cananites
Cannae, Battle of, 504
Capena, Porta, 538, 539
Capernaum, 128, 133-35, 167; see also Hum, Tell
Caphtor, 95, 104, 105, 421, 422; see also Kaptara
Caphtorim, 47
Capitoline Hill, 493, 529, 545, 549
Cappadocia, 33, 233, 313, 314, 316, 332, 333, 334, 335, 336, 337, 338, 339, 382, 383, 384, 385, 422, 464
    Roman period, 385
Capua, 500-502, 505, 536
Carbon 14 method, 9
Carcer, 549; see also Mamertine prison
Carchemish, 221, 223, 228, 233, 237, 323
    Battle of, 208
Carcopino, J., 550, 551
Caria, 314, 334, 370, 375, 385
    coast, 330
    colonists of, 211
    people of, 60, 211
    pirates, 297
Carmel, Mount, 99, 100, 101, 116, 122, 123, 129, 185, 220, 221, 237
Carmel Range, 100, 102, 116, 117

Carpenter, Rhys, 206, 213, 260, 479, 483, 484, 487, 488
Carrhae, 43, 222, 231, 275; see also Haran
Carthage, 196, 206, 210, 211, 333, 435, 446, 501, 503, 504, 505, 507, 515, 533
Carthaginians, 209, 335, 437, 496, 497, 501, 532
Cary, M., 220, 260, 404, 487, 488
Casius, Mount, 218, 243; see also Akra, Jebel
Caspian Sea, 238, 263, 264, 265, 269, 270, 274
Cassander, 332, 457
Cassius, 337, 343, 359, 447, 450, 451, 457, 516
Casson, Lionel, 191, 198, 213, 290, 309
Casson, Stanley, 309, 487, 488
Castor, god, 354, 534
Castor and Pollux, temple of, 544
Catiline, 512
Cato Marcus the Elder, 302, 507
Cato the Younger, 212, 302, 344
Caucasus Mountains, 6, 13, 237, 266, 270, 271, 314
Caviglia, Giovanni, 67
Cayster
    River, 357, 360, 398
    Valley, 315
Celts, 332, 354, 383, 496, 498, 504
Cenchraea-Corinth road, 478
Cenchreae, 414, 478, 486
Cephisus River, 413, 462, 475
Ceram, C. W., 404
Cestrus, 316, 347
Ceyhan. See Pyramus
Chadwick, John, 418, 420
Chaeronea, 442
Chalcedon, 314, 387, 451
Chalcidice, 449, 456-57
Chalcis, 413, 431, 445, 534
Chalcolithic age, 124, 221, 271, 317, 495
Chaldean Empire, 7, 28, 277; see also Neo-Babylonia empire
Chaldeans, 215, 223
Charadra River, 438
Chedorlaomer, 179
Cheops, 68, 79; see also Khufu, Great Pyramid of
Chicago, University of, 6, 323; see also Braidwood, Robert, 44
    Oriental Institute, 8
Chiera, Edward, 43
Childe, V. Gordon, 190, 213
Chios, 330, 367, 368, 429; see also Khios
Chipiez, Charles, 213, 306, 309
Chittim, 299
Chorazin, 135, 167; see also Kerazeh
Chorokh River, 313; see also Coruh

Chosroes, 63, 270. See Khosrau II
Chosroes I, 252; see also Khossau I
Chosroes II, 63, 270; see also Khosrau II
Christian era, 321
Christianity, 528-29
Christians, 529, 548
Chrysorrhoas River, 177; see also Barada
Church Divinity School of the Pacific, 149
Cicero, 302, 343, 369, 377, 473, 475, 513, 514, 516, 535
Cilicia, 241, 245, 302, 306, 314-18, 334, 336-44, 353, 368, 384, 442, 446
    Pedias, 339-42
    Tracheia, 338-39
Cilician Gates, 314, 316, 317, 331-32, 339-40, 342, 354, 357, 376
Cilician plain, 317
Cimmerians, 266, 271, 329-30, 354, 358
Cincinnati, University of, 319
Circus Maximus, 539-40, 548
Citium, 301; see also Kition
City of Salt, 162, 163
City-states, 1, 41, 177, 190, 197
    Asia Minor, 239
    Canaan, 225
    Corinth, 414
    Cos, 373
    Cyprus, 300
    Egypt, 19, 192
    Greece, 239, 245, 407, 409, 412, 418, 429, 431-34, 442, 446, 507, 533
    Hittite, 233-34, 326
    Pergamum, 393
    Phoenician, 194, 204, 208, 212, 224, 239
    Roman, 497
    Sumerian, 6, 13-21
    Syrian, 241, 326
    Ur, 6-7
Claudian
    aqueduct, 538
    family, 522
Claudians, 514
Claudius I, 101, 248, 337, 338, 344, 362, 373, 448, 461, 466, 482, 493, 494, 523, 524, 535, 538, 540
Cleanthes the Stoic, 365, 434
Clement (early church father), 547
Cleopatra, 59, 62, 302, 338, 343, 393, 443, 447, 514, 516-17
Cnidus, 330
Cnossus, 416; see also Knossos or Gnossus
Cobbam, Claude D., 293, 309
Cobern, Camden M., 308-9, 349, 364, 404, 533, 550, 551
Cocheba, Bar, 98, 162, 165

Der 'aa, 175; *see also* Edrei
Derbe, 339, 351-55, 357, 376
Deutsche Orientgesellschaft, 12, 31-32
Diana, goddess, 305, 307, 315, 345, 361-62
  temple of, 359-60
  see also Artemis
Dibon, 178-79; *see also* Dhiban
Dickson, William P., 212-13, 220, 261, 460, 487, 488
Didyma, 371-72
Dikaois Parphyrios, 299, 304
Dill, Samuel, 550, 551
Dilmun, 21
Diocletian, 63, 212, 383, 385, 388, 530
Diodorus, 273, 282
Diodorus Siculus, 71, 84
Dionysus, god, 395, 465, 474-76
  temple of, 126, 250, 395
  theater of, 464
  see also Iacchus
Diospolis, 103; *see also* Tydda or Tod
Diospolis Magna, 81; *see also* Thebes
Dipylon Gate, Athens, 462, 475
Diyala River, 14
Djoser, Pharaoh, 49, 50, 70
Dodanim, 294
Dodecanese Islands, 374
Dog River, 186, 195; *see also* el Kelb, Nahr
Dog River Pass, 186
Domus Augustana, 541
Dominican Ecole Biblique in Jerusalem, 142
Domitian, 363, 380, 402, 521, 528-29, 543
  buildings of, 541
Dor, 102, 117
  town of, 101
Doria, 299, 330-31, 421, 428, 431, 433, 479
Dorians, 344, 375, 403, 417
  occupation of Rhodes and Cos, 330
Doric dialect, 418
Dorpfeld, Wilhelm, 319
Dotha, Tell, 143; *see also* Dothan
Dothan, 123, 143-44, 299; *see also* Dotha, Tell
Downey, Glanville, 244, 248, 249, 260
Drangiana, 264, 280
Drew University. See American Schools of Oriental Research
Druze, Jebel, 175, 219; *see also* Hauran Mountains
Dublal-mah (Sumerian "Great House of Tablets"), 19
Dunand, Maurice, 196, 213
Dura-Europos, 220
Dur-Sharrukin, 39; *see also* Khorsabad
Dussaud, Rene, 213, 217, 242, 260

Dust storm (Idayay), 5
  lower Mesopotamia, 5
Duweir, Tell ed-, 113, 115; *see also* Lachish
Dyrrhachium, 396, 455

E

Eannatum, 20, 40
East Berlin Museum, 394
Ebal, Mount, 135, 137, 142, 168
Ebenezer, 152
Ebir-nari, 238
Ebro River, 504
Ecbatana, 263, 267, 273-74, 443; *see also* Hamadan
Eden, four rivers of, 1
Edom, 92, 106, 172, 175, 178, 179-81, 236
Edomites, 147, 201, 236
Edrei, 175; *see also* Der' aa
Edwards, Amelia B., 93
Edwards, I. E. S., 93
Eglon, 114, 170
Egnatian Way, 407, 452, 454-57, 459; *see also* Via Egnatian
Egypt, 1, 2, 6, 21, 33, 42, 43, 47-93, 103, 106, 119, 120, 122, 144, 146, 153, 155, 173, 196, 202, 203, 207, 208, 210, 211, 215, 219, 221, 225, 227, 232, 237, 238, 239, 240, 244, 252, 257, 259, 268, 272, 274, 277, 278, 284, 291, 292, 296, 297, 298, 300, 301, 306, 318, 323, 325, 326, 332, 333, 336, 353, 359, 366, 368, 369, 370, 373, 375, 386, 397, 417, 419, 420, 421, 423, 425, 431, 436, 438, 442, 443, 444, 445, 506, 514, 417, 518, 519, 520, 521, 530, 540
  Amarna Age, 194
  Brook of, 90; *see also* Arish, Wadi El
  Chalcolithic period, 78
  Early Dynastic Period (or Thinite Period), 54
  Empire Period, 42, 51, 55, 86, 106, 131, 186, 193, 195-96, 422; *see also* Egypt, New Kingdom
  Exploration Fund, 56-58, 74
  Exploration Society, 76
  historical outline, 54-55
  Hyksos period, 207
  Ice Age, 51
  land and its people, 47-54
  language, 53
  Lower, 54-55, 63-64, 66, 71
    map of, 56
  Middle Kingdom, 54, 75, 86, 192, 226, 230
  name of, 47
  Neolithic period, 71
  New Kingdom, 48, 55; *see also* Egypt, Empire Period

Nile, 47-51
  Old Kingdom, 54, 68, 75, 86, 87, 96, 190, 192; *see also* Egypt, Pyramid Age
  Paleolithic period, 51
  Persian period, 55
  Ptolemaic era, 61-62, 71
  Pyramid age, 54; *see also* Egypt, Old Kingdom, 68, 86, 96
  regional surveys, 55-93
  southern, 192
  Thinite period, 54; *see also* Egypt, early dynastic period
  Upper, 48, 50-51, 54-55, 66, 74-88, 190
    map of, 74
Egyptians, 35, 118, 188, 194, 205, 215, 223, 298-99, 315, 340, 443, 450
  freighters, 190-91
  gods, 193
  outpost, 169
  tablets, 230
  ware, 226
Eilat, 172
Eiselen, Frederick C., 210, 213
Ekron, 105, 109, 110, 205
El, 145-46, 207, 225
Elagabalus, 253; *see also* Heliogabalus
Elah, vale of, 112, 113; *see also* Terebinth Valley
Elam, 25, 284-86
el 'Amarna, Tell, 82; *see also* Akhetaton
Elamite
  language, 272, 280, 285
  land of Anshan, 267
Elamites, 25
El 'Arish, Wadi, 88, 90; *see also* Brook of Egypt
El-Askar, 142; *see also* Sychar
Elath, 236; *see also* Ezion-Geber
Elba, 495, 535
El Bahnasa, 75; *see also* Oxyrhynchus
El Bika, 218, 221, 237, 241; *see also* Beqa and Coele-Syria
Elburz Mountains, 264, 265
El Buseira, 181; *see also* Bozrah
Elemelech, 160
Elephantine Island, 60, 86, 87, 273
Eleusinian
  mysteries, 445, 475
Eleusis, 414, 474-76
Eleusis, Bay of, 475
Eleutheropolis, 113
El-Fara'in, Tell, 64
El-Heir, Tell, 89
El-Husn, Tell, 169; *see also* Scythopolis
Eleakim, 110
Eli, 143
Eliezer, 133
Elijah, 100, 109, 208
Elim, oasis of, 90
Eliot, C. W. J., 487, 488

Elis, 414
Elisha, 143, 294
El Jib, 148, 149; see also Gibeon and Jib
El Kebeer, Nahr, 218; see also Kebeer River
El-Mashkuta Tell, 58,; see also Per-Atum
El Muqayyar, Tell, 14
El Muqenna, 110; see also El-tekeh
El-'Ojjul, Tell, 107; see also Beth-eglaim
El-Tahun, 64, 71
Eltekeh, 110; see also el-Muqenna
Eluleus, King of Tyre, 205; see also Luli
El-Uqsur, 80; see also Luxor
El-Yahudiya, Tell, 59, 60, 298; see also Yahudiya, Tell el-
Elymas, 277, 307
Emery, Walter B., 93
Emesa, 218-19, 228, 231, 240, 253, 257; see also Homs
Endor, 124
Engannim, 123; see also Jenin
En-gedi, 162, 164, 165, 166
Oasis of, 147; see also Ain Jidi
Engelbach, R., 65
Enhil, 13
Enkomi, 297-99, 304
Enlil, 13, 32; see also Nippur
temple of in Ashur, 33
Epaminondas, 413, 441
Epaphros, 378, 380-81
Epeiros, 511; see also Epirus
Ephesians, 372
Ephesus, 305, 307, 315, 316, 317, 330, 331, 333, 334, 340, 347, 356, 357-65, 370, 371, 376, 377, 378, 382, 386, 387, 389, 390, 391, 392, 397, 400, 402, 446, 457, 461, 463, 486, 506, 516, 521, 539, 548
Arcadian Way, 362
Magnesian Gate, 361
map of, 358
Ephraim, 104, 111, 135, 137
Ephron, 161
Epictetus, 380
Epicureanism, 444
Epicureans, 472
Epicurus, 444
Epidaurus, 304, 392, 407
Epiphanes, Antiochus IV, 59, 98, 158, 273, 295, 371, 463. See Antiochus IV
Epiphania, 233, 253; see also Hama
Epirus, 407, 409, 412, 413, 417, 425, 445, 446, 448, 501, 505, 511, 515
Equites, 503, 508-9, 511, 516
Erastus, 484
Eratosthenes, 62, 293, 321
Erbil, 274; see also Arbela

Erech, 2, 6, 10-11, 13, 284; see also Uruk and Warka, modern
Erechtheum (Athens), 466
Eretria, 330-31, 435
Eridu, ancient, 6, 10-11; see also mound of Tell Abu Shahrain
Erimi, 295
Er-Rameh, plain of, 129
Er-Retaba, Tell, 58, 59
Esarhaddon, 25, 35, 38, 66, 109, 205
Esculapius, 373; see also Asclepius, temple of, 371
Esdraelon, 102, 123, 135, 139, 220
district of, 148
Plain of, 102, 116, 117, 122, 123-24, 126, 129
Valley of, 95, 116-26, 147
Esdud, 107; see also Ashdad or Azotus
Eshmun, 207
Eshmunein, 77; see also Hermopolis
Eshmunezer, 102
Eshnunna, 14; see also Tell Asmar
Esh-shaghur, fault of, 129
Esh Sham, 231
Eshtaol, 110-11
Esquiline Hill, 493, 541
es-Safi, Tell, 112; see also Tibneh or Blanchegarde
Essenes of Qumran, 162-64
Esther, 263, 268, 273, 286
Etham, 89
Ethbaal, 189, 199, 207, 234; see also Ithobalus
Ethiopia, 21, 65, 83, 277
Ethiopian Plateau, 49
Ethiopians, 87
Ethiopic language, 221
Etna, volcano, 493
Etruria, 494, 496-97, 500-501
Etruscans, 311, 435, 496-500
Et-Tell, 146; see also Ai
Et-Tur, 135. See Gerizim
Euboea, 244, 367, 411, 413
gulf of, 413
Euergetes, 85; see also Ptolemy III
Eulaeus River, 284; see also Ulai and Karun
Eumenes (Macedonian general), 332
Eumenes I, 385, 392
Eumenes II, 62, 333-34, 393-94, 446, 465, 466
Eupator, 59; see also Antiochus V
Euphrates River, 2, 3, 7, 11, 20, 21, 42, 43, 51, 55, 80, 96, 175, 193, 196, 204, 217, 220, 221, 223, 228-29, 232, 233, 237, 240, 245, 252, 257, 275, 313, 316, 325, 331, 340, 347, 376, 382, 384

lower, 10
middle, 131
upper region, 208
Europe, 2, 278, 321
Eurotas River, 415, 431
Eusebius, 91, 103, 110, 153, 274, 402
Evagoras, 210, 300
Evans, Arthur, 198, 418
Exodus, the, 179; route of, map, 90
Ezekiel, 55, 67, 120, 189, 209, 211
prophecy of, 210
Ezion-geber, 95, 99, 173, 180, 201, 236; see also Elath
Ezra, 263

F

Fair Havens, 415
Fairservis, Walter A., Jr., 93
Faiyum, 50, 64, 70-74; see also Birket Qarun
Far'a River, 168
Far'a, Tell el-, 142; see also Tirzah
Fara'in, Tell el-. See El-Fara'in, Tell
Fars, 280; see also Persis
Feiran, Wadi, 91
Felix, 103
Fertile Crescent, 1-6, 12-13, 44, 88, 217, 222, 227, 231
geographical features, 2, 3
map of, 2
rainfall, 1
Festus, 482, 532, 541, 546
Field, Henry M., 403-4
Filson, Floyd V., 249, 363, 404
Finegan, Jack, 222, 237, 257, 260, 352, 404, 452, 474, 482, 487, 550
Finley, M. I., 487, 488
Fisher, Clarence, 118, 124, 125
Five Hundred, Council of, 470
Flamininus, 446, 486
Flood, biblical, 14
Fogg Art Museum of Harvard, 399
Forum, Roman, 517, 521, 540, 543-46, 548
France, 252, 431, 495, 513
Frank, Tenney, 215, 261, 404, 487
Frankfort, Henri, 14
Free, Joseph P., 143, 299

G

Gabinian Law, 512
Gabinius, Aulus, 107, 140, 141
Gabriel, M. A., 328
Gad, tribe of, 169, 175
Gadara, 177
Gades, 206; see also Gadir or Cadiz
Gadir, 206; see also Cadiz or Gades
Gaius Caesar Caligula. See Caligula

Gaius, younger brother of Tiberius, 509
Galba, 526
Galatia, 335, 337, 338, 344, 346-48, 350, 351, 382, 384, 518, 547
people of, 314, 334, 383, 387
Phrygia, 355
province of, 354-57
Galen, 393
Galerius, Arch of, 459
Galilee
district of, 98, 101, 126-35, 148, 178, 217, 220, 221
mountains of, 116, 187
sea of, 95, 128-30, 133, 135, 167-69, 175, 177; see also Tiberias, Sea of
Gallio, 482, 486
Gallipoli Peninsula, 320
Gangites (Gangas), 452
Gardiner, Alan, 58, 63, 93
Gardiner, E. Norman, 485, 487
Garrod, Dorothy, 96, 100
Garstang, John, 75, 108, 131, 146
Gate of the Lions, 426
Gath, 105, 109, 235
Gaugamela, 274, 443
Gaugamela
Battle of, 282
Gaul, 259, 277, 504, 513-17, 519, 521, 525-27, 547
Cisalpine, 514
people of, 141, 332, 354, 383, 392, 394, 444, 467, 496, 500
Gaulanitis, 175
Gawra, Tepe, 11
Gaza, 1, 88, 105-10, 174, 220, 237
Gazna, 276; see also Takht-I-Sulaiman
Gebal, 54, 187, 190-91, 194, 205, 208; see also Byblos, and Jubayl, modern
Gedaliah, 59, 114, 149, 152
Gediz River, 398; see also Hermus River
Valley, 313
Gedrosia, 264
Gelb, I. J., 324
Gerar, 105, 113; see also Jemmeh, Tell
Gerasa, 177; see also Jerash
Gerizim, Mount, 135, 137, 138, 139, 168
Germa, 396
German Oriental Society, 323
Germanicus, 525
Germany, 324, 513, 526, 528
Geshem, 115
Geshur, 231
Geshurites, 173
Gestrus River, 345
Garden of Gethsemane, 158-59
Gezer, 59, 120, 207, 221
Ghirshman, Roman, 271, 277, 280, 284, 287
Ghor, 168; see also Aulon
Ghutah, 219, 236

Gibeah, 151-52; see also el-Ful, Tell
Gibeon, 114, 148-53; see also El Jib
Gibeonites, 149
Gideon, 123, 137, 169
Gilboa, Mount, 123-25, 169
Gilbratar, 201-2, 368, 495; see also Pillars of Hercules
Gilead, 175-76, 235, 246
Gilgal, 171
Gilgamesh and Agga, legend of, 13
Ginsberg, H. Louis, 230, 286
Giza, pyramids of, 68, 70
Gjerstad, Einar, 297, 309
Glanville, S. R. K., 190
Glueck, Nelson, 173, 181
Gnossus, 416; see also Knossos or Cnossus
Gnosticism, documents, 78
Gobryas, satrap, 238
Goetze, Albrecht, 328, 404
Goldman, Hetty, 323, 344
Goliath, 109, 113
Gomel, Tell, 274
Gomer, 266
Gomorrah, 171
Goodspeed, Edgar J., 260, 404
Gordium, 328-29, 332, 354
Gordon, Cyrus H., 20, 420, 487
Goshen, 53, 55
Goths, 359, 361, 480
Götze, Albrecht, 324
Gozan, 10; see also Halaf, Tell
Graham, James Walter, 487
Graindor, Paul, 461, 487
Granicus River, 210, 239, 331, 442
Great Pyramid, 50, 68
Greco-Persian wars, 197, 435
Greco-Roman
community, 487
culture, 431
period, 143
world, 248
Greece, 13, 44, 105, 209, 240, 296, 297, 298, 300, 304, 320, 331-33, 336, 356, 366, 407, 407-88, 495, 505, 507, 511, 514, 516, 525-26, 530
Apostle Paul, 449-87
Athenian Empire, 437-39
boundaries, 407
Bronze Age, 424, 478
Early, 417
Middle, 417, 424-25
city-states, 239, 245, 334, 407, 409, 412, 418, 429, 431-34, 442, 446, 507
classical age, 418, 429, 435-41
climate, 410-11
colonization, 342, 383, 431
dark ages, 428, 429, 433
empire of, 2
Formative Age, 429-31
geographical features, 407-11
Helladic periods, 424
history of, 418-87
immigration, 329

Indo-European invasion, 417
Iron Age, 428
language, 245, 401
map of, 408
mercenaries, 341
Middle Age, 196
Minoans, 418-23
mountains, 409
Mycenaean age, 424-29
Mycenaeans, the, 423-28, 495
natural resources, 411
Neolithic period, 416-17, 424
Paleolithic remains, 416
Panhellenic cooperation, 437
peninsula, 418
peoples, 416-18
Persian interference, 441
Persian threat, 435-37
rivers, 409-10
Roman conquest, 445-48
Roman Imperial Period, 413, 448, 451, 460-61
under the Roman Republic, 447
Greek mysteries, 475
Greeks, 118, 206, 215, 223, 230, 268, 314, 329, 331, 340, 341, 342, 354, 366, 373, 375, 398, 415, 416, 418, 435, 436, 447, 496, 497, 498, 501
in Italy, 501
Gregorian calendar, 246, 519
Gudea, 20, 38, 285
Gudelisin, 352
Gurney, O. R., 260, 324-26, 404
Guterback, Hans, 323
Gutians, 18, 285
Guy, P. L. O., 118, 122
Gyges, 330

H

Habiru, 76, 96, 114, 194
Habor River, 2, 228; see also Khabur
Habu temple, Medinet, 83
Hadad, 96, 222; see also Baal, Adad and Rimmon
Hadad-Baal, temple of, 253
Hadad-nirari III of Assyria, 235-36; see also Adadnirari III
Hadrian, 177, 351, 359, 367, 448, 462-64, 475, 477, 522
Hagar, 88, 91, 173
Haggai, 157
Haifa, 99-101
Halaf (Gazan), Tell, 10-11, 223
people of, 10
period of, 10
see also Gozan
Haleb, 220, 252; see also Aleppo or Beroea
Haliacmon plain, 412
Halicarnassus, 330-31, 439
Halys River, 266, 313, 316, 330, 334, 354, 382, 384, 398; see also Kizil Irmak
Ham, 47, 190

Hama (Hamath), 218, 232-35, 237, 253, 323; see also Epiphania
Hamadan, 263, 273-74; see also Ecbatana
Hammond, M., 550
Hammond, N. G. L., 294, 309, 420, 440, 487
Hammurabi, 5, 7, 20, 23, 32, 38, 40, 215, 222-23, 227, 285, 297, 325
code of, 23, 284, 286, 327; empire, map of, 23
Hamun, Lake, 279
Hanfmann, George M. A., 399
Hannibal, 240, 446, 504-5, 507-8, 514, 533-34
Haran (or Harran), 1-2, 35, 43, 222-23, 231, 237, 275; see also Carrhae and Paddan-Aram
Harding, G. Lankester, 163, 181
Hariri, Tell, 40, 131; see also Mari
Harmhab, 82
Harod, 124
Harosheth, 116
Harun al-Rashid, 274
Harun Jebel, 179; see also Hor
Harus, 63, 73, 85
Harvard University, 43, 140, 399
Hasbany, Nahr, 167
Hasmonaeans, 126, 138, 140, 158, 164, 274
Hassuna, Tell, 9, 38
Hastings, James, 405, 536, 550
Hathor, goddess, 90
Hatshepsut, 82, 85
Hattusas, 325, 327
Hattusilis III, 325
Hatweret-Amenemhet, 78
Haupert, Raymond S., 115
Hauran
Jebel, 175, 219, 246; see also Druzes
Hauran-Bashan, 175
Hauran
Plateau, 219; see also Auranitis or Bashan
Hawara, 64, 72, 73
Hayes, Doremus A., 462, 487, 488
Hazael, 109, 235
Hazor, 105, 116, 120, 130-32, 226
Hebrew
culture, 213
language, 116, 221
script, 141
Hebrew University, 131, 140
Hebron, 88, 95, 110-11, 113-14, 147, 153, 160-62, 170, 181, 231
Heichelheim, Fritz M., 215, 246, 253, 260, 498, 525, 550
Heir, Tell el-. See El-Heir, Tell
Heleb, 222; see also Aleppo
Heliopolis, 59, 64-66, 218, 245, 253-55; see also Baalbek

Helladic culture, 296, 424
Hellas, 336, 417-18, 424-25, 435, 481; see also Greece
Hellenic League, 437
Hellenism, 55, 152-53, 169, 258, 330, 379, 384, 387, 401
in Pergamum, 395
in Rome, 507
Syria, 242
Hellenistic Empires, map of, 239
Hellenistic remains, 399
Hellespont, 210, 239, 331, 334, 354, 356, 366, 435, 437, 442, 448, 506, 511; see also Dardanelles
Helots, 431, 433
Hephaestus, god, 471
Hera, goddess, 63, 427
temple of, 369, 395; see also Juno
Heracleopolis, 74, 75, 79; see also Neni-nesu
Heracles, 207
Heraklion, 416; see also Candia
Herculancum, 528
Hercules, god, 207, 225, 394, 471
Hermes, 352, 427; see also Mercury and Thoth
Hermon, mount, 129, 166-67, 175, 219; see also esh Sheikh Jebel
Hermonthis, 65; see also Beth-shemesh or On
Hermopolis, 77; see also Esh-munein
Hermus
Mountains, 313
River, 354, 387, 396, 398, 400
valley, 315, 391, 396, 400
Herod Agrippa I, 141, 524, 542, 546
Herod Agrippa II, 103, 382, 515
Herod Archelaus, 542
Herod the Great, 98, 103-4, 108, 140, 155, 158, 161, 164, 166, 170, 181, 245-46, 252, 291, 383, 519, 521
Herod of Judaea, 249
Herodes Atticus, 462
Odeion of, 465
Herodotus, 28, 30-31, 47-50, 56-57, 60, 63-64, 66-68, 71-73, 107, 197, 202, 277, 370, 381, 435, 439
Herzfeld, Ernst E., 9, 274, 280-82, 287
Hesa, Wadi, 95; see also Arnon River
Heshbon, 175, 179
Heth, 322, 327
Hezekiah, 25, 157, 205
Hezion, 232
Hiddekel River, 2; see also Tigris River
Hierapolis, 376, 379-81
charonion, 381
Middle Ages, 380
Plutonium, 381
hieroglyphics
Cretan, 420

Egyptian, 90, 121, 272
Hittite, 323, 326
Hill, George, 294, 298, 309
Hincks, Edward, 272
Hinnom, Valley of, 154
Hippodamus, 371, 439
Hiram I (the Great), 102, 197-201, 428
successors of, 199
Hiram II of Tyre, 204, 299
Hissarlik, 319, 322
Hitti, Philip K., 189, 192, 194, 202, 212-13, 221-22, 226, 252, 260
Hittite, 314, 320, 324, 327, 328, 341, 354
sites (at Troy), 320
city-states, 233
Empire, 105, 321, 422
influence, 36
names, 139
remains, 281
settlement, 253
tablets, 230
Hittites, 24, 42, 161, 194, 195, 196, 215, 223, 229, 230, 232, 233, 252, 297, 298, 299, 319, 328, 340, 385, 417, 422, 428
Asia Minor, 322-27, 383
Hivites, 148
Hogarth, D. G., 198, 361
Holy Grail, 249
Home, Gordon, 294, 298-99, 309
Homer, 81, 197, 299, 368, 390, 418, 428-29
Homs, 218-20, 222, 228, 231, 240, 253; see also Emesa
Hophra, 55, 208
Horites, 42
Hor, Mount, 92, 179; see also Harun, Jebel
Horeb, Mount, 91; see also Sinai, Mount
Horites, 41, 155, 277; see also Hurrians
Horus, Egyptian god, 63, 73, 85
Hrozny, Bedrich, 322-24, 404
Hrozny, F., 123
Hule, Lake, 95, 130-32, 167; see also Merom, Waters of
Hum, Tell, 134; see also Capernaum
Humann, Karl, 380, 394
Hurrians (Horites), 41-43, 96, 155, 227, 228, 230, 325, 327
language, 41
tablets, 230
see also Horites
Husn, Tell el-. See El-Husn, Tell
Hyde, 317
Hyksos, 51, 53, 54, 55, 57, 80, 81, 96, 107, 110, 114, 124, 132, 139, 192-93, 227-28, 230, 297, 298, 417
Hymettus Range, 462
Hyrcania, 263, 274; see also Asterabad Province

246, 249, 277, 454, 461, 539
  birth of, 519, 537
  the Messiah, 163
  time of, 390, 533
  Olivet discourse, 159
Jewish Christians, 391
Jews, 290, 291, 342, 348, 350-52, 363, 376, 391, 397, 451, 458-59, 468, 477, 523-24, 526-27, 529, 541, 546
Jezebel, 100, 124, 185, 189, 199, 207, 213, 397
Jezreel
  river, 168
  valley of, 116, 123, 124, 126, 169; see also Zerin
Jib, El. See El Jib
Joab, 149, 167, 176
Joash, 111, 236
Job's well, 154, 155; see also En-rogel
John, 311, 316, 358, 359, 361-63, 376, 378, 382, 387, 389-403, 529
Johnson, Sherman E., 380, 404
Jokneam, 116-17; see also Qeimun Tell
Jonah, 38, 102
Jonathan, 110, 164
Jones, A. H. M., 242, 260, 340, 386, 404, 487
Jones, Tom B., 227, 260, 321, 404, 433, 487, 488, 550
Joppa, 99, 102, 104, 200; see also Jaffa
Jordan
  kingdom of, 99
  River, 99, 128, 135, 173, 175-76, 219, 231, 235
  valley of, 95, 122, 124, 129, 153, 166-72
Joseph, 50, 53-54, 65, 74, 143, 491
Josephus, 59, 128, 138, 165, 196-201, 205, 291, 294, 348, 363, 532, 536
Joshua, 96, 101, 105, 111, 112, 113, 114, 115, 119, 125, 130, 132, 133, 135, 137, 145-46, 148, 161-62, 168-69, 170, 173, 175
Josiah, 120, 145, 237
Joy, Mount, 153; see also Nebi Samwil
Jubayl, 187, 222; see also Byblos and Gebal
Judaea, 95, 103, 114, 126, 178, 181, 205, 245, 418, 519, 522, 524, 526, 541
  mountains of, 162
  people of, 263
  wilderness of, 162-66
Judah, 25, 35, 147, 148, 153, 155, 172, 173, 205, 207, 231, 234, 236-37
  armies of, 113
  highlands of, 148
  hill country, 147-62
  mountains of, 110
Judah, Rabbi, 130

Judaism, 271, 376, 381, 528
Judas
  of Galilee
    Zealot, 128
  the Maccabean, 98, 152
Judges, period of, 105-6, 122-23, 130, 145, 170, 176, 231
Judith 1:1-14, 273
Jugurthine war, 510
Julia, 135, 522
Julia, Basilica, 543
Julian
  calendar, 248
  family, 522
  municipal law, 515
Julio-claudian line, 522
Julius, captain of the Praetorian Guard, 541-42
Julius Caesar; see Caesar, Julius
Julius, temple of, 521, 544
Juno, goddess, 369, 498; see also Hera
Jupiter, 352, 463, 498
  temple of, 250, 255, 529, 540
  see also Zeus
Justinian, 91, 252, 341, 359
Justus Titus, 482

K

Kabir, Nahr al, 187
Kadesh, 195, 226, 229-30, 252, 325
Kadesh-barnea, 91; see also En Mishpat
Kalakh, 35; see also Calah or Nimrud
Koldewey, Robert, 31, 32
Kali Limenes, 415
Kanesh, 322, 324, 325
Kanish, 33
Kaptara, 105; see also Caphtor
Karalis, Lake, 316, 350
Karaman, 314, 352
Karkar, 122, 204; see also Qarqar
Karnak, 55, 82, 83, 101, 111, 118
  temple of 82, 83
Karpas Peninsula, 290, 292, 293, 298
Karun River, 284; see also Eulaeus
Kashan Oasis, 277
Kassites, 7, 24, 41, 270, 274, 417
Kaufmann, Yehezkel, 18, 146
Kavir, Dasht-i (Desert), 264
Kavalla, 450
Kebeer River, 218
Kedesh, 132
Kedesh-Naphtali, 132; see also Qades, Tell
Kefr Kenna, 130
Keftiu, 420
Keil, Josef, 361, 386, 404
Keilah, 110
Kelb, Nahrel, 186, 187; see also Lycus and Dog rivers
Kelso, J. L., 145, 171

Kemet, 47; see also Egypt, name of
Kenyon, Kathleen, 96, 182
Kerazeh, 135; see also Chorazin
Kermanshah, 270-71
Kerti Hüyük, 352
Khabur River, 10, 40, 42, 228; see also Habor
Khafre, 69, 70; see also Khephren
Khasrau II, 270
Khasroes, 39
Khasti, 78
Khatyn-Serai, 351
Khenti-Amentiu, god, 79
Khephren; see Khafre
Khirbet el Muqenna', 110; see also Ekron
Khirokitia, 295
Khnumhotep, 75
Khorsabad, 39; see also Dur-Sharrukin
Khufu
  engineers of, 70
  Great Pyramid of, 68, 70, 78
  see also Cheops
Khurasan (Khorasan)
  mountains of, 265
Kidron Valley, 154
King, L. W., 36, 272
King's Highway, 179, 246
Kirjath-Arba, 161; see also Hebron
Kirjath-jearim (Kuriet el-'Enab) 112, 143; see also Abu Ghosh
Kirjath-sepher, 110; see also Debir
Kirkuk, 42
  modern, 8
Kish, 14
Kishon River, 116, 187; see also Muqatta, Nahr al and Qishon
Kitchen, J. Howard, 92, 182
Kition, 294, 299, 300, 301, 305; see also Citium
Kittim (Chittim), 294
Kizil Irmak, 266, 316, 382; see also Halys River
Knossos, 227, 297, 416, 418-23; see also Cnossus
Knox, John, 260
Kokhba, Bar, 98; see also Cocheba, Bar
Kolonos Agoraios, 470
Konya, 319, 350; see also Iconium
Kouklia, 305; see also Nea Paphos or Paphos
Kramer, Samuel Noah, 44
Krio, Cape, 415
Kullab, village of, 12; see also Uruk
Kültepe, 33, 318, 322, 324
Kurdistan, 42, 274
Kurds, 270, 274
Kush Range, 265
Kuwait, gulf of, 220
Kynosura, 435; see also Cynosura

Kyrenia, 305
Mountains, 292, 293, 295

L

Laban, 43, 168
Labarnas, King, 324
Lab 'ayu, 137
Lachish, 110, 113, 114, 115;
    see also Duweir, Tell ed-
    Letters, 113, 116
Laconia, 411, 415, 431
    plain of, 415
Lade, 369, 370, 371, 372
Lagash, city-state of, 6, 10, 20,
    285; see also Shirpurla and
    Telloh, mound of
Langdon, Stephen, 14
Laodice, wife of Antiochus II,
    377
Laodicea, 217, 242, 252, 271,
    314, 315, 316, 356, 376-79,
    381, 389, 390; see also
    Latakia
Lapithos, 296
Laranda, 314, 317; see also
    Karaman
Larissa, 411
Larnaca, 299
Larsa, 5, 22
La Spezia, 494
Latakia, 217, 218, 220, 252; see
    also Laodicea
Latins, 496, 499, 510
Latium, 494, 497-501
Latonian Gulf, 370, 372
Laurium, 413, 436
Law codes
    Sumerian, 44; see also Ham-
    murabi, Code of
Layard, Austen Henry, 31, 32,
    35, 36
Lebanese littoral, 195, 197
Lebanon, 54, 129, 175, 185,
    189, 193, 194, 195, 215,
    221, 237, 240
    cedars of, 188, 191
    mountains, 95, 166, 185, 187,
    188, 192, 217, 218, 219,
    253
Lechaeon, 478
Lechaeon Road, 482-83
Lechaeum, 414
Lemnos, Island of, 318
Leontes River, 129, 166, 186;
    see also Litani, Nahr el
Lepidus, Marcus Aemilius, 512,
    515, 516
Lerna, fountain of, 484
Lesbos, 318, 329, 365, 366, 367,
    391, 392; see also Mytilene
Leuctra, 441
Libnah, 112; see also Tell es-
    Safi and Blanchegarde
Libya, 202, 368, 431
Libya
    Desert, 47, 51
    kings of, 56
    tableland of, 70
Liguria, 495

Limnai, Lake, 316, 347, 374
Linear A, 420-21
Linear B, 418, 420, 421
Lioness, tomb of, 426
Lisan peninsula, 171
Litani, Nahr el, 186, 187, 218;
    see also Leontes River
Lithinos, Cape, 415
Livia, villa of, 394
Lloyd, Seton, 317, 319, 322,
    328, 404
Loftus, William K., 284
Lucius Caesar; see Caesar, Lu-
    cius
Lucullus, 336, 383, 512
Lugal (or Ensi), 13
Lugalbanda, 12
Lugalzaggisi, 20, 222
Lugdunum, 521; see also Lyons
Luke, the Apostle, 302, 338,
    344, 347, 351, 352, 355,
    357, 364, 367, 409, 449,
    451, 452, 454, 482, 524,
    532, 537
Luli
    king of Sidon, 100
    king of Tyre, 205
    see also Eluleus
Lullubi tribe, 270
Luristan, 271, 274
    plain of, 284
Lurs, people of, 271
Lut, Dasht-i (desert), 264
Luwians, 319, 324, 326
Luxor, 55, 78, 80, 82, 85; see al-
    so El-Uqsur
Lycabettus, 462
Lycaonia, 334, 337, 338, 339,
    350, 351, 355
Lyceum, 441
Lycia, 331, 334, 337, 344, 375
Lycian coast, 376
Lycian league, 337
Lycians, 344
Lycurgus, 465
Lycus, 357, 360, 379
    plain of, 377
    River, 186, 314
    valley of, 376, 377, 381, 389
Lydda, 102, 103; see also Dio-
    spolis
Lydia, 263, 267, 329, 344, 371,
    385, 391, 396, 401, 435,
    452
    kingdom, 365, 398
Lydian
    language, 401
    people of, 328-30, 341, 358,
    398
Lysimachus, 332, 359, 367, 391,
    392
Lystra, 316, 346, 351, 352, 353,
    354, 355, 357, 376, 482

M

Maacah, 231, 232
Macalister, R. A. S., 59, 112,
    182

Maccabean
    period, 101, 111, 176
    revolt, 240-41
    state, 126
    wars, 162
Maccabeans, 128, 177
Maccabaeus, Judas, 158
Maccabaeus, Simon, 126
Macedonia, 239-40, 330, 334,
    356, 359, 365, 367, 373,
    375, 396, 397, 407, 409,
    411, 412, 424, 425, 436,
    441, 442, 444, 445-46, 447,
    448, 449, 450, 451, 454,
    455, 456, 457, 459, 474,
    479, 501, 505, 506, 507
    control, 445
    people of, 400
    soldiers of, 244
    war, second, 506
    war, third, 375, 507
Machpelah, Cave of, 162, 323
MacKendrick, Paul L., 357, 361,
    373, 395, 404, 487, 488,
    549, 550
Maeander
    Mountains, 313; see also
    Menderes
    River, 315, 334, 347, 357,
    360, 371, 372, 376, 387
    Valley, 316, 356, 391
Magdala, 134; see also Tarichea
Magi, 276, 277
Magna Mater, temple of, 540;
    see also Cybele
Magnesia, 334, 347, 348, 350,
    354, 359, 377, 380, 385,
    397, 507
Magnesian Range, 409
Magnus, Leonard A., 550
Magus, Simon, 277
Ma 'in, Khirbet, 147
Maiuri, Amedeo, 550
Malian Gulf, 437
Mallawan, M. E. L., 35, 38
Mallia, 297, 422
Malta, 415, 531, 532, 533, 534
    Neolithic Age, 532
Maltese Islands, 531
Mamertime Prison, 549-50; see
    also Carcer
Mampsis (Mamshit), 174
Manasseh, 101, 119, 205
    tribe of, 122, 123, 135, 141,
    175
Manetho, 68, 78
Mangoian, L. and H. A., 309
Mannai people, 276
Marah, 90
Marathon, 33, 407, 435, 436,
    466
    Plain of, 435, 462
Marcus Aurelius, 391, 522
Marduk, god, 21, 23, 31, 32,
    286
Marduk
    statue of, 25
    temple of in Babylon, 25
Marduk, Mushe-zib, 25
Mareotis Lake, 61
Mareshah, 113

N

Nabataean period, 172, 174, 179
Nabataeans, 173, 179-80, 240-41, 245, 256, 257
Nablus, 135, 138, 139, 207; *see also* Neapolis Flavia and Shechem
Nabonidus, 20, 29, 43, 238, 267
Nabopolassar, 25, 28, 35, 208, 237, 267
Naharaim, Aram, 231; *see also* Nahor
Nahor, 231; *see also* Aram Naharaim
Nahor, town of, 43
Naphtali, 116, 126, 131
Naram-Sin, 38, 231, 265, 270, 285, 286
Narmer, 78
Nasbeh, Tell en, 152-53; *see also* Mizpah
Naucratis, 61, 63, 366
Naville, Edouard, 56, 58, 59, 74, 79
Nazareth, 127, 128, 129, 130, 134
Nea Paphos, 299, 305; *see also* Paphos or Kouklia
Neapolis, 350, 396, 407, 450, 451
Neapolis, Flavia, 138; *see also* Nablus
Nebi Samwil, 153; *see also* Joy, Mount
Nebi Yunus, mound of, 36
Nebuchadnezzar I, 266, 286
Nebuchadnezzar II, 7, 20, 28, 31, 60, 97, 98, 108, 112, 113, 114, 115, 116, 145, 146, 148, 152, 155, 157, 208, 209, 237, 263, 267, 273, 286
   armies of, 145
   hanging gardens of, 28, 31
   palace of, 32
Necho, 55, 57, 120, 202, 237
Nefertiti, Queen, 77
Negeb (Negev), 95, 147, 172-74
Nehemiah, 107, 149, 158, 263, 268, 286
Neni-nesu, 74; *see also* Heracleopolis
Neo-Babylonian Empire, 7, 28, 263; *see also* Chaldean Empire
Neo-Hittite kingdoms, 326
Neolithic Age, 6, 9, 169, 173, 221, 278, 295
   Greece, 416, 417, 424
   Italy, 495
   Malta, 532
   Mesopotamia, 9
Neo-Persian Empire, 269
Neriglisar, 28
Nero, 254, 257, 324, 337, 344, 346, 374, 378, 380, 383, 448, 460, 461, 478, 483,
486, 519, 524, 525, 526, 535, 536, 538, 541, 542, 546, 548
Nerva, 402, 522, 529, 543
Nessana (Uja-el-Hafir), 174
Nestar, 343, 344
Nestos
   plain, 412
   River, 412, 450
Neocaesarea, 383
New Testament, 212, 220, 231, 512, 529
   history of, 2, 246
   narrative, 311
   period, 249, 252, 255, 341
Nibshan, 162
Nicaea (Nice), 388, 521
   council of, 213, 308
Nicator, Seleucus, 347
Nicias, 440
   peace of, 456
Nicomedes I, 354, 383, 387
Nicomedes II, 387
Nicomedes III, 335, 336
Nicomedes IV, 388
Nicomedia, 317, 382, 387, 388, 521
Nicopolis, 383
Nicosia, 292, 294, 295
Nihawand, 271; *see also* Nehavend
Nile River, 47-49, 54, 56, 57, 70, 75, 78, 83, 99, 192, 202, 203, 229
   Bahr Yusuf tributary, 7
   Blue, 49
   canopic mouth of, 61
   cataracts, 47, 48, 51, 54, 68, 74, 86, 87
   Damietta branch of, 64
   Delta, 48, 54-64, 66, 68, 83, 88, 89, 99
   food and famine, 49
   land of, 228
   map of, 48
   mouth of, 56
   Pelusiac branch, 60
   Rosetta branch, 63, 64
   source of, 48, 49
   Tanaitic branch, 57
   valley 1, 8, 50, 51, 53
   White, 49
Nimrod, 2, 21, 38
Nimrud, 35; *see also* Calah or Kalakh
Nin-egal, 223
Nineveh, 3, 7, 10, 11, 22, 28, 31, 32, 35, 36, 38, 39, 43, 67, 80, 83, 102, 114, 208, 221, 223, 227, 237, 266, 267, 273, 443; *see also* Ninus
Ningal, goddess, 13, 19
Ninlil, 13, 32
Ninus, 223; *see also* Nineveh
Nippur, 6, 13, 32; *see also* Enlil
No (No-Amon), 80; *see also* Thebes
Noah, 221
   ark, 3, 6
Noph, 66; *see also* Memphis

North Africa, 47
Nubia, 48, 54, 86, 87
Nusayriyah Mountains, 187, 218; *see also* Bargylus Mountains
Nuzi (Nuzu), 32, 42, 227
   Tablets, 43
Nymphs, Hill of, 462

O

'Obeid, Tell, 6, 10, 12, 14; *see also* Arpachiya
Ochus, 210, 274; *see also* Artaxerxes III
Octavian, 62, 141, 337, 338, 447, 451, 457, 459; *see also* Augustus Caesar
Octavius, 515, 516, 517
'Ojjul, Tell el-. See El-Ojjul, Tell
Old Testament, 208, 222, 224, 230, 236, 246; *see also* Septuagint, history of, 2
Olives, Mount of, 154, 158-59
Olmstead, A. T., 44, 223, 261, 287
Olympia, 370, 414
Olympic Games, 415;
   of Antioch (Syria), 247
Olympus, Mount, 292, 366, 387, 409, 412, 457
Omri, 36, 122, 124, 135, 139, 140, 142, 234
   dynasty, 120
On (On-mehit), god, 65; *see also* Beth-shemesh and Hermonthis
Ophel, 155
Oppian Hill, 548
Orientgesellschaft, Deutsche; *see* Deutsche Orientgesellschaft
Orontes
   range, 166
   River, 187, 194, 195, 218, 220, 226, 228, 229, 233, 241, 243, 247, 249, 250, 252, 289, 323, 325
   Valley, 242
Osarkon I, Pharaoh, 113
Osiris, god, 64, 78, 79, 445,
Osiris-Apis, Egyptian god, 62; *see also* Serapis
Ostia, 493, 494, 524, 535
Ostraca, 115
Ottoman Empire, 252, 311
Oxus River, 275; *see also* Amu Darya
Oxyrhynchus, 75; *see also* El Bahnasa
Oxyrhynchus Papyri, 75

P

Pactolus River, 330, 398, 399
Paddan-Aram, 2, 43, 135, 144, 231; *see also* Haran (Harran)

Philip the Evangelist, 103, 107, 380
Philip the Tetrarch, 135, 166
Philippi, 365, 396, 407, 450-54, 456, 458, 460, 474, 516, 546
Battle of, 459
Plain of, 412, 451, 452, 454
Philistine period, 104
Philistine Plain, 104, 112, 113
Philistines, 99; *see also* Sea Peoples, 101, 105, 110, 111, 112, 114, 118, 124, 125, 143, 144, 152, 169, 173, 195, 197, 205, 235, 421
Philometor, 59; *see also* Ptolemy VI
Philometor, 509; *see also* Attalus III
Phoenicia, 7, 54, 61, 96, 99, 100, 101, 126, 185-213, 217, 224, 225, 232, 234, 237, 238, 241, 245, 253, 257, 266, 274, 299, 300, 340, 353, 375, 376, 428, 444, 496, 503, 530, 532
Assyrian period, 196, 203-8
barriers to communication, 186
Byzantine period, 196
cedars of Lebanon, 188
cities, 130, 187
city-states, 208, 212, 239
coastal plain, 185
colonies, 206
commercial activity in Cyprus, 299
conquest of, 193
decline of Egyptian control, 194
early relations with Egypt, 190-92
Egyptian Empire period, 193
the Egyptian Middle Kingdom period, 192
geographical features, 185-88
Greek period, 196, 210-12
historical developments, 189-213
Hyksos, 192-93
language, 221
map of, 187
Neo-Babylonian period, 208-9
Persian period, 209-10
purple dye, 203
religion, 207
rivers of, 185
the Roman period, 212-13
ships and sea power, 198, 241
shoreline, 187
Phoenician alphabet, 205-7
Phrygia, 266, 315, 316, 321, 326, 332, 335, 337, 340, 347, 348, 350, 351, 354, 355, 356, 357, 378, 381, 383, 385, 398, 400
Low, 357
Phrygian mountains, 313
Phrygians, 314, 328-30, 348, 357

Phygellus, 548
Pi-beseth, 55, 56; *see also* Bubastis
Pieria, Mount, 242
Pilate, 103, 522, 546
Pindus, Mount, 409, 412
Pion, Mount, 359, 360, 362
Piracy, 340, 353, 375, 505, 517
Piraeus (Peiraieus), 371, 414, 436, 438, 439, 440, 446, 460, 462, 511
Pisidia, 337, 344, 346, 347, 348, 355
Pisistratids, 434, 435
Pisistratus, 369
Pithom, 58, 59
Plataea, 331, 427, 437, 448, 479
Plataean infantrymen, 436
Plato, 75, 441, 429
Plebians, 503
Pliny the Elder, 277, 538
Pliny the Younger, 384, 386
Plutarch, 497
Pluto, god, 381
Plutonium, 381
Pnyx, the, 462, 465
Po
    region, 497
    River, 493, 510
    Valley, 494, 495, 496, 497, 498, 500, 501
Poidebard, Father, 198
Polemon, 337, 350, 383
Poliochni, 318, 319
Pollux, god, 534
Polybius, 2, 446, 507
Polycrates, 369, 370
Pompeii, 528, 540
Pompeiopolis, 317
Pompey, 98, 107, 140, 158, 176, 212, 241, 244, 302, 336, 337, 338, 342, 343, 344, 367, 383, 385, 386, 388, 447, 459, 511, 512, 513, 514, 515
Pontus, 313, 314, 316, 317, 332, 333, 334, 335, 336, 337, 377, 380, 382, 383, 384, 388, 447, 511, 512
Porcius Festus, 103
Porta Capena, 538, 539
Poseideion, town of, 233-34; *see also* Mina, Al
Poseidon, god, 427, 466, 478, 484
    temple of, 414, 486
Potiphar (Potipherah), 65
Pozzuoli, 491, 494, 534; *see also* Puteoli
Praetorian guard, 522, 523, 526, 528, 529, 542
Precipitation, Mount of, 129
Princeton University, 249
Pritchard, J. B., 50, 75, 149, 171, 182, 230
Propontis Sea, 356, 357, 387, 392
Propylaea Gateway, 466
Prusias I, 387
Prusias II, 387

Psamtik, 107; *see also* Psammetichus
Ptah, god, 66, 75
Ptolemaic period, 80, 375
Ptolemais, 100, 130, 187, 212; *see also* Accho, or Acre
Ptolemies, 87, 98, 107, 177, 211, 240, 300, 301, 302, 307, 371, 445
Ptolemy I (Soter), 61, 62, 158, 240, 300, 332, 443
Ptolemy II (Philadelphus), 57, 61, 62, 71, 85, 87, 101, 176, 333, 375
Ptolemy III (Euergetes I), 85, 240
Ptolemy VI (Philometor), 240
Ptolemy, Claudius (geographer), 177
Pul, 34, 140; *see also* Tiglath-pileser III
Punic War, First, 445, 504, 533
Punic War, Second, 240, 504, 505, 506, 507, 509, 510, 533
Punic War, Third, 505
Punic Wars, 503-5
Punt, 85; *see also* Somaliland
Puteoli, 491, 494, 534, 535-36; *see also* Pozzuoli
    Gulf of, 535
Pydna, 446, 451
    Battle of, 507
Pylos, 420, 424, 425, 427
Pyramid, Great, of Khufu, 68, 70, 78; *see also* Cheops
Pyramids, 49, 50, 68
Pyramus (Ceyhan), 339, 353, 384
Pyrenees Mountains, 504
Pyrgoteles, 301
Pyrrhus, 412, 501, 505
Pythian Games, 413

Q

Qades, Tell, 132; *see also* Kedesh-Naphtali
Qadesh, 228
Qarqar, 34, 204, 234; *see also* Karkar
Qatna, 194, 222, 223, 228
Qedah, Tell el, 131
Qelt, Wadi, 170
Qumran, 147, 162, 163, 164
Quyunjiq, mound of, 36

R

Rabbah (Rabbath-Ammon), 176; *see also* Amman
Rabbath, 176; *see also* Philadelphia
Rabbath-Ammon, 177, 179; *see also* Philadelphia and Amman
Ramah, 152, 234
Rameh, er-. See Er-Rameh
Rameseum (Ramses II), 83

Scipio
the family, 538
the general, 505
Schmidt, Aage, 143
Schmidt, Erich F., 281, 282
Scopas, 361, 540
Scramuzza, Vincent M., 488
Scranton, Robert L., 488
Scullard, H. H., 551
Scythians, 7, 237, 266, 271, 335
Scythopolis, 177
Sea Peoples, 195, 196, 197, 299;
   see also Philistines
Sebastea, 383
Sebastiyeh, 140; see also Samaria
Seele, Keith C., 190
Segesta, 440
Seir, Mount, 179
Seleucia, 217, 233, 234, 242,
   246, 268, 289, 290, 314,
   359, 377, 391, 444, 506
   plain of, 243
Seleucid
   Empire, 269
   fleet, 333
   outpost, 397
   period (Syria), 252, 253
   successors, 311
Seleucids, 7, 98, 107, 158, 177,
   211, 212, 217, 244, 249,
   254, 268, 270, 271, 274,
   280, 332, 340, 342, 345,
   350, 354, 371, 399, 443,
   506, 507
Seleucus I (Nicator), 7, 30,
   234, 240, 242, 244, 250,
   252, 268, 332, 342, 348,
   397, 443
Seleucus II, 240, 244
Seljuk Mediterranean fleet, 353
Seljuk period (Asia Minor), 353
Seljuk Turks, 378
Sellin, Ernst, 123, 138, 139
Semites, 6, 13, 74, 75, 96, 190,
   496, 503
Senate, Roman, 507, 509, 517,
   518, 519, 521, 522
Senate House (Rome), 545
Senate Office Building, 545
Seneca, 482, 524, 546
Sennacherib, 25, 28, 34, 35, 38,
   43, 100, 101, 107, 108, 109,
   112, 114, 148, 157, 205,
   286
Septimius Severus; see Severus
Septuagint, 2, 61, 431
Serabit el Khadim, 90, 91, 115
Serapis, god, 62, 381; see also
   Osiris-Apis
Sergia Paulla, 308, 349
Sergius Paulus, 308, 349
Sesostris, mythical Egyptian
   king, 60, 61
Sesostris I, 65
Sesostris II, 71
Seth, god, 85
Seti I, 78, 79, 82, 85, 89, 124,
   131, 195, 228, 325
   temple of, 78-80

Severus, Lucius Septimuis, 529,
   543
Seyhan, city of, 233; see also
   Adana
Seyhan River, 339; see also
   Sarus
Shabaka, 25
Shallum, king, 142
Shalmaneser I, 35
Shalmaneser III, 25, 33, 34, 36,
   122, 204, 234, 235, 252
   Black Obelisk of, 341
Shalmaneser V, 33, 34, 140, 205
Shamash-eriba, 29
Shammai, Rabbi, 133
Shamshi-Adad I, 33, 40, 222
Shapur I, 283
Shapur II (the Great), 279
Shapur III, 270
Sharon, the Plain of, 99, 102-4,
   117
Shatt-al-Arab River, 5
Shechem, 135, 138, 139, 142,
   144, 153, 170, 207; see also
   Nablus and Balata, Tell
   pass of, 137
Shedet, 71; see also Medinet el-
   Faiyum and Arsinoë
Sheikh Madhkur, Tell esh, 110
Shem, 221, 231, 285
Shephelah, 95, 105, 110-16, 147,
   172; see also Palestine,
   Shephelah
Sherwin-White, A. N., 488, 542,
   546, 550, 551
Sheshonk I, 111, 122, 149, 157;
   see also Shishak
Shiloh, 143-44
Shinar, land of, 2
Shirpurla, 285; see also Lagash
Shishak, 56, 111, 113, 122, 149;
   see also Sheshonk
Shubad, 15
Shur
   district, 173
   Wilderness of, 90
Shushan, 263, 268, 274, 284;
   see also Susa
Sicily, 206, 292, 368, 374, 415,
   425, 429, 431, 440, 476,
   479, 491, 494, 495, 496,
   501, 503, 504, 516, 531,
   533, 534
   theater of, 533
Sicyon, 250, 429, 431, 484
Side, 344, 345
Sidon, 99, 185, 186, 187, 189,
   190, 194-96, 197, 200, 203,
   204, 205, 209, 210, 211,
   212, 213, 239
   harbor of, 198
   see also Zidon
Sihon, 175, 178, 179
Silas, 353, 354, 356, 388, 451,
   452, 453, 458, 460, 474
Sile, 88, 89
Silpius, Mount, 243, 244, 249,
   250
Silvanus, temple of, 453
Simbel, Abu, 48
Simons, J., 146, 182

Simyra, 193
Sin, Wilderness of, 90
Sinai
   Desert, 217
   Mount, 90, 91, 218, 245; see
      also Mount Horeb and
      Musa, Jebel
Sinai Peninsula, 51, 54, 88-92,
   115, 172, 173, 238
Sinope (Sinop), 62, 314, 382,
   383, 384
Sisera, 116
Sizma, 348
Smith, George Adam, 36, 153,
   182, 261
Smith, James, 532, 534, 551
Smith, William, 405, 487, 488,
   551
Smyrna, 315, 317, 329, 331,
   357, 359, 371, 386, 387,
   389, 390-92, 400, 429
   gulf of, 390, 391
   see also Izmir
Socoh, 113; see also Khirbet
   'Abbad
Sodom, Mount, 171; see also
   Usdum, Jebel
Solomon, 33, 55, 58, 95, 96, 99,
   107, 120, 125, 131, 138,
   144, 155, 157, 176, 180,
   185, 188, 189, 196, 198,
   199, 200, 201, 202, 217,
   232, 233, 236, 253, 258
   temple of, 120, 143, 155, 188,
   198-201, 209
Somaliland, 85; see also Punt
Sommer, Ferdinand, 323
Sophocles, 439, 465
Sorek Valley, 111, 112
Soter, 61, 62, 291; see also Ptol-
   emy I
Souter, A., 355
Soviet Socialist Republic, Geor-
   gian, 31
Spain, 201, 203, 206, 259, 374,
   431, 495, 504, 510, 512,
   513, 517, 527, 535, 546,
   547
Sparta, 268, 331, 358, 369, 410,
   415, 429, 431-33, 435-42,
   445-49, 456, 479, 506
Speiser, E. A., 16
Speiser, Ephraim, 11
Sphercheius River, 437
Sphinx, 68
Spiers, R. Phené, 487, 488, 551
Sporades Islands, 402
Stapfer, Edmond, 182
Starcky, Jean, 257, 261
Stark, Freya, 405
Starkey, James L., 115
Starr, Chester G., 290, 309, 417,
   420, 487, 488, 551
Steindorff, George, 93, 190
Step Pyramid, 49
Stephen, 212, 291
Stevenson, G. H., 261
Stillwell, Richard, 261
Stoicism, 212, 343, 444, 472,
   527

THE WYCLIFFE HISTORICAL GEOGRAPHY OF BIBLE LANDS

Strabo, 2, 62, 71, 73, 84, 212, 217, 277, 303, 359, 366, 369, 383, 384, 533
Straight, street called, 256
Stromboli, volcano, 493
Strymon
    Gulf, 455
    Plain of, 455
    River, 412, 455
Sturtevant, E. H., 324
Succoth, 89, 169; see also Akhsas, Tell
Sudan, 49
Suetonius, 524, 525
Suez
    Canal, 1, 56, 88, 201
    Gulf of, 1, 89, 90
Sulla, 336, 368, 447, 460, 511, 512
Sultan, Tell es, 169
Sumer, 3, 6, 13, 32, 54
    classical age, 14
    dynastic age early, 14
    law codes, 44
    literary works, 32
Sumeria
    city-states of, 6, 13
    tablets, 230
Sumerians, 5, 6, 9, 13
Suppiluliumas, 42, 194, 229, 325
Surrentine pottery, 535
Susa, 10, 41, 263, 268, 274, 284, 286, 443; see also Seleucia-on-Eulaeus and Shushan
Susiana, 263, 284
Swain, Joseph W., 405, 488, 551
Swedish expedition, 297
Sychar, 142; see also Askar el
Syene, 47; see also Aswan
Symbolon Hills, 451
Syracuse, 429, 440, 479, 498, 503, 505, 533
Syria, 1, 7, 9, 34, 55, 99, 101, 110, 176, 185, 189, 190, 192, 193, 194, 195, 203, 204, 205, 207, 208, 210, 211, 215-61, 266, 275, 292, 295, 297, 298, 299, 316, 317, 323, 325, 326, 331, 332, 333, 336, 339, 340, 343, 353, 359, 365, 369, 373, 375, 376, 386, 420, 425, 428, 442, 444, 446, 463, 506, 512, 513, 517, 520, 530
    Amorite period, 221-23
    Aramaens, 231
    Assyrian period, 237
    boundaries, 217
    Canaanite period, 224-26
    city-states, 241, 326, 442
    climate, 220
    coast of, 96
    Egyptian control, 223, 228
    general geographical features, 217-20
    Greater, 195
    Hebrew advance, 231-32, 234-36
    Hellenism in, 242

Hittites, 229, 233-34
Hyksos period
    Map of, 216
    Mitanni, 228-29
    Neo-Babylonian period, 237-38
    Persian period, 238-39
    regions of, 217-20
    Roman peace, 244-60
    Roman period, 212, 215, 219, 233
    Seleucid control, 217, 233, 240-44, 253
    strategic position of, 215
    term or word, 217; see also Amurru, land of
    trade routes, 220
Syrian desert, 217, 220, 256
Syrian Gates, 218, 340, 353, 357; see also Beilan Pass
Syrians, 126, 157, 230, 443, 507
Syro-Arabian desert, 231
Syro-Iraqi desert, 220

T

Taanach, 100, 116, 119, 122, 123
    letters, 123
Ta 'annak, Tell, 122
table of nations, Genesis, 189
Tabor, Mount, 116, 117, 122, 129
Tabrimon, 232, 234
Tacitus, 306, 367, 525
Tadmor, 257; see also Palmyra
Taharka, 83, 205; see also Tirhakah
Tahpanhes, 60; see also Defenneh Tell and Daphnae
Tahun, El-. See El-Tahun
Tainat, Tell, 323
Takht-I-Sulaiman, 276; see also Gazna
Tanis, 57, 60, 83, 89; see also Avaris
Taranto, 494; see also Tarentum
Tarentum, 425, 494, 501, 537
    Gulf of, 501, 510
Tarquins, 497
Tarqumiya, 110; see also Iphtah
Tarshish, 201; see also Tharshish
Tarsus, 103, 221, 256, 302, 311, 313, 314, 316, 317, 318, 319, 323, 332, 337, 338, 339, 340, 341-44, 353, 354, 357, 397, 539
    University of, 344
Tartessus, 201, 203
Tatta, Lake, 316, 384
Taurus Mountains, 5, 21, 188, 217, 218, 223, 233, 245, 313, 331, 334, 339, 340, 344, 346, 353, 356, 382, 384; see also Zagros Mountains
Tavium, 354
Taygetus Range, 415

Tehran, 270, 273, 274, 275, 276-80
Tel Aviv, 99, 104, 112
Telloh, mound of, 20; see also Lagash
Temnos, 313
Temnus, Mount, 356
Tempe, 437
Tepe Gawra, 11
Tepe Siyalk, 277-79
Terebinth Valley, 112; see also Elah, Vale of
Teucer, 303
Teucrid family, 338
Tharshish, 201; see also Tarshish
Thasos, Island of, 411, 450
Theban rulers, 193
Thebes, 35, 55, 71, 76, 80, 81, 82, 83, 123, 413, 427, 431, 437, 441, 442, 479, 484
    map of, 81
    see also Diospolis Magna
Themistocles, 436, 437, 438, 464
Theopharastus, 366
Theophilus, 62
Thermaic Gulf, 457
Thermopylae, 331, 333, 436, 442, 479
    Battle of, 507
Thessalian basin, 411
Thessalians, 410
Thessalonica, 396, 407, 411, 448, 449, 454, 456-59, 468, 474, 482, 539
Thessaly, 407, 409, 411, 412, 413, 416, 418, 424, 425, 436, 448
Thinis, 54, 78 (This)
Thoth, god, 77, 102; see also Hermes, Greek god
Thracia, 141, 275, 318, 328, 330, 332, 333, 354, 366, 368, 387, 407, 409, 412, 435, 436, 446, 451, 454, 507, 524
Three Taverns, 458, 537; see also Tres Tabernae
Thucydides, 439, 441
Thurii, 501
Thutmose I, 81, 193, 228
Thutmose II, 193
Thutmose III, 65, 78, 82, 85, 96, 102, 117, 118, 122, 131, 193, 226, 228, 252, 294, 325, 420
Thutmose IV, 70, 82
Thyatira, 389, 390, 396, 397
    Roman period, 396
Tiberias
    city of, 98, 128, 134, 167
    Sea of, 128, 133
    see also Galilee, Sea of
Tiberius, 249, 250, 257, 337, 344, 359, 378, 385, 391, 399, 401, 402, 448, 508, 509, 522, 524, 538, 540, 542
    Arch of, 545
    palace of, 540
Tiber River, 247, 493, 494, 497

Tibur Quarry (Tivoli), 495
Tiglath-pileser I, 7, 24, 32, 33, 43, 196, 203, 273, 328
Tiglath-Pileser III, 33, 34, 107, 108, 112, 131, 132, 133, 140, 204, 205, 234, 236; see also Pul
Tigranes the Great, 241, 335, 336, 337, 342, 383, 385
Tigris River, 2, 3, 9, 21, 32, 35, 36, 223, 268, 269, 284; see also Hiddekel
plain of, 263
Timnah (Timnath), 111
Timothy, 354, 358, 451, 474
Timsah, Lake, 53, 55, 90
Tiranë, 412
Tirhakah, 205; see also Taharka
Tiryns, 420, 424, 425, 427
Tirzah, 138, 139, 142; see also Far 'a Tell el
Titus Justus, 482
Titus, Roman general, 88, 98, 103, 152, 250, 386, 527-28
Tmolus Mountains, 313, 314, 398, 400
Tobias, 274
Trabzon, 314, 383; see also Trapezus and Trebizond
Tracheia, 338, 342
Trajan, Emperor, 179, 257, 258, 384, 462, 522, 535, 543, 549
Transjordan
country, 99, 126, 147, 173
desert 95, 175-81
plateau, 95, 177
see also Abarim
Trapezus, 314, 331, 383
Trebizondo, 314, 383; see also Trabzon and Trapezus
Tres Tabernae, 537; see also Three Taverns
Tripoli, 187, 212, 239
Tripylon, 281
Troad, 314, 329
Troas, 356, 365, 366, 396, 400, 449, 548, 550
Trogyllium, 370
Trojan War, 105, 425, 429, 449, 479
Troodos Mountains, 292, 293
Troy, 105, 196, 197, 299, 318, 319, 320, 331, 418, 428, 444
Tudhaliyas II, 325
Tudhaliyas IV, 326
Tukulti-Ninurta II, 33
Tumilat, Wadi, 53, 55, 57, 58, 89
Tunisia, 514, 531
Turkey, 33, 274, 308, 313, 317, 318, 322, 323, 403, 407
Turks, 99, 130, 308, 311, 378, 399
Tushratta, 42
Tutankhamen, 84
Twelve Gods, Assembly of, 471
Twelve Tables, 503
Tyana, 233, 384, 474
Tyche, goddess, 250

Tychicus, 358
Tyre, 43, 99, 101, 102, 129, 185, 187, 189, 190, 193, 195, 196, 197, 198, 199, 200, 201, 203, 204, 205, 207-13, 226, 234, 238, 239, 245, 253, 299, 300, 376, 428, 535
map of, 211
see also Palaetyrus
Tyropoeon Valley, 155

U

Ugarit, 41, 111, 207, 217, 224, 225, 229-31, 297, 298, 420; see also Ras Shamra
Ugaritic
sacrificial system, 230
texts, 230
Ur, 1, 4, 6, 10, 11, 14-20, 43, 222, 285, 297
ancient tombs of, 5
golden age of, 6
Ningal temple, 20
"Royal cemetery," 15
third dynasty of, 3, 18, 19, 20, 22, 33, 40, 285, 297
Urartaeans, 233, 329
Urartu, 1, 3, 233, 236, 275; see also Armenia and Ararat
Urfa, 20; see also Edessa
Uriah, 176, 233
Urmia, 275; see also Rezaieh
lake, 275-76
Ur-Nammu, 18, 19, 21
stele of, 18
Uruk, 11, 12, 13, 222, 275; see also Erech and Warka
Urukagina, 20
Usdum, Jebel, 171; see also Sodom, Mount
Uzziah, 109, 236

V

Valerian, 63
Valerio-Horatian laws, 503
Van, Lake, 9, 236, 275
Vardar
Plain of, 412
River, 412, 457
Varmion Mountains, 459
Veii, 500
Venetians, 308
Ventris, Michael, 418, 420
Venus, goddess, 305, 306
temple of, 255
Vergil, 497
Veroia, 458; see also Beroea
Vespasian, 138, 145, 246, 344, 367, 369, 379, 385, 401, 448, 526, 527, 543
Vesta, temple of, 543
Vesuvius, mount, 493, 528, 535
Via Egnatian; see also Egnatian Way, 407, 452, 454-57, 459
"Victory of Samothrace," 450
Volos, Gulf of, 412

W

Wampler, J. C., 153
Warka, 284; see also Erech
Warmington, B. H., 197, 206, 213
Waters of Merom, 130; see also Merom, Waters of
Wellcome-Marston Archaeological Expedition, 115
Wen-Amon, Egyptian legendary figure, 101
Wen-Amon, Pharaonic envoy, 195
Wheaton Archaeological Expedition, 143
Wheaton College Archaeology Conference, 352
Wheeler, Mortimer, 551
Wilson, John A., 93, 192
Winckler, Hugo, 323
Wood, J. T., 360
Woolley, Sir Charles Leonard, 10, 14, 15, 16, 17, 18, 19, 182, 226, 227, 233, 261, 297, 323

X

Xanthus River, 375
Xenophon, 38, 39, 331, 340, 341, 343, 373, 381, 383, 392, 441
Xerxes, 7, 29, 263, 268, 281, 282, 283, 300, 331, 381, 398, 436, 437, 474; see also Ahasuerus

Y

Yahudiya, Tell el-. See El-Yahudiya, Tell
Yalias, 292; see also Idalia
Yarkon River, 104
Yarmuk River, 95, 175, 219
Yazilikaya, 328
Yigael Yadin, 118, 122, 131

Z

Zagros Mountains, 5, 264, 266, 270, 273; see also Taurus Mountains
Zaretan, 169
Zered River, 175, 178, 179
Zerka, Nahr ez, 101; see also Crocodile River
Zerqa, Wadi, 95, 168; see also Jabbok River
Zeus, 81, 252, 304, 352, 353, 395, 416, 418, 427, 457, 467, 476; see also Jupiter
altar of, 393, 394, 395, 396
statue of, 475
stoa of, 471
temple of, 174, 178, 250, 328, 370, 390, 434, 462
Zeus, Olympian, 463

Zeus Phratrios, 471
Zidon, 185, 197, 239; *see also*
    Sidon

Ziklag, 173
Zimri-Lim, 40
Zin, Wilderness of, 91

Zinjirli, 233, 323
Zoan, 57
Zobah (Zoba), 231, 232

Scripture Index

Index to Maps

Benjamin, Gate of 1
Beon 6, **Y5**
Beroea 8, **D2**
Bersabe (Beersheba) 7, **W6**
Berytus 5, 8, **G4**
Besor, Brook 3, 4, **W6**
Beten 6, **X3**
Beth-anath 3, 6, **X2**
Beth-anoth 6, **X5**
Bethany 7, **X5**
Betharamphtha 7, **Y5**
Beth-aven (Bethel) 6, **X5**
Beth-baal-meon 3, 6, **Y5**
Beth-dagon 3, 6, **W4**
Beth-diblathaim 6, **Y5**
Beth-eden (Bit-adini) 5, **G3**
Bethel 3, 4, 6, **X5**
Bethesda, Pool of 9
Beth-gilgal (Gilgal) 6, **X5**
Beth-haccherem 6, **X5**
Beth-haggan 3, **X3**
Beth-hanan 4, **X5**
Beth-haram 6, **Y5**
Beth-hoglah 6, **X5**
Beth-horon, Lower 3, 4, 6, **X5**
Beth-horon, Upper 3, 4, 6, **X5**
Beth-jeshimoth 3, 6, **Y5**
Bethlehem: Galilee 3, 6, **X3**
Bethlehem: Judah 3, 4, 6, 7, **X5**
Beth-meon 6, **Y5**
Beth-nimrah 3, 6, **Y5**
Beth-peor 3, 6, **Y5**
Beth-rehob: region 4, **Y1**
Beth-rehob: town 3, 4, **Y2**
Bethsaida-Julias 7, **Y2**
Beth-shan (Beth-shean) 6, **X3**
Beth-shean 3, 4, 6, **X3**
Beth-shemesh: Issachar 6, **Y3**
Beth-shemesh: Judah
 3, 4, 6, **W5**
Beth-tappuah 6, **X5**
Bethul (Bethuel) 3, **W6**
Bethzatha, Pool of 9
Beth-zur 3, 6, **X5**
Betogabri 7, **W5**
Betonim 3, 6, **Y4**
Bezek 3, 6, **X4**
Bezer 3, **Y5**
Bezetha 9
Bit-adini (Beth-eden) 5, **G3**
Bithynia & Pontus 8, **F2**
Black Sea 5, **F2**
Borsippa 5, **H4**
Bosphorus 8, **E2**
Bosporan Kingdom 8, **G2**
Bozkath 6, **W5**
Bozrah 2, **U2**
Brundisium 8, **C2**
Bubastis 2, **Q2**
Busiris 2, **Q2**
Byblos (Gebal) 5, **G4**
Byzantium 8, **E2**

C

Cabbon 6, **W5**
Cabul 3, 4, 6, **X2**
Caesarea: Palestine 7, **W3**
 also 8, **F4**
Caesarea (Mazaca) 8, **G3**

Caesarea Philippi 7, **Y2**
 also 8, **G4**
Calah 5, **H3**
Callirrhoe 7, **Y5**
Calno 5, **G3**
Canaan 2, **T1**
Canopus 8, **F4**
Canusium 8, **C2**
Capernaum 7, **Y2**
Caphtor (Crete) 5, **D3**
Cappadocia 8, **G3**
Capreae (Capri) 8, **B2**
Capua 8, **B2**
Carchemish 5, 8, **G3**
Carmel 4, **X6**
Carmel, Mt. 3, 4, 6, 7, **X3**
Carrhae (Haran) 8, **G3**
Caspian Sea 5, **K3**
Catana 8, **C3**
Cauda 8, **D4**
Cenchreae 8, **D3**
Chephar-ammoni 6, **X4**
Chephirah 3, 6, **X5**
Cherith, Brook 6, **Y3**
Chersonesus 8, **F2**
Chesulloth 6, **X3**
Chezib (Achzib) 6, **W5**
Chinnereth 3, 6, **Y2**
Chinnereth, Sea of 3, 4, 6, **Y3**
Chios 8, **E3**
Chisloth-tabor 6, **X3**
Chorazin 7, **Y2**
Cilicia (Khilakku) 5, **F3**
Cilicia & Syria 8, **G3**
Cilicıa Trachea 8, **F3**
City of David 1
City of Salt 6, **X5**
Cnidus 8, **E3**
Colchis 8, **H2**
Colonia Amasa (Emmaus) 7, **X5**
Colossae 8, **E3**
Comana 8, **G2**
Commagene 5, 8, **G3**
Corcyra 8, **C3**
Corinth 8, **D3**
Cos 8, **E3**
Court of Gentiles 9
Court of Israel 9
Court of Women 9
Crete 5, 8, **D3**
Croton 8, **C3**
Ctesiphon 8, **H4**
Cuthah 5, **H4**
Cyprus: island 5, 8, **F3**
Cyprus: Palestine 7, **X5**
Cyrenaica 8, **D4**
Cyrene 8, **D4**
Cyzicus 8, **E2**

D

Dabbesheth 6, **X3**
Daberath 6, **X3**
Dalmatia (Illyricum) 8, **C2**
Damascus 3, 4, 7, **Z1**
 also 5, 8, **G4**
Damascus Gate 9
Dan (Laish) 3, 4, **Y2**
Dan: tribe 3, **Y2**, **W5**
Danube, R. 8, **D2**

Dead Sea 7, **X6**
Debir: Judah 3, 4, **W6**
 also 2, **T1**
Debir: N.E. Judah 6, **X5**
Decapolis 7, **Y3**
Dedan 5, **G5**
Derbe 8, **F3**
Dibon 2, **U1**; 3, 4, **Y5**
Dion 7, **Y3**
Diyala, R. 5, **H4**
Dophkah 2, **S3** and inset
Dor 3, 4, 6, **W3**
Dora 7, **W3**
Dorylaeum 8, **F3**
Dothan 6, **X3**
Dumah 5, 8, **G5**
Dura-Europus 8, **H4**
Dur-sharrukin 5, **H3**
Dyrrhachium 8, **C2**

E

Eastern Sea 5, **J5**
Ebal, Mt. 3, 4, 6, 7, **X4**
Eben-ezer 6, **W4**
Ecbatana 5, **J4**
Edessa 8, **G3**
Edom 2, **U2** and inset; 3, 4, **Y7**
 also 5, **G4**
Edrei 3, **Z3**
Eglon 3, 6, **W5**
Egnatian Way 8, **D2**
Egypt 2, **Q2**; 5, 8, **F5**
Egypt, Brook of 2, **S1**
Egyptian Port 2, **S3**
Ekron 3, 4, 6, **W5**
Elah, V. of 3, **W5**
Elam 5, 8, **J4**
Elath 5, **F5**
Elealeh 6, **Y5**
Elon 4, 6, **X5**
Eltekon 6, **X5**
Emesa 8, **G4**
Emmaus (Nicopolis or
 Colonia Amasa) 7, **X5**
Enam 6, **X5**
En-dor 3, 6, **X3**
Engaddi (En-gedi) 7, **X6**
En-gannim 3, 6, **X3**
En-gedi 3, 7, **X6**
En-haddah 6, **X3**
En-rogel 1
En-shemesh 6, **X5**
En-tappuah 6, **X4**
Ephesus 8, **E3**
Ephraim: town 4, 6, **X4**
Ephraim: tribe 3, 4, **X4**
Ephraim, Hill Country of 6, **X4**
Ephron (Ophrah) 3, 6, **X4**
Epiphania 8, **G3**
Erech (Uruk) 5, **J4**
Eshtaol 6, **X5**
Eshtemoa 3, **X6**
Essenes, Gate of 9
Etam 3, 6, **X5**
Ether 6, **W5**
Ethiopia 5, **F6**
Euphrates, R. 5, 8, **H3**
Europus (Carchemish) 8, **G3**
Euxine Sea 8, **F2**

Ezion-geber 2, **T3** and inset; 5, **F5**

F

Fair Havens 8, **D4**
Farah, Wadi 6, **X4**
Forum of Appius 8, **B2**
Fullers' Tower 9

G

Gabae (Hippeum) 7, **X3**
Gabbatha 9
Gad: tribe 3, **Y4**
Gadara: Decapolis 7, **Y3**
Gadara: Perea 7, **Y4**
Galatia 8, **F3**
Galilee 6, 7, **X3**
Galilee, Sea of 7, **Y3**
Gamala 7, **Y3**
Gangra 8, **F2**
Gath: Philistia 3, 4, 6, **W5**
Gath (Gittaim): Benjamin 6, **W5**
Gath-hepher 6, **X3**
Gath-rimmon 3, 4, 6, **W4**
Gaulanitis 7, **Y2**
Gaza 2, **T1** and inset; 3, 4, 7, **V5**
also 5, 8, **F4**
Gazara 7, **W5**
Geba 4, 6, **X5**
Gebal (Byblos) 5, **G4**
Gederah 6, **W5**
Gedor 6, **X5**
Gennath Gate 1, 9
Gennesaret 7, **Y2**
Gerar 2, **T1**; 4, **W6**
Gerasa 7, **Y4**
Gerizim, Mt. 3, 4, 6, 7, **X4**
Geshur 4, **Y2**
Geshur 6, **Y3**
Gethsemane 9
Gezer 3, 4, 5, **W5**
Gibbethon 3, 6, **W5**
Gibeah 3, 4, 6, **X5**
Gibeon 3, 4, 6, **X5**
Gihon Spring 1
Gilboa, Mt. 3, 4, 6, **X3**
Gilead 3, 4, 6, **Y4**
Gilgal (nr. Jericho) 3, 4, 6, **X5**
Gilgal: Ephraim 6, **X4**
Gilgal: Sharon 6, **W4**
Giloh 3, 4, 6, **X5**
Gimarrai (Gomer) 5, **F3**
Gimzo 6, **W5**
Gittaim (Gath) 6, **W5**
Golan 3, **Y3**
Golgotha: Jerusalem 9
Gomer (Gimarrai) 5, **F3**
Gophna 7, **X4**
Gordion (Gordium) 5, 8, **F3**
Gordyene 8, **H3**
Goshen: Egypt 2, **Q2**
Goshen: Palestine 3, **W6**
Gozan 5, **G3**
Great Bitter Lake 2, **R2**
Greater Syrtis 8, **C4**
Great Plain, The 7, **X3**
Great Sea, The 2, **S1**
also 3, 4, **W3**; 5, **E4**

H

Habor, R. 5, **H3**
Hadashah 6, **W5**
Hadid 6, **W4**
Halhul 6, **X5**
Halys R. 5, 8, **G3**
Ham 6, **Y3**
Hamath 5, **G3**
Hammath 6, **Y3**
Hananel: Jerusalem 1
Hannathon 6, **X3**
Haran 5, 8, **G3**
Harim 6, **W5**
Harosheth-ha-goiim 3, 6, **X3**
Hattina 5, **G3**
Hauran 5, **G4**
Havvoth-jair 3, 4, **Y3**
Hazar-addar 2, **T2**
Hazar-shual 3, **W6**
Hazor: Galilee 3, **Y2**
Hazor: Benjamin 6, **X5**
Hebron 2, **U1**; 3, 4, 6, 7, **X5**
Helam 4, **Z3**
Helbon 5, **G4**
Heleph 6, **X3**
Heliopolis (On) 2, **Q2** and inset
also 5, 8, **F4**
Helkath 6, **X3**
Hepher 4, 6, **W4**
Heraclea 8, **F2**
Hermon, Mt. 3, 4, **Y1**
Hermopolis 5, **F5**
Hermus, R. 5, **E3**
Herod, Kingdom of 7
Herodium 7, **X5**
Heshbon 3, 4, 6, **Y5**; 2, **U1**
Hezekiah's Conduit 1
High Place 4, **X5**
Hinnom Valley 1, 9
Hippeum (Gabae) 7, **X3**
Hippicus: Jerusalem 9
Hippos 7, **Y3**
Holon 6, **X5**
Horeb, Mt. 2, **S4**
Hormah 2, **T1**; 3, **W6**
Hukkok 6, **X2**
Hyrcania 7, **X5**

I

Iadanna (Cyprus) 5, **F3**
Ibleam 3, 6, **X3**
Iconium 8, **F3**
Idumea 7, **W6**
Illyricum (Dalmatia) 8, **C2**
Iphtah 6, **X5**
Iphtah-el 6, **X3**
Israel 6, 4, **X4**; 5, **G4**
Israel, Hill Country of 3, **X4**
Issachar: tribe 3, 4, **X3**
Istros 8, **E2**
Italy 8, **B2**
Ituraea 7, **Y1**

J

Jabbok R. 3, 4, 6, 7, **Y4**
Jabesh-gilead 3, 4, 6, **Y3**
Jabneel: Galilee 6, **X3**

Jabneel (Jamneh, Jamnia):
Judah 3, 6, 7, **W5**
Jahaz 6, **Y5**
Janoah 6, **X4**
Japhia 6, **X3**
Jarmuth (Ramoth): Issachar 6, **X3**
Jarmuth: Judah 3, 6, **W5**
Jattir 3, **X6**
Javan 5, **E3**
Jazer 4, 6, **Y4**
Jebel Helal 2, **S2**
Jericho 3, 4, 7, **X5**; 2, **U1** and inset
Jerusalem 3, 4, 6, 7, **X5**
also 2, **U1** and inset; 5, 8, **G4**
Jerusalem in O. T. times Map 1
Jerusalem in N. T. times Map 9
Jeshanah 6, **X4**
Jezreel: Judah 3, **X6**
Jezreel, V. of 3, 4, 6, **X3**
Jogbehah 3, **Y4**
Jokneam (Jokmeam) 3, 4, 6, **X3**
Joppa 3, 4, 6, 7, **W4**; 8, **F4**
Jordan, R. 3, 4, 6, 7, **Y4**
Jotbah 6, **X3**
Judah: Kingdom & region 4, 6, **X5**; 5, **F4**
Judah: tribe 3, 4, **X5**
Judah, Hill Country of 3, **X5**
Judah, Wilderness of 4, 6, **X5**
Judea: region 7, **X5**; 8, **G4**
Judea, Wilderness of 7, **X5**
Juttah 2, **U1**

K

Kabul (Cabul) 6, **X2**
Kabzeel 3, 4, **W6**
Kadesh 5, **G4**
Kadesh-barnea 2, **T2** and inset
Kamon 3, 6, **Y3**
Kanah, Brook of 6, **W4**
Karkor 3, **Z6**
Kedar (Qidri) 5, **G4**
Kedemoth 3, **Y5**
Kedesh 3, **Y2**
Keilah 3, 6, **X5**
Khilakku (Cilicia) 5, **F3**
Khirbet Qumran 7, **X5**
Kidron, Brook 6, **X5**
Kidron Valley 1, 9
King's Highway 2, **U3**
Kir-hareseth 2, **U1**; 4, **Y6**
Kiriathaim 3, 6, **Y5**
Kiriath-arba (Hebron) 6, **X5**
Kiriath-jearim 3, 4, 6, **X5**
Kishon, R. 3, 4, 6, **X3**
Kumukhu (Commagene) 5, **G3**

L

Lacedaemon (Sparta) 8, **D3**
Lachish 2, **T1**; 3, 6, **W5**
Lahmam 6, **W5**
Laish (Dan) 3, **Y2**

Laishah 6, **X5**
Lakkum 3, 6, **Y3**
Laodicea 8, **E3**
Larissa 8, **D3**
Larsa 5, **J4**
Lasea 8, **D3**
Lebanon 5, **G4**
Lebanon, Mt. 3, 4, **Y1**
Lebanon, V. of 3, **Y1**
Lebonah 3, 6, **X4**
Lehi 6, **X5**
Leontes, R. 7, **X1**
Lesbos 8, **E3**
Lesser Armenia 8, **G3**
Libnah 3, 4, 6, **W5**; 2, **T1**
Libya 5, 8, **E4**
Little Bitter Lake 2, **R2**
Lo-debar 4, 6, **Y3**
Lod 6, **W4**
Lower Beth-horon 3, 4, 6, **X5**
Lower Sea 5, **J5**
Lower Zab; riv. 5, **H3**
Lowland, The 3, 4, **W5**
Lycia 8, **E3**
Lycopolis (Siut) 5, **F5**
Lydda 7, **W4**
Lydia 5, **E3**
Lystra 8, **F3**

M

Maacah 4, **Y2**
Maarath 6, **X5**
Macedonia 8, **D2**
Machaerus 7, **Y5**
Madai (Medes) 5, **J3**
Madmannah 3, **W6**
Madon 3, 6, **X3**
Maenader, R. 5, **E3**
Magadan (Taricheae) 7, **X3**
Mahanaim 4, 6, **Y4**
Makaz 4, 6, **W5**
Makkedah 3, 6, **W5**
Malta 8, **B3**
Mamre 6, **X5**
Manasseh: tribe 3, 4, **X4**
Manasseh: tribe 3, **Y3**
Manasseh's Wall 1
Mannai (Minni) 5, **J3**
Maon 3, **X6**
Mare Internum 7, **W4**
    also 8, **D4**
Mare Nostrum 8, **D4**
Mareshah 3, 6, **W5**
Mariamme: Jerusalem
    Map 9
Marisa 7, **W5**
Masada 7, **X6**
Mazaca (Caesarea) 8, **G3**
Medeba 3, 4, 6, 7, **Y5**
    also 2, **U1**
Medes (Madai) 5, **J3**
Media 8, **H3**
Media Atropatene 8, **H3**
Mediterranean Sea 7, 8
Megiddo 3, 4, 6, **X3**
Megiddo, Plain of 6, **X3**
Melita (Malta) 8, **B3**
Melitene 5, 8, **G3**

Memphis (Noph) 2, **Q3** and inset
    also 5, 8, **F5**
Menzaleh, L. 2, **Q1**
Meribah 2, **T2**
Merom 3, 4, **X2**
Merom, Waters of 3, 6, **X2**
Mesembria 8, **E2**
Meshech (Mushki), 5, **F3**
Mesopotamia 8, **H3**
Messana 8, **C3**
Michmash 3, 6, **X5**
Middin 3, 6, **X5**
Midian 2, **U3**
Migdol 5, **F4**
Migron 6, **X5**
Miletus 8, **E3**
Milid (Melitene) 5, **G3**
Millo: Jerusalem 1
Minni (Mannai) 5, **J3**
Misrephoth-maim 3, **X2**
Mitylene 8, **E3**
Mizpah 3, 6, **X5**
Mizpeh 6, **W5**
Moab 2, **U1** and ·inset; 3, 4, **Y6**
    also 5, **G4**
Moab, Plains of 6, **Y5**
Moesia 8, **D2**
Mons Casius 2, **R1**
Moreh, Hill of 3, 6, **X3**
Moresheth-gath 6, **W5**
Mount Baalah 3, 6, **W5**
Mushki (Meshech) 5, **F3**
Musri 5, **G3**
Myra 8, **F3**

N

Naarah 3, 6, **X4**
Nabataean Kingdom 7
    also 8, **G4**
Nahaliel, R. 4, 6, **Y5**
Nahalol 3, 6, **X3**
Nairi 5, **H3**
Naissus 8, **D2**
Naphath-Dor 3, **X3**
Naphtali: tribe 3, 4, **X2**
Naucratis 8, **F4**
Nazareth 7, **X3**
Neapolis: Italy 8, **B2**
Neapolis: Macedonia 8, **D2**
Neapolis: Palestine 7, **X4**
Neballat 6, **W4**
Nebo: Judah 6, **X5**
Nebo: Moab 6, **Y5**
Nebo, Mt. 3, 6, **Y5**; 2, **U1**
Negeb, The 2, **T1**; 3, 4, **W6**
Neiel 6, **X2**
Netophah 4, 6, **X5**
Nezib 6, **X5**
Nibshan 3, 6, **X5**
Nicaea 8, **E2**
Nicephorum 8, **G3**
Nicomedia 8, **E2**
Nicopolis: Greece 8, **D3**
Nicopolis (Emmaus) 7, **X5**
Nile, R. 5, 8, **F5**
Nineveh 5, **H3**
Ninus 8, **H3**
Nippur 5, **J4**
Nisibis 8, **H3**

Nob 6, **X5**
Noph (Memphis) 2, **Q3**
    also 5, **F5**

O

Oboth 2, **U2**
Odessus 8, **E2**
Oescus 8, **D2**
Olives, Mt. of 1, 9
On (Heliopolis) 2, **Q2**
    also 5, **F4**
Ono 6, **W4**
Ophel: Jerusalem 1
Ophlas: Jerusalem 9
Ophrah (Ephron) 3, 6, **X4**
Orontes, R. 5, 8, **G3**
Osroëne 8, **G3**
Ostia 8, **B2**
Oxyrhynchus 8, **F5**

P

Paestum 8, **B2**
Palace: Jerusalem 1
Palmyra 8, **G4**
Pamphylia 8, **F3**
Paneas 7, **Y2**
Panormus 8, **B3**
Paphos 8, **F4**
Parah 6, **X5**
Paran, Wilderness of 2, **T3**
Parthian Empire 8, **H3**
Patara 8, **E3**
Pekod (Puqudu) 5, **J4**
Pella 6, 7, **Y3**
Pellusium 2, **R1** and inset;
    5, 8, **F4**
Peniel (Penuel) 3, 6, **Y4**
Perea 7, **Y5**
Perga 8, **F3**
Pergamum 8, **E3**
Perusia 8, **B2**
Pessinus 8, **F3**
Petra 8, **G4**
Phasael: Jerusalem 9
Phasaelis 7, **X4**
Philadelphia: Asia 8, **E3**
Philadelphia (Rabbah):
    E. of R. Jordan 7, **Y4**
Philippi 8, **D2**
Philippopolis 8, **D2**
Philistia 6, **W5**
Philistia, Plain of 2, **T1**
Philistines 3, 4, **W5**
Phoenix 8, **D3**
Phrygia 5, **F3**
Pi-beseth 2, **Q2**
Pirathon 3, 4, 6, **X4**
Pisgah, Mt. 3, 6, **Y5**
Pisidia 8, **F3**
Pithom 2, **Q2**
Pompeii 8, **B2**
Pontus Euxinus 8, **F2**
Pools: Jerusalem 1, 9
Praetorium: Jerusalem 9
Prusa 8, **E2**
Psephinus: Jerusalem 9
Ptolemais 7, **X2**; 8, **G4**

Punon 2, **U2**
Puqudu (Pekod) 5, **J4**
Puteoli 8, **B2**

Q

Qantir 2, **Q2**
Qarqar 5, **G4**
Qidri (Kedar) 5, **G4**
Qumran, Khirbet 7, **X5**

R

Raamses 2, **Q2** and inset
Rabbah: Judah 6, **X5**
Rabbah (Rabbath-ammon):
  Ammon 3, 4, 7, **Y4**
Rakkath 6, **Y3**
Ramah: Benjamin 3, 6, **X5**
Ramah (Ramathaim-zophim):
  Ephraim 6, **X4**
Ramathaim-zophim 3, 6, **X4**
Ramath-mizpeh 6, **Y4**
Ramoth 6, **X3**
Ramoth-gilead 3, 4, **Y3**
Raphana 7, **Z2**
Raphia 2, **T1** and inset
  also 5, **F4**; 7, **V6**
Red Sea 2, **R3** & **T4** and inset;
  5, 8, **F5**
Rehob 3, 6, **X2**
Remeth (Ramoth), 6 **X3**
Reuben: tribe 3, **Y5**
Rezeph 5, **G3**
Rhegium 8, **C3**
Rhodes 5, 8, **E3**
Rimmon: Galilee 3, 6, **X3**
Rimmon: Benjamin 3, 6, **X5**
Rogelim 4, 6, **Y3**
Roman Empire 8
Rome 8, **B2**
Royal Porch: Jerusalem 9
Rumah 6, **X3**

S

Saba (Sheba) 5, **G6**
Sais 5, 8, **F4**
Salamis 8, **F3**
Salecah 5, **G4**
Salmone 8, **E3**
Salonae 8, **C2**
Salt, V. of 4, **X6**
Salt Sea 2, **U1**; 3, 4, 6, **X5**
Samal 5, **G3**
Samaria: town 6, 7, **X4**
  also 5, **G4**
Samaria: region 7, **X4**
Samos 8, **E3**
Samosata 8, **G3**
Samothrace 8, **E2**
Sangarius, R. 5, **F-2**
Sanhedrin: Jerusalem 9
Saqqarah 2, **Q3**
Sardica 8, **D2**
Sardis 5, 8, **E3**
Sarepta 7, **X1**
Sarid 6, **X3**

Scodra 8, **C2**
Scupi 8, **D2**
Scythopolis 7, **X3**
Sebaste (Samaria) 7, **X4**
Secacah 3, 6, **X5**
Sela 2, **U2** and inset; 5, **G4**
Seleucia: Asia Minor 8, **F3**
Seleucia: Mesopotamia 8, **H4**
Sepharad (Sardis) 5, **E3**
Sepphoris 7, **X3**
Serabit el-Khadim 2, **S3**
Shaalbim 3, 4, 6, **W5**
Sharon, Plain of 4, 6, 7, **W4**
Sheba (Saba) 5, **G6**
Shechem 3, 4, 6, **X4**
Shephelah 4, **W5**
Shihor-libnath 6, **W3**
Shikkeron 3, 6, **W5**
Shiloh 3, 4, 6, **X4**
Shimron 3, 6, **X3**
Shittim 3, 6, **Y5**; 2, **U1**
Shunem 3, 6, **X3**
Shur, Wilderness of 2, **S2**
Shushan (Susa) 5, **J4**
Sibmah 6, **Y5**
Sicily 8, **B3**
Side 8, **G2**
Sidon 3, 4, 7, **X1**; 5, 8, **G4**
Sidonians 4, **X2**
Siloam: Jerusalem 1
Siloam, Pool of 9
Simeon: tribe 3, **W6**
Sin (Pelusium) 2, **R1**
Sin, Wilderness of 2, **S3**
Sinai: region 2, **S3** and inset;
  5, **F5**
Sinai, Mt. (?) (Jebel Helal) 2, **S2**
Sinai, Mt. (Mt. Horeb) 2, **S4**
  also 8, **F5**
Singidunum 8, **D2**
Sinope 8, **G2**
Sippar 5, **H4**
Sirbonis, L. 2, **S1**
Sirmium 8, **C2**
Siut (Lycopolis) 5, **F5**
Smyrna 8, **E3**
Socoh: Israel 4, 6, **X4**
Socoh (Soco): Judah
  3, 6, **W5**
Solomon's Pool 9
Solomon's Porch 9
Solomon's Wall 1
Sorek 3, 4, 6, **W5**
Sparta (Lacedaemon) 8, **D3**
Strato's Tower 7, **W3**
Succoth: Egypt 2, **R2** and inset
Succoth: Palestine
  3, 4, 6, **Y4**
Suez, Gulf of 2, **R3**
Susa (Shushan) 5, **J4**
Syene 5, **F6**
Syracuse 8, **C3**
Syria 4, **Z1**; 5, **G4**
Syria, Province of 7, **Y1**

T

Taanach 3, 4, 6, **X3**
Tabal (Tubal) 5, **G3**

Tabbath 3, 6, **Y4**
Tabor, Mt. 3, **X3**
Tadmor (Tadmar) 5, **G4**
Tahpanhes 5, **F4**
Tamar 4, **X7**
Tanis 2, **Q2**; 5, **F4**
Tappuah 3, 6, **X4**
Taralah 6, **X5**
Tarentum 8, **C2**
Taricheae (Magadan) 7, **X3**
Tarracina 8, **B2**
Tarsus 8, **F3**
Tavium 8, **F3**
Tekoa 4, 6, **X5**
Tell el-Yahudiyeh 2, **Q2**
Tema 5, 8, **G5**
Teman 2, **U2**
Temple: Jerusalem 1, 9
Thamna 7, **X4**
Thebes 5, **F5**
Thebez 3, 4, 6, **X4**
Thessalonica 8, **D2**
Thrace 8, **E2**
Three Taverns 8, **B2**
Thyatira 8, **E3**
Tiber, R. 8, **B2**
Tiberias 8, **G4**; 7, **Y3**
Tigranocerta 8, **H3**
Tigris, R. 5, 8, **H4**
Til-garimmu 5, **G3**
Timnah: Hill Country
  of Judah 3, 6, **X5**
Timnah: Dan
  3, 6, **W5**
Timnath-serah (Timnath)
  3, 6, **X4**
Timsah, L. 2, **R2**
Tipsah 5, **G3**
Tirzah 3, 6, **X4**
Tishbe 6, **Y3**
Tjaru (Zilu) 2, **R2**
Tob 3, 4, **Z3**
Togarmah 5, **G3**
Tomi 8, **E2**
Topheth: Jerusalem 1
Trachonitis 7, **Z2**
Trapezus 8, **G2**
Tripolis 8, **G4**
Troas (Alexandria Troas)
  8, **E3**
Tubal (Tabal) 5, **G3**
Turushpa (Tuspar) 5, **H3**
Tyre 3, 4, 7, **X2**; 5, 8, **G4**

U

Ulatha 7, **Y2**
Upper Beth-horon
  3, 6, **X5**
Upper Sea, The 5, **E4**
Upper Zab: riv. 5, **H3**
Ur, 5, **J4**
Urartu (Ararat) 5, **H3**
Urmia, Lake 5, 8, **J3**
Uruk (Erech) 5, **J4**
Ushu 5, **G4**
Usiana 5, **F3**

V

Van, Lake 5, 8, **H3**
Viminacium 8, **D2**

W

Western Sea, The 5, **E4**

Y

Yarmuk, Wadi 6, 7, **Y3**
Yehem 6, **X3**
Yiron 3, **X2**

Z

Zaanannim 6, **X3**

Zab, Upper & Lower 5, **H3**
Zair (Zior) 6, **X5**
Zanoah 6, **X5**
Zaphon 3, **Y4**
Zarethan 3, 4, 6, **Y4**
Zebulun: tribe 3, 4, **X3**
Zela 3, **X5**
Zemaraim 6, **X5**
Zered, Brook 3, 4, **Y7**
Zeredah: Ephraim 4, 6, **X4**
Zeredah (Zarethan):
  Jordan valley 3, 6, **Y4**
Zererah: Jordan valley 6, **Y4**
Zereth-shahar 3, 6, **Y5**

Zeugma 8, **G3**
Ziddim 6, **Y3**
Ziklag 3, 4, **W6**
Zilu (Tjaru) 2, **R2**
Zin, Wilderness of 2, **T2**
Zion, Wall of 1
Zior (Zair) 6, **X5**
Ziph: Hill Country of Judah
  3, **X6**
Ziph: Negeb 3, **W7**
Ziz, Ascent of 6, **X5**
Zoan 2, **Q2**; 5, **F4**
Zobah 4, **Z1**
Zorah 3, 6, **W5**

MAP 1

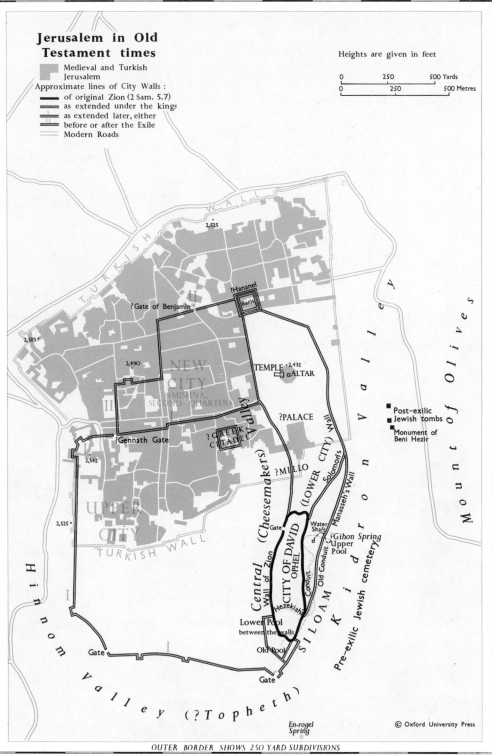

Jerusalem in Old Testament times

Medieval and Turkish Jerusalem

Approximate lines of City Walls:
- of original Zion (2 Sam. 5.7)
- as extended under the kings
- as extended later, either before or after the Exile
- Modern Roads

Heights are given in feet

0 — 250 — 500 Yards
0 — 250 — 500 Metres

2,525

?Hananel

?Gate of Benjamin   Baris

2,583

2,490   NEW CITY (MISHNA, SECOND QUARTER)   TEMPLE · 2,435 □ ALTAR

?PALACE

■ Post-exilic Jewish tombs
■ Monument of Beni Hezir

?Gennath Gate   ?GREEK CITADEL

?MILLO

2,542

Gate   Water Shaft   Gihon Spring   Upper Pool

2,525   UPPER CITY

TURKISH WALL

Central (Cheesemakers') Valley

?CITY OF DAVID   OPHEL

Wall of Zion   Hezekiah's   Old Conduit   Conduit

Manasseh's Wall   Solomon's (LOWER CITY) Wall

Mount of Olives

Kidron Valley

Pre-exilic Jewish cemetery

Lower Pool between the walls

Old Pool

Gate

Gate

Hinnom Valley (?Topheth)

En-rogel Spring

© Oxford University Press

OUTER BORDER SHOWS 250 YARD SUBDIVISIONS

MAP 2

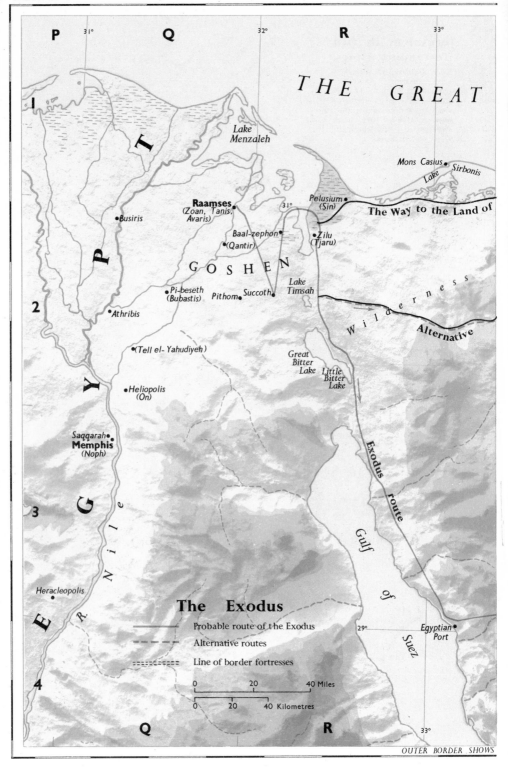

P 31° Q 32° R 33°

1

THE GREAT

Lake Menzaleh

Mons Casius • Sirbonis
Lake

E G Y P T

•Busiris

Raamses
(Zoan, Tanis, Avaris)

31°

Pelusium
(Sin)

The Way to the Land of

Baal-zephon•
•(Qantir)

•Zilu
(Tjaru)

G O S H E N

Lake Timsah

2

•Pi-beseth
(Bubastis)

Pithom• •Succoth

Wilderness

Alternative

•Athribis

•(Tell el- Yahudiyeh)

Great Bitter Lake

Little Bitter Lake

•Heliopolis
(On)

Exodus route

Saqqarah•
Memphis
(Noph)

3

R. Nile

Gulf

of

Heracleopolis
•

The Exodus

————— Probable route of the Exodus

— · — · — Alternative routes

▪▪▪▪▪▪▪ Line of border fortresses

29°

Egyptian•
Port

Suez

0   20   40 Miles

0   20   40 Kilometres

4

Q R 33°

OUTER BORDER SHOWS

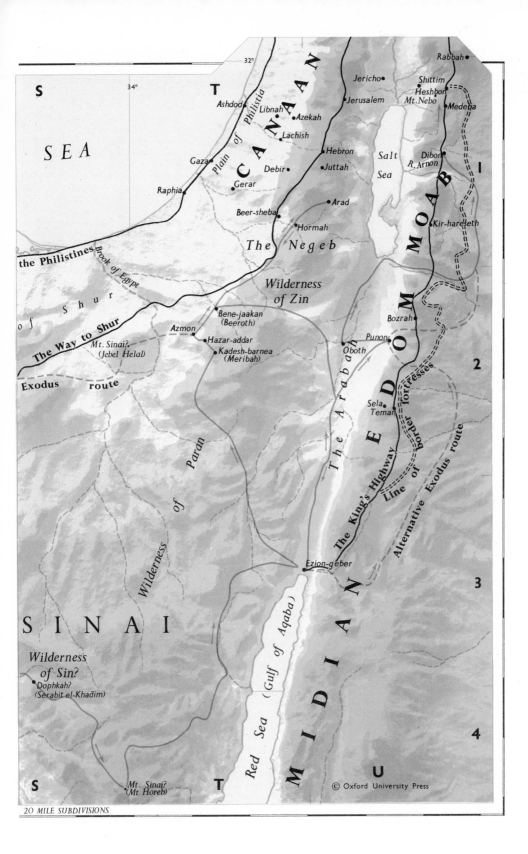

S T

S

34°

32°

SEA

Rabbah •

Jericho •

Jerusalem •

Ashdod •

Shittim
Heshbon
Mt.Nebo

Libnah •
Azekah •

Medeba •

Lachish •

Plain of Philistia

CANAAN

Gaza •

Hebron •

Salt
Sea

Dibon •
R.Arnon

Debir •

Juttah •

Gerar •

Raphia •

Beer-sheba •

• Arad

Kir-hareseth •

Hormah •

MOAB

the Philistines

Brook of Egypt

The Negeb

of Shur

Wilderness
of Zin

Bene-jaakan
(Beeroth)

Bozrah •

The Way to Shur

Azmon •

Mt. Sinai?
(Jebel Helal)

Hazar-addar •
Kadesh-barnea •
(Meribah)

Punon •

EDOM

Oboth •

Exodus   route

Line of border fortresses

2

Sela •
Teman •

Paran

of

The Arabah

The King's Highway

Alternative Exodus route

Wilderness

Ezion-geber •

3

SINAI

Red Sea (Gulf of Aqaba)

Gulf of Aqaba

MIDIAN

Wilderness
of Sin?

• Dophkah?
(Serabit el-Khadim)

4

S

T

U

Mt. Sinai?
(Mt Horeb)

© Oxford University Press

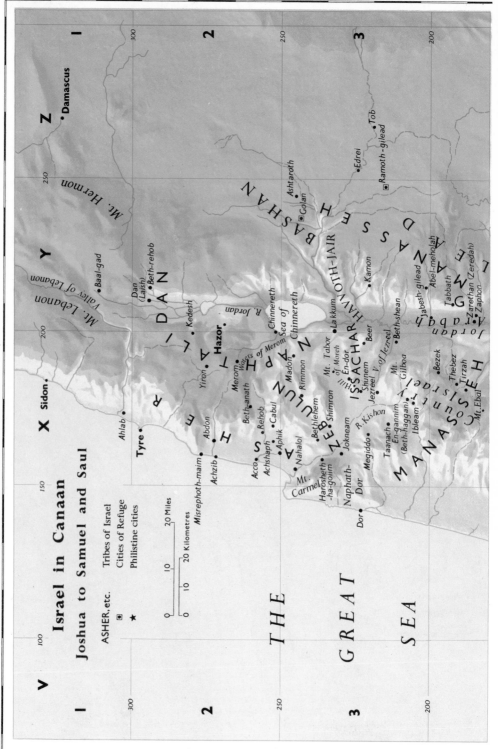

MAP 3

Israel in Canaan

Joshua to Samuel and Saul

ASHER, etc.   Tribes of Israel
               Cities of Refuge
               Philistine cities

0   10   20 Miles
0   10   20 Kilometres

Damascus

Mt. Hermon

Sidon

Baal-gad

Valley of Lebanon
Mt. Lebanon

Tyre

Ahlab

Dan (Laish)
Beth-rehob
Kedesh

Hazor

Misrephoth-maim
Achzib
Acco
Achshaph
Aphik
Nahalol
Mt. Carmel
Harosheth-ha-goiim
Naphath
Dor
Dor
Megiddo

Abdon
Rehob
Cabul
Bethlehem
Shimron
Jokneam
R. Kishon
Taanach
En-gannim
(Beth-haggan)
Ibleam

Yiron
Beth-anath
Merom
Waters of Merom
Madon
Rimmon

R. Jordan
Chinnereth
Sea of Chinnereth

Mt. Tabor
of Moreh
En-dor
Shunem
Jezreel
V. of Jezreel
Mt. Gilboa
Beer
Lakkum

Ashtaroth
Golan
Karnon

Edrei
Ramoth-gilead
Tob

Jabesh-gilead
Beth-shean
Bezek
Thebez
Tirzah
Mt. Ebal

Abel-meholah
Tabbath
Zarethan (Zeredah)
Zaphon
Arabah
Jordan

Country of Israel

DAN
NAPHTALI
ZEBULUN
ISSACHAR
MANASSEH
ASHER
HAVVOTH-JAIR
BASHAN
MANASSEH

THE
GREAT
SEA

V   X   Y   Z
1   2   3

100 150 200 250 300
300 250 200

MAP 3

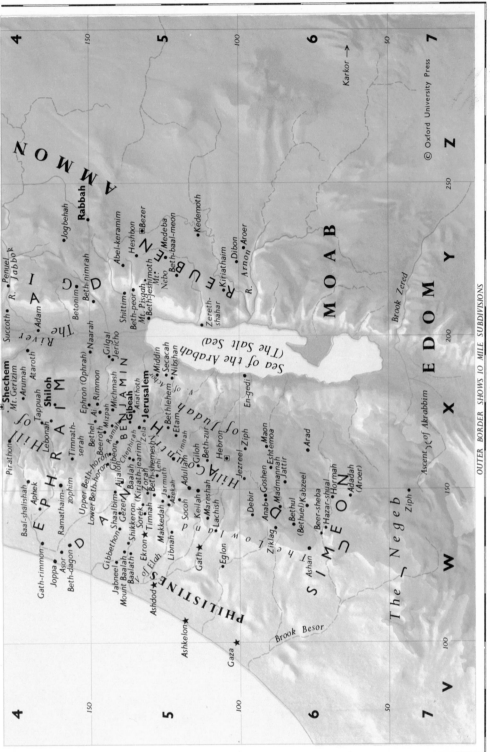

OUTER BORDER SHOWS 10 MILE SUBDIVISIONS

AMMON

Penuel
R. Jabbok
Succoth
Adam
The River
GILEAD
Betonim
Beth-nimrah
Jogbehah
Rabbah
Abel-keramim
Heshbon
Bezer
Medeba
Beth-baal-meon
Kedemoth
Kiriathaim
Arnon
Aroer
Dibon
R. Arnon
REUBEN
Mt. Nebo
Beth-jeshimoth
Beth-peor
Mt. Pisgah
Shittim
Naarah
Gilgal
Jericho

MOAB

Brook Zered

EDOM

Shechem
Mt. Gerizim
Arumah
Ataroth
Tappuah
Shiloh
Timnath-serah
Lebonah
Pirathon
Baal-shalishah
Aphek
EPHRAIM
Ramathaim-zophim
Asor
Joppa
Gath-rimmon
Beth-dagon
Upper Beth-horon
Lower Beth-horon
Bethel
Ephron (Ophrah)
Rimmon
Ai
Michmash
Mizpah
Ramah
Gibeon
Beeroth
BENJAMIN
Gibeah
Anathoth
Jerusalem
Nob
Kiriath-jearim
Chephirah
Zela
Bethlehem
Lehi
Beth-shemesh
Timnah
Adullam
Giloh
Jezreel
Hebron
Ziph
Ziph
Etam
Beth-zur
DAN
Shaalbim
Gibbethon
Jabneel
Gezer
Baalah
Ekron
Shikkeron
Sorek
Timnah
Zorah
V. of Elah
Gath
Makkedah
Jarmuth
Azekah
Socoh
Keilah
Mareshah
Lachish
Libnah
Eglon
Debir
Anab
Goshen
Maon
Eshtemoa
Jattir
Arad
Ziklag
Bethul (Bethuel)
Kabzeel
Beer-sheba
Hazar-shual
Hormah
Adadah (Aroer)
Ziph
JUDAH
SIMEON
The Shephelah
PHILISTINES
Ashdod
Ashkelon
Gaza
Brook Besor
The Negeb
Baalath
Mount Baalah

Middin
Secacah
Nibshan
V. of Achor
En-gedi
Jerusalem
Hill Country of Judah

Sea of the Arabah
(The Salt Sea)

Ascent of Akrabbim

Z

Y

X

W

V

Karkor →

50
100
150
200
250

4
5
6
7

MAP 4

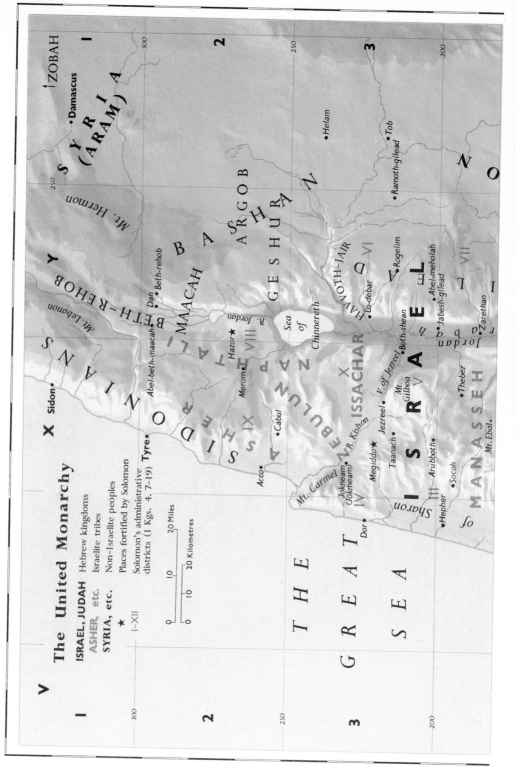

The United Monarchy

ISRAEL, JUDAH	Hebrew kingdoms
ASHER, etc.	Israelite tribes
SYRIA, etc.	Non-Israelite peoples
★	Places fortified by Solomon
I–XII	Solomon's administrative districts (1 Kgs. 4. 7–19)

Scale: 0 — 10 — 20 Miles
0 — 10 — 20 Kilometres

MAP 4

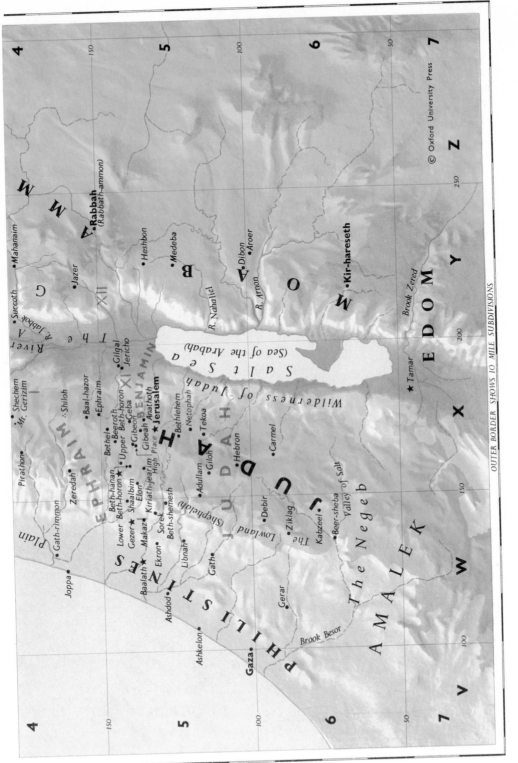

OUTER BORDER SHOWS 10 MILE SUBDIVISIONS

MAP 5

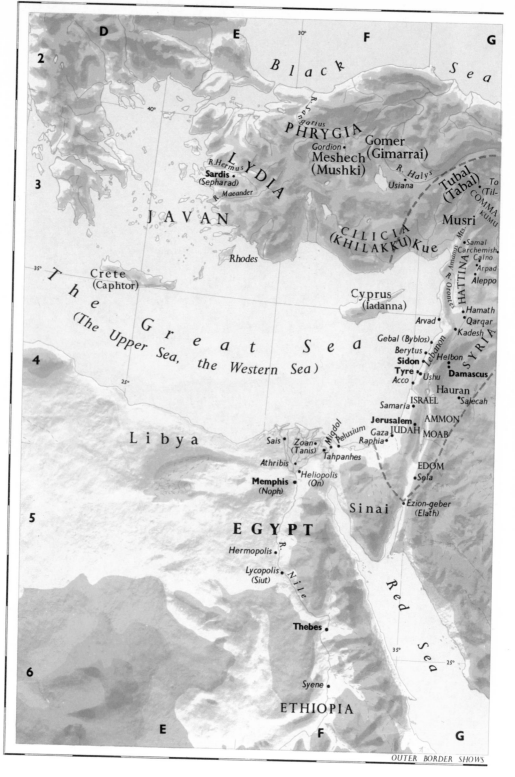

D E 30° F G

2

Black   Sea

40°

R. Sangarius

PHRYGIA

Gordion•   Gomer
Meshech•   (Gimarrai)
(Mushki)

R.Hermus   LYDIA   R. Halys   Tubal   To
Sardis•   Usiana•   (Tabal)•   (Til-
(Sepharad)   COMMA
3   R. Maeander   Musri   KUMU

JAVAN   CILICIA   Mss.
(KHILAKKU)Kue   •Samal
Carchemish•   •Calno
•Arpad
Rhodes   •Aleppo

35°   Crete   Cyprus   •Hamath
(Caphtor)   (Iadanna)   •Qarqar
•Kadesh
T h e   G r e a t   S e a   Gebal (Byblos)•   Helbon•
Berytus•   •Damascus
(The Upper Sea, the Western Sea)   Sidon•   Ushu
Tyre•   SYRIA
25°   Acco•   Hauran
4   Samaria•   ISRAEL   Salecah•

Libya   Jerusalem   AMMON
Migdol   JUDAH   MOAB
Sais•   Zoan•   •Pelusium   Gaza• Raphia•
(Tanis)   Tahpanhes•
Athribis•   EDOM
•Heliopolis   •Sela
Memphis•   (On)
(Noph)   Sinai   •Ezion-geber
(Elath)
5
EGYPT
Hermopolis•   R.
Lycopolis•   Nile   Red
(Siut)
Sea
Thebes•   35°   25°

6
Syene•

ETHIOPIA
E   F   G

MAP 5

The Near East

in the time of the

Assyrian Empire

– – – – Approximate extent of Assyrian domination
in the latter part of the 8th. century.

(Later, under Esarhaddon (681-669), Assyria conquered Egypt.)

| 0 | 100 | 200 Miles |
| 0 | 100 | 200 Kilometres |

© Oxford University Press

100 MILE SUBDIVISIONS

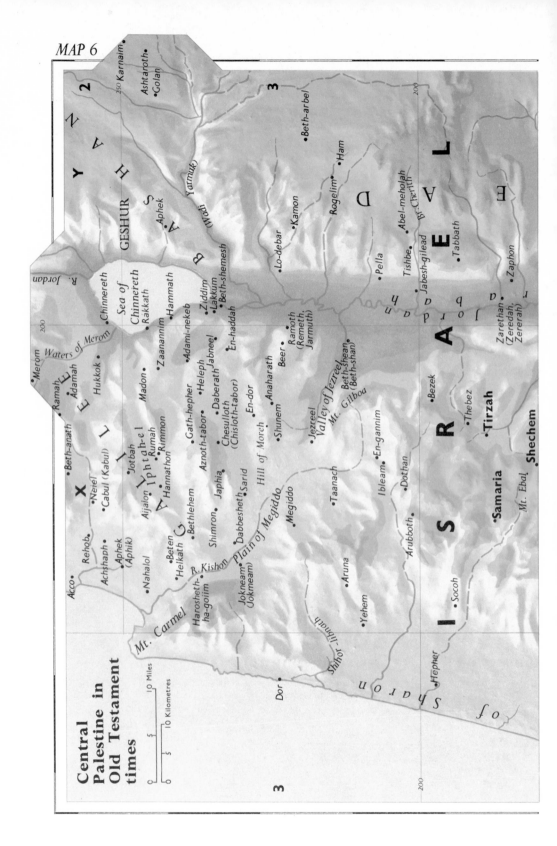

MAP 6

Central
Palestine in
Old Testament
times

MAP 6

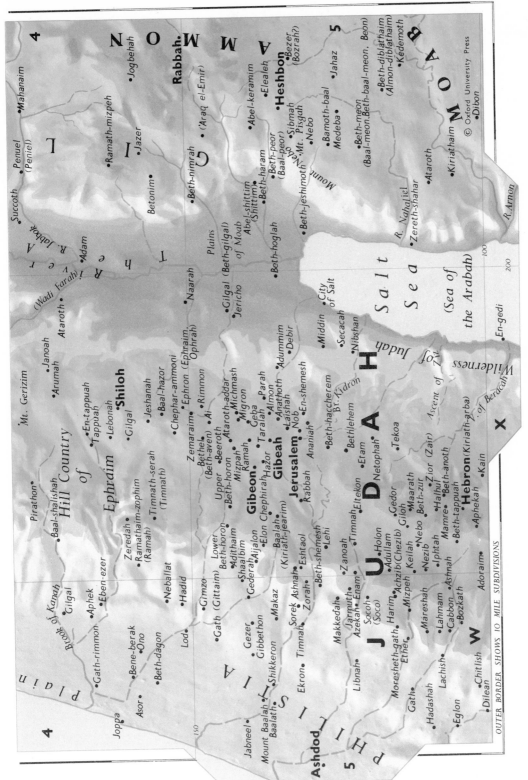

© Oxford University Press

OUTER BORDER SHOWS 10 MILE SUBDIVISIONS

MAP 7

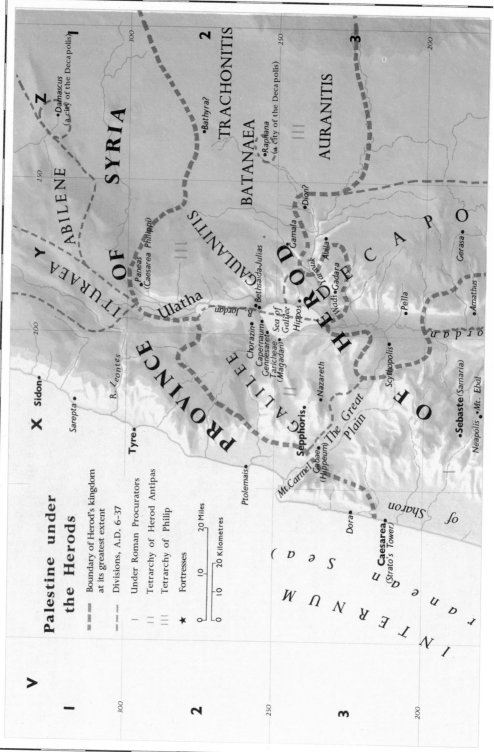

Palestine under the Herods

- ▬▬ Boundary of Herod's kingdom at its greatest extent
- ▭ ▭ Divisions, A.D. 6-37
  - | Under Roman Procurators
  - || Tetrarchy of Herod Antipas
  - ||| Tetrarchy of Philip
- ★ Fortresses

Scale: 0 — 10 — 20 Miles
0 — 10 — 20 Kilometres

MAP 7

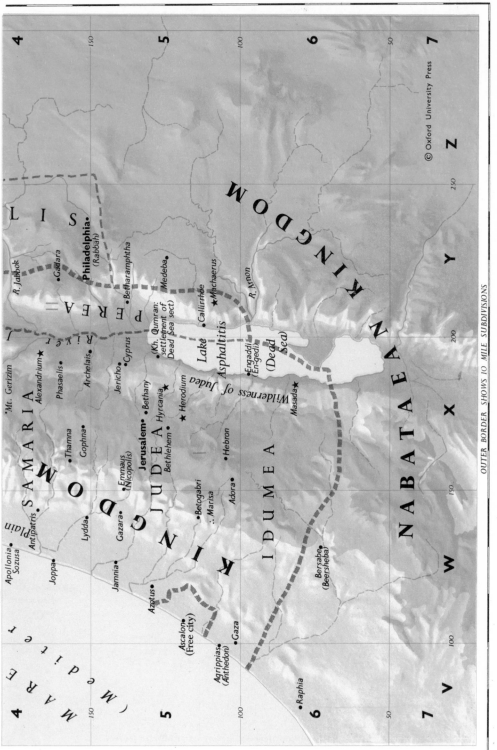

OUTER BORDER SHOWS 10 MILE SUBDIVISIONS

MAP 8

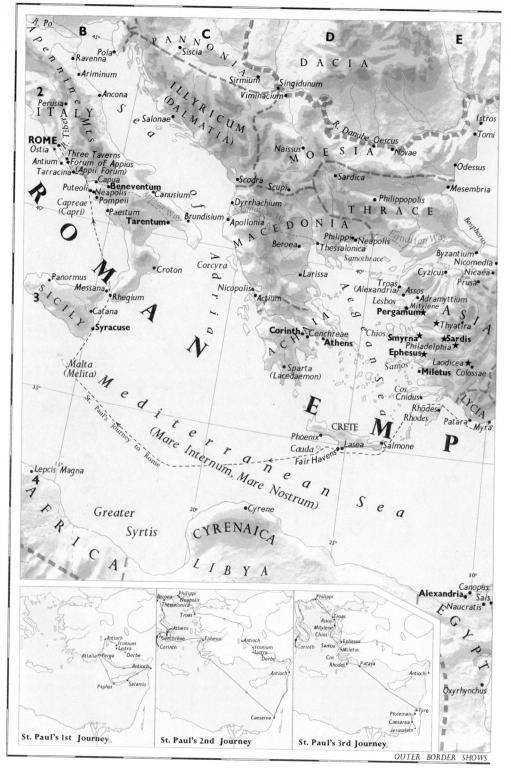

B   45°   C   D   E

R. Po
Apennines Mts.
•Ravenna   •Pola
•Ariminum
PANNONIA
•Siscia
DACIA
•Sirmium   •Singidunum
•Viminacium
2
Perusia•   •Ancona
ILLYRICUM
(DALMATIA)
ITALY   R. Tiber
•Salonae
Adriatic Sea
R. Danube   Oescus   •Istros
•Naissus   •Novae   •Tomi
MOESIA
ROME
Ostia•   •Three Taverns
Antium•   •Forum of Appius
Tarracina•   (Appii Forum)
•Capua   •Beneventum
Puteoli•   •Canusium
Neapolis•   Appian Way
Pompeii•
Capreae•   •Paestum
(Capri)   •Tarentum   •Brundisium
•Scodra   Scupi•
•Dyrrhachium   Egnatian Way
•Apollonia
MACEDONIA
•Sardica
THRACE
•Philippopolis
•Odessus
•Mesembria
40°
ROMAN
•Croton
Corcyra
Panormus
Messana•
•Rhegium
SICILY
Catana•
•Syracuse
•Beroea   •Philippi   •Neapolis
•Thessalonica   Egnatian Way
Samothrace   Bosphorus
•Larissa   40°   Byzantium•
Nicomedia•
•Cyzicus   Nicaea•
Troas   •Prusa
(Alexandria)   Assos•
Lesbos   •Adramyttium
Mitylene•   ASIA
Pergamum★
★Thyatira
•Chios   Smyrna★   ★Sardis
Ephesus★   Philadelphia★
•Miletus   Laodicea★
Colossae
•Samos
•Nicopolis
•Actium
ACHAIA
Corinth•   •Cenchreae
Athens•
Aegean Sea
•Sparta
(Lacedaemon)
EMPIRE
35°
Malta
(Melita)
St. Paul's journey to Rome
Mediterranean   Sea
(Mare Internum, Mare Nostrum)
Cos•
Cnidus•
•Rhodes
Rhodes•   •Patara
•Myra
LYCIA
CRETE
Phoenix•
Cauda•   Lasea•   •Salmone
Fair Havens
•Lepcis Magna   15°
4
AFRICA
Greater
Syrtis   20°   •Cyrene
CYRENAICA
LIBYA
25°

30°
Canopus•
Alexandria•   •Sais
•Naucratis
EGYPT
•Oxyrhynchus

St. Paul's 1st Journey
Antioch
Iconium
Lystra   •Derbe
Attalia•   Perga
Antioch
Paphos   Salamis

St. Paul's 2nd Journey
Beroea•   Philippi
Neapolis
Thessalonica
Troas•
Athens•
Cenchreae•   Ephesus•
Corinth   Antioch
Iconium
Lystra
Derbe
Antioch
Caesarea

St. Paul's 3rd Journey
Philippi
Assos•   Troas
Mitylene•
Chios•
Samos   Ephesus•
Corinth   •Miletus
Cos•
Rhodes•   Patara
Antioch
Ptolemais•   •Tyre
Caesarea•
Jerusalem•

MAP 8

★   Seven Churches of Asia (Rev. 1–3)

  Boundary of Roman Empire (c.A.D. 65)

  Provincial boundaries (c.A.D. 65)

ASIA, etc.   Roman Provinces

  Selected Roman roads (route between Rome and the East)

0   100   200 Miles

0   100   200 Kilometres

S c y t h i a n s

BOSPORAN KINGDOM

Chersonesus•

E u x i n e   S e a

(Pontus   Euxinus)

30°
45°
35°
40°
45°

COLCHIS

Amastris•
BITHYNIA and PONTUS
•Sinope
•Amisus
•Side
•Trapezus
Heraclea.
•Gangra
•Amasea
Comana
Dorylaeum•
•Ancyra
Tavium•
•Gordium
Lesser Armenia
•Pessinus
R. Halys

KINGDOM

OF

ARMENIA

•Artaxata
R. Araxes
•Tigranocerta
L. Van
L. Urmia
MEDIA ATROPATENE

GALATIA
Caesarea (Mazaca)•
CAPPADOCIA
•Archelais
Melitene•
Antioch•
•Iconium
PISIDIA
•Lystra
•Derbe
PAMPHYLIA
Perga•
Attalia•
Cilicia Trachea
Tarsus•
Seleucia•
CILICIA and SYRIA
Commagene
Samosata•
Zeugma•
Europus (Carchemish)•
OSROENE
•Edessa
Carrhae (Haran)•
•Nisibis
GORDYENE
ADIABENE
•Ninus
•Arbela
MEDIA

•Nicephorium
Nicephorium
R. Euphrates

IRE

Antioch•
R. Orontes
•Apamea
•Epiphania
•Emesa
Palmyra•
•Dura-Europus
MESOPOTAMIA
R. Tigris
PARTHIAN

EMPIRE

CYPRUS
•Salamis
Paphos•
35°
Tripolis•
Arca
Berytus•
Sidon•
Abilene
Tyre•
•Damascus
•Caesarea Philippi
Ptolemais•
Tiberias•
Caesarea•
Samaria•
Judea
Joppa•
•Jerusalem
Gaza•
•Pelusium

ELAM →

Seleucia•
•Ctesiphon
•Babylon

A r a b i a n
D e s e r t

Nabataean Kingdom

•Heliopolis
•Babylon
Memphis•
R. Nile
•Petra
Dumah•

Aila (Aelana)•

Mt. Sinai
•

Red Sea
35°

•Tema

**The Background
of the
New Testament**

Rome and the East

(including St. Paul's Journeys)

© Oxford University Press

MAP 9

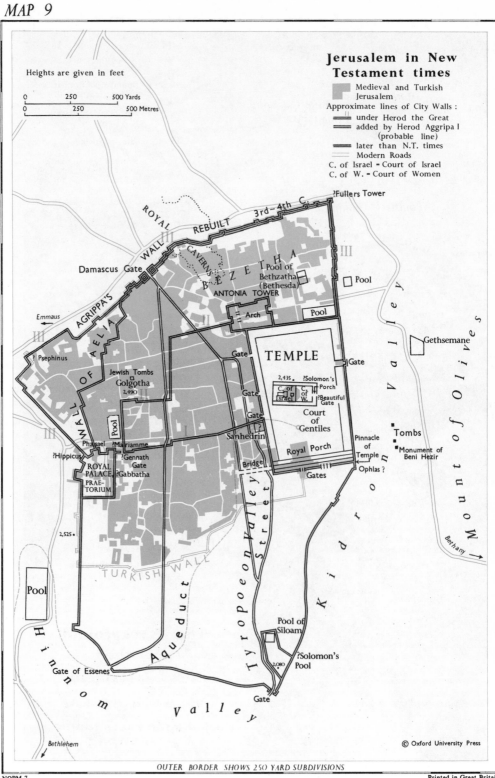

Heights are given in feet

250   500 Yards
250   500 Metres

Jerusalem in New Testament times

Medieval and Turkish Jerusalem

Approximate lines of City Walls :

under Herod the Great

added by Herod Aggripa I (probable line)

later than N.T. times

Modern Roads

C. of Israel = Court of Israel
C. of W. = Court of Women

?Fullers Tower

ROYAL WALL REBUILT 3rd–4th C.

CAVERNS

Damascus Gate

BEZETHA

Pool of Bethzatha (Bethesda)

ANTONIA TOWER

Pool

Emmaus

AGRIPPA'S WALL OF AELIA

Arch

Pool

Pool

III

?Psephinus

Gate

TEMPLE

Gate

Gethsemane

Jewish Tombs
Golgotha
2,490

2,435 ?Solomon's Porch

C. of Israel | C. of W.

?Beautiful Gate

Gate

Court of Gentiles

Gate

Pool

Sanhedrin

Royal Porch

Tombs

Monument of Beni Hezir

Phasael ?Mariamme

Bridge

Pinnacle of Temple

?Hippicus ?Gennath Gate

Gates

Ophlas ?

ROYAL PALACE. ?Gabbatha
PRAE-TORIUM

2,525

TURKISH WALL

Pool

Pool of Siloam

?Solomon's Pool

2,080

Hinnom Gate of Essenes

Aqueduct

Tyropoeon Valley Street

Kidron Valley

Mount of Olives

Bethany

Valley

Gate

Bethlehem

© Oxford University Press